SAINTS' LIVES AND
WOMEN'S LITERARY CULTURE
*c.*1150–1300

Saints' Lives and Women's Literary Culture
*c.*1150–1300

Virginity and its Authorizations

JOCELYN WOGAN-BROWNE

OXFORD
UNIVERSITY PRESS

OXFORD
UNIVERSITY PRESS

Great Clarendon Street, Oxford OX2 6DP

Oxford University Press is a department of the University of Oxford.
It furthers the University's objective of excellence in research, scholarship,
and education by publishing worldwide in

Oxford New York

Athens Auckland Bangkok Bogotá Buenos Aires Cape Town
Chennai Dar es Salaam Delhi Florence Hong Kong Istanbul Karachi
Kolkata Kuala Lumpur Madrid Melbourne Mexico City Mumbai
Nairobi Paris São Paulo Shanghai Singapore Taipei Tokyo Toronto Warsaw

and associated companies in Berlin Ibadan

Oxford is a registered trade mark of Oxford University Press
in the UK and certain other countries

Published in the United States
by Oxford University Press Inc., New York

© Jocelyn Wogan-Browne 2001

British Library Cataloguing in Publication Data

Data available

Library of Congress Cataloging in Publication Data

Wogan-Browne, Jocelyn.
Saints' lives and women's literary culture c. 1150–1300 : virginity and its authorizations
/ Jocelyn Wogan-Browne.
Includes bibliographical references and index.
1. English literature—Middle English, 1100–1500—History and criticism. 2. Women
and literature—England—History—To 1500. 3. Virginity—Religious
aspects—Christianity—History of doctrines—Middle Ages, 600–1500. 4. Christian
literature, English (Middle)—History and criticism. 5. English literature—Women
authors—History and criticism. 6. Women—England—Books and reading—History—To
1500. 7. Christian women saints—Legends—History and criticism. 8. Women—Religious
life—England—History—To 1500. 9. Christian saints in literature. 10. Virginity in
literature. 11. Hagiography.
PR275.W6 W64 2001 820.9′352042′0902—dc21 00–050420

ISBN 0–19–811279–3

1 3 5 7 9 10 8 6 4 2

Typeset by Graphicraft Limited, Hong Kong
Printed in Great Britain
on acid-free paper by
T.J. International Ltd,
Padstow, Cornwall

TO

D. M. AND G. G. W.-B.

F. J. R.

H. M. R.

without whom these
Authorized Virgins
could not have been produced

Acknowledgements

Without the help of the British Academy and the Humanities Research Council whose award of leave in 1998 provided a year of full-time research, the present book would have remained impossible to complete, and I am very grateful for this support. A term's fellowship in 1995 at the Humanities Research Centre, Australian National University, Canberra, and more recently a semester at the Institute for Advanced Study, Princeton, have been crucial both for this and other work and are deeply appreciated.

The patience and skill of many librarians has been another *sine qua non* and I thank staff at the British Library, London; Bibliothèque Albert 1er, Brussels; Cambridge University Library; Cardiff Public Library; the Sydney Jones Library, University of Liverpool; Nottingham University Library; the Bodleian Library, Oxford; the Bibliothèque Nationale, Paris; St John's College, Cambridge; the Library of the Taylor Institute, Oxford; Trinity College, Cambridge. For the opportunity to see Anglo-Norman manuscripts at the Vatican I thank Professor Teresa Pàroli and the Università di Roma 'La Sapienza'.

A much-delayed book accumulates heavy debts to the patience and kindness as well as the scholarship of its friends and helpers. If the number and calibre of the people to whom I am indebted were of itself a guarantee of quality in writing, I would be happy indeed.

In francophone medieval studies I thank especially Elspeth Kennedy, Glyn Burgess, Simon Gaunt, and Sarah Kay, and, for their welcome into a field so largely created by their fine editions for the Anglo-Norman Text Society and their other scholarship, I thank Tony Hunt, Bill MacBain, Duncan Robertson, and Delbert Russell. Most particularly I am grateful to Ian Short, the doyen of Anglo-Norman studies: so rich a field can seldom have owed so much to one scholar, and his alertness to and constructive critique and support of Anglicist work in the area is a small but characteristically vigilant part of the wide range of scholarly activity inspired and improved, to say nothing of personally produced, by him. In some countries, one can imagine, such a scholar would be kept from bureaucratic burdens and treated as a national asset.

In Anglicist medieval studies, I thank Bella Millett for inimitable but inspiring scholarship and for much generosity in rigorous attention to and encouragement of others' work. Alexandra Barratt's superb scholarship and pioneering retrieval of women's texts is equally inspiring. Geraldine Barnes, John Fletcher, Andrew Hamer, Lesley Johnson, David Mills, and Rosalynn Voaden have been exemplary scholars and critics and have provided long-enduring support and stimulus. I would also like to thank Margaret Clunies Ross, Margaret Harris,

viii Acknowledgements

Diane Speed, and Jane Tibbetts Schulenberg, whose generous interest helped more than they may have realized. Sally Thompson's kindness and her remark that she first took her children to nunnery sites in pushchairs and that they were grown up before she finished her work has remained with me for many years. She and Virginia Blanton-Whetsall, Sarah Salih, Finn Sinclair, John Frankis, and Elisabeth van Houts have sent material, published and forthcoming, for which I warmly thank them.

I owe special debts to those who read and commented on the typescript: Helen Phillips and Tom Head generously took on particular chapters, giving the benefit respectively of a superb ear and prose style and inimitable hagiographic scholarship. Simon Gaunt and Sarah Kay exchanged typescripts and ideas and my intellectual debts to them bulk large in these pages. To Nicholas Watson I remain profoundly grateful for longstanding and tireless intellectual support for the book, and above all for the insane but crucial generosity with which he gave up several precious days of an archival trip to pulling out supernumerary chapters and making the book writable (for its readability or otherwise I of course take responsibility).

I have had much skilful and kind help in preparing the typescript, and thank Gwen Jones, Elizabeth Wall, and Lillian Ashworth for bibliographical checking and indexing. Frances Whistler at Oxford University Press has shown saintly patience as well as kind and constructive professionalism, including arranging for me to have the privilege of Dorothy McCarthy's indispensably brilliant, patient, and supportive copy-editing. I am responsible for all remaining errors as I am for the many excised from the typescript by all these people in the limited periods for which I was able to leave it in their care.

Among many colleagues and friends I owe particular intellectual and personal debts to Ian Britain, Iain Bruce, the late Colette Murphy, Vera Morton, Penelope Pollitt, Catherine Rees, Anne Savage, Jean and Ian Shearman, Barbara Smith, Lorna Stevenson, Margarita Stocker, and more recently Mary Erler, Constance Hassett and Maryanne Kowaleski for encouragement, suggestions, and many other kinds of help. I thank Julia Bagguley, Julia and Simon Boyd, Francis Ryan, and Peter Woods for generous hospitality close to major research libraries. The opportunity to participate in the Strasbourg conferences on the History of Women and Christianity in Europe (1992–8) has been uniquely valuable and I am very grateful to all colleagues involved.

One of my very greatest debts is shared with many other similarly indebted people. Without Felicity Riddy's trenchant, sometimes fearsome, but always energizing interest in one's work, without her profound intellectual and personal generosity, her own brilliant interdisciplinary scholarship and most particularly her model of constructive ways to behave in a system under great stress, not only work but existence as an academic would often have seemed impossible in recent years. Many scholars have been sustained by her personal concern with their work and well-being, while her model of rigorous but inclusive scholarship and the newly alive, inquisitive, non-hierarchical social and institutional matrices she creates for its production have redefined what is possible and what to aim for.

Other supreme debts are acknowledged, with more gratitude than can adequately be expressed here, in the dedication.

Some paragraphs from Chapters 2 and 6 have appeared in 'Re-Routing the Dower: The Anglo-Norman Life of St Audrey by Marie [of Chatteris?]', in Jennifer Carpenter and Sally-Beth MacLean (eds.), *Power of the Weak: Studies on Medieval Women* (Urbana and Chicago: University of Illinois Press, 1995), and several in Chapter 1 have appeared in Sarah Kay and Miri Rubin (eds.), 'Chaste Bodies: Frames and Experiences', in *Framing Medieval Bodies* (Manchester: Manchester University Press, 1994). I thank the publishers for permission to re-use this material. Material from *Reading the Romance: Women, Patriarchy, and Popular Literature* by Janice A. Radway, copyright © 1984, 1991 by the University of North Carolina Press, is used by permission of the publisher. The photographs of Saint Faith in Illustration 1 were taken by Marilyn Deegan as part of the large on-going research project on this saint by Kathleen Ashley and Pamela Sheingorn: I am deeply grateful for the generous readiness of all involved to allow their use for the different purpose to which they are put here. For permission to reproduce part of one of the Becket leaves as Illustration 2, I thank Sir Paul Getty, KBE, Wormsley Library, England, and for permission to reproduce the illustration from London, BL MS Additional 24686, f. 3r on the jacket, I am grateful to the British Library. I have modernized manuscript punctuation and word division for Anglo-Norman and transliterated Early Middle English wherever possible for ease of reading. Translations are my own unless otherwise acknowledged. Original text is quoted wherever possible, but in the interests of space, translations alone are used on occasion.

Contents

Illustrations

Figures

Abbreviations

AA.SS.	*Acta sanctorum quotquot toto orbe coluntur . . .*, ed. J. Bollandus and G. Henschenius, (Antwerp, 1643–); *Acta sanctorum: Editio novissima*, ed. J. Carnandet *et al.* (Paris: Palmé, 1863–)
AB	*Analecta Bollandiana*
AHDLMA	*Archives d'histoire doctrinale et littéraire du Moyen Âge*
ANCL	M. Dominica Legge, *Anglo-Norman in the Cloisters* (Edinburgh: Edinburgh University Press, 1950)
AND	*An Anglo-Norman Dictionary*, ed. Louise W. Stone, William Rothwell *et al.* (London: MHRA, 1977–92)
ANLB	M. Dominica Legge, *Anglo-Norman Literature and its Background* (Oxford: Oxford University Press, 1963; repr. Westport, Conn.: Greenwood Press, 1978)
ANS	*Anglo-Norman Studies*
ANTS	Anglo-Norman Text Society
Bell	David N. Bell, *What Nuns Read: Books and Libraries in Medieval English Nunneries*, Cistercian Studies 158 (Kalamazoo, Mich.: Cistercian Publications, 1995)
BHL	Bibliotheca Hagiographica Latina
Binns	Alison Binns, *Dedications of Monastic Houses in England and Wales 1066–1216* (Woodbridge and Wolfeboro, NH: Boydell Press, 1989)
BL	British Library
BN	Bibliothèque Nationale
CFMA	Les Classiques français du Moyen Âge
CP	*The Complete Peerage* by G. E. Cokayne: revd. edn. V. Gibbs, H. A. Doubleday, Lord Howard de Walden, G. H. White, and R. S. Lea (London: St Catherine's Press, 1963–82)
CPR	Calendar of Patent Rolls
CR	Close Rolls
EETS es	Early English Text Society Extra Series
EETS os	Early English Text Society Original Series
EGM [I]	Nigel J. Morgan, *Early Gothic Manuscripts, i: 1190–1250*, Survey of Manuscripts Illuminated in the British Isles, Part I (London: Harvey Miller, 1982)

EGM [II]	id., *Early Gothic Manuscripts, ii: 1250–85*, Survey of Manuscripts Illuminated in the British Isles, Part II (London: Harvey Miller, 1988)
FMLS	*Forum for Modern Language Studies*
GP	William of Malmesbury, *De gestis pontificum Anglorum libri quinque*, ed. N. E. S. A. Hamilton, RS 52 (London, 1870)
GR	William of Malmesbury, *De gestis regum Anglorum libri quinque*, ed. W. W. Stubbs, 2 vols., RS 90 (London, 1887–9)
HBS	Henry Bradshaw Society
Herbert	*The French Text of the 'Ancrene Riwle': British Museum MS Cotton Vitellius F vii*, ed. J. A. Herbert, EETS os 219 (London, 1944)
HSJ	*Haskins Society Journal*
JEGP	*Journal of English and Germanic Philology*
JMEMS	*Journal of Medieval and Early Modern Studies*
JMH	*Journal of Medieval History*
Jones	'St Richard of Chichester: The Sources for his Life', ed. and tr. David Jones, *Sussex Record Society*, 79 (1995), 83–159
Knowles and Hadcock	D. Knowles and R. N. Hadcock, *Medieval Religious Houses, England and Wales* (2nd edn., London, 1971)
MED	*Middle English Dictionary*, ed. H. Kurath and S. M. Kuhn (Ann Arbor: University of Michigan Press, 1956–)
MHRA	Modern Humanities Research Association
Millett and Wogan-Browne	*Medieval English Prose for Women: Selections from the Katherine Group and Ancrene Wisse*, ed. Bella Millett and Jocelyn Wogan-Browne (Oxford: Oxford University Press, 1990; pbk. 1992)
MLR	*Modern Language Review*
Mon.	*Monasticon Anglicanum*, ed. William Dugdale, rev. J. Caley, H. Ellis, and B. Bandinel (London: Bohn, 1846)
NMS	*Nottingham Medieval Studies*
OE	Old English
PL	*Patrologiae cursus completus . . . series latina*, ed. J.-P. Migne (Paris, various years)
PMLA	*Publications of the Modern Language Association of America*
Rev. bén.	*Revue bénédictine*
RHS	Royal Historical Society
RMS	*Reading Medieval Studies*
RS	Rolls Series
RTAM	*Recherches de théologie ancienne et médiévale*

SATF	Société des anciens textes français
SCH	*Studies in Church History*
SEL	*The South English Legendary*
ST	Aquinas, *Summa Theologiae*
Tolkien	*Ancrene Wisse: MS Corpus Christi College Cambridge 402*, ed. J. R. R. Tolkien, EETS OS 249 (London, 1962)
Trethewey	*The French Text of the 'Ancrene Riwle': Trinity College Cambridge MS R. 14.7*, ed. W. H. Trethewey, EETS OS 240 (London, 1958)
VCH	*Victoria County History of England*
ZRPh	*Zeitschrift für romanische Philologie*

Introduction: Women's Literary Culture in Twelfth- and Thirteenth-Century England

The literary culture of women in earlier medieval England is far from being a mere pre-history for women's writing in the fourteenth and fifteenth centuries. Nor is it simply a poor relation in comparison with Continental women's writing. In twelfth- and thirteenth-century England women's writing is part of a complex, polyglot, and still only partially mapped literary history, in which the shapes and periodizations from the earlier to the later Middle Ages are relatively uncharted. What is clear is that women, whether in secular households or religious communities, engaged in literary activity: they were patrons and dedicatees (sometimes personally engaged in the selection, treatment, or transmission of material); they were audiences, readers, scribes, and copyists, and, not least, composers of texts.[1] Though the class range of women for whose literary culture there is evidence is largely (though not exclusively) confined to gentry, nobility, and urban élite groups, the books and the genres associated with women's literary culture in Anglo-Norman England embrace a wide range.[2] Little

---

[1] On patronage, the major study is Ian Short, 'Patrons and Polyglots: French Literature in Twelfth-Century England', *ANS* 14 (1992), 229–49. On women's patronage see further the works listed in Ch. 1, n. 125: for a general survey of women patrons see Karen K. Jambeck, 'Patterns of Women's Literary Patronage in England, 1200–ca. 1475', in June Hall McCash (ed.), *The Cultural Patronage of Medieval Women* (Athens: University of Georgia Press, 1996), 228–65, and for a revisionist account of the vernacular patronage of the Angevin court see Karen M. Broadhurst, 'Henry II of England and Eleanor of Aquitaine: Patrons of Literature in French?', *Viator*, 27 (1996), 53–84. For examples of female scribes see Pamela Robinson, 'A Twelfth-Century Scriptrix', in P. R. Robinson and Rivkah Zim (eds.), *Of the Making of Books: Medieval Manuscripts, Their Scribes and Readers: Essays Presented to M. B. Parkes* (Aldershot: Scolar Press and Brookfield, Vt.: Ashgate, 1997), 73–93; Duncan Robertson, *The Medieval Saints' Lives: Spiritual Renewal and Old French Literature* (Lexington, Ky.: French Forum, 1995), Appendix. For examples of copying see Bella Millett, '"Women in No Man's Land": English Recluses and the Development of Vernacular Literature in the Twelfth and Thirteenth Centuries', in Carol M. Meale (ed.), *Women and Literature in Britain, 1150–1500* (Cambridge: Cambridge University Press, 1993; 2nd edn. 1996), 86–103 (95).

[2] In addition to vernacular narrative genres such as saints' lives and romance, and the major doctrinal and instructional genres (sermons, treatises, devotional manuals, etc.), genres with examples of female patronage, dedication, and manuscript ownership include letters, lyrics, miracle collections, medical collections, lapidaries, bestiaries, encyclopaedias, apocalypses, biblical paraphrase, biblical commentary, historiography, estates, and other handbooks. See Ruth J. Dean, with the collaboration of Maureen B. M. Boulton, *Anglo-Norman Literature: A Guide to Manuscripts and Texts*, ANTS OP 3 (London, 1999). M. Dominica Legge, *Anglo-Norman in the Cloisters* (Edinburgh: Edinburgh University Press, 1950) and her *Anglo-Norman Literature and its Background* (Oxford: Oxford University Press, 1963; repr. Westport, Conn.: Greenwood Press, 1978) remain the basic literary histories: see also William W. Calin, *The French Tradition and the Literature of Medieval England* (Toronto: University of Toronto Press, 1994).

other than scholastic academic prose is excluded (and that itself was not debarred to the learned and Latinate women of some convents).

Current interest in late medieval women's reading and writing in England is not yet matched by attention to the earlier Middle Ages, partly because modern disciplinary boundaries make the principal language of this literary culture, Anglo-Norman, largely inaudible.[3] But women writers and readers in the England of the twelfth and thirteenth centuries inhabit a polyglot world of at least two languages, so that study of their literary culture must move across modern divisions between French and English. The literary history of women from the late twelfth to the early fourteenth century in England also suffers, as that of the late fourteenth and fifteenth century does not, from the lack of named and known women writers working in English. The one woman writer from this period who is generally known, Marie de France, is usually treated as a 'French Studies' writer.[4] Until very recently she has also been seen principally as a writer of 'secular' courtly literature (her visionary poem, *L'Espurgatoire seint Patrice*, and her collection of short moral tales, the *Fables*, form a good proportion of her extant corpus of some 13,000 lines, but have had less attention). In the context of Anglo-Norman England, Marie de France is but one of several named women writers: she should surely be seen alongside other francophone women writers—and franco- and anglophone female audiences—in insular culture. In spite of all the interdisciplinary thinking characteristic of work on medieval women's writing, it is still hard to hold together across the various linguistic and disciplinary boundaries a literary world in which we can view Marie de France's work alongside the devotional and doctrinal literature produced for and by her contemporaries in England—a world which includes both Marie's *Lais* and the *Guide for Anchoresses* (*Ancrene Wisse*), *L'Espurgatoire seint Patrice* and the Katherine Group.

The genre in which twelfth- and thirteenth-century women writers of Anglo-Norman have left the most substantial records is, as far as we currently know, the saint's life: three hagiographic biographies by women in Anglo-Norman England

[3] 'Anglo-Norman' usually means the French used in speech and literary composition in England from the Conquest until the 14th c. (though in fact French documents are composed in England for much longer in some genres). 'Anglo-Norman' is sometimes internally periodized by references to Norman French (immediately afer the Conquest); Anglo-Norman (the French roughly of the Angevins and the early Plantagenets); Anglo-French (the later medieval French of England). In this book it has often proved clearest to use 'Anglo-Norman' as a global term for French composed at any date in England, just as it has sometimes been necessary to use 'Anglo-Norman' to refer to the whole post-Conquest period. The context makes the particular extent of the term clear in these usages.

[4] David Wallace (ed.), *Cambridge History of Medieval English Literature: Writing in Medieval Britain 1066–1547* (Cambridge: Cambridge University Press, 1999) has, however, provided an important new platform for interdisciplinary work: see especially Susan Crane, 'Anglo-Norman Cultures in England, 1066–1460', 35–60. For Marie de France, see Glyn S. Burgess, *Marie de France: An Analytical Bibliography* (London: Grant and Cutler, 1977; *Supplement* No. 1, 1986; *Supplement* No. 2, 1997).

add a further 17,000 lines to the 13,000 lines known to have been written by Marie de France. Many more saints' lives were written for and owned, heard, or read, or, in the case of some anonymous works, possibly composed, by women: saints were also prayed to and culted in a range of ways that leave further records in women's books, such as the illuminations and the suffrages and other prayers of psalters and books of hours. Beyond these sources again there is much evidence from material culture testifying to women as patrons, devotees, and clients of saints, whether in shrine pilgrimage, the cult of relics, or in the dedications and iconography of church and convent foundations.

The present book focuses mainly on vernacular hagiography, principally in its textual manifestations. Together with saints' lives and their importance for women, a primary concern is the pervasiveness of virginity as a cultural ideal and a form of exemplary biography for women. Treatises on how to become a consecrated virgin are nearly as old as Christianity itself, and virgins and the life of consecrated virginity are highly authorized both in the sense of being prestigious and being much written about. Throughout the medieval centuries, a patristic corpus of letters and treatises on virginity by St Jerome and others was repeatedly drawn on to authorize new virginity letters and guides to various kinds of holy lives for women. In medieval England, these exist in English and French as well as Latin. For its clerical writers, this virginity literature offers in many ways a liberatingly unofficial writing-space where professional knowledge is informally deployed—often (especially in the later Middle Ages) in a different language from the Latin of clerical institutional identity. But the politics of writing and authority are complex here, not a straight top-down mediation of Latin authority to vernacular ignorance. What is phrased as learned response to female requests for information and guidance may well dignify clerics, chaplains, and confessors writing on command for women patrons as authoritative interpreters and mediators of texts. The textual construction of authorized virginity has frequently conferred authority on its producers, but it provides for an audience whose requirements and responses also leave their mark.

In addition to its treatises, letters, and rules for living, virginity has a major narrative form in the virgin saint's life. The hagiographic genre of the virgin martyr passion extends through two millennia, in Latin and all the European vernaculars. It is a, perhaps *the*, major Western form of representing women.[5]

---

[5] As the *Corriere della Sera* (25 Apr. 1994, p. 14) remarked of the beatification of Gianna Berretta Molla (a doctor who had died in 1962 at the age of 39 rather than accept the risk to the foetus she was then carrying of a cancer operation): 'It has never come about that the husband and children should be present at a woman's beatification. There have always been other extraordinary cases: in 1947 at the beatification of Maria Goretti the mother was present, in 1982 at the canonization of Maximilian Kolbe there was present the man he had saved from death. But husbands and wives have never been present because married saints are still a rarity.' As Anneke Mulder-Bakker points out, in the Middle Ages, 'saints who were mothers . . . were honoured . . . despite rather than because of their children' (Anneke B. Mulder-Bakker (ed.), *Sanctity and Motherhood: Essays on Holy Mothers in the Middle Ages* (New York: Garland, 1995), 3–30 (4, see also 9)). In medieval

One of the earliest virgins to be recognized by the church is the fourth-century Roman Agnes, martyred at the age of 12; one of the latest is Maria Goretti of Ancona (1890–1902, canonized 1950): in between these two figures there is no European language without its versions of the virgins of the universal church and its own examples of virgin saints. Similarly the literary career of a virgin saint's *passio* (usually represented as occurring in the persecutions of the early Christian centuries) frequently extends from early medieval Latin rewriting (often incorporating traces of earlier Greek as well as Latin sources) to further eleventh- and twelfth-century Latin and vernacular versions; to incorporation in the most influential of all legendaries, the late thirteenth-century *Legenda aurea* by Jacobus de Voragine, Archbishop of Genoa (d. 1298); to a continuing career, in insular culture, in late medieval vernacular versions by Caxton and others, and (with some gaps in England's post-Reformation culture) on into the late sixteenth-century virgin martyr lives by Lady Falkland, the seventeenth-century female legendary of Robert Buckland, the work of Alban Butler, and the retellings by Mrs Jameson, Sabine Baring-Gould, and Agnes Dunbar (whose 1904 *Dictionary of Saintly Women* remains an impressive work).[6]

To its medieval audiences, virginity literature seems to have offered versions of autonomy—of a kind. Virginity texts announce themselves as seeking to

Britain, women saints are underrepresented as compared with male saints, and among women saints virgin martyrs are overrepresented: thus, for instance, as in the earliest manuscript of the *South English Legendary* [henceforth *SEL*] (London, BL, MS Laud 108, late 13th c.), so in its latest and most comprehensive (Oxford, Bodleian Library MS Bodley 779, 15th c.): 135 items include 21 lives of women, among which, counting the 'elleue þousend uirginis' as one item, there are 11 virgin martyrs, 2 repentant harlots, 6 British abbesses, one housewife/hostess (Martha), and the Virgin's mother Anne.

[6] For later medieval lives and legendaries in English see Charlotte d'Evelyn and Frances A. Foster, 'Saints' Legends' in *Manual of the Writings in Middle English 1050–1500*, gen. ed. Albert E. Hartung (New Haven: Connecticut Academy of Arts and Sciences, 1970), ii. 410–57; 553–649: for a recent edition of a late medieval legendary, see *The Kalendre of the Newe Legende of Englande Edited from Pynson's Printed Edition of 1516*, ed. Manfred Görlach, Middle English Texts 27 (Heidelberg: Carl Winter, 1994): see also Görlach's study, *Middle English Saints' Lives* (Tübingen: Francke, 1998). Literary histories of medieval hagiography in English with further detail are Theodor Wolpers, *Die englische Heiligenlegende des Mittelalters: eine Formengeschichte des Legendenerzählen von der spätantiken lateinischen Tradition bis zur Mitte des 16 Jahrhunderts* (Tübingen: Niemeyer, 1964) and G. H. Gerould, *Saints' Legends* (Boston and New York: Houghton Mifflin, 1916). Karen Winstead has recently treated virgin martyr lives: see her *Virgin Martyrs: Legends of Sainthood in Late Medieval England* (Ithaca: Cornell University Press, 1997). For Lady Falkland (1585–1639) see Joseph Gillow, *Bibliographical Dictionary of the English Catholics* (London: Burns and Oates, 1885–1902), ii, Additions and Corrections, pp. ix–xiv. For Buckland, see *Lives of Women Saints of Our Contrie of Englond, (c.1610–1615)*, ed. Carl Horstmann, EETS os 86 (London, 1886). *Lives of the Saints* by Alban Butler (1711–73) is edited by Herbert Thurston and Donald Attwater (Westminster: Christian Classics, 1956): Anna Jameson's retellings are collected in her *Sacred and Legendary Art*, 2 vols. (London, 1848; Boston and New York, 3rd edn.: Houghton Mifflin, 1857). In addition to his studies of Celtic and Cornish saints, the Revd Sabine Baring-Gould produced a female legendary, *Virgin Saints and Martyrs* (London: Hutchinson, 1900); more comprehensive is Agnes B. C. Dunbar, *Dictionary of Saintly Women*, 2 vols. (London: G. Bell, 1904–5).

sustain professed and vowed women with a romance script where the virgin is not only the object of quest, but in part the subject, the active selector of her bridegroom, Christ. This incontestably superior and self-chosen marriage is also offered as aristocratic freedom from drudgery: as, for example, a life which includes authorized spaces for reading and contemplation. The virgin is none the less potentially recontained: if she combats the earthly patriarchy's demands for her marriage and child-bearing, it is in order to enter into spiritual patriarchal marriage with a top-ranking bridegroom and a truly omnipotent Father and Lord. For defying her pagan father, suitor, judge, or governor and his pagan gods, the virgin martyr is tortured, dismembered, and finally executed before she proceeds triumphantly to her Christ bridegroom in heaven. Death and transcendence take the role of marriage in romance closure here, while torture and execution greet the virgin's eloquent resistance. The romance of virginity is thus in complex relation with its constructed and historical audiences. For issues of representation, violence, autonomy, and recontainment in the history of romance and women's reading of it, virgin martyr narratives offer both an important field in themselves, and pertinent comparisons with many other genres—not only with chivalric romance and the novel, but, for instance, Harlequin (Mills and Boon) romances and slasher movies. A further, valuable complication is that, like these other genres, medieval virginity literature was written not only for, but in some cases by, women (some of the earliest uses of the medieval term for courtly love, fin'amor, for instance, are to be found in a twelfth-century virgin saint's life written by a woman in England, suggesting that a rather different account of this term could be given from that of much twentieth-century discussion of medieval chivalric romance).[7]

The thematics of *passio* can seem depressing, part of a powerful patriarchal metanarrative about women in which death thematizes the principal nexus of the maiden to European conventions of representation. If this is the case, matters are perhaps not much helped when women themselves engage with this genre. Yet, as will be exemplified in the chapters following, the pervasiveness of a representational code is a different matter from the politics and possibilities of its particular instantiations. What looks potentially dreary or appalling at the aerial-survey level of genre-history takes on life, multiplicity, and nuance at the level of particular texts in their context. The virgin life and its narrative representation constitute an arena where the relation between the genre and its realizations is surprisingly various and flexible.

There are interesting gaps between the texts owned by women and the wider cultural prominence of virginity among monastic and clerical writers. Although many individual lives of virgin saints make the virgin the heroine of a spiritual nuptial romance, very few collections of lives focus on this without further

---

[7] See William MacBain, 'Some Religious and Secular Uses of the Vocabulary of *fin'amor* in the Early Decades of the Northern French Narrative Poem', *French Forum*, 13 (1988), 261–76.

inflection. The exception is one of the saints' lives collections best known today, the Early Middle English Katherine Group. This was compiled, in association with *Ancrene Wisse*, the *Guide for Anchoresses*, in the early thirteenth century in the West Midlands for anchoritic and other groups of women in religious lives.[8] It is a specialized miniature female legendary consisting only of three semi-legendary virgin martyrs of the universal church, Katherine, Juliana, and Margaret, each life closely aligned with the others in terms of its structure and motifs, in a compilation designed for the spiritually demanding anchoritic life. No other legendary in twelfth- or thirteenth-century England so intensively presents the female saint as virgin martyr and romance heroine.[9]

Though deservedly given much attention in anglophone scholarship for its remarkable linguistic and literary properties, the Katherine Group is atypical in the context of women's post-Conquest ownership of saints' lives, where a large proportion of texts are of Anglo-Norman composition or are Anglo-Norman copies of Continental French texts. Not only the predominance of English texts in the Katherine Group manuscripts but the exclusivity with which they present female sanctity as virgin martyrdom is almost without parallel. Most collections were more varied: most women readers and female audiences had several kinds of saints in their manuscript collections, to say nothing of their psalters and books of hours. The three Anglo-Norman saints' lives known to be by women (all women within or associated with female communities) are all, like the Katherine Group, about virgin saints, but exemplify a much wider range in the ideal of virgin sanctity. One is Clemence of Barking's life of the virgin martyr and patron saint of learning, St Catherine of Alexandria; the other two are an anonymous life of Edward the Confessor as a virgin king, and a life of St Audrey (Latin: Etheldreda) of Ely, twice-married queen and abbess as well as virgin. Unlike the Katherine Group manuscripts, none of the books in which these Anglo-Norman lives appear contains only virgin martyrs as its saints.

The largest extant compilation of Anglo-Norman lives known to have been owned by a female community, and a major focus of interest in the present book, is a manuscript from the Augustinian priory of Campsey (founded 1195), in Suffolk. This nunnery was among the richest in the diocese of Norfolk. The manuscript

---

[8] For the history of scholarship on these texts see Bella Millett, '*Ancrene Wisse*', *the Katherine Group and the Wooing Group: A Bibliographical Guide*, Annotated Bibliographies of Old and Middle English Literature ii, gen. ed. T. L. Burton (Cambridge: Brewer, 1996), 5–45.

[9] For a good characterization of the specialized quality of these lives, see Anne Savage, 'The Solitary Heroine: Aspects of Meditation and Mysticism in *Ancrene Wisse*, the Katherine Group and the Wooing Group', in W. Pollard and R. Boenig (eds.), *Mysticism and Spirituality in Medieval England* (Woodbridge and Rochester, NY: Brewer, 1997), 63–84, and for an argument for the fluidity and polysemy of these texts in their construction of virginity, see Sarah Salih, 'Performing Virginity: Sex and Violence in the Katherine Group', in Cindy L. Carlson and Angela Jane Weisl (eds.), *Constructions of Widowhood and Virginity in the Middle Ages* (New York: St Martin's Press, 1999), 95–112.

is late thirteenth century and was certainly at Campsey by the early fourteenth century, when the earlier of two ownership inscriptions declares it to have been given for use in meal-time reading, and when three further Anglo-Norman lives were added to its collection.[10] The Campsey manuscript includes texts of all the hagiographic works currently known to have been composed by women, was very possibly commissioned by a noblewoman, Isabella, Countess of Arundel, and certainly contains saints' lives of individual and collective female patronage.[11] Unlike the *South English Legendary* (the largest thirteenth-century collection of Middle English metrical legends, extant in various recensions from the late thirteenth to the late fifteenth century), it does not represent a legendary based on the church calendar. Nor is it a collection focused on the convent's own particular dedication, since this was to the Virgin.[12] Virgin martyrs figure, but do not dominate, in the Campsey book: only one (Catherine) is a virgin martyr of the universal church after the pattern exemplified in the Katherine Group: the second (Faith) is almost a local virgin martyr, since she represents a version of *passio* from south-central France which is here further translated to the insular, indeed specifically East Anglian, cult of this figure. Also included in the manuscript's thirteenth-century section are the lives of three British abbesses (all virgins, though two are married and one a martyr), two post-Conquest English archbishops (one a martyr) and one bishop, and one Anglo-Saxon king. The only remaining non-native saint is a repentant harlot, the Magdalen, who again has a cult thoroughly translated into north-west Europe, and one that represents her as the member of a holy household or family group. The early

[10] London, BL, MS Addit. 70513 (*olim* MS Welbeck I.C.1.), f. 265va: 'ce livre deviseie [est] ala priorie de kanpseie de lire amengier' (inscription of gift). There is a later inscription of ownership on f. 1r, 'Cest liuere est a couent de campisse'. This is a bookhand inscription similar to that in another Campsey manuscript, a psalter now Cambridge University Library MS Addit. 7220, f. 2r, 'Cest livere est al couent de campisse', also a 14th-c. inscription added to a 13th-c book. The names of Edmund of Canterbury and Modwenna of Burton, two saints represented in the Campsey saints' lives collection in MS Addit. 70513, have been added into the calendar of this psalter on f. 4r and f. 5r respectively. For Campsey's books see David N. Bell, *What Nuns Read: Books and Libraries in Medieval English Nunneries*, Cistercian Studies Series 158 (Kalamazoo, Mich.: Cistercian Publications, 1995), s.v. Campsey, and Alexandra Barratt, 'Books for Nuns: Cambridge University Library MS Additional 3042', *Notes and Queries*, NS 45 (Sept. 1997), 310–19. A valuable study of women's houses in the later Middle Ages including Campsey is Marilyn Oliva, *The Convent and the Community in Late Medieval England: Female Monasteries in the Diocese of Norwich, 1350–1540*, Studies in the History of Medieval Religion 12 (Woodbridge and Rochester NY: Boydell Press, 1998): see 69 for continuing bequests of French books to Campsey in the later Middle Ages.

[11] On the manuscript see the important forthcoming study by D. W. Russell, who combines the distribution of the manuscript's illuminated capitals and other codicological data with the historical dates of its saints to argue for the thematics of its arrangement. I was privileged to hear a version of this study (given at the Anglo-Norman Colloquium, St Peter's College, Oxford, April 1998, where I was myself discussing the Countess of Arundel as a possible patron of the manuscript), and while we differ on whether and how the manuscript can be read thematically, I remain indebted to him for shared information and discussion.

[12] *VCH, Suffolk* ii. 121.

Fig. 1. Types of saints in the Campsey Manuscript (in order of occurrence in the manuscript)

Saint	Activities and modern categorizations	Commemorations	MS term for saint and biography
(early 14th c. texts)			
Elisabeth, Elisabeth of Hungary	biological mother, ascetic, charity worker (1207–31)	canonized 1235, feast 17 (19) Nov.	'seynte' 'vie'
Panuce, Paphnutius	desert father (?4th c.)	none	'seynt' none
Paule le hermite	first hermit, desert father (d. c.345)	feast 10 Jan.	'seint' 'vie'
(late 13th c. texts)			
Thomas de Cantorbéry, Thomas Becket	Archbishop of Canterbury (1162–70), martyred Dec. 1170	canonized 1173, feast 29 Dec., translation 7 July	'saint' 'vie'
Marie Magdalene	1st c., cult at Vézelay from 11th c.	feast 22 July, translation 4 May	'sainte' 'romanz'
Edward, Edward the Confessor	Anglo-Saxon king (1003–66)	feast 5 Jan., translation 13 Oct.	'saint . . . rei' 'romanz'
Eadmund, Edmund of Canterbury	Archbishop of Canterbury (1233–40)	canonized 1246, feast 16 Nov., trans. 9 June	'confessur arcevesque' 'vie'
Audree, Etheldreda of Ely	Anglo-Saxon widowed princess abbess (d. 679)	feast 23 June, translation 17 Oct.	'noneyne' 'vie'
Osith of Chich, Aylesbury, Hereford	semi-legendary Anglo-Saxon married princess abbess (d. ?c.700)	feast 7 October, multiple translations	'virge e martire' 'vie'
Fey, Faith of Agen and Conques	semi-legendary young girl, culted from 11th c. at Horsham	feast 6 Oct., translation 14 Jan.	'virgine e martire' 'vie'
Modwenne, Modwenna of Britain	semi-legendary Irish princess abbess (?7th c.), culted at Burton, 12th c.	feast 6 July	'noneyne' 'le romanz de la vie'
Richard evesque de Cycestre	Bishop of Chichester (1244–53)	canonized 1262, feast 3 April, translation 16 June	'seint . . . evesque' 'vie'
Katerine Catherine of Alexandria	semi-legendary virgin (?4th c.)	feast 25 Nov.	'sainte' 'vie'

fourteenth-century lives added to the manuscript (all by the Franciscan, Bozon) comprise two desert fathers, and one contemporary married woman saint (see Figure 1). The categories of saint unrepresented here, but elsewhere available in vernacular lives, are apostles, male martyrs, popes, hermits, abbots, and male child saints.[13] Some of the Campsey lives are unique survivals but none are holographs: all the texts must have been elsewhere represented and some are still extant in manuscripts other than the Campsey book. The manuscript, that is, represents a significant selection—about half—of the kinds of saints' lives available in Anglo-Norman England, chosen from a broad typological and diachronic range, though its ensemble is at the same time distinctive and focused. It is strongly, but not exclusively, concerned with saints culted in East Anglia, and has many ties and interconnections with East Anglian and Essex communities.[14] It has possible precedents and possible imitators (though none with so many saints in such a specific combination).[15]

[13] For editions of texts in the Campsey manuscript, see the Bibliography of Primary Sources under the names of the saints tabulated in Figure 1. Approximately 60 Anglo-Norman verse saints' lives from the late 12th to the 14th c. are extant: see M. Thiry-Stassin, 'L'Hagiographie en Anglo-Normand', in Guy Philippart (ed.), *Hagiographies*, Histoire internationale de la littérature hagiographique latine et vernaculaire en Occident des origines à 1550, I (Turnhout: Brepols, 1994), 407–28; Jocelyn Wogan-Browne, ' "Clerc u lai, muïne u dame": Women and Anglo-Norman Hagiography in the Twelfth and Thirteenth Centuries', in Meale (ed.), *Women and Literature in Britain 1150–1500*, 61–85, with a bibliographical list at n. 4 (75–8); for a prose legendary, see *Le Légendier apostolique anglo-normand*, ed. D. W. Russell (Montréal: Presses de l'Université de Montréal, 1989); Dean and Boulton, *Anglo-Norman Literature* give detailed listings of Anglo-Norman lives and manuscripts. The list by Paul Meyer ('Légendes hagiographiques en français', *Histoire Littéraire de la France*, Académie des Inscriptions et Belles Lettres (Paris: Imprimerie Nationale, 1906), xxxiii. 328–458) includes Continental lives and prose legendaries. For Middle English vernacular lives see d'Evelyn and Foster, 'Saints' Legends'. Numbers are approximate because boundary criteria for lives are not firm: I have not for instance here counted stories of holy figures in Anglo-Norman Marian miracle collections; others would not include, for instance, Brendan, as a saint's life *strictu sensu*. Numbers of saints are not a guide to numbers of lives: St Margaret for instance has 8 extant distinct Anglo-Norman lives, St Modwenna one.

[14] Most Anglo-Norman manuscripts of saints' lives are anthologies mixing hagiography, biblical narrative, devotional treatises, etc., as, for example, in the two 13th-c. manuscripts in which the *Vie de Saint Laurent* is extant, London, BL, MS Egerton 2710 (owned by nuns: see Bell, s.v. Derby) and Paris, BN f. fr. 19525. For descriptions see *La Vie de saint Laurent: An Anglo-Norman Poem of the Twelfth Century*, ed. D. W. Russell, ANTS 34 (London, 1976), 1–6: on the probable Oxford origin of the second manuscript in association with William de Brailes, see François Avril and Patricia Stirneman, *Manuscrits enluminés d'origine insulaire viie–xxe siècle* (Paris: Bibliothèque Nationale, 1987), no. 107, p. 67, and for a de Brailes psalter for a female parishioner of St Lawrence, Oxford, see Claire Donovan, *The de Brailes Hours: Shaping the Book of Hours in Thirteenth-Century Oxford* (London: British Library, 1991). Even considered as an exclusively hagiographic collection, Campsey retains its distinctiveness. If an East Anglian book, it is striking for *not* including a life of the Anglo-Saxon Edmund king and martyr, whose cult centre was at Bury (Campsey's Edmund Life concerns the 13th-c. archbishop of Canterbury): it offers, rather, a beheaded female Anglo-Saxon royal saint in the figure of St Osith (see Ch. 2.1 below and *passim*). The manuscript's 13th-c. inclusions concentrate on female saints and lives of contemporary medieval churchmen of direct interest to particular women and female communities. For more detail on the affiliations of individual Campsey texts and the communities represented in and by them, see Ch. 5.1 below.

[15] Campsey perhaps has a Latin precedent in an early to mid 12th-c. collection of *vitae* owned and possibly produced by Barking (Cardiff, Public Library MS 1.381, ff. 81–146: see N. R. Ker, *Medieval Manuscripts in British Libraries*, ii (Oxford: Clarendon Press, 1977), 348–9). Here, two Barking foundress biographies (Ethelburga and Hildelitha) are joined by lives of Edward, king and

With virgin martyr *passio* but one among its range of hagiographic genres, this manuscript contextualizes the Katherine Group's romanced use of saints' lives prescribed for the reading of women in religious lives. Only three of Campsey's saints are not British: it most frequently represents saints of insular and often specific regional significance. The bulk of the manuscript is concerned with figures who belong to insular historiography as well as to hagiography. Especially in its context of Anglo-Norman traditions of women's patronage, commissioning, and composition, the Campsey manuscript is testimony to the range with which Anglo-Norman women themselves used saints' lives: as exemplary biography (both of women and the clerical men associated with them), as historiography, as devotional and theological meditation and argument, as a way of representing their communities, and, arguably, of mapping their time and place, specifically East Anglian and Essex, but also north-west European as it was, through images of élite figures in British and international European culture.

The manuscript is specially important in that its texts link the two major female communities of Barking and Campsey, through the inclusion, in late thirteenth-century copies in the Campsey book, of the vernacular texts composed by women at Barking, or supported by the abbess and community there, in the twelfth century. The Campsey book thus contains several layers of women's texts: thirteenth-century copies of earlier lives composed by women (Catherine, Edward), together with a thirteenth-century life of female composition (Audrey); a thirteenth-century copy of a text given patronage by twelfth-century female religious (Thomas Becket); late thirteenth-century lives associated with a noblewoman patron (Edmund of Canterbury, Richard of Chichester); and early fourteenth-century lives added while the manuscript was in the possession of a female community (Paul, Paphnutius, Elisabeth of Hungary). The remaining texts in the manuscript, although so far lacking known connections with specific women patrons or female communities other than Campsey, are of significant insular or European female figures: Osith, Modwenna, Faith, and the Magdalen. From

martyr, Goscelin's life of Edith of Wilton, Ricemarch's David of Wales, Hildebert of Lavardin's metrical life of Mary of Egypt, and the life of St Ebrulfus. The Cardiff manuscript thus combines lives of abbesses, an Anglo-Saxon king, male ecclesiastical saints, a repentant harlot, and, in the shape of St Ebrulfus [Evroul], a married layman whose wife entered a nunnery while he himself became an eremitic saint. The Campsey manuscript includes some Latin (for instance, a Latin quotation rubricated in the life of Edmund of Canterbury, f. 95rb, a Latin closing prayer retained in its life of Modwenna, f. 222ra), but its vernacular lives function (as I shall be arguing in this book) in specific ways centred in a primarily vernacular (though polyglot and Latin-aware) literary culture (and distinctive in further ways, as suggested in n. 14 above). A collection which shares something of Campsey's interests is the principal manuscript of Bozon's saints' lives, London, BL, MS Cotton Domitian A. XI (early 14th c.): the manuscript contains Denis Piramus's life of Edmund (Anglo-Saxon king and martyr); Guernes de Pont-Ste-Maxence's Becket (leading churchman and martyr); Bozon's six virgin martyr lives and his three 'honorary virgin' saints (see further Ch. 4.2 below); a Gospel *catena* (*Le evangel translaté*), and narratives from Herman de Valenciennes' '*Bible*'. Since the manuscript is an anthology of different genres in the manner of those mentioned in n. 14 above, and since it has a proportionately large concentration of saints of the universal church, this compilation is only partially reminiscent of Campsey: it also throws that manuscript's distinctiveness into further relief.

the texts of Benedictine Barking in the twelfth century to the reading of Campsey's late thirteenth-century Augustinian canonesses to the Franciscan additions to the manuscript at the turn of the thirteenth and fourteenth centuries, the Campsey book constitutes an important representation of women's conventual literary culture for the entire period.

But the selection of saints in the Campsey manuscript has a further significance in that it embodies overlaps in lay and professed female reading also found in many more kinds of books and texts in the post-Conquest centuries.[16] In this respect, women's literary culture of the twelfth and thirteenth centuries shows significant parallels with that of the fourteenth and fifteenth centuries. Although women's reading often has an institutional context, it is not necessarily part of 'official' institutional culture: coded as informal and personal, texts produced for women have a different history from standard monastic texts, even, in fact especially, when they are texts of specific religious obligation or regulation. Their matrix has frequently to be traced in the personal ties and family and social networks important both outside and within female communities. Like the networks of book-ownership, reading, audition, and composition currently being explored for later medieval English women, women's writing in the earlier period can in part be thought of as a 'female subculture', though, given the rank and power of the noblewomen around whom most of what we can so far identify as evidence clusters, it is a subculture with overlaps and shared interests with ecclesiastical and lay seigneurial culture.[17]

[16] Even if Isabella of Arundel, texts of whose patronage are included in the manuscript, had become a vowess (see further Ch. 5.1 below), she would still exemplify the category of semi-religious important in later medieval female reading communities, and the presence of her saints in the manuscript, as of others common to professed and secular reading (Becket, the Magdalen, Catherine) would still testify to the overlap of professed and laywomen's interests (see Ch. 5.1 and Ch. 5 n. 55 below). Many other manuscripts without specific provenance compile texts which elsewhere occur in both nunnery and secular manuscripts: for example, the 13th-c. compilation in Cambridge, University Library Ee.6.11 places a life of St Margaret alongside Marie de France's *Espurgatoire St Patrice* and her 'Aesop' of beast fables, making a collection which could be assigned on grounds of content alone to either milieu. In Paris, BN, nouv. acq. fr. 4503, hagiographic texts of nunnery reading (*Vie de ste Catherine*, *Vie st Alexis*) are compiled with the Anglo-Norman *Brendan*, dedicated to Henry II's queen.

[17] For the term 'female sub-culture', see Felicity Riddy, ' "Women talking about the things of God": A Late Medieval Female Sub-Culture', in Meale (ed.), *Women and Literature*, 104–27. The valuable deployment of the term in this article has inspired much further work. However, the term is both useful and in need of careful negotiation. Even among women hearing and reading in the vernacular(s) alone, participation in female sub-culture(s) does not exclude, and often coexists with, participation in a dominant culture: a gentrywoman reading devotional texts with her relatives and servants may also hear romances and chançuns in mixed audiences in her hall. Similarly 'women's literary culture' is a slippery category: manuscripts and texts made for women were read by men; only in some kinds of reading and social contexts were women segregated; texts not specially directed to women might be read or heard by them, and so on. Some women were Latinate: 'women's literary culture' is not coterminous with vernacular literary culture. (Much Anglo-Norman vernacular literature is indeed written for men, and not only for laymen: there are vernacular texts in too many monastic manuscripts for these texts not to have been used and demanded by male religious, whether for pastoral purposes or to supplement their own varying competences in Latin, or for novice reading.)

The history of women's engagement with saints' lives and the ideals inculcated in them has, then, as with other genres of text, to be sought in the books, texts, and other traces of a broad, loosely defined literary culture which includes both female communities and the laywomen who were so often, in the twelfth and thirteenth centuries, their foundresses and patrons or who shared family and other ties with them. While it is unfortunately not possible to be completely precise about the patronage and production of the Campsey book in the current state of our knowledge, the manuscript combines some features importantly suggestive for the nature of this literary culture. On the one hand Campsey's choice of saints conforms to no discernible schematic principle of selection or of reading across the manuscript's texts, while, on the other, many of its texts have specific origins in particular East Anglian and Essex communities and interests or associations with particular women. Some categories of particular interest are evident in the manuscript (for example, female saints, with special attention to abbesses and to preaching saints, and churchmen saints of high status both at court and as ascetics), but particular selections are most likely to have been produced by contingent factors of affiliation and interests. Rather than a scheme *for* women's reading, the manuscript seems more likely to represent texts *of* women's reading in a series of choices by a particular woman or women made within specific seigneurial, family, monastic, and ecclesiastical networks. Many other kinds of text collections exist within twelfth- and thirteenth-century women's literary culture, but the Campsey manuscript is particularly suggestive for the complexities of mapping women's agency in medieval literary history.

As far as the question of the languages of twelfth- and thirteenth-century saints' lives and virginity treatises is concerned, this book deals with the issue by trying to ignore it. By this I mean that as far as possible, the presuppositions of monoglot literary histories and of histories ranking the vernacular as derivative from Latin are consciously evaded, and texts are simply dealt with according to their prominence for women readers.[18] Thus the *Guide for Anchoresses,*

---

[18] Even as she excavated huge riches of principally English and also French vernacular evidence from nunneries in England, Eileen Power, their great later medieval historian, saw their history as one of decline and fall toward the Dissolution and away from earlier, higher levels of Latinity. In this view, relatively well-equipped Anglo-Saxon nunneries, technically *litteratae* because of their ability to work in Latin, give way to nunneries with mixtures of French, English, and ever less Latin and ever more dissoluteness (*Medieval English Nunneries c.1275–1535,* Cambridge: Cambridge University Press, 1922). Sally Thompson's recent fundamental work on post-Conquest female foundations still does not fully allow in its framing assumptions for how much the relative informality and liminality of female communities escapes conventional records (though its scrupulous documentation allows this to emerge: see *Women Religious: The Founding of English Nunneries After the Norman Conquest,* Oxford: Clarendon Press, 1991). Historiographical gloom is reinforced by a venerable tradition of moralizing women's history that dates back beyond the antiquarian accounts of the 16th and 17th c. to the 14th-c. bishops' registers and 12th- and 13th-c. letters and treatises of direction. Exceptionally, scandals occurred in enclosed female communities as in male houses, but the ecclesiastical historiography of medieval female communities speaks more loudly of the anxieties and the vested interests of those who found it necessary to control or to 'reform'

a text given relatively intense critical attention in its English versions, is here usually quoted in Anglo-Norman.[19] Thirteenth-century English versions of this text were undeniably important to women: but it is also a text with a significant Anglo-Norman career, and a text that was still being exchanged in French by women in fifteenth-century England.[20] Earlier twentieth-century desire for nationalizing linguistic origins (so glowingly pursued by the *Ancrene Wisse* and Katherine Group scholars Tolkien and Chambers) is still strong in our sense of how post-Conquest texts mean. Gayle Margherita's brilliant and provocative book, *Desire for Origins*, has recently refocused a usefully politicized attention on the question of what it might mean for the Katherine Group saints' lives to be in English, but, even here, the tracing of possible horizons of desire is conducted as if medieval culture were monoglot.[21] If we ask who in thirteenth-century England might have required the Katherine Group to be in English, one immediate answer is not Tolkien's heroically surviving West Midlands squirearchy of English speakers (who, according to Tolkien, show that the language could still be a gentleman though conquered), but, rather, speakers of French.[22] On the analogy of the contemporary *Brut* by Laȝamon—with its telling allusion to Queen Eleanor (of Aquitaine? or even, perhaps, to Eleanor of Provence, wife of Henry III, the extant *Brut* manuscripts being no earlier than the mid-thirteenth century); its self-proclaimed pedigree from Bede and 'Albin' as well as from Wace's Anglo-Norman *Brut*; and the *faux* archaizing of its language in its Caligula manuscript version—the people most anxious to assert English origins and continuities were the Anglo-Normans.[23]

nunneries than of these communities as experienced by the women within and associated with them. As John Tillotson points out, the surge in recorded disciplinary offences in nunneries after Boniface's notorious 'Periculoso . . .' bull of 1298 attempted to reinforce enclosure is partly a matter of the attention drawn to nunneries by the bull and of changing bureaucratic practices associated with this ('Visitation and Reform of the Yorkshire Nunneries in the Fourteenth Century', *Northern History*, 30 (1994), 1–21, 9–10).

[19] The earlier Anglo-Norman version in London, BL, MS Cotton Vitellius F VII is preferred (*The French Text of the 'Ancrene Riwle'*, ed. J. A. Herbert, EETS os 219, London, 1944): the later version in Cambridge, Trinity College MS R.14.7 (*The French Text of the 'Ancrene Riwle'*, ed. W. H. Trethewey, EETS os 240, London, 1958) is used where Vitellius is not running.

[20] MS Cotton Vitellius F VII (14th-c.) was given by Joan of Kent (wife of the eighth earl) to Eleanor Cobham, Duchess of Gloucester, between 1433 and 1441 (see Herbert, *French Text*, xii–xiii; H. Emily Allen, 'Eleanor Cobham', *Times Literary Supplement*, 22 Mar. 1934, 214). This late manuscript of the earlier Anglo-Norman version specifies French reading where the early English versions specify French or English (see Ch. 1 below, n. 50). For a possible use of French texts of *Ancrene Wisse* even by those involved in transmitting or borrowing from English versions, see F. N. M. Diekstra, 'Some Fifteenth-Century Borrowings from the *Ancrene Wisse*', *English Studies*, 71 (1990), 81–104 (98).

[21] Gayle Margherita, *The Romance of Origins: Language and Sexual Difference in Middle English Literature* (Philadelphia: University of Pennsylvania Press, 1994), 43–61.

[22] J. R. R. Tolkien, '*Ancrene Wisse* and *Hali Meiðhad*', *Essays and Studies*, 14 (1929), 104–26 (106).

[23] For the possibility of Laȝamon as an Anglo-Normanizing reviser of his own work, see Christopher Cannon, 'The Style and Authorship of the Otho Revision of Laȝamon's *Brut*',

The Katherine Group cannot be derived either from Ælfric's or Wulfstan's late Old English alliterative prose, nor from Old English verse: Bella Millett, who has done most to clarify this situation, has suggested that they are as likely to have synchronic connections with the contemporary early Middle English alliterative verse of the Harley lyrics.[24] On all counts they are written in a koiné of, and designed for, their own time, a koiné whose business it partly was to suggest their traditionality (the kind of linguistic strategy one might expect from, say, a Paris-trained cleric back in England, anxious to provide newly translated texts with a local pedigree). And while the style of the Katherine Group does not derive from French models (and very consciously evokes English registers), French models may well have suggested the choice of text for translation, models such as, for instance, the *Vie sainte Juliane*, perhaps composed in Liège, and certainly in circulation with a popular Anglo-Norman Judgement Day text.[25] The Royal manuscript, one of the only two we have that contains all three texts in the Katherine Group and possibly the earliest surviving manuscript of them, introduces its lives of Juliana and Margaret by announcing 'Her cumseð þe *uie* of seinte iuliane . . . ant telleð of liflade', and by asking its audience to 'Her [hear] seinte marherete *uie* þe meiden + *martir.* her' (London, British Library, MS Royal 17 A xxvii, ff. 37r, 56r, italics mine). The generic name for the texts of

Medium Ævum, 62 (1993), 187–209 (203–4). For a further example (from Thomas of Kent), see Ian Short, '*Tam Angli quam Franci*': Self-Definition in Anglo-Norman England', *ANS* 18 (1996), 153–75 (155–6). The point has been demonstrated for post-Conquest saints' lives by Susan J. Ridyard, *The Royal Saints of Anglo-Saxon England: A Study of West Saxon and East Anglian Cults* (Cambridge: Cambridge University Press, 1988): in the late 12th and 13th c., the continuing preoccupation of English royalty with the cult of Edward the Confessor is further testimony: see Frank Barlow, *The Life of King Edward Who Rests at Westminster* (London and New York: Nelson, 1962; 4th edn., Oxford: Clarendon Press, 1992), Appendix D, 'The Development of the Cult of King Edward'; Paul Binski, 'Reflections on the *Estoire de seint Aedward*: Hagiography and Kingship in Thirteenth-Century England', *JMH* 16 (1990), 333–50.

[24] See 'The Saints' Lives of the Katherine Group and the Alliterative Tradition', *JEGP* 87 (1988), 16–34.

[25] *Li ver del Juïse*, ed. Hugo von Feilitzen (Uppsala: Edv. Berling, 1883), Appendix 1, 1–24. See further Juliette Dor, 'Post-dating Romance Loan Words in Middle English: Are the French Words of the *Katherine* Group English?', in Matti Rissanen, Ossi Ihaleinen, Terttu Nevalainen, and Irma Taavitsainen (eds.), *History of Englishes: New Methods and Interpretations in Historical Linguistics*, Topics in English Linguistics 10 (Berlin and New York: Mouton de Gruyter, 1992); and on the contemporary 13th-c. creativity of these lives, Ursula Schaefer, 'Twin Collocations in the Early Middle English Lives of the Katherine Group', in Herbert Pilch (ed.), *Orality and Literacy in Early Middle English*, ScriptOralia 83 (Tübingen: Gunter Narr, 1996), 179–98. It is worth remembering that even though pre-Conquest French people in England tended to concentrate in the south and east of the country (see C. J. Lewis, 'The French in England Before the Norman Conquest, *ANS* 17 (1995), 123–44, at 135), the West Midlands, Tolkien's outpost of native resistance to the Conquest, was in the 12th and 13th c. an area where at least four languages were used (Welsh, French, English, and Latin) and of early Flemish communities: see Michael T. Clanchy, *England and Its Rulers: Foreign Lordship and National Identity 1066–1272* (Totowa, NJ: Barnes and Noble, 1983).

the lives is given in French.[26] At this date, as indeed the manuscript seems to expect, lives of saints for women would have been as likely to have been written in French as in English.[27]

Manuscripts belonging to individual women and to female communities in Anglo-Norman England include all the possible variations among the three main languages used in England at this date: all in French, all in Latin, all in English, bilingual and trilingual. Interpreting this evidence is complex, with different levels of interplay between the linguistic competences of manuscript users and the registers of particular texts and documents to be taken into account.[28] The

[26] As also happens in later 13th-c. manuscripts: for example the narratorial self-inscription in the life of Marina in London, BL, MS Harley 2253 as 'He þt made & wrot þis *vie*' (*Sammlung Altenglischer Legenden*, ed. Carl Horstmann (Heilbronn: Henninger, 1878), 173/227, italics mine) or the authorship attribution in 'Meidan Margarete' (Cambridge, Trinity College MS B.14.39): 'imai tellen ou . . . þe *vie* of one meidan' (italics mine), f. 20r; 'Theo*dric*us þe clerc. he wrot hire *uie*' (italics mine), f. 23v, and in the concluding prayer to Christ: 'for feire margcrete loue. of us haue me*rcie*. | Amen amen. checun die amen', f. 24r (the last line is a conventional ending in French narrative and is immediately followed by a double prayer to 'Jhesu cr*ist* le fiz marie cil ke tut le munde fist' and to 'Lord crist' who 'madest al þis world of nou3t').

[27] The *SEL*'s earliest extant manuscripts date from the late 13th c. In addition to the continued circulation of Ælfrician lives, there are some individual late 11th- and early 12th-c. lives (notably of Giles and Margaret) which reflect (in late Old English) the stimulus of intensified Continental French cults (see D. A. G. Scragg and Elaine Treharne, 'The Three Anonymous Lives in Cambridge, CCC 303', 231–4 (appendix d. A. G. Scragg, 'The Corpus of Anonymous Lives and Their Manuscript Content', 209–30), in Paul E. Szarmach (ed.), *Holy Men and Holy Women: Old English Prose Saints' Lives and their Contexts* (New York: Garland, 1996), 209–30. Nevertheless, on the evidence so far available, new vernacular hagiographic composition in 12th-c. England is overwhelmingly in Anglo-Norman, with lives of Alexis, Brendan, Catherine, Edmund the Martyr, Edward the Confessor, George, Giles, Gregory the Penitent, Lawrence, Margaret, Mary of Egypt, Mary Magdalen, Osith, Thomas Becket. For summaries of Anglo-Norman and Continental 12th-c. lives, see Phyllis Johnson and Brigitte Cazelles, *Le Vain Siècle guerpir: A Literary Approach to Sainthood Through Old French Hagiography of the Twelfth Century*, North Carolina Studies in the Romance Languages and Literatures 205 (Chapel Hill: University of North Carolina Press, 1979).

[28] For example, London, BL, Cotton Claudius D III, an early 13th-c. manuscript belonging to Wintney (a Benedictine Hampshire nunnery with some Cistercian affiliations), includes a short Anglo-Norman treatise on the use of the calendar (f. 3r–v), the calendar in question being used for Bede's (Latin) martyrology (ff. 4r–49v). An early Middle English copy of the Old English version of the Benedictine Rule, set out by chapter turn about in Latin and English and with adapted pronouns and other inscriptions of a female audience, is also present (ff. 50r–138r). This book continued in active use in the monastery: its mortuary roll (ff. 138v–160v) contains names from the 15th c. (a note of the death of Alice Preston 'professa et refectora*trix*' is in the calendar at f. 157r: a list of her effects on f. 3rb dates her death to 1436). (On the manuscript and its copy of the Benedictine Rule, see the works cited in Ch. 6, n. 7 below.) To the Waverley witnesses in the foundation charter and the obit of a Waverley abbot in the Wintney obituary roll (see Thompson, *Women Religious*, 108–9) can be added the verses of brother Simon of 'le cuvent de Wauerle' (copied on a blank leaf of the Wintney martyrology, f. 3v (ed. P. Meyer, 'Bribes de littérature anglo-normande', *Jahrbuch für romanische und englische Literatur*, 7 (1866), 37–57; for Simon of Waverley see *Annales monastici*, ed. H. R. Luard, RS 36 (London, 1864–9), ii. 253, 284–5, 304, 309–12, 315, 321, 327). Simon writes, 'enfebli . . . *par* maladie', to beg the prioress of 'Wintoni' 'en chapitre me

bulk of manuscripts and texts from this earlier period of women's literary culture are in French however, and this book most often deals with French texts, then English and Latin. In this way it replicates the hierarchy of use that seems to have prevailed among women readers and writers in twelfth- and thirteenth-century Britain overall (though the modes and proportions of each language in use at any one time or place during this period vary considerably). Some elements have perforce been more or less completely neglected, however. The most pervasive of these is the extent to which French and English audition and reading must have occurred, for twelfth- and thirteenth-century women, in a sound-world regularly marked by the repetitions of liturgical and recitational Latin.[29] Many women reading or hearing hagiographical and other texts in the vernaculars will have used psalters and books of hours: apart from nodding occasionally at these and at the current interdisciplinary work rethinking their roles, I have had space to do little other than assume them as a background. Other languages which women in medieval Britain used or knew of—Gaelic, Welsh, Irish, Cornish, Flemish, Hebrew (and, more restrictedly, Greek)—have also been left out.

As with languages, so with cultural traditions. 'Although women have historically borne the burden of representing immanence for others . . . "women do not have particular forms of representation that are exclusively their own, but only particular relations to cultural representation and discourse".'[30] Without simply essentializing virginity into separate meanings for women and men, it is necessary both to recognize the dominant cultural patternings of virginity in historiography and other writings by men, and, given that these are inevitably part of the cultural environment of women, to consider the overlaps and distinctivenesses of virginity's history for women. For post-Conquest sources, such attention quickly suggests that the extent to which laywomen's and professed religious women's experiences have been conceptualized as separate realms in modern scholarship has obscured some salient versions of personal autonomy and participation in religious culture taken up by women, and that, in this, a fundamentally monastic virgin mythology has played its part.

receuer | E de estre frere me granter | E ke mun nun. e mun obit | En ceste liure seit escrit' (f. 3v/18–20). The request was granted only through the copying of these verses it seems; there is no Simon of Waverley in the manuscript's calendar or mortuary roll. For an example of linguistic mixtures within an individual text, see the 'Salut et solace par l'amour de Jésu' (where, for instance, women religious are assured that, when they come to the 'bon ostel' of 'la curt ihesu crist', they 'salt fare swyþe wel'): Betty Hill, 'British Library, MS Egerton 613–II', *Notes and Queries*, NS 25/223 (Dec. 1978), 492–501 (498).

[29] For a sense of this sound-world see the excellent account by Christopher Baswell, 'Latinitas', in Wallace (ed.), *The Cambridge History*, 122–51 (143–5).

[30] Sarah Beckwith, 'Passionate Regulation: Enclosure, Ascesis, and the Feminist Imaginary', *South Atlantic Quarterly*, 93 (1994), 803–24, quoting Henrietta Moore, *Space, Text and Gender: An Anthropological Study of the Marakwet of Kenya* (Cambridge, 1986).

The first chapter therefore compares representations of idealized female communities as outside or above historical process with the rhetorical and social history of virginity and the historiography of female communities to argue that virginity does indeed have a history, or rather histories. An influential high medieval romance version of virginity has, I argue, produced images of enclosure, of female community, and female readers which partly represent but partly obscure the audiences of virginity literature and their preoccupations. In the first chapter I am primarily concerned with the ideology of virginity in prescriptive treatises: the remaining chapters examine various narrative virginities and audiences in the hagiography of twelfth- and thirteenth-century England. The second chapter considers post-Conquest virgin saints and foundresses within textual and social paradigms of gift-giving (an anthropological model of particular usefulness given the importance of gift-exchange both in saints' cult and in post-Conquest and Anglo-Norman society). This chapter proposes that nuptiality is a surface trope of virgin sanctity, the rhetorical face of more complex narratives concerned with what I am calling 'dotality', the virgin's capacity to be given and to give. The importance of wholeness and fecundity in virgin figures of foundation and patronage, I argue, is underestimated in modern concern with the dismemberment and partition of virgin bodies, as is the agency ascribable to these figures. Romance, and with it rape, has often been seen in recent criticism as the most obvious aspect of virgin martyr narratives, but my argument that romance and nuptiality are surface aspects of more complex dotal structures compels me to defer consideration of these aspects till the third chapter. Here the meanings of *raptus* and of romance in virgin martyr *passio* are further explored. Concentrating on the virgin–pagan conflict, the third chapter argues that the *passio*'s refraction of the social anxieties focused on and mediated by the virgin resists readings of the virgin simply as object in these narratives. A complex literary form of special importance in the twelfth and thirteenth centuries, the *passio* allows for the virgin's scrutiny of what she is offered by clerical and lay patriarchy, and it is hospitable to a range of desires in its various audiences.

The fourth chapter returns to ideas developed in the first to examine ways in which, both within and beyond the dominant virgin martyr *passio* narrative, lives of honorary virginity and the honorary martyrdom of asceticism may be represented and the concerns of maternity and householding voiced. The fifth chapter considers the career of a prominent widow and patroness, Isabella, Countess of Arundel (d. 1279), and the overlap in her texts with those of female community on the one hand and the court on the other. This chapter explores the common concerns of women and churchmen with the discourse of male continence and asceticism, especially in the representation of contemporary ecclesiastical courtier saints. Widows were prominent in the patronage of communities as well as texts, and, often working with churchmen, founded, supported, and sometimes led significant communities in twelfth- and thirteenth-century Britain. The sixth chapter examines the representation of professed virginity, its authority and its communities, and examines virgin abbess lives as a historiography offering precedents, role models, and accounts of their own histories to women. Saints' lives are also important as stagings of doctrine and debate, and the question of how far female audiences could systematically study, debate, and place the doctrinal implications of saints' lives is considered in the final chapter, together with some related consideration as to whether insular culture is really as deprived in regard to women visionaries as is often suggested. A vision of history, I argue, is certainly discernible in a professed virgin's biography of a virgin English king composed at Barking Abbey. Finally, a brief Conclusion attempts some preliminary characterization of the literary culture of women in the period and suggests directions for further research.

Virginity is thus, as premissed in the ideological ambitions of prescriptive virginity treatises, an important aspect of women's literary as well as their social and cultural history. Whether in the romance of the nuptial and nubile virgin, the role of the virgin as treasure, the honorary virginities of maternity and householding, or the powers of older, established virgins, virginity as exemplary biography leads us into the social matrixes of women's literary culture and offers many ways of rereading and reimagining the literary history of both women and men in medieval Britain.

I

The Virgin Estate

Virginity treatises of the twelfth and thirteenth centuries in England construct an eternal future as heavenly brides for their audiences and propose enclosure away from historical process as the proper position of virgin audiences on earth. The virgin heroine is imaged as an enclosed and solitary reader in a way that occludes female collectivity and the common experience of lay, professed, and semi-religious women. This chapter uses Anglo-Norman manuscript and other material to argue that the conceptual morphology and the social circumstances of virginity are always much more labile than such models suggest. If we search for virgin visionaries and holy women in the image of the youthful romance heroine, we will find relatively few sources in the post-Conquest period. If we read through the ideological agendas of virginity texts to their relation with their social context, a more complex and variously peopled world emerges, in which virginity and its histories represent and are used by women both individually and collectively. To argue this case and to provide background for later discussions, this chapter surveys five topics: the construction of virginity as timelessly youthful; the enclosure of women, secular and lay; images, prescriptions, and practices in the occupations of enclosed women; the interrelations of virginity with other kinds of lives; and the historiography of female communities.

I.I. FROM HISTORY TO ETERNITY

Only fallen women age, claims an Anglo-Norman beauty book of the thirteenth century. Eve was given *bauté . . . pardurable* (v. 3) when God drew her from Adam's side, but lost it when she ate the apple (vv. 1–5). As a result, women's beauty is now transient, and marriage brings with it the mortal contamination of the fall, the loss of the 'perfect beauty of the white maiden', and the need for repair and recipes.[1] Virginity alone recalls the pristine loveliness that was once Eve's: so Aldhelm

---

[1] *L'Ornement des Dames. Ornatus mulierum: Texte anglo-normand du xiiie siècle*, ed. Pierre Ruelle, Université libre de Bruxelles, Travaux de la Faculté de philologie et de lettres t. 36 (Brussels: Presses Universitaires de Bruxelles, 1967), 32. The theology of maquillage is also present in earlier virginity writing, usually as a topos of denunciation: see especially Tertullian, *De virginibus velandis*, PL2.887–914; Cyprian, *De habitu virginum*, PL4.451–78; Jerome (e.g. F. A. Wright, *Select Letters of St Jerome* (London: Heinemann, 1933), nos. 22: §116, 32, 38: §4, 54: §7, 107: §5, 127: §3–4), and for a modern study see Lynda L. Coon, *Sacred Fiction: Holy Women and Hagiography in Late Antiquity* (Philadelphia: University of Pennsylvania Press, 1997), esp. 36–44; also R. H. Bloch, *Medieval Misogyny*

(cited as an authority in post- as in pre-Conquest works) in his *De virginitate* for the nuns of Barking:

O excellent grace of virginity, which like a rose grown from thorny shoots blushes with a crimson flower and never withers with the defect of dread mortality . . . virginity alone in the manner of happy youth continually flourishes and is constantly growing.[2]

Similar themes are sounded in many of the virginity letters and treatises written for women by their spiritual advisers. This literature has been aptly christened the 'literature of spiritual formation' by Barbara Newman, and characterized as occupying 'a middle ground between monastic rules and mystical writing'.[3] Its conceptions of virginity are very different from the twentieth-century sense of virginity as primarily a state of negation, of absence of sexual knowledge. The amplitude of myth echoes through virginity writing: virginity symbolizes a lost primal wholeness, a haunting image of eternity experienced in mortal life. Such images are made still more resonant by being given longevity

and the Invention of Western Romantic Love (Chicago and London: University of Chicago Press, 1991), 93–112 (esp. 99, 108–9). In the high Middle Ages, see *inter alia* Marbode of Rennes (a writer well known in insular culture through his lapidary), 'Ad reginam Anglorum', PL171.1660. Vernacular versions of these topoi have received less attention, but for a Continental French text of 1249 which builds on Genesis 6 to explain that shortly before the Flood, women began calling attention to their bodies by using cosmetics and clothing to cause lust in men, see J. L. Grigsby, '*Miroir des Bonnes Femmes*: A New Fragment of the *Somme le Roi* and a *Miroir des Bonnes Femmes*, a hitherto unnoticed text', *Romania*, 82 (1961), 458–81 (469): see also *Traduction en vers français du xiie siècle de l'épître de saint Jérôme à Eustochium*, ed. T. Nurmela (Helsinki: Société de la littérature finnoise, 1947). An important 13th-c. Anglo-Norman compilation of treatises (see below, n. 93) uses the authority of Jerome to warn holy maidens against the company of women who are proud of their hair and headdresses, sleeves close-fitting or ruched, buttons, garlands, and such vanities ('femmes ki de lur cheueulurs sunt orgoilleuses e de lur testes, ne de manches estreites ne ridees, ne botons ne de garlandesches ne de teles uanitez', Paris BN f. fr. 6276, f. 102r cols. a–b).

[2] 'De virginitate', tr. Michael Lapidge in *Aldhelm: The Prose Works*, tr. Michael Lapidge and Michael Herren (Ipswich and Totowa, NJ: Brewer, 1979), 51–132 (74). On Aldhelm manuscript traditions see J. A. Kiff-Hooper, 'Class Books or Works of Art? Some Observations on the Tenth-Century Manuscripts of Aldhelm's *De laude virginitatis*', in Ian N. Wood and G. A. Loud (eds.), *Church and Chronicle in the Middle Ages: Essays Presented to John Taylor* (London and Rio Grande: Hambledon Press, 1991), 15–26. Aldhelm's post-Conquest reputation was kept high by William of Malmesbury's respect for the former abbot of his house: although Aldhelm is not a virginity authority in the *SEL* texts of his life, he continued to be regarded so in more academic traditions, although never with the status of Jerome, Augustine, Ambrose, or other patristic writers. Aldhelm's account of Pope Clement (d. 100) in the *De virginitate* is quoted in a 13th-c. manuscript of the Clementine *Recognitiones* (Oxford, Bodleian, MS Bodley 870, f. 4v): in the 14th c., Ranulph Higden's *Polychronicon* and its translation by Trevisa cite Aldhelm as writing a book, the foremost of his 'egregios libellos', on virginity for St Ethelburga of Barking Abbey (*Polychronicon Ranulphi Higden Monachi Cestrensis* ed. J. Rawson Lumby, RS 41 (London, 1846), vi. 124, 182). Aldhelm is also represented as an encratic hero: when tempted he would have 'a faire mayde in his bed while he seide þe sawter' right through (ibid. 178–9).

[3] 'Flaws in the Golden Bowl: Gender and Spiritual Formation in the Twelfth Century', *Traditio*, 45 (1989–90), 11–147; repr. in her *From Virile Woman to WomanChrist: Studies in Medieval Religion and Literature* (Philadelphia: University of Pennsylvania Press, 1995), 19–45 and 313–16.

and traditional status: the early church fathers are constantly invoked in order to construct virginity as a timeless and permanent form of ideal Christian living. The texts of high medieval virginity are sprinkled with references to Ambrose, Augustine, Cyprian, Jerome and to more contemporary figures, such as Bernard of Clairvaux, deemed to possess comparable authority.[4] Living the 'life of the angels' on earth without marrying or giving in marriage (Luke 20: 35), the medieval virgin, like her predecessors in the early Christian centuries, continues to exemplify Augustine's account of virginity as 'the perpetual contemplation of incorruption in our corruptible flesh'.[5] The virgin while on earth carries 'balsam in a fragile vessel', as she bears the eternal treasure of virginity and its resemblance to God through the fallen, mortal territory of the 'land of unlikeness'.[6] Virginity makes its strongest claims through a rhetoric of eternity and timelessness.

As far as the representation of women is concerned there seems at first sight an alarming price to be paid for this mythic amplitude. If virgins are vessels, they are precious but fragile. If they are flawless and eternally youthful, inhabiting bodies without menstrual and menopausal phases, then they are also excluded from historical process. Leading a life of silent veiled enclosure, 'dead to all earthly desires', virgins' real existence is in heaven, enclosed beyond mortal action and change, and they have no history.[7] But different virginities exist for different genres, times, and audiences, and there are synchronic dissonances as well as overlaps between the prescriptive representations of virginity in the literature of spiritual formation and its narrative examples in the virginities of saints' lives. Cloistered virgins may be represented as fragile vessels: virgin martyrs in the public spectacle of their passions are rarely this, their undaunted wills and remembered bodies often eloquently triumphant. Different aspects of the iconography of eternity are tailored to various reading groups and inscribed audiences. Osbert of Clare, Prior of Westminster, (*c.*1139–63), for instance, chooses gem and flower imagery for his nieces in Barking Abbey, but offers a series of mature virginal and vidual figures to the abbess of Barking to whom he also

---

[4] On patristic traditions as used in 12th- and 13th-c. virginity see *Hali Meiðhad*, ed. Bella Millett, EETS os 284 (London, 1982), pp. xxiv–xlv. For a list of 12th- and 13th-c. Latin texts, see Newman, 'Golden Bowl', Appendix.

[5] 'In carne corruptibili incorruptionis perpetuae meditatio', *De sancta virginitate*, I, ch. 13, PL40.401, but widely quoted in later works: see for example the *Summa virtutem de remediis anime*, ed. Siegfried Wenzel (Athens: University of Georgia Press, 1984), 300. From the now large literature on late antique and earlier medieval Christian virginities and women's lives and letters, see Kate Cooper, *The Virgin and the Bride: Idealized Womanhood in Late Antiquity* (Cambridge, Mass. and London: Harvard University Press, 1996); Jane Tibbetts Schulenberg, *Forgetful of Their Sex: Female Sanctity and Society ca 500–1100* (Chicago: University of Chicago Press, 1998).

[6] On these figures see Newman, 'Golden Bowl', 126; Robert Javelet, *Image et ressemblance au douzième siècle* (Paris: Le Touzey et Ané, 1967), chs. 1, 5, 7.

[7] The phrase is William of Malmesbury's, used of the virgin saint Cutburga (*fl.* AD 709): see *De gestis regum Anglorum libri quinque*, ed. W. W. Stubbs, 2 vols., RS 90 (London, 1887–9), i. 35–6 (henceforth *GR*).

writes.[8] Although high medieval ideals of virginity pretend to be, and to some extent are, long-lived descendants of earlier virginities, they are culturally specific. Virgins had always been brides of Christ as well as *vir*-agos, but in the late twelfth and thirteenth centuries they live in eternity as elegant young noble-women at God's high medieval court, just as the iconography of heaven itself shifts from that of paradise garden to celestial city.[9] In the early thirteenth-century *Hali Meiðhad* (*Letter on Virginity for the Encouragement of Virgins*), virgins circle close to God in an exclusive courtly ring dance, while in the Franciscan Nicholas Bozon's vernacular legendary near the end of the century, the 'karole de virgines', as Bozon calls it, proceeds on its eternal decorous way in heaven, a stably revolving garland of elegant young women in the 'bal au ciel'.[10] *Hali*

[8] *The Letters of Osbert of Clare, Prior of Westminster*, ed. E. W. Williamson (London: Oxford University Press, 1929), nos. 21, 22, 42. For a translation of Osbert's letters to these three women, see *Heavenly Brides and Holy Mothers: Texts from Twelfth-Century Convents in England and France*, tr. and introd. Vera P. Morton (Boydell and Brewer, forthcoming). Osbert's nieces, Margaret and Cecilia, are given individual selections of virginity imagery appropriate to their names and with different thematic emphases, while Matilda of Darenth and Ida of Barking (probably a niece of Henry I's queen Adeliza) to whom Osbert also writes are addressed differently again (see *Letters of Osbert of Clare*, ed. Williamson, nos. 40, 41).

[9] In earlier 12th-c. Latin writing, as Newman shows, female audiences are inscribed in terms of female gender stereotypes, but virginity is very frequently recommended as a form of virile spirituality ('Golden Bowl', 120–1, 126–30). But in the 13th-c. vernacular virginity writings which draw on and claim to continue the 12th c.'s revivals of patristic virginity, virgins become more exclusively feminine and romanced. On the shift in the figuring of heaven (further confirmed by the more urban conception of heaven among the mendicant orders of the 13th c.), see Colleen McDonnell and Bernhard Lang, *Heaven: A History* (New Haven and London: Yale University Press, 1988) 72–80; on the earlier varieties of patristic paradise, see 67. The inhabitants of heaven change too, moving from paradisal nakedness (still featured in Honorius's *Elucidarius*) to full courtly clothing. These are broad tendencies rather than precisely datable changes: in Goscelin's late 11th-c. *Liber confortatorius* for the recluse Eve, formerly of Wilton, Wilton is clearly envisaged as a community (*urbs*): Goscelin sees it as a jewelled casket, a reliquary and ark of virgins, at its most splendid when the Bridegroom returns at the end of time, for his mother's formal courtly presentation of his brides and peoples to him ('The *Liber confortatorius* of Goscelin of Saint Bertin', ed. C. H. Talbot, in *Analecta monastica*, series 3, ed. M. M. Lebreton, J. Leclercq, and C. H. Talbot, Studia Anselmiana, 37 (Rome: Pontifical Institute of St Anselm, 1955), 1–117 (113–15)).

[10] For *Hali Meiðhad* see Bella Millett and Jocelyn Wogan-Browne (eds. and trs.), *Medieval English Prose for Women: Selections from the Katherine Group and 'Ancrene Wisse'* (Oxford: Oxford University Press, 1990), 11/1–4 (henceforth cited by page and line number in the text): for Bozon's 'karole' see his Life of St Agnes, in *Seven More Poems by Nicholas Bozon*, ed. Sr M. Amelia Klenke, Franciscan Institute Publications Historical Series 2 (St Bonaventure, New York: Franciscan Institute, 1951), 95, v. 73. Alan Fletcher discusses the courtly nature of the *carole*, paralleled, as he points out, in the *Roman de la rose* ('The Dancing Virgins of *Hali Meiðhad*', *Notes and Queries*, NS 40 (1993), 437–9). For a full development of the 'bal au ciel' topos, see *La Court de Paradis, Poème anonyme du xiiie siècle*, ed. Eva Vilamo-Pentti, Annales Academiae Scientiarum Fennicae Ser. B, t. 79.1 (Helsinki: Société de la littérature finnoise, 1953); a verse account of the ball given by God for All Saints ('La Feste de Touz Sainz et la Querole de Paradis', ibid. 24), in which the various heavenly ranks sing refrains from love poetry. For the liturgical context see Susan J. Rastetter, ' "Bot mylde as maydenes seme at mas": The Feast of All Saints and *Pearl*', *Bulletin of the John Rylands Library*, 74 (1992), 141–54, and for the cosmology of the heavenly ring-dance (notably from Plato's *Timaeus* 40a–d, see Ch. 7, n. 18 below), James L. Miller, *Measures of Wisdom: The Cosmic Dance in Classical and Christian Antiquity* (Toronto: University of Toronto Press, 1985).

Meiðhad's virgins wear, like good *vir*-agos, the 'kempene crune' (p. 11/17), the champions' crown, in the heavenly court, but among their 'priuileges' have the extra crown of those seeking perfection, a 'gerlondesche' engraved with flowers and gems.[11] These scenes invoke a specifically high medieval ideal of the aristocratic heroine, one shared to a large extent with courtly literature and secular romance.[12]

The intensified courtly troping of virginity in the high Middle Ages cannot be read in any simple way as recording an increase in the powers and opportunities of women in the virgin life, and the apparently high valuation of the virgin stands in problematic relation to the lived history of women.[13] The nuptial and courtly presentation of virgins as young queens of heaven, aristocratic and powerful, cannot be directly correlated with an increase in the powers of queenship.[14] Although the Virgin queen of heaven joins her son to be crowned in heaven at this period, she is usually represented on a slightly lower throne, receiving her crown and a delegated sovereignty from her son.[15] On the other hand,

---

[11] The courtly privileges of the virgins are designated by French words, the general crown by the English *kempene* (gen. pl. from OE *cempa*, 'warrior, champion'). On the two crowns see *Hali Meiðhad*, ed. Millett 10/9n. and 11/17–20n.: also p. 105 below, and Edwin Hall and Horst Uhr, 'Aureola super auream: Crowns and Related Symbols of Special Distinction for Saints', *Art Bulletin*, 67 (1985), 567–603 (567–72).

[12] This shift is partly in tandem with that described by Newman, *From Virile Woman to WomanChrist*. See also Bruce L. Venarde, *Women's Monasticism and Medieval Society: Nunneries in France and England 890–1215* (Ithaca and London: Cornell University Press, 1997), 81–128 (92). On virginity and youth see Kim M. Phillips, 'Maidenhood as the Perfect Age of Women's Life', in Katherine J. Lewis, Kim M. Phillips, and Noël James Menuge (eds.), *Young Medieval Women* (Gloucester: Sutton, 1999), 25–46. For an excellent account of the complexities of gendering desire for God and of configurations other than compulsory heterosexual femininity for the virgin, see Sarah Salih, 'Queering *Sposalia Christi*: Virginity, Gender, and Desire in the Anchoritic Texts', *New Medieval Literatures*, 5 (forthcoming).

[13] On women's loss of rights over chastity vows in Gratian's Decretals see Dyan Elliott, *Spiritual Marriage: Sexual Abstinence in Medieval Wedlock* (Princeton: Princeton University Press, 1993), 156–8. (Elliott's point seems truer of Latin prescriptive works than of how the vows get worked out/imagined in vernacular literary texts and in social practice.) John Gillingham argues that late 12th- and early 13th-c. changes in inheritance law allowing daughters to inherit principalities and kingdoms are linked with the increased emphasis on youthful heroines at the centre of dramas of household establishment and succession ('Love, Marriage, and Politics in the Twelfth Century', in his *Richard Coeur de Lion: Kingship, Chivalry and War in the Twelfth Century* (London and Rio Grande: Hambledon Press, 1994), 243–55 (this has as much to do with keeping patrimonies intact as adding to women's rights).

[14] See Laura Wertheimer, 'Adeliza of Louvain and Anglo-Norman Queenship', *Haskins Society Journal*, 7 (1995), 101–15; Lois L. Huneycutt, 'Intercession and the High Medieval Queen: The Esther *topos*', in Jennifer Carpenter and Sally-Beth MacLean (eds.), *Power of the Weak: Studies on Medieval Women* (Urbana and Chicago: University of Illinois Press, 1995), 126–46; John Carmi Parsons, 'The Queen's Intercession in Thirteenth-Century England', ibid. 147–77.

[15] See Penny Schine Gold, *The Lady and the Virgin: Image and Experience in Twelfth-Century France* (Chicago: Chicago University Press, 1985), 51–68; Roberta Gilchrist, ' "Blessed art thou among women": The Archaeology of Female Piety', in P. J. P. Goldberg (ed.), *Woman is a Worthy Wight: Women in English Society, c.1200–1500* (Stroud: Sutton, 1992), 212–26 (221). Pamela Sheingorn has argued that narratives of the Virgin are used to socialize young women towards the acceptance of elderly husbands, 'The Maternal Behavior of God: Divine Father as Fantasy Husband', in John Carmi Parsons and Bonnie Wheeler (eds.), *Medieval Mothering* (New York: Garland, 1996), 77–99.

the status of saint and the role of heavenly patroness can make a virgin a very powerful figure. Although the question of whose interests a virgin represents is usually complex and will vary greatly from one context to another, some versions of virginity provide models and precedents which are both culturally powerful and useful to and adopted by women. The very intensity of the attempt to place the virgin in an imaginative *gynaceum* encodes a transferred and suppressed awareness of the critical vitality of women's roles in both biological and cultural reproduction and transmission. Such residual anxiety and awareness helps make the whole cultural 'imaginary' of virginity not settled, but dynamic and productive. The use of figures of virginity as validating images of integrity and stasis outside historical change and decay partly masks and partly reveals their importance as fecund figures of transmission and translation.

I.2. THE ROMANCE OF VIRGIN ENCLOSURE

If the rhetoric of eternity separates the virgin in her permanent youthfulness from time and history, the imagery of enclosure with which virginity is closely associated asserts a separation of her life from other people and their social structures. Because she carries such precious liquor in a fragile vessel, the virgin must be 'hors de presse', safely enclosed, in her tower, bower, chamber, cave, or cell, and, most powerfully, within her own internalized sense of shame and decorum.[16] Enclosure images are present throughout Christian tradition, but gather particular intensity in insular culture in the high Middle Ages.[17] In the twelfth-century psalter associated with the recluse and prioress Christina of Markyate, the Virgin Mary becomes, as Michael Clanchy has pointed out, domesticated: the Annunciation takes place in a private interior chamber, not a public space.[18]

[16] Herbert, 134/37: for another text with a rhetorically brilliant repertoire of enclosure and decorum topoi, see *Hali Meiðhad*, in Millett and Wogan-Browne (eds. and trs.), *Medieval English Prose for Women*.

[17] For the early medieval history of female enclosure see Jane Tibbetts Schulenberg, 'Strict Active Enclosure and its Effects on the Female Monastic Experience (ca. 500–1100)', in John A. Nichols and Lillian T. Shank (eds.), *Distant Echoes: Medieval Religious Women* I, Cistercian Studies Series 71 (Kalamazoo: University of W. Michigan Press, 1984), 51–86.

[18] See M. T. Clanchy, *From Memory to Written Record: England 1066–1307* (London: Edward Arnold, 1979; 2nd edn. Oxford and Cambridge, Mass.: Blackwell, 1993), 191–2. According to R. W. Southern, the image of the Virgin Mary as herself an enclosure from Luke 10: 38 ('intravit in quoddam castellum') becomes widely used in insular preaching after a sermon by Archbishop Ralph d'Escures, 1114–22, translated into English in the early 12th c. (*Robert Grosseteste: The Growth of an English Mind in Europe* (Oxford: Clarendon Press, 1986), 226). René Metz suggests that enclosure becomes a more intensely normative image for consecrated women in the high Middle Ages: 'Avant le IXe siècle, il était admis que les vierges consacrées vécussent isolées dans le monde. Mais dans la suite ce mode de vie se fit de plus en plus rare. En fait, à partir de la fin du IXe siècle, toutes les femmes qui avaient fait profession publique vivaient en communauté', 'Le Statut de la femme en droit canonique médiéval', in id., *La Femme et l'enfant dans le droit canonique médiéval* (London: Variorum Reprints, 1985), article IV, 85–6. The rite for virgins living in the world

The Virgin can be pictorially represented in other kinds of spaces in the high Middle Ages (in the porch of Fra Angelico's famous Annunciation at San Marco in Florence, for instance), but the insular Virgin is enclosed: Gabriel finds the Virgin 'toute seule: ele fu nule part hors, mes fu dedenz fer[m]ement enclose' ('completely alone: she was in no way outside, but was securely enclosed').[19] The enclosed woman is also particularly associated with the special prevalence of anchoritism as a form of religious life in England. As Ann Warren has shown, reclusion, the most dramatically complete form of enclosure, was largely female in the late twelfth and thirteenth centuries in Britain, with nearly twice as many women undertaking it as men.[20]

The image of the recluse has remained powerful in a number of ways in both medieval and modern reception. The solitary woman in her cell was a specially attractive image for modelling the self and the soul in medieval reception.[21] It has also often been exploited in post-medieval versions of the medieval as the Gothic (and abjected) foundation of the psyche: thus Alexander Pope explores a new sense of the individual by figuring Heloise (formidably successful and efficient administrator of the abbey of the Paraclete and its six daughter houses as she was) as apparently alone and entombed in her convent.[22] In the nineteenth century, England's medieval rules and treatises for recluses and anchoresses were rediscovered just as Pusey and others were beginning to compose *regulae* for Anglican sororities in the 1840s and 1850s, and when a vigorous tradition of representing professed women within the sexualized, death-like embrace of the cell had flourished for several decades in the paintings of Millais and others.[23] But medieval uses of enclosure imagery should not be simply assimilated to such neo-Gothic reworkings of reclusion and religion. Images of the recluse as a

---

was again suppressed in *Castitatis Sponsa Christi*, 21 November 1950 (at the peak of the Goretti cult, see p. 4 above): see Metz, 'Les Conditions juridiques de la consécration des vierges dans la liturgie latine, des origines à nos jours', *La Femme et l'enfant*, article VI, 279–80.

[19] Herbert, 131/34–7 (punctuation modified). For the Early Middle English version ('in anli stude al ane . . . nahwer ute, ah . . . biloken faste') see *Ancrene Wisse: MS Corpus Christi College, Cambridge*, ed. J. R. R. Tolkien, EETS os 249, (London, 1962), f. 43b/12–13 (84) (henceforth referenced as 'Tolkien', by folio and line number).

[20] See Ann K. Warren, *Anchorites and Their Patrons in Medieval England* (Berkeley: University of California Press, 1985), 20, table I: male and female recluses occur in similar numbers in the 12th c. (48 women and 30 men), but in the 13th c., 123 women recluses are recorded, as against 37 male and 38 of unknown gender.

[21] See Linda Georgianna, *The Solitary Self: Individuality in the 'Ancrene Wisse'* (Cambridge, Mass. and London: Harvard University Press, 1982).

[22] Pope, 'Eloisa to Abelard'. For recent studies of Heloise, see Bonnie Wheeler (ed.), *Listening to Heloise: The Voice of a Twelfth-Century Woman* (New York: St Martin's Press, 2000).

[23] See Martha Vicinus, *Independent Women: Work and Community for Single Women 1850–1920* (Chicago: University of Chicago Press, 1985), 46–84; Susan P. Casteras, 'Virgin Vows: The Early Victorian Artists' Portrayal of Nuns and Novices', *Victorian Studies*, 24 (1981), 157–84. James Morton's edition of *Ancrene Wisse* was published as *The Ancrene Riwle: A Treatise on the Rules and Duties of Monastic Life. Edited and Translated from a Semi-Saxon MS of the Thirteenth Century*, Camden Society Publications 57 (London, 1853).

solitary entombed figure are less a guide to the medieval contexts and meaning of the practice of reclusion than they are a tribute to the rhetorical brilliance of virginity and enclosure texts, most especially the *Guide for Anchoresses* (*Ancrene Wisse*) and associated Katherine Group texts, which, among all the early literature of spiritual formation in England, seem most eloquently to have imaged enclosure for both modern and medieval audiences.[24]

Enclosure is often thought of as the characterizing practice of women's religious lives, and certainly English churchmen in the twelfth and thirteenth centuries, like their colleagues in the later Middle Ages, sought to maintain and intensify the enclosure of women religious as much stricter than that of men.[25] But our sense of what and how this means should not depend only on virginity writings and on the accounts of female houses in bishops' registers (documents which can to some extent be seen as continuations of twelfth- and thirteenth-century letters and treatises on female enclosure and virginity in their use of the ideology of virgin enclosure).[26] The social practices and representations of enclosure embraced laywomen as well as religious: *all* good virgins' lifecycles begin in voluntary self-cloistering in a chamber, include a briefly public moment of display in nuptial exchange, and continue to enclosure as the bride either of Christ or of an earthly man in the convent cell or the household— 'virgo manet in thalamis'.[27] Whether as bride of Christ or some other groom, the woman contemplating enclosure is veiled and given a nuptial ring.[28] Anglo-

---

[24] The *Guide* was translated into French and Latin, as well as being adapted in its Middle English versions for various religious and lay audiences, and was printed in the early 1490s (as the *Tretyse of Loue*) by de Worde. For an account of the medieval versions and the scholarly 19th- and 20th-c. receptions of these texts see Millett, '*Ancrene Wisse*', *the Katherine Group and the Wooing Group*, General Introduction; on later medieval reception of the *Guide*, see F. N. M. Diekstra, 'Some Fifteenth-Century Borrowings', and Nicholas Watson, in *Companion to 'Ancrene Wisse'*, ed. Yoko Wada (Boydell and Brewer, forthcoming).

[25] On earlier medieval enclosure see Schulenberg, 'Strict Active Enclosure'. In England enclosure for nuns was reaffirmed throughout the 13th c.; at the Council of Oxford in 1222; the legatine council in London of 1268; Archbishop Pecham's Lambeth provincial council of 1281; and in Boniface's papal bull, *Periculoso*, of 1298: see Elizabeth Makowski, *Canon Law and Cloistered Women: Periculoso and its Commentators 1298–1545* (Washington, DC: Catholic University of America Press, 1997), see esp. ch. 7 on the English canonists. For 13th-c. ecclesiastical legislation regulating anchorholds and candidates for them see Warren, *Anchorites and their Patrons*, ch. 3.

[26] See, for example, Pecham's letter to Barking, endorsing the Bishop of London's 1279 visitation (*Registrum epistolarum fratris Johannis Peckham Archiepiscopi Cantuariensis*, ed. Charles Trice Martin, RS 77 (London, 1882), i. 81–6 (with special insistence on claustration, control of ingress and egress, 84–5)).

[27] According to Giles of Rome, both religious and secular little girls are to be shut up (*De regimine principum*, Bk. II, pt. ii, ch. 19 (with a full range of enclosure topoi from physical confinement to internalized custody of the senses)): see the 13th-c. French version (tr. Henri de Guachi) and see *Li livres du gouvernement des rois*, ed. Samuel P. Molenaer (New York and London: Macmillan, 1899), 225–30.

[28] See René Metz, 'La Couronne et l'anneau dans la consécration des vierges. Origine et évolution des deux rites dans la liturgie latine', in id., *La Femme et l'enfant*, article VII; Jean-Baptiste Molin and Protais Mutembe, *Le Rituel du mariage en France du XIIe au XVIe siècle* (Paris: Beauchesne, 1974), 28–9, 35–7, and ch. 6: for a description see Goscelin, *Liber confortatorius*, ed. Talbot, II, ch. 2. On rings see further Ch. 2.3 below.

Norman marriage ceremonies used a canopy, held over both the bride and groom, but marking the wife's enclosure within a structure of husbandly control.[29] As the figure of God says to Eve of the archetypal marriage in the twelfth-century *Jeu d'Adam* (italics mine):

> Il est marid e tu sa mulier
> A lui soies tot tens encline
> *Nen issir de sa discipline.*

He is the husband and you are his wife: always be obedient to him and do not leave [*lit.* go out from] his governance.[30]

In the same way the nun at her consecration enters within the shadow or shelter of the veil. This, according to one Anglo-Norman treatise for nuns of, probably, the early thirteenth century, signifies both the enveloping grace of the Holy Spirit and the discipline of the senses:

> You should not forget the veil which gives you the name of nun. The veil, which is placed over the head and provides a shelter ['adumbre'] for the ears and the face and drapes lightly over the shoulders, signifies, together with the rest of the habit, the shadow ['l'umbre'] of the holy spirit which descends spiritually on the nun when she takes the veil, and shelters ['umbre'] her from the heat of vice and folly.[31]

The metaphor of *umbre* ('shadow, shelter') for all these processes invokes the nuptiality of the Song of Songs 2: 3 for the nun, while the *Jeu d'Adam*'s Eve is bidden within a less romantic enclosure, but both nun and wife are in their own ways *femmes couvertes*, veiled from the world.

Not only the professed nun or consecrated virgin, but the married laywoman are thus in some respects both symbolically asserted to be dead to the world. Enclosure as entombment is associated with the ritual of reciting the office of the dead over the recluse as she formally entered her anchorhold.[32] But

---

[29] Molin and Mutembe, *Le Rituel du mariage*, 25–6 (for controversy as to whether only the woman or both spouses were veiled) and 228–33 for variations in practice. From the 12th c., in some rituals, it was customary to place children born before the marriage under the pallium, which had the effect of legitimating them in canon law, though Grosseteste argues that 'bastardus sub palio . . . surgit bastardus', *Roberti Grosseteste Epistolae*, ed. H. R. Luard, RS 25 (London, 1861), *Ep.* 24, 96. For a 13th-c. Anglo-Norman account, see *Corset*, ed. K. V. Sinclair, ANTS 52 (London, 1995), vv. 435–40, 459–64.

[30] *Le Jeu d'Adam*, ed. W. van Emden, British Roncesvals Society Publications I (Edinburgh, 1996), 4, ll. 34–6. Although the play is no longer thought to have been staged in the church porch, marriage ceremonies took place in this liminal zone. In the 12th-c. movement to verify the absence of impediments and the freedom of consent to marriage, there was a 'transposition devant la porte de l'église, juste avant la messe, d'usages, pratiqués jusque-là à la maison' (Molin and Mutembe, *Le Rituel de Mariage*, 31–2). Like the bishop's questioning of the recluse, this signifies a moment of public verification prior to enclosure.

[31] Tony Hunt, 'An Anglo-Norman Treatise on Female Religious', *Medium Ævum*, 64 (1995), 205–31 (219–20, vv. 487–98).

[32] For the enclosure ritual see Warren, *Anchorites and their Patrons*, Appendix, and for a 12th-c. example, *The Pontifical of Magdalen College*, ed. H. A. Wilson, HBS 39 (1910), Appendix, 245–6.

enclosure imaged as entombment or death does not achieve a simple separation of religious from lay lives: it applies equally to the secular romance heroine:

> When the turuf is thy tour
> and the put is thy bour
> Thy wel and thy white throte
> Shulen wormes to note
> What helpet thee thenne
> All the worilde wenne?[33]

In this thirteenth-century lyric, the romance heroine in her tower is always already underground in the enclosure of death, and her bower (her very heroinehood) is already the pit. The poem is the lyric equivalent of a double-tomb sculpture, or the *memento mori* narrative accounts of the feminine as the mortal, at once sealed and enclosed in the romance location of tower and bower, and yet finally permeable and consumable.[34] So, too, if the anchoress shows herself, she is both the man of the Old Testament who uncovers the pit and has to suffer a penalty if an animal falls into it (Exodus 21: 33–4) and the pit is her own 'fair face and . . . white neck and . . . light eye, and . . . her hands' if she shows them, and her speech 'is also a pit'.[35] The anchoresses' fair hands (the very marker of romance) should not be looked at by her, and should 'each day scrape up the earth of their grave where they will rot'.[36] Again, in the Anglo-Norman thirteenth-

---

[33] Cambridge, Trinity College MS B.14.39, f. 47b (with a Latin version, 'Cum sit gleba tibi turris'): see *Religiöse Dichtung in englischen Hochmittelalter: Untersuchung und Edition der Handschrift B.14.39 des Trinity College in Cambridge*, ed. Karl Reichl, Texte und Untersuchungen zur Englischen Philologie, Band I (Munich: Wilhelm Fink, 1973), 444–5. I have used here the transliteration of Maxwell S. Luria and R. L. Hoffman (*Middle English Lyrics* (New York: Norton, 1974), 223) and have marked alliteration in bold to bring out the play of sound against meaning in the lyric's chiastically inverted collocations.

[34] Notable literary examples include the Lady and her duenna in *Sir Gawain and the Green Knight*, other versions of the Dame Ragnell figure, and Henryson's Cresseid as leper and erstwhile 'flour of womanheid' (for a powerful account of what is at stake in representing decay and corruption in female bodies see Felicity Riddy, ' "Abject odious": Feminine and Masculine in Henryson's *Testament of Cresseid* ', in Helen Cooper and Sally Mapstone (eds.), *The Long Fifteenth Century: Essays for Douglas Gray* (Oxford: Clarendon Press, 1997), 229–48).

[35] 'le puz est sa bele face, son blanc col, son legier oil, ses mains si ele les tent hors en vewe domme. Vnquore sunt ces paroles puz', Herbert, 41/30–34.

[36] 'Eles deussent chescun ior gratinner sus la terre de lour fosse la ou eles punirunt [*sic* for purrirunt] dedenz', Herbert, 95/30–3 (with reference to the custom of an open grave being kept in the corner of anchoritic cells). A rule for male recluses is even more insistent on this theme, however: in the rule written by Walter, an elderly Augustinian canon ('sexagenarius', 81), *c.*1280, ch. xv on the recluse's sepulchre not only suggests that the recluse should be able within the cell 'nightly and daily to see whither they are bound' but asks, 'What do the lips of the grave cry out except "Hither, hasten, hasten, come . . . ?" ' ('Regulae reclusorum Angliae et quaestiones tres de vita solitaria saec. xii–xiv', ed. Livarius Oliger, *Antonianum*, 9 (1934), 37–84 (67–8)). Read literally, the lyric quoted above images male sexuality as the activity of greedy little worms: in its pit imagery for women, the *Guide for Anchoresses* similarly, as Anne Savage has pointed out, figures male sexuality as a stray dog ('The Translation of the Feminine: Untranslatable Dimensions of the Anchoritic Works', in Roger Ellis and Ruth Evans (eds.), *The Medieval Translator*, 4, Medieval and Renaissance Texts and Studies 123 (Exeter: University of Exeter Press, 1994), 181–99).

century treatise earlier referred to, nuns are told that, of their two surplices, the black one denotes contempt of the world and signifies that 'you will be buried in the black habit when your body returns to the earth and becomes earth'.[37] But a version of enclosure is equally part of lay rituals of death: the practice of putting on monastic habit at one's deathbed was prevalent in the twelfth and thirteenth as in later centuries and embraced by lay upper-class women among others.[38]

If lay and secular experience are less separate than enclosure imagery asserts, so too the solitudes of enclosure are rhetorical, and the place even of the recluse (as also of the nun or female householder) can be much more public, normative, and privileged than a literal reading of enclosure literature and rituals suggests. Like the early stylitic saints, at once remote on the pillars and yet highly visible in the centre of their communities, the ascribed liminality of the recluse's position gives her power and a public role: she is an important part of the *imaginaire* of her community and also of its socio-economic life.[39] The very success with which the *Guide for Anchoresses*, that most influential text of virgin reclusion, created (and creates) an image of its audience as women who are solitary, and contained in a cell and in their own body, masks the selectivity with which the image inscribes its own audience.[40] The three gentry sisters addressed in the *Guide*'s early version were not solitary in terms of the physical and social arrangements which supported them: they had their patron, spiritual director,

---

[37] 'Que el neir serrez ensevelie | Quant vostre cors revertirat | A terre e terre devendrat' (Hunt, 'Anglo-Norman Treatise on Female Religious', 219, vv. 484–6).

[38] Though later considered an abuse, the practice was widespread and respected in earlier centuries (Dante may have taken the habit of Friars Minor at Ravenna). All possessions had to be renounced, the three vows of religion taken, and if the postulant happened to recover and went back to the world, they were deemed apostate (Dom Louis Gougaud, *Devotional and Ascetic Practices in the Middle Ages*, English edition prepared by G. C. Bateman (London: Burns, Oates and Washbourne, 1927), 141, and see 132–3). Janet Burton notes that some great Anglo-Norman ladies achieved permission to have Cistercian clothing on their deathbeds (*Monastic and Religious Orders in Britain 1000–1300* (Cambridge and New York: Cambridge University Press, 1994), 217). See further Brian Golding, 'Burial and Benefactions: An Aspect of Monastic Patronage in Thirteenth-Century England', in W. M. Ormrod (ed.), *England in the Thirteenth Century: Proceedings of the 1984 Harlaxton Symposium* (Woodbridge and Dover, NH: Boydell Press, 1986), 64–75, and 'Anglo-Norman Knightly Burials', in Christopher Harper-Bill and Ruth Harvey (eds.), *The Ideals and Practice of Medieval Knighthood* (Woodbridge: Boydell Press, 1986), 35–48.

[39] In practice, any recluse, once she had obtained permission for this difficult and respected form of spiritual life, lived within overlapping ecclesiastical and lay social structures and networks. She had a lay public of patrons and clients, whose socio-economic support was exchanged for her prayers and her counsel. She answered ultimately to the bishop of her diocese, intermediately to her spiritual director and confessor (and also to her abbess if she were the rarer form of recluse, a nun embarking on a solitary life within a convent rather than a laywoman proceeding to reclusion after episcopal investigation): see Warren, *Anchorites and their Patrons*, esp. chs. 3 and 5–8; ibid., 'The Nun as Anchoress'; Patricia J. Rosof, 'The Anchoress in the Twelfth and Thirteenth Centuries', in John A. Nichols and Lillian T. Shank (eds.), *Peaceweavers: Medieval Religious Women*, II, Cistercian Studies Series 72 (Kalamazoo: University of Michigan Press, 1987), 123–44.

[40] In its terminology for itself, the *Guide* is not exclusively addressed to a lone recluse, but is the 'riwle [rule]' or 'wisse [guide]' of *ancrene* (genitive plural), a *Guide for Anchoresses*.

each other, their servants (specified as of two kinds, indoor and outdoor). Their anchorhold had at least three cells, a parlour, perhaps some kind of yard or garden, probably a servants' room.[41] Rhetorically all this is subordinated to the dependence of the individual recluse on her *Guide*, but on that text's own evidence we should see here not only the single enclosed female body, but a miniature female community: these women are not living so much in solitary cells as in a small household which contains individual rooms.[42] In so far as virginity is constructed as heterosexual nuptiality, female collectivities can be rendered so culturally invisible that a woman can be perceived, as in one strand of the *Guide*'s address, to be solitary, but solitude in post-Conquest texts for women means 'unappended to an earthly husband' rather than literal aloneness.

The high socio-economic levels from which twelfth- and thirteenth-century women recluses usually come is significant (recluses at this period were often women who could have afforded other forms of life). In the wake of the monastic orders' late twelfth-century refusal of female recruits, women who could sought enclosure, sometimes in the face of opposition, sometimes at considerable expense, and anchoritism became an important way for laywomen to live a holy life.[43] It is untenable to see women's desire for enclosure simply as the fruit of female masochism and internalized misogyny. Certainly, religious enclosure, as

---

[41] On the physical organization of anchorholds see Warren, *Anchorites and their Patrons*, 29–36; her figures do not distinguish male and female recluses at this point, but it is clear that two and even three recluses were by no means unusual in an anchorhold, and most of the sites with more than one inhabitant discussed by Warren are those of anchoresses. Eric J. Dobson discusses the households for whom early texts and copies of the *Guide* were created (*The Origins of Ancrene Wisse* (Oxford: Clarendon Press, 1976), 253–5). On the representation of the household in the *Guide* and its associated texts, see Nicholas Watson, 'The Methods and Objectives of Thirteenth-Century Anchoritic Devotion', in Marion Glasscoe (ed.), *The Medieval Mystical Tradition in England: Exeter Symposium IV* (Cambridge: Brewer, 1987), 132–53, esp. 146–7, and for the social context of the recluse, Warren, *Anchorites and their Patrons, passim*.

[42] Even now, Christina of Markyate is remembered as a recluse rather than the foundress and prioress of Sopwell. Texts for women include household as well as cell allegories: see e.g. *Sawles Warde* (Millett and Wogan-Browne (eds. and trs.), *Medieval English Prose for Women*, 86–109); the *Jerarchie* (pseudo-Dionysius translated by Archbishop Pecham for Eleanor of Provence), ed. M. Dominica Legge, 'John Pecham's *Jerarchie*', *Medium Ævum*, 19 (1942), 77–84; *The Abbey of the Holy Ghost*, ed. N. F. Blake, *Medieval English Religious Prose*, York Medieval Texts (London: Edward Arnold and Evanston, Ill.: Northwestern University Press, 1972), 88–102, and for *The Abbey* and its companion text, *The Charter of the Holy Ghost*, see further Robert R. Raymo, 'Works of Religious and Philosophical Instruction', in *Manual of the Writings in Middle English*, vii (1986), nos. 184–6, 2545–8. Such allegorical buildings are also associated with monastic and scholastic treatises of the late 12th and 13th c. which use architectural tropes for ordering and memorizing doctrine and theology: i.e. they are part of the wider culture as well as powerfully feminized (see Christiania A. R. Whitehead, 'Making a Cloister of the Soul in Medieval Religious Treatises', *Medium Ævum*, 67 (1998), 1–29).

[43] On the rising 13th-c. rate of noble support for recluses, see Warren, *Anchorites and their Patrons*, ch. 4 (188). Royal support was institutional, though fluctuating according to the interests of individual kings (ibid., ch. 5 and see also her 'The English Anchorite in the Reign of Henry III', *Ball State University Forum*, 19 (1978), 21–8). See also Rosof, 'The Anchoress in the Twelfth and Thirteenth Centuries'.

a practice claiming to protect women—from external violence and from the purported frailties of their own nature—is designed at least in part for the comfort and reassurance of men, locking away potential victims from potential aggressors in preference to restricting male rights and powers. (It should be noted that a form of female enclosure of men was nevertheless possible: so, for instance, the abbess and convent of Elstow, though lacking episcopal powers of control over enclosure, could and did act as patron in presenting Walter the chaplain to the reclusory of Kempston and undertaking to support him there in food and clothing.)[44] Resistance to enclosure (memorably symbolized by the nuns of Markyate throwing a copy of Pope Boniface's 1298 bull on the subject at the retreating back of Bishop Dalderby) was read in early modern scholarship as confirmation of the unruliness of women, but can be read differently as a history of women's responses and achievements in the face of institutionalized underfunding and restriction.[45]

For women, enclosure might be paradise and punishment, entombment and escape, or any and all of these things. Religious enclosure's secular counterpart, life within the marital household, is both restrictive and attractive, a domain, in some of its imagery, of female containment, and also (since nuptial enclosure is the route to the territory of the matron), a domain of female power. (As Anneke Mulder-Bakker has pointed out, both maternity and age (*pace* the eternal youthfulness of virgin heroines), can importantly transform women's experiences of gender-based restriction.)[46] Like romance heroines *and* virgin martyrs, nuns *and* married women might be the subject of punitive enclosure: both Henry II's wife and his mistress were locked away at different times, while solitary confinement was a standard punishment in nunneries.[47] On the other hand Amis's wife, in the Anglo-Norman version of the Amis and Amiloun romance, thinks

---

[44] *Rotuli Roberti Grosseteste episcopi Lincolniensis, AD mccxxxv–mccliii*, ed. F. N. Davis, Canterbury and York Society 10 (London, 1913), 320.

[45] First treated by Power, *Medieval Nunneries*, 351–2: see also Makowski, *Canon Law*, 114–15 (n. 25 above). Some individual cases of breaking cloister are discussed by F. Donald Logan, *Runaway Religious in Medieval England c.1240–1540* (Oxford: Clarendon Press, 1996), see esp. ch. 3.

[46] Anneke Mulder-Bakker, '"The Prime of Their Lives": Women and Age, Wisdom and Religious Careers in Northern Europe', in Juliette Dor, Lesley Johnson, and Jocelyn Wogan-Browne (eds.), *New Trends in Feminine Spirituality: The Holy Women of Liège and their Impact* (Turnhout: Brepols, 1999), 215–36.

[47] Eleanor of Aquitaine was imprisoned for fifteen years before Henry II's death released her; Rosamund Clifford, his mistress, was sent to Godstow nunnery. Eleanor of Brittany, Prince Arthur's sister, was captured by John in 1202, and held in perpetual custody in England at Bristol 1224–34, and from 1238/9 till she died in 1241 (*Bristol Accounts of the Castle Constables*, ed. M. Sharpe, *Bristol Record Society*, 34 (1982), pp. xxvii–xxix). In Pecham's letter to Godstow the punishment for a disobedient nun is 'quinze jours enclose en une chambre en penaunce' (*Registrum*, ed. Martin, iii. 852): for a celebrated case involving the punitive enclosure of a noblewoman see Ch. 4, n. 18 below. Virgin martyr saints are conventionally represented as imprisoned in dungeons to think over their stance towards the pagan tyrant. Standard nunnery punishments included, in addition to solitary confinement, fasting and disciplines, deprivation of contact (including letters), deprivation of the veil, and saying of extra psalters (Burton, *Monastic and Religious Orders*, 13).

of hiding from her returning husband in a nunnery; Abbess Isabel of Wherwell sought and stayed in perpetual seclusion; and the semi-legendary abbess Modwenna takes seven years of anchoritic reclusion: for older women with the considerable cares of the abbess's office, reclusion may have functioned as a kind of retreat or sabbatical.[48] In a woman religious's account of a secular bride, virgin enclosure sounds more like a productive and busy life than a living death. The anonymous nun of Barking's late twelfth-century account of Edward the Confessor's queen Edith says that

God had adorned [Edith's] person with manners, virtue and beauty. In her youth she was as wise as if she were of mature age ['de grant eage']. Wantonness and worldliness was never loved by her. She remained quietly ['sutivement'] in her chamber where she produced her beautiful work. She knew how to work in a very wonderful way, sewing with silk and embroidering with gold thread. She knew how to portray everything and how to imitate in depiction. When she was wearied with sewing, she took pleasure in fine books ['en beaus livres se deduieit']. She was never found idle or without concern for every good thing. She was replete with all the virtues of good actions and good living.[49]

The history of enclosure is thus a history of women's choices as well as of women's difficulties. It remains fascinating not only because of the powerful liminality of its imagery, but because enclosure as a social phenomenon strongly exemplifies the dilemmas of recontainment and autonomy that have so often affected women: reclusion offers a kind of personal liberty to women of socio-economic privilege or achievement, but does not necessarily entail political transformation of the institutions by which it is supported.

I.3. THE OCCUPATIONS OF ENCLOSURE

These tensions also inform the occupations represented for women in the texts of virgin enclosure. Reading, a prestige activity requiring economic investment both in the production of the book and the leisure of the female reader, is the primary activity envisaged for the woman enclosed in cell or bower. In the influential *Guide for Anchoresses*, it is valued equally with prayer: 'as you read, when the heart is pleased, a devotion arises which is worth many prayers'.[50] Almost

[48] See *Amys e Amyllyoun*, ed. Hideka Fukui, ANTS Plain Texts Series (London, 1990), 28, vv. 1155–7, and see 29, vv. 1208–23 for the wife's subsequent imprisonment; *VCH, Hampshire* ii. 134 (Abbess Isabel); *St Modwenna*, ed. A. T. Baker and Alexander Bell, ANTS 7 (Oxford, 1947), vv. 5817–28.

[49] *La Vie d'Edouard le confesseur: poème anglo-normand du XII siècle*, ed. Ö. Södergård (Uppsala: Almqvist & Wiksell, 1948), vv. 1272–88.

[50] 'En mie lieu de la lescon quant li queor sei delite, sourd vne deuocion qe vaut mult d'oroisons' (Herbert, 200/22–4; Tolkien, f. 78a/15). Part Eight of *Ancrene Wisse* recommends daily reading from the *Guide* (Herbert, 317/13–15; Millett and Wogan-Browne, 148/9), while Part One recommends daily psalter recitation, reading of the Gospel or holy meditations in French

equally often envisaged as the occupation of the enclosed is embroidery or sewing of one kind or another. The production of elegant gold embroidery is a topos in the twelfth- and thirteenth-century representation of holy and royal women, such as Queen Edith in the Latin and vernacular lives of Edward the Confessor, the Anglo-Saxon princess saint Etheldreda, St Margaret of Scotland (d. 1093) in the *vita* commissioned by her daughter (Henry I's queen Matilda), or Christina of Markyate and the famous pair of slippers embroidered by her for Pope Adrian IV.[51] Although the *opus anglicanum* of female religious and the paid embroidery work of non-professed women produced valuable and treasured artefacts, the economic value of women's sewing is subordinated to its image-making function in representations of enclosure.[52] Henry of Huntingdon's epigrams mention an abbot who ordered nuns to sew and resew garments like Penelope:

> A saintly father once proclaimed a rule for holy nuns
> To sew their clothes, and then unstitch the finished work again,
> And then repeat the task, and thus perform a pleasing work.[53]

Aelred of Rievaulx's treatise on the enclosed life conflates textiles and reading in encouraging the recluse to meditation on her altar cloth, embroidering its plain whiteness with an allegory of penitential cloth production. This meditative

('versiller en psalter, lire euangeiles ou en francoys seinte meditacions', Herbert, 29/8–10—not, as in the English text, 'redunge of englisc oðer of frensch', Tolkien, f. 11a/22–3). For a full account of anchoritic reading and literacies, see Millett, ' "Women in No Man's Land" '.

  [51] For Edith, see Aelred, *Vita Aedwardi*, PL195.747, Matthew Paris, *La Estoire de seint Aedward le rei*, ed. Kathryn Young Wallace, ANTS 41 (London, 1983), vv. 1159–66; anonymous nun of Barking, *Vie d'Edouard*, ed. Södergård, vv. 1278–82: the 7th-c. Etheldreda's embroidery is not in Bede's account of this saint (*Bede's Ecclesiastical History of the English People*, ed. Bertram Colgrave and R. A. B. Mynors (Oxford: Clarendon Press, 1969), iv. 19), suggesting that this is a 12th-c. perception of her. For Margaret of Scotland see AA.SS. Iun. ii (1867), 329A: on Christina of Markyate's embroidery see *The Life of Christina of Markyate: A Twelfth Century Recluse*, ed. and tr. C. H. Talbot (Oxford: Clarendon Press, 1959), 9–10.

  [52] See A. G. I. Christie, *English Medieval Embroidery* (Oxford: Clarendon Press, 1938), Appendix I for a list of medieval embroiderers. Kay Staniland, *Embroiderers*, Medieval Craftsmen series (London: British Library, 1991), includes colour reproductions of major works of *opus anglicanum*: for embroidery used in a lay context see Frédérique Lachaud, 'Embroidery and the Court of Edward I', *NMS* 37 (1993), 33–52. By 1295 the Vatican had over a hundred *opus anglicanum* pieces in its treasury: on the dissemination of English embroidery, see Christie, 1–4. Images of saints and narrative cycles were produced by women on liturgical vestments, as in for example the Vatican cope (*c.*1260, no. 51 in Christie); the Piacenza cope (Christie no. 95 and pl. 19; Staniland, endleaves); the Bologna cope (Christie 11; Staniland, endleaves). A mitre of 1180–1210 with Becket and Stephen the protomartyr is repr. Staniland, pl. 7. Many of these pieces involved considerable investment of capital, skill, and time, whether the production of convents or lay embroideresses. It is no part of my case to deny the artistic and economic significance of this work, but rather to argue that it is represented in particular ways in the texts under discussion.

  [53] Quoted by A. G. Rigg, *A History of Anglo-Latin Literature 1066–1422* (Cambridge: Cambridge University Press, 1992), 38–9: full text ('De veritate libri') in *Historia Anglorum: The History of the English People*, ed. Diana Greenway (Oxford: Clarendon Press, 1996), 778–9.

activity in turn becomes in Aelred's imagery the spiritual production of a golden-fringed bridal robe of virtues for the enclosed woman.[54]

Although images of reading and embroidery as the occupations of enclosure give us some incidental information about these activities, their presence in treatises and saints' lives is not simply a transcription of contemporary social practice. In showing the heroine as a reader and embroidery as both her text and her occupation, treatises and saints' lives reveal their agenda of image-making. Women's time in enclosure is constructed as repetitive stasis, in which women are at once producers of images and icons themselves. Their socio-economic productivity is occluded in these representations, just as the socio-economic success of many female communities, surviving on resources that would be exiguous by the standards of many male houses, is occluded in the representations of enclosure and solitude discussed earlier. How far these representations were constraining, negotiable, or even, in some ways, enabling is a matter for debate: the nun of Barking's representation of the future Queen Edith, as noted above, does not make her sound unhappy. Julia Kristeva has characterized 'women's time' (in comparison with the linear time of [masculine] historicity, of time as project and teleology) as repetition and eternity 'whose regularity and unison with what is experienced as extra-subjective time, cosmic time, occasions vertiginous visions and unnameable *jouissance*'.[55] But, as Henry of Huntingdon's epigram suggests, the representation of women's time and life-cycle as a busy stasis might serve ecclesiastics' anxieties to regulate women within household and conventual enclosure, as much as women's own agendas.

The enclosure heroine is both reader and an image of reading as the route to romance heroinehood.[56] The Early Middle English *Seinte Katerine* (an early account of a saint important to post-Conquest women and to become of still greater importance as a model for later medieval women's reading) further suggests that the curriculum of these feminized enclosed times and spaces is one or another

---

[54] On this image in Aelred see further Jocelyn Price, ' "Inner" and "Outer": Conceptualizing the Body in *Ancrene Wisse* and Aelred's *De institutione inclusarum*' in Gregory Kratzmann and James Simpson (eds.), *Medieval English Religious and Ethical Literature: Essays in Honour of G. H. Russell* (Cambridge: Brewer, 1986), 192–208.

[55] See Julia Kristeva, 'Women's Time', in Catherine Belsey and Jane Moore (eds.), *The Feminist Reader: Essays in Gender and the Politics of Literary Criticism* (London: Macmillan, 1989), 197–217, originally published in translation in *Signs*, 7 (1981), 13–35: see also the discussion by Tina Chanter, 'Female Temporality and the Future of Feminism', in John Fletcher and Andrew Benjamin (eds.), *Abjection, Melancholia, and Love: The Work of Julia Kristeva*, Warwick Studies in Philosophy and Literature (London and New York: Routledge, 1990), 63–79. I thank John Fletcher and Finn Sinclair for illuminating written and other discussion of Kristeva: for an application of these theories to 12th- and 13th-c. literature, see Finnuala Sinclair, *Blood and Milk: Motherhood and Matrix in Old French and Occitan 'chansons de geste'* (Peter Lang, forthcoming).

[56] The *Guide for Anchoresses* brilliantly exploits the thematics of nuptiality, enclosure, reading, and containment and (because of its relatively early date, its vivid and traceable afterlife among a range of medieval audiences, and its 19th-c. reception) is a good candidate for the originary text of women's romance reading in English (though it is preceded by Anglo-Norman psalters, saints' lives, and *lais*).

form of romance.[57] Katerine will not learn or listen to 'love songs or love stories', but keeps her eyes and her heart ('most often both together') on holy writings.[58] Yet these, it emerges, are also a form of romance, the only one fit for the woman reader's heart. *Katerine* and the *Guide for Anchoresses* are but two among many texts promoting a nuptial spirituality in which, following the efflorescence of twelfth-century commentary on the Song of Songs (the 'luue boc' or 'liuere de amours' as the *Guide* calls it), religious texts are 'romanced', and the female reader is positioned in a pre-nuptial moment and trained in 'the eroticization of waiting'.[59] 'He shut them away from the world's clamour and the sight of men, so that having entered the king's chamber, they might be free in solitude for the embrace of the bridegroom alone', says St Gilbert's *Book* of his enclosure of women at Sempringham.[60] The Anglo-Norman reworking of William of Newburgh's *Explanatio* on the Song of Songs (*c*.1190), is called by its narrator a 'chaunt . . . d'amur de seinte marie'.[61] The exemplum of the lover-knight as a figure for the bridegroom of the soul is present in numerous 'contes' and lyrics 'of the king who loved a lady' ('du roy k'aveit unc amie'), as well as in the famous dramatized *exemplum* of Part Seven of the *Guide*, while Bozon's 'Le evangel translaté de Latin en Franceys' is effectively a collection of passages on love: a 'romanced' Gospel.[62] *Li romanz de Dieu et de sa mere* is the manuscript title of Hermann de Valencienne's 'bible', itself based on the liturgy, and Grosseteste's *summa* in vernacular theology is the *Chasteau d'amour*.[63] The late twelfth-century commentary on Psalm 44 written for Marie de Champagne and in insular circulation calls itself a 'chançun' and is structured as an epithalamion for a courtly wedding feast, a heavenly 'joie de la court', to which King David gains access as jongleur.[64] This is also a text offering itself, in its claim to the customary medieval understanding of the psalter as the Bible in miniature, as teaching 'le fondemant de nostre loi' (v. 2072). Romance and regulation are linked in the positioning of its audience as those who, in hearing its word, school their hearts ('Mout met son cuer a bone escole | Qui volentiers ot sa parole', vv. 2093–4). The famous linking of romance and regulation with which the *Guide for Anchoresses* opens, punning on the Song's '*recte* diligunt te' (1: 3), is but the most incisive of many linkings of romance and rule in the period.[65]

Devotion, indeed doctrine itself, is here 'romanced' in every sense, vernacularized *and* made nuptial. Even the liturgical practices envisaged for anchoresses

---

[62] Wilbur Gaffney, 'The Allegory of the Christian Knight in *Piers Plowman*', *PMLA* 46 (1931), 155–68. As Michael Evans points out, in England the lover-knight became a commonplace of vernacular poetry, and is powerfully linked in various meditational schemae with the *scutum fidei* ('An Illustrated Fragment of Peraldus' *Summa* of Vice: Harleian MS 3244', *Journal of the Warburg and Courtauld Institute*, 45 (1982), 14–68 (21)). On the *Guide* and Marie de France's use of this figure, see further Ch. 4.1 below. For the Gospel poem attributed to Bozon, see *Seven More Poems*, ed. Klenke, 19–43.

[63] For this poem's basis in the liturgy see Ina Spiele, *Li Romanz de Dieu et de sa mere d'Herman de Valenciennes* (Leyde: Presse Universitaire de Leyde, 1975), 1–5 and ch. 1; André de Mandach, '*The Creation* of Hermann de Valenciennes: An Unpublished Anglo-Norman Mystery Play of the Twelfth Century', in Ian Short (ed.), *Anglo-Norman Anniversary Essays*, ANTS OP 2 (London, 1993), 251–72. The poem also uses *chanson de geste*, romances, saints' lives, and Peter Comestor's *Historia scholastica* (see further James H. Morey, 'Peter Comestor, Biblical Paraphrase and the Medieval Popular Bible', *Speculum*, 68 (1993), 6–35 (16, 26) and on the importance of both Hermann de Valenciennes and Grosseteste's *Chasteau* for Middle English literature, John Thompson, 'The Cursor Mundi and its French Tradition', in O. S. Pickering (ed.), *Individuality and Achievement in Middle English Poetry* (Cambridge: D. S. Brewer, 1997), 19–37 (33–4): on the manuscripts of the *Chasteau* (an important text in nunnery and lay reading) see C. W. Marx, *The Devil's Rights and the Redemption in the Literature of Medieval England* (Cambridge: D. S. Brewer, 1995), Appendix 4, 160–70).

[64] *Eructavit: An Old French Metrical Paraphrase of Psalm XLIV*, ed. T. A. Jenkins, Gesellschaft für romanische Literatur, Bd. 20 (Dresden: Gesellschaft für romanische Literatur, 1909). This verse paraphrase and commentary, probably written before 1187, is extant in fourteen manuscripts (including Paris, BN f. fr. 902, which was copied in England in the 14th c. and contains the first 558 lines, ff. 159rb–162rb). For an argument against the assignation of the poem to Adam de Perseigné, see J. F. Benton, 'The Court of Champagne as Literary Centre', *Speculum*, 36 (1961), 551–91 (583–4).

[65] 'Li dreiturels vous aiment. Ceux sunt dreiturels qe viuent apres reule', Herbert, 1/15–18 (Tolkien, f. 1a/11).

in their *Guide* climax in what is presented as the nuptial embrace of the mass ('with shining love embrace your beloved who has descended from heaven into the chamber of your heart and hold him fast until he has granted you whatever you wish').[66] In his *Speculum Ecclesie* or *Mirour de seinte eglise*, probably written in 1213–14 and, like the *Guide for Anchoresses*, continuingly influential in Latin, Anglo-Norman, and Middle English versions, St Edmund of Abingdon, Archbishop of Canterbury, shapes a scheme of passion meditation on the seven canonical hours that women religious sing 'in the minster', so that 'you can spend no hour in which your heart is not sweetly busy'.[67] As much or more than medieval 'secular' narrative romance, such texts offer women formation in the new high medieval politics of romance and household, [hetero]sexuality and subordination, in a combination of 'reactionary [social and cultural] structures and private sexual radicalism' such as has been argued to inform some modern mass-produced romance.[68] Reading her book, reciting her hours, or producing and reading textile imagery, the new post-Conquest chaste reader exemplifies what has become our standard picture of the romance reader as a solitary female consumer of the very cultural script that contains her: a model of reading as feminine and enclosing.

Such images of reading seem to have been attractive for both male and female medieval readers. Part of the seductiveness of enclosure comes from the way in which erasure of a historical sense of place and identity can align a romance self with the selves of eremitic reform so much focused on in twelfth-century and later monasticism. The cell of the isolated reader, endlessly fashioning herself to her rule's aspirational directions and to her Christ bridegroom's taste, is related,

---

[66] 'od estencelant amour embracez vostre ami, qen la chambre de vostre piz est descendu du ciel. et le tenez tout ferm desquil vous eit tout grante quanqe vous volez', Herbert, 23/11–15 (Tolkien, f. 8b/18–23). For the liturgical day of the anchoress see *Ancrene Riwle: Introduction and Part One*, ed. R. W. Ackermann and Roger Dahood, Medieval and Renaissance Texts and Studies (Binghamton: SUNY, 1984), and the helpful Notes to Part I, *Anchoritic Spirituality*, tr. Savage and Watson, 342–7; Bella Millett, '*Ancrene Wisse* and the Book of Hours', in *Writing Religious Women*, ed. Denis Renevy and Christiania Whitehead (Cardiff: University of Wales Press, forthcoming).

[67] 'Pur ço lé [i.e. aspects of God's humanity as subjects for meditation] vus ay jo ci destincté par les set hures del jur ke vus chauntez a muster, ke nul' hore ne vus puse passer ke vus ne eez docement ocupé vostre quor' (*Mirour de Seinte Eglyse: St Edmund of Abingdon's Speculum Ecclesie*, ed. A. D. Wilshere, ANTS 40 (London, 1982), ch. 20 of the version for 'dames religieuses', 58/13–15). See further Mother Mary Philomena SHCJ, 'St Edmund of Abingdon's Meditations Before the Canonical Hours', *Ephemerides Liturgicae*, 3 (1964), 33–57.

[68] Janice Radway, *Reading the Romance: Women, Patriarchy and Popular Culture* (Chapel Hill: University of North Carolina Press, 1984). Much of the modern iconography of romance (for example, the role of the ring) owes even more to 12th-c. romanced spirituality than to classical sources. On medieval romance reading see Roberta Krueger, *Women Readers and Gender in Old French Romance* (Cambridge: Cambridge University Press, 1993). Michael Camille has argued that vernacular reading was frowned on because it 'encouraged a new privatisation in the reading experience', but in the case of reading imagined as specifically for women, this seems often to be a desired effect ('Seeing and Reading: Some Visual Implications of Medieval Literacy and Illiteracy', *Art History*, 8 (1985), 26–49).

as a cultural space, to the desert, equally closely associated with experiences of reform and renewal.[69] In complex ways, both comfort and a sense of power might be derived from this by women readers. Equally, images of the reclusive female reader create internalizable images of solitude and isolation which were taken up as empowering models of male attention to the self and continued, more ambiguously, to construct models of female selves.[70] But isolated reading is hardly the whole story.

As Bella Millett has shown, the thirteenth-century texts associated with enclosed women are historically early examples of literature in the modern sense of the word, 'vernacular works composed with readers not just hearers in mind'.[71] But, precisely because of the retrospective naturalization we tend to apply here, we are less likely to register the selectivity of this reading model or its ideological ambitions in its original context: it has become our norm, but was not initially so in the anchoresses' culture. Like the reading of secular gentry and noblewomen with their relatives and servants in their chambers, the reading of recluses and other women religious is also a group activity, at times audiate and oral rather than silent and solitary.[72] If the clerically authored Early Middle English *Katerine* cited above sees its heroine as a solitary reader of divine romance, Clemence of Barking (whose own reading in Latin and the vernacular in her wealthy Benedictine nunnery must have been considerable) does not sexualize Catherine's reading. In her late twelfth-century life of the saint, Clemence shows Catherine's learning and heroinehood by making her a dialectician, a public speaker,

[69] See Gerhardt Ladner, 'Images and Terms of Renewal', and Giles Constable, 'Renewal and Reform in the Religious Life: Concepts and Realities', in Robert L. Benson and Giles Constable with Carol D. Lanham (eds.), *Renaissance and Renewal in the Twelfth Century* (Oxford: Clarendon Press, 1982), 1–33 and 37–67 (esp. 48–51) respectively, and Ch. 4 below.

[70] On the culturally powerful model whereby solitude demands not disconnection but a radical shift of relation with the world, see Georgianna, *The Solitary Self*, ch. 2: for a 'male' version of the solitary reading model, see Jocelyn Wogan-Browne, 'Chaste Bodies: Frames and Experiences', in Sarah Kay and Miri Rubin (eds.), *Framing Medieval Bodies* (Manchester University Press, 1994), 24–42 (31–2).

[71] ' "Women in No Man's Land" ', 99.

[72] In the *Guide*, solitary reading and recitation within the cell is one among many practices in a whole spectrum of reading, hearing, and telling. During their blood-letting, the anchoresses are advised to exchange 'edifying stories' ('Mes daliez de paroles od voz meschines et od honestes countes solacez vous ensemble', Herbert, 311/4–7); they read aloud some of the rule to their servants once a week until they know it ('petite parcel lire a [v]oz meschines chescune symeyne vne foiz desqatant qil le sachent', Herbert, 315/37–316/3), and though they each have copied out their own service books for individual use, they will probably have had the *Guide* in a single shared manuscript (see Millett, ' "Women in No Man's Land" ', 95). In the Trinity version, the reading instructions (in a reworking for brothers and sisters in the life of religion—'freres e suers en deu', Trethewey, *The French Text*, 159/5, 9 etc.) envisage reading or hearing read: 'ke vus regardez cest escrit isci au comencement souent e deske a la fin ententiuement. E a tret le lisez ou deuant vus lire facez' ('that you often look upon this text here at the beginning and with careful attention through to the end. And read it at length, or have it read before you'), ibid. 160/25–9 (Vitellius not running at this point).

rather than a private reader.[73] In Edmund of Canterbury's *Mirour* it is clear that hearing, discussing, and enquiring about texts, rather than solitary reading of them, is the basis of much female devotional learning. In the 'Sermon a dames religioses' version of the *Mirour*, women are advised that

quantk'est escrit poit estre dit . . . si vus ne savez entendre quantk'est escrit, oez volunters le bien ke l'en vus dist, quant vus oez rien de seint' escripture, u en sermon commun, u en privee collaciun.[74]

Whatever is written can be spoken . . . if you do not know how to understand something written, listen willingly to what is beneficial in what people tell you when you hear anything of holy scripture, whether in public discourse or private conversation.

Moreover, whatever ambitions to textual enclosure are to be credited to the writers of *regulae* and other treatises, and however seductive and absorbing their constructions of 'the solitary self', the matters and modes of prescribed reading are not the same thing as that which is read and understood. Just as enclosure itself both seeks to control women and yet guarantees some notions of female autonomy, so too even silent reading (in both modern and medieval theory) is simultaneously immobilizing and yet capable of autonomous deployment by the reader (whose will and responses may be scripted but are not therefore determined).[75] A whole spectrum of response to reading as enclosure can be seen in

---

[73] See *The Life of Saint Catherine by Clemence of Barking*, ed. William MacBain, ANTS 18 (Oxford, 1964), vv. 141–4; Jocelyn Wogan-Browne and Glyn Burgess (trs.), *Virgin Lives and Holy Deaths: Two Exemplary Biographies for Anglo-Norman Women* (London: Everyman, 1996), 5. For the Latin source of these passages in both the Early Middle English and the Anglo-Norman Lives see *Seinte Katerine*, ed. d'Ardenne and Dobson, 148/82–9.

[74] *Mirour*, ed. Wilshere, 4 (for the manuscript title), and 22. For Wilshere's dating of the *Speculum* to 1213–14, see pp. xix–xx: the Anglo-Norman version may be anything up to 30 years or so later.

[75] For a modern theoretical recuperation of fantasy see Jean Laplanche and J.-B. Pontarlis, 'Fantasy and the Origins of Sexuality', tr. and repr. in Victor Burgin, James Donald, Cora Kaplan (eds.), *Formations of Fantasy* (London: Methuen, 1986), and, for an example, Cora Kaplan, '*The Thornbirds*: Fiction, Fantasy, Femininity', ibid. 142–66. Modern and medieval theories of reading have some convergences here. As Mary Carruthers argues, indeterminacy of meaning is indissociable from the reading process considered as recollective gathering of exemplary *loci* of conduct (*The Book of Memory: A Study of Memory in Medieval Culture* (Cambridge: Cambridge University Press, 1990), 169–83): while Kaplan and others, drawing on Laplanche's post-Freudian rethinking of fantasy, argue that romance importantly mobilizes the position of the spectator. Female solitaries will rarely if ever have had access to systematic memorial learning: when the *Ancrene Wisse* author thinks of 'anyone who does not know' her prayers or hours, he does not offer systematic training such as Hugh of St Victor writes for young boys for learning the psalms, but recommends having 'what you do not know written out on a scroll' (Tolkien, 25, f. 10b/21–2), while if someone does not know Matins, they are to substitute pater nosters and other prayers (f. 12a/3–4). Access to formal systems of organization ('distinccions' that you call 'dalen', Tolkien, f. 4a/20–1) is limited, though some mnemonic experience is indissociable from saying the office, and the various prayers (in groups of 5's, 7's, 4's, etc.) in *Ancrene Wisse*. For women's unscripted use of modern Harlequin romance as a source of information (travelogue and historical detail), see Radway, *Reading the Romance*, 112–13: similar possibilities abound in medieval romance. For an illuminating account of anchoritic reading as holding in its very repetitiousness the possibility of readers producing meanings for their own use, see Savage, 'The Translation of the Feminine'.

post-Conquest texts. At one end of this spectrum, reading becomes direct inscription on the body. The author of the *Guide* seems to have known some women whose response to enclosure was that of self-mutilation: 'Do not mutilate yourselves with cuts' ('na keorunge ne keorue') he tells his audience in Part Eight's practical regulations.[76] Some women in modern British prisons and related institutions slash their flesh with knives; some women have their fat cells vacuumed out or their stomachs stapled under medical supervision: both practices are intelligible as responses respectively of internalized violence and of the infinite desire to remake the body to models perceived as culturally powerful. But genre is important: there is no simple division between practical regulation and the ideology of the whole text, and we cannot here assume innocent transcription of social practice. In the saints' lives associated with the *Guide*, the slashing of chaste bodies is an important signifying process: it produces spectacle and cultural meaning as virgin martyrs are flogged, torn, raked with flesh-hooks, and burnt all over with tapers, in tortures principally confined to body surfaces and expressive of pagan tyrants' attempts at inscribing their law and power on flesh that has become a discursive site—the field of argument between virgin and tyrant, Christian and pagan. These saints are also starved for weeks at a time in dungeons, only to emerge looking more beautiful than ever. The *Guide* itself suggests that, since 'the bird with little flesh flies higher', spiritually elegant anchoresses, their soul 'enclosed in an unnatural place in a strange land . . . in a charnel house', are *slim*.[77] Ascetic control becomes explicitly a substitute for martyrdom: 'rather than asking [for more delicate food] she should die as a martyr in her discomfort . . . one should die rather than commit any deadly sin' (here, the sin of causing comment on food preferences).[78] Whether the *Guide*'s exemplified responses can be read as records of willed choices or of internalized oppression is as undecidable as the case of a punk nose-ring worn on a twentieth-century face. What is certain is that they represent only a few points on a wide spectrum of women readers' and hearers' responses. Other reading possibilities are explored in the rest of this book.

1.4. VIRGINS, WIVES, WIDOWS

It is sometimes claimed that virginity moves from being technical to honorary in the later Middle Ages.[79] But this understates the essentially rhetorical nature

---

[76] Millett and Wogan-Browne, 136–7 (Tolkien, f. 1136/7). No direct equivalent in the earlier French version (Herbert, 308/32–7); later Trinity version not running.

[77] 'Ces oyseles volent bien qe ount poi de char . . . Ele est ici en estrange lieu boutee en vne prisone enclosee en vne mesone de mortalite', Herbert, 108/18–20, 115/33–6 (Tolkien, f. 36a/11 and f. 38b/9–10; *Anchoritic Spirituality*, tr. Savage and Watson, 101, 97).

[78] 'Mes auant ceo qe de tiele demande lieue nule esclaundre, auant moerge martire en sa miseise', Herbert, 88/26–9 (Tolkien, f. 28b/5–6; Savage and Watson, tr., 87).

[79] See Clarissa W. Atkinson ' "Precious Balsam in a Fragile Glass": The Ideology of Virginity in the Later Middle Ages', *Journal of Family History*, 8 (1983), 131–43.

and endemic turbulence of virginity as a construct: there is no time at which virginity is fixed, no time at which it is not changing into honorary forms. Even the model of female virginity as anatomically marked destabilizes and disappears on closer inspection (the hymen is periodically reinvented in Western anatomical discourse as an identifiable and normatively intact seal, but is in fact bi-labial and perforate in its normal growth and difficult to identify as a discrete anatomical feature).[80] The relations between 'technical' and 'spiritual' virginity are constantly and revealingly negotiable. So Anglo-Norman *pulcele* and *virgine*, as also Middle English *virgine* and *mayden*, are all used both interchangeably and on occasion oppositionally within each language to make distinctions between 'physical' and 'spiritual' virginity (distinctions which, in the orthodox texts most likely to come down to us, routinely stop short of heterodox dualism).[81]

Virginity is often defined as a kind of dynamic stasis which, like the construction of women's time in this literature, is both absorbing and confining for its female practitioners. No sooner is virginity defined as inhering in technical bodily intactness, than it is shifted to inhering in the will, so that even a woman who could feel sure about her virginity in a technical sense is encouraged to remain fearful about the state of her volition, and given many points to watch for in order to remain truly virgin. Virginity can be undermined and negated by lustful thoughts or even by spiritual pride in being a virgin. So Christina of Markyate, after years of sustained resistance in which she preserved her virgin status against parental violence and enforced betrothal before finally escaping into her religious career, is represented, on the verge of profession, as anxious about

what she should say, when the bishop enquired during the ceremony of consecration about her virginity. For she was mindful of the thoughts and stings of the flesh with which she had been troubled, and even though she was not conscious of having fallen

[80] See Giulia Sissa, 'Une virginité sans hymen: le corps féminin en Grèce', *Annales économies sociétés civilisations*, 39 (1984), 1119–39; ead., *Le Corps virginal: la virginité féminine en Grèce ancienne* (Paris: Vrin, 1987); Jocelyn Wogan-Browne, 'The Virgin's Tale', in Ruth Evans and Lesley Johnson (eds.), *Feminist Readings of Middle English Literature: The Wife of Bath and All Her Sect* (London and New York: Routledge, 1994), 165–94. Experimentally in lectures and workshops on the history of the hymen to the Association of Women in Medicine in Great Britain, I found that women physicians can still internalize this construction as part of training in the (astonishingly loaded) language of their anatomy textbooks (see *Women in Medicine*, Workshop Reports, Wogan-Browne, London, July 1993, 6–7). As Salih points out, in virginity discourse the hymen is 'invoked as a physical reality in order to be treated as a metaphor', 'Performing Virginity', 107.

[81] See H. Kurath and S. M. Kuhn (eds.), *Middle English Dictionary* (Ann Arbor, 1956–); L. W. Stone and W. Rothwell (eds.), *Anglo-Norman Dictionary* (London: MHRA, 1977–92). The view in Wogan-Browne, 'The Virgin's Tale', that 'maydenhod' and 'virginite' in Middle English respectively represent technical and spiritual virginity is too categorical: this is a matter of tendencies rather than a stable conceptual opposition. For an example of heretical virginity, see further Ch. 3.2 below.

either in deed or in desire ['neque actu neque voluntate'], she was chary of asserting that she had escaped unscathed ['integram evasisse'].[82]

But virginity can also be restored through repentance: a fair young girl whose will assents to 'delit de lecherie' can 'recover her virginity by repenting her will to evil'.[83] Physical testing for virginity by midwives or juries of matrons had been condemned by Augustine on the grounds that it risked destroying the very thing it sought to validate, but the interior spiritual condition of virginity is conceptualized as requiring constant inspection and maintenance.[84]

   Not only the virgin state itself, but its interrelation with other conditions is continually renegotiated. The recuperation of virginity for widows and wives is perhaps the single most dynamic aspect of virginity's history. By this I mean not just the quasi-technical ability of penance to restore virginity (see further Chapter 4 below), or conceptual movement between technical and spiritual virginities, but the interactive construction of virginity and other states for women. Not even rhetorically can virginity be sustained as an exclusive state, and neither technical intactness nor a form of professed religious life is a prerequisite for being affected or targeted by virginity texts. So vigorous, indeed, is lay and female interest in the religious life that the church had frequently to insist that the belief that only virgins could be saved was heretical.[85] And no sooner is the separateness of virginity asserted than other states are rewritten back into it:

Ne tele thu nawt ethelich, al beo thu meiden, to widewen ne to iweddede . . . is betere a milde wif other a meoke widewe then a prud meiden.

Though you may be a virgin, do not undervalue widows and married women . . . a modest wife or a meek widow is worth more than a proud virgin.[86]

Or, as the Middle English *Vices and Virtues* puts it, 'there are many in paradis that han lyud [lived] in mariage and widowhode that ben wel nere [nearer] God than many virgines'. (All this text can save as virginity's exclusive prerogative is the claim that 'neuer the later [nevertheless] the virgines han a speciale coroune'.)[87]

---

[82] *Life of Christina*, ed. Talbot, 126–7. See also *Hali Meiðhad*, in Millett and Wogan-Browne, 36/20–38/19.

[83] 'Ele peust recouerer sa *virginite par* repentance de sa male volunte', *Compileisun des dis comandemenz*, ch. 5 (the three orders of salvation) in Oxford, Bodleian Library, MS Bodley 654 (f. 137ra). The treatise adds a warning that once corrupted by the deed of lechery, *pucelage* (as opposed to *virginité*) cannot be recovered.

[84] See Sissa, 'Une virginité sans hymen', 1136. Ambrose is also indignant about midwives touching Christian virgins, PL16.891–8.

[85] See Thomas Head, 'The Marriages of Christina of Markyate', *Viator*, 21 (1990), 75–101. See also Michel Riquet SJ, 'Christianity and Population', in Orest and Patricia Ranum (eds.), *Popular Attitudes to Birth Control in Pre-Industrial France and England* (New York, 1972), 21–44.

[86] *Hali Meiðhad*, in Millett and Wogan-Browne, 38/19–20 and 23–4.

[87] *The Book of Vices and Virtues*, ed. W. N. Francis, EETS os 217 (London, 1942), 260/7: this is a Middle English version of Friar Laurent's *Somme le roi* of 1280 (which also circulated in French in England): see Ellen Virginia Kosmer, 'A Study of the Style and Iconography of a Thirteenth-Century *Somme le roi* (British Museum MS Add. 54180), with a Consideration of Other Illustrated *Somme* Manuscripts of the Thirteenth, Fourteenth and Fifteenth Centuries' (Ph.D. thesis, Yale

Virginity is also positioned relationally as the best of three in a gradational hierarchy of estates of the flesh (marriage, chastity, virginity), which uses the parable of the sower in Matthew 13: 4–9 to image virginity as the human condition with the highest spiritual yield. This use was established in patristic writing and further developed in the literature of spiritual formation and the proliferating occupational taxonomies of the twelfth and thirteenth centuries. Although the triad moralizes rather than reveals women's economic and social importance, it involves more direct address and consideration of their lives than other estates schema, which frequently omit or elide women altogether. So Honorius 'Augustodunensis' is one among many twelfth-century writers to develop the basic Isidorean three occupations (labouring, fighting, praying) of the early Middle Ages: the estates of his influential twelfth-century *Speculum Ecclesie* are priests, judges, rich, poor, soldiers, farmers, married people.[88] The earliest vernacular 'estates handbook', probably written between 1168 and 1178 by Bishop Etienne de Fougères (a former chaplain of Henry II) for Cecily, Countess of Herford, does include women, but while dividing men by occupation (clergé, chevalier, bourgeois) places women within moral categories—good (stable and faithful married women, given, like the countess herself, to good works) and bad (adulterous, lesbian).[89] Aquinas's account of estates theory deals only with male ecclesiastics and religious laymen, not women in religion.[90]

University, 1973: University Microfilms, Ann Arbor). *Miroir du monde* texts also transmit this kind of material in French and English (Raymo, *Manual of the Writings in Middle English*, vii, nos. 10–11).

[88] *Speculum ecclesie*, PL172.807–1108. A 12th-c. handbook of monastic orders exceptionally mentions nuns and recluses but is unfinished: see Giles Constable and Bernard Smith (eds.), *Libellus de diversis ordinibus et professionibus qui sunt in aecclesia* (Oxford: Oxford Medieval Texts, 1972). On the three estates, see further Matthäus Bernards, *Speculum virginum: Geistigkeit und Seelenleben der Frau im Hochmittelalter* 2 Auflag (Cologne and Vienna: Böhlau, 1982), 40–59; Atkinson, '"Balsam"'; Georges Folliet, 'Les Trois Catégories de chrétiens: suivie d'un thème augustinien', *L'Année théologique augustinienne*, 14 (1954), 81–96. For the education of children including girls in the virgin status in the 12th and 13th c. see Jenny Swanson, 'Childhood and Childrearing in *ad status* Sermons by Later Thirteenth-Century Friars', *JMH* 16 (1990), 309–31; see also Alain de Lille's model sermons to married people, virgins, and widows in his *De arte praedicandi* (PL210.109–98, tr. Gillian Evans, *Alain de Lille: The Art of Preaching*, Cistercian Studies Series 23, Kalamazoo, Mich.: Cistercian Publications, 1981), model sermons xlv, xlvi, and xlvii (PL210.193–5). See also Jenny Swanson, *John of Wales: A Study of the Works and Ideas of a Thirteenth-Century Friar* (Cambridge: Cambridge University Press, 1989), ch. 5, esp. 135–6.

[89] *Le Livre des Manières*, ed. R. A. Lodge (Geneva: Droz, 1979). On the probable author, see 13–15; on the dedicatee ('Contesse de Hierefort', vv. 1205), see 17–18: there is a portrait of her as a virtuous and charitable woman upholding her husband's rank, vv. 1205–24.

[90] *Summa Theologiae* (London and New York: Blackfriars with Eyre & Spottiswoode and McGraw-Hill, 1964), xlvii, *The Pastoral and Religious Lives (2a2ae 183–9)* (London: Blackfriars, 1973), 183–9. In satiric works, such as the *Ordre de bel ayse* of which there is a copy in MS Harley 2253, the nuns of 'Simplingham' (Sempringham, Britain's post-Conquest double order) are extensively satirized, but even then only as part of a salaciously understood notion of double monasteries: nuns are often omitted from anti-clerical satire as in 'Sur les états du monde' (*Anglo-Norman Political Songs*, ed. Isabel S. T. Aspin, ANTS 11 (Oxford, 1953), no. XII, 130–42, see esp. 133, vv. 31 ff. and 135, vv. 115 ff.).

As an account of the three 'orders of salvation', the threefold hierarchy of the flesh becomes part of the extensive literature of compilations and manuals, for both clergy and laypeople, developing from Lateran III onwards and given still further impetus by Lateran IV. It is found in various combinations—with explications of the ten commandments, with the Anselmian gifts of the spirit and the flesh, the joys of heaven and pains of hell and purgatory, and lists of vices and virtues. A relatively early example is found in an Anglo-Norman poem which positions virginity first as 'seven times brighter than the sun in summer, always seeing Christ face to face', but which also defends marriage as an 'ordere enclose' in Christ and a worthy state, even if inferior to virginity and chastity.[91] The estates of the flesh also inform much preaching, notably in *ad status* sermons, which are often addressed not only to occupational estates such as the clerisy or the military but to the wedded, the widowed, and the virgin lives.[92] In detailed articulation, however, these estates of the flesh tend to disappear as a hierarchy of three distinct 'orders' and to become a continuum. The late thirteenth-century Anglo-Norman *La Compileison*, an important compilation of treatises for 'brothers and sisters in God', devotes a chapter to 'the five degrees of chastity which are found in virginity and in widowhood', and its calibrations of virginity are constructed in reference to marriage:

[1]. 'Li primer degré est li plus haut par deuant Deu: si est uirginité de quor e de cors par vo[u] p[ro]mis a Deu en ferme uolunté de garder sei en netteté.
[2]. Li secund degré si est en cele ki ad ceste volunté de uiure en uirginité. Mes ele ne veut pas p[u]r ceste uirginité par promesse de bouche ne par vou sa uolonté a deu confermer.
[3]. Li tierce degré si est en cele ki n'est pas oncore certeine ne purpensee si de se veut fere marier ou uiure en uirginité. Mes si com Deu mettra en sa uolunté ceo uou ora ele fere garder.
[4]. Li quart degré en est cele ki de mariage ne de uirginité n'en a ausi com pou ou nient pensee, mes cele ke ele memes desira ceo fra ele qant ele uoudra.
[5]. Li quint degré est de cele ki est oncore en virginité e ad certein purpos de estre marie[e] e auer delit de sa char en esposailles, mes ele ne set pas a ki <ele> se veut copler. Cest ne est pas plus haut(e) deuant Deu mes plus basse ke bone femme ki est marie.

---

[91] 'Plus cler vii feiz | ke n'est en esté li solaiz: face a face tout jors veit Crist', 'Poème anglo-normand sur le mariage, les vices et les vertus, par Henri (XIIIe siècle)', ed. Jacques Monfrin, in *Mélanges de langue et de littérature du Moyen Age et de la renaissance offerts à Jean Frappier, par ses collègues, ses élèves et ses amis* (Geneva: Droz, 1970), ii. 845–67 (857, vv. 25–9; 858, v. 61). This and related themes are also treated extensively by Bozon: see his 'Lettre de l'empereur Orgueil', ed. Johann Vising, *Deux poèmes de Nicholas Bozon: Le char d'orgueil; La lettre de l'empereur Orgueil* (Göteborg: Elander, 1919), and in anonymous estates poems (F. J. Tanquerey (ed.), *Deux poèmes moraux anglo-français: Le Roman des romans et le Sermon en vers* (Paris: Champion, 1922)).

[92] See D. L. D'Avray and M. Tausche, 'Marriage Sermons in *ad status* Collections of the Central Middle Ages', *AHDLMA* 47 (1980), 71–119.

Car ele ne seet pas ki ele ueut auer, e la femme ki est marie[e] ne quiert autre fors celui a ki ele est acoplee.[93]

[1]. The first degree is the highest before God and is virginity of heart and body promised by vow to God with a stable will to keep oneself in purity.

[2]. The second degree is to be found in that woman who wishes to live in virginity. But she does not wish to confirm her will to this virginity before God by verbal promise or vow.

[3]. The third degree is found in the woman who is not yet certain or resolved whether she wishes to be married or live in virginity. But according to how God inclines her will, that vow from thenceforth she will keep.

[4]. The fourth degree is found in the woman who has so far given little or no consideration to virginity or marriage, but will do that which she wants when she chooses.

[5]. The fifth degree is in the woman who is still virgin and has it in mind to marry and to have the pleasure of her flesh in her nuptials, but she does not know to whom she wishes to be joined. This degree is not higher before God but lower than that of a good married woman. For she does not know whom she wishes to have and the woman who is married does not seek anyone other than him to whom she is joined.

Earlier texts can show a similar recuperation of virginity's exclusions: in the twelfth century, for instance, St Hugh of Lincoln teaches that the married will obtain the same glory in heaven as virgins and celibates.[94] The *Compileison* extends its recuperations to the mothers of virgin daughters: the daughters will be bright and shining stars in heaven (providing they stay humble), but the mothers will

---

[93] From the fourth treatise in the Anglo-Norman 'compileisun' of five treatises on penance and confession: *Compileisun des dis comandemenz*, cap. 15, 'De treis ordres de sauuacion', Paris, MS BN f. fr. 6276, f. 102va (collated with Cambridge, Trinity College MS R.14.7, f. 119ra, diacritics and paragraphing added, word-division and punctuation modernized).
  The later Anglo-Norman version of the *Guide for Anchoresses* (*Ancrene Wisse*) is the source for this compilation's fifth treatise (the *Vie de gent de religion*) and for much of the first and second (*Compileison de set morteus pecches, Compileison de seinte penance*). The *compileison* amounts to over 29,000 lines of manuscript text: it is dated to 1257–74 (Trethewey, *The French Text*, p. xxiii). Parts of it are repeatedly recompiled in English translation in major later works such as *The Pricke of Conscience* and the *Book of Ghostly Bataylle*. Hope Emily Allen argued that although it includes five treatises, it was designed as a single compilation, based on an expanded version of *Ancrene Wisse*, and serving as a religious manual for both professed and lay people ('Wynkyn de Worde and a Second French Compilation from the *Ancrene Riwle* with a Description of the First', in *Essays and Studies in Honor of Carleton Brown* (New York: New York University Press, 1940), 182–219: see also Marcel Thomas, 'Une compilation anglo-normande de la fin du xiiie siècle: "La vie de gent de religion"', in *Recueil de travaux offerts à M. Clovis Brunel* (Paris: Société de l'école des chartes, 1955), ii. 586–98. On the third treatise (the *Compileison des peines de purgatorie* ascribed to Grosseteste) see Robert J. Relihan, '*Les peines de purgatorie*: The Anglo-Norman and Latin Manuscript Traditions', *Manuscripta*, 22 (1978), 158–68. Other parts of the first and second 'compileisun', and the whole of the fourth (*Compileison des dis commandements*) need a great deal of further work, as does the whole compilation. The Paris manuscript cited above is the fullest for the non-*Ancrene Wisse* sections of the *compileison* (manuscripts containing the *Vie de gent de religion* are described by Trethewey, *The French Text*, pp. xii–xvi).
[94] *Magna vita sancti Hugonis (The Life of St Hugh of Lincoln)*, ed. and tr. Decima L. Douie and David Hugh Farmer (Oxford: Clarendon Press, 1961; repr. with corr., 1985), i. 9: and cf. p. xviii.

shine 'like dark stars'.[95] A mid-thirteenth-century text composed for a married woman, the *Miroir ou évangiles des domnées* by Rober the chaplain for Elena de Quenci, wife of Lord Alain la Zouche, bestows on its patroness a metaphorical flower of virginity, which can, in the trope of virgin fecundity, bear fruit:

> Deu raime des espus la flur
> Qui se tenent en chaste amur,
> Qu'il ne.l sunt pas pur lecherier
> Mes pur seinz enfanz engendrer,
> Qui soeffrent icest mundeine fais
> En pacience, en ben, en peis.
> E s'il mesfunt par charnalité
> Tant s'amendrunt de lur gré.
> L'espusaille qui ben flurist
> Mut avera gent merite od Crist.[96]

God restores the flower of spouses who maintain themselves in chaste love (providing they are not married for lechery's sake but to beget children in blessing) and who suffer the accidents of this world in patience, good will, and peace. And if they err in the flesh, so much the more they may make amends through their good will. The marriage that flourishes will receive great reward with Christ.

Some churchmen went further again. Jacques de Vitry, writer of the influential life of the married but celibate Marie d'Oignies in early thirteenth-century Liège, preaches that 'the virtue known as Virginity is not lost on marriage, but retained with a new name, *castitas matrimonialis*, so long as people do not violate the marriage bed'.[97] A late twelfth-century English treatise on the vices says that those who have lost their 'likamliche maidenhad' can still have *continentia*,

---

[95] 'Mes seint Augustin dist ke la file pucele est meillor de sa mere mariee. e si eles seient ambedeus umbles eles serrunt ambedeus en ciel coronees. La fille pur virginité serra si come vne esteile luisante e clere, e la mere si come une esteile oscure. Mes si la mere seit omble, ele auera líu en ciel, e la fille pucele, si ele seit orgoilleuse, n'en auera nul líu fors ou le diable, ki illoc chai par orgoill', *Compileisun des dis comandemenz*, ch. 5, Paris, BN f. fr. 6276, f. 101r ('St Augustine says that the virgin daughter [pucele] is better than her married mother and if they are both humble they will both be crowned in heaven. Because of her virginity [virginité] the daughter will be like a shining and bright star and the mother like a dark star. But if the mother is humble, she will have a place in heaven and if the virgin daughter [pucele] is proud she will have no place other than with the devil, who fell thence through pride'). For Aquinas's endorsement of such views in the 13th c., see *ST*, 2a2ae, 152.5 (Blackfriars, 1967), xliii. 184–7.

[96] *Miroir ou Les Évangiles des domneiches: edizione di otto domeniche*, ed. Saverio Panunzio (Bari: Adriatrica Editrice, 1967), 1–9, 115, vv. 60–9. See further Keith Val Sinclair, 'The Anglo-Norman Patrons of Robert the Chaplain and Robert of Greatham', *FMLS* 27 (1992), 193–208. Similar reassurance is offered to non-virgin nuns: see *Le Sermon en vers de la chastéé as nonains de Gautier de Coinci*, ed. Tauno Nurmela (Helsinki: Société de la littérature finnoise, 1937), 145, vv. 383–8.

[97] D'Avray and Tausche, 'Marriage Sermons', 88 n. 70, quoting from BN lat. 17509 f. 137vb: 'virtus illa, que virginitas appellatur ante matrimonium, non amittitur sed retinetur, et castitas matrimonialis in coniugibus nuncupatur, quando thorum immaculatum et honorabiles nuptias conservare procurant'. See further Carolyn Muessig, 'Paradigms of Sanctity for Thirteenth-Century Women', in Beverly Mayne Kienzle *et al.* (eds.), *Models of Holiness in Medieval Sermons*, Textes et études du Moyen Age 5 (Louvain-la-Neuve: Fédération internationale des instituts d'études médiévales, 1996), 85–102.

pudicitia, and *castitas*.[98] Medieval chaste marriage does not mean marriage without sex, but marriage with ordinary licit sexual relations for the purpose of procreation. Marriage is thus on a spectrum with virginity, not just in opposition to it, and the division between the two is not always constituted by sexual activity.

In the same way, widowhood is not simply a fixed outer form of occupation, but an unstable interior condition, dependent on the grace of God and liable to the ruinous effects of spiritual pride. In Elena de Quenci's Gospel homilies, those who live in pious widowhood present a beautiful flower to Christ, but the fruit of charity is only cultivated with humility.[99] In the Anglo-Norman *Compileison* and the French *Somme le roi*, as in their various Middle English descendants and analogues, widowhood is given as many specific gradations as virginity: 'vidual chastity ['chastete de uedeté'] has . . . five degrees ['cinc maneres de degrez']', as the *Compileison* puts it.[100] The widow who confirms the 'chastity of her heart and her promise to God by her mouth's vow has a higher chastity before God than others who do not wish to vow themselves', but such others are not so much excluded from holy widowhood as encouraged to go further in it: in any case, 'no man or woman can have chastity or keep or acquire any other virtue without the special grace of God'.[101] This kind of spiritual articulation of the estate of widowhood has the same enclosing force as the vision of the virgin's life as dynamic but interior and contained stasis. But, given the tendency of maternity and age to confer an authority that could cut across gender-based restrictions, and given that widows had the greatest opportunities for control of property of their own, this containment is more striking as an aspiration of texts inscribing widowhood than as an account of widows' lives. Although the numbers of widows who have left traces of their religious lives, texts, and foundations in the sources of post-Conquest Britain form, as far as can be estimated, a quantitatively small proportion of the population, they are visible in greater numbers than women who had not been married, and their significance as cultural patrons is qualitatively high.[102] If widowhood is a

---

[98] *Vices and Virtues*, ed. F. Holthausen, EETS os 89 (London, 1888), 131/20–2: in the Middle English *Vices and Virtues* quoted above, marriage provides the third and fourth of five degrees of chastity, of which the first is youthful premarital virginity, the second repented loss of chastity, and the fifth dedicated virginity (*Vices and Virtues*, ed. Francis, 243–60): a sixth degree is clerical celibacy and a seventh the religious life (ibid. 260–72).

[99] *Évangiles des domnées*, ed. Panunzio, 118/296–303.   [100] Paris, BN f. fr. 6276, f. 102va.

[101] 'Cele uedue ki *con*ferme de queor e de *pro*messe a Deu *par* vou de bouche sa chasteté est plus haute deva*n*t Deu ke ne sunt autres ki ceo ne volent voer. Mes ceo sachez ke nul home ne nule fe*m*me poet chasteté aver ne garder ne autre uertu purchacer sanz especiale *grac*e de Deu', ibid.

[102] On vidual patronage, see further Chs. 5 and 6 below: for the proportion of households with a single (widow or widower) head, John S. Moore gives 'about one in eight' ('The Anglo-Norman Family: Size and Structure', *ANS* 14 (1992), 153–96 (188)). Henrietta Leyser suggests 10% of medieval English households would 'at a conservative estimate' be headed by widows (*Medieval Women: A Social History 450–1500* (New York: St Martin's Press, 1995), 168). For never-married women attempting a religious career and foundation, the case of Christina of Markyate suggests that ecclesiastical friendships and institutional affiliations were needed to substitute the power of family and kinship groups if a female foundation was to stabilize as a religious house.

version of death to the world, it is one in which, like the saints themselves, women could have a significant afterlife of activity.

The gradations between all the estates of the flesh, then, are both more nuanced and more unstable than at first appears, and the argument that there is a late medieval change in the relation of technical and volitional virginity needs refining. Virginity does indeed seem to have been too powerful and prestigious a cultural ideal to be ignored or discarded: rather, women negotiated with and redefined it so as to allow wives and mothers status as honorary virgins. But this is not of itself new: virginity is *always* recouped, *always* extended so as not to exclude wives and widows. This is in the interest both of churchmen and of women. Churchmen had always to take account of women's actuality in their pastoral work as in their soliciting of donations. Virginity's constant conceptual modification and inflection towards the other estates suggests not only its own dynamic lability, but also that laywomen never ceased wresting some of its territory for themselves. Together with asceticism it confers prestige on regimes of household and personal conduct which are often more readily accessible to women than institutional and occupational status.

1.5. FEMALE COMMUNITY AND ITS HISTORIES

Virginity theory's strenuous occlusions of history and collectivity for women make the representation of female community a matter of particular political significance. In the light of the arguments above, it is almost unnecessary to insist that, although the inhabitants of the 150 or so female foundations in post-Conquest England may on occasion in the twelfth and thirteenth centuries be addressed as if they were identikit young consecrated virgins, the social composition of female communities is much more varied. As the work of Thompson, Riddy, and Gilchrist has made clear, however firmly convents may be enclosed in the theories and representations of the churchmen responsible for them, monastic life included a range of options of less than strict segregation, and was frequently permeable as between lay and professed women.[103] Women enter and sometimes re-enter communities as virgins, wives, and widows at different stages of their lives and for different reasons.[104] Although by the thirteenth

[103] Sally Thompson, *Women Religious*, esp. chs. 2–4 and 9–10; Roberta Gilchrist, *Contemplation and Action: The Other Monasticism* (London and New York: Leicester University Press, 1995); Felicity Riddy, '"Women talking about the things of God"'. At Ickleton Priory, in 1278, the Archbishop's Vicar-General forbade the reception of married laywomen for holidays, and enjoined that secular women should not stand in the choir during the singing of the canonical hours or while mass was celebrated (*VCH, Cambs.* ii. 224). For other attempts at stricter segregation which reveal the presence of laywomen in convents, see Makowski, *Canon Law and Cloistered Women*, ch. 7.

[104] As against Christina of Markyate's desire to enter a religious community, compare the famous involuntary veiling of Gunnhilda, Harold Godwineson's daughter: see A. Wilmart, 'Une lettre inédite de St Anselme à une moniale inconstante', *Rev. bén.* 40 (1928), 319–32.

century there were episcopal prohibitions against veiling women younger than 15, small girls might be present for education and/or safe-keeping, and small boys were also sometimes taught initially in nunneries.[105] Far from severing family ties, female religious houses functioned in the service of family lineage requirements—as *gynacea* for surplus women or safe-keeping for women whose dynastic potential was to be held in reserve, as repositories of family identity and commemoration, as sources of intercession and other benefits in spiritual exchange on behalf of both living and dead. Although the monastic *vita* of Christina of Markyate represents her as bitterly opposed by her family (and as leaving it for a pronouncedly eremitic form of life in the first instance), many women did become inhabitants of female communities without irrevocably leaving their family milieu, especially in houses founded by family members. Lay women's involvement in professed career virginity had long been institutionalized in the responsibilities of pre-Conquest queens for nunneries laid down in the *Regularis Concordia* of the 970s.[106] It was also powerfully represented in the *vitae* of virgin Anglo-Saxon queens, abbesses, and foundresses written before and after the Conquest, and continued in the patronage of élite nunneries and in the vocations of women in semi-religious lives.[107]

Important as royal or aristocratic leadership was in the identity of monastic houses, the class composition of female communities was also varied: lay sisters and servants inhabited most kinds of religious community, providing an element of class mix even in 'solitary' anchoritic groups. In tracing the families of donors

---

[105] Child oblation became a less regular practice during the 12th c. (though Cecilia, daughter of William Marshall, was a child oblate at Holy Trinity, Caen, see Thompson, *Women Religious*, 178). On oblation see John Doran, 'Oblation or Obligation? A Canonical Ambiguity', in Diana Wood (ed.), *The Church and Childhood*, SCH 31 (1994), 127–41 (141). In the 13th c., Archbishop Pecham forbade veiling virgins before the age of 15 (*Registrum*, ed. Martin, ii. 653). Nuns had the right to protest parental oblation at the 'age of intelligence' if forcibly oblated as a child. But they had to protest at the appropriate time (Doran, 'Oblation or Obligation?', 136).

[106] See Thomas Symons, '*Regularis concordia*: History and Derivation', in David Parsons (ed.), *Tenth-Century Studies: Essays in Commemoration of the Millennium of the Council of Winchester and the 'Regularis Concordia'* (London and Chichester: Phillimore, 1975), 37–59; Barbara Yorke, 'The Secular Context of Anglo-Saxon Nunneries', lecture, Nov. 1998, Oxford.

[107] On the range of religious and semi-religious lives for women in pre- and post-Conquest England see Jean A. Truax, 'From Bede to Orderic Vitalis: Changing Perspectives on the Role of Women in the Anglo-Saxon and Anglo-Norman Churches', *HSJ* 3 (1991), 35–51; Patricia Halpin, 'Women Religious in Late Anglo-Saxon England', *HSJ* 6 (1994), 97–109; Carol Neumann de Vegvar, 'Saints and Companions to Saints: Anglo-Saxon Royal Women Monastics in Context', in Szarmach (ed.), *Holy Men and Holy Women*, 51–93; Barbara Yorke, 'Sisters Under the Skin', *RMS* 15 (1989), 95–117. The writings of Archbishop Wulfstan of York and Worcester (d. 1023) voice a recurrent concern with the disposition of widows and the law codes formulated by him portray the good widow as very similar to later vowesses (*Die 'Institutes of Polity, Civil and Ecclesiastical', Ein Werk Erzbischofs Wulfstans von York* (Bern: Francke, 1959), ed. K. Jost, I Polity, D 2, 91 'Be wuduwan' (136–7)). For OE 'nonne' in the sense of vowess, see Mary Clayton, 'Ælfric's Judith: Manipulative or Manipulated?', *Anglo-Saxon England*, 23 (1994), 215–27 (225–7). The lay/religious virgin/chastity permeabilities discussed above may thus be as characteristic of Anglo-Saxon as of Anglo-Norman England.

to post-Conquest Shaftesbury, for example, Kathleen Cooke has found that the familial origin of the nuns themselves spans a wide class range beyond Anglo-Saxon and Norman nobles, with an overlap between class groups in landowners and in urban mercantile and administrative élites.[108] This is not to say that distinctions were not sometimes made: in 1298, for instance, the Augustinian canonesses of Chatteris fed and clothed one woman, Idonea, as a lay sister, refusing her any more prestigious rank—she was illiterate (i.e. insufficiently Latinate to sing the offices) and Archbishop Winchelsea had insisted she be received as a choir nun (the objection here may have been as much to the bishop's imposition as to Idonea's *illetterata* status, with its implication of low rank).[109] But it is to insist that the burden of recent research suggests that we should and can think of convents as miniature polities rather than, in the imagery of ideal virginity, as the celestial ballrooms of young debutantes.

Fluidity of conceptual and social distinction between virgins, wives, and widows is repeated between anchoresses, nuns, vowesses, laywomen, as it is in the material composition and the history of female foundations. Female communities embodied this permeability of lay and religious life for women in an architecture that tended to interpret institution as household. Nunneries and gentry houses shared planning features, and small *familiae* groups developed in nunneries.[110] Only exceptionally grand convents could aspire to anything like large monastic corporate building programmes. And even so, when, for instance, the wealthy house of Elstow was rebuilt so as to approximate to a male house, the nuns insisted on arranging themselves in the way familiar from castles.[111] (The mother of an Elstow nun also got herself privately housed at the aristocratic French convent of Marcigny in spite of Lateran IV's prohibitions of women living in private dwellings in religious houses and wanting to be called nuns while not strictly under rule.)[112] Such groups are not only fluid in their internal social structures, but labile in their institutional identity. With a few privileged exceptions, female houses rarely have long and stable institutional histories. Although bishops strove to tighten the notion of the enclosed community both conceptually and in terms of the regulation of behaviour, post-Conquest female communities continued their long existence as the partly hidden history of lay as well as religious women.

Many aspects of the history of female houses are obscured both in medieval and in some modern accounts. In monastic hagiography and historiography, the

---

[108] 'Donors and Daughters: Shaftesbury Abbey's Benefactors, Endowments and Nuns c.1086–1130', *ANS* 12 (1990), 29–45.

[109] *VCH, Cambs.* ii. 220.

[110] Roberta Gilchrist, *Gender and Material Culture: The Archaeology of Religious Women* (London and New York: Routledge, 1994). On the growth of anchorholds into larger communities, see Sharon K. Elkins, *Holy Women of Twelfth-Century England* (Chapel Hill and London: University of North Carolina Press, 1988), 45–54, 150–60; Thompson, *Women Religious*, ch. 2.

[111] Gilchrist, *Gender and Material Culture*, 126, 168.   [112] Thompson, *Women Religious*, 90.

representation of female virgin saints tends to express the needs of monastic institutions, rather than being a portrait of female power as such.[113] Monastic accounts of virgin foundation, moreover, partly reveal and partly mask the translation of resources from female communities to male. The assertion of continuous male monastic ownership can doubly conceal a history of repeated losses of female institutional resources, both in the Anglo-Saxon past (as in the case of female houses 'reformed' by Bishop Æthelwold in the tenth and by the Cluniacs in the eleventh centuries), and in post-Conquest losses of socio-economic power for women. Denial or expropriation of female institutional resources is both a pre- and a post-Conquest story, and, as Pauline Stafford has argued, the temptation to view the Conquest as a refoundation story behind which lurks a lost golden age for Anglo-Saxon women is itself part of a nostalgic nationalizing myth and should be resisted.[114] For post-Conquest kings as well as monks, 'reform' remained a useful way of legitimating refoundations: the nunnery of Reading, for instance, was turned into a Cluniac house by Henry I and was said to be much the better for it.[115] Part of Henry II's reparation for the murder of Becket was obtained through the 'reform' (and dispossession) of women when the Benedictine nunnery of Amesbury was found to be in so scandalous a state as to require Henry's refoundation of it as a Fontevrault house (significantly, the abbess, although accused of being the mother of three children, was given a pension at the refoundation).[116] (It is much rarer for a male house to be expropriated for the use of women: Christina of Markyate's eventual transformation of Roger's hermitage into a female priory is one well-known example, and one other example is discussed in Chapter 6 below.) On the other hand, the new foundation at Amesbury did benefit from its links with the royal family, links maintained and developed over the following two centuries.

Foundation on ideal virgin sanctity is more frequently claimed for male than female communities. In most of the Anglo-Saxon female houses which continued to exist after the Conquest, women foundresses are appended to a male founder, either as the queen to the king (Polesworth, Romsey, Shaftesbury, Winchester), or the sister to the bishop (Barking, Chatteris). When, exceptionally, women

[113] As Bruce Venarde has recently argued, the growth of female monasticism in north-west France and England cannot necessarily be charted by following the patterns of contemporary male monasticism and its reforming movements: female communities are often independently affected by wider social and economic changes as well as group and individual monastic aspiration (Venarde, *Women's Monasticism*, p. xi).

[114] 'Women and the Norman Conquest', *Transactions of the Royal Historical Society*, 6th ser. 4 (1994), 221–49.

[115] *De gestis pontificum Anglorum libri quinque*, ed. N. E. S. A. Hamilton, RS 52 (London, 1870), 193 (henceforth *GP*). Not only kings: 'in urbe fuit ex antiquo sanctimonialium monasterium, nunc per Hugonem Cestrensem comitem monachis repletum' as William of Malmesbury remarks of the monastery supposedly founded by Wulfhere for his daughter St Werburga in Chester (*GP* 308). See further Jane Tibbetts Schulenberg, 'Women's Monastic Communities 500–1100: Patterns of Expansion and Decline', *Signs*, 14 (1989), 261–92.

[116] Discussed by Elkins, *Holy Women*, 146–7 and Venarde, *Women's Monasticism*, 152–6.

are represented as foundresses in their own right, there is often a price to pay for such representation. Judith, widow of Waltheof, Count of Northampton and Huntingdon, and niece of William the Conqueror, is said to found Elstow Abbey in the late eleventh century in penance for betraying her husband (executed in 1076 after the failed rebellion of the earls against the Conqueror). Waltheof, a major benefactor of Crowland abbey, was culted there in the late eleventh century, and it is in Crowland traditions that his putsch against William becomes the treachery of his wife.[117] Ælfthryth, widow of Æthelwold and subsequently queen of his brother Edgar (king of Wessex, AD 959–75), is said in post-Conquest sources to have founded the nunneries of Amesbury and Wherwell in penance for the murder of her stepson Edward (supposedly killed on her orders so that her son by a previous marriage could take the throne at Edgar's death).[118] Gaimar, writing the *Estoire des Engleis* near Lincoln for Lady Constance Fitzgilbert in the early twelfth century, does not directly accuse Ælfthryth of Edward's death, but nevertheless states that she entered Wherwell in penance.[119] For William of Malmesbury, Ælfthryth becomes the knowing seductress of King Edgar after he has married her to his brother Æthelwold, and she murders her stepson herself; Henry of Huntingdon retails stories of her as murderess and Walter Map knows that she first poisoned Edward, then had him killed.[120]

---

[117] *The Ecclesiastical History of Orderic Vitalis*, ed. M. Chibnall, 6 vols. (Oxford: Oxford University Press, 1969–80), ii ('per delatinem Judith uxoris suae accusatus est'), 320. Judith's foundation was very successful: Elstow was one of the wealthiest houses at the Dissolution, and by 1160 already had over 48 properties (Thompson, *Women Religious*, 167 n. 44: see also S. Wigram, *Chronicles of the Abbey of Elstow* (Oxford and London: Parke and Co., 1885)).

[118] The other Anglo-Saxon nunnery founded by a royal widow is Minster in Kent: the 11th-c. foundation story uses not penitence, but an ancient legendary motif. Offered as much land as an oxhide will cover, the foundress Dom Eafe cuts the hide into thin strips and encloses the island of Thanet for her foundation and establishes a saintly lineage of abbesses for herself and her daughters (see David W. Rollason, *The Mildrith Legend: A Study in Early Medieval Hagiography in England* (Leicester: Leicester University Press, 1982)). Her successor, Abbess Quendritha, however, comes down to post-Conquest history and hagiography as having plotted the death of her brother, the child martyr Kenelm (see *Three Eleventh-Century Anglo-Latin Saints' Lives: 'Vita Sancti Birini', 'Vita et miracula Sancti Kenelmi' and 'Vita Sancti Rumwoldi'*, ed. and tr. Rosalind Love (Oxford: Clarendon Press, 1996), 54 n. 1 and 70–3; *The South English Legendary*, ed. Charlotte d' Evelyn and Anna J. Mill, 3 vols., EETS os 235, 236, 244 (London, 1956–9), i (1956), 290–1, ll. 337–66).

[119] On stepmothers and their strategies for dynastic power, see Pauline Stafford, 'The King's Wife in Wessex, 800–1066', in Helen Damico and Alexandra Hennessey Olsen (eds.), *New Readings on Women in Old English Literature* (Bloomington and Indianapolis: Indiana University Press, 1990), 56–78. For Ælfthryth's penance see Gaimar (*L'Estoire des Engleis*, ed. Alexander Bell, ANTS 14–16 (Oxford, 1960), vv. 4076–86 and for discussion, pp. lxvii–lxviii). Ælfthryth's murder of her first husband is also assumed by *VCH, Hampshire* ii. 132: for a judicious account of the Wherwell foundation stories and of modern revisionary readings of them, see Diana K. Caldicott, *Hampshire Nunneries* (Chichester: Phillimore, 1989), 15–19.

[120] *GR* 183–4, and see 175, 131, 129; Henry of Huntingdon, *Historia anglorum*, ed. Greenway, 167; *Walter Map, De nugis curialium. Courtiers' Trifles*, ed. and tr. M. R. James, rev. C. N. L. Brooke and R. A. B. Mynors (Oxford: Clarendon Press, 1983), 412–13. Such representations seem

Nunneries needed historiography as much as monasteries, but, as Sally Thompson's important study of post-Conquest nunnery documents has shown, there are fewer, less well-preserved sources for women's houses (especially if these are sought among the genres and texts of male monasticism).[121] But there are a number of ways in which this lack can be at least partly remedied. The historiographical interests and practices of female communities in the post-Conquest period are partly less well-evidenced because they have been less thoroughly studied. Among the four baronially ranked nunneries of Anglo-Saxon foundation, for instance, twelfth-century patterns of Latin hagiographic commissioning along the lines of male monastic houses are discernible, while the formidable achievements of some thirteenth-century abbesses suggest there may have been still more, even though traces are often all that now survive.[122] Moreover, not only are the (relatively) exiguous Latin sources for women's houses still in need of more attention than they have had, but they can be supplemented by vernacular documents and by more attention to the texts and genres used by Anglo-Norman women. The widely circulating tale of 'Le Miracle de Sardenei', for instance, shows an anchoress developing a pilgrimage hostel and eventually a double monastery around her acquisition of a wooden image of the Virgin which grew a coating of flesh.[123] The nuns of Delapré kept an Anglo-Norman chronicle in which the abbey's patrons, the earls of Huntingdon, are shown (to the advantage of the house) to be feoffees of the king of Scotland, not England, and in which the lives of Earl Waltheof and his father Siward are told (also retold

to be a convention, not a matter of individual misogyny: William of Malmesbury for instance gives high praise to Ælfgyva, wife (probably) of Edmund of Essex, mother of Edwy and Edgar, d. 944, and foundress (after Alfred) of Shaftesbury (where Edward's body was a relic), and he wrote verses in honour of her miracles (*GP* 186–7).

[121] 'Why English Nunneries had no History: A Study of the Problems of the English Nunneries Founded after the Conquest', in Nichols and Shank (eds.), *Distant Echoes*, 131–49: see also her *Women Religious*, 7–15.

[122] For example, although two of Goscelin of St Bertin's lives of Barking's abbesses (including that of the foundress, Ethelburga) are dedicated to Bishop Maurice of London (Marvin L. Colker, 'Texts of Jocelin of Canterbury which Relate to the History of Barking Abbey', *Studia Monastica*, 7 (1965), 383–460, 388) it is difficult to believe that Ælfgyva, then abbess of Barking, was not involved, the more so as she was extensively rebuilding the abbey at the time (see Ch. 6.2, n. 21 below); it is also probable that Shaftesbury had some role in commissioning the life of its patron saint Edward the Martyr (*Edward King and Martyr*, ed. Christine E. Fell, Leeds Texts and Monographs, NS (University of Leeds: School of English, 1972), pp. xix, xxv), while Amesbury almost certainly commissioned the 12th-c. *vita* of its Breton child saint Melor when it was refounded as a Fontevrault house ('The Life of Saint Melor', ed. A. H. Diverres, in Ian Short (ed.), *Medieval French Textual Studies in Memory of T. B. Reid*, ANTS OP 1 (London, 1984), 41–53).

[123] Gaston Raynaud, 'Le Miracle de Sardenai', *Romania*, 11 (1882), 519–37 (536, vv. 343–7); *Romania*, 14 (1885), 82–93. Raynaud suggests that cedar wood could exude sap and produce 'une sorte de croûte' over the image in 'un espece d'incarnation' (529), but the thematic relevance of an image becoming embodied in a community is also significant here. In a late 12th-c. Latin version of this tale, an *abbess* procures the image for herself from Jerusalem: in the 13th-c. vernacular versions (during a major period of female anchoritism in insular culture) a *recluse* sends a monk for the image.

is the story of Countesse Ivetta [Judith]'s accusation ('encusement') of her husband; William I's offer of her in marriage to Simon de Senlis; her flight from her dower lands of Huntingdon, and the eventual marriage of Simon with her daughter).[124] A francophone woman user of the Anglo-Norman *Compileison* could learn from the *Livere de reis* which accompanies it in Cambridge, Trinity College MS R. 14. 7 (ff. 163r–198) that Queen Ælfthryth had founded 'vn abbeye de noneines' after the death of her husband Edgar to expiate *his* sins, or that 'Wulfride', whom Edgar took from her abbey ('prist de sa abbeye') to be his concubine, and her daughter St Edith both became 'noneines a Wyltone' (f. 168ra).

Recent scholarship on royal and noble women has revealed a strong tradition of historical and hagiographical patronage dating from before the Conquest, in which women and their interests were vitally engaged in the production of ecclesiastical and family history (including Latin history).[125] Family histories are an important aspect of institutional history, especially for upper-class women who so often entered family foundations. Elizabeth van Houts's recent study of

---

[124] N. Denholm-Young, 'An Early Thirteenth-Century Anglo-Norman Manuscript', *Bodleian Quarterly Record* (1929–31), 225–30; the chronicle was written probably between 1220 and 1240 under abbess Cecilia de Daventry (ibid. 225; K. J. Stringer, *Earl David of Huntingdon: A Study in Anglo-Scottish History* (Edinburgh: Edinburgh University Press, 1985), 144–5). It is now extant only in Dugdale's transcript (Oxford, Bodleian Library, MS Dugdale 18, ff. 27rb–29r). The chronicle names only 'Richard le Chauntour de Notyngham' as a source for Earl Siward's exploits (f. 27vb). It begins with a legendary history of ancestors which seems to borrow from the Norse myths of Sigurd and Fafnir (here Earl 'Syward' slaying a dragon in 'Orkeine'), and moves rapidly to establish the pre-Conquest creation of the earldom by Edward the Confessor.

[125] Emma, Cnut's queen, and Edith, wife of Edward the Confessor, protected their own positions at court by commissioning biographies: see Pauline Stafford, *Queen Emma and Queen Edith: Queenship and Women's Power in Eleventh-Century England* (Oxford: Blackwell, 1997); on Anglo-Norman patrons, Jean Blacker, *The Faces of Time: Portrayal of the Past in Old French and Latin Historical Narrative of the Anglo-Norman Regnum* (Austin: University of Texas Press, 1994), ch. 3, esp. 136–8. Adela, Countess of Blois and daughter of William the Conqueror, 'litteris erudita', is one of the dedicatees of Hugh of Fleury's ecclesiastical history (for which Jerome's letters to Paula and Eustochium are cited as precedents: see PL163.822 and André Wilmart, 'L'Histoire ecclésiastique composeé par Hugues de Fleury et ses destinataires', *Rev. bén.* 50 (1948), 293–305; also Gerald A. Bond, *The Loving Subject: Desire, Eloquence and Power in Romanesque France* (Philadelphia: University of Pennsylvania Press, 1995), 131–6. Adela's sister-in-law, Matilda, wife of Henry 1, 1100–18, and correspondent of Archbishop Anselm, was William of Malmesbury's patron for *GR*: she also requested a genealogy of the West Saxon kings from him (Rodney Malcolm Thomson, 'William's Kulturkreis', in his *William of Malmesbury* (Woodbridge and Wolfeboro, NH, Boydell Press, 1987), 34). For the hagiographic *vita* of her mother (Margaret of Scotland, 1046–93) commissioned by Matilda, see Lois L. Huneycutt, 'The Idea of the Perfect Princess: The *Life of St Margaret* in the Reign of Matilda II (1000–1118)', *ANS* 12 (1990), 81–97. On vernacular patronage see Diana B. Tyson, 'Patronage of French Vernacular History Writers in the Twelfth and Thirteenth Centuries', *Romania*, 100 (1979), 180–222; Ian Short, 'Gaimar's Epilogue', *Speculum*, 69 (1994), 323–43, and his 'Patrons and Polyglots'; Jean Blacker, '"Dame Custance La Gentil"': Gaimar's Portrait of a Lady and her Books', in Evelyn Mullally and John J. Thompson (eds.), *The Court and Cultural Diversity* (Cambridge: Brewer, 1997), 109–19, and the works cited in the Introduction, n. 1.

memory and gender argues that, rather than a male monastic institutionalization of memory, a history of 'continuous collaboration between monastery and lay world' in which the stories and texts of men and women are both important is to be discerned in the post-Conquest period.[126] However poor the survival of records for female communities, we cannot assume that their inhabitants were not interested in their own history, or that they did not require precedents and examples for successful conduct of their affairs. In the Anglo-Norman life of Etheldreda (Audrée), as the saint works to establish herself and a religious community on her dower island of Ely, her priest Hunus shows her 'lives of saints and true prophecies'.[127] So too a secular queen must be concerned with saints and history: in the thirteenth century, when continuity with Edward the Confessor, the last (and childless) Anglo-Saxon king, was a well-established legitimating trope for the regnal family, Matthew Paris dedicates his 'estoire' of 'Saint Edward the King' to 'Alianor, riche reïne | D'Engletere', proclaiming that

> En mund ne est, ben vus l'os dire,
> Païs, rëaume, ne empire
> U tant unt esté bons rois
> E seinz cum en isle d'Englois,
> Ki apres regne terestre
> Ore regnent reis eu celestre.[128]

In all the world, I dare tell you, there is not a country, realm, or empire where there have been so many good kings and saints as in the isle of the English, who after their terrestrial reign now reign as kings in the celestial kingdom.

If, as has been suggested, the illustrated version of this life of Edward the Confessor was originally designed as a presentation copy for Eleanor of Provence's marriage to Henry III, the dedication of the life to Eleanor suggests that sacralizing the house and the dynasty continued to be seen as the business of women, secular or religious. Representation of the patron saints of her husband's kingroup was important in the ritual of Eleanor's own entry to it, and remained important for her daughter-in-law Eleanor of Castile.[129] A ranging history of Europe and her own family was produced by Nicholas Trevet for Eleanor of Provence's granddaughter, Princess Mary, daughter of Edward I, who entered the nunnery of Amesbury as a child.[130]

---

[126] *Memory and Gender in Medieval Europe 900–1200* (Basingstoke: Macmillan, 1999), 13–14.

[127] *Audrée*, ed. Södergård, vv. 1611–14.

[128] Matthew Paris, *La Estoire de Seint Aedward le Rei*, ed. Wallace, vv. 1–6.

[129] John Carmi Parsons, 'Of Queens, Courts, and Books: Reflections on the Literary Patronage of Thirteenth-Century Plantagenet Queens', in June Hall McCash (ed.), *The Cultural Patronage of Medieval Women* (Athens: University of Georgia Press, 1996), 175–201 (176–7); Margaret Howell, *Eleanor of Provence: Queenship in Thirteenth-Century England* (Oxford and Malden, Mass.: Blackwell, 1998), 91.

[130] 'The Anglo-Norman Chronicle of Nicholas Trivet', ed. A. Rutherford, Ph.D. thesis, University of London, 1932.

For all virginity's rhetoric of eternity, female communities both have histories and interests in historiography. Rather than looking for virgin lives modelled on male monasticism and seeking sharply defined communities of virgins isolated from the family and household lives of Anglo-Norman England, it seems that we should attend to a fluid, relational, untidy, provisional, under-resourced history of (often abjected and erased) activity and enterprise by women, if we are to think about the history of women and their literary culture. The women about whose interests in hagiography most can be shown by attending to French sources in the twelfth and thirteenth centuries include women in Benedictine and other religious houses but also women in pious lay or para-religious lives outside the enclosure of the convent. Virginity's powerful models of enclosure and intactness have partially revealed, but also partially occluded, the history of female community as well as the collective history of women.

2

Virginity and the Gift

de femmes vient les pruesces
Les onurs e les hautesces,
Les biens, les joies, [tut] a un mot.
Dunc m'est auis, [q']il fest cum sot
Ke de eles se feist haïr
('Les aprises Salomon li sage',
vv. 57–61)[1]

From women come [the possibility of] acts of prowess, honours and noble
deeds, goods and pleasures, in a word, everything. In my opinion whoever
makes himself hated by them is a fool.

Virginity's ideology of enclosure, as discussed in Chapter 1, is important, but is
by no means the only way in which virginity informs practices and representations. Virginity and virgins are also foundational gifts and important nexuses of
transmission and exchange.

The Latin hagiography of eleventh- and twelfth-century post-Conquest England
which provides much of the source material for twelfth- and thirteenth-century
and later vernacular virgin lives is intensely engaged in embodying legitimacy and
continuity for monastic houses in the rewritten lives of founding virgins of Anglo-
Saxon England. The perennial association of women and territory has particular
resonance in Anglo-Norman society, where landholding moved from acquisition by conquest to a vigorous marriage and inheritance market, trading among
lineages and territories. Anglo-Norman culture is preoccupied with many forms
of translation and exchange and its cultural and social structures imply conceptions
of personhood in which reification in exchange is not necessarily accompanied
by commodification. Virgins are patronesses, not only objects of exchange. In
the Anglo-Norman cultural context, I argue, we should focus less on virginity
and sexuality than on the virgin's 'dotality', her capacity to be given and to give.

2.1. POST-CONQUEST RE-INVENTIONS OF VIRGINITY

Virginity is a long-standing trope of foundation, both classical and Christian.
The cultural fecundity of virgins is a leading motif in European stories of

[1] Oxford, MS Bodley 82, f. 3b/9–14 (miscellany manuscript of French and Latin, written in
England: see E. Stengel, 'Handschriftliches aus Oxford', *Zeitschrift für französische Sprache und
Literatur*, 14 (1892), 127–60 (151)).

translatio imperii et studii in the high Middle Ages. Neoclassical traditions join with Christian historiography in the creation of royal and seigneurial post-Conquest identities in Britain. As many high medieval clerks knew from Martianus Capella's account of the seven liberal arts and as laymen could hear in the twelfth-century *romans d'antiquité*, Troy had been founded by the virgin goddess Pallas Athene. The passage of dominion from Troy to Rome is marked by the removal of Troy's Palladium, a sacred image of the virgin goddess: 'she will transfer with herself the seat of empire', says Ovid.[2] For Augustine, the Palladium, like any heathen idol, was a material object unable to help itself: kept in the virgins' temple of Vesta in Rome where it supposedly guaranteed the safety of the city, the image had had to be rescued by human hands from the fires during the first Punic war.[3] For Benoît de Ste-Maure however, in his *Chroniques des ducs de Normandie* for his twelfth-century Angevin patrons, Pallas is 'deuesse de chevalerie' (v. 25,390) and her image has been sent down from heaven ('del ciel i fu tramis', v. 25,396).[4] The statue is a founding virgin gift for the European history that would culminate in the Norman expansions and invasions.

In the Trojan-Roman diaspora, Britain itself, according to post-Conquest traditions, was officially founded by Brutus, but had a proto-foundation by a group of virgin women, Albina and her sisters.[5] Bede's only poem in the *Historia Ecclesiastica* is a hymn to virginity in which he replaces Helen of Troy's role in European culture with Christian virgin fecundity and redemption. He begins with the Virgin herself, giving birth both to her own creator and indirectly to a glorious lineage of virgin martyrs from the early Roman church—Agatha, Eulalia, Agnes, Cecilia. England is linked into this succession via St Etheldreda of Ely: her sixteen years of incorruption between death and the translation of her body are hymned by Bede as a sign of pure and constant virginity. The poem has been read as an intensely personal expression of Bede's private reverence for chastity, but its introduction of virginity as a factor in history is of wider significance.[6] Where Helen, for Bede, is the figure of a destructive exchange between Greece and Troy, Etheldreda powerfully and harmoniously links British historiography to the universal Roman church (as celebrated in the liturgy and in Prudentius' *Peristephanon*) and images the continuing workings of grace in English

---

[2] Ovid, *Fasti*, VI. 427. In addition to Virgil (*Aeneid*, II. 164 ff.) and Ovid's accounts of the Palladium, medieval clerical culture knew Pallas as foster sister to Athena, goddess of wisdom, from Martianus Cappella's *De nuptiis philologiae*.

[3] *City of God*, tr. H. Bettenson (Harmondsworth: Penguin, 1984), III. 18.

[4] *Le Roman de Troie par Benoît de Sainte-Maure: publié d'après tous les manuscrits connus*, ed. Léopold Constans, SATF iv (Paris: Firmin-Didot, 1898), 123, 124.

[5] See Lesley Johnson, 'Return to Albion', *Arthurian Literature*, 13 (1995), 19–40, on the Anglo-Norman version (probably the earliest extant) of this story.

[6] *Bede's Ecclesiastical History*, ed. Colgrave and Mynors, iv. 20, 298–400. J. M. Wallace-Hadrill argues that 'Bede merely reports the miracle of Caedmon, whereas his song to virginity is his personal contribution' ('Bede and Plummer', in Gerald Bonner (ed.), *Famulus Christi: Essays in Commemoration of the Thirteenth Century of the Birth of the Venerable Bede* (London: SPCK, 1976), 366–85 (378)).

history. Bede's originary link here was foundational for post-Conquest historiography: his authority, together with the prestige of Etheldreda's ancient dynasty and her important foundation at Ely, made her the leading post-Conquest British virgin as she had been the leading Anglo-Saxon princess saint. She heads William of Malmesbury's twelfth-century account of the five completely incorrupt saints of the realm, and remains a paradigmatic figure in the pervasive concern of insular historiography with the translation of powers and identities.[7]

Virgin bodies become the stuff of history in several powerful ways. They share at a general level in the abjection of the female body which marks so many foundation narratives, and, equally, they return to haunt narratives of foundation and propagation as patriarchal creation by an exclusively agnatic (i.e. male-filiated) Trinity or its human analogue in the succession from seigneur to son.[8] But the liminal and numinous complement provided by the feminine in narratives of foundation is specially resonant in the case of virgin saints. This is partly because, as virgins, they already signify originary wholeness, and partly because, as saints, they share in the role of the male holy dead as powerful presences, patrons, and protectors for the communities of the living. Historians of hagiographic cult have convincingly shown how far the bodies of saints are from being simply material objects. Infused with narrative meaning, objectifying communal memory, saints' relics are signs, nexuses of relationships, and pledges of continuing commitment in heaven to their client communities on earth.[9] Virgin saints are identity, sustenance, treasure, territory, and revenue for communities textual and social, as well as important to individual devotees. Participants in virgin cults throughout medieval Europe collect, touch, kiss, wear, treasure tiny pieces of body and text, each fragment understood as transmitting the power of originary wholeness embodied in virgin cult. Female saints form a small proportion of Anglo-Saxon (as of most other) hagiography.[10] But in Anglo-Saxon England to be royal was in effect to be saintly, and the royal virgins of pre-Conquest

---

[7] *GR* ii. 207 (259–60, 517–18); *GP* iv. 184, 323–5. Jean Truax points out that, though her Anglo-Saxon and nationalizing identity remains unimpaired, Etheldreda's virginal marriage becomes less valued in Anglo-Norman chroniclers in comparison with lay noblewomen such as Margaret of Scotland (Truax, 'From Bede to Orderic Vitalis', 51). Etheldreda's celibate marriage continues to be valued in post-Conquest vernacular hagiography however.

[8] A notable insular example is the 'haunting' of the Brutus narrative by that of Albina (see n. 5 above). On seigneurial lineage, see Elisabeth Schmid, *Familiengeschichten und Heilsmythologie: Die Verwandtschaftsstrukturen in den französischen und deutschen Gralromanen des 12 und 13 Jahrhunderts* (Tübingen: Niemeyer, 1986), esp. 24–30. On saints and lineage, see André Vauchez, 'Beata stirps: sainteté et lignage en occident aux XIIIe et XIVe siècles', in G. Duby and J. Le Goff (eds.), *Famille et parenté dans l'Occident médiéval* (Paris, 1974), 397–406.

[9] See Thomas Head, *Hagiography and the Cult of the Saints: The Diocese of Orléans 800–1200* (Cambridge: Cambridge University Press, 1990), 11–15.

[10] On the under-representation of women saints, see Jane Tibbetts Schulenberg, 'Sexism and the Celestial Gynaceum, from 500–1200', *JMH* 4 (1978), 117–33, and her *Forgetful of Their Sex*, 403–15. On Anglo-Saxon sanctity, see David Rollason, *Saints and Relics in Anglo-Saxon England* (Oxford: Blackwell, 1989).

Britain were figures to reckon with, even more in death than while living. Virginity is thus fertile in the production of institutional identities, and, for all its apparent defiance of genealogical filiation, has powers of transmission and succession.

Such powers cannot be used as a simple index to the historical visibility and power of women. The presence of female saints, particularly in royal dynasties, is quite likely to be a sign of the holiness of the lineage itself, rather than of female power in it. Nevertheless, there is a post-Conquest efflorescence of virgin martyr foundresses in Anglo-Norman England of particular interest and importance, in which saintly Anglo-Saxon virgins old and new are found, or rediscovered, as patronesses.[11] As Susan Ridyard has shown for post-Conquest Latin *vitae* of native saints, the Anglo-Normans, after the first generation or so, became less interested in replacing than in co-opting native saints for their own monastic and dynastic interests in Britain.[12]

The initial reinvention of Anglo-Saxon virginity for Anglo-Norman interests takes place in monastic Latin alongside the hagiography of established and new male saints during the late eleventh and the twelfth centuries. It partly feeds (and is partly left behind by) vernacular hagiography in Anglo-Norman (from around the mid-twelfth century on).[13] Some virgin foundress and abbess lives were rewritten in the late eleventh century by Goscelin of St Bertin (Mildred of Minster in Thanet, Ethelburga, Hildelitha, and Wulfhilda of Barking, Sexburga of Sheppey, Edith of Wilton), and these continued to be copied in twelfth- and

[11] As Antonia Gransden remarks, 'the chroniclers of the post-Conquest foundations are remarkable for the way they ransacked their houses, libraries and archives for pre-Conquest material', *Historical Writing in England c.550–c.1307* (London: Routledge & Kegan Paul, 1974), 273, and see further chs. 13, 'Local History from the Reign of King Stephen to John', and 14, 'Sacred Biography'. Robert Bartlett notes the uninnovative nature of Angevin hagiography, arguing that of 30 male Latin lives produced between 1180 and 1220, only 7 deal with saints who died after 1150 ('The Hagiography of Angevin England', in P. R. Coss and S. D. Lloyd (eds.), *Thirteenth Century England V* (Woodbridge: Brewer, 1995), 37–52 (48–9)). But rewriting *vitae* and translating them makes new meanings as validly as new saints, and the vernacular hagiography of the 12th and 13th c. is rich and inventive whether reworking established saints or writing new lives.

[12] Ridyard, *The Royal Saints of Anglo-Saxon England*. This is also witnessed to in the continuing post-Conquest compilation of lists of saints' resting places. For Anglo-Saxon lists, see Felix Liebermann, *Die Heiligen Englands: Angelsächsisch und Lateinisch* (Hanover: Hahn'sche, 1889); for Anglo-Saxon and later lists, David Rollason, 'Lists of Saints' Resting Places in England', *ASE* 7 (1978), 61–94 (esp. 69); Alexander Bell, 'The Anglo-French *De Sanctis*', *Notes and Queries*, 12th ser. 5 (1919), 281–3. See also John Frankis, 'Views of Anglo-Saxon England in Post-Conquest Vernacular Writing', in Herbert Pilch (ed.), *Orality and Literacy in Early Middle English*, Scriptoralia 9 (Tübingen: Narr, 1996), 227–47.

[13] Many lives from this period remain without proper editions: as E. Gordon Whatley points out, the best-known texts from this efflorescence of hagiographical-historiographical writing are the least typical ones, being lives of contemporaries such as Anselm and Christina of Markyate (*The Saint of London: The Life and Miracles of St Erkenwald*, Medieval and Renaissance Texts and Studies 58 (Binghamton: SUNY, CMERS, 1989), 72). See now Paul Antony Hayward, 'Translation-Narratives in Post-Conquest Hagiography and English Resistance to the Norman Conquest', *ANS* 21 (1999), 67–93. For attention to the literary qualities of Anglo-Latin lives of male saints, see David Townsend, 'Anglo-Latin Hagiography and the Norman Transition', *Exemplaria*, 3 (1991), 385–433. For editions and a study see Love, *Three Eleventh-Century Anglo-Latin Saints' Lives*, esp. pp. xi–xlviii.

thirteenth-century manuscripts (and later collections).[14] Twelfth-century rewrit-
ings include, in addition to the continued reworking of lives of Etheldreda, Hild,
Ebba, and other saints based on Bede's *Historia*, *vitae* 'discovered' or rewritten
for Brigid of Kildare, Cuthburga of Wimborne, Edburga of Pershore, Elfleda of
Romsey, Ermenilda of Sheppey and Ely, Frideswide of Oxford, Kyneburga of
Gloucester, Milburga of Wenlock, Tibba of Peterborough, Werburga of Chester,
Winifred of Flintshire, and others, as well as the monastic dossier created for
Modwenna at Burton, and the lives propagating Osith's cult at Chich and
Hereford.[15] Female patron saints preside over a small proportion of the British
houses, but are not negligible: in his *Gesta Regum* and *Gesta Pontificum*, for instance,
William of Malmesbury deals in various ways with over twenty-five of them,
while Gaimar's Anglo-Norman version of the Anglo-Saxon lists of 'Resting Places
of the Saints' mentions Aldre (Etheldritha) and her sisters Wiburc (Witburga)
and Sexburga of Ely, Osith of Aylesbury, Werburga of Chester, St Sitha of Exeter,
St Edith of Polesworth, and Milburga of Wenlock.[16]

[14] For Goscelin's lives see Susan J. Millinger, 'Humility and Power: Anglo-Saxon Nuns in
Anglo-Norman Hagiography', in Nichols and Shank (eds.), *Distant Echoes*, 115–29: Richard
Sharpe, *A Handlist of the Latin Writers of Great Britain and Ireland before 1540*, Publications of the
Journal of Medieval Latin I (Turnhout: Brepols, 1997), s.v. Goscelin.

[15] For bibliography on these saints see D. H. Farmer, *The Oxford Dictionary of Saints* (Oxford:
Clarendon Press, 1978; 4th edn. 1992). On Modwenna, see Robert Bartlett's edition of the *vita* by
Geoffrey of Burton (Oxford University Press, forthcoming). For Osith see n. 18 below.

[16] For the houses surviving the Conquest or founded between 1066 and 1216, Alison Binns
tabulates 10 dedications to native virgin saints as against 6 of all other kinds of female dedications
(apart from the Virgin Mary who has 235 dedications, including all Cistercian houses) (*Dedications
of Monastic Houses in England and Wales 1066–1216* (Woodbridge and Wolfeboro, NH: Boydell
Press, 1989), 18–19). The Benedictines, well-established before the Conquest, unsurprisingly have
the greatest number of such saints (Bega, Eanswith, Edburga, Etheldreda, Modwenna, Werburga,
Wulfrida, Binns, 34–5), followed by the Augustinians (Edburga, Frideswide, Osith, 37), the
Cluniacs (Milburga, 35), and the Premonstratensians (Werburga, 38). Male saints receive over 300
dedications of whom at least 50 are native British figures (18–19). For Gaimar's list see *Lestorie des
engles solum la translacion Maistre Geffrei Gaimar*, ed. T. D. Hardy and Charles Trice Martin, RS 9
(London, 1888), pp. xxxix–xlii; Bell, 'The Anglo-French *De Sanctis*'. Among the pre-Conquest
foundresses/abbesses dealt with by William of Malmesbury (whose chronicling of women in
religion would itself make a study of interest) are: in *GR* i, Cuthburga (who leaves her husband
for Hildelith's Barking, 35), Bridget of Ireland (27), Edburga of Pershore and Winchester, Edith
of Wherwell, Edith of Wilton, Ercongota (daughter of Sexburga, goes to the nunnery of Chelles
(see Bede, *Historica Ecclesiastica*, iii, ch. 8), 15–6, 267), Ethelburga of Barking, Etheldritha and
the abbesses of Ely, Ethelfleda (born in Gloucester), Frideswide of Oxford, Hild of Whitby (her
relics at Glastonbury, 56), Hildelitha at Barking, Kineburga (as nun), Milburga of Wenlock, Mildred
at Canterbury, Mildritha of Canterbury (78), Werburga of Chester (78, 267); in *GP* iv he mentions Cutberga of Wimborne (379), Ebba of Coldingham (231–2), Edburga of Winchester (174)
and of Pershore (298), Edith of Wilton (30, 188–91), Elfleda of Romsey (175), Ercengota (daughter of Sexburga, niece of Etheldreda, 323), Ermenhilda of Ely (323, 308), Ethelburga of Barking
(143), Etheldreda (323–4 for her genealogy, 325 her translation), Frideswide of Oxford (315),
Kinedrida of Petersborough (317); Kineswida (celibately married virgin, 317), Milburga of Wenlock
(306), Ealhswide, Hilda, Hildelitha of Barking (143), Osith of Chich (146), Sexburga of Ely and
Minster in Sheppey (308, 323), Werburga of Chester (308–9, 323), Witburga (324–5), Wulfhildis
of Barking (143), Wultrud of Wilton (190–1). In many cases, as noted in Ch. 1.5 above, the houses
of these patron saints had become male houses by the 12th c.

Historians of English monasticism have worked hard to sift history out of legend in these materials, and have sometimes been dismissive about the gaps and confusions in the evidence for these new-found founding virgins. The Augustinian canons at their new house of Chich in twelfth-century Essex, for instance, are scolded by David Rollason for producing 'an inept account of their patron Osyth', which 'muddled her career with that of a certain Osyth of Aylesbury and set her life in the seventh century while attributing her death to the Viking invasions of the ninth'.[17] Certainly, Osith was culted not only at Chich but at Aylesbury and at Hereford, and her life blends various, often legendary, traditions and motifs, as well as competing feast days.[18] Both Latin and vernacular lives give the saint a pagan husband from seventh-century East Anglia (against whom she maintains her virginity and from whom she secures endowments for her community) and martyrdom by decapitation at the hands of marauding ninth-century heathen Danes. She also becomes a cephaloric saint, depositing her own head on the altar of her church at Chich (in the *caput*, so to speak, of her canons' honour). But, as has been recently more widely realized among historians of monasticism, foundation legends, whatever their historical basis, have a great deal to say about the communities that produce them.[19] In the twelfth-century conflation of Osiths, as Christopher Hohler points out, 'Aylesbury could offer [to Chich] distinguished ancestry . . . to Aylesbury, Chich could offer royal marriage and a cephaloric martyrdom'.[20] Whoever had the best claim—that is, the most convincing account (and hence the account that sounded most like every other royal Anglo-Saxon princess saint's biography)—had a valuable possession. The condensation of times and territories in the canons' *vita* asserts possession of the past and hence the present, with Osith's intact virginity authorizing the canons' landholding at Chich as continuous British history, legitimated in opposition to the claims of the rival cult at Aylesbury. Martyred in heathen

[17] Rollason, *Saints and Relics*, 235.

[18] On the Aylesbury and Chich traditions see Christopher Hohler, 'St Osyth and Aylesbury', *Records of Buckinghamshire*, 18, pt. 1 (1966), 61–72. Denis Bethell, 'The Lives of St Osyth of Essex and St Osyth of Aylesbury', *AB* 88 (1970), 75–127 compares in detail all the extant Latin and the vernacular lives to reconstruct their textual relations with the lost life by William de Vere, Bishop of Hereford (1186–98). De Vere's mother Alice took Osith as her patron and retired to Chich: see Julia Barrow, 'A Twelfth-Century Bishop and Literary Patron: William de Vere', *Viator*, 18 (1987), 175–89 (177–8). The life discussed by Rollason (*Saints and Relics*, 235) is extant in Oxford, MS Bodley 285, s. xiii, and is one of three lives related to the lost life by de Vere (now extant only in Leland's notes and lessons in the Hereford Breviary: see Bethell, 'Lives of St Osyth', 77 and Appendix III).

[19] See Jörg Kastner, *Historiae fundationum monasteriorum* (Munich: Arbeo Gesellschaft, 1974); Amy G. Remensnyder, *Remembering Kings Past: Monastic Foundation Legends in Medieval Southern France* (Ithaca: Cornell University Press, 1995); Penelope D. Johnson, 'Pious Legends and Historical Realities: The Foundations of La Trinité de Vendôme, Bonport and Holyrood', *Rev. bén.* 91 (1981), 184–93; Dominique Iogna-Prat, 'La Geste des origines dans l'historiographie clunisienne des xi et xii siècles', *Rev. bén.* 102 (1992), 135–91. On the white stag in Osith's *vita* see further Ch. 3.1 below.

[20] Hohler, 'St Osyth', 67.

raiding, Osith also takes on something of the broad cultural authority possessed by King Edmund the martyr: she differentiates illegitimate (pagan) plundering of Britain from Christian succession, and she is a sign that it was always already legitimate and providential that Britain should be in the hands of its post-Conquest rulers. As a newer monastic house, Chich needed a prestigious, royal, martyred Anglo-Saxon saint comparable with neighbouring Bury's celebrated King Edmund, and both the relative historical underdocumentation of women and their cultural role as figures of foundation conduce to producing a female foundress.

Although she is a composite virgin, Osith for all important purposes is indistinguishable from a 'historical' royal virgin saint like Etheldreda (see Figure 2.1). My term 'composite' does not imply a simply cynical creation of virgins, but rather that in long-attested *vitae* as well as those with less well-evidenced traditions, whatever materials can be found or borrowed are brought together in the attempt to fill out a powerful post-Conquest hagiographical template of Anglo-Saxon royal sanctity. In this template, the saint's personal history is important for the continuity and specific identity it confers on a monastic house, while a properly authoritative royal virgin will also confer dynastic associations. The ancient Mercian lineage represented by St Etheldreda of Ely, with her sisters and abbatial successors at Ely, is the most potent of holy female kinships; Milburga, Mildred, Mildgyth represent the Kentish dynasty; a Mercian sub-dynasty is more confusedly recorded in the competing traditions of Kyneburga and Kyneswith of Castor and their kinswoman Tibba.[21] In her Latin *vita*, Osith is given Kyneburga and Edburga as aunts and Werburga, Edburga, Elftreda, and Elgida as cousins, while in her late twelfth-century Anglo-Norman life she learns chastity from the example of her aunts Keneburg and Eadburc, themselves purportedly virgin abbesses.[22] All these are names redolent of sanctity, while the presence of alliterative and shared onomatopoeic elements signals dynastic connection: Osith's composite holy kinship is a very passable version of historical models.[23]

Twelfth- and thirteenth-century hagiography and historiography are shot through with these semi-legendary genealogical systems, which remain important in vernacular as in Latin hagiography, though the precise ways in which they signify vary over time and in different contexts. In the thirteenth century, for instance, an interpolation in Osith's twelfth-century Anglo-Norman life links her into the Warwickshire and Staffordshire network focused around the

[21] See William of Malmesbury on female royal spiritual dynasties, *GR*, bk. 8, ii, §§214, 218. On Cyneburga, Cyneswitha, Cuthburga see the bibliography in Elliott, *Spiritual Marriage*, 75, nn. 93, 94, and also Paul Grosjean, 'Saints Anglo-Saxons des marches Gauloises', *AB* 79 (1961), 161–9 (167–8). Milburga's dynasty is studied by David Rollason, *The Mildrith Legend*.

[22] 'An Anglo-French Life of St Osith', ed. A. T. Baker, *MLR* 6 (1911), 476–502, vv. 151–2.

[23] Hohler points out that these names appear among the queens and abbesses' names in the Durham *Liber vitae*, and that, although St Werburga of Chester is made a great-granddaughter instead of a granddaughter of Penda, Elftreda, Elgida, and Edburga probably represent respectively Ælfthryth abbess of Repton, a saint buried at Bishop's Stortford, and a saint buried at Bicester ('St Osyth', 63).

FIG. 2.1. Monastic foundress virgins

A 'historical' virgin: Etheldreda of Ely

King Anna of E. Anglia (d. 654) = Hereswitha

Etheldreda* (d. 679) (Audrée) (1) = Tonbert, prince of the S. Gyrwas (2) = Ecgfrid of Northumbria	Ethelburga* (d. 664) (nun of Farmoutier-en-Brie)	Witburga* (d. *c.*745) solitary of E. Dereham	Sexburga* = Erconbert (d. *c.*700) of Kent
• founds Ely • succeeded as abbess by Sexburga* Ermenilda* Werburga*			Ermenilda* = Wulfhere of Mercia Werburga* (d. *c.*700) (of, briefly, Ely, Hanbury, and Chester)

A 'composite' virgin: Osith of Chich (and Aylesbury)

King Penda of Mercia (d. 654)

K. Fredewald = Wilburga
     Osith* = Sighere, K. of
        E. Anglia
	Peada	Kyneburga* (of Castor? and sr of Tibba*?) (of Gloucester?)	Edburga* (of Bicester)

Other connections in *vitae*: • brought up by aunt Edith* ?(of Aylesbury) • (in 13th-c. interpolation) sent by Edith* ?(of Polesworth) to Modwenna* of Burton		Other descendants of Penda named in Osith's genealogy: granddaughters Mildred* of Thanet (sr of Mildritha* and Milburga* of Wenlock) Werburga* of Hanbury and Chester Elstreda*? (of Repton?) Elgida*? (Bishop's Stortford)	

---

* = also culted

semi-legendary abbess, Modwenna of Ireland and Burton, and a shadowy Anglo-Saxon one, Edith of Polesworth.[24] While the borrowing of legendary motifs to negotiate transitions and to indicate different thematic areas in part attests to

---

[24] Bethell, 'Lives of St Osyth', 79, 83–4, 104–6; A. T. Baker, 'An Episode from the Anglo-French Life of St Modwenna', in Mary Williams and James A. de Rothschild (eds.), *A Miscellany of Studies in Romance Languages and Literatures Presented to Leon E. Kastner, Professor of French Language and Literature in the University of Manchester* (Cambridge: Heffer, 1932), 9–21. In another context, that of the users of the Campsey manuscript, the interpolation could be read as pulling Modwenna into the Chich-centred orbit of Osith in Essex.

the paucity of other styles of sanctity for women in this period, the virgin martyr-foundress is a powerful model, incorporating into itself a relatively wide range of behaviour and concerns. The extent to which the writers of such lives worked to conform semi-legendary and fully historical virgins to the same pattern is an indication of its power and importance, not a measure of historiographical inadequacy.

The virgin pantheon of post-Conquest Britain endures, though it does not remain static, throughout the English Middle Ages. Few lives of contemporary women in medieval England supplement the pantheon as formulated in the post-Conquest period.[25] Nevertheless, this initially monastic reinvention continues to feed the large and varied corpus of Anglo-Norman and later English vernacular lives. The *vitae* reinvented in the eleventh- and twelfth centuries become the basis for later reworkings into the sixteenth century and even beyond, by which time they have contributed strongly to nationalizing legendaries from the fourteenth century onwards (see Figure 2.2).[26] The pattern is not of an originally complete and settled historical pantheon suffering gradual attrition in the processes of transmission. The most prolific Middle English collection of saints, the *South English Legendary*, for instance, shows *increased* numbers of native Anglo-Saxon and British virgin saints in its *later* manuscripts.[27] In the enduring sacred chorography of England, new-old virgins continue to be found or reinvented for new purposes.[28]

[25] It is symptomatic that the extant manuscript of the life of Christina of Markyate, one of the few historical 12th-c. holy women to be given a contemporary monastic *vita*, is the 14th-c. manuscript of John of Tynemouth's *Sanctilogium Angliae* to which Christina's *vita* has been added at the end of the manuscript (*Life of Christina*, ed. Talbot, 1).

[26] So, for example, St Osith's later medieval career produces a new conflation of Osith and Sitha (St Zita, the servant saint of Lucca): see Sebastian Sutcliffe, 'The Cult of St Sitha in England: An Introduction', *NMS* 37 (1993), 83–9. For another example of continued reworking of a virgin life going back to Goscelin's 11th-c. *vita*, see Jocelyn Wogan-Browne, 'Outdoing the Daughters of Syon?: Edith of Wilton and the Representation of Female Community in Early Fifteenth-Century England', in Jocelyn Wogan-Browne, Rosalynn Voaden, et al. (eds.), *Medieval Women: Texts and Contexts in Late Medieval Britain* (Turnhout: Brepols, 2000), 399–415.

[27] The *SEL* was first composed in the late 13th c. and is extant in several recensions and variant manuscripts through the 14th and 15th c. The latest of these, Oxford, Bodley MS 779 (15th c.), is the fullest manuscript and contains the largest number of abbess lives. (The addition of British foundresses to the *SEL* is most easily seen in Carl Horstmann's tabulation of manuscripts in his *The Early South English Legendary: MS Laud 108*, EETS os 87 (London, 1887), pp. xiii–xxiv: see also the fuller account in Manfred Görlach, *The Textual Tradition of the South English Legendary*, Leeds Studies in English Texts and Monographs, ns 6 (University of Leeds: School of English, 1974), 306–9). On the representation of British abbesses, see Jocelyn Wogan-Browne, 'Queens, Virgins, and Mothers: Twelfth and Thirteenth-Century Hagiographic Representations of the Abbess in Medieval Britain', in Louise Fradenburg (ed.), *Women and Sovereignty* (Edinburgh: Edinburgh University Press, 1992), 14–35.

[28] By the late 15th and 16th c., the topographical and regional significance of Anglo-Saxon virgin foundresses amalgamates into an early-modern and explicitly English nationalism where the narratives of Brigid of Kildare and Modwenna of Ireland, Scotland, and Burton, and Margaret of Scotland continue to be renarrated because their long association with the foundational virgin pantheon assists the elision of Britain into England. See for example Richard Pynson's *The Kalendre of the Newe Legende of Englande*, ed. Görlach.

FIG. 2.2. The virgin pantheon of England

Date	Writers	Virgin foundress/abbess lives
11th c.	Goscelin of St Bertin, *fl.* 1080–1114	EDITH of Wilton d. 984, ETHELBURGA d. 675, HILDELITHA d. *c.*712, WULFHILDA of Barking d. *c.*1000: other *vitae* (not all accepted as by Goscelin) of abbesses ERMENILDA of Ely d. *c.*700, ETHELDREDA of Ely d. 679, MILBURGA of Wenlock d. 715, MILDRED of Minster-in-Thanet d. *c.*700, SEXBURGA of Minster-in-Sheppey d. *c.*700, OSITH of Chich d. *c.*?700, WERBURGA of Hanbury and Chester d. *c.*700, WITBURGA of East Dereham and Ely d. *c.*745.
12th c.	various authors	William of Malmesbury, FRIDESWIDE of Oxford d. ?727, brief mentions of most women in this column (see Ch. 2, n. 16); Turgot, MARGARET of Scotland d. 1093: Osbert of Clare (*fl.* 1120–40) EDBURGA of Winchester d. 960; Robert of Shrewsbury (*c.*1138) WINEFRIDE of Flintshire, d. 7th c.; anon. of St Albans (*c.*1155–66) CHRISTINA of Markyate; William de Vere (bishop of Hereford, 1186–98), OSITH.
13th c.	anon	*South English Legendary*: BRIDE (BRIGID)
late 13th c.–early 14th c.	various authors	*South English Legendary*: AELDRI (ETHELDREDA), BRIGID, EADBORW (EDBURGA), FRIDESWIDE, MILDRIDE *MS Lansdowne 436*: CUTHBURGA of Wimborne d. *c.*725, EBBA of Coldingham d. 683, EDBURGA of Minster in Thanet d. 751, ETHELFLEDA *fl. c.*960 and MERWENNA 10th c., of Romsey, ETHELDREDA of Ely ('et sororibus suis'), HILDA of Whitby d. 680, MILBURGA of Wenlock d. 715, MODWENNA of Burton ?7th c., ?9th c., OSITH, WERBURGA, WINEFRIDA.
14th–15th c.	John of Tynemuth (1290–1349): rearranged by Capgrave (15th c.)	*Sanctilogium Angliae* and *Nova Legenda Anglie*: BRIGID of Kildare, d. *c.*525, CUTHBURGA of Wimborne, EANSWIDA of Folkestone d. 640, EBBA of Minster of Coldingham, EDBURGA of Minster in Thanet, EDITH of Wilton, ELFLEDA of Whitby d. 714, ERMENILDA, ETHELBURGA of Barking, ETHELDREDA, FREDISWIDA, HILDA of Whitby, HILDELITHA, KYNESWYDA, KYNEBURGA and TIBBA of Castor, Peterborough, and Thorney d. *c.*680–90, MARGARET of Scotland, MILBURGA, MILDRED, MODWENNA, OSITH, SEXBURGA, WALBURGA of Heidenheim, d. 779, WERBURGA, WLFHILDA. [Extant Life of CHRISTINA of Markyate d. 1155–66? added at end of *Sanctilogium* MS.]
1516	de Worde	*Nova Legenda Anglie* printed with 15 additional lives, incl. ETHELBURGA of Lyming d. 647, ETHELFLEDA.
1521	Pynson	*Kalendre of the New Legende of Englande*: BRIDGET, CUTBERGA, EANSWITHA, EBBA, EDBURGA, EDITH, ELFLEDA, ERMENHILDA, ETHELBURGA, ETHELDREDA, FRIDESWIDE, HILD, HILDELITH, KYNEBURGA, MILBURGA, MILDRED, MODWENNA, OSITHA, SEXBURGA, WALBURGA, WERBURGA, WITHBURGA, WLFHILDA.
1521	Bradshaw, pr. Pynson	WERBURGA of Chester, RADEGUNDE (?Bradshaw)
1610–15	Ralph or Robert Buckland	*Lives of Women Saints of our Contrie of England* (based on Capgrave): BRIGID, CUTHBURGA, EANSWITHA, EBBA, EDBURGA, EDITH, ELFLEDA, ERMENHILDA, ETHELBURGA, ETHELDREDA, FRIDESWIDE, HILDA, HILDELITHA, KINEBURGA, KINESWIDA, MARGARET of SCOTLAND, MILBURGA, MILDRED, MODWENNA, OSITHA, SEXBURGA, TIBBA, WERBURGA, WITBURGA, WALBURGA, WLFHILDE.

2.2. ENDURING BODIES: THE GIFT OF THE VIRGIN

Foundation, survival, and the power to confer and defend identity are the dominant features of the virgin saints of post-Conquest England. Inviolable and continuous identities are underlined not only in their lives, but even more importantly in their post-mortem careers. In some ways this is less readily apparent in reading the *vitae* of the virgin martyrs of the universal church, such as Bede's Agatha, Eulalia, Agnes, Cecilia, or Ælfric's Agnes, Agatha, Cecilia, Lucy, Euphemia. Lives of many of these figures, and others, such as Margaret and Catherine, whose cults intensified after the Conquest, continued vigorously to be produced in both Middle English and Anglo-Norman, but although such lives often include particular intercessions and very explicitly inscribe a devotional community around the saint, their heroines are universal patronesses from whom particular favour is claimed, not specific topographical and communal identities asserted or contested within Britain. These *vitae* tend to occur grouped in legendaries, liturgies, or other calendrical forms, not in the *libelli* and dossiers especially characteristic, from the eleventh century onwards, of saints with local habitations, and they seldom include detailed and localized miracle collections. They therefore rarely assume the diptych form of saint's life characteristic of native saints, and tend instead to give only the first half of the diptych, the saint's *passio*. Her cult and afterlife is implied but not narrated in her closing prayers. (This concentration on only the first half of the diptych in the lives of the better-known universal saints has obscured some of the relations and functions of saints from literary criticism, and promoted essentialist readings of hagiography as rape and pornography.)[29]

In the lives of native virgins, the dead saint's patronage of specific groups, as illustrated in her miracles, is often allocated as much narrative space as her *passio*. In addition to cures, visionary appearances, and other demonstrations of special powers of intervention, ferocious vengeance miracles are directed against transgressive inspections of virgin bodies. Thus, invading Danes are killed or immobilized at St Etheldreda's tomb in Ely, while other miracle stories show the punishment of canons and monks who peep into her shrine to see if she is intact. These tales vigorously proclaim the continuing presence of Etheldreda's body at Ely. Vigour was needed, since Ely was in fact anything *but* continuously owned, either by the reforming Benedictines of the tenth century or by the Norman abbots and priors of the eleventh and twelfth. The Ely monks' twelfth-century *Liber Eliensis*, compiled largely in order to assert the continuity of monastic tradition at Ely against baronial depredation, presents Etheldreda's uncorrupt virgin body as the embodiment of the house's tradition and proprietorship: as

---

[29] See Kathryn Gravdal, *Ravishing Maidens: Reading Rape in Medieval Literature and Law* (Philadelpha: University of Pennsylvania Press, 1991), 21–41, for an influential argument for *passio* as rape script.

Ridyard shows, 'guardianship' of Etheldreda's relics conferred 'guardianship' of '[her] church and lands'.[30]

Whether explicitly present as the continuing history of her celestial life (as with local saints' miracles), or inscribed only in the concluding intercessory prayers of the saint or the exemplary petitions of her narrator, the double nature of a saint's career has important implications for the relations between fragmentation and wholeness in saints' lives. The fragmentation of relics enables maximum participation in a saint's cult and virgin bodies produce identity, treasure, territory, and revenue in an endlessly fecund process of dissemination and translation.[31] But the smallest fragment transmits the power of the whole identity of the martyr (so that, for instance, acquired relics can suffice to create a whole identity for groups lacking any buried founding body of their own). Wholeness, not dismemberment, is the crucial desire of saints' lives, and fragmentation and translation (the term for the removal of a saint's relics from their place of burial to a shrine) are useful in providing occasions for asserting originary integrity, especially in a post-Conquest culture so aware of its own shifts and transpositions. A telling instance is that of St Werburga of Hanbury, Chester, and Repton, whose body is seen not to be intact during her translation. Werburga's late eleventh-century *vita* explains that her body fell to powder during Danish raiding rather than risk violation by the impious hands of enemies, unbelieving and ungrateful as these are about God's miracles.[32] The saint thus redefines her wholeness, removing it to another plane, and maintaining it as the condition from which all fragmentation proceeds.

[30] Ridyard, *Royal Saints*, 191. See also Edward Miller, *The Abbey and Bishopric of Ely: The Social History of an Ecclesiastical Estate from the Tenth Century to the Fourteenth*, Cambridge Studies in Medieval Life and Thought, NS 1 (Cambridge: Cambridge University Press, 1951). The *Liber Eliensis*, put together between 1131 and 1174, and incorporating earlier lives of the saint, is both the source for the Anglo-Norman Life and the principal text of Etheldreda's post-Conquest cult (*Liber Eliensis*, ed. Blake: the sources are discussed on pp. xxviii–xxxiv). In post-Conquest England, following its early support of Hereward's uprising, the abbey's relations with William the Conqueror had been uneasy, and the demands of land-hungry Norman barons did not cease, so it is unsurprising that 12th-c. Ely should so strongly have reasserted its claims, or that these should focus on Etheldreda: see further Ridyard, *Royal Saints*, 196–210. Monika Otter proposes a sexualized reading of the monks' conduct here ('The Temptation of St Æthelthryth', *Exemplaria*, 9 (1997), 139–64). While this essay forcefully testifies to the interest of the monks' representation, I cannot myself, for the reasons argued in this chapter and in Ch. 3 below, accept sexuality as an inevitable hermeneutic key or founding desire in saints' lives.

[31] For the importance of partible relics from the 11th c. onwards, see Nicole Herrmann-Mascard, *Les Reliques des saints: formation coutumière d'un droit* (Paris: Klincksieck, 1975), esp. 62–70. For the dialectic between fragmentation and reasserted wholeness as a major category of medieval culture see Caroline Walker Bynum, *Fragmentation and Redemption: Essay on Gender and the Human Body in Medieval Religion* (New York: Zone Books, 1991); ead., *The Resurrection of the Body in Western Christianity 200–1336* (New York: Columbia University Press, 1995).

[32] 'Tunc demum vitalis gleba voluit cedere mortali legi, atque resolvi, ne impiis manibus eam contingerent hostes, miraculorum Dei increduli et beneficiorum ingrati', *The Life of Saint Werburge of Chester by Henry Bradshaw*, ed. Carl Horstmann, EETS os 88 (London, 1887), p. xxv. This polemic of course assimilates rival claimants to the saint to Danes and pagans.

Wholeness, continuity, and the social circulation of value are contextually much more important originary desires in the representation of founding virgins than the dismemberment of virgins often taken as the most signal feature of virgin *passio* in modern scholarship. To explore some of the implications here for conceptions of personhood, agency, and the relationships and desires focused through the figure of the virgin martyr, I turn to the Anglo-Norman Life of St Faith, in which the notion of gift—the giving of and by—the virgin saint can be closely observed. Written about 1200, this life concerns a saint from the early Gallic persecutions: Faith is purportedly a girl of 12 years, martyred in the Aveyron by the provost Decius under Diocletian. This is itself already a translation from the conventional virgin martyr setting among the Roman and Eastern Empire persecutions, and Faith herself is very much a figure of medieval translation and transmission. Her Anglo-Norman Life was composed by Simon of Walsingham, a Benedictine monk of Bury born in or near the principal English cult centre of the saint, Horsham St Faith in Norfolk (itself not far from Walsingham), who probably composed the Life *c.*1205–10 in connection with Abbot Samson of Bury's renovation of Bury's chapel of St Faith.[33] The Anglo-Norman Life preserves much of Faith's post-mortem career, not just her *passio*.[34] An important dimension of this life is its staging of its narrator's investment in Faith's cult for an inscribed male audience—Simon's monastic senior (probably Thomas of Walsingham, also Norfolk-born) and the supplier of the Latin source material (named as 'danz Benjamin', v. 444).[35] But since the text survives only in the late thirteenth-century section of the collection of Anglo-Norman lives owned

---

[33] 'Vie anglo-normande de sainte Foy par Simon de Walsingham', ed. A. T. Baker, *Romania*, 66 (1940–1), 49–84 (50–2): for the suggestion of the Bury renovations, see *ANCL* 10–11. A 12th-c. manuscript provenanced by Ker to St Augustine's Canterbury (London, BL, MS Arundel 91, the companion to Oxford, Bodleian Library MS Fell 2) includes the Latin *passio*, an account of Caprais's martyrdom and Bernard of Angers's letter to Fulbert of Chartres on Faith's miracles and his *Liber miraculorum* ('Vie anglo-normande', ed. Baker, 54; N. R. Ker, *Medieval Libraries of Great Britain: A List of Surviving Books*, 2nd edn. (London: Royal Historical Society, 1964), 42).

[34] The *Liber miraculorum* concerning Faith's miracles for the monks of Conques is not translated, though the narrator promises 'en ses miracles orrez | Quant greigniur leisir averay' (vv. 968–9), suggesting that an account of the miracles on the model of Anglo-Norman lives of British saints (such as *Osith*) was contemplated. But even if the text in the Campsey manuscript represents only part of a larger planned diptych of life and miracles, the point holds that the *passio* of the saint is far from the end of her narrative: the foundation story of Conques (vv. 931–62), Faith's translation from Agen and triumphal entry and continuing miracles at Conques (vv. 977–1241) are part of her identity. For the miracles, see *Liber miraculorum sancte Fidis critica et commento*, ed. Lucca Robertini (Spoleto: Centro italiano di studi sull'alto medioevo, 1994); *The Book of Sainte Foy*, tr. Pamela Sheingorn (Philadelphia: University of Pennsylvania Press, 1995); Kathleen Ashley and Pamela Sheingorn, *Writing Faith: Text, Sign, and History in the Miracles of Sainte Foy* (Chicago: University of Chicago Press, 1999).

[35] As Baker points out, a Thomas of Walsingham and his relative Simon of Walsingham, both Norfolk-born, are among the monks sent to the pope in 1214 during the contested election of Abbot Hugh of Northwold ('Vie anglo-normande', 51–2: see also *The Chronicle of the Election of Hugh Abbot of Bury St Edmunds and Later Bishop of Ely*, ed. R. M. Thomson (Oxford: Clarendon Press, 1974), 37 n. 7, 188).

by the Augustinian canonesses of Campsey, it is a text read and heard in a manuscript used by women and possibly commissioned by a woman.[36] It is also a text offering an account of a male saint imitating a female saint, perhaps thus inscribing the new attention to female holiness characteristic of the late twelfth and early thirteenth centuries, as well as figuring an ancient tradition of syneisactic relations between men and women in holy lives.

For the purposes of this chapter, my argument subordinates the text's self-proclaimed genesis in male–male relations in favour of attention to its claimed origins in female saintly patronage, and tries to read it as a text heard in a female community of seigneurial rank. It is also worth noting that female patronage is prominent in the cult of Faith as well as in the reception context of the extant copy of the Anglo-Norman Life. The priory of Horsham St Faith, the initial centre of Faith's cult in Britain, was established as a dependent cell of Conques by Robert and Sybil Fitzwalter on their return from pilgrimage in the early eleventh century.[37] A series of late thirteenth-century wall-paintings in the former priory church depicts Robert and Sybil's journey and the foundation story.[38] Sybil gave her marriage portion of land at Redham to the foundation: her family, the de Cheneys [de Caineto], were of sufficiently higher rank than the Fitzwalters for her sons to take her name rather than her husband's, and she may well have been the major patron.[39]

[36] On this manuscript see Introduction, n. 10. For the Countess of Arundel as possible patroness of the manuscript see Ch. 5.1 below.

[37] On the priory see W. R. Rudd, 'The Priory of St Faith', *Norfolk Archaeology*, 23 (1929), and *VCH, Norfolk* ii. 346. For a 16th-c. account of the 1105 [or 1107] foundation of Horsham St Faith by Sibyl and her husband, see *Mon.* iii. 636, no. I. For other English dedications to Faith see A. Bouillet and L. Servières, *Sainte Foy. Vierge et martyre* (Rodez: E. Carrere, 1900), 348–55: for a cell of Longueville Ste Foi, founded by Walter Giffard in 1102, see Binns, 115. For Faith as patron of a chapel in St Paul's, London (mentioned in the *Miracula sancti Erkenwaldi* of 1141), see Whatley (ed.), *The Saint of London*, 25 and 158–9.

[38] On the wall-paintings see Dominic Purcell, 'The Priory of Horsham St Faith and Its Wall Paintings', *Norfolk Archaeology*, 35 (1970–3), 469–73; David Park, 'Wall Painting', in Jonathan Alexander and Paul Binski (eds.), *The Age of Chivalry: Art in Plantagenet England 1200–1400* (London: Royal Academy of Arts in association with Weidenfeld & Nicolson, 1987), 313, and plates 1 and 2. I am grateful to Dr David Park for generously sharing his knowledge of St Faith and for confirming that the figure supervising building work in the frescoes is almost certainly male and not a representation of Sybil de Cheney.

[39] Sybil was heiress to Ralph de Cheney (see Julian Eve, *A History of Horsham St Faith, Norfolk: The Story of a Village* (Norwich: Catton Printing, 1992; rev. edn. 1994), 10). Horsham's 'Genealogia fundatoris' begins, unusually, with 'Domina Sibilla' (*Mon.* iii. 636, no. II). For the gift of 'nominatim terram de Rodeham quam Sibilla uxor praefati Robertis dedit', i.e. Sybil's marriage portion, see *Cartulaire de l'Abbeye de Conques en Rouergue*, ed. Gustave Desjardins, Documents historiques publiés par la Société de l'École des chartes (Paris: Picard, 1879), no. 519 [de Rodeham]). Adela de Blois gave to Conques in 1101 and 1108 (ibid., nos. 470, 486) and Walter Giffard and 'mater ejus Agnes' visited Conques and donated to Horsham after 1107 (ibid., no. 497). I am grateful to Pamela Sheingorn for confirming (pers. comm.) that her researches show the cult of Faith in the British Isles to have been particularly strong among aristocratic women. (I know of no evidence to show whether the women of Campsey had any knowledge of Sybil de Cheney's role in the cult.)

At first glimpse the Life of Faith offers some grounds for the modern concern that virgin martyr lives are the product of clerical sexual fantasy, of 'near-pornographic' representations. When Faith defies the pagan provost's demand for her conversion, she is stripped and burned on a bed of brass. This scene is viewed twice in the text, first by the narrator of the Life in some detail (vv. 381–412) together with a crowd of pitying spectators (vv. 413–42) and then by Faith's companion St Caprais, as he hides in the hills above Agen:

The blessed martyr Caprais, who himself was to suffer tortures for the son of Mary, *looked* [*esguarda*] towards God's beloved, who was bound to the gridiron and surrounded with dreadful flames, and *saw* [*vit*] a white dove descending from heaven, such as he had never *seen* [*vit*]: never had he ever *beheld* [*vit*] with his own eyes so white or so very beautiful a dove, for he had never *seen* [*vit*] any flower in summer nor any snow on frost of such whiteness or of so delightful a colour. [The dove] carried a crown of gold: he had never *beheld* [*esguarda*] so rich a one. The crown was adorned with costly precious stones, with luxurious gems, and gave forth greater light than the sun in summer at the height of the solstice, in the hour when it shines most strongly in the clearest part of the firmament. [The dove] placed this very beautiful crown on the head of the maiden who had suffered so much in this martyrdom for God that she well deserved it. He *saw* [*veit*] her clad in white garments, with new bright robes, shining beautifully and splendidly. Then he *saw* [*vit*] and understood that Jesus Christ in his mercy had already given her victory in his eternal glory, so that her torments were gone and her joys begun. The white dove which came down from heaven *as you have heard* flew around the blessed martyr and comforted her with its gentle flight: caressing her with its soft wings it shielded her from the flame, and, by the blessed grace of Jesus, quenched the fierceness and strength of the flame and the gridiron and the burning and the hurt as if by a shower, so that the blessed saint Faith felt no pain or suffering, our Lord be praised for it! When the blessed Caprais, who *saw* [*vit*] all the secrets of heaven, *looked at* [*esguarda*] the maiden and *saw* [*vit*] her whole and beautiful, and not at all harmed by the torment she had endured—she shone in this torment like a star in the firmament, made very beautiful and certainly very joyful by the crown which Jesus Christ sent her through his angel . . . he no longer wished to hide himself, but wanted to share the pains which Saint Faith, God's beloved, suffered for the son of Mary. (vv. 523–96, my italics)[40]

---

[40] Capraisse li seint martir | Ke memes les peines suffrir | Deveit pur le fiz Marie, | Esguarda vers la Deu amie | Ke en grëil esteit liée | D'orible flamme environée, | E si vit descendre del ciel | Un blanc columbe, unk ne vit tel, | Unkes si blanc ne si tres bel | Ne vit (mes) des oiz de columbel; | Kar nule flur [en tens] d'estée | Ne [unkes] neif sur la gelée | Ne vit mes de tele blanchur | Nul si delitable colur. | Une corone d'or porta, | Dunc tant riche ne esguarda; De riches peres preciuses, | De gemmes tres deliciuses | Ert la coronë aurné | E si dona greignur clarté | Ke ne fet (li) soleil en esté | Al jur quant est plus haut levé | A l'ure quant il meuz resplent | En le plus cler del firmament. Icele corone tres bele | Mist [il] au chief de la pucele | De cel martir ke tant suffri | Pur Deu ke bien li meri; | Vestue la veit a cele ure | D'une tres blanche vestëure, | De noeve vestëure clere [MS noeve vesteure blanche e clere] | E bien lusant de grant manere; | Dunt il vit bien e entendi | Ke Jhesu Crist par sa merci | Li aveit ja doné victoire | En sue parurable gloire, | Ke ses peines furent passées | E ses granz joies comencées. | Le blanc columb ke descendi | Del cel cum vus avez oy, | Entur la seinte martir volat | [E] de son duz voil li confortat; | De ses [deus] eles la blandi | Et de la flamme defendi; | (E) par la seinte grace Jhesu | Esteint la force e

Faith's bath of flames on this fiery bed and the double frame of male narratorial and spectatorial gaze gives some initial credence to the notion of
scopic/erotic fantasy as a motivation or goal for the narrative.[41] But the scopic
here is also the visionary: the insistent verbs of perception (*esguarda* largely in
the sense of ordinary physical perception and *vit* in the sense of spiritual perception of sensory manifestations) suggest Caprais is as much visionary witness
as voyeur.[42] The narrative's earlier account of the scene (vv. 385–412) admittedly
stresses Faith's tender limbs (v. 389, 399–400), her youth (v. 399), her nakedness
(v. 387), and her undismayed suffering (vv. 403, 409–10), but the terms of this
first shorter account are correctively expanded and transformed in St Caprais's
more authoritative witness. Here it is the transformation by which Caprais sees
flesh as gem that is the point and the narrative is as intent on the gem-imagery
of virginity and celestial vision and on Faith's crowning as on her body. In effect
Caprais's vision is an encounter with a *Pearl*-maiden, although, unlike that great
Middle English dream-vision, it is on earth rather than in the heaven partially
entered by the narrator of *Pearl*.[43] Faith's white robes and golden gemmed crown
are Caprais's privileged vision of her permanent incorruptible body as a great
lady of heaven, manifested to him just before the dove's wings temper the flames'
heat to leave Faith's earthly body whole and unmarked on the gridiron. (The
gridiron's connotation here need not be primarily of an erotically inflected bed,
so much as a tool for the hagiographic testing of relics, which were customarily
tried by fire.)[44]

la vertu | De la flamme e del grëil | E si del fu e del peril | Cume ceo fust d'une rosée; | Dunt
seinte Fey la bonurée | Ne senti peine ne dolur; | Loé [en] seit nostre seigniur! | Quant Capraisse
li bonurez | Ki de cel vit [tuz] les secrez | Esgarda devers la pucele | Si la vit entire e bele, | E ke
de rien n'esteit blecé | Del turment k'ele out enduré; | Ausi luseit en cel turment | Cum fet esteile
en firmament; | De la corone ke Jhesu Crist | Par son angele li tramist | Esteit tree bele e certes
lée ... Ne se voleit plus long tapir, | Mes as peines voleit partir | Ke seinte Fey la Deu amie | Soffri
[la] pur le fiz Marie', 'Vie anglo-normande', ed. Baker, vv. 523–96.

[41] It would be possible to argue for Anglo-Norman here, as Gayle Margherita does in an
exhilarating Lacanian account of the early Middle English *Seinte Iuliene*, that the 'discursive integrity
of the Faith, linked to the integrity of the "original" language is shown to depend on the specu-
lar and spectacular disintegration of woman as body' (*Romance of Origins*, 55). In so far as every
virgin *passio* encodes linguistic desire for the pre- and post-discursive wholeness figured by
virginity this reading applies to them all. But each *passio* is also different and culturally specific.

[42] Only angels, in medieval visual theory, can see God directly, but as Augustine argues (*De
Trinitate*, III. x–xi, PL42.879–86), miracles and signs are used to announce aspects of God to humans.
These may include the eucharist, or other means, such as the dove and crown conventional to
virgin martyrs often witnessed by text-internal spectators. (I thank Professor Bernard Martin of
the English Department, University of Sydney, for helpful discussion of the visionary/scopic in
this Life.)

[43] Since John of Gaunt, Duke of Lancaster, owner of Tutbury Castle in the *Gawain/Pearl*-poet's
territory, took a special interest in Horsham St Faith, requesting its denization (and hence freedom from the fines of alien priory status) in 1390 (*VCH*, *Norfolk* ii. 347), historical links between
the two poems may not be beyond the bounds of possibility.

[44] See Thomas Head, 'Saints, Heretics, and Fire: Finding Meaning through the Ordeal', in Sharon
Farmer and Barbara H. Rosenwein (eds.), *Monks and Nuns, Saints and Outcasts: Religion in Medieval
Society: Essays in Honor of Lester K. Little* (Ithaca: Cornell University Press, 2000), 220–38.

The Anglo-Norman Life alternates flesh and gem in the very structure as well as the rhetoric and thematics of its diptych narrative: Simon of Walsingham's saint is not only a nubile nuptial tortured virgin but the fierce hieratic reliquary prayed to by Robert and Sybil Fitzwalter on their way home to Norfolk and still today in the treasury at Conques and represented in the Horsham wall-paintings (see Illustration 1). She is studded with eye-like gems, efficacious and powerful (her blessed name and her meaning, says Walsingham, fit 'better than a gem in a ring', vv. 25–8). The relation between the virgin and her reliquary statue here involves understanding both as persons and both as treasures. To see Faith's statue as simply material would be, certainly for the St Augustine so dismissive of Pallas's effigy, to exhibit a pagan literal-mindedness. Such a reading is offered in the Life when Faith is seen as and compared with the statue of 'seinte Dyane' as a 'goddess of love' (vv. 320, 322), but it is a reading made by the pagan tyrant Decius. In Faith's famous *translatio* narrative, retold in the Anglo-Norman Life by Walsingham (vv. 976–1232), Faith's reliquary statue becomes a Helen of monastic competition, stolen by the monastery of Conques from the sacristy at Agen, the original site of her martyrdom. Agen eventually accepted the theft as a valid translation, and Conques' pilgrimage revenues began, Faith's gems and jewels multiplying themselves many times over.[45] When the statue arrives at Conques in Walsingham's version it is celebrated as 'the arrival of the maiden' ('la venue de la *pucele*', v. 1208, italics mine).

If Faith's statue has the kind of presence and influence we associate with personhood, the maiden Faith is also herself an object, a very valuable one. A glorious, effulgent gem, who radiates more light the harder Decius tries to extinguish her (vv. 205–20), Faith is acclaimed as 'this bright *polished* gem, this *well-refined* gold' ('Cele gemme tant cler polie, | Cel fin or tant bien esmeré', vv. 820–1). The life's imagery and epithets activate in newly significant ways the conventional association of virginity and precious gold and gems.[46] When, in the rhetoric of romance heroinehood, Walsingham's narrative celebrates Faith as the most beautiful maiden and of 'highest lineage' (vv. 123–4), the 'most

[45] Patrick Geary, *Furta Sacra: Thefts of Relics in the Central Middle Ages* (Princeton: Princeton University Press, 1978), 70–6; Benedicta Ward, *Miracles and the Medieval Mind: Theory, Record and Event 1000–1215* (rev. edn. Aldershot: Wildwood House, 1987), 36–42.

[46] For discussions of such imagery see Claude A. Luttrell, 'The Medieval Tradition of the Pearl Virginity', *Medium Ævum*, 31 (1962), 194–200; Barbara Newman, 'Flaws in the Golden Bowl'; Margaret Ashton, 'Gold and Images', in *The Church and Wealth*, ed. W. J. Sheils and Diana Wood, *SCH* 24 (1987), 189–207. Marbod of Rennes's lapidary had wide circulation in Anglo-Norman culture and influenced the highly stylized meditations for women of the Early Middle English Wooing-Group (see Elizabeth Salter, ed. Derek Pearsall and Nicolette Zeeman, *English and International: Studies in the Literature, Art and Patronage of Medieval England* (Cambridge: Cambridge University Press, 1988), 73–4), as did vernacular versions of it and associated works (Paul Studer and Joan Evans, *Anglo-Norman Lapidaries* (Paris: Champion, 1924), 1–11). Precious stones also share in the therapeutic aspects of saints' cult, being themselves valued medicinally (*Marbode of Rennes (1035–1123): De Lapidibus considered as a Medical Treatise with Text, Commentary and C. W. King's Translation; together with Text and Translation of Marbode's Minor Works on Stones*, ed. John M. Riddle (Wiesbaden: Franz Steiner, 1977), 23–5).

ILLUST. 1. The virgin as treasure and the treasure as virgin. Sainte Foy: Conques reliquary statue (10th c. and later). St Faith: Wall-painting from Horsham St Faith, Norfolk (13th c.).

beautiful of all the province' (v. 122), Faith's heavenly existence as patroness of her region does indeed make her Agen's treasure. The narrative's rhetoric is simultaneously romance hyperbole and hagiographic truth-claim. And when, in a play on virginity literature's standard comparison between virginity and gold refined in a furnace, Faith is said to love 'chastity better than fine gold and humility better than treasure' ('Chasté ama plus ke fin or | Humilité plus de tresor', vv. 147–8), the narrative's rhetoric becomes tautologous: the virgin who is a gem treasures the gem of chastity. These are not simple gestures of commodification, but suggest more fluid relations and boundaries between persons and things than in our own paradigms. In this virginity rhetoric, the very notion of treasure is much less closely associated with monetary value than it is for us. As Jacques Godbout has argued of the archaeologists' 'paleomoney', 'the significance of archaic money is . . . not found in its relationship to things but in . . . the relationship it forges between persons living, dead, or to be reborn, with animals and with the cosmos'.[47]

Faith's role as personified relic and treasured person is not that of an object of exchange, but a gift. In Marcel Mauss's famous anthropological examination of oblationary systems, gift-giving customs involve not a mechanical exchange of a neutral medium, but a moral transaction in which what is exchanged is 'itself a person or pertains to a person'. The gift relates persons, not things, is coded as gratuitous and free, but entails reciprocity and exchange and itself has an ineradicable spiritual dimension which persists in all circulation. 'It is groups and not individuals which carry on exchange, make contracts and are bound by obligations' and 'the obligation attached to a gift itself is not inert. Even when abandoned by the giver it still forms a part of him'.[48] This model, though derived from anthropological analysis of 'archaic' societies, is suggestive for the circulation of the saintly virgin, and retains its value when considering a society neither entirely archaic nor entirely like later European societies.[49] It has been

[47] Jacques T. Godbout, with Alain Caillé, tr. Donald Winkler, *The World of the Gift* (Montreal: McGill-Queen's University Press, 1998), Part Two, 'From the Archaic to the Modern Gift', 116.

[48] Marcel Mauss, *The Gift: Forms and Functions of Exchange in Archaic Societies*, tr. Ian Cunnison, introd. E. E. Evans-Pritchard (London and New York: Norton, 1967), 10, 3, 9, and see chs. 3, 4; and Evans-Pritchard, 'Introduction', p. ix; Godbout, *World of the Gift, passim*. In the Anglo-Norman context, the notion of the 'royal love' (the king's giving) as both pragmatic, fiscal, and emotional is analogous to the conceptualization of Faith's powers and functions: see Stephanie Mooers Christelow, 'The Royal Love in Anglo-Norman England: A Fiscal and Courtly Concept', *HSJ* 8 (1996), 29–42, and Ch. 7, n. 89 below.

[49] Gayle Rubin, 'The Traffic in Women: Notes on the Political Economy of Sex', in Rayna R. Reiter (ed.), *Towards an Anthropology of Women* (New York and London: Monthly Review Press, 1975), 157–210; Henrietta L. Moore, *Feminism and Anthropology* (Cambridge: Cambridge University Press, 1988), esp. 12–41: Marilyn Strathern, *The Gender of the Gift: Problems with Women and Problems with Society in Melanesia* (Berkeley: University of California Press, 1988). Jacques Derrida argues that the gift is impossible: 'for there to be a gift, there must be no reciprocity, return, exchange, countergift or debt', and that a gift only becomes possible by tearing apart 'time as circle': see his 'Given Time: The Time of the King', *Critical Inquiry*, 18 (1992), 161–87 (170, 168). The double

persuasively deployed by Sarah Kay in reading the period's *chansons de geste*, and applies with even greater closeness to contemporary narratives of virgin saints, whom the imagery of treasure encodes as a particularly valuable form of gift.[50] When Simon of Walsingham calls Faith 'refined gold', or when (to take an early Middle English example) Thomas of Hales in his early thirteenth-century 'Letter of Love', *Luuve Ron*, calls virginity the gemstone of the maiden's bower, set 'in heouene golde' and 'ful of fuyn amur' (ll. 181–2), they are not simply paraphrasing sexual desire, but evoking a set of relationships between persons in which the virgin is nexus, sign, and participant.[51] In the rhetoric of virgin sainthood and treasure, the principal tropes of nuptiality and dotality connote not just privatized sexual fantasy but a range of social meaning.

As Simon Gaunt argues in his analysis of the Occitan version of the legend, Faith's virginity (and sanctity) makes her a sign of value transmitted between men.[52] Homosocial links and relations around the saint are certainly stressed in Simon of Walsingham's narrative both as environment and stimulus for the Life. In addition to the conventional declaration of obedience to a Benedictine superior (v. 46), the narrator jests about the stature of the colleague and compatriot who has asked for the work (his friend is 'a man . . . of small stature but full of virtues', for whom, 'in affection and fellowship', the work has been undertaken, vv. 79–82, 88–9). Before making her choice between the pagan tyrant and Christ, and her choice of client communities, the Anglo-Norman Faith circulates between the male narrator and his male God and between the male narrator and his monastic colleagues as a way of authorizing the narrator's devotion and his translation from the Latin *vita*. Even more fully than in the Latin source material, the saint in Simon of Walsingham's version is thus a gift given by the Lord to his faithful servants, firstly in visionary knowledge to St Caprais, witness to and emulator of Faith's passion, then to particular monastic houses,

career of the virgin saint, both dead and continuingly alive in historical time because of her eternal existence, makes her both the gift of temporal social circulation and a 'true' gift as in Derrida's model. For a generally illuminating study of medieval gift-giving, see Stephen D. White, *Custom, Kinship, and Gifts to Saints: The 'laudatio parentum' in Western France* (Chapel Hill: University of North Carolina Press, 1988). For insular culture, see John Hudson, *Land, Law and Lordship in Anglo-Norman England* (Oxford: Clarendon Press, 1994), esp. ch. 5.

[50] *The Chansons de Geste in the Age of Romance: Political Fictions* (Oxford: Clarendon Press, 1995), to which I am much indebted. As Kay points out, relations of commodification are not excluded in 12th- and 13th-c. transactions, but are subordinate in the period's conceptualizations (43–4).

[51] For the *Loue Ron* (literally 'rune', 'secret'), see *Moral Love Songs and Lyric Laments*, ed. Susanna Greer Fein, TEAMS (Kalamazoo, Mich.: Medieval Institute Publications, 1998), 11–56.

[52] *Gender and Genre in Old French Literature* (Cambridge: Cambridge University Press, 1995), 188–90. Literary and hagiological functions of the virgin body are congruent here: as Head argues, '[relics] did not serve as a direct conduit of . . . thaumaturgic [forces]. Rather, personal relationships formed between the living and the dead, relationships which were balanced on the delicate fulcrum of the saint's pledges or relics, allowed the saint to exercise his *virtus* on behalf of his living servants' (*Hagiography and the Cult of Saints*, 12).

then to Walsingham's monastic superiors, the 'cumpaignun' (v. 79) who commands the translation and 'danz Benjamin' (who transmits the Latin material to Walsingham, v. 444), and then by Walsingham himself to those who cannot understand Latin (vv. 93–4).

Although Faith is thus transmitted by men, it is both possible and necessary to speak of Faith herself as choosing and giving in seigneurial gift and patronage exchanges. She gives power and value to the men who exchange her, paradigmatically so in the narrative's acquisition of these things as it circulates her (and with her the identity of her devotee, Simon of Walsingham). But they do not simply use her: she is a self-donating gift. 'I have given myself' ('me rendi', 'me doinz', vv. 295, 299) she explains, 'to Christ, who has this earth in his power' ('an baillie', v. 298). With her relation to Christ authoritatively crowned in martyrdom, Faith, like the Virgin herself (whose Coronation becomes a prominent iconographical motif at this time in north-west Europe), is seen to be the beloved of the highest king ('seinte amie a plus haut rey', v. 884) with all that implies for her powers of intercession and gift-granting.[53] The saint gives an enduring identity to the group who hold her: her monastic house is itself a gift to her, is dedicated to her.[54] The Life includes an account of Caprais's rejection of Decius's worldly courtly honours (offered to him as a 'beautiful and comely' youth, v. 658) in favour of Christ, the giver, as Caprais asserts, of all goods ('de tuz biens . . . dunëur', v. 697). It includes the conversion and martyrdom of Primus and Felicianus, moved by the angelic beauty of Caprais's unswerving loyalty in his passion. But this agenda of homosocial loyalties is framed and articulated by the example of Faith's passion, the foundational gift to Christ that enables these further circulations of value.

As with the *Pearl*-poet's narrator and his 'luf-daungere', the vision both of Caprais and the narrator is inflected in the Life of Faith by longing and desire, but by a range of desires for a fecund treasure as polysemous as the Pearl. Certainly, a personal and affective relation to the saint is included: Simon of Walsingham's narrator must specially honour and serve Faith, he claims, because his own birth was on the day of her death (6 October, Faith's feast day):

---

[53] The culminating wish of the narrator's prologue is that God will admit us to his father's kingdom through the holy intercession of Faith (vv. 105–6). On the coronation of the virgin, see Gold, *The Lady and the Virgin*, 61–5. The Virgin's sovereignty is derived from her son, of course, not held in her own right, but as recent studies of medieval queenship have shown (see esp. Parsons, 'The Queen's Intercession'; id., 'Of Queens, Courts, and Books'; Huneycutt, 'Intercession and the High Medieval Queen'; Howell, *Eleanor of Provence*) this does not obviate important powers of gift and intercession.

[54] For these exchanges between saint and community see the works by White and Hudson cited in n. 49 above. For an account of Faith's statue and the rituals focused on it as serving the political ends of various groups in the 11th c., rather than creating a single or unproblematic notion of community, see Kathleen Ashley and Pamela Sheingorn, 'An Unsentimental View of Ritual in the Middle Ages, or, Sainte Foy was no Snow White', *Journal of Ritual Studies*, 6 (1992), 63–85.

> Cum de ses peines s'en parti,
> Gié a mes peines [ci] nasqui;
> Al jur ke ses travailz finerent,
> Este vus les mens comencerent;
> Al jur k'ele reçut (joie e) honur
> Nasqui a(d) peine e a(d) dolur;
> Ele ad joïe e ad leesce
> E jeo ay plur e ay tristesce.
>
> (vv. 55–62)

As she quitted her torments, I was born to mine; the day when her labours finished saw the beginning of mine; on the day she received joy and honour, I was born to anguish and grief; she has joy and bliss, and I have weeping and sadness.

These wistful, envious (and finely chiastic) lyrical inversions on the part of the narrator, 'serf Marie a seint Eadmun' (v. 100) as he identifies himself, form one strand of the narrator's stance towards his youthful female patron. As the play on birth pains and labour in the passage quoted above suggests, the poem is also interested in the feminized and infantilizing positions offered by the modesty topics commonly found in hagiographic prologues. The narrator is, he says, a humble figure hardly able to use the prestige vernacular of French ('povrement enromancé', v. 38), he has little learning ('guere lettré', v. 37), and he writes out of devotion to the saint and out of his relationship with his Benedictine colleague (v. 88). Perhaps these claims had a historical basis in a meritocratic career for a brother from Horsham entering the wealthy old community of St Edmunds, but there is nothing in the text to bear them out and it is dangerous to read them literally. One might compare Adam of Eynsham, for example, in his biography of St Hugh of Lincoln (completed *c.*1212) claiming that he is 'sensibus parvulum et sermone imperitum . . . in utero et post uterum miserum . . . peccatorem' ('a child in understanding and completely without eloquence . . . from the womb and ever after a pitiful . . . sinner'), and fathering the *vita* on his superiors who have inspired and commanded it.[55] The position of a child is especially appropriate for the narrator of Faith's Life, given the youth of the saint. Childlikeness seems also to have been capable in this period of connoting, if ambivalently, the unimpaired volitional wholeness by which virginity and faith are mutual symbols of each other in so much virginity literature, here underlined by the identity of Faith's name and meaning.[56] The narrator's attribution of infantile status to his own vernacular language is thus not simply humble, but a move to align its truth-telling capacities with her integrity and power.

---

[55] *Magna vita sancti Hugonis*, ed. and tr. Douie and Farmer, 1–2.

[56] On 12th-c. perceptions of childhood see Jane Gilbert, ' "Boys will be . . . what?": Gender, Sexuality, and Childhood in *Floire et Blancheflor* and *Floris et Lyriope*', *Exemplaria*, 9 (1997), 39–62.

In so translating Faith from the Latin, from the Aveyron and from Horsham to Bury, Simon of Walsingham seems both to have explored his own allegiances and claimed, in 'cele pucele | Apres Marie la plus bele' (vv. 47–8), the most powerful and precious personal patron for them. His narrative stages its teller's devotion as personal rather than institutional (the monastic house of Walsingham is not mentioned, and the narrative finishes with the triumphal procession by which Faith enters Conques). In composing this text, its lexical surface covered with gold and gem imagery and with puns on Faith's name (see especially vv. 1–32, 121–50, 208–16, 276–80, 819–22), its thematics asserting integrity, and its narrative stance re-presenting and memorializing his own relation to the central figure, Walsingham may well have thought of himself as creating a devotional and ritual object, a linguistic reliquary crafted to embody and announce the meaning and powers of the saint. As Amy Remensnyder has written of the relics in the treasury at Conques: 'the precious materials from which reliquaries were typically constructed symbolically made visible what was hidden, and transformed it. The actual relic was a bodily fragment, something identifiably human. The gold, silver, and precious stones of the reliquary interpreted that fragment and revealed to the viewer what could not be seen even were the relic visible: the other and true nature.'[57] The Anglo-Norman Life of Faith, 'povrement enromancé' (v. 38), but lavish in homage, desire, and treasure imagery, participates in this poetics of revelation concerning the human body and the powers of the vernacular as well as in monastic politics of identity. Functioning, in the Campsey manuscript, as material for a community of upper-class women's audition, the life's staging of monastic devotion to a powerful professionally virgin patroness speaks many desires and many possibilities of exchange. To use displaced clerical heterosexual desire as the fundamental hermeneutic of such narratives is to elide a much richer range of desires and social relations, and also to erase a conceptualization of personhood that deserves more investigation, not assimilation to our own assumptions.

2.3. VIRGIN EXCHANGE: DOTALITY IN ANGLO-NORMAN CULTURE

In addition to the many affective and volitional meanings of her name, Faith is, then, both romance virgin *and* enduring treasure, nubile courtly heroine (as

---

[57] Remensnyder, 'Legendary Treasure at Conques: Reliquaries and Imaginative Memory', *Speculum*, 71 (1996), 884–906 (890). Again the archaeologists' 'paleomoney' is suggestive for how treasure means in such contexts: '[paleo]money's primary function is not to measure the value of things but of people . . . in a society without writing, money is the privileged record-keeper that helps shore up the collective memory . . . it embodies and makes visible an entire series of intersecting debts and obligations linking each individual to all' (Godbout, *World of the Gift*, 115–16). By the time of Walsingham's Life of Faith, insular culture, as Michael Clanchy has shown (*From Memory to Written Record*), is hardly a society without writing, but it *is* (as argued by Brian Stock, *The Implications of Literacy: Written Language and Models of Interpretation in the Eleventh and Twelfth Centuries* (Princeton: Princeton University Press, 1983)) a culture much closer to an a-literate society than our own.

in the Horsham frescoes) and powerful, hieratically magnificent gold (as in the Conques reliquary). The exchanges of *La vie sainte Foy* have many parallels and resonances in Anglo-Norman socio-economic arrangements, and in the ethical and sacramental implications of gift-giving in this culture, both within and around saints' lives. The giving of both women and land in Anglo-Norman England takes particular and complex forms.[58] Contra those critics who have argued for completely separate ideologies as informing hagiography and romance, it is important, if the particular social embeddedness and the full resonance of virgin-martyr narratives in high medieval Britain are to be appreciated, to acknowledge the continuities and overlaps in the exchanges of women and territory for both secular and ecclesiastical purposes.[59] These exchanges are both economic and spiritual-affective: at the heart of feudal relations of exchange and gift, the basic terms of *amor* and *feodus* ('contract, treaty') are related to *fides* and *fidus*, and a pledge is *foedus amoris*, as well as *pignus*.[60]

One of the most pertinent examples from monastic discourse is Hugh of St Victor's *De arrha anime* (The Bride-Price of the Soul), a dialogue between a man (*homo*-Christ-bridegroom) and his soul constructed on the metaphor of bridal *dos* in the nuptial contract, and exploring the mystical relation between God and the soul.[61] Creation itself here becomes the dowry of the soul. Conversely, in marriages between humans, dotal charters from the tenth to the twelfth centuries include statements of theological formation as well as of contract for

---

[58] See Eleanor Searle, 'Women and the Legitimization of Succession at the Norman Conquest', *ANS* 3 (1981), 159–70; Judith A. Green, *The Aristocracy of Norman England* (Cambridge: Cambridge University Press, 1997). Charlotte A. Newman, *The Anglo-Norman Nobility in the Reign of Henry I: The Second Generation* (Philadelphia: University of Pennsylvania Press, 1988) stresses the importance of marriage as a strategy for advancement, above even the opportunities available for 'new men' in the royal *domus* and the *curia regis*. John Hudson has argued that although the crucial formulations and shifts of Anglo-Norman land transactions occurred in the 12th c., they continued to influence the developments of the 13th c. (*Land, Law, and Lordship*, esp. chs. 8 and 9).

[59] So for instance Susan Crane in her excellent study of Anglo-Norman romance narratives insists (wrongly in my view) on ideological opposition between hagiography and romance as a necessary concomitant of Anglo-Norman social structures (*Insular Romance: Politics, Faith and Culture in Anglo-Norman and Middle English Literature* (Berkeley: University of California Press, 1986), 94–104). I take it rather to be a rhetorical strategy used by vernacular hagiographers.

[60] See Bond, *The Loving Subject*, ch. 2 (65). Marriage is founded on an equally double exchange: the *maritalis affectio* of canon law referring both to feeling itself and to the readiness to give property.

[61] The *De arrha* (PL176.950–700) was several times translated into French and figures in a manuscript owned by Barking in the early 15th c. (Oxford, Magdalen College, MS Lat. 41), as well as being incorporated into Philippe de Mézières' early 14th-c. treatise on marriage, the *Livere . . . du sacrement de mariage*: see Geneviève Hasenohr, 'Aperçu sur la diffusion et la réception de la littérature de spiritualité en langue française au dernier siècle du Moyen Age', in Norbert R. Wolf (ed.), *Wissensorganisierende und wissensvermittelnde Literatur im Mittelalter*, Wissensliteratur im Mittelalter. Schriften des Sonderforschungsbereichs 226 Würzburg/Eichstatt (Wiesbaden: Reichart, 1987), 57–90.

the couple (as does the Anglo-Norman *Jeu d'Adam*).[62] Material and conceptual forms of gift and giving interchange: betrothal was confirmed with a kiss in the early Middle Ages, and *osculum* comes to mean the dotal charter itself.[63] The theological dimensions of the lexis of gift-giving further illuminate the complexities and slipperiness of medieval boundaries between persons and things and their interrelations. The doctrine of the gifts of the body and spirit was at the centre of a contemporary debate as to whether virtues are gifts or qualities, a debate in which grace, gifts, and talents join estates theory in consideration of the endowments and obligations of the human being. Two important gifts, dowry and dower (the gift given with the bride and the gift given to the bride), have appropriately complicated legal histories and Anglo-Norman morphologies (*dower, doaire, doeire,* etc. slip easily into *deurie, duarie*). Christ himself is sometimes a confusing giver. As the bridegroom of the virgin or the chaste soul, he brings the creation itself, or gifts of body and spirit (*dotes spiritualis et corporalis*) such as life, movement, sensory powers, etc.[64] The bliss of the body in both its mortal and eternal form is increased by this endowment (the *dotes spiritualis* include absolute powers of movement, intensity of joyful feeling, etc. in heaven). But which kind of gift does Christ give? If he gives *dowry,* is it a gift or talent in the woman? If *dower,* is it something she can claim from him? The Early Middle English *Guide for Anchoresses* (*Ancrene Wisse*) construes Christ's gifts (space, light, and freedom in heaven for the bride reclusively enclosed on earth) as the Germanic *dos ex marito,* or *Morgengab,* 'marhe ȝeouen' (this had become equated to *dower* in canon law). The earlier Anglo-Norman version of the *Guide* renders these as the 'doweires' of recluses, then later generalizes them as the 'duaries de bone gent de religion', a metaphoric version of the *dowry* for entering a religious house, and explains their special applicability to enclosed women religious.[65]

In Anglo-Norman England, the lord of all lay and ecclesiastical donors was the king, the principal owner in Britain of land and of unappended women through his right of ward over heiresses and orphans (lists of whom were kept from 1185).[66] The gift ceremonies developed for the giving of land in the creation of monastic foundations attend to secular as well as spiritual overlordship. These complex ceremonies included ritual countergifting (a public assertion of exchange and relationship between donor and donee which made it harder to retract gifts), counsel and consent from relatives, particularly heirs, and also from the donor's

---

[62] See Philip Lyndon Reynolds, 'The Dotal Charter as Theological Treatise', *RTAM* 61 (1994), 54–68; Willem Noomen, 'Le *Jeu d'Adam*: Étude descriptive et analytique', *Romania,* 89 (1965), 145–93.

[63] Reynolds, 'Dotal Charter', 56 n. 6.

[64] On the seven gifts see A. Gardeil, in A. Vacant, E. Mangenot, *et al., Dictionnaire de théologie catholique* (Paris: Letouzey et Ané, 1908–50), IV, pt. 2, s.v. 'Dons du seint esperit', cols. 1738–77, 1765–71, 1771–7.

[65] Tolkien, ff. 7b/28; 24b/17, 28; Herbert, 78/2, 22; Trethewey, 197/29–198/13.

[66] *Rotuli de dominabus et pueris et puellis de XII comitatibus (1185),* ed. J. H. Round, Publications of the Pipe Roll Society 35 (London: St Catherine's Press, 1913).

lord.[67] As with giving for the purposes of monastic foundation, so too in secular marriage's household formation: *dos* (dowry), in the shape of lands and income from them, comes attached to the bride in the transaction between father and groom. But a mode of countergift to the bride herself is included even though the exchange is framed as between men. If the bride herself is a gift to be given, she is also sufficiently a subject in the transaction to receive a gift, even in the very moment of her exchange between one kin group and another. Her gift is the provisional one of dower (AN *douarie*) given by her husband, which she will be able to claim as a widow. Like monastic donations, these exchanges are complicated and have ramifying 'vertical' dimensions in relations antecedent to as well as proceeding from the new nuptial contract (*dos*, dowry, for instance is concerned not only with the disposal of the bride, but with protecting primogeniture and allowing older generations to exert control on the formation of new households).[68] And these gifts also interact in a network of shame and honour distinctions, activated by the requirement for open giving—for dower to be given publicly, *ad ostium ecclesiae*, at the door of the church.[69] In this giving, conceptual oppositions between seigneurial honour and seigneurial spirituality are tellingly difficult to make. Correct behaviour in the exchange is part of seigneurial *fraunchise* and *largesse*.

This can be readily seen in the earliest known Anglo-Norman exposition of the seven sacraments for a lay patron. The *Corset* (the title metaphorically renders the sacraments as a protective covering enveloping the human body and soul) was composed, probably in the mid-thirteenth century, by Rober le Chapelain for Alain la Zouche (d. 1270).[70] It states that a woman can only be honourably given in marriage by her father and her lineage, or, in their absence, by someone who has known her from infancy (vv. 233–40). To guarantee seigneurial identity through purity of lineage, a wife's body needs, so to speak, a certificated narrative, much as a virgin saint's needs to be able to signal past and future integrity of identity and proprietorship for her monastic household. But the bride is owed something herself as well. Rober explains the marital giving of 'dower' to the bride as a spiritual obligation for men. As a 'membre del corps Crist' (v. 308) a man ought not to use whoredom ('se mest en puterie',

---

[67] For gift-giving ceremonies, see Binns, 11–18; Hudson, *Land, Law, and Lordship*, chs. 5, esp. 164–6 on countergifting, and 7.

[68] On the development of *dos*, dowry, see Jack Goody, *The Development of the Family and Marriage in Europe* (Cambridge: Cambridge University Press, 1983), Appendix; Diane Owen Hughes, 'From Bride Price to Dowry in Mediterranean Europe', *Journal of Family History*, 3 (1978), 262–96; Searle, 'Women and the Legitimization of Succession'.

[69] Anglo-Norman marriages were conducted outside the church door (Molin and Mutembe, *Rituel du mariage*, 35–7, and see Ch. 1, n. 30).

[70] *Corset: A Rhymed Commentary on the Seven Sacraments by Rober le Chapelain*, ed. Keith Val Sinclair, ANTS 52 (London, 1995), henceforth cited by line number in the text. For the identification of Rober's patrons, see Sinclair, 'Anglo-Norman Patrons', and *Corset*, Introduction, 15–21.

v. 309), but should love his wife as Christ does the church (vv. 127–8 and Ephesians
5: 25). The guarantee against whoredom, and the sign of Christian love, is to
exchange treasure for one's bride:

He [the bridegroom *in facie ecclesiae*] gives her dower ['li done le duaire'] so that she
has no fear that anything will be done wrongly, and so that he has without a doubt
bought her ['l'achatee'] when he has endowed her with his chattels. He has bought her
in chastity ('en chastée'), so that she does not fall into any sin. May such a purchase
['achate'] be blessed by God who creates all that is good and overthrows all evils! And
yet it is not really a purchase ['achat'], but a stable form of love ['estable druerie'] for
honouring the lady ['la dame bien honurer'], for it is very honourable to give and a
man should give to his friends and take away from his enemies ['il est grant honour de
doner | Et l'ome soult doner a ses amys | Et tolir a ses enemys'].

Then the donor ['li donour'] must take her by the hand and give her to her lord
['baillier son seignour'], so that no one can remark any rapine or compulsion ['ravine
ne force'], only just possession ['dreite saisine']. (*Corset*, vv. 325–42)

The husband's gift is further glossed in the exchange of rings in the marriage.
These (like Faith's name and meaning) connote a version of eternity and are a
sign of female purity: their roundness symbolizes refined and enduring love ('fin'
amour ke ne fine mie', v. 378), their shining the openness and honour of the
nuptials whereby the woman is not married in 'obscurté' (v. 396), and the whiteness of their fine silver signifies that (like Faith's dove) the woman is 'as white
in chastity as a lily in summer' (vv. 403–4). A seigneur who doesn't marry in
this way, Rober adds, is worse than a dog and is behaving like a Jew (vv. 441,
447).[71]

   Chaste marriage is notably close here to being a form of virginity, and the
handbook made for Lord Alain further shows that (as argued in Chapter 1) the
conceptual boundaries between spiritually fecund virginity and bodily fecund
chastity in wives are less sharp, or at least differently accented, than we might
think. What appears to be a sexually grounded distinction operates primarily as
a shame and honour one.

   The overlap between secular and religious nuptiality and dotality is explicitly
made in another way in St Nicholas's concern with dowry. By the end of the
twelfth century dowry was a category of charitable bequest. The cult of St Nicholas,
early popular in Anglo-Norman England, has as one of its most frequent icono-
graphic representations the saint's gift of dowry for the three daughters of an
impoverished man of status.[72] The legend implausibly but tellingly claims that
had the saint not given these dowries, the daughters would have had to become
prostitutes. Prostitution is here unlikely to be a literal account of the daughters'

---

[71] Analogously, in some dotal charters, clandestine marriage is heathen (Reynolds, 'Dotal
Charter', 57).

[72] For an account of this motif in the development of Nicholas's cult, see Charles W. Jones,
Saint Nicholas of Myra, Bari and Manhattan: Biography of a Legend (Chicago: Chicago University
Press, 1978), 53–78, 144–54.

fates, and suggests rather the co-option of the saint's cult in the maintenance of a newly intensified shame and honour distinction based on the patriarchal ability to give dowry or not.[73] Conversely, in the romance economics of the ecclesiastical and social satire, 'Plainte d'Amour', Love inverts teaching such as that given Lord Alain by his chaplain to claim that

> Jeo fiz marier gentil femme
> Sanz doner or ou riche gemme
> Mult noblement.
>
> (vv. 187–9)[74]

I cause well-born women to be married very nobly without the giving of gold or rich gems.

True love, not simony, will inform entry to the religious life to provide spiritual rather than material dowry. But the poem is not proposing alternative values to the seigneurial honour and shame model: it is inverting it, within a shared framework of assumptions.

For the bride of Christ, spiritual dower from her Christ bridegroom is one part of her donation, but she also needs dowry from her earthly father. A whole discourse of honourable and shameful giving develops around Anglo-Norman religious dowry, comparable with that around lay marriage as prescribed in *Corset*. In the exchange of women in chivalric narrative, as Roberta Krueger has shown, romance glosses the socio-economics of the exchange as acceptable and inevitable for women.[75] So, too, canon law and hagiography's stress on the freely willed vow by which the consecrated virgin (accompanied by the freely given parental donation) gives herself to God glosses the socio-economics of religious *gynaceum* as a system of personal choice, of the voluntarism distinguishing honour from shame.[76] Religious dowry became increasingly regarded as simoniacal in the later twelfth century and by Lateran IV had been specially mapped onto women religious: in the Council's 64th canon, nuns are said to be infected with simoniacal stain.[77] However, the practice of requiring gifts on entry to a

---

[73] As Peter Coss has shown, over the late 12th and into the 13th c., the marriage market became increasingly open to professionals as well as to various forms and ranks of knighthood and nobility (*Lordship, Knighthood, and Locality: A Study in English Society 1180–c.1280* (Cambridge: Cambridge University Press, 1991)).

[74] *La plainte d'amour, poème anglo-normand*, ed. Johan Vising (Göteborg: Göteborg Högskola Aarsskrift Text XI, App. crit XIII, 1905–7), stanza 33.

[75] 'Love, Honor, and the Exchange of Women in *Yvain*: Some Remarks on the Female Reader', *Romance Notes*, 25 (1985), 302–17, and *Women Readers and the Ideology of Gender*, esp. chs. 1 and 2.

[76] On the ambiguities here as they affect the question of monastic oblation see Doran, 'Oblation or Obligation? A Canonical Ambiguity': for the complexities of lexis and interpretation surrounding the act of profession for both women and men, see John van Engen, 'Professing Religion: From Liturgy to Law', *Viator*, 29 (1998), 323–43.

[77] See Joseph H. Lynch, *Simoniacal Entry to Religious Life 1000–1260* (Columbus: Ohio State University Press, 1976), 192–4. The solution offered by the papacy for the problems caused by the prohibition was to limit the number of permitted novices in nunneries.

nunnery persisted. This practice rephrases shamefully obligatory trading into honourable and freely given gift exchange (between the nunnery and the parents, king, or other guardian).[78] The free will of young women is a prestige symbol for their male kin, since it denotes a political and economic mastery so complete (on the part of their fathers, brothers, and uncles) that young women's choices can be afforded. It was the baronial fathers of young women and men who were most anxious for seigneurial controls in marriage and who in Magna Carta extracted guarantees from the king against marital disparagement (marriage to persons of lower status) for the heiresses and widows whom the king held in wardship.

Nevertheless, the early thirteenth-century virginity letter, *Hali Meiðhad* (closely contemporary with Magna Carta) can make capital for virginity and female choice out of precisely this situation:

When it is like this for the rich, what do you expect for the poor, who are wretchedly married and ill provided for?—like almost all gentlewomen living at present who do not have the wherewithal to buy themselves a bridegroom of their own rank, and give themselves up to the service of a man of lower rank with all that they own. Alas, Lord Jesus, what a dishonourable bargain! ['unwurðe chaffere']! It would be better for them if they were brought to burial on their wedding day.[79]

Like much other virginity literature, the *Letter* claims to reveal the socioeconomic realities of marriage purportedly disguised in other genres. This is done in the service of its own reinscription of spiritual nuptiality with Christ as superior and capable of conferring greater freedom and dignity—more serious powers of self-donation—on the virgin than lies within marriage to ordinary men. So, too, St Gilbert's first enclosed protégées at Sempringham are said to be self-trading young women, giving themselves in exchange for the immortal gem of consecrated virginity: 'In the minds of these women there gleamed the image of a valuable pearl, which they bought, giving themselves and their possessions for it.'[80] And when Ralph of Meltonby placed his daughter Alice in the nunnery of Wilberfoss between 1170 and 1180, his charter stated:

---

[78] Gifts may be offered *after* reception into a community, but are felt to be tainted if force or previous agreement is involved (Lynch, *Simoniacal Entry*, 215). On the Lateran IV distinction between reception through 'pact' and through 'love', see Janet Burton, 'Yorkshire Nunneries in the Middle Ages: Recruitment and Resources', in John C. Appleby and Paul Dalton (eds.), *Government, Religion and Society in Northern England 1000–1700* (Stroud: Sutton, 1997), 104–16. For many nunneries, accepting entrants without financial provision was a ruinous option and gifts remained a necessity, however glossed (Cooke, 'Donors and Daughters'; Thompson, *Women Religious*, 187–90; Penelope D. Johnson, *Equal in Monastic Profession: Religious Women in Medieval France* (Chicago: University of Chicago Press, 1991), 25). As Thompson points out, avoiding the implication of simony is one reason for obscuring the link between nunnery entry and donation by the kin-group of the new nun (*Women Religious*, 181, n. 149).

[79] Millett and Wogan-Browne, 8/1–6.

[80] *Book of St Gilbert*, ed. and tr. Foreville and Keir, 32: 'Fulsit enim in earum mente species preciose margarite pro qua et se et sua dederunt et eam comparauerunt (cf. Matt 13: 46)'.

I have offered ['obtuli'] this charter with my daughter Alice ['hanc cartam cum filia mea Aaliz'], to whom my inheritance belongs, on the altar of St Mary of Wilberfoss, at the instance and prayer of my daughter herself ['concessu et prece ipsius filie mee'], whom the aforesaid nuns have accepted into their fellowship, to serve God there all the days of her life, as she herself has vowed in the presence of God ['sicut ipsa coram Deo vovit'].[81]

Though the daughter is here 'offered' by the father together with the charter, the wording expressive of his will carefully attends to the role of her volition in the transaction. In all these genres of virgin exchange the claim that the women exercise a freely willed choice is a saving gloss on a much more constrained and complex transaction, but not therefore only a disguise for straightforward commodification.

<h2 style="text-align:center">2.4. THE GIVING OF WOMEN</h2>

In saints' lives, the role of the virgin woman, as very pointedly in the case of St Faith, is potentially always ideal, more allegorical than historical, an idea to think male institutional identity and desire with. But, as we have seen, the role of the virgin saint-patroness complicates the possibilities, inadvertently or otherwise, for the represented participation and volition of women. Women's experiences of being given in marital exchange have for some time been seen as a relevant context for the representation of virgin martyrs. But so too are their experiences of giving.

In the Anglo-Norman Life of St Osith, the gift of the saint to God embraces territory and martyrdom:

> [seinz Deu] guerpirent terre e honur
> Et tut le mund pur Deu amur,
> Et soffrirent hunte e esclandre.
> Pur Deu firent lur sanc espandre;
> En bone entente e (en) bon espeir
> *Mort donerent* pur vie aveir.
> (vv. 39–44)

[God's holy ones] abandoned land and honour and all the world for the love of God and suffered shame and calumny. They shed their blood for God: with good purpose and in good hope they gave death in order to have life. [punctuation and italics mine]

This gift becomes key in a series of reciprocal obligations. Osith's gift of herself, expressed by vowing her maidenhood to God (v. 174), is given a territorial correlative in the claim that no grass grows in the place of her birth, which has become sacred (vv. 191–4). This claim creates obligations for God. Osith

<hr/>

[81] *Early Yorkshire Charters*, 3 vols., ed. W. Farrer (Edinburgh, 1914–16), i, no. 444, quoted by Janet Burton, *The Monastic Orders in Yorkshire 1069–1215* (Cambridge: Cambridge University Press, 1999), 167.

requires of him 'as her lord that she should never be violated' ('Et cil requist
come seigniur | Ke violée ne seit nul jur', vv. 175–6, also vv. 403–10). When
God keeps his part of the exchange by sending a white stag to divert her husband Sigher from pursuit of her virginity, Osith carries out her commitment
by veiling herself as a consecrated virgin during her husband's absence. This is
particularly marked in the vernacular Life as an act of self-donation, since the
priests sent with Osith by her mother at her marriage are shown as too fright-
ened to veil her.[82] The consecration of a virgin normally required a bishop to
officiate. It is therefore very clearly Osith's own willed act, one described in
careful ceremonial detail (vv. 668–72), when she donates herself to God. Her
legal right to do so in canon law would stem from her prior vow of virginity
(which makes God and not Sigher her real husband and lord), as has been shown
for the case of Christina of Markyate by Thomas Head.[83] The Anglo-Norman
Life draws even more strongly than Christina of Markyate's *vita* on the status
of this vow. Osith's self-consecration is not only accepted by Siger, but ratified
by his gift to her of various manors for her religious foundation and by his
decree that she is to have the second daughter of every count and baron in
his kingdom to be veiled and given ('donéez', v. 748) to religion with her
(vv. 735–48).

Osith's self-donation confers power over her own life and also power over
and for others. God, the narrative assures the audience, continues to respond
to Osith's martyrdom for his sake in the 'miracles gentils e granz'(v. 849) that
he does for her. Osith thus becomes a figure with whom the audience can enter
into various forms of exchange.[84] Instead of a procession of transient ancestors
('U sont nos aels [grandfathers] e nos peres | U sont nos uncles e nos meres?'
asks the prologue, vv. 23–4), audience attention to the Life will secure the favour
('gré', v. 120) of a patroness, who is to be respected and who knows how to
avenge insult (vv. 109–13). The form of gift-exchange inscribed for the audiences
of *Osith* is land donation: not only the saint, but '*whoever* gives up territory
['guerpist terre'] in his name, God gives to them heaven in reward' (vv. 7–8).
In the later Life of St Lucy by the Franciscan Bozon (*c.*1300), the saint
argues for less specific benefits (which could include inheritance, or moveable
property):

[82] Most Latin versions of the Life say that the priests ('bishops' in Ramsey's manuscript and
Bury's lectionary) agreed to veil her: only in the lost Life commissioned by William de Vere, Bishop
of Hereford (reconstructed from Leland's notes by Bethell, 'Lives of St Osyth', Appendix III), is
it said that they were unwilling (ibid. 87). Their position in the vernacular Life—you are joined
to your lord, we do not dare change your clothing (vv. 651–4)—was in practice often taken, since
one spouse's vow of virginity or chastity required the consent of the other.

[83] 'The Marriages of Christina of Markyate', esp. 91–100.

[84] These include exchanges, as Duncan Robertson has suggested, of pain and commemoration
('The believer transfers his suffering to the martyr, but remembers, devotedly and in detail, the
pain the latter underwent for his sake', Robertson, *The Medieval Saints' Lives*, 72), but still of necessity ascribe agency and patronage to the saint.

Ne est pas asez de Dieu doner
Ceo ke meymes ne poez aver;
A la mort, ceo ke vus durrez,
A force covent ke vus le lessez;
Co est la reson ke dunc le donez,
Ke aporter od vus ne le poez.
Meis si vus volez a Dieu paer
Des *biens* li donez ke pussez user [italics mine].[85]

It is not enough to give God that which you cannot have yourself. What you give away at death is what you are forced to leave behind. You give it away then for the reason that you cannot carry it with you. But if you wish to please God, give him goods of which you can have the use.

While a focus on 'biens' rather than the 'terre' of Osith is perhaps unsurprising in a late thirteenth-century mendicant poem, the continuing, adapted rhetoric of gift is noteworthy. Women's gift-giving powers, and their patronage, continue as a significant strand in the representation of virgin martyr lives.

Women's powers of donation are usefully borne in mind in considering the lives' representations not only of narratorial and seigneurial desire but of the desires of the saint. When a virgin says yes to Christ, she is not necessarily being masochistic and she does not simply confirm her wooer's identity. Rather she escapes from dotal control to make a gift of herself, a sacrifice. No one can die someone's own death for them: but saints dedicate themselves to God in a gratuitous and voluntary gift to a lord who does not need it for himself, but with whom it enables a relation of reciprocity to be established.[86] St Faith argues that, 'since he [Christ] suffered death for me, I ought to die for him' (vv. 371–2). The power to give, as Jo Ann McNamara points out, is one sought by many medieval women both as a prestige activity and for the sake of charity; saints' lives show that giving upwards spiritually is as important as giving downwards.[87] Clemence of Barking's St Catherine both concedes that 'I shall never be able to suffer so much for him [as he for me]' ('Ja pur lui ne sufferai tanz', v. 1404), and yet continues to donate her suffering: 'You will never be able to plan so much torment that I shall not be able to bear more', she says to the pagan emperor (vv. 1407–8). In freely deciding to give her own suffering and death, Catherine evolves a way not of equalling but of allowing God's foundational gift to continue to circulate. God does not need Catherine's death in the way she does his, nor does she need to die in order for God to love her. Her giving thus reciprocates God's in being gratuitous and freely willed: their voluntarily conformed wills permit honourable exchange even when their powers are unequal. Christ,

[85] *Seven More Poems*, ed. Klenke, vv. 84–91.
[86] I am grateful to Simon Gaunt for discussion of this point.
[87] 'The Need to Give: Suffering and Female Sanctity in the Middle Ages', in Renate Blumenfeld-Kosinski and Timea Szell (eds.), *Images of Sainthood in Medieval Europe* (Ithaca and London: Cornell University Press, 1991), 199–221.

Catherine says, is so 'cuveitus' for her love they have made a 'cuvenant' (vv. 1358–9), and things of differing value can be exchanged: 'through his death he turned my death back to life, and I shall gladly die for him' ('ma mort par sa mort revesqui | e pur lui volentiers murrai', vv. 1940–1). Catherine's account of the relation is Bernardine in tone ('douce' love is a major feature), but Bernard at his most Anselmian.[88] This is a theory of martyrdom as union, but not the union of masochism or romantic *Liebestod*: it is, rather, the honourable and free union of two wills in the 'covenant' of seigneurial gift-giving.[89] For Catherine, it is explicitly an assertion of honour, agency, and free will: as the narrative comments, Catherine 'rewarded ['guereduna'] God as far as she had the power ['poeir'] to do so: no part of her will ['voleir'] remained unexpressed' (vv. 2682–4).

In spite of such examples, self-disposition of course rarely lay wholly within the power of virgin daughters, and only extraordinarily persistent women could resist or avoid parental, kinship, or royal disposal in monastic *oblatio* (offering, sacrificial gift) on the one hand, or *desponsatio* (betrothal) on the other, should the arrangements made for them happen to run counter to their own desires.[90] Significantly few of the foundress virgins discussed earlier in this chapter are contemporary, historical figures in post-Conquest England. Women wishing not to marry needed to be able to pay substantial amounts not to do so, and widows, rather than young virgins, had the best basis for participation in their own exchange as *sponsa Christi*. If they were able to retain their dower and dowerlands, they could pay not to marry and pay to enter a female community or live in chaste widowhood in vowess lives (or even, perhaps, as I shall argue of one especially significant case (Chapter 5, below), simply to live without being enclosed in any one religious category's rights and obligations). One setting that

[88] The term 'fin'amor' is not used in *Catherine*, though it is a feature of the Barking *Edouard* (see Ch. 7 n. 89 below): love of Christ is characterized as 'sweet' in Catherine's account of what the pagan queen will enjoy in marriage to Christ ('duz . . . douz . . . duçur . . . endulci . . . douçur', vv. 2290–6). On 'fin'amor' and on the Anselmian dimensions of *Catherine*, see further Ch. 7. For St Bernard's conception of martyrdom as union not through the mingling of two natures but through the will to love, see Javelet, *Image et ressemblance*, ii. 303.

[89] Christ and Catherine have a personal and intense mutual contract, but a dignified and publicly maintained one. Christ's visit to Catherine's dungeon is with a full court of angels and virgins: at her execution the saint goes not to a private heavenly love-bower (as in many other virgin martyr passions) but to the 'great gate' of heaven (v. 2597), where its court and choir of virgins awaits her (a formal entry into a public space perhaps not unlike some of Barking's own, especially following the rebuilding of its choir and church at Abbess Ælfgyva's 11th-c. translation of her great predecessor abbess saints: for Goscelin's account of this see Colker, 'Texts of Jocelin of Canterbury', 388, 435–54).

[90] On marriage to Christ and marriage to men, see Head, 'The Marriages of Christina of Markyate'. Canon law's stress on the free will of both partners to a marriage was often observed more in theory than practice, and the vowing of virgin daughters, known to the Middle Ages from Roman law as well as the Old Testament, remains a close analogue to the politics of patriarchal marital disposal of daughters. (There was also a continuing conflict between the free will of male oblates and their parents' disposal of them, a potential strand in the allegiances of women and celibate men.)

recurs for widowhood in post-Conquest sources is that of an island, a location which can signify a version of enclosure with female proprietorship. This is shown negatively in the Anglo-Norman Life of St Clement, where the saintly pope's mother lives on an island defined as a form of economic marooning. She and her companion widow are too arthritic to spin enough for their support, and they are rescued by St Peter.[91] But for a widow with the claim to the prerogatives of virginity, an island can signify a secure refuge from undesired ties and obligations on her own territory. Thus in the thirteenth-century Anglo-Norman Life of Etheldreda of Ely by Marie [of ?Chatteris], King Egfrid, the saint's second husband, is said in his negotiations with the (still virgin) saint's family to acquire the saint as his bride ('sainte Audrée [i.e. Etheldreda] *porchacier*', v. 1381, my italics), but Audrée, being already a widow, can use the Ely land given her in dower by her first husband to negotiate her own disposal.[92] Pursued by her second husband, this virgin widow is first miraculously cut off in ascetic retreat on St Ebb's Head with her handmaidens, and then, as the foundress-abbess of Ely, becomes the wielder of the island territory of her dower.[93] Audrée establishes herself in the religious life with still greater freedom than St Gilbert's maidens, for she is able to found her own female community rather than have one founded for her by a benevolent churchman: 'Bone est ceste *marchandise* | Ke la virge ha de Deu conquise' (vv. 2810–11, my italics), comments Marie's narrative. Many of the women reading or hearing Simon of Walsingham's *Vie de sainte Foy* in the wealthy Augustinian nunnery of Campsey were in exactly this position. In the complex gift transactions of Anglo-Norman *sponsae Christi*, there is indeed a purchase for the bride's own participation and desire, but to be truly sure of her freedom of choice, she should become a widow before she becomes a virgin.

[91] The Anglo-Norman Life of St Clement is edited by Nora K. Willson, 'La Vie de seint Clement pape' (Ph.D. thesis, University of Cambridge, 1952): for a study see Jocelyn Wogan-Browne, ' "Bet . . . to rede on holy seyntes lyves . . .": Romance and Hagiography Again', in Carol M. Meale (ed.), *Readings in Medieval English Romance* (Cambridge: Brewer, 1994), 83–97. See Willson, 'La Vie', 125–31, Book VII, chs. 13–14, vv. 5878–6102 for Clement's mother's narrative of her shipwreck and life on the island.

[92] Ed. Södergård. On the legal capacities of widows in Anglo-Norman law see further John Walmsley, 'The Early Abbesses, Nuns, and Female Tenants of the Abbey of Holy Trinity, Caen', *Journal of Ecclesiastical History*, 48 (1997), 425–44 (438–40) (as the foundation of William I's daughter this house's practices have many implications for Anglo-Norman nunneries); Janet S. Loengard, '*Rationabilis dos*: Magna Carta and the Widow's "Fair Share" in the Earlier Thirteenth Century'; and Sue Sheridan Walker, 'Litigation as Personal Quest: Suing for Dower in the Royal Courts, circa 1272–1350', in ead., *Wife and Widow in Medieval Europe* (Ann Arbor: University of Michigan Press, 1993), 59–80 and 81–108 respectively. Seigneurial widows are considered in more detail in Ch. 5 below.

[93] *Audrée*, ed. Södergård, vv. 1293–6 (Audrée's flight to her dower island), vv. 1325–1400 (her escape to St Ebbs's Head), vv. 1597–1714 (establishment of her Ely foundation).

3

Virgin Passions: Romance, *Raptus*, Ritual

Use against my body all the torments you can devise, for God calls me through martyrdom as his humble handmaiden. For my sake God made an offering of himself to his father: it is right that I should repay him for it . . . Do whatever you want, for you will find me ready for anything. I desire my bridegroom so much that to me the pain will be sweet to suffer.

(*Life of St Catherine* by Clemence of Barking, vv. 1933–8, 2501–4)

Nes seinte Peter & seinte Andrew . . . istraht o rode? Sein Lorenz o the gridil & lathlese meidnes the tittes itoren of, tohwitheret o hweoles, heafdes bicoruen? . . . heo weren ilich theose yape children the habbeth riche feaderes, the willes & waldes toteoreth hare clathes forte habbe neowe.

Was not St Peter, and St Andrew, stretched on the cross, St Lawrence on the gridiron, and did not innocent maidens have their breasts torn off, were they not whirled to pieces on wheels, and their heads cut off? . . . they were like those sly children who have rich fathers and who wilfully and wantonly tear up their clothes in order to have new ones.

(*Guide for Anchoresses*, ed. Geoffrey Shepherd, p. 9/23–5)

The concern for teaching humane orthodoxy does not, however, suffice to justify the seemingly gratuitous, wildly exuberant dolorism of the passion genre . . . The more the tortures are multiplied and detailed, the more unreal and seemingly pornographic the literature becomes.

(Duncan Robertson, *The Medieval Saints' Lives*, p. 69)

In this chapter I will try further to place the romance of virgin martyr hagiography by looking not only at the virgin's nuptial and dotal relation with Christ but at her argument with the pagan tyrant. This involves attention both to historical development and to literary structural analysis of the *passio*. I will argue that by the later twelfth century the central conflict of hagiography is shifting to a conflict seen in gender rather than generational terms, in what is generally understood as a romancing and feminizing development. This partly reflects the importance of women and land in the social structures of Anglo-Norman society already discussed in Chapter 2, but it also has further resonances. The contest between virgin and pagan at the heart of so much post-Conquest hagiography opposes an integral virgin body to a despised and dismembered pagan body in a society whose insular boundaries are tightly patrolled and whose authorities boast of freedom from heresy. I borrow from René Girard's theorizations of violence, the sacred, and sacrifice, to explore further the 'vertical' and transcendent aspects of *passio* narrative structure and to look at some of the collective preoccupations articulated in the complex mirroring inversions of the high medieval *passio*'s relations with its context. The virgin–pagan conflict in the *passio* may have been serviceable in many ways to Anglo-Norman women (legitimated resistance to enforced marriage and coition is one implication of its representation, for instance). However, since the virgin–pagan exchange also maps a range of collective preoccupations, and, since women of seigneurial classes are not simply 'sub-cultural' as women, but for many purposes share in dominant seigneurial discourses, this chapter also argues that we should be prepared to find politically incorrect women readers of *passio*.

3.1. THE VIRGIN HEROINE AND THE PROPERTIES OF ROMANCE

It is often argued that the high Middle Ages brought a fundamental change in the representation of saints—from admirable to imitable, from figures who were as distant as possible to figures closer to the lives and aspirations of their audiences—and that this involved a 'feminization of sanctity'.[1] As with 'courtly love' and the 'discovery of the individual', this formulation usefully points to important issues for which it remains an inadequate label. The efflorescence of vernacular virgin *passio* in the twelfth and thirteenth centuries is difficult to see as a straightforward measure of increased visibility and power for women, even though, as argued in Chapter 2, it has resonances with the importance of female patronage and the role of women in securing land and lineage in Anglo-Norman society. As has long been recognized, such resonances tend to be expressed in the rewriting of established figures of female sanctity, not in the veneration of contemporary medieval women.[2] Nevertheless, change as well as continuity is observable in the representation of virgin martyrs.

For Ælfric (d. 1004), pre-eminent writer of vernacular hagiography in late Anglo-Saxon England, the virgin is the leading type of female sanctity, and the narrative morphology of his representation of virgin martyrs is often very similar

---

[1] André Vauchez, 'Les Fonctions des saints dans le monde occidental (IIe–XIIIe siècle)', *Actes du colloque organisé par l'École française de Rome avec le concours de l'université de Rome 'La Sapienza'* (Rome: École Française de Rome, 1991), 161–72.

[2] Post-Conquest Britain venerated disproportionately small numbers of contemporary holy women. Only St Margaret of Scotland (d. 1093) and Christina of Markyate (d. *c.*1155/66) received *vitae*, and Christina remains uncanonized, as do the only two women candidates from England in Michael Goodich's 'Master List of Thirteenth-Century Saints' (*Vita Perfecta: The Ideal of Sainthood in the Thirteenth Century* (Stuttgart: Hiersemann, 1982), Appendix), Ela of Lacock and Margaret of Catesby (see further Ch. 6 and Ch. 5, n. 58 below). On the under-representation of women as saints see Schulenberg, 'Sexism and the Celestial Gynaeceum'. For lists of post-Conquest vernacular lives, see the works cited above, Introduction, nn. 6 and 13.

to that of post-Conquest *passio*.[3] Unlike saints' relations with their families in later *passio*, and unlike Anglo-Saxon models of more eremitic styles of sanctity, however, Ælfric's lives carefully omit or reduce their Latin source's representations of social disruption consequent on saints' cults.[4] Ælfric's virgins, as one might expect from a royalist partisan of monastic reform, are representations designed to defend the disposition of genealogical and territorial capital to the church, figures of Benedictine churchmanship.[5] They illustrate, to borrow Stephanie Hollis's formulation, the tendency of late Germanic societies to assimilate women to men, as opposed to high medieval alterization of women.[6] Very differently from Simon of Walsingham's Faith and Caprais (Chapter 2.2 above), Ælfric's aristocratic saintly partnerships reinscribe a model of Anglo-Saxon social order focused on the king's royal household: the women are complementary (Anglo-Saxon nunneries were under the queen's patronage in subordination to the king's patronage of the monasteries) and die either with their husband or quietly with their female attendants in a coda to his death.[7]

Later saints are indeed more 'other', that is to say, more feminized, than Ælfric's but this change cannot be seen in isolation from other shifts. Change in the thematics of female sainthood is complemented, for instance, by shifts in

---

[3] Ælfric's saints' lives continued to circulate in post-Conquest manuscripts and women's reading (see Joyce Hill, 'The Dissemination of Ælfric's *Lives of Saints*: A Preliminary Survey', in Szarmach (ed.), *Holy Men and Holy Women*, 235–60). For a Rochester manuscript containing Ælfrician pieces modernized in the 12th to 13th c. alongside French sermons, see Mary P. Richards, 'MS Cotton Vespasian A. XXII: The Vespasian Homilies', *Manuscripta*, 22 (1978), 97–103 (102). Ælfric's *Catholic Homilies* were in female ownership in the 12th c.: London, MS Cotton Vespasian D xiv (which also contains Ælfric's letter on chastity to Sigeferth) adds a 12th-c. prayer to the Virgin by her 'ancilla' (N. R. Ker, *Catalogue of Manuscripts Containing Anglo-Saxon* (Oxford: Clarendon Press, 1957), 271–7 (esp. 277 and 276, art. 54)). Etheldreda (Ælfthryth) is Ælfric's leading native female saint, as she had been for Bede (Ch. 2.1 above). Among his 47 saints' lives, Ælfric includes 7 virgin martyrs of the universal church, two abbesses (one transvestite, one British), and two chaste female consorts. All of Ælfric's lives of female saints concern virgins (though not all of Ælfric's virgins are female). For a valuable survey, see E. Gordon Whatley, 'Late Old English Hagiography, ca. 950–1150', in Philippart (ed.), *Hagiographies*, 429–99.

[4] Evidence for this point is assembled in a comparison of Ælfric's virgins and their sources in my unpublished paper, 'Ælfric's Virginities', given to the Italian National Association for Germanic Philology, Udine, 1991. See now the excellent studies cited in n. 7 below; on non-Ælfrician lives see Hugh Magennis, 'St Mary of Egypt and Ælfric: Unlikely Bedfellows in Cotton Julius E.vii?', in Poppe and Ross (eds.), *The Legend of Mary of Egypt*, 91–112.

[5] For Ælfric's world as 'deeply divided about the wealth and role of the churches', where the realignment of property following the Benedictine-driven church reform was bitterly resented by many Anglo-Saxon nobles (though supported by others such as Ælfric's patron Æthelweard), see Eric John, *Orbis Britanniae and Other Studies* (Leicester: University of Leicester Press, 1966), 203.

[6] Stephanie Hollis, *Anglo-Saxon Women and the Church: Sharing a Common Fate* (Woodbridge and Rochester, NH: Boydell Press, 1992), 10–12.

[7] See further Clare Lees, 'Engendering Religious Desire: Sex, Knowledge, and Christian Identity in Anglo-Saxon England', *JMEMS* 27 (1997), 17–45 (44 n. 46); Catherine Cubitt, 'Virginity and Misogyny in Tenth- and Eleventh-Century England', *Gender and History*, 12 (2000), 1–32.

conceptions of childhood and parenthood. Ælfric was writing in a world where child oblation—the gift of a living sacrifice, *hostia viva*—was a common practice and one still deemed on the whole meritorious: by the time of Lateran IV in 1215 the theory and practice of oblation was disputed and uncertain.[8] The imagery of the virgin saint as treasure reveals this shift together with the changing focus of conflict. Ælfric's Eugenia is recurrently shown as gold: as a statue of gold made by her mourning parents, as a woman adorned with gold after her trial and recognition scene, as a gold-adorned saint seen by her mother in a heavenly vision.[9] The meanings of gold develop from image to image, accreting all the tensions, ambivalences, and competing desires inscribed in Eugenia, as social and spiritual capital is reassigned from her pagan family to the church in the Life's reformulation of that family as a church-supporting Christian entity. Ælfric's Eugenia signifies differently from a later virgin such as Simon of Walsingham's Faith. As a golden statue, she represents the desire of her parents to withhold her from the church in quasi-idolatrous attachment to a mortal child. Faith is represented as treasure not to her parents but to rival sexual and ideological suitors, the emperor Dacien and Christ, and to the rival monasteries of Agen and Conques. Ælfric's Eugenia resolves conflict by leaving the parental household to enter an abbey in disguise as a monk. Unlike post-Conquest virgins she does not seek intensified occupation of the *sponsa Christi* role as a defence against her parents and, again unlike them, she converts her father in the end. In post-Conquest lives, not only are there almost no new vernacular lives of transvestite saints,[10] but the idolatrous overvaluation of a female child functions to paganize courtly love, rather than to reproach parental retention of possible oblates. Thus the golden statue of St Catherine proposed by the pagan emperor Maxentius is an offer to put Catherine's image on a pedestal for worship (and is duly mocked by the saint). Although the disposition of the resources represented in a child remains a common concern in Ælfric's and in post-Conquest virgin lives, lives of post-Conquest composition focus on conflict as between patriarchy (i.e. suitor and father), and daughter, rather than between generations.[11]

---

[8] Permanent oblation seems to have declined at different rates for male and female children in the 12th and 13th c. (see Lynch, *Simoniacal Entry*, 36–50 (39, 42), and more generally John Eastburn Boswell, '*Expositio* and *Oblatio*: The Abandonment of Children and the Ancient and Medieval Family', *American Historical Review*, 89 (1984), 10–33). On earlier medieval attitudes to oblation see Janet Nelson, 'Parents, Children, and the Church', in Diana Wood (ed.), *The Church and Childhood*, SCH 31, 81–114 (107–12), also the works cited in Ch. 1, n. 105, Ch. 2, n. 76 above.

[9] See *Ælfric's Lives of Saints*, ed. W. W. Skeat, EETS os 76 and 82 (London, 1881 and 1885; repr. as one vol. 1962), 30/112–32/115; 40/253; 48/416–18.

[10] An exception is the 14th-c. Middle English Euphrosyne in the Vernon manuscript: a French life may also have had some insular circulation (see Florence McCulloch, 'Saint Euphrosine, Saint Alexis and the Turtledove', *Romania*, 98 (1977), 168–85).

[11] Paul Hayward notes the tendency in 8th-c. and later texts to assimilate the Holy Innocents to the one hundred and forty-four thousand of Revelation 14: 1–5 and to see the martyred infants as examples of active virginity ('Suffering and Innocence in Latin Sermons for the Feast of the Holy Innocents', in Wood (ed.), *The Church and Childhood*, 67–80 (78–9); ibid., 'The Idea of

Given the persistence of Ælfric's lives alongside new lives in the vernaculars and in Latin, audience experience in the twelfth century must have been capable of considerable variation depending on what books and texts were in question.[12] Nevertheless, twelfth- and thirteenth-century virgin *passio* can in general be said both to be romanced in newly intense and different ways from the earlier instantiations of this long-enduring model and to become itself inter-textual with romance.[13] The white stag who distracts St Osith's pagan husband from his climactic assault on her virginity is present in earlier Latin *vitae*: he has a literary pedigree in monastic foundation legends and their sacralizing of monastic sites and identities, and he is also associated with the hermit saints of the eleventh- and twelfth-century eremitic reform.[14] Mystic and sacred propert-ies for the stag ('whiter than snow') are signalled in the Latin's brief evocation. But in the later twelfth-century vernacular Life, rather as the 'birth' of Arthur-ian romance can be mapped onto Chrétien de Troyes' white stag, we may take this animal as a metonym of the shift to romance.[15] The Anglo-Norman text's greatly expanded account of the 'aventure'(v. 547) of the 'completely white' stag (v. 558) shows the sacred received within the register of courtly quest and love hunt as the stag deflects the pagan king-ruler-bridegroom's pursuit of Osith's

Innocent Martyrdom in Late-Tenth- and Eleventh-Century Hagiography', in Diana Wood (ed.), *Martyrs and Martyrologies*, SCH 30 (1993), 81–92). Barbara Newman's brilliant account of later representations is concerned with the 'shift from father to mother as the parent whose child is required of her' which becomes prominent in 13th- and 14th-c. hagiography and somewhat undervalues the capacity of child sacrifice to change in significance in the earlier period, seeing its meaning as 'fairly constant from antiquity onward' (*From Virile Woman to WomanChrist*, 76–107 (77)).

[12] Shifts in virgin martyr thematics are also accompanied by and to an extent part of the 12th-c. development of eremitic saints: Christina of Markyate's monastic Latin *vita* (which is in part a way of claiming both virgin and eremitic prestige for a figure associated with Benedictine monasticism) is an example (see Kristine E. Haney, 'The St Alban's Psalter and the New Spiritual Ideal of the Twelfth Century', *Viator*, 28 (1997), 145–73), as also are the vernacular traditions of Alexis, Giles, and Mary of Egypt.

[13] The most famous post-Conquest case is Clemence of Barking's use of the *Tristan*: see William MacBain, 'Anglo-Norman Women Hagiographers', in Ian Short (ed.), *Anglo-Norman Anniversary Essays*, ANTS OP 2 (London, 1993), 235–50 (243–6); Duncan Robertson, 'Writing in the Textual Community: Clemence of Barking's Life of St Catherine', *French Forum*, 21 (1996) 5–28 (18–23), and Ch. 7 below.

[14] On the stag as epiphany see Remensnyder, *Remembering Kings Past*, 58–65. The Anglo-Norman *Vie de saint Gilles* includes one such stag: it leads Charlemagne to the saint's hermitage, and eventually to confession, penance, and full social reincorporation in a classic *vita* of eremitic reform (see G. Paris and A. Bos (eds.), *La Vie de saint Gilles*, SATF (Paris, 1881) and (for Charlemagne's charter of forgiveness), L. Brandin, 'Un fragment de *La vie de saint Gilles*', *Romania*, 33 (1904), 94–8). Stags often signal saints' ability to restore the right Adamic relations between humanity and the created world: they can also be benevolent helpers for young saints (for an insular example, see the *vita* of Wulfhad and Ruffinus, ed. P. Grosjean, 'Codicis Gothani Appendix', *AB* 58 (1940), 177–204 (184, §§3–4)).

[15] Claude Luttrell, *The Creation of the First Arthurian Romance: A Quest* (Evanston, Ill.: Northwestern University Press, 1974).

virginity.[16] King Sigher has never seen a stag 'of such whiteness', but it vanishes before his eyes in the sea at Dunwich, leaping out of his grasp for ever (vv. 625–6). As well as Sigher's desire, the stag signifies God's: it is providentially sent by him to save his bride Osith from the pagan rival, whose grasp and territory is thereby shown as limited. But, equally, the stag represents not only the person of Osith but what she herself wants by way of conforming her desire to God's. Female desire and dissent are stressed well beyond anything in Ælfric or earlier hagiography.[17]

The courtly and nuptial virgin is the heroine of 'rumanz' in both its major Anglo-Norman meanings: she is the predominant *vernacular* female saint and her passion is an extended and stylized display of romance constancy to the highest-ranking bridegroom of all.[18] Her *passio* can be related both to chivalric courtly romance and to the romance modes of modern popular culture. It is worth briefly pursuing this latter comparison for what it reveals of the dynamics of romance in the medieval *passio*.[19] With virgin martyr *passio* identified as romance, the question of gendered violence and the role of rape in the *passio* has become an issue both in accounts of the genre and in discussion of the roles of saints in the reading of medieval women.[20] It is important here to see what kind of narrative structure and encoding characterizes the *passio* as well as to consider historically its relations with its contexts and audiences.

The principal difference between the *passio* and the modern form of nuptial romance (see Figure 3) lies in the distribution of the suitor role. In the modern romance the hero ('sign of the patriarchy, enemy and lover', as Jan Cohn calls the romance and novel hero) is a single figure, offering emotionally warm and emotionally cruel behaviour to the heroine in turn.[21] (His cruelty is later

---

[16] 'An Anglo-French Life of St Osith', ed. Baker (who prints the Latin text, see 483). On the courtly troping of this stag see Delbert Russell, 'The Secularization of Hagiography in the Anglo-Norman *Vie seinte Osith*', *Allegorica*, 12 (1991), 3–16, 5–10.

[17] In the 13th-c. Anglo-Norman life of Bede's Etheldreda, *La vie sainte Audrée*, the opposition of virgin and suitor is also sharpened: unlike the 'good' Ecgfrid of Bede or Ælfric, the post-Conquest husband is inflected towards the pagan suitor model and keeps attacking his wife's plans, trying to throw ('geter') her out of his aunt's monastery (*Audrée*, ed. Södergård, vv. 1281, 1321–2).

[18] Such a point is part of the case made by Karl Uitti, 'Women, Saints, the Vernacular and History in Early Medieval France', in Blumenfeld-Kosinski and Szell (eds.), *Images of Sainthood in Medieval Europe*, 247–67. But Uitti's argument concerns the image and properties of the vernacular seen as a feminized language, not its capacities as a medium of women's agency and subjectivity.

[19] See Radway, *Reading the Romance*, ch. 3; Krueger, 'Love, Honor and the Exchange of Women in *Yvain*', and her *Women Readers and the Ideology of Gender*, esp. chs. 1 and 2.

[20] See Gravdal, *Ravishing Maidens*; and for objections Katherine J. Lewis, ' "Lete me suffre": Reading the Torture of St Margaret of Antioch in Late Medieval England', in Jocelyn Wogan-Browne *et al.* (eds.), *Medieval Women: Texts and Contexts in Late Medieval Britain* (Turnhout: Brepols, 2000), 69–82; Evelyn Burge Vitz, 'Re-reading Rape in Medieval Literature: Literary, Historical and Theoretical Reflections', *Romanic Review*, 88 (1997), 1–26; Diane Wolfthal, *Images of Rape: The 'Heroic' Tradition and its Alternatives* (Cambridge and New York: Cambridge University Press, 1999), esp. ch. 4.

[21] *Romance and the Erotics of Property: Mass-Market Fiction for Women* (Durham, NC: Duke University Press, 1988), 8.

'revealed' as not really intended to damage her and as a sign of his vulnerability/love/need.) The medieval *passio* uses Christ and the pagan for these opposed aspects of the hero role. Christ sums up all aspects of the romance hero role in himself. The Campsey manuscript's life of Paphnutius explains that it is a mark of Christ's gentleness ('douzour') that he prefers a gentle heart ('un quer pitous') and disapproves of ravishment ('ravyne', in its senses both of abduction and rape).[22] But although presented as a gentle spouse and supremely courtly lover, Christ can also resort to emotional blackmail and threats of violence at which a pagan might blush and which suggest an area of identity between the male rivals in the suitor role.[23] Christ can boast bigger and longer-lived fires and more torturers in hell than any pagan empire can command, as well as a bigger, better, and higher-ranking court in heaven and an unchallengeable role as the most powerful and desirable bridegroom in the universe. (That Christ is also so often represented as a maternal healer and nourisher, comforting and feeding heroines in their dungeons, completes the romance parallel: modern romance heroes are also both superheterosexual heroes and, at the peripeteia of the narrative, the providers of maternal nurture and care.)[24]

As in the classic analyses of Mills and Boon (Harlequin) romance by Janice Radway and of chivalric romance by Roberta Krueger, the virgin's opposition to her father-suitor-ruler in hagiography is an opposition that triangulates desire: the virgin is the medium of male exchange through which the hero competes with (and is bonded to) other men in order to gain the heroine. Acting as the medium of rivalry between Christ and the pagan, the virgin enables their relation and their difference. In this exchange, patriarchal violence to women is both represented and masked in the separating out of good and bad aspects of the suitor-hero role. The ambiguities of the heroine's position, considered as the representation of a female subject, and the question of how far she can represent female agency, are complicated issues. Even as it incorporates the triangulation of desire endemic to romance, the historically prior genre of hagiography provides the grounds for a critique of romance, at least in the secular form attributed

---

[22] 'Vie de saint Panuce', ed. A. T. Baker, *Romania*, 38 (1909), 418–24 (416, vv. 72–4).

[23] Christ's wooing speeches in the *Guide for Anchoresses* combine emotional blackmail and threats of violence in all 13th-c. versions (Herbert, 290/35–293/13; the Trinity Anglo-Norman version (with an added rubric, 'Si uostre amur seit a rauir, nostre seignur la deit auer', Trethewey, 148); Millett and Wogan-Browne, 118/37–122/3). See also Hugh of St Victor, *De arrha anime*, PL176.950–70 (and see Ch. 2 above, n. 61), where emotional suasion in wooing is explicitly within a gift-giving paradigm.

[24] See Bynum, *Jesus as Mother: Studies in the Spirituality of the High Middle Ages* (Berkeley and London: University of California Press, 1982); Radway, *Reading the Romance*, ch. 4 (and, for the application of Nancy Chodorow's theory of the reproduction of mothering to romance, 135–40). For Christ's crucifixion as a mother's sacrificial bath of blood see *Guide for Anchoresses*, Part Seven (Millett and Wogan-Browne, 118/9–28): he is frequently represented as visiting virgin martyrs in their dungeons and offering consolation, spiritual food, and healing (so for example the lives of Agatha in the *SEL* and Bozon, and of Catherine in Anglo-Norman, the Katherine Group, and *SEL*).

FIG. 3.1. Hagiographic romance

1. The heroine is young, beautiful, rich and noble [i.e. nuptial], and brought up in a pagan household. Her social [pagan] identity is thrown into question by her own and the audience's knowledge of her true [Christian] identity.

2. When approached by an aristocratic [pagan] male suitor/tyrant, she refuses him (she has already accepted an aristocratic [Christian] male suitor/lord).

3. The pagan insists that he loves/honours/desires her and that she must give in to him.

4. The heroine interprets his insistence as evidence of idolatrous [sexual] interest in her [as opposed to the Christian [romance] interest in her of her Christ bridegroom].

5. She responds with anger and coldness.

6. The [pagan] bridegroom-hero responds by punishing the heroine, often by having her stripped, whipped, and thrown into a dungeon in order to bring her to compliance.

7. The heroine and [pagan] bridegroom-hero are now physically separated.

8. The [Christ] bridegroom-hero gives the heroine care and nurture in the dungeon [angels or Christ himself appear to feed her/tend her wounds].

9. The heroine responds warmly to the [Christ] bridegroom-hero.

10. The heroine interprets the duality of the bridegroom [pagan/Christian; cruel/kind; idolatrously sexual/romantically desirous] as a function of the fallen world's sinfulness, for which the [Christ] bridegroom has previously suffered enormous hurt [on the cross].

11. The [Christ] bridegroom now openly invites the heroine into his heavenly bower, while the [pagan] bridegroom demonstrates his unwavering committment to [lacerating, dismembering, and consuming] the heroine, and openly threatens her with beheading.

12. The heroine says yes to the bower/beheading of the [Christ]/[pagan] bridegroom.

13. The heroine's eternal identity is confirmed as she becomes what she was always going to be, a bride of Christ and a saint in heaven.

in the *passio* to pagan desire. This is revealed as a delusion and rejected as such by the virgin, who is free to enjoy feminized romance with Christ, leaving the 'pagan' concomitants of socialized heterosexuality behind her. In this form there are none of the *molestiae* of secular sexual desire—Christ is a supremely acceptable and adequate lover, and one who poses no risk of pregnancy. Transferred from being pagan, illegitimate, and male, desire becomes Christian, licensed, and female. We need not see women's romance reading of *passio* as their textual containment, a fantasy of desire without political implication. While the romancing of the *passio* is an ambiguous and problematic measure of its importance and attraction for women, its complex version of romance is hospitable to a number of reading positions. An important potential of the genre is the decoding and reinscription of courtly desire in favour of the virgin heroine, a feminizing or romancing of passion that includes female subjects.

FIG. 3.2. Popular romance

1. The heroine's social identity is thrown into question.

2. The heroine reacts antagonistically to an aristocratic male.

3. The aristocratic male responds ambiguously to the heroine.
4. The heroine interprets the hero's behaviour as evidence of a purely sexual interest in her.
5. The heroine responds to the hero's behaviour with anger or coldness.
6. The hero retaliates by punishing the heroine.

7. The heroine and hero are physically and/or emotionally separated.
8. The hero treats the heroine tenderly.

9. The heroine responds warmly to the hero's act of tenderness.
10. The heroine reinterprets the hero's ambiguous behaviour as the product of a previous hurt.

11. The hero proposes/openly declares his love for/demonstrates his unwavering commitment to the heroine with a supreme act of tenderness.

12. The heroine responds sexually and emotionally.
13. The heroine's identity is restored.

Source: Radway, *Reading the Romance: Women, Patriarchy, and Popular Literature*, Table 4.2: an analysis of Harlequin [Mills and Boon] romances.

But it also remains important that, though coded as personal and individual, romance in the medieval *passio* is a way of figuring (and glossing as desirable and inevitable) a complex series of social transactions focused on women and territory and occurring in a society whose exchange systems are located more in gift-giving than in commodity exchange. To put this in the terms which Chapter 2 has argued are especially pertinent to twelfth- and thirteenth-century insular *passiones*, 'nuptiality' in the virgin heroine figures the broader structure of 'dotality' in a gift-giving society. Just as 'nuptiality' is part, but not the whole, of 'dotality', so, in addressing the issue of sexualized violence, it is useful to remember that what may appear to be a representation of *stuprum* (the defloration of virgins) is dealt with in the *passio* within a framework of *raptus*. A primary meaning of *raptus* is the incorrect disposition of treasure/property in marriage arrangements. In thirteenth-century England, *raptus* remained largely a crime against male property rather than a crime against the female person, a matter of trespass and not felony.[25] There are cases of *raptus* by guardian widows: there are also cases where *raptus* serves the interest of the abducted woman if she wishes to marry her abductor against her parents' wishes.[26] Most pagan tyrants, even when considering rape and/or *raptus*, have a socially inflected sense of the relations of person and property in their transactions rather than a private rape fantasy in mind: although the saint is an unarmed woman and they have a militia at their command, they still consider the terms on which they may acquire the noble virgin. So in St Margaret's many insular lives, even though Olibrius sends his soldiers to fetch the saint once he has seen her, he still works out a scale of treatment according to class distinctions, for example:

> s'ele ert de fra[n]c lingnage
> Tout l'esposeroit sans mariage,
> Et s'ele fu ancele et de basse gent né [*sic*]
> Avoir li dorroit a grant plenté,
> Et ele seroit sa soignante
> Et il le feroit riche et manante.[27]

If she were of free rank he would marry her without dowry and if she were a handmaid born of low family he would give goods for her in great plenty and she would be his concubine and he would make her rich and powerful.

While the pagan here provides the virgin with yet another opportunity for transcending his terms (Margaret responds with the *ancilla Dei* topos to say that

---

[25] Sue Sheridan Walker, 'Punishing Convicted Ravishers: Statutory Strictures and Actual Practice in Thirteenth and Fourteenth-Century England', *JMH* 13 (1987), 237–50. I am arguing here for a range of connotations in the hagiographic representation of *raptus*: I do not, of course, deny that *raptus* could and did involve rape or that medieval conceptions of *raptus* as theft of property could elide and silence rape victims and fail to address rape as a crime against women (see further Gravdal, *Ravishing Maidens*, ch. 1; and, for a detailed study of the continuing ambiguities of the terminology, Henry Ansgar Kelly, 'Meanings and Uses of *Raptus* in Chaucer's Time', *Studies in the Age of Chaucer*, 20 (1998), 101–65. On spiritual aspects of ravishment, see Dyan Elliott, 'The Physiology of Rapture and Female Spirituality', in Peter Biller and A. J. Minnis (eds.), *Medieval Theology and the Natural Body*, York Studies in Medieval Theology (York: University of York Medieval Press, 1997) 141–74).

[26] An Anglo-Norman woman accused of *raptus* is Alice Beauchamp, sued for ravishment of her female ward, by marrying her to Alice's own son, in 1279: see Sue Sheridan Walker, 'Free Consent and Marriage of Feudal Wards in Medieval England', *JMH* 8 (1982), 123–34 (128).

[27] For the (late 13th-c.) text of this life, see Paul Meyer, 'Notice du ms. Sloane 1611 du Musée Britannique', *Romania*, 40 (1911), 541–58 (542, vv. 63–8). For other Margaret lives see the manuals listed in Introduction, n. 13 above. For 'mariage' in the sense of dowry as used in v. 64 here, see *AND mariage*; cf. also *maritage*, 'dower', as defined in the *Rotuli Parliamentorum*, i. 453, 'que a veve tantost aprés la mort son baron soit rendu son heritage & son maritage' (wrongly glossed as *dowry* rather than *dower* in *AND*). *Soignante* (for Latin *concubina*), omitted from *AND*, but given here in v. 67, must mean 'concubine, attendant' (cf. Wace, *La Vie de Sainte Marguerite*, ed. Elizabeth A. Francis, CFMA (Paris, 1932), 9/vv. 102–3, 'Por ço qu'ele ert et gente et bele | En sognantage la tendroit', also (like the Sloane Margaret Life) following 'si vero ancilla est, dabo precium pro ea et erit michi concubina; bene enim erit ei in domo mea propter pulchritudinem eius').

she is nobly born, but also a handmaid of God), his terms are still significant in themselves. The pagan's power to take is complicated by the relation of nuptial and sexual desire to the social code of gift-exchange. It is also located in a transaction to which heaven and earth are party, and in which a number of relations of patronage and donation are refracted and echoed.

One of the saintly figures in whose *passio* rape is most explicitly thematized is the fourth-century virgin martyr, Lucy of Syracuse. In the mid-thirteenth-century *South English Legendary* Life, as in the later thirteenth-century or early fourteenth-century Anglo-Norman Life by Bozon, Lucy refuses to marry her pagan fiancé and to sacrifice to the pagan gods, and is sentenced to the public brothel by the judge Paschasius. She cannot, however, be dragged to the brothel by 'ropes strongue i-nouȝ', by 'a thousand men with al heore main', or by 'Oxene mani on' (Bozon: 'mil double des boufes forz'), nor does trying to burn her where she stands succeed, and a sword through her throat does not hinder her preaching to the spectators and announcing the death of the pagan emperor-tyrants Diocletian and Maximian before she herself goes to heaven.[28]

The argument between Lucy and the judge Paschasius arises as a property dispute. Lucy has persuaded her mother to give her her inheritance, rather than keeping it for her dowry, arguing (in what in the Bozon version becomes an eloquent piece of Franciscan mendicant rhetoric) that what her mother has set aside to be given to Lucy's bridegroom should go to the poor (vv. 68–71, 82–95). In Bozon's striking elaboration of his *Legenda Aurea* source, Lucy asks her mother never to appoint for her a husband or corruption of her body, or to seek from her 'bodily fruit by way of mortal children' ('ja ne nomez a moy barun | Ne a mon cors corruptiun | Ne frut ne querez de mon cors | Par enfanz ki serrunt mors', vv. 64–7). What persuades the mother to agree is the efficacy of Lucy's prayers in curing her of four years of bloody flux when they visit the tomb of St Agatha of Catania and hear at mass the gospel of Christ's healing of the Hemorrhissa (the bleeding woman of the Gospels, cured by touching Christ's robe, Matt. 9: 20, Mark 5: 21, Luke 7: 42, explicitly alluded to in the *SEL* version, ll. 27–30). When Lucy's pagan fiancé realizes she has given everything to the poor, he takes her before Paschasius on the charge of being a Christian. The *SEL* judge claims that Lucy's prior obligation is to her pagan betrothed: Lucy claims that her betrothed is Christ, to whom she is pledged in her baptismal vows ('I-wedded ich was to Ihesu crist . . . tho ich was i-baptized', ll. 91–2). To the deployment of her inheritance in Christ's service, she declares, she will add her body: the judge can do what he likes but her every limb will be a sacrifice to Christ (l. 82). The judge accuses her of having spent her goods 'In hore-dom and In lecherie' (l. 86) and claims that when she speaks of following her

[28] Middle English quotations are from *Early South English Legendary*, ed. Horstmann, 104/111, 105/133, henceforth referenced by line number in the text; Bozon is quoted from *Seven More Poems*, ed. Klenke, 56/v. 142, henceforth referenced by line number in the text. For Lucy's prayer and prophecy, see *SEL* 105/155–106/170; Bozon, 57/vv. 158–67.

emptied purse with her body she is speaking as a whore who means to forsake her wedded lord (ll. 87–90).[29] He declares that Lucy will be made to forsake the spouse she claims for herself by being sentenced to the brothel (in Bozon's version this is explicitly linked with the question of ideological faithfulness: the charge is of being secretly a Christian, v. 105, and the threat of the brothel is the punishment for not giving it up, vv. 115–17).

When Paschasius sentences Lucy, it is quite true that he is asserting rape and property rights in her body as a cornerstone of patriarchal control. He is not just trying (like Christina of Markyate's parents) to get Lucy deflowered by her bridegroom as a technical matter of ensuring her submission. In threatening her with the common brothel, he asserts a common right of men in women as property. It is also true that, although his rule is purportedly illegitimate and pagan, it mirrors Christian patriarchy's stances towards its daughters and their disposition in wedlock. Nevertheless, this is an argument about the disposition of property, in the person and in the dowry, and not simply a voyeuristic and covert expression of a sexual desire not otherwise representable. Lucy is accused of whoredom not simply because she is a nubile virgin whom Paschasius or his narrator wishes to make imaginatively available for rape, but because she has given away her dowry to an unsanctioned bridegroom, with all that connotes for shame/honour distinctions and lineage propagation.

Even as Paschasius reasserts a fundamental appropriation of women as property, the Lucy legend offers footholds for women to resist being traded or to trade themselves. The dispositions of selves and property represented here, while serving a clerical patriarchy's rewriting of secular Anglo-Norman property concerns as pagan, none the less coincide with agendas historically pursued by upper-class women in Anglo-Norman England. The virgin–pagan confrontation here is part of an action which begins in a female household, and it may be significant that in so far as Lucy is initially opposed by her mother, persuasion and conversion of the saint's opposition is possible (as not for the fathers of Agnes, Agatha, Juliana, Christine, Margaret). Although only a small proportion of households in Anglo-Norman England are estimated to have been headed by widows or other *femmes seules*, the high profile of many aristocratic widows and the conventions of cultural and ecclesiastical patronage and almsgiving by women of high rank make such women significant figures.[30] In the Bozon version especially, it might be objected that to argue in this way merely makes Lucy and her mother objects of clerical economic instead of sexual desire. While it is true (here as in Ælfric's and any other hagiography) that church agendas shape the *passio*, these texts, especially but not exclusively in their vernacular versions, must

---

[29] In the *Legenda Aurea* the legal status of Lucy's acts rather than a sexual motivation for the charges against Lucy underpin such accusations: she is acting 'contra leges Augustorum' (*Legenda Aurea, vulgo Historia Lombardica dicta*, ed. T. Graesse (Bratislava, 1890, 3rd edn. 30), accused that 'patrimoniam tuam cum corruptoribus expendisti et ideo quasi meretrix loqueris', 31).

[30] On the proportions of Anglo-Norman households with single heads, see Ch. 1, n. 102 above.

function in and respond to a society whose ecclesiastical and secular members are constantly negotiating the disposition of land and lineage between their over-lapping and competing interests. It is the women's as well as the church's agenda which triumphs here: the church, even if sometimes more accidentally than on purpose, could serve Anglo-Norman women in allegiance against secular patri-archy, *clerc* versus *chevalier*. And if the church is represented in the legend, so too is a certain amount of female networking, role-modelling and co-operation. These are household-centred (mother, daughter, nurse, peer-group female saint and spiritual sister), but, as with the religious patronage of Anglo-Norman women, not without public implication. Lucy's course of action, especially in Bozon's version, is inspired by a vision of St Agatha and the argument that her virgin-ity equips her to propagate Christian faith in her community and become its patron saint (vv. 35–57). Taught by her sister saint, the daughter teaches the mother here: once the end of her sexo-biological duties is survived and marked in the cessation of bloody flux, Lucy's mother learns to redistribute dowry and to lead an independent life.

The canon law status of vowed virginity as a prior betrothal endorses the 'vertical' plot separations of hagiographic romance in which the apparently metaphoric marriage with Christ is more 'real' than the literal suit of the pagan, and Lucy draws on this in claiming Christ as her true groom (*SEL*, ll. 91–2).[31] However, in the later twelfth century, consummation had begun to be regarded as definitive of marriage, and even a consummation secured by rape could invalidate prior betrothal as *sponsa Christi* and transfer a woman's rights of self-dedication to her husband. If Lucy were to lose her virginity to her earthly fiancé, her option of consecrated career virginity would be lost, not so much through the loss of virginity itself as through changed legal status.[32] The potential use-fulness for women of the church's stake in the disposition of their property and themselves nevertheless emerges in an alternative reading of women's persons. To Paschasius' sentence of the brothel, the *South English Legendary*'s Lucy replies:

> Ne mai no wumman . . . of hire maiden-hod beo ido
> For no dede that men deth the bodie: bote [h]ire herte beo therto.

---

[31] Thomas Head, 'The Marriages of Christina of Markyate', 91,100. Contemporary canon law required at least in theory the free assent of both parties in marriage, but constraint could be brought to bear on women for purposes of dynastic exchange and affiliation. See further John T. Noonan, 'Power to Choose', *Viator*, 4 (1973), 418–34; Michael M. Sheehan, 'Choice of Marriage Partner in the Middle Ages: Development and Mode of Application of a Theory of Marriage', *Studies in Medieval and Renaissance History*, NS 1 (1978), 1–33.

[32] The role of consummation in confirming a marriage (and hence in locking women into careers as wives and mothers) shifted in the 12th and 13th c. Whereas, in the early 12th c., Hugh of St Victor had argued betrothal to be a complete sacrament in itself, Peter Lombard and others later argued that consummation completed and could even constitute marriage, with the result that it became much harder to dissolve a consummated marriage (Head, ibid.; A. Esmein, *Le Mariage en droit canonique*, 2nd edn. with R. Genestal (Paris: Recueil Sirey, 1929–35), t. I, 1ère partie, chs. 1 and 2).

> For the more that mi bodi ayein mi wille: here defouled is
> The clenore is mi mayden-hod: and the more mi mede, i-wis.
>
> (ll. 99–102)

No woman can be deprived of her virginity through any deed men do to her body, unless her heart consents. For the more my body is defiled here against my will, the purer will be my virginity, and the greater, indeed, my reward.

while Bozon's Lucy is equally firm:

> N'ert ja perdue virginité
> Ne ja mon cors n'ert soilé
> Fors par assent de volenté
> (vv. 119–21)

Virginity will not be lost, nor my body defiled except through the assent of my will.

This is a position ultimately based on Augustine's discussion of the relations between virginity and chastity, rape, and martyrdom, and one reiterated in contemporary medieval virginity theory.[33] The late thirteenth-century Anglo-Norman *Compileison* decrees that the will to virginity is

tant pre*c*ius . . . ke se par force e de tut encontre sa uolunte fust une pucele co*rru*mpue ele nekedent serreit entre les uirgines de deu en ciel corone. si ele se gardast fermem*ent* apres en purpos de chastete e de uirginite.[34]

so precious . . . that if a maiden were to be corrupted by force and completely against her will, she would nevertheless be among the virgins crowned by God in heaven, as long as she firmly kept her will to chastity and virginity thereafter.

For Augustine, purity is a matter of the will, not just of the body.[35] Ironically enough, the choice of death rather than dishonour is therefore not of itself martyrdom, but needs extra evidence that it is a choice taken for the sake of Christian faith. In the thirteenth century, Aquinas builds on this position in discussion of whether death is essential to the definition of martyrdom. He explains that 'if a woman loses her physical virginity, or is condemned to lose it, because of her Christian faith, it is not clear to other people whether she suffers this for love of the Christian faith or because she puts little stock in chastity'.[36] The grounds on which Lucy can claim double merit in being violated as well as put to death are therefore not that loss of virginity alone constitutes one martyrdom and execution another one, but that *if in the judgement of God the martyred woman is losing her virginity for the sake of the faith*, this loss can be considered for extra reward in addition to that merited by the loss of life in martyrdom for the faith. Aquinas concludes that Lucy has a case in claiming,

---

[33] See *City of God*, i. 26 (PL41.39) and cf. Ambrose, *De virginibus*, iii. 7 (PL16.229–32): Augustine values martyrdom above virginity (*De sancta virginitate*, 45, PL40.423).

[34] Paris, BN f. fr. 6276, f. 101va (on this manuscript and text see Ch. 1, n. 93 above).

[35] See *City of God*, i. 18, 28, also xiv. 1–6.

[36] 'Utrum hoc mulier patiatur propter amorem fidei christiana, vel magis pro contemptu castitatis', *ST* 2a2ae, 124, 4, resp. 2 (xlii, Blackfriars, 1966), 53–5.

as she does in the *Breviary* and in the *Legenda Aurea*, that her chastity 'will be crowned twice over' (*ST* 2a2e. 124, 4.2, pp. 52–3). It is unspecified by Aquinas whether this means that Lucy will continue to have the special crown normally worn in heaven by virgins (since her will to virginity is unchanged by threats of rape), and that she will also gain a martyr's crown, or whether it means that God will judge both the rape and the execution as martyrdom and give her two virgin-martyr crowns. As defined by Aquinas, in this situation only God can judge how many of which sort of crown any woman deserves. The reading of the virgin's volition is thus confided to a transcendent force (to which she has, at least theoretically, privileged access).

Lucy's argument cannot overturn the medieval legal and social codes whereby a deflowered bride of Christ could be repossessed by her earthly bridegroom. Nevertheless, it is an argument with doctrinal underpinning, some ecclesiastical support, and something to offer to female readers. In the vernacular lives, it makes a much clearer space for women's wills than Aquinas's statement that it may not be clear whether a woman suffers death 'from love of the Christian faith or because she puts little stock in chastity', a view that leaves women no middle position between martyrdom and whoredom.[37] Seen alongside patristic and sometimes legally institutionalized beliefs that, for instance, pregnancy as the result of rape showed consent to the rape (since conception was theorized as impossible without pleasure), this virgin martyr legend has a lot to offer. It articulates a position where 'no' means 'no', even if that 'no' cannot of itself prevent rape. A courtly heroine of romance, if she is to exercise her courtly *pité* and *mercy*, has no position from which to say a final 'no', unless her suitor is already publicly characterized as a 'losengier' or in some other way unworthy.[38] To the pagan tyrant suitor on the other hand, the virgin martyr can return a 'no' of unusually strong legitimation for a courtly heroine. As with the *molestiae nuptiarum* rhetoric of virginity treatises, saints' lives can offer a more subversive place than many romances in which to represent enforced betrothal and marriage.

Sarah Kay argues that the Saracen princess figure in the *chansons de geste* 'does not merely ventriloquize a controlling masculine fantasy: she helps to shape it,

---

[37] Ibid. 124, 4.2 (52–3). As Andrew Galloway has shown, in 14th-c. commentaries on Lucretia, the best that can be done for her in the much-discussed Augustinian question of whether she felt pleasure in the rape and if this precipitated her suicide is Ridewall's account of her as 'the victim of the paradoxes and inadequacies of the [Roman and pre-Christian] ideology in which she lives' ('Chaucer's *Legend of Lucrece* and the Critique of Ideology in Fourteenth-Century England', *ELH* 60 (1993), 813–32 (821)). Vernacular hagiography arguably has more to offer female audiences here.

[38] This is not to say that the heroine can say an immediate 'yes', either: what is required is reluctance (which enables a verbal taxonomy of deferral articulating the hero's *gentillesse*) and certain eventual submission: see Felicity Riddy, 'Engendering Pity in the *Franklin's Tale*', in Evans and Johnson (eds.), *Feminist Readings in Middle English Literature*, 54–71, and Susan Crane, *Gender and Romance in Chaucer's Canterbury Tales* (Princeton: Princeton University Press, 1994), 55–92 (61–6).

and thereby disrupts assumed hierarchies'. The princesses' choice of their own husbands confuses the distinction between persons and things and elicits 'the potential for irony and ambiguity in a gift economy.'[39] This is even more the case in virgin *passio*. The virgin not only chooses her own husband, but simultaneously occupies the positions of the Other (as woman and object of desire) and of the rival, Christ, for whom she speaks. These roles are normally distributed between a female figure and a male chivalric one, not combined in a single woman. The virgin's confrontation with the pagan throws all exchanges and desires askew even as it reconfirms the potential of women as gift, setting up disturbing and disruptive inversions as it seeks to settle binaries of good and evil, legitimate and illegitimate. If a treasure and gift can negotiate its own status and speak from a subject position the romance triangle is made unstable: rejecting one's suitor is, so to speak, to reinvent one's father and his household. Although this is arguably less subversive than refusing to choose any suitor, the identities which the *passio* strives to fix are still brought into question. Not only does the heroine's power to give receive endorsement, the powers of the pagans—who may be fathers, suitors, husbands, clerical and ecclesiastical associates, and/or heathen raiders—can all be looked at again with a critical scrutiny. When the foot is tutor, inversion and outright *bouleversement* are never far away.

3.2. THE VIRGIN AND THE PAGAN: DEBATE AND TORTURE

Virgin martyr saints' lives use a romance script, but we cannot see hagiography simply as another version of romance. In the *passio*, ranking Christ and the pagan as rival suitors is part of the narrative strategy (but no part of the teleology) of a genre which takes Christ's superiority as its premiss. Hagiography begins where chivalric literature leaves off: it is the retrospective display by the victor (God) of his rights to the virgin and his control of the rival. Christ's mode of combat is not to prevent the assault of the pagan on the virgin, but to transform its meaning, or rather, to reveal himself as always already having been in charge of a larger framework of meaning of which the pagan commands only a tiny metonymic parody.

At the heart of the *passio*, the combat is a contest not of strength, but of meanings. This is signalled in the *passio*'s use of another major literary mode, debate. The twelfth- and early-thirteenth century *passio* stages debate theatrically and spectacularly. It also tends to elaborate torture and debate much further than Old English hagiography. It is doubtful whether this can be causatively attributed to changes in juridical practice and the morphology of

---

[39] *Chansons de geste in the Age of Romance*, 46, 45.

torture in contemporary interrogation or execution.[40] As we might surmise from its narrative production in debate, the *passio*'s represented torture is less juridical than rhetorical and epistemological. This is not to argue that represented torture is not to be distinguished from represented argument at various signifying levels. But it is to argue that neither verbal violence nor represented dismemberment function as a simple substitute for male violence against women. The *passio*'s triangle of desire does not stably align male pursuit on one side and a female object of desire on the other: the triangle can, so to speak, be viewed with female desire and volition as its defining apex. Nor is the action of the *passio* simply an instance of the flesh's ritual submission to the word: the prominence of debate, prayer, and eloquence speaks to the importance of the word, but the body of the saint is reconstituted and endures past the words (and the body) of the pagan. The virgin is partner to, not only object of, this exchange. Torture as the pagan's mode of producing meaning is opposed and answered both by the virgin's own arguments and prayers and by God's production of miracles for the saint: a particularly explicit example is the prayer of St Margaret, when faced with boiling in a vat, that immersion should be a baptism to her.[41] What the pagan tyrant intends as a literal inscription of will on the saint's body is answered and transcended by the conversion of acts of pagan torture into Christian meaning. It is no mere *façon de parler* to claim that words and blows are interchangeable as well as interchanged in the *passio*. The pagan tears up the virgin's body and she dismembers his arguments.

René Girard's theory of violence, as applied in Kay's study of the *chansons de geste*, can be usefully extended to hagiography. To take Girard's formulation, 'only the introduction of some transcendental quality that will persuade men of the fundamental difference between sacrifice and revenge, between a judicial system

---

[40] See Edward Peters, *Torture* (Oxford: Blackwell), 1985, esp. ch. 2, and on the reappearance of juridical torture in the 13th c., his Appendix I, '*Res fragilis*: Torture in Early European Law', in *The Magician, the Witch and the Law* (Hassocks: Harvester, 1978), 183–95; Robert Bartlett, *Trial by Fire and Water: The Medieval Judicial Ordeal* (Oxford: Clarendon Press, 1986); for its English replacement, H. R. T. Summerson, 'The Early Development of the *peine forte et dure*', in E. E. Ives and A. H. Manchester (eds.), *Law, Litigants, and the Legal Profession* (London: RHS, 1983), 116–25; Klaus P. Jankofsky, 'Public Executions in England in the Late Middle Ages: The Indignity and Dignity of Death', *Omega*, 10 (1979), 43–57. Thomas H. Bestul suggests in his excellent *Texts of the Passion: Latin Devotional Literature and Medieval Society* (Philadelphia: University of Pennsylvania Press, 1996) that development of the Inquisition and its adoption of juridical torture may lead to the increase in represented torture, but as Caroline Walker Bynum points out, the papal inquisition (never established in England, see Peters, *Torture*, 58–9), permitted only pressure and stretching of its victims' bodies, not the dismemberment so frequently represented in saints' lives ('Material Culture, Personal Survival, and the Resurrection of the Body: A Scholastic Discourse in its Medieval and Modern Contexts', in *Fragmentation and Redemption*, 239–97 (272–6)). On contemporary attitudes to juridical torture, see now Edward Peters, 'Destruction of the Flesh—Salvation of the Spirit: The Paradoxes of Torture in Medieval Christian Society', in Alberto Ferreiro (ed.), *The Devil, Heresy and Witchcraft in the Middle Ages: Essays in Honor of Jeffrey B. Russell* (Leiden: Brill, 1998), 131–48.

[41] See Millett and Wogan-Browne, 76/5–13.

and vengeance, can succeed in by-passing violence'. Only ritualized violence of an uncontestedly sacred character can put an end to violence, for 'as soon as the essential quality of transcendence—religious, humanistic, or whatever—is lost, there are no longer any terms by which to define the legitimate form of violence and to recognize it among the multitude of illicit forms'.[42]

Hagiographic narratives claim a superordinate level of reference both by metaphor and metonymy: the saint is a sign of and a contact with God as her opponent is for and with the devil. In Girard's terms, a hagiographic *passio* would ritually eliminate violence by establishing vertical differentiation (as between rival suitors, good and bad, heaven and earth, God and the devil) in the final referents for the saint's and the pagan's debating positions and between the mirrorings of pagan tortures and saintly miracles. The violence of saints' lives stems structurally from the articulation of transcendence, rather than from covert desires for pornography (itself in any case not a fixed entity).[43] The premiss of the genre is not that it opposes heaven and earth and Christian and pagan in order to represent torture, but that it represents torture in order to distinguish revenge and sacrifice, earth and heaven, pagan and Christian. Torture is not *the* grounding but *a* narrative hermeneutic in saints' lives. The ritual production of vertical differentiation, of transcendence, is a better candidate for the fundamental desires of hagiographic narrative than the fulfilment of clerical sexual fantasy. Moreover, ritual, as recent work on hagiographic miracles has made clear, is not automatic or invariant repetition, but is performative and transformative of the materials selected for it.[44] The rich strangeness, the wild exuberance of the tortures by which the dolorism of Christianity is expressed in *passio* (to borrow Duncan Robertson's suggestive phrase quoted as epigraph above) may be pornographic from the point of view of a pagan tyrant hopelessly trying to actualize a fantasy of power. But the *passio*'s graphic fecundity of invention is better caught by the *Guide for Anchoresses*' image of the martyrs as gleeful children improvidently tearing up their robes—their bodies—because their rich father—God—can easily give them others (see epigraph). Torture is not a static sign of desire: it has no stable taxonomy from one legend to another, and its meaning is not instrumental but enacted, produced in front of us in each legend's narrative exchange.

Kay critiques Girard's assumption of sameness in the positions ritually differentiated by violence: his emphasis on the ontological 'sameness' of antagonists,

---

[42] René Girard, *La Violence et le sacré* (Paris: Grasset, 1972), trans. Patrick Gregory as *Violence and the Sacred* (Baltimore and London: Johns Hopkins University Press, 1977), 24: I draw gratefully here on discussions with Sarah Kay.

[43] See Suzanne Kappeler, *The Pornography of Representation* (Cambridge: Polity Press, 1986): for a lucid argument against reading torture as pornography see Lewis, ' "Let me suffre" ' (cited in n. 20 above).

[44] See Catherine Bell, *Ritual: Perspectives and Dimensions* (New York and Oxford: Oxford University Press, 1997); Ashley and Sheingorn, 'An Unsentimental View'.

she argues, obscures the political importance of unequal access to resources (such as force) and the resulting distribution of antagonists into the politically opposed categories of oppressor and oppressed.[45] Virgin martyrs sometimes comment on such unequal distributions. Clemence of Barking's Catherine wryly points out that the emperor is giving large professional rewards to the clerks speaking against her, but (in a manner most improper for a feudal lord) has promised her no gift for her part in the debate (vv. 645–52). At another level, however, these categories are not settled once we have noted the obvious differences of military and political resource, since the virgin is fighting on the side of an already transcendent figure, at the narrative's referential limit, while the pagan stumbles in a darkened arena of misperception. Martyrs and virgins most often taunt their tyrants with their inability to make a difference: they transcend the pagan's limits of exchange by transforming and converting whatever he offers them.

As dialectic between virgin and pagan, debate and torture produce reciprocal bodies, bodies of flesh and bodies of belief. If the virgin's body is seen by her persecutor as stubborn, mute, resistant, so his idols are seen by her as dumb, inanimate, and disposable. St Faith's argument rhetorically dismembers the bodies of Dacien's gods—they have mouths, hands, ears, eyes, and feet and can use none of them (vv. 341–6)—and disrupts his reward and punishment scheme for administering Agen. The persecutor's attempts to dismember the virgin are frequently followed by his own dismemberment: he tears himself to pieces in his fury, or is trampled into fragments by wild horses or suddenly explodes with disease.[46] Dacien, twisted with anger, swells up like a serpent unable to disgorge its venom (vv. 803–6). The body of the pagan, as of his shattered idols, is torn up and discarded as rubbish, while the body of the virgin endures as territory and treasure, and is fecundly reproduced by its very fragmentation, a version of plenitude. Both parties are capable of representing inversion to and of the other: both represent a number of desires and tensions internal to Christian patriarchy and both can function as a device for abjecting or incorporating the Other in a range of territorial, ethnic, and psychic identities in a way that serves to create (or to express, at least, the wish to create) ordered and controllable Christian communities.

The inversions of the *passio*, especially in the thirteenth century, are endlessly productive in annexing these areas of cultural tension. Matthew Paris's brilliant Life of St Alban (like the *Vie seinte Osith*, intertextual with *chanson de geste*) was written probably *c.*1230–40 and is associated with baronial women readers of

---

[45] *Chansons de geste in the Age of Romance*, 59.

[46] Alain Boureau, *La Légende dorée: le système narratif de Jacques de Voragine (+1298)* (Paris: Éditions du Cerf, 1984) looks at 'l'évanescence des opposants' and concludes that opposition to the saints on the part of devils, pagans, Jews, or heretics is nugatory: they are either defeated or 'se laissent facilement conduire à la vérité' (178, 181). This has been a commonly held view, and it is of course true that the pagan never wins and the saint always does. But the easy defeat of pagan opposition is not the same issue as what the opposition is doing in the narrative.

the court of Eleanor of Provence. Its narrating persona is revealed as a reformed
Saracen, and its narrative successively inverts and mirrors a number of conversion, battle, clothing, and doctrinal topoi.[47] This Life demonstrates the range
of the *passio*'s powers of annexation through inversion whereby almost any
discourse or thematic territory can be placed, so to speak, within inverted com-
mas and given as a mirror image of itself. Again, in some thirteenth-century
lives, Thomas Becket's mother becomes a Saracen princess, 'rescued' and married by his merchant father: one prospect offered by the image of the power of
the martyred archbishop would seem to be the ability to neutralize and contain the contamination of the Other in trade and annexation in pagan territories.[48] By the same token, demons preach orthodoxy when defeated by
virgin martyrs, ending up telling it like it is in God's universe, however much
they desire differently. Closely concerned with the ordering of violence and in
some ways permitting interrogation of the violence of order as the *passio* is,
there is much at stake in its stylizations and inversions. They can be socially
and historically mapped onto the Crusades (within and outside Europe), onto
church concern with heterodoxy and heresy, the extended programmes of
pastoral control developed from Lateran III in 1179 to their consummation in
Lateran IV's focus on the confessional narration of individual desire, and the
expansion and recontainment of female monasticism. In the era of the Crusades
and following the Arabic reconquest, there is a heightened Western awareness
of the foreigner, the outsider as the Other, as well as intensified alterization of
women as Other.[49]

Both sides of this debate, however, are attended with anxiety. Not only fragmentation but originary wholeness requires reiteration and assertion. Virgins and
pagans have not only reciprocal, but potentially interchangeable bodies. Some
especially interesting contemporary evidence for the reversibility of the virgin–pagan
dialectic comes from the chronicler Ralph of Coggeshall, who famously tells of
the encounter of the encyclopaedist Gervase of Tilbury with a virgin outside
Rheims sometime between 1176 and 1180. Propositioning the girl, the English
cleric immediately perceives from her arguments against him and for her
virginity that she is a heretic, a woman manifesting a gnostic overvaluation of
virginity: 'if I lost my virginity and my body was once corrupted, there is no
doubt that nothing could save me from eternal damnation' (heresy here, as Robert
Moore has shown, being as so often a strenuous version of orthodoxy, rather

[47] *La Vie de seint Auban: An Anglo-Norman Poem of the Thirteenth Century*, ed. A. R. Harden,
ANTS 19 (Oxford, 1968). On the links of this text with women readers see Ch. 5.1 below.
[48] The story is found in the *Quadrilogus* (the 13th-c. compilation of hagiographic accounts of
Becket, PL190.346–9, 'De ortu mirabili beati Thomae'), and in the *SEL* (ed. d'Evelyn and Mill,
610/1–612/54).
[49] See Robertson, *The Medieval Saints' Lives*, ch. 1, for a helpful survey of *passio* development
and the suggestion that the crusades 'inspired a renewal of interest in the traditional passion' (73).
See also Steven F. Kruger, 'Conversion and Medieval Sexual, Religious, and Racial Categories', in
Karma Lochrie, Peggy McCracken, and James A. Schultz (eds.), *Constructing Medieval Sexuality*,
Medieval Cultures 11 (Minneapolis and London: University of Minnesota Press, 1997), 158–79.

than its conceptual opposite).[50] Taken into the town, incarcerated, examined, this virgin is revealed as a member of the *Publicani* sect, and, proving obstinate, she is burnt at the stake. Ralph of Coggeshall, in his version of the incident, comments that in her endurance of the fire's torments she was the image of the martyrs ('sed disparili causa', p. 123), who in former times were slaughtered for the sake of the Christian religion by the pagans. This inverted martyrdom—a heretical virgin killed by orthodox Christians—makes pagan suitor-persecutor-torturers of the Christian clerics who desire and murder her. Inversion here so shadows the orthodox version of martyrdom that one sees why so much energy is invested in interrogation's naming and fixing of the different as the other. Not only the young woman, but her older *magistra* and tutor are interrogated. The older woman is 'bombarded by the archbishop and his clerks with questions and citations of the holy scriptures to convince her of the greatness of her errors', but she 'perverted all the authorities which they brought forward with such subtle interpretations that it was obvious to everybody that the spirit of all error spoke through her mouth. She replied so easily, and had such a clear memory of the incidents and texts advanced against her, both from the Old and the New Testament, that she must have had great knowledge of the whole Bible, and had plenty of practice in this kind of debate: she mixed truth with falsehood, and distorted the true explanation of our faith with evil intelligence' (p. 123).[51] Difference is firmly reasserted by Ralph of Coggeshall: 'there is nothing in common between [this] stubbornness and the constancy of Christ's martyrs, for contempt of death is the result of piety in the one case and mere obstinacy in the other'.[52] But this pronouncement could be made, with minimal alterations, by a pagan rhetor or a Christian narrator commenting on a virgin martyr.

The behaviour of the clerics here is echoed elsewhere in chronicle and anecdote, as well as in the capacity of the hagiographic pagan tyrant to represent the cleric. It offers confirmation that the pagan can indeed shadow and express illicit clerical desire.[53] But the story of Gervase and the virgin is still more significant

---

[50] On heresy see R. I. Moore, *The Formation of a Persecuting Society: Power and Deviance in Western Europe 950–1250* (Oxford and New York: Blackwell, 1987) and Herbert Grundmann, *Religiöse Bewegungen im Mittelalter* (1934; now tr. by Steven Rowan as *Religious Movements in the Middle Ages* (Notre Dame, Ill. and London: University of Notre Dame Press, 1995). For the Gervase of Tilbury story see Ralph of Coggeshall, *Chronicon Anglicanum*, ed. J. Stevenson, RS 66 (London, 1875), 121–5 (further references by page number in the text); R. I. Moore, *The Origins of European Dissent* (London: Allen Lane, 1977), 183–4 and id., *The Birth of Popular Heresy: Documents of Medieval History* (London: Arnold, 1975), 86–8.

[51] Tr. Moore, *Birth of Popular Heresy*, 87.

[52] 'sed nihil simile habent martyrum Christi constantia et istorum pertinacia, quia mortis contemptum in illis pietas, in istis cordis duritia operatur', Ralph of Coggeshall, *Chronicon Anglicanum*, 124.

[53] While identifications between the gaze of the courtly lover, the cleric, and the pagan tyrant can certainly be made, there is no reason to privilege this as the dominant and necessary reading of the texts. For valuable work on the use of rape narratives in the formation of medieval clerics, see Marjorie Curry Woods, 'Rape and the Pedagogical Rhetoric of Sexual Violence', in Rita Copeland (ed.), *Criticism and Dissent in the Middle Ages* (Cambridge: Cambridge University Press, 1996), 56–86.

for its display of the inversion and the lability of the virgin–pagan/orthodox–heterodox categories. Similarly, saints' lives are not triumphal patriarchal statement, but a struggle to fix contested and anxiety-ridden categories. Since difference, however desired and asserted, is never finally fixable, all categories oscillate wildly with their own inversions within and around the *passio*.

The virgin's own position as bride of Christ is shadowed by heterodoxy. Her resistance has an analogue not only in the reluctance of the romance heroine, but in the pagan idols of the *passio*. Michael Camille has argued that, for the high Middle Ages, the Virgin Mary replaces Venus as the locus of desire and he shows many examples of ambivalent linking between the two.[54] A comparable duality emerges most clearly in insular saints' lives around the figure of Diana, classical goddess of chastity and hunting, already demoted to a heathen idol in Ælfric's *De falsiis diis* and herself in some functions an inversion of the Virgin. Her role in the Troy story, where she presides over Brutus's quest for a land to inhabit, makes her a figure for insular historiography in both English and French as well as Latin. She is Geoffrey of Monmouth's answer to Bede in his alternative foundation narrative: as Bede's only poem in the *Historia Ecclesiastica* hymns his counter to Helen of Troy and principal example of English virginity, Etheldreda of Ely, so in the *Historia Regum Britanniae* Geoffrey's only poem is offered by Brutus to Diana.[55] In Simon of Walsingham's Life of Faith of *c.*1200, Diana is the oppositional term for Faith: the pagan tyrant Decius tells the saint, 'You should worship [Diana] for she is the goddess of love: believe me and adore her, for she and you are alike' (v. 324). Though he later expressed his regret for comparing Faith 'to statues of Venus or Diana', the possibility that the virgin might be the pagan was also a doubt Bernard of Angers represents himself as overcoming before writing his *Liber Miraculorum* for Faith's reliquary statue in Conques.[56] In Wace's *Roman de Brut* Diana is a sorceress and a devil deceiving people through enchantment, and in his *Vie de seint Nicolas* she becomes 'a very deceptive goddess and traitress' (vv. 349–50), disguises herself as a nun and (in a further signal of virginity's conceptual entanglement with the Magdalen, discussed in Chapter 4.2 below) offers anointing oil for Nicholas's church.[57] The

[54] Michael Camille, *The Gothic Idol: Ideology and Image-Making in Medieval Art* (Cambridge: Cambridge University Press, 1989), 220–41 (240–1).

[55] *The Historia Regum Britannie of Geoffrey of Monmouth*, ed. Neil Wright (Cambridge: Brewer, 1985), i. 9, §16. Etheldreda, as noted in Ch. 2.1 above, is Bede's principal example of English virginity, as against Helen [of Troy] and her 'wantonness'. See also P. J. Frankis, 'Laȝamon's English Sources', in *J. R. R. Tolkien, Scholar and Storyteller* (Ithaca and London: Cornell University Press, 1979), on Laȝamon's use of Ælfric's 'De falsiis diis', 64–5 and, on Diana, Michael Camille, *The Gothic Idol*, 107–14. In the 13th c., Matthew Paris retells the story of Brutus and Diana's temple (*Chronica majora*, ed. H. R. Luard, RS 57 (London, 1872–80), i. 19–20).

[56] *Liber miraculorum sancte Fides*, ed. Robertini, 113; *Book of Ste Foy*, tr. Sheingorn, 10, 78.

[57] 'une divineresse: | diables esteit, ki la gent | Deceveit par enchantement' (*Le Roman de Brut de Wace*, ed. Ivor Arnold, SATF, 2 vols. (Paris, 1938–40), vv. 636–8): 'un diesce | Mult deceivante et tricheresce' (*La Vie de saint Nicolas par Wace*, ed. Einar Ronsjö (Lund and Copenhagen: Gleerup and Munksgaard, 1942), vv. 349–50).

saint exposes the oil as dangerously inflammable 'Mediacon' (i.e. oil of Medea, i.e. petroleum, v. 376) capable of setting the sea alight (vv. 405–44, esp. 425–8). The fire lurking under the nun's veil and the deceptive promise of beneficent oil which becomes the blazing liquid of the *tricheresse* is close kin to the *vitae patrum* illustrations of the pious or beautiful woman at the cell-door, one devilish claw-foot showing under her cloak.[58] In Wace's *Nicolas*, Diana thus suggests the ways in which even religious women are secretly pagan, illicit, carnal beings underneath. Her action echoes both Mary Magdalen's box of unguent and the 'Greek fire', the twelfth-century liquid incendiary, used in the *Guide for Anchoresses*' metaphorics of love to figure blazing love for Christ.[59]

The potential heterodoxy of the virgin is echoed in a more general heterodoxy of women, itself serving as a carrier of anxiety about territorial and ideological boundaries in what are, after all, accounts of conquest and rule, *translatio* narratives par excellence. When their queens are converted by virgin martyrs, the anxiety of pagan emperors knows no bounds. As handbooks of seigneurial formation teach and romance implies, a good queen or empress is a helpmeet:

> Quel pru, quel socors
> Frunt as amperurs
> Lur femmes gentils

What support, what help their noble wives afford to emperors

(and so on, through 'reine', 'cuntesse', 'dameisele'), all supposed as extensions rather than oppositions for the seigneurial self.[60] In the Anglo-Norman lives of Saints Catherine and George, the emperors Maxentius and Dacien revenge themselves on their wives with special viciousness and point by having their breasts torn out with iron nails (in the *South English Legendary*, with its interest in constructing pastoral images of a calendrically regulated and ordered Christian community, these are said to be used like 'woolcombs').[61] Simund de Freine's late twelfth-century *Vie de saint Georges* shows the Emperor Dacien begging his queen not to renounce her pagan affiliations for the sake of her love for him ('Duce, pur l'amur de mei, | Ne reneez vostre lei', vv. 1276–7), only to have her 'make' him hang her up by the hair, and 'cause' him to have her body publicly tormented (v. 1285). The emperors' savagery has an equivalent in the romance

---

[58] See e.g. Alison Elliott, *Roads to Paradise: Reading the Lives of the Early Saints* (Hanover, NH: University Press of New England for Brown University Press, 1987), plate opp. p. 112.

[59] See Geoffrey Shepherd (ed.), *Ancrene Wisse, Parts Six and Seven* (London: Nelson, 1959; rev. edn. Exeter: Exeter University Press, 1985), 65, n. to 27/11 ff.; for Greek fire's use in naval warfare and a recipe, see Mildred Leake Day (ed.), *The Rise of Gawain, Nephew Of Arthur: De ortu Walwanii nepotis Arturi* (New York: Garland, 1984), pp. xx–xxi, 68–76.

[60] *Roman des romans*, ed. F. J. Tanqueray, in *Deux poèmes moraux anglo-français: Le Roman des romans et le Sermon en vers* (Paris: Champion, 1922), sts. 25–6.

[61] *Early South English Legendary*, ed. Horstmann, 99/246.

and the legal punishments for adulterous women, especially royal women.[62] Some of the earliest-known uses of the phrase 'fin'amor'—refined, courtly love—describe the empress's feeling for Christ in these situations (so Dacien's empress, unsurprisingly, feels 'amur fine' for God as opposed to the relations offered her by her husband, vv. 1323, 1366). These are situations as intimately connected with the politics of rule as anxieties focused on the adulteries of an Isolde or Gwenevere.[63]

The profoundly resented intimacy of the rebellion of wives and daughters has its obverse in patriarchy's use of virgins and wives as ideological infiltrators. The Venomous Virgin of chivalric romance is sent in to Alexander the Great and to King Arthur bearing poison in herself or her gift of a cloak.[64] In Pierre DuBois's treatise for Edward I on the recapture of the Holy Land (1307), it is proposed that educated Christian virgins be sent in to marry Saracen princes and convert them in pillowtalk (on the authority of 1 Cor. 7: 14, 'the unbelieving husband is sanctified by the wife').[65] Closer to home, in the late twelfth- and thirteenth-century confessional manuals studied by Sharon Farmer, programmes for priests to use wives to persuade their husbands to Christian virtue are routinely proposed.[66] Women both are, and make the link to the Other, and the post-Conquest oppositions of Faith and Diana, virgin and Venus, relic and idol are so gripping not because they are fixed but because they are oscillatory. It is significant that Gervase of Tilbury's story is told of himself by an English cleric outside the tightly patrolled borders of England. 'Heresie, Godd haue thonc, ne rixleth nawt in Englelond', declares the *Guide for Anchoresses*, but the anxieties capable of producing and detecting it certainly did.[67]

[62] Gwenevere is sent to the stake in Arthurian tradition, and Isolde to a leper colony (in Béroul and some later versions). Cutting off the nose is a punishment for women in Marie de France's *Bisclavret* (ed. Ewert, *Lais*, 49–57, v. 235), and is invoked in Thomas's *Tristan* (ed. Stewart Gregory, *Thomas of Britain: Roman de Tristan* (New York: Garland, 1991), v. 1541). On representations of women inflicting this punishment on themselves see n. 72 below.

[63] See Peggy McCracken, 'Body Politics and the Queen's Adulterous Body in French Romance', in Linda Lomperis and Sarah Stanbury (eds.), *Feminist Approaches to the Body in Medieval Literature* (Philadelphia: University of Pennsylvania Press, 1993), 38–64.

[64] See e.g. *Le Mantel mautaillié*, ed. F. A. Wulff, *Romania*, 14 (1885), 343–80; Margaret Hallissy, *Venomous Woman: Fear of the Female in Literature*, Contributions in Women's Studies (Westport, Conn.: Greenwood, 1987), 120–1 (for the virgin as weapon in the *Secreta Secretorum*: see more generally ch. 2 on the figure of the *venefica*). As has often been noted, the Germanic word for poison is 'Gift'. A hagiographic parallel for the venomous virgin is the use of serpentine maidens against St Chrysanthus: see Skeat, *Ælfric's Lives of the Saints*, ii, no. 35, 380–1, ll. 51–70 ('næddran', 58, 63).

[65] Pierre DuBois, *De recuperatione sanctae terrae*, ed. C. V. Langlois (Paris: Picard, 1891), pt. I, ch. 86, p. 83.

[66] Sharon Farmer, 'Persuasive Voices: Clerical Images of Medieval Wives', *Speculum*, 76 (1986), 517–43.

[67] Tolkien, f. 21a/12–13. There is a lacuna in the Vitellius manuscript at this point: only the words 'Heresie . . . [Eng]leterre' survive (Herbert, 68/26–8): Trinity reads 'heresie, deus en soit a orrez, ne regne pas. en engletere' (Trethewey, 189/14–15). English women heretics seem to have been active abroad, however: see Peter Biller, 'The Earliest Heretical Englishwomen', in Wogan-Browne *et al.* (eds.), *Medieval Women*, 363–76.

In order to see the virgin or her married converts as heterodox, a reading position somewhere near a pagan viewpoint, and somewhere near clerical misogyny, has to be adopted. But it is also possible to reverse direction and look with the virgin at the figure of the pagan (a possibility frequently thematized by gaze in saints' lives: the virgin is not only sign and spectacle but herself looks at others).[68] The *passio* thus becomes a genre in which a range of male behaviour is submitted to the scrutiny of the virgin, and in which it is possible for her to see the paganity of clerics, just as much as clerics may see the heresy of a virgin. Like courtly love poets, the male hagiographic narrator both gazes upon and rhetorically dissects the virgin: his witness is shadowed by idolatry. Clerical knowledge itself, like the pagan tyrants' false idols, is potentially heterodox human manufacture in a world made by God.[69] The pagan also allows exhibition of the desire for writing and of the allegiance between desire and rhetoric: he is a would-be inscriber of bodies and hence aligned with the subordinate creativity of the human writer in a world officially signifying God in all its created parts and creatures. While virginity letters and treatises often offer monitory portraits of clerical seducers, the *passio* dramatizes academic male vanity and the seduction of knowledge. Pagan figures permit the exhibition and recontainment of Christian clerical desires, and also their evaluation.

In the lives of forcibly betrothed and married native virgin saints, the pagan tyrant role is filled by unwanted British husbands. The unhappy Burthred of Christina of Markyate's *vita* is joined by vernacular accounts of Ecgfrid (*Audrée*) and Sigher (*Osith*), and, as noted above, a fierce internal dissent is envisaged on the part of the virgin (and, in these exemplary biographies for women, it is a legitimated dissent).[70] The pagan may also have served as a way of articulating

[68] So, for example, Bozon's St Juliana looks at a demon who flees her gaze ('Kant ele regarda si vers li | Le diable tost s'en fuy', *Seven More Poems*, ed. Klenke, vv. 148–60); Seinte Iuliene's gaze makes her demon duck away 'as for a schoten arewe ['arrow']' and reduces him to the status of a small hobgoblin-like creature: 'gripe ha me eanes ['Once she catches me']', he says, 'ne ga i neauer mare threfter o grene ['I'll never be able to walk the earth again']' (*Þe Liflade ant te Passiun of Seinte Iuliene*, ed. S. R. T. O. d'Ardenne, EETS os 248 (London, 1961), 65 (emended text)). Clemence of Barking's Catherine is shown seeing ('veit' v. 195) the pagan emperor in a more ordinary act of perception (his own gaze is more compulsive and arrested, his eyes fixed on her beautiful face, 'En sun bel vult ses oilz ficha', v. 222), but her intellectual scrutiny of him continues throughout the Life.

[69] This point is made in word-play by several saints, most notably in an extensive confrontation of 'faiture' with 'creature' in the Anglo-Norman *Laurent* (*La Vie de saint Laurent: An Anglo-Norman Poem of the Twelfth Century*, ed. D. W. Russell, ANTS 34 (London, 1976), vv. 429–63, tr. Wogan-Browne and Burgess, 52, and see p. xlviii).

[70] For Burthred see *Life of Christina*, ed. Talbot, 44–6, 48–54. How far Christina's *vita* was read by women is unknown (it would be surprising if the inhabitants of Christina's priory did not know it in some form: as Talbot points out, the *Gesta abbatum* I. 105 mentions a manuscript of the Life 'preserved at Markyate', *Life of Christina*, 3). The extant rule for Sopwell is from the 14th c. and in Anglo-Norman: it prescribes attention to the 'psalter, prayers and other devotions', and to 'le Dieu service', but mentions no other texts. See 'Anglo-Norman Rules for the Priories of St Mary de Pré and Sopwell', ed. Tony Hunt, in Stewart Gregory and D. A. Trotter (eds.), *De mot en mot: Aspects of Medieval Linguistics. Essays in Honour of William Rothwell* (Cardiff: University of Wales Press and MHRA, 1997), 93–104 (100–4).

aspects of women's individual and communal histories. Danish invasions, mass burnings, and rapes were remembered in English nunneries, and violent raiding even from, perhaps specially from, local landowners was a perennial possibility: the pagan embodies not only a legendary but a historical and contemporary threat to nunneries and to nuns.[71] St Osith is martyred by heathen raiders who decapitate her as she bathes with her four handmaidens at a 'secree fontaine' (v. 799), and can partly be seen (together with her stag) as a version of Diana discovered (her *passio*, as pointed out in Chapter 2.1 above, is a careful, rich and significant pastiche of virgin foundress elements). The raiders, pagan dogs who actualize a threat to her life analogous to her husband's hunt for the white stag and her virginity, do not themselves suffer Actaeon's fate, but move from archetype to history. Though unnamed in the Latin *vita*, they are specified in the Anglo-Norman Life as the Danish raiders Ynguar and Ubba. In insular tradition these were figures well known from Bede, the Anglo-Saxon Chronicle, and other sources. In *Audrée*, Ingar and Hubbe are among the raiders who burn and pillage the abbey and kill all the nuns at Ely (vv. 2410–11, 2420–5). The Danes of these lives thus historicize and localize pagan violation, and Osith's death updates the virgin-martyr convention of beheading-as-closure.

A virgin martyr *passio* such as Osith's arguably deals with this in a more satisfactory way for women readers than chroniclers and clerics' exemplary stories of self-mutilation as a way of avoiding rape.[72] Updating the legendary pagan Roman tyrant to Danish raiding is both the refurbishing of a stereotype (one could compare the move from redskins to rednecks in modern American horror films as analysed by Carol Clover), and a change of register.[73] In the life of Modwenna the figure of the pagan raider becomes still more contemporaneous since the saint is shown dealing with the raids of both outlaws and local lords on her convents. (St Modwenna's response is less desperate than self-mutilation: against a band of raping robbers, she leads her nuns in a burying

---

[71] See, for example, 'Texts of Jocelin of Canterbury', ed. Colker (no. 1: cap. 13, cap. 20, 413–14, 416; no. 6: cap. 2, 455–6) for 11th-c. accounts of 9th-c. raiding. (I am grateful to Dr C. E. Lewis for giving me access to his account of Earl Swein's abduction of the abbess of Leominster, which will figure in his forthcoming book.) Awareness of pre-Conquest Danish raiding (such as e.g. the pillaging and burning of Ely and Soham in 870, *VCH, Cambs.* ii. 199) was supplemented by more recent accounts (see Power, *Medieval Nunneries*, 423–35).

[72] See Schulenberg, 'The Heroics of Virginity: Brides of Christ and Sacrifical Mutilation', in Mary Beth Rose (ed.), *Women in the Middle Ages and the Renaissance* (Syracuse: Syracuse University Press, 1986), 26–72, for such stories in the period 500–1000 AD, and see n. 62 above. Insular sources of the 12th and 13th c. by churchmen and chroniclers also use this convention in representing pre-Conquest female communities. Matthew Paris, for instance, retails a story of Coldingham in which abbess Ebba leads her nuns in cutting off her nose in order to deter Danish raiders (*Chron. maj.* i. 391–2). (There is no foundation for this at all in Bede, though disciplinary problems in the community are represented in the *Historia Ecclesiastica*, iv. 25.) No text known to be by a woman, so far as I am aware, retells stories of self-mutilation as a strategy for dealing with rape. See further Ch. 6, n. 48 below.

[73] *Men, Women and Chain Saws: Gender in the Modern Horror Film* (Princeton: Princeton University Press, 1992), 134–6.

raid for their murdered chaplains ('martyrs', v. 918), causes the would-be rapists and plunderers to fall asleep at the sign of the cross, and then converts them.)[74]

It is thus possible to argue that readings by women of the *passio* could involve recuperating masculinist fantasy into history, or perhaps herstory.[75] That virgin passion can function as insular history is signalled in the prologue to *Osith*: 'la veraie estoire' (v. 97) of hagiography is opposed in this 'romanz' (i.e. 'vernacular') version (v. 75) to the *chanson de geste*.[76] Such readings of representations of violence to women are strengthened by the seriousness with which a woman writer takes the figure of the pagan tyrant. In Clemence of Barking's late twelfth-century *passio* of St Catherine the pagan emperor Maxentius is by far the most fully developed version of this figure. This Life offers a doubled female viewing of male desire, staged by the narrator and watched by her heroine. Clemence most fully shows what the *passio* affords by way of a position from which the virgin can examine what is offered her in her world. Clemence critiques not only power and desire, but the ways in which the licensing of bullying and irrationality creates a parody courtoisie. (Her Catherine *passio* also offers one of the most elaborate and witty deconstructions of courtly idolatry in the treasuring of women.)[77] Moreover it is behaviour as represented in other genres, and also recognizable as normative social patterns: the violence and anxiety that attend some forms of male authority and desire and their encoding in chivalric romance are strongly and thoroughly critiqued here. In Clemence of Barking's innovative (and, as I shall argue in Chapter 7.2, theologically profound) rethinking of *passio*, it is quite impossible to see the genre simply as male fantasy visited upon women.

[74] During their sleep they view various punishments in a miniature heaven-and-hell tour (*Saint Modwenna*, ed. Baker and Bell, vv. 917–1104). See also Modwenna's vengeance miracles against raiders, Ch. 6.3 below.

[75] The move is comparable with that made when Chaucer for a moment considers Criseyde as a potential anchoritic reader of saints' lives: 'It satte me wel bet ay in a cave | To bidde and rede on holy seyntes lyves' (*Troilus and Criseyde*, II. 117–19). Criseyde's alternative to Pandarus's romance script gives her a position outside the fantasy reading of herself as romance heroine (for failing to respond to which C. S. Lewis famously condemned her). Her reply to Pandarus's announcement of important news ('is then th'assege awey?') is a rational response for a besieged Trojan citizen, not simply a failure of heroism. The particular model for Criseyde's image may well be Mary of Egypt or Mary of Magdalen, both figures of penance inflected towards anchoritism in their insular lives (see further Ch. 4).

[76] 'ge le vus di seurement, | Meuz vaut oir ici entour | Ke de la geste paenur, | De Guercedin e de Saisons, | Deu enemis e felons' (vv. 88–92: 'I tell you that, assuredly, it is better to hear about [St Osith] here than stories of the pagans, of Guercedin and of the Saracens, wicked men and enemies of God'). The Life does in fact deal with pagans in Osith's martyrdom, but the point is precisely that these are 'true' hagiographic pagans, not romanced ones.

[77] See Catherine Batt, 'Clemence of Barking's Transformations of *cortoisie* in *La vie de sainte Catherine d'Alexandrie*', in Roger Ellis (ed.), *Translation in the Middle Ages, New Comparisons*, 12 (1991), 102–33; St Catherine's deconstruction of the emperor's idolatry is explicitly signalled as a 'gab', a jest (v. 1304): see Jocelyn Wogan-Browne, 'Saints' Lives and the Female Reader', *FMLS* 27 (1991), 314–32 (328).

3.3. REVOLTING READERS: HAGIOGRAPHIC NARRATIVE AND WOMEN'S ANTI-SEMITISM

Although pagans are represented in virgin martyr *passio* exclusively as Romans or heathens, the most immediately 'other' category in purportedly 'heresy-free' late twelfth- and thirteenth-century England is that of Jewishness. Jewishness and virginity are intimately opposed in the construction of symbolic purity and filth. In *Cursor Mundi*, the thirteenth-century compilation of Anglo-Norman, Latin, and English texts that became the layperson's biblical and salvation history, the foundational purity of the Virgin's body is the fulcrum of redemptive history, and its antitype, as so often in Marian cult, is the collective body of Jewish culpability for the crucifixion.[78] In treatises for women, virginity's stereotypes inscribe class valuation and are associated with or aspire to aristocratic virtue, while 'Jewishness' is made its antitype for women of refinement. The *Guide for Anchoresses* proclaims itself unworried about heresy, but warns its audience of well-born women that failing in ardour for Christ is to become one of 'the envious Jews' (envy being a pre-eminently uncourtly quality as well as an especially deplored sin).[79] In Matthew Paris's *Vie seint Auban*, the Jews are declared in the conversion discourses of Amphibalus to Alban to be a kingless people after Christ's death ('sanz rei', v. 164) and to be released serfs who refuse to accept God's gift ('present e dun', vv. 306–15) of freedom.[80] The political illegitimacy of the Jews is thus asserted in a context that must have been resonant for Paris's monastic and baronial audiences (many of the latter women). As a people both chosen and dispossessed, and as mythically licensed hate-figures, the Jews are a crucial figure of the Other in twelfth- and thirteenth-century constructions of the nation as the Christendom of England (a matter of equal urgency in different ways both for the *South English Legendary* and for the Angevin and Plantagenet dynasties).

Given these endemic constructions of purity and filth (which continue with undiminished virulence long after the deportation), the absence of an explicit Jewish presence in virgin martyr *passio* is all the more striking. Jews were often linked with 'Saracens', as in Lateran IV's insistence (in canon 68) that both Jews and Muslims be distinguished in dress from Christians.[81] Yet unlike the Saracens, Danes, and Romans, the *passio*'s pagan others never include Jews

---

[78] Briefly discussed in Johnson and Wogan-Browne, 'National, World and Women's History', in Wallace (ed.), *The Cambridge History*, 107–8.
[79] Millett and Wogan-Browne, 124/16, and see 124/32, 'Giwes make' (with a pun on 'mate' and 'equal'), also 116/22–6.
[80] *Vie saint Auban*, ed. A. R. Harden. See further Sophia Menache, 'Matthew Paris's Attitudes Toward Anglo-Jewry', *JMH* 23 (1997), 139–62.
[81] On the tendency to call perceived 'Others' Mohammedans, see further Jennifer Bray, 'The Mohametan and Idolatry', in W. J. Sheils (ed.), *Persecution and Toleration*, SCH 21 (Oxford: Blackwell, 1984), 89–98, and Diane Speed, 'The Saracens of *King Horn*', *Speculum*, 65 (1990), 564–95.

as the persecutors of virgins. Instead, notoriously, in the twelfth and thirteenth centuries, the Jews are represented as a persecuting community who re-enact *passio* in a literal way by crucifying children. Pre-Conquest child martyrs such as the murdered royal innocents Kenelm and Melor continued to have their passions reworked in the twelfth and thirteenth centuries (and were part of women's reading—Kenelm is widely diffused in the *South English Legendary*, and Melor's Anglo-Norman Life is associated with the nunnery of Amesbury).[82] But new child martyrs in twelfth- and thirteenth-century Britain were represented as children from a wider class range and as martyred by Jews.[83] In one way, the *raison d'être* for this is all too clear: such stories begin circulating after the earliest English pogroms in the twelfth century.[84] But their existence raises questions about virgin martyr *passio*: what depth of repression and intensity of 'othering' in the genre is signalled by the exclusion of Jews as persecutors of virgins? And what is being said about the over-valuation of female children (only male children are represented as child martyrs)?

Here again Girard is helpful: his theorized attention to violence and sacrifice considers the role of the persecutors/the pagans seriously, as does the twelfth- and thirteenth-century *passio*. In the *passio* the willing self-donation of the saint officially ends the exchange of violence and enables transcendence: a voluntary victim is scapegoat and also hero[ine].[85] But, as Girard argues, there are relations between real and imaginary violence. Represented persecution is not only persecution mania, but a story about persecution, one in which it is possible for the text to function without actually naming its referent. It is not just a matter of decoding the persecutors' representation of what they are doing, but asking further what their text is about, something Girard's theory enables us to do in collective and not just individual psychosexual terms. His argument is suggestive for saints lives' mimesis of a historical layering of their knowledge. In Girard's terms, these are texts claiming to look at the scapegoating mechanisms of other communities (usually figured as antecedent heathen communities) and to invert the persecutors' meanings.[86] In such dramas, Girard argues, we

---

[82] See Hayward, 'The Idea of Innocent Martyrdom'. On Kenelm, see Love, *Three Eleventh-Century Anglo-Latin Saints' Lives*; for Melor, see 'The Life of St Melor', ed. A. H. Diverres, in Short (ed.), *Medieval French Textual Studies*, 41–53, and Conclusion below.

[83] Michael Goodich notes a comparable shift between the 12th and 13th c. in miracle stories, with a large increase in child beneficiaries occurring: *Violence and Miracle in the Fourteenth Century: Private Grief and Public Salvation* (Chicago: University of Chicago Press, 1995), 86.

[84] The earliest such story, St William of Norwich (d. 1144), is mentioned in the 1155 Peterborough continuation of the Anglo-Saxon chronicle, and a full Latin *passio* had been written by *c*.1150 (Gavin I. Langmuir, 'Thomas of Monmouth: Detector of Ritual Murder', *Speculum*, 59 (1984), 820–46, 821).

[85] René Girard, *Le Bouc émissaire* (Paris: Grasset, 1983), trans. Yvonne Freccero as *The Scapegoat* (Baltimore: Johns Hopkins University Press, 1986), 43, and see esp. chs. 1–3, and 9.

[86] Girard argues that, unlike myth, the Gospels *know* that the victim of collective murder is a scapegoat: 'they know not what they do' and Pilate's inability to find 'a cause' reveal the origins of culture in collective violence (117). They recall this origin in order to revoke it, acheiving thereby

need to distinguish between theme and structural principle, between scapegoat *in* and *for* the text and the scapegoat *of* the text:

> The scapegoat released to us by the text is a scapegoat both *in* and *for* the text . . . the scapegoat that we must disengage from the text for ourselves is the scapegoat *of* the text. He cannot appear in the text though he controls all its themes: he is never mentioned as such. He cannot become the theme of that text that he *shapes*. This is not a theme but a mechanism for giving *structure*. (p. 118, pp. 119–21)

Thus the scapegoat released in and for the text is the Christian martyr, but (given that this is a representation of an Other antecedent community and the persecutors' meanings are inverted) the scapegoat for the medieval Christian audience is also the pagan Roman or Dane (the linking of Christ and the pagan as suitor so readily observable at the level of romance thematization further underlines this). It is important that the pagans are abjected and fragmented so that the integrity of Christian ideology and community can be asserted. If we ask what the scapegoat *of* the text is here, the pagans, in all the ways detailed earlier in this chapter, become inverse figures of patriarchy, of Christian clerisy, of ecclesiastical and secular authorities—with all their uneasy and threateningly dynamic labilities of resemblance to the pagan Other—but the Jews do not.

If the virgin martyr *passio* can permit this much exploration and recontainment of the unspeakable in the society that writes and hears it, there would seem nevertheless to be issues it cannot touch even obliquely. Female sacrifice in the virgin–pagan confrontation is tolerable and representable. But the sacrifice of male children, together with Christian society's most intense practice of the 'violence of order' against the Jews, is displaced into a less reputable subgenre of *passio*, that of Jewish ritual murder. A further dimension of Girard's argument is suggestive here for the theology of the *passio*. The ultimate claim of the Christian victim-hero is that of innocence (Oedipus on the other hand really *is* a parricide as well as a sacrifice, just as the gods of Greek myth are culpable gods). But if Christ, the model for martyrs and the scapegoat for the world, is not a parricide, his Father can look dangerously like a filicide. Hence the *passio* must commit energy to distinctions that absolve God from this charge and allow the innocent victim to be innocently donated even if culpably killed. They must to a greater or lesser extent draw on the resources of Christian theology (primarily among them the doctrine of the Trinity and of the two natures, human and divine, in Christ) to make these distinctions. This provides a model of the Godhead that will clear God of infanticide. This God is both like and unlike the parents in the Ælfrician hagiography discussed at the beginning of

---

not myth but the Word, and the persecutors' representation of persecution fails, with exemplary force. The Gospels use the same drama—that of passion—to give birth to new myths which present the perspective of the persecutors and also to present the perspective of a victim dedicated to the rejection of the illusions of the persecutors (*The Scapegoat*, ch. 9).

this chapter: he commits child sacrifice, *hostia viva*, in the right Christian oblatory rather than the pagan culpable spirit (coded as for mere material gain). Doctrine in saints' lives is not just extraneous teaching thrown in to improve the occasion: it is intrinsic to the question of what kind of God is demanding or permitting a sacrifice and the identity of the community articulated in the ritual and performative drama of a *passio*. A Christian patriarchal god who would demand real (i.e. male) children for sacrifice must, with profound irony, be a Jew: the community of this god must be persecutory, violent, and to be feared—and ought to be rejected. No wonder these perceptions remain largely unspeakable in the virgin *passio* (in Anglo-Norman this is on the whole an élite and aristocratic genre) and are inverted into Jewish ritual murder stories and the inverse *passio* represented by the *Vengeance nostre seignur* cycles of the twelfth and thirteenth centuries.

Aristocratic female audiences must often have been complicit in the oppositions of Christian aristocratic ladyhood and Jewishness. The royal women of Henry III's and Edward I's households suggest over several generations how closely and how ambivalently the English crown engaged with Jewish finance and with anti-Semitism before the 1290 deportation (so too did baronial families and monasteries).[87] Edward I's mother, Eleanor of Provence, suppressed Jewries at Canterbury, Gloucester, Marlborough, and Worcester even against her own interests as a landed proprietor in these places: she also acquired encumbered Jewish estates cheaply and was reproached by Archbishop Peckham in a personal letter and ordered 'devaunt Dieu e devaunz la curt du ciel' not to retain the profits of usury.[88] Writing for Edward's daughter in her nunnery at Amesbury in the early fourteenth century, Nicholas Trevet salutes her father's Christian prowess: Edward joins the long line of great English kings because, in his mass deportation of English Jewry in 1290, he 'enchacea touz lez Judeus d'Engleterre'.[89]

---

[87] William Marshal himself contracted such debts, see David Crouch, *William Marshal: Court, Career and Chivalry in the Angevin Empire 1147–1219* (London and New York: Longmans, 1990), 169. Rose Graham notes that smaller barons in the 13th c. often had monasteries take over their debts to Jews in exchange for grants of land, and many monasteries had debts to Jews (*St Gilbert of Sempringham and the Gilbertines: A History of the Only English Monastic Order* (London: Elliot Stock, 1901), 123–5. Jocelin of Brakelond complains that Jews can go into monastic shrines, have their money safekept by monastic houses and, in time of war, their wives and children lodged in monasteries (*Chronica Jocelini de Brakelonda*, ed. J. G. Rokewode (London: Camden Society, 1840), 8). Sophia Menache argues that the kings were not strongly supported over the expulsions and that there was a new awareness of how the monarchy manipulated the idea of Jewry for its own ends ('The King, the Church and the Jews: Some Considerations on the Expulsions from England and France', *JMH* 13 (1987), 223–36).

[88] See *Registrum*, ed. Martin, ii. 619: also *Recueil des lettres anglo-françaises 1265–1399*, ed. F. J. Tanqueray (Paris: Champion, 1916), no. 37, 37–8. On the problems of distinguishing anti-Semitism and anti-Judaism, see Langmuir, *History, Religion and Antisemitism* (London and New York: Tauris, 1990), ch. 14. On the association of Jewish financiers and queen's gold, see Howell, *Eleanor of Provence*, 277–8, and on Eleanor's attitudes to Jewry, 299.

[89] See Trivet, *Chronicle*, ed. Rutherford, 342.

The manuscripts and texts of women readers include not only treatises of reflex anti-Semitism such as the *Guide for Anchoresses* but texts devoted to anti-Semitism. Purported child murders and other anti-Semitic tales circulate in the texts and manuscripts of women's reading. Paris, BN MS f. fr 902, for example, compiles exegetical commentary on the *Eructavit* psalm for the Countess of Champagne with the Anglo-Norman legend of the Jewish ritual murder of Little St Hugh of Lincoln.[90] So, too, the compensatory horror stories of the *Vengeance nostre seignur* narrative, in which Saints Veronica and Clement are involved in Vespasian and Titus's vengeful crusade against Jerusalem. Jewish veins, slit by avenging soldiers, are discovered here to run with silver and gold instead of blood (a discovery also made in English social practice, to go by the example of Eleanor of Provence).[91] Early vernacular versions of the *Vengeance nostre seignur* are among the texts read by women in nunnery and gentry manuscripts.[92]

In the shifts and developments of the high Middle Ages, virgin martyr *passio* intensifies its romancing, its own articulation in tortures and debates, and remaps the gendering and ethnicity of the sacrificeable child. A great deal is happening in and around the *passio* over the twelfth and thirteenth centuries. Women as mothers and childbearers are occluded in the *passio* genre (as will be further discussed in Chapter 4.1), but they can be implicated as well as targeted in the *passio*'s constructions. In a genre so rich and protean as virgin martyr narrative turns out to be, no reading position is guaranteed in advance.

[90] *Eructavit*, ed. Jenkins; *Hugues de Lincoln: Recueil de ballades anglo-normandes et écossoises relatives au meurtre de cet enfant commis par les juifs en mcclv*, ed. F. Michel (Paris: Silvestre and London: Pickering, 1834); Gavin I. Langmuir, 'The Knight's Tale of Young Hugh of Lincoln', *Speculum*, 47 (1972), 459–82.

[91] Alvin Ford (ed.), *La Vengeance de Nostre Seigneur: The Old and Middle French Prose Versions: The Version of Japheth*, Studies and Texts 63 (Toronto: Pontifical Institute of Mediaeval Studies, 1984), 175/955–176/962. Anglo-Norman and French versions of the *Vindicta Salvatoris* circulated vigorously in north-west Europe and also form one of the most widely disseminated *matières* among Middle English legends.

[92] Examples of nunnery manuscripts containing the *Vengeance* are London, BL, MSS Egerton 613 and 2710, and Paris BN f. fr. 19525 (all 13th c., though it is not certain that Egerton 2710 was owned by the nuns of Derby before the 15th c.). They are assigned by Ford to his textual families of I and D (*La Vengeance*, 24). For editions see Alvin Ford, *La Vengeance de Nostre Seigneur: The Old and Middle French Prose Versions* (Toronto: Pontifical Institute of Mediaeval Studies, 1993), 56–64.

4
Honorary Virginities

Although she was never put to death, she bore in her flesh the cross where
Jesus Christ suffered death, when Longinus struck him. In fasting, vigils,
and weeping, she tormented her body night and day . . . There was as much
virtue in this lady as if in the time of Diocletian and Nero when they
carried out the slaughter of Christians in their cruel rage, she did not fear
martyrdom; she was joyful and glad in the torments she had. She was a
martyr without bloodshed, she was a martyr in vigils, in weeping, in her
desire, in hunger, in thirst and in nakedness.

(*La vie sainte Audrée* by Marie [of Chatteris?],
early–mid 13th century)[1]

Behold the rose of martyrdom, the flower desired by God, which does not
refuse its heart to Jesus because of the prick of any thorn, Jesus who was
born incarnate in this world as a rose grows from a thorn and has a sweet
tenderness without the sting [i.e. original sin] of his begetting. [This rose]
smells so much the sweeter the more severely she is pricked: it is those who
suffer martyrdom and shed their blood without anger, those who suffer
violence and do not worry about bodily harm: those religious who have
left everything for Jesus; those people in poverty, indeed, to whom riches
are a torment; those who languish with desire in good hope of God's love.
All who are badly treated, when they suffer gladly for God and for no other
reason, present to God a beautiful rose, and they will have the fruit of their
faith with Christ who suffered wholly for our sake.

(*Évangile des Domnées* for Lady Elena de Quenci, mid-13th century)[2]

---

[1] 'Ja soit iceo ke ele ne fust occise, | Si out ele sur sa char mise | La croiz ou Jhesu Crist
sueffri | La mort, quant Longis le feri. | En jonne, en veillie et en plur | Tormentoit son cors nuit
et jur . . . En ceste dame out si grant bien | C'el tens que Dioclicien | Eust esté et en tens Neron, |
Kant il firent le occision | Des cristiens de cruel ire, | Ele ne dota pas le martire; | Denz tormenz
com ele avoit | Joieuse et lee se fesoit. | Senz sanc espandre fu martir | En veillie, en plur et en
desir, | En feim, en soif, et en nuesce' (vv. 1469–91), *Audrée*, ed. Södergård, 94–5.

[2] 'Veëz la rose de martire | Ço est la flur que Deu desire, | Qui pur pointe de nule espine | Sun
quor de Jesu ne decline; | Qui charnelment en cest mund nest | Cume rose del espinel crest, | E
ad en sei duce tendrur | Sanz pointe de sun genitur. | Qui de tant flaire plus suef | Cum ele seit
pointe plus gref, | Ço sunt cil que soffrent martire | E lur sanc fundent sanz ire; | Ço sunt cil que
soffrent tolage | E ne curent charnel damage; | Ço sunt cil de religün | Que tut unt lessé pur
Jesum; | Ço sunt, en veir, la poure gent | A qui les riches sunt turment; | Ço sunt qui soffrent
langur | En bon espeir pur Deu amur. | Trestuz qui sunt malmenez, | Quant il le soffrent de lur
grez | Pur Deue pur nul altre chose, | A Deu presentent bele rose | E lur frut averunt de fi | Od
Crist qui tut pur nos suffri' (*Évangile des domnées*, ed. Panunzio, 116/270–117/295).

This chapter is concerned with the relations between virginity and maternity especially as mediated by penance and asceticism. The imaging of the female reader, secular or religious, as virgin heroine of nuptial romance values the suffering of martyrdom and asceticism over women's experiences of maternity (the socio-economic value of women's production being in any case occluded and refigured as spiritual in virgin representations). The chapter explores continuities between religious and secular lives to argue, first, that some female writings and receptions of cultural maternity represent it as productive again for women. Secondly, I argue that the very intensity with which penance is required of non-virgin women makes its powers also useful to women. Hagiographic repentant harlots and *vitae patrum* figures are in various and potentially misogynist relations with contemporary reformulations of imagined cultural spaces, most especially the 'authorized' associations of virginity with the spiritually valuable desert of twelfth-century eremetic reform. Nevertheless, this literature also serves women by providing in effect templates and handbooks on the prestige of penance. Penance and asceticism become modes in which widows and mothers can claim the powers of the virgin-martyr ideal for lives within and outside the enclosures of convents and households. Over the thirteenth century, new models of female sanctity and piety are created in which the relations of holy women with the wider cultural and fiscal economy are reimagined. An increasing number of honorary virginities join the figure of the virgin martyr. At the same time, the extension of virginity to a socio-economically indispensable audience of married and widowed women helps maintain the status of professional virginity as a relevant and powerful ideal in the laicization of thirteenth-century spirituality.

4.1. RESPONSES TO ENCLOSURE: VIRGIN ROMANCE AND MATERNITY

'Holy virgins seek their true spouse in blood', as Hildebert of Lavardin says in his letters to women, while in one Anglo-Norman *Tristan*, Isolde, like a heroine of asceticism, wears an iron corselet ('bruine a sa char nue') during her marriage, so as to share the exiled Tristan's suffering.[3] The notion that female enclosure is both a form of martyrdom and a proper response to the shedding of blood by Christ constructs powerful links between romance, suffering, and reading. Invoked as a model of infinite and immeasurable suffering, Christ is also a figure of control and desire. Since Christ's sinless virgin flesh was more sensitive to pain than any other human's, his suffering always relativizes any-

---

[3] 'Holy virgins and widows . . . have offered their bodies as a living sacrifice, consecrated, pleasing to God, yielding with reason their compliance. So it is that amidst the fire Agnes gave thanks, in the torture of her breasts Agatha praised God, other holy virgins sought their true spouse in blood, choosing rather to follow the Lamb wherever he might go, than a man who followed evil' (Hildebert of Lavardin, Letter of *c*.1131, 'For the encouragement [*confortatio*] of a nun', PL171.191); for *Tristan* see *Thomas of Britain: Tristan*, ed. Gregory, 104, v. 2029.

thing of which an enclosed woman might wish to complain ('Lady, nothing ought to seem hard to you, for he sends you nothing he has not faithfully suffered himself', says one treatise for Anglo-Norman nuns couched as a love-letter of greeting and comfort through the love of Christ, the 'Salut et solace par l'amour de Jésu').[4] An infinitely expanding economy of desire and perpetual aspiration thus underpins and maintains the dynamic stasis in which the enclosed woman reads her own romance heroineship. What is often at stake for the heroine is a physically contained self whose psychic boundaries indefinitely recede in absorption and identification with others. Nevertheless, as argued in the previous chapters, some representation of agency is possible in female suffering, viewed as a gift to Christ. Further versions of agency emerge in the applications and appropriations of the virgin model for other kinds of women.

The converted queens of the late twelfth-century *passiones* discussed in the previous chapter suffer even more graphically than their virgin role-models. They are one example of the honorary virginities and martyrdoms of the twelfth and thirteenth centuries. For the virgin-wife-widow-princess-foundress-saint Audrée in the thirteenth-century Life by Marie quoted at the head of this chapter, asceticism is a martyrdom without blood. For the married Elena de Quenci martyrdom is shown as a sliding scale of assimilations from courage under torture to the stifling of longing and unhappiness. By the end of the passage quoted above, marital or any other discontents of Elena's privileged life can be given structure and purpose as a version of martyrdom.

Many of the forms and powers of household and maternity are represented in the conventions of virginity and martyrdom, and this particularly applies to the penitential and purgative aspects of female secular and religious enclosure in its late twelfth- and thirteenth-century forms. But such representation is often indirect. The suffering most distinctively experienced by women is represented in oblique ways. Women are generally represented as grieving for their children and relatives more than for themselves. Their grief is given a high cultural value as a form of exchange between the living and the dead, less directly valued as women's experience.[5] Childbirth and its associated fears and agonies are testified to in women's shrine attendances and pilgrimages; are silenced in the perfection and painlessness of the Virgin; reappear as grief in her com-passion at the crucifixion; are mentioned as a deterrent in virginity treatises and addressed in gynaecological handbooks. Many saints, including male saints, are consulted over fertility and over problems of deformity and illness in children. But, apart from the pain-exempt Virgin herself, no childbearing woman presides over this most pressing and recurrent female need for saintly intercession. Vernacular lives of saintly biological mothers first emerge in England in the later thirteenth

---

[4] 'Dame, ren ne *vus* deít sembler dur. kar reen ne *vus* enveit/ ke il memes [ne] suffry leuament': see Betty Hill, 'British Library, Ms. Egerton 613—II', *Notes and Queries*, NS 25/223 (Dec. 1978), 492–501 (498, §12).

[5] See Barbara Newman, '"Cruel Corage"' and 'On the Threshold of the Dead: Purgatory, Hell, and Religious Women', in her *From Virile Woman to WomanChrist*, 108–37.

century, in the Bozon legendary discussed later in this chapter, while the 'official' and most intensely culted helper of women in childbirth from the late twelfth century onwards is St Margaret, a virgin martyr.[6] (In the thirteenth century, Margaret is joined, in Anglo-Norman, by St Francis, who has a number of vernacular lives and whose miracles are often associated with maternal and infant needs.)[7] Most of the numerous twelfth- and thirteenth-century versions of Margaret's Life stage martyrdom in part as a version of birth: Margaret emerges triumphant from an engulfing demonic dragon, a boiling cauldron, an earth-quake. The dragon threatening her in her enclosure—the cell to which she is consigned by her pagan tyrant—is a spectacular Hammer horror creature and seems at first sight, with his glaring eyes and sword-like tongue, a consuming phallic monster, the confrontation of saint and monster like that of Andromeda and the monster from the sea-depths. But the dragon's gendering is less fixed than this suggests since he also functions as the birthing body from which Margaret's spiritual life emerges.[8] If such a reading makes hellish dragons of birthing bodies, it seems none the less to have articulated the experience of birth for many women: Margaret's Life was read aloud to, or worn as amulets by, women in labour.[9]

However, as recent studies have also increasingly elucidated, maternity is not only an extremely dangerous occupation for medieval women, and one

---

[6] See further Jocelyn Wogan-Browne, 'The Apple's Message: Some Post-Conquest Hagiographic Accounts of Textual Transmission', in A. J. Minnis (ed.), *Late Medieval Religious Texts: Essays in Honour of A. I. Doyle*, York Manuscripts Conferences, Proceedings Series 3 (Cambridge: Brewer, 1994), 39–54 (to the instances cited in this article there can be added Eleanor of Provence's invocation of Saint Margaret in childbirth and subsequent naming of her daughter as Margaret, *Chron. maj.* iv. 48: compare the very different role of saints at Eleanor's wedding suggested in Ch. 1, n. 128 above).

[7] Extracts edited by Janice M. Pindar, 'The Lives of St. Francis of Assisi contained in MSS BN f. fr. 19531, 2094, 13505' (D.Phil. thesis, University of Oxford, 1985): edition for ANTS by D. W. Russell forthcoming. For a 13th-c. Continental French life, see Janice M. Pindar (ed.), *The Life of Saint Francis of Assisi: A Critical Edition of the Ms Paris, Bibl. Nat. fonds françaises 2094* (Rome: Archivum Franciscanum Historicum, 1995).

[8] Rather than a phallic sea-monster, one might think here of medieval alternations of women and dragons, as in the Melusine story, or the iconography of the Virgin Mary trampling the siren (see Laurent Harf-Lancner, *Les Fées au Moyen Age: Morgane et Mélusine. La naissance des fées* (Paris: Champion, 1984), chs. 4–5).

[9] Margaret's re-emergence, frequently illustrated in women's psalters and books of hours as it is, is very much a view of birth from outside a body capable of it, so that the saint emerges, as in a Caesarean birth, from the dragon's split belly (see Renate Blumenfeld-Kosinski, *Not of Woman Born: Representations of Caesarean Birth in Medieval and Renaissance Culture* (Ithaca and London: Cornell University Press, 1990)). Birth is used to figure redemption in the influential sermons of Maurice Sully (extant in Anglo-Norman manuscripts): for example, Sermo 18 (Easter Sunday), 'La femme com ele doit enfanter, si est triste . . .', where the pain of childbirth is compared with the apostles' joy in the resurrection (see C. A. Robson (ed.), *Maurice de Sully and the Medieval Vernacular Homily* (Oxford: Blackwell, 1952), 123/16–21). See also Simon of Walsingham's identification with Faith's birth-death day, Ch. 2.2 above, and for the crucifixion as birth in medieval lyric, *Moral Love Songs*, ed. Fein, 92–4.

represented in constrained ways in the portrayal of women and the holy, but also a significant form of power.[10] There is a great deal of testimony, some of it by negation and abjection, to this. The *Guide for Anchoresses*, for instance, is tellingly careful to ascribe maternity only to Christ and not to its own female audiences and to subordinate maternal imagery to romance imagery in the experience it scripts for them. In its seventh section, on Love, the *Guide*'s famous image of Christ as a mother shedding a bathful of her own blood to save her sick child is offered *en route* to a romance climax, where the anchoress's response is figured as a blazing liquescence kindled by the courtly and violent Christ-bridegroom (see Chapter 3.1 above). The anchoress is Christ's child, but, unlike the texts of so many women visionaries, Christ is never shown as hers: affectivity and maternity accrues to Christ, but the symbolic 'reproduction of mothering' is not imagined for his brides.[11] The maternity of women is also figured as absence (in a way associated by Freud with the infant's exploration of the death drive) when the *Guide* shows Christ-as-mother playing Freud's *fort-da* game:

our Lord when he allows us to be tempted, is playing with us like a mother with her little child. She runs away from him and hides herself, and lets him sit alone and look eagerly about crying 'Mother!' and crying for a while: and then with open arms she jumps out laughing, and hugs and kisses him and wipes his eyes. So our Lord sometimes lets us be alone and withdraws his grace, his comfort, and his support . . . and yet at the same time our dear father does not love us any the less.[12]

Maternity and death are further linked for the *Guide* through Christ's enclosure in the womb and in the tomb: the anchorhouse must mean death to the world if it is to be a nurturant spiritual enclosure.[13] Many other post-Conquest

[10] Mulder-Bakker, Introduction to ead. (ed.), *Sanctity and Motherhood*; Parsons and Wheeler (eds.), *Medieval Mothering* (esp. Introduction and the essays by Chibnall, Huneycutt, Lo Prete, Parsons).

[11] Links between romance as the normalizing form for heterosexual household-formation and a particular construction of maternal nurture have been persuasively argued for, both in modern psychoanalytic theory and in modern readings of medieval and modern romance. Using Nancy Chodorow's theory of the pre-Oedipal stage for women, Janice Radway argues that romance mediates the relations of the female self with husband and mother as constituted within patriarchy, and offers 'spectacular masculinity as heterosexual lover, confirming the completeness of the reader's rejection of her childlike self, while at the same time [the hero's] capacity for tenderness and gentle nurturance allows her to return to the primary love and total security of pre-Oedipal relation with her mother' (*Reading the Romance*, 147; see further 140, 138).

[12] 'Nostre seignour quant il soeffre qe nous soioms temptez, il se iue od vous [*sic*] ausi come la mere od son cher enfansonet: ele se enfut de li et se musce et le lest seer soul et regarde ententiuement entour sei, apeler "dame" et plurer vne piece, et dunqe, od braz estenduz, salt auant riant, l'acole et boise et tert ses eoilz. En ceste maniere nostre seignour nous lest ascune foiz sul a couenir et retret sa grace, son confort, et son solaz . . . et nepurquant en cel meisme point ne nous eime ia le meins nostre cher piere', Herbert, 154/13–34 (Tolkien, f. 62b/6–16; *Anchoritic Spirituality*, tr. Savage and Watson, 132).

[13] See Herbert, 274/34–275/4; Tolkien, f. 102b/2–5. For a more positive view of the *Guide*'s tactics here, see Catherine Innes Parker, 'Fragmentation and Reconstruction: Images of the Body in *Ancrene Wisse* and the Katherine Group', *Comitatus*, 26 (1995), 27–52.

texts make comparable associations between death, maternity, and enclosure. So, for instance, Herman de Valenciennes' *Bible*, or 'Romanz de Dieu et de sa mere', where the lament for Henry II associates womb, cloister, grave:

> Molt est hom feble chose et de feble nature
> Qant est dedans la mere molt a povre clouture
> Il n'i oit ne ne veit, molt est la chambre oscure,
> Molt travaille la mere, n'en set nule mesure
> Car qant il naise et ist de sa povre clouture
> Ne se puet removoir, chiet sor la terre dure.[14]

> Man is a feeble creature with a weak nature:
> When he is inside his mother he is poorly cloistered
> He neither hears nor sees, the chamber is dark:
> The mother knows no measure in her labour [for him]
> For when he is born and comes out of his wretched cloister
> He cannot move for himself, but falls on the hard earth.

The maternal body here is figured as profoundly *unheimlich*, a much less comfortable cloister than that of a monastery.[15]

Maternity seems differently viewed and valued in the writings of women in the twelfth and thirteenth centuries. A woman writer who may herself have had a career both at the Angevin court and in the cloister reworks the figure of the lover-knight of treatises and *passio* in a work dealing with secular marriage as enclosure.[16] Marie de France's *lai* of *Yonec* has often been read as a courtly love tale standardly preoccupied with adultery as 'fin'amor', focusing its important issues around the dramatic eruption of the lover-knight into the heroine's imprisonment in her tower. This has made the *lai*'s Corpus Christi imagery, enlisted as it is in the representation of desire for a love better than marital, problematic for early twentieth-century secular 'courtly love' scholarship: how blasphemous is refined adultery allowed to become?[17] The *lai* has an unnamed

[14] *Li Romanz de Dieu et de sa mère*, ed. Spiele, 315–16, vv. 5648–54. This circulates widely in insular manuscript collections of the 12th to 14th c.: see ibid. 144–57 for a list, to which Maureen Boulton has recently added Dublin, Trinity College MS 374 (paper given to the Anglo-Norman Colloquium, St Peter's College, Oxford, Apr. 1998).

[15] Not all representations of enclosure and maternity involve such abjections. Nicholas Bozon, for instance, develops the nuptial mysticism of the king's bride with theological precision and delicacy to include the Virgin's role in the incarnation. In his haunting version of the allegory 'Du roy ki aveit jadis une amie', the king is armed for the rescue of his lady by 'une damoysele' in her chamber (vv. 40–1), where she gives him the borrowed armour 'de un son bacheler | Qe Adam fu nomé' (vv. 38–9): a jerkin of pure white flesh padded not with cotton but with blood; for cuisses and greaves, groin and thighs; for leg-plates, well-fitting bones: see *The Anglo-Norman Lyric: An Anthology*, ed. David L. Jeffrey and Brian J. Levy (Toronto: Pontifical Institute of Mediaeval Studies, 1990), 'Coment le fiz Deu fu armé en la croyz', 186–91.

[16] For a useful summary of studies on the identity of Marie de France, see Yolande de Pont Farcy (ed.), *L'Espurgatoire seint Patriz: Nouvelle édition critique accompagnée du De Purgatorio Sancti Patricii* (Louvain and Paris: Peeters, 1995), Introduction.

[17] For an excellent critique of the older scholarship, see Arlyn Diamond, 'Engendering Criticism', in *Thought*, 64 (1989), 298–309.

heroine who spends her married life locked in a tower by a wealthy old husband.[18] He is lord of the fief of Caerwent and has married in order to have an heir. It is noted that though there are other women in the establishment, they are in a separate room and the heroine (more solitary than the reading anchoress) is not allowed contact with them. She first develops resistance to her ferocious elderly duenna and her husband in the spring by remembering romance tales of knights and ladies: musing over these in her enclosure she articulates her sorrow for her exclusion from romance and desire. As in the *Guide for Anchoresses*, this contemplation produces a vivid and present evocation of a lover, not the wooing Christ lover-knight who explodes rhetorically into the solitary woman's chamber in Part Seven of the *Guide*, but a lover who flies through the barred window as an aristocratic hawk-knight. When he has taken communion *in the shape of the heroine* to reassure her, they become lovers. (Communion is at first denied the heroine, but, by feigning mortal sickness, she succeeds in having a priest brought in to adminster it, thus, like many other medieval women, successfully combating restricted access to the eucharist.)[19] When her happier demeanour alerts her husband and duenna to the change in her, they place sharpened stakes in the window of the heroine's chamber and the hawk is mortally wounded. As he leaves her for the last time, the distraught heroine leaps from the chamber window and follows the trail of blood left by her dying lover to his beautiful kingdom within a mountain. He gives her his sword to keep for the son she will have by him and sends her back for her own safety, together with the promise that her old husband will not remember or reproach her for what has happened. This indeed is the case: the heroine manages to steal back inside her enclosure and she and her old husband bring up her son, who is greatly prized by them both. When he comes of age, the boy slays his official father in revenge for his mother's chosen lover's death. There is no condemnation or sanction for this act: the son becomes the lord of his father's people, while his mother, swooning on her lover's tomb and dying while still unconscious, is buried with honour.

It is significant that in all but one of the extant manuscripts this *lai* is titled after the child, Yonec, not after the hawk-lover, Muldumarec.[20] Critical

[18] *Yonec*, in *Marie de France: Lais*, ed. Alfred Ewert with Introduction and Bibliography by Glyn S. Burgess (Oxford: Blackwell, 1944; repr. London: Bristol Classical Press, 1995), 82–96. For examples of secular imprisonments of wives, see Ch. 1, n. 47 above. As Cecily Clark has shown, the case of the imprisoned Agnes de Vere is of special interest in relation to *Yonec* ('La Vie féminine en Angleterre au temps d'Aliénor d'Aquitaine', *Cahiers de civilisation médiévale*, 29 (1986), 49–51).

[19] Bynum, 'Women Mystics and Eucharistic Devotion', repr. in her *Fragmentation and Redemption*, 119–50. *Ancrene Wisse* limits communion to 15 times a year on the grounds that 'people care less about what they have often' (Millett and Wogan-Browne, 131 (Vitellius, 302/31–2) and see Bella Millett, 'The Origins of *Ancrene Wisse*: New Answers, New Questions', *Medium Ævum*, 61 (1992), 206–28 (209–10)).

[20] 'Yonec' is also the title by which the *lai* is known in the Southern Version of the *Cursor Mundi*: see Sarah M. Horrall (gen. ed.), *The Southern Version of the Cursor Mundi*, 5 vols. (Ottawa: University of Ottawa Press, 1978–2000), i. 33, line 19, and 342 n. 19.

readings of the *lai* privileging male subjects and their amatory and sacrificial pain focus on the status of the hawk and the question of whether courtly adultery is being endorsed or not. But if the heroine's desire is taken as the focus, the *lai* falls into line with its title to suggest that the production of a loved child and the replacement of her husband by her son in her affections is the most constructive thing the heroine can do with her situation. She is isolated, imprisoned in her household and marriage, her communication with other women more restricted than that of anchoresses. She can only love and act through her child, and producing a child is both what she has been married for and her major route to power in the household and to some kind of affective life. Whether we are to see the hawk-knight as a figure for a literal affair (the shape-shifting encoding the elements of fantasy and socially unsanctioned desire) with the husband willing to forget the adultery in his need for heirs, or whether we are to see the hawk-knight as a bird onto whom a fantasy is mapped which enables the woman to endure her husband and to conceive by him seems to me relatively unimportant (though the second alternative is more precise): either reading runs with the narrative actualization of the woman's desire, and it is this which provides the crucial perspective in the *lai*'s narrative structure and which moves past the suffering and passion of male lovers to the production of children. The passionate, bleeding, caring hawk-lover and his desirable realm of power within her husand's fief encode a vestigially glamorous version of marriage as offering fulfilled heterosexual desire and the power of landed property to women. But the unnamed woman heroine and reader of the *lai* thinks on past the romance of marital enclosure: she reads, uses, and transforms its power relations in a paradox of subversion and fulfilment. In this account by a woman writer of how a woman might make the restrictive conditions of her marriage bearable enough to herself to be able to become fecund in them, we get a narrative of female desire which suddenly illuminates by implication how occluded the pain and suffering of women may be. It is less rhetorical but in some ways more eloquent than the graphic accounts of the horrors of maternity and the woes of marriage which become such fecund topoi in writings on virginity such as *Hali Meiðhad* (the early thirteenth-century *Letter on Virginity for the Encouragement of Virgins*) and its Latin analogues.

In the *lai* of *Yonec*, marriage is as much an enclosure as any form of spiritual life offered to post-Conquest women as an alternative, and there are many crossovers between 'secular' and 'spiritual' romance for women. The production of maternity by women is also observable from places of enclosure and darkness in spiritual romance, for example. One might compare, from (probably) about the same date as *Yonec*, Clemence of Barking's Anglo-Norman *St Catherine*, which transforms the saint's imprisonment by adding maternity to the Latin *vita*'s equation of dungeon and cloister:

Christ placed himself in a narrow dungeon when he took our humanity. He whom the whole world cannot contain lay for a long time in a womb. But he encompasses the entire world and all creatures within it . . . For love of him, I shall gladly accept the darkness of this dungeon which I see here, for he did much more for me. I must tell you that in return for this darkness such light will be given to me that no tempest or chill wind will ever dim it.[21]

This is very different from the topos as deployed by the *Guide* or Hermann de Valenciennes. So too the contemporary holy woman Christina of Markyate is represented as dealing with heterosexuality via maternity. Christina finds that her wedding-night retelling of the legend of the virgin wife and martyr St Cecilia to the bridegroom forced on her by her parents is insufficent defence against forced consummation. She then, like the heroine of *Yonec*, leaps out of her enclosure in the (wrong) nuptial chamber. She jumps a high fence 'with amazing ease', and flees into an anchorhold.[22] After difficulties worthy of a virgin martyr she becomes established in her religious career, and it is just at this point of relative security that she is represented as most tempted, and as resolving a martyrdom of sexual desire by spiritual maternity:

She violently resisted the desires of the flesh, lest her own members should become the agents of wickedness against her. Long fastings, little food, and that only of raw herbs, a measure of water to drink, nights spent without sleep, harsh scourgings . . . She called on God without ceasing not to allow her, who had taken a vow of virginity and had refused the marriage bed, to perish for ever . . . Then the Son of the Virgin looked kindly down upon the low estate of His handmaid and granted her the consolation of an unheard-of grace. For in the guise of a small child He came to the arms of his sorely tried spouse and remained with her a whole day, not only being felt but also seen . . . Who shall describe the abounding sweetness with which the servant was filled by this condescension of her creator? From that moment the fire of lust was so completely extinguished that never afterwards could it be revived.[23]

This is a monastic text and one with a strong interest in representing its heroine's influence on the author's abbot as that of chaste spiritual *amicitia*, but it again demonstrates a contextual incorporation of maternity in virginity.

If the leaky female body requires sealing and enclosure, it must also open as the body of (re-)production. The question of productivity from within the enclosure arouses powerfully ambivalent responses and much masking of the socio-economic value of women's labour of (re-)production.[24] Yet if there are male fears and abjections shaping representational codes here and providing psychic imperatives for the policing of enclosure and the claustration of women's bodies, the very force of these drives also allows cultural prestige and urgency to accrue to the penitential roles of female bodies. Prostrate and hair-shirted

---

[21] *Life of Saint Catherine*, ed. MacBain, vv. 1441–6, 1449–56. For the Latin source here ('ego tenebrosi carceris horrorem amplecti gaudeo . . . per has lux perpetua michi paratur') see *Seinte Katerine*, ed. Dobson and d'Ardenne, 178/651–5.
[22] *Life of Christina*, ed. Talbot, 52.   [23] Ibid. 114–18.
[24] For an account of this masking in 14th-c. texts, see Nancy Bradley Warren, 'Pregnancy and Productivity: The Imagery of Female Monasticism Within and Beyond the Cloister Walls', *JMEMS* 28 (1998), 531–52.

among the ashes while lyrically pleading entry to the inner chamber of bridal bliss, David the jongleur-psalmist of the Countess of Champagne's *chançun* is in part a figure of the pious woman's devotional recitation: penitence is the way to the nuptial enclosure of a reconstructed virginity.[25]

4.2. REPENTING AT LEISURE: VIRGINITY, HARLOTRY, HOUSEHOLDING

> 'Religiun', dient, 'vodrunt entrer
> Mes nos baruns nel uolenint granter.
> Nos volers volum meuz lesser
> Qe nos mariz corucer.'
> (Waddington, *Manuel des pechés*)[26]

'We wanted', [the virtuous wives] said, 'to enter religion, but our husbands would not agree. We would rather give up our own wishes than make our husbands angry.'

For the late twelfth and thirteenth centuries, the model of the penitent, purgatorial, and purged woman has special value and creates its own subgenres of reading, concerned indirectly or directly with maternity and the profound ambivalences aroused by the indispensably fecund and non-virgin female body. The reforming canons and monks of the eleventh and twelfth centuries—the Augustinians and Premonstratensians and the Cistercians—gave renewed power to patristic images of the desert as a source of spiritual renewal and themselves created many fresh sites for foundation in an increasingly urbanized twelfth-century Europe. Further impelled by the insular precocity in confessors' manuals and treatises on penance (written before as well as after Lateran IV in 1215), an efflorescence of vernacular treatises and exempla inculcating the value of confession and penance appears during the thirteenth century.[27] The cultural significance of the desert as a trope of foundation and spiritual renewal has been well studied for male monasticism, but has its own particular inflections in the history of women's texts, where it is closely associated with the anchoritic cell and a life of penitential prayer.

Connections between female bodies, purgation, and anchoritic enclosure are explicit in a late twelfth-century Life of the penitent harlot saint, Thaïs. When the abbot Paphnutius has converted her from her career of successful courtesanship,

---

[25] See *Eructavit: An Old French Metrical Paraphrase of Psalm xliv*, ed. T. A. Jenkins (Dresden: Gesellschaft für romanische Literatur, 1909), 7–9, vv. 149–53, 201–4. On this figure see Isabelle Marchesin, 'Les Jongleurs dans les psautiers du haut moyen âge: nouvelles hypothèses sur la symbolique de l'histrion médiéval', in *Cahiers de civilisation médiévale*, 41 (1998), 127–39.

[26] Printed in *Handlyng Synne*, ed. F. J. Furnivall, EETS os 119 (London, 1901), 71, vv. 2471–94.

[27] Jean-Charles Payen, *Le Motif du repentir dans la littérature française médiévale* (Geneva: Droz, 1968), esp. 62–88. On the expanding use of the *exemplum* in the 13th c. see J. Th. Welter, *L'Exemplum dans la littérature religieuse et didactique du Moyen Age* (Paris and Toulouse: Occitania, 1927), 83–108.

Par soi en une petite celle la ferma,
E l'us de la celle de plum enseela,
E un poi d'ewe e de pain cum il li mesura
Parmi une fenestre doner li comanda.
E quant li abas Panuncius devoit aler,
Dunc li comença Thaisis a demander:
'Coment doi je, bel pere, Dampnedeu preer?
E u doi je me naturelement espurger?'
E il diseit: 'En la cell t'espurgeras,
E la mesaise que tu es digne sufferas'.[28]

[He] enclosed her by herself in a small cell, and he sealed the doorway of the cell with lead, and ordered a little bread and water, as he apportioned for her, to be given her through a window. And when Abbot Paphnutius had to leave, Thaïs asked him, 'How should I, good father, pray to God? And where should I relieve myself as nature demands?' and he said to her, 'You will relieve yourself in the cell and suffer the discomfort you deserve'.

The cell is to contain both Thaïs's straying female body and its exudations in penitential disciplines of prayer and purgation. (That this may not have been how women viewed the question of cell hygiene is suggested by Christina of Markyate's twelfth-century biography, for which she herself must have supplied much of the material.[29] It is mentioned as a source of distress to Christina—and hence as a point of ascetic heroism—that 'she could not go *out* until the evening to satisfy the demands of nature'.[30] In any case, the standard Anglo-Norman polite word for lavatory, *chambre foreine*, assumes a separate external lavatory as normative, as is also envisaged in the thirteenth-century English *The Owl and the Nightingale*, possibly written for or at the nunnery of Shaftesbury.)[31]

Excrement in the *vitae* of the repentant harlot has been linked with the ill-gotten gains of prostitution, but if so, this is only the beginning of its significance. As argued in earlier chapters, prostitution is more likely in insular saints' lives

[28] 'Henri d'Arci: The Shorter Works', ed. R. C. Perman, in E. A. Francis (ed.), *Studies in Medieval French Presented to Alfred Ewert* (Oxford: Clarendon Press, 1961), 284, vv. 65–74. This life is included in the *Vie des pères* collection made for (not, as was once thought, by) the Templar Henri d'Arci of Temple Bruer, Lincoln, *c*.1160–1180, see ibid. 279, and for an edition see n. 39 below.
[29] For the creation of saints' biographies through a combination of observation, reminiscence, and dictation by the saint herself, see Aviad M. Kleinberg, *Prophets in Their Own Country: Living Saints and the Making of Sainthood in the Later Middle Ages* (Chicago and London: University of Chicago Press, 1992). For the composition of the life of Christina of Markyate, see *Life of Christina*, ed. Talbot, 6–7.
[30] Ibid. 105.
[31] Roberta Gilchrist points to the relative modesty of nunnery lavatories compared with the grandeur of male monastic latrines (*Gender and Material Culture*, 113–15, 125–6): the *Guide*'s image envisages a small communal lavatory ('dous parties de chambre priuee', Herbert, 191/38–192/1; '*deus trous d'une* chambre foreine', Trethewey, 2/10). For Shaftesbury and *The Owl and the Nightingale* see Alexandra Barratt, 'Flying in the Face of Tradition: A New View of The Owl and the Nightingale', *University of Toronto Quarterly*, 56 (1987), 471–85.

to signal a shame/honour distinction concerned with sanctioned ways of disposing of women and territory.[32] Thaïs is upper-class: her prostitution a matter of misplaced desire, not economic necessity. The purgation of the body is most important here for signalling Thaïs as anchoress (a connection underlined when Paphnutius seals Thaïs's penitential cell with lead: this was a standard aspect of the ritual of enclosure by which anchoresses began their life of consecrated penance).[33] Like Thaïs, the anchoress is a producer of ordure, *is* ordure:

En mie lieu del honour de vostre face qest la plus bele partie de vostre corps, entre le gust de la bouche e odorement de la nes, ne portez vus ausi come dous parties de chambre privee? (Herbert, p. 191/32–192/1)[34]

In the middle of your lovely face which is the most beautiful part of you, between your mouth's ability to taste and your nose's to smell, do you not bear the two holes of a latrine?

Spiritually, she is, like Thaïs, to void herself in the cell:

La deit ele baler [Trethewey: uomisse; Tolkien: speowe] hors plenerement tout cele merueilles. La od ouertes paroles l'ordure solum ceo qele est plenerement defoler. (Herbert, p. 347/31–3)[35]

There she should sweep [vomit] all these things out [in confession]. There with plain words she should openly dishonour the ordure [of her sins] according to what it is.

But both Thaïs and the anchoress are also images of purgation for their society as a whole: their prayers have special value, and their self-abasement and humility is a strong, if inverted, form of prestige.[36]

---

[32] So Ruth Mazo Karras, 'Sex, Money, and Prostitution in Medieval English Culture', in Murray and Eisenblichler (eds.), *Desire and Discipline*, 207. (Karras deals principally with later medieval English texts in making this argument.)

[33] *Ancrene Wisse*, ed. Shepherd, pp. xxxiv–xxxv; Warren, *Anchorites and their Patrons*, 97–8, and, on the blocking of the cell door as symbolic, 98 n. 15.

[34] See Tolkien, f. 75b/11–13. For the Middle English term 'drawing chambre', see L. C. Salzman, *Building in England: A Documentary History Down to 1542* (Oxford: Clarendon Press, 1952), 484.

[35] Vitellius translates cryptically here (compare 'culle al the pot ut; ther speowe ut al that wunder; there with fule wordes that fulthe efter that hit is tuke al towundre', Tolkien, f. 93b/16–19), and perhaps takes 'ordure' not as excrement but in a more polite general sense of 'refuse, rubbish' to arrive at its verb *baler*, 'to sweep' (where Trinity and Tolkien have 'she should *vomit*'). The verb 'defuler' can also mean 'trample, defile, ill-treat', so the penitent may in Vitellius be envisaged as trampling rubbish underfoot in using filthy words for the filth of sin. Trinity vigorously elaborates female confession ('There in front of her confessor she should vomit everything out and throw out all the venom and filth and monstrousness ['le uenimet tute la ordure e toute la merueille'] that she has thought, spoken, handled, and done in the order of her sin, of weakness by night and likewise by day, as it has befallen her', see Trethewey, 113/18–24), but is more restrained for male confession ('If you have been incontinent, that is, unchaste in either mind or body, repent of this and confess it as soon as possible', Trinity, 111/33–112/2).

[36] On the prestige of reclusion, see Ch. 1.1 above. Warren, *Anchorites and their Patrons* is the most comprehensive study: for penitential intercession as exchange with the afterlife see Joel C. Rosenthal, *The Purchase of Paradise: Gift Giving and the Aristocracy 1307–1485* (London: Routledge & Kegan Paul, 1972); for a Continental comparison, Anneke B. Mulder-Bakker, 'Lame Margaret of Magdeburg: The Social Functions of a Medieval Recluse', *JMH* 22 (1996), 155–69; for women's engagement in this exchange see the essays by Barbara Newman cited in n. 5 above.

Thaïs is also, like anchoresses, associated with the desert fathers, and her Life often circulates in compilations of the *vitae patrum* or *vie des pères*.[37] The *vitae patrum* vernacular collections, recognizable as behavioural and biographical exempla though they are, are very different from the 'high' formal genres of monastic hagiographic and historiographic *vitae*.[38] But they seem to have functioned as an ancilliary and 'informal' hagiographic genre, part-way between the *vita* and the conduct book, and to have provided models not only for the professional religious, but for semi-religious and lay people. Latin versions of such texts had long been used as texts of male monastic socialization, but they become feminized in a number of ways over the late twelfth and thirteenth centuries. *Vitae matrum* lives figure increasingly in the collections: for instance, the desert mothers Sarre and Sincletica join the Thaïs life quoted above in the manuscript of the Anglo-Norman *vie des pères* made for the Templar Henri d'Arci of Temple Bruer, Lincoln. Sincletica, although eremitic, is clearly envisaged as the leader of a small community, preaching to her household of 'sorors' and 'non-ains' on chastity, on the medicine of confession, on the control of food desires and the custody of the senses.[39] *Vitae patrum* tales figure in the books of lay as well as professed women in newly translated and recycled forms, and the asceticism of the desert fathers becomes associated with female pious lives, even and especially the lives of married women.[40] The Thaïs life included in Lady Elena

[37] *Vitae patrum*, PL73.661–3; *The Exempla of Jacques de Vitry*, ed. T. F. Crane (London: Nutt for the Folklore Society, 1890), nos. 256–7 (108, 244–5); *Legenda Aurea*, ed. Graesse, cap. clii.

[38] See Constance L. Rosenthal, *The 'Vitae Patrum' in Old and Middle English Literature* (Philadelphia: Graduate School of the University of Philadelphia, 1936). The *vitae patrum* are often supplemented by or circulate with e.g. Cassian's *Collationes*, Gregory the Great's *Dialogues*, and, later, Caesarius of Heisterbach's *Dialogus Miraculorum*. On the *vitae patrum* and their posterity see Elliott, *Roads to Paradise*, chs. 3–6.

[39] *Vitas Patrum: A Thirteenth-Century Anglo-Norman Rimed Translation of the Verba Seniorum*, ed. Bro. B. A. O'Connor (Washington DC: Catholic University of America Press, 1949), vv. 5396–5433, 6559–72. Sincletica also discourses ('sermun dist', v. 5289) on temptations after the noviciate (vv. 5290–5305) to an apparently male audience (female audiences, however, could be included and even represented by male pronouns); and on treasuring up one's good deeds for God, not public display (vv. 6357–74). K. V. Sinclair argues for a date before the late 1170s for the *Vie des pères*, *Thaïs*, and related works ('The Translations of the *Vitas Patrum*, *Thaïs*, *Antichrist*, and *Vision de saint Paul* made for Anglo-Norman Templars: Some Neglected Literary Considerations', *Speculum*, 72 (1997), 741–62 (761) and suggests they were made in London by a priest, 762).

[40] In an insular context the figure of Thaïs is inflected as an anchoress: on the other side of the Channel in Flanders she was already explicitly a figure of confession and penitence, her life interpolated in the influential Walloon *Poème moral* of *c*.1200 in the most frequently transmitted section of the poem and specifically addressed to women (*Le Poème moral: Traité de vie chrétienne écrit dans la région wallone vers l'an 1200*, ed. Alphonse Bayot, Académie Royale de langue et de littérature françaises de Belgique, Textes anciens, I (Brussels: Palais des Académies, 1929), 'La vie de sainte Thaisien, uns bons exemples as dames ki soi orguillent de lor bealteit', Distinctio primum, cap. vii. 32)). Bayot thinks the poem pre-Lateran IV (it inserts a confession treatise in the Thaïs Life (vv. 761–1108) but without specifying how many times to confess in a year). Thaïs Lives, like much else, cross the Channel in women's books: for example, a translation of the *Vie des pères* was made for Blanche of Navarre, Countess of Champagne, between 1199 and 1229, a late 13th-c. copy of which came (in Paris, MS BN f. fr. 1038), to Barking Abbey in the early 15th c.: it includes the exemplum 'D'une fole fame q'avoit nom Tays' told in the first person (no. cxxii in table of

de Quenci's *Évangile* presents the pious practices of desert hermits indistinguishably
from those of chaste matrons and continent widows: they consist of 'veilles,
junes, afflictiüns' ('vigils, fasts, mortifications') and habitual reading of 'ympnes,
psalmes e de chant'.[41] In a fine late thirteenth-century book for Baroness Joan
de Tateshul, illustrated *exempla* from the *Manuel des pechés* attributed to
William of Waddington include that of the desert father Macharius. His holiness is brought into explicit comparison with the piety of married women when
he learns he is less virtuous than some of them, even though they have been
unable to follow a professionally eremitic and penitential life.[42] A similar story
of a married couple's superior virtue revealed to desert fathers is included as a
precedent for Sainte Audrée and her first husband in Marie's thirteenth-century
reworking of Etheldreda material as *La vie sainte Audrée*.[43] The early fourteenth-
century addition of lives by Nicholas Bozon to the manuscript of the
Augustinian canonesses at Campsey consists of the Life of the contemporary
married saint Elisabeth of Hungary (d. 1231) alongside two desert father lives,
Paul and Paphnutius.[44] These lives include particularly graphic versions of the
misogyny and misogamy topics common in *vitae patrum* lives (in the Life of
Paul, for instance, being tied to a silken bed and tempted with a maiden is a
torture equivalent to being whipped raw, smothered in honey, and exposed to

contents, f. 3v, and f. 95r). For a study of Continental French manuscript compilations including
Thaïs, see Pamela Gehrke, *Saints and Scribes: Medieval Hagiography in its Manuscript Context* (Berkeley,
Los Angeles, and London: University of California Press, 1993), ch. 2 (Paris, BN f. fr. 2162). Pelagia
seems to have been less well known in medieval insular vernacular sources, though present in the
Old English Martyrology and in the *Northern Homily Cycle* text in the Vernon manuscript (see
J. E. Cross, 'Pelagia in Medieval England', in *Pélagie la pénitente: métamorphoses d'une légende*
(Paris: Études Augustiniennes and CNRS, 1984), ii. 281–93 (287)).

[41] M. Y. Aitken, *L'Évangile des Domnées* (London, 1926): Thaïs, no. XIV, 170–2, vv. 15437, 15477–8.
I am grateful to Mrs Gill Lewis of Nottingham University Library for allowing me to see the Wollaton
Hall manuscripts of the *Évangile*, which has yet to receive a full edition.

[42] The exemplum (quoted at the head of this section) suggests that married women prefer celibacy,
but that the two in question have nobly renounced this desire rather than contravene their husbands' wishes: see n. 26 above. On Joan Tateshul's book see Adelaide Bennett, 'A Book Designed
for a Noblewoman: An Illustrated *Manuel des Péchés* of the Thirteenth Century', in Brownrigg
(ed.), *Medieval Book Production*, 163–81. For the *Manuel des pechés* and its manuscripts, largely
copied between 1275 and 1325, see E. Arnould, *Le Manuel des péchés: étude de littérature religieuse
anglo-normande (XIIIme siècle)* (Paris: Droz, 1940), and Matthew T. Sullivan, 'The Original and
Subsequent Audiences of the *Manuel des pechés* and its Middle English Descendants', D.Phil.
thesis, University of Oxford, 1990 (Sullivan argues for a primarily clerical distribution, with only
two manuscripts specifically designed for lay use (11): however, the uses for which clerics themselves require such a text are pastoral. A manuscript of the *Manuel* was bequeathed to one nunnery
in the late 14th c.: see Bell, s.v. Malling, 153).

[43] *Audrée*, ed. Södergård, vv. 413–62.

[44] For editions see 'La Vie de sainte Elisabeth d'Hongrie', ed. Ludwig Karl, *ZRPh* 24 (1910),
295–314 (the Campsey text of the Elisabeth Life: see also n. 65 below); 'Vie de saint Panuce', ed.
Baker, 418–24, and 'An Anglo-French Life of Saint Paul the Hermit', ed. A. T. Baker, *MLR* 4
(1908–9), 491–504 (with 'frere Boiun' mentioned as its author in v. 299): henceforth referenced
by line number in the text.

desert flies, and is endured at the cost of biting out one's own tongue rather than yielding (vv. 33–62, 13–20)). But their contextual convergence with a contemporary holy woman in the reading of a prestigious female community of canonesses and vowesses once again suggests that these lives could offer ways of appropriating the powers of penitential asceticism to female holiness.

Such stories underline the significance of penitence, humility, and penance, and although confession and internalized penance are very much an official church programme (especially after Lateran IV), these stories also offer important mediations for women of the impossibilism of the virgin role-model.[45] The figure of the repentant harlot saint renders viable the spirituality of the honorary virgin, while allowing a measure of restored virginity to women who have had to postpone celibacy till after marriage. The repentant harlot makes such women, who may have wished to remain continent or even virgin, valid as well as licit in religion, and gives encouragement and increased visibility to the spirituality of married women. These developments are with justice attributed to the mendicant orders, established in 1224 in England (with advice and help from an anchoress, the Countess of Leicester, who lived in reclusion at Hackington for 44 years).[46] But the need to articulate extra-conventual and semi-religious lives for women was intensified, rather than produced, by Lateran IV's prohibition on the formation of new female orders: women's desires for religious lives and texts had already led, in the Anglo-Norman world, to the foundation of Fontevrault and the Gilbertines, as also to the feminization of anchoritism in thirteenth-century England.[47]

Alongside their circulation in collections of short tales, female penitents become still more prominent in late twelfth- and thirteenth-century vernacular hagiographic lives.[48] Newly reworked lives of Mary of Egypt and Mary Magdalen

---

[45] As discussed in Chs. 2.3 and 1.4 above, relatively few women, especially heiresses, can have been allowed to enter convents when young: such a waste of an asset would have seemed dynastic suicide for most upper-class families (as indeed Christina of Markyate's father is represented as making abundantly clear in her *monastic*-authored *vita*: see *Life of Christina*, ed. Talbot, 66–8).

[46] F. M. Powicke, 'Loretta, Countess of Leicester', in J. Goronwy Edwards, V. H. Galbraith, and E. F. Jacob (eds.), *Historical Essays in Honour of James Tait* (Manchester: private subscription, 1933), 247–72 (268–9).

[47] See e.g. Jacqueline Smith, 'Robert of Arbrissel: *procurator mulierum*', in Derek Baker (ed.), *Medieval Women* (Oxford: Blackwell, 1978), 175–84; Marjorie Chibnall, 'L'Ordre de Fontevrauld en Angleterre au XIIe s.', *Cahiers de civilisation médiévale*, 29 (1986), 41–7; Brian Golding, *Gilbert of Sempringham and the Gilbertine Order* (Oxford: Clarendon Press, 1995); Warren, *Anchorites and their Patrons*, ch. 1.

[48] Although these figures are not unknown in Anglo-Saxon vernacular hagiography, their post-Conquest development is more intense and differently thematized. Such development is traced in Erich Poppe and Bianca Ross (eds.), *The Legend of Mary of Egypt in Medieval Insular Hagiography* (Dublin and Portland: Four Courts Press, 1996). For an argument associating the pre-Conquest Mary of Egypt primarily with male institutional spirituality see Magennis, 'St Mary of Egypt and Ælfric . . .', ibid., 99–112. The distinction between full lives and exempla or *contes* is for these purposes an artificial one, too often observed in editions using monastic hagiography as a normative model. In a valuable exception, all the French lives of Mary of Egypt, including not

circulated in Anglo-Norman from the twelfth century and in English from the later thirteenth century.[49] Like virgin martyrs, none of the women in these repentant harlot lives is presented as anything but noble: the Magdalen is lady of Magdala ('la sue cité . . . par heritage | Si estait de grant ligneage') and her brother Lazarus is explicitly not a leper, but a knight (vv. 10–15, Bozon's version; 'of kinges kunne', l. 2, *SEL*). Like Thaïs, these saints are prostitutes by choice, not by economic necessity (further suggesting that literal concern with the representation of prostitution is not necessarily what is at stake here).[50] As in the narrative of Thaïs, the Life of Mary of Egypt uses a pronounced diptych structure, confronting desert and city, worldliness and reform. The anchoritism of the female penitent and the coenobitism of the male confessor are counterbalanced. In her desert reclusion, the repentant harlot is both ministered to and sought by the monk as a figure of counsel and spiritual superiority: he brings her the eucharist, but regards her as holier than himself. This says something of the relations of women and men in religion, much as the *vitae* of early thirteenth-century Liège explore and stage the spiritual and ecclesiastical agendas of men such as Jacques de Vitry and Thomas of Cantimpré. (In presenting holy women as figures of superior standards of humility, affectivity, penance, and spiritual insight, the exemplary value of the models becomes inseparable from their articulation by clerical directors and admirers.)[51] It also speaks to the interchangeability of cultural spaces,

only discrete lives but long short stories from collections, are edited by Peter Dembowski in his *La Vie sainte Marie l'Egyptienne*, Publications romanes et françaises 144 (Geneva, 1977). The Magdalen also frequently appears in miracle and other tales (on miracle collections see Carol M. Meale, 'The Miracles of Our Lady: Context and Interpretation', in Derek Pearsall (ed.), *Studies in the Vernon Manuscript* (Cambridge: Brewer, 1990), 115–36): collective editions similar to Dembowski's challenging the distinction between formal and informal hagiographic lives could readily be made for her, Thaïs, and the other saints discussed here. See further on these saints, Ruth Mazo Karras, *Common Women: Prostitution and Sexuality in Medieval England* (Oxford and New York: Oxford University Press, 1996), ch. 6.

[49] Lives of Mary of Egypt circulated in Anglo-Norman and French manuscript collections in Britain and Northern France (see Dembowski (ed.), *La Vie*, 281–2, 16–17 and Duncan Robertson, 'The Anglo-Norman Verse Life of St Mary the Egyptian', *Rom. Phil.* 52 (1998), 13–44). For the Middle English versions see d'Evelyn and Foster, 'Saints' Legends', *Manual of the Writings in Middle English*, ii, s.v. Mary of Egypt; on the Anglo-Norman versions see Judith Weiss, 'The Metaphor of Madness in the Anglo-Norman Lives of St Mary the Egyptian', in Poppe and Ross (eds.), *Legend of Mary of Egypt*, 161–73. On Mary Magdalen see, for Anglo-Norman lives, *Three Saints' Lives by Nicholas Bozon*, ed. Sr. M. Amelia Klenke (St Bonaventure, NY: Franciscan Institute: 1947), pp. xx–xxiii; for the Middle English versions, see d'Evelyn and Foster, 'Saints' Legends', s.v. Mary Magdalen and for the *SEL* version, *The South English Legendary*, ed. d'Evelyn and Mill (Magdalen lives quoted from Klenke and *SEL* by line number in the text).

[50] The *SEL* alone of the insular lives suggests a motif other than pleasure: the Magdalen has been deprived of her bridegroom John the Evangelist when Christ calls him forth (because John 'was clene maide', 303/13). Even so, she is still explicitly said to be 'so ioiuol . . . of hure folie þat heo ne wilnede no part þo | Of hure eritage' (*SEL*, ed. d'Evelyn and Mill, i. 303/29–304/30).

[51] For study of such relations, see e.g. John Coakley, 'Friars as Confidants of Holy Women in Medieval Dominican Hagiography', in Renate Blumenfeld-Kosinksi and Timea Szell (eds.), *Images of Sainthood in Medieval Europe* (Stanford: Stanford University Press, 1992), 222–46; Else Marie Wiborg Pedersen, 'The In-carnation of Beatrice of Nazareth's Theology', in Dor *et al.*, *New Trends in Feminine Spirituality*, 61–79.

of the way in which desert imagery is used both to refresh the spiritual force of the *urbs* constituted by large monastic communities and to state the claims of monasticism against the new mendicant orders of the cities. Thaïs's repentance is signalled by enclosure, while Mary of Egypt becomes a female desert solitary. The cell as a cultural space is not neutral, but a version of the desert, figuring the eremitic basis of reform. Desert and cell are each other's obverse and continuum: both can figure penance and reform, inward retreat and flight from the city to the clean spaces of the waste land.[52] The lability of this narrative structure explores the relations and complementary or competing values of male and female figures of spirituality, as well as of the roles of men and women in religion: it is available both for the institutional church's thinking-through of newly feminized styles of spirituality and for women's own various identifications.

The penitent harlot saints, then, look like and, in terms of their religious lives, behave like upper-class women of the later twelfth and thirteenth centuries. Thaïs, as noted above, becomes an anchoritic figure in her penance: the Magdalen too, in Bozon's late thirteenth-century poem, leads a penitential life in a rock outside Marseilles for thirty years (v. 369, a figure which no doubt signals ascetic fortitude, but which was also quite often the length of pious noble Anglo-Norman widowhoods: see Chapter 5.1 below and Figure 4). In this context the lavish description of Mary of Egypt's penitential body could be read not as echoing by inversion the eroticism of her initial state, but as imaging a welcome post-sexual and especially post-parturition condition for women readers. This thin, long-nailed Mary of Egypt, her hair no longer blonde but ermine, her feet pierced by thorns as she heedlessly traverses the desert wastes, her limbs carrying no more flesh than a glove, her naked breast and belly sunken and sun-darkened, rejoices in every thorn and every affliction as helping one more sin to fall away. She looks more like an athlete of asceticism than a body punished for male erotic delectation.[53] This particular version of the Life shares one of its manuscripts with the *Conte du Graal* (a chivalric spiritual quest in which aristocratic recluses also figure, and in which, like the repentant harlot sought by Zozimas in the desert, they give counsel to knights from their forest cells).[54] In another manuscript, a woman scribe adds a prayer to the Virgin, the Magdalen, and Mary of Egypt.[55] That the penitential value of Mary of Egypt was directly associated with the socio-spiritual functions of women is further suggested by a juxtaposition of stories in Adgar's *Gracial*, a collection of miracles of the Virgin probably

[52] The cell itself becomes a site of *peregrinatio in stabilitate*, a place of interiorized quest and contemplation, at this period: see Jean Leclercq, 'Monachisme et pérégrination du IXe au XIIe siècle', *Studia Monastica*, 3 (1961) 33–52 (51).

[53] Dembowski (ed.), *La Vie*, Version T, vv. 621–2. For erotic readings, see Gaunt, *Gender and Genre*, 219; Robertson, 'Poem and Spirit: The Twelfth-Century French "Life" of St Mary the Egyptian', *Medioevo Romanzo*, 7 (1980), 305–27 (321).

[54] Dembowski (ed.), *La Vie*, 25–6.

[55] See Robertson, *Medieval Saints' Lives*, Appendix, 262–8, who shows that the prayer was probably composed by the female scribe of a Picard manuscript (Paris, BN f. fr. 23112) containing a 12th-c. life of Mary of Egypt and Clemence of Barking's Life of St Catherine.

composed between 1150 and 1170 for the abbey of Barking (whose abbess from
c.1175, Maud, illegitimate daughter of Henry II, may be the 'dame Mahaut', v.
60, of its prologue).[56] In the miracle immediately following the story of Mary
of Egypt (whose conversion is effected by the Virgin), a nun dies before she can
do enough penance for her lost virginity. Her abbess is reassured by the Virgin
that the community's prayers will rescue the nun from purgatory.[57] Again the
implication that lost virginity is recoverable, or at least recoverable from,
emerges along with the stress on the value of intercessory prayer, both major
aspects of the exotic figure of the penitent Egyptian harlot, and both encoding
contemporary concerns for women readers.

The Magdalen extends the logic of the repentant harlot's ability to figure
the redeemability of women with a past. She mediates not only widowhood and
other forms of honorary virginity but the contradictions of motherhood for all
those who, unlike the Virgin, cannot reproduce without losing their virginity. The gift of tears (Bozon's Magdalen washes Christ's feet in 'chaude lermes a
plenté', v. 79, where the Latin more coolly has only *lacrimis*) and penance (especially the penitential life of the anchoress) restores fallen women and biological
mothers to honorary virginity.[58] Penitence, tears, and devotion are as heavily
inscribed in motherhood roles as in those of professed virgins. As Nigel Morgan
points out, in the devotional images added at the end of the superb Lambeth
Apocalypse made either for Margaret Ferrers or for Elena de Quenci, Countess
of Winchester, in the later thirteenth century, the illustrations of the figure of
the penitent, the patron, and the Magdalen are remarkably similar.[59] Married
women had particular reasons for identification with a figure occupying high
social and celestial rank and yet so strongly mediating the unattainable perfection of the Virgin (next to whom the Magdalen is usually found in litanies, suffrages, and other devotional forms in the books of hours used by women and
laypeople). The development of her cult stemmed from the twelfth-century translation to Vézelay of Magdalen relics for monastic purposes, but it is significant

[56] Dembowski (ed.), *La Vie*, Version W, 153–7 (extant in London, BL, MS Egerton 612);
for the whole miracle collection see *Le Gracial*, ed. Pierre Kunstmann (Ottawa: Éditions de l'Université
d'Ottawa, 1982), 14. Barking also owned a late 12th- or early 13th-c. copy of Hildebert of
Lavardin's metrical Latin *vita* of Mary of Egypt, see Introduction, n. 15 above.

[57] *Le Gracial*, ed. Kunstmann, nos. XL and XLI.

[58] As Benedicta Ward remarks, virginity is not only restored, but created, by tears (*Harlots of
the Desert: A Study of Repentance in Early Medieval Sources* (Oxford: Mowbray, 1987), 103): see also
K. L. Jansen, 'Mary Magdalen and the Mendicants: The Preaching of Penance in the Later Middle
Ages', *JMH* 21 (1995), 1–25.

[59] The penitent woman is also a major component in an allegorical diagram on penitence specially added at the end of this Apocalypse for its female patron's meditation: see N. J. Morgan,
The Lambeth Apocalypse: MS 209 in Lambeth Palace London: A Critical Study (London: Harvey
Miller, 1990), ii [London, Lambeth Palace MS 209], ff. 40r (the patroness), 48r (the crucifixion
with Magdalen), 49r (Mary Magdalen and Christ in the garden), 53r (allegorical female figure of
repentance).

that its later medieval forms involved the Magdalen as a member of one or more holy kinships. In the early thirteenth-century Anglo-Norman Magdalen Life by Guillaume le Clerc (extant in a nunnery manuscript and a nunnery collection) Mary Magdalen is head of a transplanted holy household, including not only her own kinship of Martha and Lazarus, but other disciples such as 'la curteise Marcilla' (v. 87) who had blessed Christ and 'the womb that bore him and the breasts at which he suckled' (vv. 19–20).[60]

Guillaume's life also, as the later thirteenth-century versions in the *South English Legendary* and by Bozon were to do, includes new miracle stories making the Magdalen a figure of special maternal significance, associated with the remission of barrenness and the protection of mothers and children. Following the apostolic dispersion after the Ascension, the Magdalen's household arrives in Marseilles and, for lack of other shelter, lives in a pagan temple, until the Magdalen's preaching and intercessions convert and fecundate the childless town magnate and his wife.[61] The lord sets off on pilgrimage to the Holy Land, and his pregnant wife refuses to be left behind in the elegant enclosure of her painted, or perhaps tapestried, chamber ('chambre depeinte', v. 180), where, her lord argues, she can be looked after ('vus ferez servir et baigner', v. 181). She gives birth prematurely on the voyage, the narrative commenting that the 'aventure' of premature birth has happened often to many women whose children have none the less survived through God's providence to live long lives (vv. 252–63). Abandoned by the ship's crew on an island as dead in childbirth, the wife's lactation is maintained through the Magdalen's intercession, and her husband, returning from the Holy Land, finds the child alive and his wife waking 'tute entiere' (v. 583) from a tranced state. Her body has not dried out (v. 441) or been attacked by wild animals or worms (vv. 455–7) and her child has been fed 'as well as if he had had several nurses' (v. 442). She explains that, thanks to God and the Magdalen, she has been everywhere with her husband: wherever St Peter has taken him in the Holy Land, Mary Magdalen has taken her and she has seen all that her husband has (vv. 635–43).

The Magdalen thus mediates household and external world, piety and fecundity, enclosure and pilgrimage. A saint noted for her holy tears, she is also responsible for the life-giving fluid which continues while the mother is in a state of

---

[60] 'La Vie de Madeleine', ed. R. Reinsch, *Archiv*, 64 (1880), 85–94. The manuscripts are Paris, BN f. fr. 19525 (a large mid-13th-c. collection of devotional and hagiographic texts closely related to the mid-13th-c. MS Egerton 2710 which was owned by the nuns of Derby certainly in the 15th c. if not before) and the Campsey manuscript (see Ludwig Karl, 'Die Episode aus der Vie de Madeleine', *ZRPh* 34 (1910), 363–70).

[61] Unlike the Middle English *SEL* version, Guillaume's life does not refer these functions to St Peter (of whom the *SEL* Magdalen says 'ich do al bi [h]is rede', ed. d'Evelyn and Mill, i. 307, l. 126). As Alcuin Blamires has noted, however, vernacular lives do generally emphasize the Magdalen's preaching more strongly than Latin *vitae* ('Women and Preaching in Medieval Orthodoxy, Heresy, and Saints' Lives', *Viator*, 26 (1995), 135–52 (144)).

suspended animation. (If this Life attempts to teach women to stay enclosed in their childbearing roles, it also suggests motherhood as a kind of *fausse mort*, permitting only visionary travel.) Bozon's late thirteenth-century Life also shows the Magdalen converting lay nobility through the remission of barrenness: that the prostitute's gift is fertility again suggests that she is more important as a figure recuperating maternity than as a prostitute as such (especially given stereotypical associations of prostitutes and *in*fertility). (Another repentant harlot, Porfire/Pelagia, in the thirteenth-century Anglo-Norman Life of St John the Almsgiver, moves into adoptive motherhood as the sign of her conversion, picking up a lost child from the street.)[62] Other aspects of the Magdalen—her importance for confession, her role as *apostola apostolorum*, her preaching— perhaps encode older women's greater permission to speak: age cancels some of the restrictions of gender in women's religious lives in the twelfth and thirteenth centuries.[63]

The later thirteenth-century development of the calendrical Middle English *South English Legendary* added a large number of saints to the vernacular lives that had been available in English near the beginning of the century. These include Martha, Mary of Egypt, the Magdalen, and one of the first wives to appear in the *South English Legendary*, Anastasia (married against her will and, for secret visiting of imprisoned Christians, put in prison by her husband, where he attempts to rape kitchen pots and pans in error for her serving maidens: Anastasia herself is eventually martyred by the emperor for refusing remarriage).[64] But I shall here pursue the development of female sanctities through the less well-known, but important Anglo-Norman lives of the Franciscan Nicholas Bozon. Nine women saints and two short *vitae patrum* lives were composed by Bozon, perhaps in Nottingham, at the end of the thirteenth century or at the beginning of the fourteenth.[65] They suggest still further possibilities for religious lives for laywomen without any enclosure other than that of the household. I have already referred to one selection from Bozon's lives, that of two desert father lives together with a thirteenth-century holy woman in the additions to the Campsey manuscript (pp. 136–7 above). Their principal extant manuscript presents nine saints in an all-female legendary. Though nothing is certainly known of patronage and audiences for these lives (aside from their presence in the Campsey manuscript),

[62] *The Life of St John the Almsgiver*, ed. K. Unwin, ANTS 38 (London, 1980), i, vv. 6275–84. Though this may seem chiefly remarkable for its sacralizing construction of motherhood as what redeems women, it also underlines the continuities between the mother and the harlot.

[63] See Mulder-Bakker, 'The Prime of Their Lives', in Dor *et al.*, *New Trends in Feminine Spirituality*, 215–36.

[64] *SEL*, ed. d'Evelyn and Mill, ii. 586–90.

[65] *Three Saints' Lives by Nicholas Bozon*, ed. Sr. M. Amelia Klenke (St Bonaventure, NY: Franciscan Institute, 1947) (Magdalen, Margaret, Martha), and her *Seven More Poems by Nicholas Bozon* (Louvain: Nauwelaerts, 1951) (Bozon's Gospel poem, Lucy, Elisabeth, Juliana, Agnes, Agatha, Christine); for Paphnutius and Paul, see n. 44 above. Bozon's Agnes is also edited as Appendix II in A. J. Denomy, *The Old French Lives of Saint Agnes and Other Vernacular Versions of the Middle Ages* (Cambridge, Mass.: Harvard University Press, 1938), 214–25.

it is probable that they were specifically designed for use with female and/or lay audiences.[66]

Bozon's dominant figure of female sanctity remains the virgin martyr and six of his nine female lives are of legendary and semi-legendary virgins of the universal church (in the order of their appearance in the principal manuscript these are Lucy, Margaret, Christina, Juliana, Agnes, Agatha). However, not only are Bozon's virgin martyr lives inflected with particular thirteenth-century concerns, as will be argued below, but Mary Magdalen (following Lucy), and Martha and Elisabeth (following Margaret) vary this virgin legendary with the lives of three non-virgin holy women.[67] The addition of the two householding female saints Martha and Elisabeth is, if anything, more striking than the inclusion of the Magdalen, the most prestigious repentant harlot. Bozon's Martha, sister to his Magdalen, is a well-born heiress (daughter of a duke but inheriting through her mother the town of Bethany, and 'de Jerusalem une partie', v. 18).[68]

---

[66] The manuscript is London, BL, MS Cotton Domitian A. XI (see Introduction, n. 15 above). Combining two major English martyrs and scriptural paraphrases with a female legendary, the manuscript would make an excellent anthology for a francophone female community in England, for pious lay reading, or for the use of clerics with female pastoral responsibilities. For the argument that its binding together with an earlier manuscript from Bec suggests its origin in the Benedictine priory of Steventon, Berkshire (an alien priory of Bec), see M. Amelia Klenke, 'Steventon Priory and a Bozon Manuscript', *Speculum*, 30 (1955), 218–21.

[67] This represents no particular historical, geographical, or calendrical order that I can discern:

Saint	Category	Date	Place	Feast
Lucy	virgin martyr	*c.*AD 304	Syracuse	13 Dec.
Magdalen	repentant harlot	1st c.	Palestine, Vézelay	22 July (feast)
Margaret	virgin martyr	?4th c.	Antioch	20 July
Martha	hostess, holy woman	1st c.	Palestine, Provence	variously (19 Jan., 17 Oct.)
Elisabeth	married ascetic	1207–31	Thuringia	17 (19) Nov.
Christine	virgin martyr	4th c.	Tyre, Bolsena	24 July
Juliana	virgin martyr	4th c.	Cumae or Naples	16 Feb.
Agnes	virgin martyr	*c.*350	Rome	21 (28) Jan.
Agatha	virgin martyr	4th c.	Catania	5th Feb.

The much-culted married virgin martyr Cecilia is interestingly absent, perhaps strengthening the possibility that Bozon's selection was made with particular patronesses in mind, but I know of no evidence for this, and a great deal more research is needed on Bozon's hagiography. Since writing this chapter I have seen Laurie Postlewate's argument that where Wace's late 12th-c. *Marguerite* emphasizes 'the ability of the soul to communicate directly and intimately with God', Bozon's Margaret 'gives examples of the power of the ordinary practice of piety' ('Vernacular Hagiography and Lay Piety', in Sandro Sticca (ed.), *Saints: Studies in Hagiography* (Binghamton, NY: SUNY, 1996), 115–30, 130): i.e. trends similar to those for which I am arguing in Bozon's honorary virgins appear in his presentation of virgin martyrs.

[68] See *Three Saints' Lives*, ed. Klenke, 'La vie seinte Martha', 45 (quotations henceforth by line number in the text). There is also a life of Martha in the 14th-c. MSS of *SEL*: see d'Evelyn and Mill, i. 348–40. She loses her heiress status in this version, but remains a 'god womman', l. 1, and Christ's 'leue ostesse', 353/127, 'oure [Christ's and Bishop Fronton's] ostesse Martha', 354/146.

Persecuted, it is claimed, by the Jews, she travels from the Holy Land to Marseilles in the mode of the accused queens of romance by rudderless boat, where, like some of the contemporary holy women of the Low Countries, she teaches, preaches, and founds a female community (in Martha's case, in the woods where she has vanquished the Tarascon dragon with the sign of the cross and her girdle, vv. 85–102). Above all, Martha is the hostess of Christ: this gives her miracle-working and visionary powers and she is received at her death as 'ma chere hostesce' (v. 221) by Christ in exchange for her hospitality to him on earth. The Franciscan interest in so representing women and their powers of gift was propagated through lives of the saint himself: 'Woman has more pity than man', says one Anglo-Norman life of St Francis, 'and gives more willingly to the poor'.[69]

Bozon's account here clearly proposes a model for the female householder's reception of the mendicant but it also endorses semi-religious lives, whether of the religious tertiary or the committed charity-giver, for women. Mary and Martha are a frequent topos for the contrast of active and contemplative and monastic and lay lives, used, for example, to urge recluses to contemplation rather than outward-directed charity.[70] But the topos could also be used in a less oppositional way in the thirteenth century, even in the life of an established virgin saint. The Life by Marie of the widowed virgin princess abbess Audrée claims that 'this queen became perfected in the service of God . . . In her life she resembled the two sisters Martha and Mary: she followed Martha in labouring and Mary in praying to God'.[71] Bozon's Martha still further rehabilitates the female religious life of active holiness, pursued without enclosure (in anything other than a household's routines and interchanges with the world) as its precondition. Nor, unlike her preaching and dragon-destroying precedessor, St Margaret, is martyrdom demanded of Martha, though she practises the asceticism of chaste matrons in her later life (prayers, vigils, weeping, restricted diet and unluxurious sleeping arrangements, intercessions, vv. 155–66). She is leader, but not, apparently, abbess of her religious community of women 'de bele manere, de bon mours' (v. 148, and see vv. 171–3). She exercises the devotional artistic patronage which seems to have been customary among urban women householders as well as women in religion by having a statue made of Christ. This is

---

[69] 'Femme est pitouse plus ke houme | E plus volunters a povres doune', see Louise W. Stone, 'Fragments d'une Vie de saint François d'Assise en vers anglo-normands', *Archivum Franciscanum Historicum*, 31 (1938), 48–58 (56). For the other Anglo-Norman and French lives of Francis, see n. 7 above, and Gehrke, *Saints and Scribes*, ch. 3 (on Paris MS BN f. fr. 2094), 'St Francis and the Mother of God: An Ascetic Ideal for the Laity'.

[70] For this topos in anchoritic rules, see Millett and Wogan-Browne, 134/19–21; Alexandra Barratt, 'Anchoritic Aspects of *Ancrene Wisse*', *Medium Ævum*, 49 (1980), 38–40: on Mary and Martha see Giles Constable, *Three Studies in Twelfth Century Spirituality* ('The Interpretation of Mary and Martha').

[71] 'Ceste roine fu parfite | En le Deu servise . . . Semblance out en la soue vie | De deuz soreurs Marthe et Marie. | Marthe ensui de travaillier, | Marie de Deu prier' (ed. Södergård, vv. 1223–4, 1229–32).

not a crucifix, but a Christ walking and clothed as he had appeared to her on earth ('en tele semblance cum ele le vist | Alant en tere e si vestu', vv. 168–9).[72] Not only is this a mendicant Christ, but Martha's patronage is a transaction and a commission, not the self-containing and solitary preoccupation with Christ's image prescribed in virginity treatises for women (see Chapter 1.2 above). Martha's relations with religious men are as from householder to upper clergy: her death is one of exemplary lay piety, borrowing from monastic ritual as she is carried outside to lie on ashes on the ground with a cross held before her (vv. 227–31).[73] A bishop attends her funeral to recite the Office of the Dead (making a visionary tour with Christ during the reading of the Epistle in his own church in order to do so, vv. 242–84). The imitable aspects of the exemplary Martha as stressed by Bozon are rooted in the household powers of women, in dispensing hospitality and counsel: the audience of Martha's life is adjured to be similarly charitable in offering hospitality either in their households, or their hearts (vv. 315–40).

The most radical of Bozon's women saints is, however, not a *femme seule* and head of her own household, but Elisabeth of Hungary, a near-contemporary medieval married woman (d. 1231), technically under obedience to her husband. Every point of her behaviour is thus of potential significance in the politics of household rule and representation, even more so, perhaps, than Bozon's virgin martyr Margaret (who 'stanched the blood of kinship when she acted against [her parents'] will').[74] Calling Elisabeth, Margravine of Thuringia (d. 1231) the 'daughter of the king of Hungary' ('fille esteit le rey de Ungarye', v. 7), as Bozon does, makes her sound like a romance heroine (though she was in fact the daughter of Andrew II of Hungary), but it is the novelty and contemporaneity of her religious life that the legend, written within a half-century of her death, chiefly emphasizes. Elisabeth is 'something new in our garden [of saints] shown to us the day before yesterday' ('novele chose en nostre verger | A nus mustra avant her', vv. 1–2).[75] Instead of spending her virtuous girlhood in the service

[72] On urban women's patronage, I have profited greatly from hearing the York Household Research Group's paper (European Science Foundation conference on Women and the Christian Tradition in Europe, Seefeld, Oct. 1998).

[73] For the penitential practice of death in ashes, see David Crouch, 'The Culture of Death in the Anglo-Norman World', in C. Warren Hollister (ed.), *Anglo-Norman Political Culture and the Twelfth-Century Political Renaissance* (Woodbridge: Boydell Press, 1997), 157–80, esp. 168, 178–9 and n. 82.

[74] Margaret 'la sanc estanchea de parenté | Kant fit encuntre lur volenté', *Three Saints' Lives*, ed. Klenke, vv. 21–2.

[75] Klenke argues that Bozon's source was not directly the 1235 *Libellus de dictis quatuor ancillarum S. Elisabethae sive examen miraculorum eius* (I.B Menckenii Scriptores Rervm Germanicarvm praecipve Saxonicarvm, tomvs II, Lipsiae, Ioannis Christiani Martini, 1728), which was the chief canonization document, but the *Legenda Aurea*'s incorporation of the *libellus* together with the letter of Elisabeth's confessor, Conrad of Marburg, to Pope Gregory IX. From a comparison of the *libellus* text with Bozon, it is indeed clear that he was using some mediated form of the handmaids' testimonies (there are significant differences of detail and of narrative ordering, and

of God in her chamber, she makes daily visits to 'les povres genz', shares what she owns with them, and asks them to pray for her (vv. 18–22). The husband to whom her parents consign her is agreeable to her patronage of a hospital and her other public works of almsgiving, fostering, and counsel, but her food asceticism and her desire to wear poor clothing remain secret practices (vv. 73–4, 188–93): it is at the points where she must represent the household's rank and its conspicuous consumption that conflict lurks. When her husband requires her presence in entertaining an important visitor, angelic intervention resolves her dilemma (spiritual and actual) about what to wear and provides a dress of extremely rich material ('de mult noble atissure', v. 236). Elisabeth's eventual widowhood of joyous poverty, humility, and spinning is interrupted by her father and friends' attempts to restore her to the dignity of her rank, till finally she finds a private place ('privee leu', v. 405) in which to serve God. That Elisabeth's asceticism and charities constitute an intervention in the socio-economic conditions of her life and that of her community is underlined by her anxiety that the food taken into her body should come from morally impeccable economic activities:

> Avant que mangeast, certeyne fut
> Ke le dener fut bien gaygné
> Dunt la viande fut achaté.
>
> (vv. 76–8)

Before she would eat it, she was certain that the money with which the food had been bought was decently procured.

Food acquired as amercement or protection or through theft ('merciment', 'pur doute a present | Ou par prey de roberye', vv. 79–81) is rejected.

The Bozon saints' lives modulate and broaden the models of female sanctity available in the vernacular in England, adding figures who authorize a wider range of female roles and occupations as exemplary. Magdalen and Martha are distant fruits of the Continental French twelfth-century reinvention of this holy kinship, when the two women and their brother Lazarus are represented as coming to Provence. This translation doubtless expresses the desires and anxieties of a crusading society as well as the ambitions of St Maximin in Provence, and, later, Vézelay in the diocese of Sens (both of which claimed relics of these saints).[76] Bozon's versions (for all their extensive use of the *Legenda Aurea* and, for

some omissions as well as reflections of the *libellus* text), but I have not been able to undertake a full study of exactly what Latin materials might have been available to Bozon. I thank Lori Pieper for information about her work on a further anonymous Latin version which may throw light on Bozon's sources (*Archivum Franciscanum*, forthcoming). Among Bozon's nine female saints, the Elisabeth life is the only one extant in more than one manuscript, being added in the early 14th-c. updating of the Campsey manuscript as well as surviving in MS Cotton Domitian A.XI.

[76] Victor Saxer, *Le Culte de Marie Magdalene: des origines à la fin du Moyen Age* (Auxerre and Paris: Publications de la Société des fouilles archéologiques et des monuments historiques de l'Yonne, 1959).

Elisabeth of Hungary, a version of Conrad of Marburg's *vita* of the saint) seem also to speak directly into, and in part to create, a more intensely urban milieu than previous English legendaries.

Although the only earlier female legendary in English, the Katherine Group from the West Midlands, is possibly not more than fifty years older than Bozon's East Midlands Anglo-Norman, it seems a world away, not only because of its alliterative, highly stylized early Middle English prose, but in terms of the themes and preoccupations of the two legendaries. There is overlap between two of their virgin martyrs (Juliana and Margaret), but the emphases are very different. The Katherine Group martyrs, Katherine, Margaret, Juliana, are all virgin martyrs, and in conformity with the early thirteenth-century anchoritic audiences for whom they were compiled, have a spectacular inner theatre in their tyrant's dungeons (a kind of interior cell-drama, comparable with *vitae patrum* desert temptations, but intensely feminized). Their tortures are spectacular too, as are their lavish speeches and prayers, these latter almost constituting a kind of feminized vernacular liturgy, or at least psalmody.[77] The penitential anchoritic ascesis encoded as heroic acceptance of torture in this specialized anchoritic legendary is a reciprocal gift in return for Christ's crucifixion and the nature of the exchange between the virgin and Christ is intensely personal and affective. The Bozon lives are more lightly worked, less intense, less spectacular, less interiorized: addressed to and representing active models of female holiness. His saints preach occupationally, as well as in theatrical debate with pagan tyrants. Martha's foundation, for all its location in the forests of Provence, sounds like the informal beguinage communities that are so marked a feature of the religious lives of women in the Low Countries and France from around the turn of the thirteenth century onwards, and, as Norman Tanner has suggested, more rarely in later medieval England (again near the east coast, in Norwich, and with possible Low Countries connections).[78] Bozon's saints, as is customary with earlier (and, for that matter, later) virgin-martyr lives, are all high-born, but tend to have urban inheritances rather than the landholdings of an Osith or an Audrée. His Agatha and Lucy are shown as patronesses of Sicilian cities. Indeed Agatha, to whom Lucy prays as to a sister, explicitly thematizes urban patronage as a role: 'just as you have seen that through me, Catania has grown in faith and Holy Church has been advanced, so the great city of Syracuse will be enhanced through you', she says.[79] The Katherine Group Katherine, Juliana, and Margaret inhabit the cities of Alexandria, Nichomedea, and Antioch respectively, but these

---

[77] For discussion of these lives, see the bibliographical listings in Millett, *'Ancrene Wisse', the Katherine Group, and the Wooing Group*.

[78] Norman Tanner, *The Church in Medieval Norwich 1370–1532* (Toronto: Pontifical Institute of Mediaeval Studies, 1984), 64–6, 131.

[79] *Seven More Poems*, ed. Klenke, *Vie seinte Lucie*, 'E sicum vus veez ke par may | Catanense est cru en fay | E Seinte Eglise par moy enhalcé, | Siracusan, la grant cité | Par vus enbeli de cristienté', vv. 51–5.

are distantly legendary locations, vaguely exotic backgrounds for pagan official-dom and crowd scenes in the intensified imaginary theatre of these texts.

It may also be significant that Bozon is not known to have written a life of Catherine, virgin-martyr patroness of learning. Catherine's legend shows the saint converting and inspiring the pagan Emperor's wife to the spiritual queenship of honorary virginity through martyrdom. But Bozon's legendary does not inscribe audiences of professionally enclosed virgins and their relatively high opportun-ities for learning, but of women mediating tower/bower/cell enclosure via the exchanges of urban, household, and hostess lives. Bozon's Magdalen is spiritu-ally certificated by her ability to figure eremitic reform, leading her life of penance on a hard rock outside Marseilles, but her represented links with her commun-ity and with the nobility of Marseilles are a reminder that, from the twelfth to the fourteenth centuries, anchoritic cells increasingly became places of urban exchange rather than of rural solitude.[80] The preoccupations of Bozon's holy women with making a good death diffuse the nuptial emphasis of the Katherine Group: this is less *Liebestod* in the embrace of the bridegroom than the death of women householders amongst their friends and relations (so Martha with her prepara-tions, her lying in the ashes, her vision of her sister Magdalen, and clergymen and Christ in attendance at her funeral, reciting the Office of the Dead, vv. 193–240, vv. 257–64). Bozon's legendary updates and extends the styles and environments of female sanctity while the anchoritically customized Katherine Group legendary conforms it to the heroinic and the antique. The two legendaries demonstrate something of the range, the prestige, and the flexibility of penance and asceticism as modes of thirteenth-century female sainthood.

Bozon's audiences, apart from the Campsey canonesses, remain largely unknown. His own probable circuits of activity from Nottingham to Oxford, the East Anglian diffusion of his saints' lives, and the particular thematic inflections of his ver-sions of female sanctity make it tempting to see his hagiography in simultane-ously regional and international terms. His saints' lives were most probably occasioned by the mendicant and pastoral duties of the Franciscans or by their female patrons, much as the Katherine Group compiles its lives for use in particular female communities. Where one community is Western and past-referenced, however, the other is Eastern and modernizing. Bozon's female sanc-tity is also permeable with Continental styles of female holiness, and possibly part of an as yet unwritten history of exchange and cross-influence in women's thirteenth-century literary culture in the region constituted by the East Anglian coast and north-west Europe. Across the Channel, a woman of class status similar to the aristocratic Campsey audience commissioned the life of Martha: Marguerite, who was countess of Flanders and Hainault from 1244 and who died in 1280. The legendary in which this poem composed at the 'commande de ma dame' is extant also includes a Life of Becket and the voyage of St Brendan,

---

[80] On the development of cell sites, see Warren, *Anchorites and their Patrons*, 37–41.

suggesting a series of English–Continental interconnections of potential significance in the earlier, as they are in the later, history of medieval women's literary and spiritual culture in England.[81] The first vernacular *Brendan*—a glorious melding of saint's life and travel literature into a kind of mobile *vita patris* inspired by Celtic voyage literature—was composed for Henry I's queen, Edith-Matilda (daughter of St Margaret of Scotland), though its patroness, actual or desired, is in one manuscript updated to Henry's second wife, Adeliza of Louvain.[82] Adeliza married William d'Albini after Henry's death in 1134/5, and when she became a widow for the second time retired to the convent of Afflighem in her Flemish homeland. Knowledge of the Anglo-Norman *Brendan*, if not of Becket, the saint murdered in 1170 at the wish of her step-son, Henry II, may well have travelled in the first place with her. The patroness of the Flandrian *Ste Marthe*, Marguerite of Hainault, was the daughter of Marie de Champagne, whose epithalamion or *chançun* on Psalm 44 circulated in England.[83] These different generations seem to coincide with the developments noted above in England: Marie de Champagne's is a twelfth-century text of nuptial romance and love casuistry, voiced by the great royal male penitent, David; Marguerite's text is the Martha, composed within a very short time of the Bozon legendary.[84]

The distinctions and perspectives sketched here are largely provisional: the widespread diffusion of the *South English Legendary* alone breaks down any easy polarization between the West where it originates and the East where it is substantially witnessed in later manuscripts. Much more detailed and integrated accounts of texts and contexts barely touched on here remain to be given. Nevertheless, it seems clear that over the late twelfth and thirteenth centuries, the figure of the penitent woman acquires public meaning and value, depend-ent on exhibiting rather than on containing her spirituality as feminine, and that this can be traced in, particularly, francophone insular sources. The penitent holy woman is an important image for and of the thirteenth-century's confessional spirituality of penance, purgation, feminization, and laicization. Although insular society lacked the beguine communities of the Low Coun-tries and the biographies of Low Countries holy women do not circulate in England until the fourteenth and fifteenth centuries, this penitentially focused

[81] For this life of Martha (prose, with a verse prologue) see Paul Meyer, 'Notice du MS Bibl. Nat. Fr. 6447', repr. from *Notices et Extraits des manuscrits de la Bibliothèque Nationale et autres bibliothèques* 35 (Paris: Imprimerie Nationale, 1896), item 68, 68–73 [500–5]. The manuscript hand is late 13th c. in this section. For other Continental influences see Rosalynn Voaden (ed.), *Prophets Abroad: The Reception of Continental Holy Women in England* (Cambridge: Boydell and Brewer, 1996).

[82] See *The Anglo-Norman Voyage of St Brendan*, ed. Ian Short and Brian Merrilees (Manchester: Manchester University Press, 1979), 4–5.

[83] See Ch. 1, n. 64 above.

[84] In the intervening generation, Blanche of Navarre, d. 1229, commissioned a prose *Vie des pères*, a copy of which came to Barking Abbey (Bell, s.v. Barking, 15, and n. 40 above).

spirituality offered women in insular culture models of anchoress, vowess, and other semi-religious lives in a variety of informal religious and semi-religious communities. The status of virginity was thereby available for non-virgin women, while the powers of maternity and household, acquired for virginity, were incorporated into models of holiness which still proclaimed virginity as the superior form. The boundaries thus remained permeable between a narrowly defined professional virginity to which in practice very few women could aspire, and the wider religious and semi-religious lives of women enclosed, but not contained, in a range of ecclesiastical and secular households.

5

Beyond Enclosure: The Lives of a Widow

This chapter looks at religious and literary patronage in the numerically small but culturally significant group of aristocratic Anglo-Norman widows who avoided remarriage. It takes as a particular example the life, literacies, and patronage of Isabella, Countess of Arundel (d. 1279). Isabella is the dedicatee of an Anglo-Norman biography of Archbishop Edmund of Canterbury and the commissioner of a Latin biography of Bishop Richard of Chichester (subsequently translated into Anglo-Norman). She was also a monastic foundress, and the subject of a dedicatory letter in the form of a chastity encomium.

Like the *vitae patrum* lives discussed in the previous chapter, ascetic biographies of male saints seem to have been of interest to élite women, inside and around female communities. The chapter looks at the represented powers of asceticism and celibacy in the lives of English churchmen after Becket, and examines the relations of these hagiographic biographies with the ideal of the courtier saint and the politics of Henry III's court. Isabella of Arundel's connections with contemporary saints, with court and convent, and her own baronial concerns suggest the inadequacy of such labels as 'pious' and 'devotional' in characterizing patronesses. She is a figure leading on the one hand to the aristocratic community of Campsey and on the other to the devotional, social, and political aspects of saints' cults at court.

5.1. 'IN MY LIEGE POWER AND WIDOWHOOD': ISABELLA OF ARUNDEL, HER LITERACIES, HER SAINTS

A discourse on vidual continence forms part of a dedicatory letter addressed by Ralph Bocking, Dominican confessor of the Bishop of Chichester, to Isabella, Countess of Arundel in or within a few years of 1272. After congratulating the Countess on her own refusal of remarriage, Bocking deplores the

contemptible and wicked example of women of noble stock, and not only the young, but also the aged whose worn-out bodies have long since lost all hope of bearing children. Nowadays the old and the aged marry the young and the youthful, the well-born marry the illegitimate, the nobility marry their servants, ladies their bondsmen, losing their own good name, shaming and dishonouring their whole line, a subject of scandal and gossip among the common people—and all this merely to satisfy their lusts. Such a person may perhaps object 'I have not done this because I could not remain continent,

but because as a weak and feeble woman I was not able and did not know how to control my dower and my inheritance from my father and my other rights and properties.'
Let anyone who speaks in this way understand how she condemns her own shame. Listen,
I say, not to me, but to St Jerome who fiercely attacks such women . . . 'No woman takes
a husband if she does not intend to sleep with him. Indeed, if it is not lust which
spurs you on, surely it is the height of madness to prostitute yourself like a harlot
simply to increase your wealth and for some paltry and passing gain to defile that
precious chastity which might otherwise endure for ever?'[1]

For all Jerome's authority, Bocking's analysis of the thirteenth-century baronial
marriage market as driven by female lust does not survive reflection on the legal
status and family positions of thirteenth-century widows. It is, rather, eloquent
indirect testimony to the strength of seigneurial fears of the dispersal of patri-
mony through widows. The common destiny of most noble widows was indeed
remarriage, though the reasons have less to do with women exercising sexual
preference than with the king's interest in the marriage market and the English
barony's need to create advantageous allegiances within as well as outside itself.[2]
Women who wanted freedom from remarriage could substitute a fine for the
king's use of them and their lands in rewards and marriage strategies. Even very
wealthy women were frequently married several times before achieving undis-
rupted widowhood. The custom of formal dedication to a semi-religious life as
a vowess (which could be used to settle the widow's position and exempt her
from the risks of childbearing, as well as to allow straightforward administration for the executors of her husband's estate, and peace of mind for her kin)
seems at this date to have been less well-established (or is less well-attested) than
it subsequently became, but it is in evidence. Becoming a vowess, founding and

---

[1] *Vita S. Richardi Episcopi Cicestrensis*, Epistola dedicatoria: text in *AA.SS.* (Antwerp, 1643–),
Apr. i (1675), 282–318 (282–3): this letter and the full text of the closing dedication are extant only
in the 14th-c. manuscript, Brussels Bibliothèque Royale MS 2057–62, ff. 2r–4v. The *vita* is dated
to *c*.1270. The letter and *vita* have been recently edited by David Jones, 'Vita sancti Ricardi Episcopi
Cycestrensis', in id., 'St Richard of Chichester: The Sources for His Life', *Sussex Record Society*,
79 (1995), 83–159, henceforth cited as 'Jones' by page number. The opening dedicatory letter is,
among other things, a small compendium of chastity texts and images (for example, Isabella is a
turtle dove in rejecting remarriage ('ad turturis similitudinem iteratam copulam maritalem
respuendo', Jones, 83; the Song of Songs and St Bernard's letter to Sophia (Ep. 113) are cited, as
is the 'laver' of chastity from Exodus 38: 8, Jones, 84). The quotation from Jerome in the passage
cited is from Ep. 54, Ad Furiam, 'De viduitate servanda', PL22.550–60 (558). Translation from
Jones, 161, and see 235, nn. a–v.
[2] S. F. C. Milsom, 'Inheritance by Women in the Twelfth and Early Thirteenth Centuries', in
M. S. Arnold, T. A. Green, S. A. Scully, and S. D. White (eds.), *On the Laws and Customs of
England: Essays in Honour of S. E. Thorne* (Chapel Hill: University of North Carolina Press, 1981),
60–89; J. C. Holt, 'Feudal Society and the Family in Early Medieval England: IV. The Heiress
and the Alien', *TRHS* 5th ser. 35 (1985), 1–28; S. L. Waugh, 'Marriage, Class and Royal Lordship
in England under Henry III', *Viator*, 16 (1985), 181–207; id., 'Women's Inheritance and the Growth
of Bureaucratic Monarchy in Twelfth and Thirteenth-Century England', *NMS* 34 (1990), 71–92
(90–2).

entering a religious house, becoming an anchoress are the most common alternatives to marriage undertaken by upper-class widows.[3]

Although women of lower social rank also acted as religious foundresses, as
commissioners of texts, books, images, and artefacts, and as administrators of
female communities, Anglo-Norman noblewomen who achieved long widowhoods are among the most visible of female cultural patrons in the late twelfth
and thirteenth centuries (see Figure 4).[4] They form a significant proportion, for
instance, of monastic foundresses acting without male kin.[5] They also exemplify
a spectrum of greater and lesser degrees of formal religious affiliation for women,
and, especially given the closely interrelated nature of English baronial and royal
families in the period, can be seen as indicative as well as personal in the nature
of their piety.

Specific connections between Isabella, Countess of Arundel, and hagiographic
lives are better exemplified in extant texts and manuscripts than for almost any
other woman in the thirteenth century, excepting royal women. Moreover, the
fact that Isabella's texts were copied into the manuscript collection of a female
community makes her an important and early example of the continuities of

[3] On vowesses see Mary Erler, 'English Vowed Women at the End of the Middle Ages', *Mediaeval Studies*, 57 (1995), 155–203; only two vows are recorded from the 13th c. A letter of 1289 from Archbishop Pecham to Edmund, Earl of Cornwall 1272–1300, testifies to the strategic use of vowing by a divorce-minded husband: vows do not invariably signal women's choices, involving as they do the interests of many other parties (*Registrum*, ed. Martin, iii. 969). On monastic foundresses see Thompson, *Women Religious*, ch. 9; on anchoritism, Warren, *Anchorites and their Patrons*, and on the high status of the anchoritic life in the 13th c., Ann K. Warren, 'The English Anchorite in the Reign of Henry III, 1216–1272', *Ball State University Forum*, 19 (1978), 21–8. For earlier para-religious lives, see Halpin, 'Women Religious in Late Anglo-Saxon England'.

[4] The information in Figure 4 is taken from *CP*; Knowles and Hadcock; Thompson, *Women Religious*; and *VCH*. The phrase in Figure 4's title is frequently used in the foundation charters of widowed noblewomen. For more detailed studies see Powicke, 'Loretta, Countess of Leicester'; on Ela of Salisbury, see Margaret Wade Labarge, 'Three Medieval Widows and a Second Career', in Michael M. Sheehan (ed.), *Ageing and the Aged in Medieval Europe* (Toronto: Pontifical Institute of Mediaeval Studies, 1990), 159–72; on Maud de Clare's family see Michael Altschul, *A Baronial Family in Medieval England: The Clares 1217–1314* (Baltimore: Johns Hopkins University Press, 1965). See further Linda E. Mitchell, 'Noble Widowhood in the Thirteenth Century: Three Generations of Mortimer Widows 1246–1334', in Louise Mirrer (ed.), *Upon my Husband's Death: Widows in the Literature and Histories of Medieval Europe* (Ann Arbor: University of Michigan Press, 1992), 169–90; RaGena DeAragon, 'Dowager Countesses 1069–1230', *ANS* 17 (1995), 87–100; Paula Dobrowolski, 'Women and their Dower in the Long Thirteenth Century, 1265–1329', in Michael Prestwich, R. H. Britnell, and Robin Frame (eds.), *Thirteenth Century England VI* (Woodbridge and Rochester, NH: Boydell Press, 1997), 157–64. For estimates of the statistical proportions of widows see the works cited in Ch. 1, n. 102 above.

[5] Thompson calculates that of the nine post-Conquest foundations for women with the rank of abbey, five were established by widows of noble rank (*Women Religious*, 172). For other women acting without male kin see ibid., Appendix A, and see further Ch. 6.1 below. It has been cal-culated that between 1200 and 1330, women inherited 43 of the 195 baronies in England in 1200 (with 33 going to sons and 22 to nephews)—a statistic testifying less to women's freedom than the importance of consanguinity in baronial identity and holdings, but also suggesting how significant women's patronage powers could become: see Waugh, 'Marriage, Class and Royal Wardship', 185–6.

Fig. 4. 'In ligia potestate et viduitate mea': some Anglo-Norman widowhoods

Name	Biographical details	Length of widowhood	Foundations	Associated texts
Loretta, Countess of Leicester	b. ?1180; m. ?after 1196; w. 1204; d. 1266. Childless. Networker for friars, adviser to Henry III.	62 years (incl. 44 as recluse)	endowed sisters at Minchin Buckland, Somerset	source of miracle of the Virgin story in Vaux de Cernay MS
Ela, Countess of Salisbury	m. 1198; w. 1226; d. 1261. Abbess of Laycock 1238. Her vision of her son Wm. Longespee's death reported by M. Paris, 1250.	35 years	1227 Henton Carthusians 1229 Lacock Augustinian Canonesses	?AN *Speculum ecclesie*; ?lost *vita* of Ela by Beatrice of Lacock
Isabella, Countess of Arundel	b. 1226/1230; m. 1234; w. 1243; d. 1279. Childless.	36 years	1249 Marham Cistercian nuns; perh. 1253 Arundel Dominican priory.	M. Paris's *Vie saint Edmond*, Bocking's *vita* Ric. Chichester
Maud de Clare, Countess of Gloucester	m. 1238; w. 1262; d. 1289. Children.	27 years	1284 Canons-leigh made female Augustinian house	Cotton Cleopatra MS of *Ancrene Wisse*
Denise de Munchesny	m. (i) Walter Langton, d. 1234; (ii) Warin de Munchesney; w. 1255; d. 1304. Children. (Marsh & Grosseteste write on her marital misery)	(i) uncertain (ii) 49 years	1270s–1290s Waterbeach (Friars minor and minoresses)	Walter Bibbesworth: *Traitié*
Margaret Ferrers, Countess of Derby*	m. 1238 to William Ferrars III, Earl of Derby, w. 1254 (son contests dower), d. 1281.	27 years	none known	perh. the Lambeth Apocalypse
Elena de Quenci,* Countess of Winchester	m. (i) William Vaux, d. by Dec. 1252; (ii) 1252 Roger de Quenci [as his 3rd wife] he d. 1264; (iii) 1267 Roger de Leybourne, w. 1271; she d. 1274.	(i)? (ii) 12 (iii) 4 = 3 short widowhoods	none known	perh. the Lambeth Apocalypse
Elena/Aline la Zouche	m. Alan la Zouche 1240/1242?, w. 1270 (Alan killed by John de Warenne). Aline d. 1296.	c.28 years	patron of Brackley Hospital	Rober le chapelain, *Évangile des domnées*
Margaret de Quincy, Countess of Lincoln	sr and coheir of Robert Fitzparnell, Earl of Leics. (d. 1235); m. Saher de Quincy; w. 1219; d. 1234/5.	c.15 years	foundress of Brackley	*Les reules seint Robard*, *Walter of Henley*; corr. with Grosseteste

* Both women were stepdaughter and stepmother to each other. Margaret was d. of Roger de Quenci, Earl of Winchester, by his 1st wife, Helen of Galloway, d. 1245; Eleanor d. of William Ferrars, Earl of Derby c.1200–54 and his 1st wife Sybil Marshal, m. 1219, d. 1237.

reading and book ownership between female lay and professed religious which have recently illuminated study of later medieval women.[6] The texts associated with Isabella of Arundel are much better known than the Countess herself, principally because of their connections with Matthew Paris, the thirteenth-century chronicler and artist of the Benedictine Abbey of St Alban's. A famous note on the manuscript of Paris's illustrated hagiographic dossier of St Alban (text 1230–40 or earlier; illustrated format later, perhaps *c.*1250) suggests that Isabella knew at least two lives—of Thomas Becket and Edward the Confessor—with whose commissioning she was not directly involved: probably she also knew the life of the English protomartyr, Alban, in which the note occurs.[7] A fourth

---

[6] Riddy, ' "Women talking about the things of God" '.

[7] Paris famously directs in a note of 1250 × 1252 that a message should go to 'the lady Countess of Arundel, Isabel, that she is to send you the book about St Thomas the Martyr and St Edward which I translated [or copied] and designed ['transtuli et protraxi'], and which the lady Countess of Cornwall may keep until Whitsuntide'. It is generally agreed that this refers either to Paris's own illustrated lives of these saints or to copies of them (such as the extant illustrated *Estoire* of Edward the Confessor and the four surviving leaves of a Thomas Becket life in a similar style). Paris's note is on f. 2 of the extant Alban manuscript, now Dublin, Trinity College MS 177 (E. I. 40): see M. R. James, *La Estoire de Seint Aedward le Rei . . . together with some pages of the Manuscript of the Life of St Alban at Trinity College, Dublin* (London: Roxburghe Club, 1920), 20. (The note may be addressed to an unknown 'G.' but 'G' is probably a paraph mark.) The Life of St Alban illustrated in the manuscript is in Anglo-Norman and is accepted as Matthew Paris's own translation from the Latin *vita* by William of St Alban's, as in this case are the illustrations (though not necessarily their French captions): see Nigel J. Morgan, *Early Gothic Manuscripts [I] 1190–1250,* A Survey of Manuscripts Illuminated in the British Isles (London: Harvey Miller, 1982–8), iv. 1, no. 85, 130–3 (Dublin, Trinity College MS 177); Florence McCulloch, 'Saints Alban and Amphibalus in the Works of Matthew Paris: Dublin, Trinity College MS 177', *Speculum,* 56 (1981), 761–85. The Anglo-Norman *Auban* may have been composed between 1230 and 1240, though an earlier date cannot be excluded (see *Vie seint Auban,* ed. Harden, p. xxvii). Since, as Paul Binski points out, there was no Countess of Cornwall between 1240 and 1243 (Sanchia, sister of Eleanor of Provence, did not marry Richard of Cornwall until 1243 and Richard's previous wife, Isabella of Arundel's aunt on her mother's side, died in 1240) the illustrated *Alban* must be later than the text ('Abbot Berkyng's Tapestries and Matthew Paris's Life of St Edward the Confessor', *Archaeologia,* 109 (1991), 81–100, 99 n. 81). Morgan dates the illustrations on stylistic grounds as nearer 1250 than 1240 (*EGM [I] 1190–1250,* iv. 2, no. 123, 94–8 (95), Cambridge, University Library MS Ee.3.59). The lives of Thomas Becket and Edward the Confessor mentioned in Matthew Paris's note are not extant in his holograph but in manuscripts which are perhaps copies of work by him. The Getty Thomas (four leaves of an illustrated Anglo-Norman Life of Becket, purchased in 1986 by Paul Getty) may be from a copy of the Becket Life mentioned in Paris's note: they are in a style close to St Alban's and contemporary London workshops and are dated to *c.*1220–40 (*The Becket Leaves,* introd. Janet Backhouse and Christopher de Hamel (London: British Library, 1988), 17): the text is edited by Paul Meyer, *Fragments d'une vie de saint Thomas de Cantorbéry en vers accouplés,* SATF (Paris, 1885)). Eleanor of Castile married the future Edward I in 1254, but did not become queen until after Henry II's death in 1272, when Paris (d. 1259) had been dead for over a decade, so the Queen Eleanor of the *Aedward* dedication has to be her mother-in-law, Eleanor of Provence (married to Henry III in 1236). M. R. James and others argued for the *Aedward* manuscript's links to St Alban's, but Morgan has argued that it is a Westminster production, dating to 1255–60 and placed it in his 'Westminster' group (*EGM [I] 1190–1250,* iv. 2, no. 123, 95–6, and see no. 124, p. 99). Binski, 'Reflections on the *Estoire de seint Aedward*' argues that the manuscript was not necessarily put together at Westminster (339), and (in 'Abbot Berkyng's Tapestries') favours

saint's life, Matthew Paris's Anglo-Norman version of his own Latin Life of St Edmund, Archbishop of Canterbury (1233–40, canonized 16 December 1246), is dedicated to 'dame Ysabele', 'honuré dame | Riche cuntesse d'Arundele'.[8] This must have been composed between Edmund's canonization and Paris's death in 1259. Since no other patron for the Latin Life is known and since Paris says that he has written the Life 'en deux langages | Par vous Cuntasse Ysabele' (vv. 1976–7), Isabella may have been behind both Latin and Anglo-Norman versions of the Life.[9] In the early 1270s Isabella commissioned Bocking's Latin *vita* of Richard, bishop and saint of Chichester (d. 1253, canonized 1262). This was approved by Robert Kilwardby, then Prior Provincial of the Dominicans in England and soon to become Archbishop of Canterbury (1272–9).[10] At least one manuscript of this fifth saint's life associable with Isabella contains dedicatory letters to and about her (including the one quoted above); she is also represented by name within the Life in one of the miracles performed by the saint (the resuscitation of her nephew, Hugh Bigod's child, some time between 1258 and 1260), and she is very probably the noblewoman friend of the saint who figures in several other incidents in the Life.[11] Bocking's Latin *vita* was translated into Anglo-Norman

a date early in Henry and Eleanor of Provence's marriage on the grounds that the Life would not appeal for more to be done after Henry's intensified promotion of Edward's cult had begun in 1245 (95). For the text of the life, composed between 1236 and 1245, see *La Estoire seint Aedward le rei*, ed. Wallace: she points out that the reference to devotions to Edward in the *Edmund* Life suggest that Paris had finished with the Edward Life by 1247 (p. xxii).

   [8] See 'La Vie de saint Edmond, archevêque de Cantorbéry', ed. A. T. Baker, *Romania*, 55 (1929), 332–81, vv. 28–30; henceforth quoted by line number in the text. For the Latin texts and a study see C. H. Lawrence, *St Edmund of Abingdon: A Study in Hagiography and History* (Oxford: Clarendon Press, 1960). The Anglo-Norman Life is not extant in any illustrated copy: for a lost text of 'La Vie Seint Edmund le Confessur translate de Latin en Romans' together with a lost 'vie seint Alban', once extant in London, BL, MS Cotton Vitellius D vii, see James, *La Estoire de Seint Aedward*, p. 18. Paris adds 'et d'Essexe' to Isabella's title in v. 1978: she was not countess of Essex but may have been called so by Paris on account of her holdings at Stanstead and elsewhere ('Vie de saint Edmond', ed. Baker, 340).

   [9] Most of Paris's surviving hagiography consists of translation (including one self-translation) into Anglo-Norman from Latin: the *Vie seint Auban* from the Latin by William of St Alban's, the *Estoire seint Aedward le rei* from Aelred of Rievaulx's *vita* of 1163, the Life of Becket (from the *Quadrilogus*) and the self-translation of the *Edmund*. A fragment from a Latin Life of Stephen Langton by Paris is also extant: see C. H. Lawrence, *The Life of St Edmund by Matthew Paris* (Stroud: Alan Sutton in association with St Edmund Hall, Oxford, 1996), 105–6 (the identification of Paris's patroness with 'Isabella de Fortibus, countess of Arundel' on p. 107 of this work is an error: Isabella de Fortibus was the Countess of Aumale, not Arundel, and the patronage of Wymondham was in the family of the husband of Isabella de Warenne, Countess of Arundel, see n. 32 below).

   [10] See *La Vie seint Richard, evesque de Cycestre*, ed. D. W. Russell, ANTS 51 (London, 1995), 8. The Life was presumably begun by 1272 at latest since it refers to Kilwardby as Prior Provincial and not as Archbishop. It would very probably have been wanted for the 1276 translation of the saint's shrine.

   [11] The closing letter of Bocking's *vita* is dedicated to a successor of Richard's as bishop, either John Climping 1253–62, or Stephen Bersted 1262–87. See Bocking, *Vita Ricardi*, Bk. ii, Ch. 3 for the miracle of Isabella's resurrected nephew (Jones, 140–1; Russell, M89–97). Bigod (Isabella's

by Pierre d'Abernon of Fetcham after 1276 and before 1293, most probably in 1277, but without mention of Isabella (who died in 1279): the commission for the translation was from the canons of Chichester for an unspecified lay audience.[12]

Isabella is therefore linked in various ways with texts of Becket (martyred in 1170), Edward the Confessor (intensely culted by Henry III as by Henry II and other English kings), and the two contemporary saints, Edmund, Archbishop of Canterbury, and Richard, Bishop of Chichester, while a note in the Life of the English protomartyr and patron of St Alban's mentions her by name (see Figure 5). This involvement with saints and their lives fits with the dates of Isabella's long widowhood, from the beginning of the 1240s to the late 1270s. It is tempting to see this widowhood as a career of progressive literacy, especially given Isabella's relations with clerical men—as a devotee of St Edmund's (whom she may have met, since he died in 1240, and of whose cult, following his 1245 canonization, she was a patron); as a patronage figure for Matthew Paris (d. 1259); and in what seems to have been a close friendship with Edmund's own ex-chancellor, Richard of Chichester (d. 1253). Robert Kilwardby is also a candidate for this list, though Isabella's connection with him could be accounted for by Bocking's mediation.

By the end of her widowhood, a full Latin *vita* might have been possible for Isabella's own audition or personal reading, in supplementation of the French and recitational Latin literacies which seem to have been characteristic of many

---

half-brother) is referred to as Justiciar (which he was from June 1258 to October 1260) in both the Latin and the Anglo-Norman accounts. See also *vita* i. 29 where Richard is said to be teaching a noblewoman dear to him ('quandam personam nobilem admodum sibi familiarem et caram', Jones, 123) to offer 'prayers, supplication, requests and thanksgiving' (Phil. 4: 6): perhaps, since Richard is also said to have told Bocking that he was inspired by a heavenly voice to use the liturgy of the Holy Trinity composed at St Amand and was then able to use this material to finish the work, Richard may have composed some devotions for this noblewoman (Jones, 123, also 123–4 for the story gathered by Bocking at St Amand on which this seems to be modelled: lacuna in Anglo-Norman text). Later in the same chapter, a noblewoman has a vision of Richard: the mysterious words spoken to her in it are explicated by the saint in a letter ('epistolam', Jones, 124 and 241 nn. 0–r: lacuna in Anglo-Norman text's exemplar). Richard visits a noblewoman friend before his last illness in an incident not present in the Brussels text of the *vita* but adopted by the Anglo-Norman Life from its fuller source text; Russell, vv. 1324–7 (see 134–5 and 1324–5n. for a reconstruction of missing lines here). Russell shows that the source for the Anglo-Norman translation was a text in the Sloane manuscript tradition of the *vita*, not the Brussels manuscript in which the dedicatory letters are fully extant; see *La Vie seint Richard*, ed. Russell, 2–4, 16–17).

[12] D'Abernon de Fetcham was in all probability the lawyer and clerk to William de March, treasurer (in 1290) of the king who died in 1293 and also author of the Anglo-Norman *Lumere as lais* and *Secré de secrez*: see *La Vie seint Richard*, ed. Russell, 8–13, and for the dating of the Anglo-Norman Life, ibid. 11, 17. For Isabella's death date see John A. Nichols, 'The History and Cartulary of the Cistercian Nuns of Marham Abbey, 1249–1536', Ph.D. diss., Kent State University, 1974, 245, no. 139. She was a tenant-in-chief of the king and Edward I's commission for a post mortem survey of her lands was in 1282 (CPR (1281–92), 49), but this would normally have been a little time after a death.

FIG. 5. Books and texts associated with Isabella, Countess of Arundel (1226/30–1279)

MS or text	Date	Nature of connection
1. Becket leaves (Getty MS)	c.1220–40	Possible copy (and only extant representative) of the lost Becket life said by Paris (in a note in 2 below) to be in the Countess of Arundel's possession.
2. Dublin Trinity College MS 177 (E.I.40)	MS c.1250, texts c.1230–40	Illustrated hagiographic dossier of St Alban composed by Paris who names the Countess in flyleaf note.
3. Cambridge University Library MS Ee.3.59	MS 1255–60, text 1236 × 45	Copy of Paris's illustrated Edward the Confessor Life, said in 2 above to be in the Countess's possession.
4. Campsey MS, AN Life of Edmund of Canterbury	1247 × 59	Translated by Paris from his own Latin Life of the saint for the Countess who is named as dedicatee in rubric and text.
5. Latin *vita* of Richard of Chichester	c.1270	Dedicated to the Countess (in dedicatory epistle now extant only in Brussels, MS Bib. roy. 2057–62; Countess's patronage also discussed in epilogue) by its composer Ralph Bocking.
6. AN Life of Richard of Chichester	c.1276–7	Extant in the Campsey MS (see 4 above). Translated from 5 above.

psalter and books of hours users.[13] With even a minimal version of the psalter-based literacy conferred by the education of upper-class women, however, Isabella would have been able to read in several ways the books of saints prepared by Matthew Paris and his forerunners and imitators. The illustrations and captions of the Edward and Thomas Lives would allow for visual and audiate participation and also for some kinds of personal reading and recitation. For example, in the extant Becket manuscript (see Illustration 2), the visual image of the sick saint is an important link between him and female audiences (of whatever literacy) since it confers prestige on the ascetic devotional practices common to the representation both of male ascetics and of chaste widows; the Latin caption in the illustration offers both a cartoon dramatization of

[13] The extant Thomas and Edward texts associated with Matthew Paris are illustrated and accompanied by running captions which themselves constitute a summary retelling: each page is open to several kinds of visual and audiate reception as well as to literate personal reading. See Paul Saenger, 'Books of Hours and the Reading Habits of the Later Middle Ages', in Roger Chartier (ed.), *The Culture of Print: Power and the Uses of Print in Early Modern Europe*, tr. Lydia G. Cochrane (Cambridge: Polity Press: 1988), 141–73; Michael Camille, 'Seeing and Reading: Some Implications of Illiteracy', *Art History*, 8 (1985), 26–49, and id., 'The Book of Signs: Writing and Visual Difference in Gothic Manuscripts', *Word and Image*, 1 (1985), 133–48.

ILLUST. 2. Becket's abstinence and the literacies of Isabella of Arundel.

what the doctor is saying about the saint's over-zealous fasting, vigils, and self-mortification *and* a visual image of a learned language for Latin-less readers; the red French captions beneath the illustration offer one kind of summarized narrative, open to more rapid perusal; the black ink verses beneath them offer the full text in a form suitable for reading aloud; and the Latin inscriptions above the illustration offer a further form of brief summary (perhaps as a key to clerical readers taking less Latinate female patrons through the narrative).

It is not clear that Isabella was *not* Latin-literate at the date of the Edmund Life. When Paris explains that he has composed this text in two languages because of Isabella, he may mean either that he has prepared the Anglo-Norman text as a second version especially for her, or that he has composed in both languages at her request (vv. 1976–7). But Paris's treatment of different languages within his Anglo-Norman *Edmund* Life for Isabella suggests slightly more strongly the first alternative, which would mean that Isabella in the 1240s–1250s heard texts, as expected, in French (her first language, but the second—after English—of the less aristocratic archbishop saint).[14]

In the Anglo-Norman Life, the words spoken to Edmund by the Christ child in the saint's vision are in Latin and are not translated: it is simply explained that 'Ceo est *Jhesus Nazarenus* | *Rex Judeorum gloriosus*' (vv. 269–70), perhaps because it is Edmund's vision and he had to be represented, especially to a lay audience, as having highly authoritative and Latinate visions. (Similarly, as noted above, the physician diagnosing Becket as very ill indeed at Pontigny speaks Latin, in what amounts to a visual image of a particular professional register for a French-literate reader.)[15] On the other hand, the words '*letare Jherusalem*' in the Lenten

---

[14] Paris's narrative for Isabella translates into French an English proverb used by St Edmund (quoted in English in Paris's Latin *vita* of the saint): 'Men seth gamen gooth on wombe. Ac ich segge, gamen gooth on herte' ('Vita Edmundi' in Lawrence, *Edmund of Abingdon*, 266). This becomes 'Puis [il] ad dit en son engleis | Ke dire vous puis en franceis | "Hem dit [suvent] que ventre feit | Munter en blandur et [en] heit: | [Mes] je di ke primes comence | Joie de quer et conscience"' (ed. Baker, vv. 1543–8). ('Then he said in his English what I may say to you in French: "It is often said that the belly flatters and cheers: but I say that joy begins in the heart and the conscience".') This proverb is also quoted in a sermon of *c*.1333 by William Herbert: see Tony Hunt, 'Anecdota Anglo-Normannica', *Yearbook of English Studies*, 15 (1985), 1–17, 12 n. 40). As a child, the English-speaking Edmund is said to be 'not from base nor from high people, but from loyal people of middling estate' (vv. 89–90). Edmund's parents, Reinald li Riches and Mabilia, are said to have an appropriate surname, Rich (with the sense of 'noble' as well as 'well-off' ('Bien fu li surnums ajustez, | Riches furent et honurez', vv. 95–6). Richard of Chichester is also said to be from 'bone gent' (*Vie seint Richard*, v. 71) though he is also shown working on his family's estate himself (see n. 63 below). The mystification of social status here is partly a function of the 'martyrdom of humilty' topos by which the meritocratic rise of the ecclesiastical saints is glossed: while none of these saints were directly from the nobility, it is implied of Becket, Edmund, and Richard that all three are of lower status than they were.

[15] The right-hand caption above the illustration reads 'apud Pontiniacum commorans pre nimio voluntario ieunio infirmatur graviter' ('while staying at Pontigny he becomes seriously ill through excessive voluntary fasting'). The report of the physician's speech within the frame of the illustration is 'infirmatur pre nimio ieiunio apud Pontiniacum sinisterque rumor auditus auget

liturgy for Edmund's consecration are explained: 'In French this is as much as to say "Jerusalem the joyful and merry"' (vv. 861–2). Paris's Anglo-Norman Life includes accounts (usually more extensive than those of his Latin Life) of Edmund's heroically ascetic study habits ('asez pesant martire', vv. 344 and 335–62), the trivium and quadrivium (vv. 411–48), Edmund's Oxford studies (vv. 509–38) and of Merton priory's library (vv. 540–50): this suggests both that Isabella was unable to read the Latin *vita* and that she was interested in study and learning.

Between the *Edmund* Life (composed between 1247 and 1259) and the commission to Bocking for the Latin *vita* of the 1270s, there is time for Isabella to have learnt a fuller Latinity than the recitational Latin literacy of psalter-reading, but whether she would have seen the need to do so is more of a question, and the available evidence is currently inconclusive.[16] The image of a given language can be understood and used for particular purposes without the necessity of full literacy in the language represented. The closing letter of Bocking's Richard *vita* is addressed to the Bishop of Chichester and his chapter: it looks past Isabella herself in its account of why they should accept a life written at the instigation of a woman. Although the opening letter directly addresses Isabella, Bocking may have expected its contents to be mediated to Isabella, perhaps by her chaplain or confessor or by himself at a presentation ceremony to the patroness and the chapter.[17]

Isabella's role in Bocking's letter and the Richard *vita* shows a form of, so to speak, general cultural and political literacy about saints' lives. This is also the

dolorem' ('he is ill through excessive fasting at Pontigny and the unfavourable opinion given increases grief'). The rubricated caption below the illustration is 'Par ses ieunes e uraisuns | Veilles e afflicciuns | Fiebles est le quor ad fade | E cuchez sen est malade | Par force de obedience | Amenda puis cele abstinence' ('He is feeble because of his fasts and prayers, vigils and mortifications: he has a weak heart and has gone to bed ill. By virtue of obedience he will then make up for this abstinence').

[16] Bocking's suggestion that Isabella is doing through others what she cannot do herself ('quod per semetipsam nequivit, alieno labore perficere procuravit', Jones, 159) need not refer to Latin reading literacy, but rather to Bocking's ability as a cleric to obtain, rewrite, and propose the reworked version of, the canonization proceedings. Paris's Anglo-Norman Life would suggest Isabella did not have more than phonetic or recitational Latin literacy early in her widowhood, but is at least a decade earlier than the Bocking *vita*. There is no evidence against Isabella's having Latin literacy at the later date of the Richard *vita*, but it is not quite assumable on the basis of the dedicatory letter alone, since Bocking is as concerned with offering a portrait of a suitable patroness to the Chichester chapter as with addressing Isabella herself. Isabella seems to have had her own clerk, Hugh de Brome, described as 'clericus et procurator nobilis domine Isabelle de Albiniaco, comitisse Arundell' when he appears in the Canterbury consistory court for her against Roger bishop of Lincoln (over the advowson of Olney, Bucks., diocese of Lincoln) after her efforts between 1263 and 1270 to present Hugh de Brome to the living had been rebuffed (*Select Cases from the Ecclesiastical Courts of the Province of Canterbury c.1200–1301*, ed. Norma Adams and Charles Donehue Jr. (London: Selden Society, 1981), 49.

[17] Although it is usually assumed that Latin letters written to upper-class laywomen and abbesses in 13th-c. England will have been interpreted by their clerks and chaplains, the evidence badly needs gathering and reassessing to take account of female 'micro-literacies' in particular family or monastic groups: see further Ch. 6 below.

case in the Life where there is more reason to expect Isabella to have (French) reading and audiate literacy, Matthew Paris's Anglo-Norman *Edmund*. The prologue invokes an understanding of saints' lives, represented as common to writer and patron, which uses texts, but values texts less in themselves than as contact-relics for saints.[18] The prologue and epilogue of Matthew Paris's Anglo-Norman version of his *Edmund* Life explains the choice of French as best suited not for Isabella's position as someone without the Latin for reading the *vita*, but for her status as a patron of Edmund's cult. For, says Paris, French is more widely used and better understood by clerks and lay people alike than Latin—the Life will benefit more people if it is in French.[19] Paris develops the standard Benedictine hagiographic topos of obedience to a superior in the production of texts to accommodate a lay female patron, simultaneously deferring to Isabella and constructing her in a figurehead role of pious *imitatio*. On the one hand, Isabella can claim the work from him as an obligation ('clamer dette', v. 43), since she is the patroness of Wymondham (a daughter house of St Alban's where the Earls of Arundel were buried) and he will perform her command to the best of his powers (vv. 44–5). On the other, he is moved to the work by Isabella's own alliance with the saint: she has made a great offering of her own life to him, she has sought and honoured the saint in pilgrimage (vv. 55–64). These themes are repeated at the close of the Life: Isabella provides the spur ('espurun', v. 1979) to making the saint available, she is the honoured lady of good repute who follows the path of St Edmund ('de saint Edmund suez la trace', v. 1984), and, as she is his patroness ('avoee dame', v. 1981), Paris makes a gift of the text to her ('De cest treté vous [faz] le dun', v. 1980).[20] However, the focal concern of Paris's

---

[18] For an account and further examples of such views of textuality, see Wogan-Browne, 'The Apple's Message'.

[19] 'Iceste estoire vus translat | De latin en franceis apert; | Ke chascun est de ceo bien cert | [Ke] plus est usée et sëue | Ke nule launge et entendue | De clers et lais et la gent tute | Ke le latins, ne mie dute. | De vostre purpos la resun | Bien crei saver et l'achaisun: | Ke ses beles vertuz et grace | Et clers et lays, chascuns les sace', vv. 32–42 ('I have translated this history for you from Latin into plain [*apert*] French, for everyone is very certain that French is more used and known than any other language and more understood by clerks and lay people and by everyone than Latin. I believe I will safeguard the meaning and the motive of your intention, so that his fine virtues and grace will be known to everyone, both clerk and lay'). The claim to have composed in 'deux langages' (v. 1976) because of Isabella is made in the closing dedication (vv. 1975–80).

[20] 'Avoee' in v. 1981 might conceivably refer to Isabella's being a vowess, but here the context and Paris's phrasing ('Vous *m'estes* avoee dame') make it more likely to refer to Isabella's patronage (i.e. holding of the advowson) of Wymondham, a dependent cell of St Alban's. Wymondham seems to have been important to Isabella: she challenged St Alban's to appoint priors there and took her suit to Rome: see *Gesta Abbatum monasterii Sancti Albani*, ed. H. T. Riley, RS 28 (London, 1867–9), i. 407–9; *Mon.* iii. 323–9 (325); Susan Wood, *English Monasteries and Their Patrons* (London: Oxford University Press, 1955), 61). Wymondham was one of three properties held by her at her death according to the inquisition *post mortem* of 1282 (Nichols, 'History and Cartulary, 3, 8). The phrasing of Bocking's letter is more ambiguous, but again does not prove that Isabella was a vowess (see further n. 44 below). The association of women patrons and the provision of horses for clerical writers (see Ch. 7, n. 92 below) may be relevant for the image of Isabella as the spur

dedication and conclusion is not literary composition so much as the network of obligations and allegiances between a monk, a monastic patron, and a saint, which may be mediated by a text. Isabella's is not only the request of a great and pious lady for private devotional reading (though that use of the Life by her would not be excluded), but has a public dimension.[21]

Similarly, in the case of Ralph Bocking's lengthy prologue dedication of the Latin Life of Richard of Chichester, much is said to and of Isabella which both includes and looks beyond her to several audiences: Bocking is both paying tribute to an influential figure of patronage, and articulating the value of her chaste widowhood in a Dominican project also sponsored by the then Dominican Prior Provincial. Bocking's account presents Isabella as seeing the need for a properly elegant and formal post-canonization *vita*. He notes (in another standard hagiographic prologue topos) that the accounts of Richard's virtues and miracles at the canonization proceedings were rough and unpolished ('rudi . . . stylo et incomposito') because they used the actual words of the witnesses, and so were written down in a disorderly way ('confuse fuerint scripta'). So, he says, Isabella has asked him to order and polish the materials 'to the honour of God and the edification of the audience', because, unworthy as Bocking is, he knew Richard well in his lifetime. Therefore, equipped by Isabella's command to her servant ('famulus') Bocking, the merits of the saint, Isabella's prayers, and the instruction of 'our reverend father the prior provincial, Brother Robert Kilwardby', Bocking will attempt the *vita*.[22]

Isabella's personal book ownership most probably included a psalter or book of hours for her personal devotions.[23] Bocking's dedicatory letter celebrates

to the Life (v. 1979). For a career with many striking parallels with Isabella's (including a very close Franciscan affiliation which seems never to have involved formal membership as a tertiary) see Hilary Jenkinson, 'Mary de Sancto Paulo, Foundress of Pembroke College, Cambridge', *Archaeologia*, 16 (1914–5), 401–46 (420).

[21] This is further suggested by the text's range of registers: these include a narratorial homily on the transitory nature of [baronial] 'honurs' (v. 1052) to 'vus pechëurs cheitifs', v. 1039.

[22] Jones 85, 163. Kilwardby became Archbishop of Canterbury in 1272: his register was lost when he died suddenly in Viterbo en route to the papal court (F. M. Powicke, *The Thirteenth-Century 1216–1307*, The Oxford History of England iv (Oxford: Clarendon Press, 1953), 471 n. 3). W. A. Hinnebusch thinks it possible that Isabella founded the Dominican Priory of Arundel in Sussex in 1253 and that Bocking was from there (*The Early English Friars Preachers* (Rome: Santa Sabina, 1951), 87: also *VCH, Sussex* ii. 93).

[23] The earliest book of hours produced in England has been dated to *c*.1240 (London, BL, MS Addit. 49999: see *EGM [I] 1190–1250*, iv. 1, no. 73, 119–21, and Donovan, *The De Brailes Hours*). I have not found any psalters or books of hours associated with Isabella: the closest is a Psalter and Bestiary from Petersborough or Norwich of *c*.1310 (Cambridge, MS Corpus Christi College 53) in Latin and French, which includes de Warenne obits, among them Isabella's brother, John de Warenne (27 Sept. 1304), but it is too late to be connected with Isabella. The book belonged to the prior of Peterborough, Hugh de Stukely, and is illustrated by the artist of Alice de Reydon's book of hours (Cambridge, University Library MS Dd.4.17): see N. J. Morgan and Peter Lasko, *Medieval Art in East Anglia 1300–1520* (London and Norwich: Thames and Hudson, Jarrold, 1974), 12.

Isabella's assiduity in 'votive masses, "spiritual songs, psalms and hymns" [Eph. 5: 19, Col. 3: 16]', which may mean that she paid for masses and went to church frequently, but equally suggests a regular user of a psalter or book of hours. She also owned saints' lives, though it is unclear how many or of what kind. Bocking says that Isabella has sought to adorn God's house and to edify the lives of the faithful 'inter specula scripture sacre et vite sanctorum que penes vos copiose habentur in unum' (translated by David Jones in his edition of the *vita* as 'with the mirror of scripture on the one side and on the other that of the Lives of the saints, which are plentifully represented in your library').[24] It is more likely that this is not a library, but a group of a few books, even perhaps a single compendium manuscript, or collection of *libelli*. As to whether these were Latin or Anglo-Norman lives, there is no more direct evidence than there is for Isabella's personal reading of the dedicatory letter. Another possible, but uncertain reference to a text may also be present: although Bocking has been immediately discussing the mirrors with which the virtuous women of Exodus adorn the temple, his reference to a 'speculum Scripturae' could be to a mirror text (for which the obvious candidate would be the *Speculum Ecclesie*, the *Mirour de seinte eglise* of Edmund of Canterbury, the very saint of the French Life dedicated to Isabella, in whose text indeed, contemplation of the scriptures is recommended for 'dames religieuses').[25]

It is worth considering further the life of this significant hagiographic patroness, which, despite much scholarly attention to Matthew Paris and his circle, has never been studied in its own right. In addition to saints' lives, one text which may very probably have been known to Isabella is the biography of her grandfather, William Marshal, written around the time of her own birth, and including an account of her mother and aunts' marriages and a portrait of her mother:

> Maheut out nom la premereine
> A cui Dex fist si bele estreine
> Qu'il mist en lui sens e largesse
> Bealté, franchice e gentillece
> E tot le bien, gel di por veir,
> Qu'en gentil feme deit aveir.
> (vv. 14917–22)[26]

---

[24] Jones, 84, 162.

[25] See *Mirour de Seinte Eglyse*, ed. A. D. Wilshere, ANTS 40 (London, 1982), 4.

[26] *Guillaume le maréchal, comte de Striguil et de Pembroke, régent d'Angleterre de 1216 à 1219*, ed. Paul Meyer, SATF (Paris, 1891–1901), 3 vols. (see vv. 14915–56 for the daughters of the Marshal: on their marriages see further Claude Thiry and Martine Thiry-Stassin, 'Mariage et lignage dans l'histoire de Guillaume le maréchal', in *Femmes: mariages-lignages xii–xiv siècles: mélanges offerts à Georges Duby* (Brussels: De Boeck-Wesmael, 1992), 349–59). Isabella's mother and aunts are commemorated in a 15th-c. Anglo-Norman Adam and Eve genealogical roll in which the women in the Marshal family seem to have been remembered as important (Diana B. Tyson, 'The Adam and Eve Roll in Corpus Christi College Cambridge MS 98', *Scriptorium*, 52 (1998), 301–16, 305,

Matilda was the name of the eldest,
To whom God gave such good endowment
That he bestowed on her intelligence, generosity,
Beauty, noble rank, and nobleness,
And every good quality, I declare in truth,
That a noble woman ought to have.

This is a conventional portrait, but does not sit badly with Isabella's own life (her charters emphasize the prestigious Marshal descent in comparison with her marital family of d'Albini). Isabella's mother, Matilda, was the co-heiress of William Marshal, first Earl of Pembroke (d. 1219), and became in 1225 the second wife of Isabella's father, William de Warenne, Earl of Surrey (d. 1240).[27] Isabella, born either in 1226 or 1230, was married very young in 1234 to Hugh d'Albini, count of Arundel (d. 1243).[28] Both her father and her husband died early (1240 and 1243 respectively). Moreover, Isabella had no children (and so no sons as well as no father to contest her dower). Her brother John, Earl de Warenne, was younger than she was and they seem to have remained on friendly terms, given that Isabella is represented as present in his castle of Lewes when Richard of Chichester's saintly powers save her nephew (v. M91).[29] The only other male with the right to interfere with her plans, Henry III, granted Isabella's marriage in 1243 to his foreign favourite Peter of Geneva, but she successfully fined to stay unmarried, and indeed spent thirty-six years or more—the greater part of her life—as a widow.[30] According to Bocking's Richard *vita*, she had a female

315–16). There was also a tradition of romance patronage in Isabella's marital family: the d'Albinis had patronized the Anglo-Norman *Boeve de Haumtone*: see Judith Weiss, 'The Date of the Anglo-Norman *Boeve de Haumtone*', *Medium Ævum*, 55 (1986), 237–40, and her 'The Power and Weakness of Women in Anglo-Norman Romance', in *Women and Literature in Britain 1150–1500*, 7–23, 18–19.

[27] Isabella's mother was first married to Hugh Bigod (who became Count of Norfolk in 1221), and whose son Hugh (d. 1266) was Justiciar of England: hence Isabella's kinship with the child resurrected by Richard of Chichester (see n. 11 above), the son of her half-brother, Hugh. The first wife of William de Warenne was Matilda d'Aubigny, d. 1215. Isabella, probably the eldest child of William de Warenne and Matilda of Pembroke, was born 1226–30 (see *CP* i. 238–9).

[28] Hugh d'Albini was also a royal ward until 1231 (see further Nicholas Vincent, *Peter des Roches: An Alien in English Politics 1205–1238*, Cambridge Studies in Medieval Life and Thought, 4th ser. 31 (Cambridge: Cambridge University Press, 1996), 319–20; and R. Eales, 'Henry III and the End of the Earldom of Chester', in P. J. Coss and S. D. Lloyd (eds.), *Thirteenth Century England I* (Woodbridge: Boydell, 1986), 100–13). In 1233 he agreed to pay a fine to have free administration of his estates in what remained of his minority. Girls could be betrothed at 7 though not married till 12 (14 for boys): Jennifer Ward, *Women of the English Nobility and Gentry 1100–1500* (Manchester: Manchester University Press, 1995), 17.

[29] Joan de Stuteville may be the attendant Joanna of this miracle: she later married Roger, Hugh Bigod's son, who inherited as Earl of Norfolk after his uncle Roger died in 1297 (Blaauw, *Barons' War*, 181 n. 47).

[30] On Henry III's arrangements for Isabella's dower and Hugh d'Albini's estates, see 'Vie de saint Edmond', ed. Baker, 340. It was specified that the dower assigned Isabella by the king should be saved to her (CPR (1232–47), 408). For Isabella's fine against marriage, see ibid. 423, also CR (1251–3), 87. Either Isabella or her fine was to go to the count, and, as Thompson suggests (*Women*

companion, Alice Tyrel, an 'honest widow of good character' and 'a dear personal friend' for much of her later life.[31] There was a tradition of male ecclesiastical patronage of male houses in both her biological and marital families (the d'Albinis, for instance, being buried at Wymondham, the daughter house of St Alban's in respect of which Matthew Paris salutes her as a patron).[32]

That Isabella would establish a foundation and that she would do so 'for the good of her parents and husband's souls' could have been expected, and so in her 'liege power and widowhood' she duly does, but her choice was unusual. On 27 January 1249 Isabella, then probably about 22 years old, had her nunnery of Marham in Norfolk dedicated to the Virgin, St Barbara, and St Edmund of Canterbury in a ceremony performed by Richard, Bishop of Chichester.[33] By 1250 she had Marham incorporated as a Cistercian nunnery,

---

Religious, 171), the fact that she did not remarry in these circumstances suggests that she preferred not to (as RaGena DeAragon has shown, after Magna Carta, 'dowager countesses who remained single in the period 1216–30 outnumbered those who remarried by two to one' ('Dowager Countesses', 98). A grant to Marham by her brother John, sixth earl de Warenne, in Isabella's memory makes it clear that she died in 1279 (Nicholas, 'History and Cartulary', no. 139, p. 245). She was thus either about 49 or 55 when she died: her thirty-six years of widowhood is long, but by no means unparalleled among 13th-c. noblewomen (see Figure 4).

[31] Possibly Alice, widow of Thomas Tyrel, a Sussex and Hampshire landholder, d. by 2 November 1248 (Jones, 242). In the *vita* (i. 39; lacuna in Anglo-Norman) Richard heals the eye of a noblewoman and dear friend and companion of the countess, 'an honest widow of upright character' ('Extitit quedam domina nobilis, Alicia nomine, cognomento Tyrel, illius nobilis et generose comitisse de Arundelya, Ysabelle de Aubeny, commensalis aliquando et quasi socia, quam etiam dicta comitissa viduam honestam et probis moribus ornatam intelligens, admodum caram habuit et acceptam', Jones, 130): this widow is also said to be particularly dear to the saint himself ('sancto, cui plurimum erat specialis et cara', Jones, 130). A Ralph Tyrel was constable of the castles of Richard Marshal in Ireland (CPR (1232–47), 53), and involved in transactions with Richard, Bishop of Chichester (CPR (1232–47), 120–1). In the dedicatory letter, Bocking warns Isabella not to tolerate in her household what she would not do herself: marriage is licit in itself but inappropriate for those who wish to live in chastity ('Credite michi, non ipsa conjugum licita commercia caste vivere volentibus conveniunt', Jones, 84): perhaps Alice wanted remarriage and hence is said to be 'commensalis *aliquando*' of Isabella.

[32] The earls of Warenne had each founded and patronized at least one (male) house (principally in Norfolk) as had every Earl Arundel except Hugh d'Albini (from whom Isabella had her right to confirm the priors of Wymondham). Paris died before Isabella's suit over Wymondham against St Alban's (see n. 20 above) began in 1262.

[33] See Nichols, 'History and Cartulary', 223, no. 8. Nichols assumes Edmund to be the major East Anglian king and martyr (d. 869) culted at Bury (ibid. 12), but given Edmund of Canterbury's recent canonization and Isabella's interest in him, the archbishop seems the better candidate for the house's dedication. According to the [14th-c.] cartulary (now NRO Hare I 232X) Isabella used her dowry from William de Warenne to Hugh d'Albini (p. 234, no. 70). Matthew Paris says she founded 'de libero maritagio suo', a term associated with dower (*Chron. maj.* v. 215, n. 3, AD 1251). In the cartulary's copy of the charter, the foundation is 'in viduitate et ligia potestate mea, pro salute animae meae, et pro anima Willelmi comitis Warenniae patris mei, Matildis comitisseae Warenniae matris meae et pro anima Hugonis comitis Arundelliae quondam viri mei et pro animabus antecessorum et successorum meorum', 223. (The Countess of Salisbury's charter for her early 13th-c. foundation of Lacock puts her husband first, founding Lacock 'pro Deo et pro anima comitis Willielmi Longespeie, mariti mei, et omnium antecessorum suorum et

one of only two female houses to achieve this status in England following the Cistercians' General Chapter statutes of the 1220s against the acceptance of any more nunneries.[34] (She thus succeeded where, for instance, the redoubtable countesses of Salisbury and Gloucester had difficulty, respectively, with their slightly later foundations of Lacock and Sandleford.)[35] Isabella seems to have been careful and strategic in her choice of affiliation: she got papal permission to enter Waverley, the English Cistercian mother house, and, according to the Waverley annalist, devoutly and successfully petitioned, 'in capitulo noster', for association— and also gave Waverley gifts of wine, pittances, and money.[36]

meorum, et pro salute mea et Willelmi Longespeie filii mei primogeniti' and also completing the establishment of his foundation at Henton before fully setting up Lacock: *Mon.* vi. 1, 502, no. VI.) The relative status of the families is a factor here and the charters are dubious evidence for these patronesses' attitudes. However, Isabella's purposefulness is suggested by her special purchases of lands for the nunnery and her continuing advocacy of its interests. A papal letter of 1250, issued at Lyons by Innocent IV, grants forty days' indulgence for all contributing to Marham, which the 'Countess of Arundel, sister of R(oger) Bigod . . . earl of Norfolk and Marshal of England, has begun to rebuild with great expense' (Jane E. Sayers, *Original Papal Documents in England and Wales from the Accession of Pope Innocent III to the Death of Pope Benedict XI (1198–1304)* (Oxford: Oxford University Press, 1999), no. 375, p. 168). Isabella continued to support this nunnery throughout her life, as did her brother.

[34] Sally Thompson argues that 'the early Cistercians at first ignored and then barely tolerated the ladies who wished to share their fervour and imitate their customs . . . even in the first half of the 13th c. the affiliation of nunneries to the order was beset by difficulties' ('The Problem of the Cistercian Nuns', in Baker (ed.), *Medieval Women*, 227–52). But the history of women and the Cistercian order is still emerging: Marham was the last Cistercian nunnery founded in England and Wales (Nichols, 'History and Cartulary', 8): three others existed after the Cistercian statutes in 1228. Gilchrist disputes Knowles and Hadcock's account of Cistercian nunneries and argues that half were founded before 1175 (*Gender and Material Culture*, fig. 7, p. 37). For assessments and counter-arguments to previous estimates of the visibility of Cistercian nuns, see Constance Berman, 'Cistercian Nuns and the Development of the Order: The Abbey at Saint-Antoine-des-Champs outside Paris', in E. Rozanne Elder (ed.), *The Joy of Learning and the Love of God: Studies in Honor of Jean Leclercq* (Kalamazoo, Mich.: Cistercian Publications, 1995), 121–56 (146, nn. 4 and 7), who argues that Thompson's figures in *Women Religious* assume that the statutes mention all houses. See also Venarde, *Women's Monasticism*, 81.

[35] Lacock was not incorporated as Cistercian till twenty years after Ela of Salisbury's foundation (see Thompson, *Women Religious*, 112, 171), and Maud de Clare's Sandleford never succeeded, though her later foundation at Canonsleigh (with the Augustinians) was successful (see Ch. 6, nn. 66–72 below).

[36] '. . . societatem ordinis in capitulo nostro devote petiit et obtinuit: iv marcas et unum dolium vini conventui ad pitancias donavit', *Ann. mon.* ii. 345, AD 1252 (where Isabella's desire to found is described as divinely guided: 'divina, ut creditur, inspiratione praeventa', 344–5). As Thompson notes, this was especially tactful since their house was on land she had inherited (*Women Religious*, 171). Everything that is known of Isabella suggests great intelligence, skill, and knowledge in the achievement of her objectives, including her management of churchmen and institutions. Marham was one of two Cistercian nunneries to remain exempt from episcopal visitation in England, although this privilege of Cistercian monasteries was not generally shared by female houses (see John A. Nichols, 'Medieval Cistercian Nunneries and English Bishops', in Nichols and Shank (eds.), *Distant Echoes*, 237–49 (239)). As a Cistercian house, Marham was excused the 1254, 1275, and 1291 taxations in the Norwich diocese: the Cistercian affiliation gained by Isabella conferred valuable privileges (Nichols, 'History and Cartulary', 122–4).

Isabella's choices and strategies regarding Marham and the Cistercians may have been due to Richard of Chichester's influence (he supported Cistercians as well as Dominicans).[37] Even more likely perhaps is St Edmund's pro-Cistercian influence and Isabella's experiences in northern France, where she travelled, and where, unlike England, St Barbara was widely culted. In spite of the Cistercian legislation against the affiliation of female houses, there was, as Constance Berman has shown, a vigorous early thirteenth-century tradition of female lay noble foundation in northern France, including at least nine female Cistercian communities affiliated as daughter houses to the major male Cistercian community at Pontigny in the diocese of Sens.[38] Pontigny was the site of Becket's exile and Edmund of Canterbury's burial: according to Paris's Life of Edmund, it was the object of Isabella's pilgrimage (perhaps with her relative Henry III in 1254, or perhaps with Blanche of Castile, her son Louis XI of France, and Richard of Chichester at the translation and the dedication of Edmund of Canterbury's Pontigny shrine in 1247).[39] In his *Chronica Majora* under 1250, the Benedictine Paris claims that the Cistercians of Pontigny cut off St Edmund's right arm (for a separate shrine just inside the church door), either because they were stirred 'by greed horrible to narrate', or because they were 'wearied by the frequent arrival of pilgrims, especially Englishwomen (for permission was not granted to any other women to do so) who flocked to the tomb of St Edmund'.[40] In 1255 the cardinal of S. Lorenzo in Lucina, Rome, sent a letter to Pontigny relaxing the ban on women from the shrine of St Edmund, though access to other Cistercian churches was to remain forbidden.[41] It is not impossible that

---

[37] In his will, bequests are made to both orders: see W. H. Blaauw, 'The Will of Richard de la Wych', *Sussex Archaeological Collections*, 1 (1848), 164–92.

[38] 'Fashions in Monastic Patronage: The Popularity of Supporting Cistercian Abbeys for Women in Thirteenth-Century Northern France', *Proceedings of the Annual Meeting of the Western Society for French History*, 17 (1990), 36–45. Berman argues that 'conscious choices for the foundation of Cistercian houses for women were influenced neither by an excess of religious vocations, nor by the closing off of religious avenues for women, but because Cistercian women were extremely popular and their prayers thought efficacious' (41).

[39] Sunday, 9 June 1247 (Lawrence, *Life of St Edmund*, 99; 'multisque Galliae et Angliae proceribus' (*Ann. mon.* ii. 339)). Or perhaps the 1249 translation of Edmund when Matthew Paris records 'praelatorum et magnatum numerosa multitudine' as present (*Chron. maj.* iv. 76).

[40] '... monachi Pontiniacenses, vel taedio affecti de frequentia peregrinorum, praecipue mulierum ad tumbam sancti Edmundi Anglicarum, (quia aliis non est concessa licentia) catervatim affluentium, vel stimulis agitati cupiditatis, brachium ejusdem sancti dextrum, quod est horribile dictu, ausu temerario absciderunt', *Chron. maj.* v. 113.

[41] 'Vie de saint Edmond', ed. Baker, 342. The ban had been lifted before, in 1204, to allow Adele, Queen of France, widow of Louis VII, and mother of Philip Augustus, with her women, to hear a sermon in the chapter room, walk in the cloister and stay two nights, but the abbot who allowed this was threatened with deposition the following year. Nevertheless Adele was buried there in 1206 (Edmund Martène and Ursinus Durand, *Thesaurus Novus Anecdotorum* III (Paris, 1717; repr. Farnborough, Hants: Gregg, 1968–9), cols. 1244–5). In 1291 a papal indult was granted to Joan, Countess of Gloucester and Hereford to enter Cistercian monasteries accompanied by eight 'honest matrons' (*Cal. Pap. Bulls*, ed. Bliss and Johnson, 525).

Isabella had had a hand in this relaxation: certainly Matthew Paris says that she 'sought, honoured and paid service to [St Edmund]' (vv. 59–60) by more than feminine efforts ('travals plus ke femenins', v. 58).

All this sounds like a woman of force and character. It is very striking that, for all the importance of female anchoritism in thirteenth-century England, Isabella was not a recluse (like the Countess of Leicester), nor, for all her lifelong support of it, did she enter her own foundation of Marham (unlike the Countess of Salisbury, who, 'according to the counsel of St Edmund archbishop of Canterbury and other wise men', took the habit in her own abbey of Lacock).[42] Nor is it clear that Isabella chose the other approved path for an Anglo-Norman widow who wished to remain unmarried, that of becoming a vowess. Edmund of Canterbury himself had consecrated no less a vowess than Eleanor, sister of Henry III, in 1231 at a ceremony also attended by Richard of Chichester.[43] However, Bocking's dedication praises Isabella for *voluntary* chastity, specifically 'non voti necessitate, sed casti proposito sola voluntate' ('not required by a formal vow, but a purely voluntary chastity').[44] There is no evidence that she affiliated with Marham in any way other than as its patron.[45] Paris also avoids explicit statement of a vow, declaring rather that Isabella has dedicated the great offering of her soul, her person, and her life to Edmund ('grant offrende | De vostre almë et cors et vie', vv. 62–3). Yet Isabella seems to have managed, throughout her long and independent life, to be perceived as a chaste and pious widow rather

[42] On the Countess of Leicester's reclusion at Hackington (1221–66), see Powicke, 'Loretta of Leicester', 263–6. Ela 'assumpsit habitum religionis apud Lacok . . . secundum consilium et auxilium S. Edmundi Cantuar. archiepiscopi et aliorum virorum discretorum' (the foundation story is in the Lacock register, printed by Dugdale: *Mon.* vi. 1, 501–2, no. II).

[43] Eleanor had vowed to remain 'permanens in viduitate' at some point between 1231 and 1238, following the death of her first husband, William Marshal II, and subsequently abandoned the vow to marry Simon de Montfort (see *Ann. mon.* iv. 65; Maddicott, *Simon de Montfort*, 21–9).

[44] Jones, 83. Baker suggests that Isabella made a vow before Richard of Chichester ('Vie de saint Edmond', 344), but there is no evidence for this. Bocking's phrasing is ambiguous and could refer to Isabella's readiness to keep a vow rather than to her ability to remain chaste without one, but given the absence of other indications and given Isabella's mobility and public appearances, the second meaning seems more likely with Isabella still unvowed when, many years into her widowhood, Bocking's *vita* was composed. (Isabella kept the Albini title of Arundel after Hugh d'Albini's death and is usually referred to as 'd'Albiniaco, comitissa Arundelliae': Isabella de Mortimer, Isabella's sister-in-law on her husband's side, seems not to have been referred to as the Countess of Arundel until after Isabella (de Warenne's) death in 1279.) Matthew Paris records the vows of Cecilia de Sandford and Joanna, Countess of Pembroke in 1251 in the presence of Edmund of Canterbury, and he also exemplifies de Sandford's steadfast adherence to her vow with her dying refusal to give up the ring of profession to the confessor (who reproaches her with dying adorned), since it is her witness before the tribunal of 'her spouse, God' (*Chron. maj.* v. 235–6). But he says nothing of Isabella's making such a vow in his account of her in the Edmund Life (see n. 20 above) or anywhere else. Mary Erler's study of vowed women shows that in the later Middle Ages, 'some women affiliated with religious communities [took formal vows], others did not' ('English Vowed Women', 156).

[45] The extant cartulary documents distinguish Isabella and the abbess of Marham (see e.g. Nichols, 'History and Cartulary', 222, no. 3).

than a woman worryingly on the loose, and this in spite of her pilgrimages and her several recorded occasions of public speaking.[46] Adam Marsh, who did not hesitate to excoriate the king's sister as a 'praevaricatrix' (when she broke her *votum castitate* in order to become Countess of Leicester and wife, from 1238, of Simon de Montfort), speaks respectfully of Isabella in a letter to the Anglican Minister General of the Friars, while the Waverley annalist says she is 'adorned to no small degree by worthy conduct' ('morum gravitate non mediocriter adornata').[47] Isabella's texts and their portrayal of her as a chaste and devout widow and pious patron must have had an immediate personal value not only to the clerics whose projects she supported but to Isabella herself in maintaining and validating her notably independent and unenclosed widowhood.

Isabella's interest in the lives of contemporary holy men is, then, both personal and specific and more than a general devotional interest. However, her interest also has important representative aspects. Her Anglo-Norman *Edmund* and the Anglo-Norman *Richard* are extant in late thirteenth-century copies in the manuscript of the Augustinian canonesses of Campsey in which Isabella herself is relatively prominent as the only named contemporary woman in the rubrics of any of the manuscript's lives and of which she is a possible patroness.[48] The thirteen lives in the manuscript (see Figure 6) suggest a series of monastic

[46] Isabella's appearance in the chapter at Waverley (n. 36 above) and her intervention at Henry III's court as represented by Matthew Paris (see further below) must both count as forms of public speaking.

[47] For Adam Marsh on Eleanor, see *Ann. mon.* iv. 65; on Isabella, *Monumenta Franciscana*, ed. J. S. Brewer, RS 4a (London, 1858), Ep. clxxxiv, 330–1 (331); for the Waverley Annalist on Isabella, *Ann. mon.* ii, AD 1252, 344–5.

[48] Campsey's rubric for the Edmund Life is: 'Ici comence la vie saint eadmund le cunfessur arceuesque de canterbire translate de latin en romanz par la requeste la cuntesse de arundel' (London, BL, MS Addit. 70513, f. 85vb). On the question of her patronage, see the forthcoming study of the Campsey manuscript by D. W. Russell (Introduction, n. 11). It would be very satisfying to identify this manuscript with the *vitae sanctorum* said to be owned by Isabella (p. 164 n. 24 above) but there is insufficient evidence and other possibilities (for example, the presence of two lives composed in Barking and one associated with it in the Campsey manuscript might suggest a patron or inmate of that abbey). As Delbert Russell points out (pers. comm., May 1998), the quiring of the Campsey manuscript precludes Isabella's own texts having been incorporated into the manuscript if, as suggested above, they were *libelli* (the manuscript in any case involves a programmatic compilation of eleven lives, not just the lives of Isabella's two churchmen). If, at the date of Bocking's dedicatory letter in 1270, Isabella owned what was to become the Campsey manuscript it would necessarily have lacked the Anglo-Norman Life of Richard (composed 1276 at earliest and a *terminus ad quem* for the manuscript), yet codicologically the Campsey text of this Life was part of the planned eleven lives of the manuscript. None of this is however incompatible with Isabella's commissioning or patronage of the manuscript: though the dates are tight (the Campsey manuscript must be after 1276, Isabella died in 1279), they are not impossible. Isabella's will might shed further light on her books, but I have so far been unable to find it (unsurprisingly in the case of a 13th-c. will, see M. M. Sheehan, *The Will in Medieval England* (Toronto: Pontifical Institute of Medieval Studies, 1983) and see his 'A List of Thirteenth-Century Wills', in M. M. Sheehan (ed.), *James K. Lafarge, Marriage, Family, and Law in Medieval Europe: Collected Studies* (Toronto: University of Toronto Press, 1996). The Bury Chronicle notices her death and her burial at Marham

FIG. 6. Texts and authors in the Campsey manuscript

Saint	Author and Date	Locations/associations
1. Elisabeth of Hungary	Bozon, end 13th–early 14th c.	Bozon probably from Nottingham, perh. Steventon Priory
2. Paphnutius	Bozon	
3. Paul the hermit	**frere boioun** (f. 8rb)	
4. Thomas Becket	**Guernes** (de Pont-Ste-Maxence, f. 48rb), 1172–6	patronage from abbess of Barking 'suer saint Thomas' claimed in Paris MS BN f. fr. 13513
5. Magdalen	**Will'** (Guillaume le clerc, f. 55va) 1180 × 91–1238	G. associated with Kenilworth Augustinian priory, known to Alexander Stavensby, bp. Coventry and Lincoln (1224–38)
6. Edward the Confessor	Nun of Barking, 1163 × 89	Barking: probable connections with Henry II's court
7. Edmund of Canterbury	Matthew Paris, 1247 × 59	**translaté de latin en romanz par la requeste la cuntesse de arundel** (f. 85vb)
8. Audrey of Ely	**Marie** (f. 134a)	?Barking ?Chatteris ?Canonsleigh (Hugh de Northwold, abbot of Bury, then Ely, translates shrine 1252)
9. Osith of Chich, Aylesbury, Hereford	anon., late 12th c.	Alice de Vere (d. 1163), mother of Bp. William de Vere of Hereford (author of a Latin version), becomes corrodian at Chich in her widowhood
10. Faith	**Symon de Walsingham** (f. 148ra) before 1214–5?	Horsham St Faith cult site, Bury St Edmunds (author's monastery), Fitzwalter patronage (intermarried with de Valoignes, late 12th c.)
11. Modwenna	anon., early 13th c.	based on Latin *vita* by Abbot Geoffrey of Burton (Richard of Bury becomes prior of Burton 1222)
12. Richard of Chichester	**Pieres de fecham** (f. 244va) 1276–7	based on Bocking's *vita* of 1270, dedicated to Isabella of Arundel
13. Catherine of Alexandria	Clemence of Barking, *c.*1170 × *c.*1200	Barking, ?Henry II's court

(*The Chronicle of Bury St Edmunds 121–1301*, ed. Antonia Gransden (London and Edinburgh: Nelson, 1964), 77, AD 1282), as does a manuscript of the *Flores Historiarum* compiled until 1304 at St Benet Holme in Norfolk (see *Flores Historiarum*, ed. H. R. Luard, RS 95, iii. 58), but there is no mention of Isabella's death and burial in the Marham cartulary. The abbess of Marham had the right of proving the wills of those who died in the abbey: this was disputed but confirmed by the bishop of Norwich, *VCH, Norfolk* ii. 370.

and family networks stretching from Essex to Norfolk (both places where Isabella owned property). The de Valoignes, founders of Campsey, had links in these places, as did the de Vere family (whose foundations included Castle Hedingham in north Essex near Campsey), while the countesses of Ufford contributed inmates and associates to Campsey at the end of the thirteenth and throughout the fourteenth century, helping it to remain the most prestigious female house in the diocese of Norfolk (see Figure 7).[49] As noted in the Introduction above, composition on the part of the women of Barking Abbey in Essex is represented in the Campsey manuscript's Edward the Confessor and Catherine of Alexandria, while its Becket Life (not Matthew Paris's, but Guernes de Pont-Ste-Maxence's) claims in one of its manuscript traditions to have had material help from the community and abbess of Barking, who at the time was Becket's sister.[50] The Life of Faith was composed by a Bury monk of Norfolk origins, Simon of Walsingham, while the Life of Etheldreda (*Audrée*) also present in the manuscript is principally set in Ely, with which, as Virginia Blanton-Whetsall has shown, Campsey had many links.[51] Other princess-abbess

[49] On Campsey, see *VCH, Suffolk* ii. 112–15; Marilyn Oliva, *Convent and Community*, 121–2, 168–9, 172–3. (Noble patronage was not exclusive: Oliva points out that Campsey received patronage from all ranks, 180.) Dr Virginia Blanton-Whetsall has suggested to me that the manuscript could have come to Campsey as a gift from Isabella de Ufford: this provides the kind of donor one would expect, but is rendered problematic by the early 14th-c. inscription of Campsey ownership. While the dating of this earlier inscription can scarcely be hard and fast, Isabella de Ufford did not enter the house until the later 14th c. (though Maud de Ufford established a chantry there in 1347, *VCH, Suffolk* ii. 113), and the earlier Isabella of Arundel is a better candidate as the commissioner/donor of the manuscript. Isabella de Ufford is, however, an excellent example of someone who could be numbered among the manuscript's later audiences: for a valuable study of this noble vowess and patron, with many implications for the future unravelling of Campsey, Barking, and Ely nexuses around the manuscript and its texts, see Virginia Blanton-Whetsall, 'St Æthelthryth's Cult: Literary, Historical, and Pictorial Constructions of Gendered Sanctity', Ph.D. thesis (SUNY, Binghamton, 1998), 272–307. (I am very grateful to Dr Blanton-Whetsall for sending me a copy of her work.)

[50] On the lives composed at Barking see further Ch. 7 below. For the revisions to the Becket life, see Ian Short, 'An Early Draft of Guernes' *Vie de saint Thomas Becket*', *Medium Ævum*, 46 (1977), 20–34. Guernes's second life of Beckett was completed in 1174 (*La Vie de saint Thomas le Martyr par Guernes de Pont-Sainte-Maxence*, ed. E. Walberg (Lund: Gleerup, 1922)). In Walberg's MS P, f. 98r–v (BN f. fr. 13513), the text is followed by an epilogue addressed to 'l'abeesse suer saint Thomas' (Appendix and see pp. xxiii–xxiv). A 13th-c. abbess of Barking, Maud de Bosham (1215–47), was a relative of another of Becket's biographers, Herbert de Bosham (d. 1186): see E. A. Loftus and H. F. Chettle, *A History of Barking Abbey* (Barking: Wilson and Whitworth, 1932), 31 n. 42.

[51] Blanton-Whetsall suggests that Hugh de Northwold, Bishop of Ely (1229–54) and formerly abbot of Bury, encouraged Marie in the composition of *Audrée* in connection with his translation of the saint's shrine in 1252 ('St Æthelthryth's Cult', 311 n. 16, 251–8). Hugh's disputed Bury abbatial election in 1214–15 concerned some of the region's major lay noblemen (Isabella's father's generation of Bigods, Marshals, Fitzwalters, and Warennes, for example: see Thomson, *Chronicle of the Election*, 83 n. 5, 168), and also monks subsequently connected with some of the communities represented in the Campsey manuscript. Simon of Walsingham, author of *La vie sainte Foy*, served on Hugh of Northwold's deputation to the pope (Ch. 2, n. 35 above); Richard, the precentor of Bury who unsuccessfully contested the election, became abbot of St Modwenna's abbey

[cont. on p. 174]

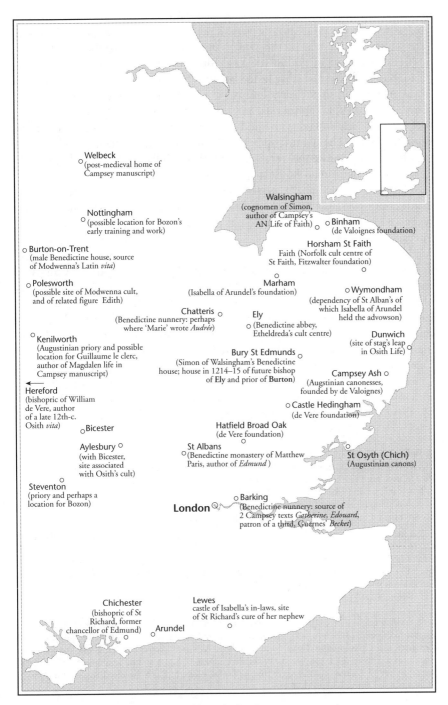

Fig. 7. Sites and communities associable with the Campsey manuscript

lives in the manuscript are Osith, associated with the priory of Chich in Essex (the retirement place of Alice de Vere, d. *c*.1163, whose son Bishop William de Vere wrote a Latin *vita* of the saint), and Modwenna (patroness of Burton-on-Trent, but brought within the Essex orbit by the thirteenth-century inter-polation of a Modwenna story in the late twelfth-century Life of Osith).[52] Added to the manuscript in the early fourteenth century are, as noted in Chapter 4.2 above, Lives of Paul, Paphnutius, and Elisabeth of Hungary by Bozon, who has been most closely linked with the Nottingham friary and whose family came from Norfolk.[53] The manuscript's Magdalen Life is by Guillaume le Clerc and together with Modwenna represents another Midlands Life (with probable links to the Augustinian house at Kenilworth).[54]

Whether or not Isabella herself was the commissioner or patron of the manuscript, overlaps between Isabella's hagiographic interests and at least two élite female communities are clear. Barking, Campsey, and Isabella all have interests in the life of Becket; Isabella's Life of Edmund of Canterbury and the Anglo-Norman version of her *vita* of Richard of Chichester (lives largely fashioned on the model of Becket's hagiography) became part of Campsey's reading; Campsey (together with Isabella if she was patron or commissioner of the Campsey manuscript) knew Barking's texts (with Barking's Edward the Confessor and Catherine of Alexandria as well as Guernes's Becket Life in its collection). In addition, in as yet undetermined relations with the texts and com-munities already mentioned, former élite female communities are imaged in the Campsey manuscript's account of Etheldreda's Ely, Modwenna's Burton, and Osith's Chich (see further Chapter 6 below): contemporary thirteenth-century relations with the male replacements of these communities (and with others, notably Matthew Paris's St Alban's and perhaps Simon of Walsingham's Bury and

of Burton on Trent in 1222; Bury's Nicholas of Dunstable subsequently became archdeacon of Ely, then bishop of Worcester, Winchester, and chancellor to Henry III (Thomson, *Chronicle of the Election*, pp. xvi, 193–4). A book from Bury's medieval library contains a letter from the niece of Hugh de Northwold, 'Lucy of St Edmund's', to her brother Nicholas the archdeacon (ibid. 192 n. 5). It is along such networks, combining monastic, ecclesiastic, and family threads, that the specific history of the Campsey book was most probably shaped.

[52] First noticed by Alexander Bell, 'Notes on Two Anglo-Norman Saints' Lives', *Philological Quarterly*, 35 (1956), 48–60 (48) and published by A. T. Baker, 'An Episode from the Anglo-French Life of St Modwenna', in Williams and de Rothschild, *Miscellany . . . Presented to Ernst Kastner*, 9–21. On Osith's own East Anglian connections, see Bethell, 'Lives of St Osyth', and for possible connections with Hatfield in Essex, n. 3 (87–8).

[53] *Three Saints' Lives*, ed. Klenke, pp. xxv–xxxii, and ead., 'Steventon Priory and a Bozon Manuscript'.

[54] Guillaume le Clerc (1180 × 91–1238) was from Normandy, but was employed by the Augustinian prior of Kenilworth on commissions and seems to have worked in the diocese of Coventry and Lincoln (*ANCL* 120), whose bishop, Alexander Stavensby (1224–38), responded to one of his poems in the 1230s. On the Magdalen Life, see Ch. 4.2 and n. 60 above; for Guillaume, see *Le Besant de Dieu de Guillaume le clerc de Normandie*, ed. Pierre Ruelle (Brussels: Éditions de l'Université de Bruxelles, 1973), 7–11.

Horsham) may also be related to the manuscript's production. A more mobile version of household is also represented in the community of the manuscript's Magdalen (Chapter 4.2 above). Three bishops, three abbesses, two virgin martyrs, a king, and the high-status penitent, Mary Magdalen, with all but two virgin martyrs and the Magdalen native to Britain, seem a combination appropriate both to aristocratic women in lay or semi-religious lives and to prestigious female communities. If Isabella herself was not responsible for the manuscript (and if she were, it might well have been designed in the first place for Marham's reading and subsequently found suitable for Campsey's), someone among these Essex and East Anglian communities who knew her may well have instigated it.

The involvement of Isabella herself (or, at the very least, the inclusion of her saints' lives) in the manuscript also allows us to see thirteenth-century continuities between nunneries and the court, for Isabella's interests are also represented there.[55] Her reading overlaps with that of royal and noble women, reading which itself could have a role in the public functions of these women (as in, for example, the necessity for Eleanor of Provence's knowledge of the cult of Edward the Confessor propagated by her husband Henry III, as mentioned in Chapter 1.5 above) as well as in their personal pieties. The note in Matthew Paris's *Auban* manuscript asks Isabella to send on the Lives of Edward and Thomas to Sanchia, Countess of Cornwall (married to the king's brother), and that these lives continued to figure in the reading of the court is suggested by the fact that Eleanor of Castile in the 1280s had her *pictor* and *scriptor* repair lives of Thomas and Edward (possibly in the case of the Confessor's Life, the presentation copy given to her mother-in-law, Eleanor of Provence).[56] The Countess of Winchester was in all probability the dedicatee of another book by Paris.[57] Isabella's lives of churchmen are the saints of at least two audiences, secular and religious, with each of whom she has many things in common.

Although élite audiences are the most visible in the records, it is unlikely that the sisters of Edmund of Canterbury, whom he had placed in the nunnery of Catesby and who successfully promoted his cult there, did not have a life of

---

[55] The manuscript's 12th-c. texts from Barking (see further Ch. 7 below) represent similar overlaps of interest between an élite female community and the court, both in the reign of Henry II when they were composed and in their continuing 13th-c. existence (especially as texts of royal and episcopal cults: even the legendary Catherine of Alexandria in the Barking *Catherine* is a royal princess converting an empress, with both saint and convert mourned by the women of the court).

[56] See n. 7 above for Paris's note in the *Auban* manuscript. On the repair of Eleanor of Castile's books, see John Carmi Parsons, 'Of Queens, Courts, and Books', 178 and n. 20.

[57] According to another note (possibly in Matthew Paris's hand) on the flyleaf of the *Auban* manuscript, a series of at least thirteen illustrations of saints accompanied by brief Anglo-Norman verses was to be prepared for inclusion 'in libro comitisse Wint' bine imagines in singulis paginis fiant sic' (James, *La Estoire de Seint Aedward*, 23; M. R. James, W. R. L. Lowe, and E. F. Jacob, *Illustrations to the Life of Saint Alban in Trinity College Dublin MS E. i. 40* (Oxford: Clarendon Press, 1924), 15–16). The countess in question is most probably the Countess of Winchester (at this date Roger de Quenci's second wife Elena or perhaps her successor).

him.[58] The Lives both of Edmund and of his chaplain Richard of Chichester are largely modelled on Becket, as are the Latin Lives of Bishop Walter Cantilupe, d. 1266 (whose cult did not suceed), and Thomas Cantilupe (who was canonized in 1320). Several versions of Becket's life were written both in England and in northern France (where Becket is well represented in manuscripts of vernacular hagiography).[59] These texts are part of the hagiographic subgenre of the ecclesiastical courtier-saint which stretches across the thirteenth century.

5.2. ASCETIC BIOGRAPHY AND BARONIAL SPIRITUALITY

Although vernacular Becket lives have always had some attention, *Edmund* and *Richard* have been little commented on. These lives of meritocratic churchmen certainly lack spectacular action: Richard's biggest miracle while alive is to leave an Oxford college dinner just before a lump of stone crashes down onto his seat (vv. 403–82), a story also told of his patron St Edmund of Canterbury. However, by trying to reconstruct their interest for their thirteenth-century audiences, especially their patroness and other female audiences, a number of interesting features emerge both of the lives and of the reading of women so inadequately labelled by the portmanteau terms of 'pious' and 'devotional' reading.

Churchmen's biographies map family relations and sexual and gender identities no less powerfully than chivalric and courtly romance or virgin martyr hagiography.[60] They can be compared with virgin martyr *passio* both in terms of

---

[58] Margery and Alice Rich developed their brother's cult at Catesby: Edmund left his cloak and his painted image of the Virgin and of Becket's passion to them (*Vie de saint Edmond*, vv. 1585–92). In the small and not very wealthy nunnery of Catesby, this inheritance was significant: Margery became prioress and a new chapel was built to house Edmund's relics. The *SEL* version of Edmund's Life claims that God has performed many miracles through these relics and that both women were buried before the high altar of a chapel built by them at Catesby in their brother's honour (*Early South English Legendary*, ed. Horstmann, 436, ll. 162–4). Catesby was chosen, according to his biographies, out of Edmund's hatred for simony, but since the practice of dower for conventual entry was virtually universal, this is much more likely to reflect an inability to fund entry to a wealthier convent, or the refusal of such convents to accept women of Edmund's sisters' birth. Edmund's brother, Robert, is cited by Matthew Paris in 1244 among other clerics as a miracle worker ('Novi sancti clarent in Angli', *Chron. maj.* iv. 378): the elevation of one brother seems to have provided religious careers for the entire family.

[59] Ian Short, 'The Patronage of Beneit's *Vie de Thomas Becket*', *Medium Ævum*, 56 (1987), 239–56; for Continental lives see Paul Meyer, 'Légendes en vers'; 'Légendes en prose'; Martine Thiry-Stassin (forthcoming study of lives of English saints on the Continent).

[60] On hagiography as a place for medieval thinking about sexuality see, for instance, Simon Gaunt, *Gender and Genre in Medieval French Literature*, ch. 9. For a study of the Anglo-Norman Life of Pope Clement as a clerical romance of psychic and social formation, see Wogan-Browne, ' "Bet . . . to . . . rede on holy seyntes lyves . . ." '. The figuration of relations and actions in churchmen's lives can be very striking: the Becket Life (*c.*1184) by Beneit images Becket's murderers as killing their father in the womb of their mother ('Kar dedens le ventre lur mere | Unt a

their treatment of desire and for the importance of speech as theme and mode of narrative action. In the *passio* of the virgin martyr, Christ is the rival bridegroom to the virgin's pagan tyrant. In ascetic biography, the bishop saint is in nuptial relation to his church, which, especially in a period of such intense commentary on the Song of Songs as the twelfth and early thirteenth century, is his bride.[61] Edmund's triumph at his (contested) accession to the archbishopric is compared with Tobit's as the successful spouse of Sarre (vv. 907–16).[62] The saint's personal virginity is already wedded to the supreme Virgin Mother: a Marian statue accepts—and hangs on to—a betrothal ring from him ('De cest anel or vus espus', v. 189) in answer to his prayer for chastity and continuing virginity ('mun quer, ma char en chasteté', v. 173; 'pucele, puceus me gardez', v. 179). Richard of Chichester also keeps 'the flower of his flesh' from all stain, so that he could 'sing the new song' to the Lamb together with those others who follow the Lamb wherever he goes and who 'have never been stained ['unt tetche . . . atret'] with women' (vv. 103–20 and Rev. 14: 4). The exchange of women, land, and marriage is dealt with in this Life in a miniature parody of secular meritocratic ascent. Richard gains land as a reward for saving his elder brother's estate by being prepared to labour on it (vv. 247–59).[63] But he returns the land once he realizes it implicates him in advantageous marriage: 'I will be as courteous ['curteis', v. 305] to you', he says to his brother, 'as you were to me: here is your land, I give it all back to you—and your charter, and the maiden, if it pleases her and her kin' (vv. 305–10), and he departs for Oxford and Paris. Like the beloved disciple John (who was supposedly the groom at the wedding of Cana), God has recalled Richard from the marriage bed (vv. 275–6). Temporal landownership is transcended by study, the route to an eternal inheritance in heaven

tort occiz lur pere | E lur pastur, vv. 2044–6) and as taking her spouse from their mother and making her a widow ('A lur mere unt toleit | Sun espus e vedve feit', vv. 2047–8), *La Vie de Thomas Becket par Beneit: poème anglo-normand du XIIe siècle*, ed. Börje Schlyter (Lund: C. W. K. Gleerup, 1941): see also vv. 751–2. Similar metaphors are also in the Becket Life by Guernes de Pont-Ste-Maxence: Becket, for instance, is said to have been martyred for his mother the church: see *La Vie de saint Thomas le martyr par Guernes*, ed. Walberg, v. 14.

[61] See E. Ann Matter, *The Voice of My Beloved*. On insular commentaries see Hunt, 'The Song of Songs', in Burgess (ed), *Court and Poet*, 189–96.

[62] Edmund's election was a fraught affair, with three previous candidates quashed before Edmund was finally successful. According to Matthew Paris, Henry none the less took much pleasure in Edmund's canonization in December 1246 (*Chron. maj.* iv. 586). This, and Edmund's mediation between the king and the barons, had happened when Isabella was not more than 8 years old, but at the time when she became a young widow, similar struggles attended the elevation of Edmund's former chancellor, Richard, as bishop of Chichester (Lawrence, *St Edmund of Abingdon*, 40–1).

[63] Richard is said to work the estate himself, harrowing and carting hay (hence his later role as patron saint of Milanese coachmen: he is one of the few saints known to have driven a cart occupationally). Although often celebrated as a 'yeoman' saint, Richard seems rather to have belonged to a minor branch of the baronial family of Chandos in Herefordshire (C. H. Lawrence, 'St Richard of Chichester', in M. J. Kitsch (ed.), *Studies in Sussex Church History* (London: Leopard's Head Press, 1981), 35–55). As with Becket and Edmund, the troping of saints' rising worldly careers as a martyrdom of humility (see n. 14 above) has caused historical confusion.

('pardurable eritage', v. 316). This opposition is further defined when Richard rejects a second virgin, the daughter and heir of his master in canon law at Bologna. She is a tempting prize who comes with 'terres ... et chasteus e vignies ... ou rentes e autres biens asez' (vv. 510–12), but the saint escapes this snare ('cest laz', v. 528).

Ascesis is assimilated to martyrdom as well as to the nuptial language of the Song of Songs. Both Edmund and Richard wear hairshirts (as was *de rigueur* among saints after the discovery of a lice-ridden hairshirt on Becket's body).[64] Richard's body at death is found to be white and shining as bodies at the resurrection will be (v. 1601), but his flesh has purple bruises and lots of blisters, vv. 1603–5, from his ascetic disciplines (the 'heyre e huiberc' and the knotted cords he had worn, vv. 1597–8):

> Culur de rose e culur de lis
> Melé resembla, ceo lur fut avis,
> Dunt Seint'Eglise put chanter de li:
> 'Blanc est e vermeil mun ami'.
>   (vv. 1608–11)[65]

[his body] seemed to them the colour of the rose and the honeyed lily: whence Holy Church was able to sing of him 'White and scarlet is my love'.

Edmund similarly imitates the reddening of Christ's virgin flesh from the knotted scourges to embellish his own whiteness with 'la rose et la violette' (v. 1621). As Jennifer O'Reilly has shown in her study of Becket lives, Christ's white breast and blood from his side (the 'Candet nudatum pectus | Rubet cruentum latus' tradition common also to Middle English and French lyrics), together with the beloved ('candidus et rubicundus') of the Song of Songs, are used in developing the trope of 'cerebrum candeus et sanguis rubens'—the brains and blood of the martyr Thomas on the floor of Canterbury cathedral.[66] Like many other Becket motifs, this is taken up with vigour in the Edmund and Richard Lives.[67]

---

[64] Herbert de Bosham sums up Becket's career thus: 'Egressus ejus a purpura ad cilicium, a cilicio ad exsilium, ab exsilio ad martyrium, a martyrium ad regnum' (*Homilia in festo S. Thomae*, PL190.1408).

[65] See also Richard's early post-mortem miracle when, at the beginning of the canon of the mass at his funeral, as witnessed by 'de clers de religiuns ... E des hauz homes e femmes ausi' (vv. M68–9), his lips gradually become 'culur de rose' and his face resumes the look of a living man (vv. M55–63).

[66] ' "Candidus et rubicundus": An Image of Martyrdom in the "Lives" of Thomas Becket', *AB* 99 (1981), 303–14. The third colour mentioned in the Anglo-Norman lives, violet, is especially associated with confessors (red for martyrs, white for virgins) so that Richard's and Edmund's bruises in 'violette' and 'purpre' are also significant marks.

[67] Others include illness, asceticism, thaumaturgy, and the colours of martyrdom, and a stay at Pontigny (Becket's Cistercian house of refuge in exile). C. H. Lawrence argues convincingly that Edmund of Canterbury in fact did not die in ineffectual exile: his illness in Pontigny en route to Rome was repatterned to conform to Becket's life (*St Edmund of Abingdon*, 180–1).

The language of ascesis thus writes continence as spiritual nuptiality, learning as the path to heavenly territory, and personal body disciplines as heroic charisma and strength in the service of God's superior kingdom and authority. Ascesis confers authority in claiming hegemonies and resources, not least among them the resources of wealthy widows. It also offers several points of identification with ascetic heroes in Edmund and Richard's lives: the penitential practices of fasting, vigils, and mortification are standardly represented as the particular hallmark and occupation of pious widows and chaste churchmen.[68] Paris represents them as taught to Edmund by his biological mother, Mabilia, who, as a virtuous widow, is an outstanding exponent (she is, in the favourite symbol of virginity discourse, a 'gem among all her neighbours', v. 122, in Edmund's hometown of Abingdon). Mabilia changes her hairshirt only in order to place iron next to her flesh in Lent and Advent (vv. 133–4). She trains her children to keep vigil, fast, wear a hairshirt and love and honour God ('veillier, juner, heire porter, | Deu amer et [Deu] honurer', vv. 141–2).

Such identifications are taken, in the Edmund Life, to the extent of showing Edmund's mother 'feminizing' his studies as pious ones, in a much more detailed account than the Latin text of the Life. When she dies, Edmund's prayers and donations to the poor of Abingdon quickly release her from purgatory, and she comes to him in a vision as he labours over the 'triangles et sercels' (v. 465) of his arithmetical studies in the Oxford quadrivium. 'What are you doing with those circles you're drawing,' she scolds, 'wasting your youth, only ever reading treatises, rules, measurements ['reule, cumpas'], withering your flesh and drying your bones, and not sleeping properly: don't you have anything better to do?' (vv. 472–9). She draws three circles on his hand, inscribed 'pater', 'filius', 'spiritus sanctus', and converts him to the study of the Trinity (in a rhetoric of oppositions—'Guerpit Euclide et Tolomeu | Pur Johan, Luc, [Marc] et Matheu | De Platun lest la veine gloire | Pur Augustin et pur Gregoire', vv. 521–4—which were in practice not mutually exclusive in the medieval curriculum).[69]

A further point of convergence between ascetics and widows is in almsgiving. This is figured in the lives as social fidelity and compassion for the poor

---

[68] So for instance Audrée 'mortified her body . . . with fasting, vigils and weeping' ('en jonne, en veillie et en plur', *Vie sainte Audrée*, v. 1473). These practices were also recommended to (and followed by) some lay people. Becket set a fashion in his extreme asceticism at Pontigny: Edmund is said also to spend his time there 'in prayer, | Fasting and mortification' ('Vie de saint Edmond', ed. Baker, vv. 1427–8). In the *SEL* version of the life, Mabilia herself is suggested as cult-worthy: she is 'flour of wuduwene' and buried in an Abingdon chapel 'in front of the cross on the south side' where 'mani Miracle' have since occurred (*Early South English Legendary*, ed. Horstmann, 435, ll. 141, 143, 145).

[69] Similar oppositions are used in the Latin Vulgate Life of St Catherine, and in some vernacular versions, as the saint anathematizes pagan learning (see *Seinte Katerine*, ed. d'Ardenne and Dobson, 162/355–163/359, and Ch. 7.1 below). My point here is the constructed nature of the opposition and the feminizing of its devotional side: it is both a monastic/scholastic and a gendered opposition where in practice a continuum existed.

(though it is also, of course, a practice that defines and maintains social hier-archies). Edmund's almsgiving relieves any clerk, burgess, or peasant who is sick, old, or poor (v. 1074), but 'gentiz hom' of such lineage that they would die rather than avow their poverty are looked after by him honourably, well, and *privately* ('si honestement, | Si bel, et si priveement', vv. 1082–4). Such tactful and hierarchical giving would also be part of the social obligations of Isabella as a wealthy widow of status, certainly in Paris's Benedictine eyes.

In the biographies of ascetic courtier saints, the role of pagan tyrant, the mistreater of the bride of Christ, is potentially available for the king as oppon-ent of the church. As Mary Ann Stouck has noted, this is a capacity that would later be exploited not only in the opposition of churchmen to the king, but (from de Montfort's death), in the sanctification of baronial figures of opposition. Chroniclers and hagiographers both 'displace political dissent into hagiography' and offer an exemplary corrective in hagiography's account of 'the ideal relation-ship between divine and human justice'.[70] The complexities and shifts of allegiance in the hagiographic oppositions of churchmen and the king make the ascetic biographies of the twelfth and thirteenth centuries as turbulent and multi-faceted as the *passio* narratives discussed in Chapter 3. In his late twelfth-century Life of Becket, for example, Beneit concludes with prayers for the king and his wife and children, but states the royal–ecclesiastical opposition uncom-promisingly as ordained power versus private caprice:

Seinte Eglise ad sa digneté,
Ke tut est plein de verité,
Ke Deus est.
E li reis ad une poüsté
Ke vait apres sa volunté
E cum li plaist.[71]

Holy Church has its high office
Which is completely verified by the truth
Which is God.
And the king has a power
Which is wielded according to his will
And as it pleases him.

The king in these lives moves in and out of his potential for anti-ecclesiastical tyranny: he cannot self-destruct and go to hell as do the pagan tyrants of female virgin martyrs. The rhetoric of nuptial passion and ascetic discipline through which

[70] Mary Ann Stouck, 'Saints and Rebels: Hagiography and Opposition to the King in Late Fourteenth-Century England', *Medievalia et Humanistica*, NS 24 (1997), 75–94 (87–8 and see 78 for suggestions of pagan tyrant in the portrayal of Richard II, a counter to Richard's own deployment of hagiology in the Wilton diptych (88)).

[71] *La Vie saint Thomas*, ed. Schlyter, 101–2, vv. 43–8. A number of other contrasts are also offered, construing the king's behaviour as *mundus inversus*: the ewe beating the shepherd, the disciple the master, the father the son, and the vassal the lord (vv. 631–6).

the saint's power is figured thus functions in part as an oppositional language negotiating for power in relation to royal and lay patriarchy. Affiliations and identifications between chaste women and churchmen can represent an allegiance against the king or against secular patriarchy or both in these lives. It is, of course, an allegiance of the élite against part of itself. However hard ecclesiastical saints' lives claim heroic austerity, charismatic body discipline, and marginal and humble status, bishops, archbishops, and well-dowered countesses are not romantic and ragged apostolic or even eremitic outsiders. Indeed, one enriching complexity of the relation between these texts and their contexts is that the texts' oppositions—celibacy/marriage, saintly simplicity/worldliness, royal/ecclesiastical power, pagan/Christian learning, British/alien—figure relationships which were socially imbricated with each other and in flux, forming and re-forming in serial allegiances according to circumstance. The ecclesiastics and the courtiers represented in saints' lives inhabit overlapping social spaces and competing interests, in which saints are also courtiers.

As these vernacular lives engage in the politics of thirteenth-century curiality, the pagan-tyrant role of improper behaviour to Christ's church-bride can thus be filled not only by the king but by certain constructions of courtliness. The rise of the courtier saint is recuperated for Edmund and Richard (as it is in Guernes de Pont Ste Maxence's Becket) as an inner martyrdom of humility: the higher the saint's position the greater his inner humility, the fiercer his secret ascetic practices. Churchmen themselves needed courtliness to get on (especially Becket, Edmund, and Richard, who, like many of the new curial civil servants, were not from the highest gentry or nobility families), and episcopal households and *curiae* were as important as royal courts in the social formation of young men.[72] Mabilia of Abingdon herself is said to be both very 'curtaise' and very holy (v. 454), and her children are represented as doubly trained in ascetic practices and social advancement: as well as the discipline of the hairshirt, she sets them to learning French and Latin (they were not intent on 'agriculture or trade ["gaignage u . . . marchandise"]', the narrative comments, vv. 105–6). Courtier bishops were supposed to be physically imposing ('a shapely leg was no disadvantage'), as was the case with Peter des Roches, Henry III's foreign hunting bishop of Winchester (and a powerful influence at both John's and Henry's court for thirty years).[73] Edmund's Life claims that he does not value vain glory and the praise of men at an apple, or rate the 'Romanz d'Oger u de Charlemeine' at 'a chestnut' (vv. 331–2), but he is also said to be always affable ('haite', v. 350), to despise avariciousness (v. 370), to be 'humbles et fraus et debonaire' (v. 715),

---

[72] On bishops' courts see C. Stephen Jaeger, *The Envy of Angels: Cathedral Schools and Social Ideals in Medieval Europe, 950–1200* (Philadelphia: University of Pennsylvania Press, 1994). For the continuities of religious and lay etiquette in insular society see Jonathan W. Nicholls, *The Matter of Courtesy: Medieval Courtesy Books and the Gawain Poet* (Cambridge: Brewer, 1985), esp. chs. 2 and 3.

[73] Vincent, *Peter des Roches*, 3.

and important in the counsels of the court because he knows the customs of great men well (vv. 943–4). Richard is likewise 'gracious in every way, virtuous in his behaviour, beautiful of body, affable of countenance, and well-endowed with every quality' (vv. 91–4). But he was also famously severe on clergy who succumbed to the contemporary fashion for combing the hair forward and using a filet to seem untonsured.[74] Edmund (who was responsible for the banishment of the tenacious and experienced courtier-bishop Peter des Roches) is represented as simple and unworldly, more attuned to scholars and priests than knights (vv. 1301–2), and ignorant about hawking, hunting, and other recreations: 'about birds, dogs, minstrels | He knew no more than a shepherd' (vv. 1305–6). However, Paris omits from the vernacular Life something included in the Latin *vita*—Edmund's dispute with Isabella's husband, Hugh d'Albini, whom Edmund had excommunicated for impounding some of the archiepiscopal pack of hounds as they coursed over Hugh's lands.[75]

In relation to the court, hagiography can be an insiders' language posing as an outsiders' one, claiming through the code of ascetic discipline special prerogatives and authorities beyond but also sometimes in tandem with the king. By the thirteenth century, English kings had, as Clanchy and others have shown, established traditions of relying, certainly for their administration and sometimes for their council, on a new kind of royal servant in the *familia regis*, the lettered and numerate civil servant. William Marshal, Isabella's grandfather, was virtually the last noble to gain high office through military and chivalric accomplishment. Baronial families of Isabella's rank often maintained their roles at court through service but were supplemented and sometimes supplanted by the 'new men'.[76] Laymen, as well as churchmen, pursued careers as *curiales*, and although 'the Church' was often a separate interest group as against the king and/or the nobles, it was also sometimes aligned with nobles against the king.[77]

[74] See Richard of Chichester's Statutes, summarized as 'Clerks, moreover, should not cultivate their hair, but should be properly tonsured in the usual circular fashion and so bear themselves that they cannot be criticised for the sin of pride' (Jones, 62, no. 57). Tonsure was unpopular with clerics, and Pecham also issued statues on it (in 1281).

[75] For Edmund's 1240 excommunication of Hugh d'Albini see *Cal. Pap. Bulls*, ed. Bliss and Johnson, 189 and Lawrence, *St Edmund of Abingdon*, 172. See further on such disputes in the 13th c. Brian Golding, 'The Hermit and the Hunter', in John Blair and Brian Golding (eds.), *The Cloister and the World: Essays in Medieval History in Honour of Barbara Harvey* (Oxford: Clarendon Press, 1996), 95–117.

[76] See Ralph V. Turner, *Men Raised From the Dust: Administrative Service and Upward Mobility in Angevin England* (Philadelphia: University of Pennsylvania Press, 1988), ch. 1.

[77] Bocking's disgusted discourse on disparagement quoted above shows (like that of *Hali Meiðhad*, quoted in Ch. 2.3 above) the potential complexity of alignments here: without being pro-baronial it must be partly anti-royal (the barons insisted on new anti-foreign rules for disparagement in 1258). On distrust of the king's foreign favourites see Huw Ridgeway, 'Henry III and the Aliens, 1236–1272', in P. R. Coss and S. D. Lloyd (eds.), *Thirteenth Century England II* (Woodbridge: Boydell, 1988), 89–99. On the importance of conciliar control at court as a recognition of the corporate interests of baronial families in royal lordship, see Waugh, 'Marriage, Class, and Royal Wardship', 206.

Just as thirteenth-century bishops are courtiers, so magnates are royalists in some of their interests and ecclesiastical or Montfortian suporters in others. The hagiography of this period can thus encode viewpoints with baronial as well as ecclesiastical endorsement. Lay audiences other than Isabella clearly responded to and tried to assimilate the powers represented in it. Hairshirts, for instance, figure in lay piety: that unsuccessfully culted baronial figure (and distant connection of Isabella's), Simon de Montfort, was said to be wearing one when he was dismembered after the battle of Evesham in 1265.

In their representation of saintly speech—debate, eloquence, and counsel—these lives interact as multifariously with their context as in their troping of power as ascesis and courtesy as humility. Courtier saints engage in intercessory roles also ascribed to women: Edmund, for instance, 'hates discord, especially among high-ranking men, for he knows that when king, count, or baron contend among themselves, it is to the destruction, death, and disinheritance of their subjects' and that strife in the baronage is 'the harm of the poor' (vv. 943–53). He therefore not only gives profitable council to the king, but

> Ne jur ne nuit ne fine jeske
> Pes mettë entre les majurs
> Ke [en] decent sur les meinurs.
>
> (vv. 954–56)
>
> did not stop by day or night
> until he brought peace between the great
> so that it descended to the humble[78]

and gives much attention to maintaining stable relations between the king and the great men of the land (vv. 1015–17). Counsel, debate, and eloquence, however, are the stuff of conflict and competition as well as of reconciliation. Guernes's Becket Life, for instance, is virtually one scene after another of the 'cunseil' (as well as the formal church Councils) of the various parties. 'Counsel' is a discourse valued by both barony and the church.[79] In the matter of Edmund's intercessions in the year of his consecration to the archbishopric,

---

[78] Scholarly response to Edmund's hagiographic representation in Latin saw him as weak and ineffectual, but Lawrence shows that Edmund was a successful and respected negotiator in the tensions between Henry and the barons (averting civil war in the very year of his consecration) and a firm resister of Henry's manipulations of episcopal elections. He was respected on both sides—the royal children were baptized in his name and his memory was also invoked by the rebel barons (Lawrence, *St Edmund of Abingdon*, 181).

[79] For the importance of counsel as social practice and romance discourse, see Geraldine Barnes, *Counsel and Strategy in Middle English Romance* (Cambridge: Brewer, 1993). The relation between speech and action in the lives of churchmen is on a spectrum with that of debate and dismemberment in *passiones*, rather than radically different in kind: in terms of its role in their *vitae*, speech is performative. The vernacular Becket lives use speech as narrative action, in scenes of council as well as of counsel: so too does the 13th-c. Life of St Clement (see Wogan-Browne, ' "Bet . . . to . . . rede on holy seyntes lyves . . ." '). See further Kay, *Contradiction in Medieval Literature* (forthcoming) and Robertson, *The Medieval Saints' Lives*, 175–99.

Matthew Paris does not shorten his vernacular narrative: far from seeing this as potentially tedious for Isabella or any other lay audience, he gives a longer account of Edmund's interventions than in his own Latin *vita* and flags the extra level of detail in the conventional way by the claim to *brevitas* ('Ke vus ferai de ceus lung cunte?', v. 1035). He includes the matter of Gilbert Marshal's inheritance after the murder of his father Richard (vv. 957–1010); and the reconciliations to the king of Hubert de Burgh, Gilbert Basset, Stephen Seagrave, and Richard Siward (vv. 1019–34), many of whom will have been known to Isabella.[80]

Isabella herself is represented by Matthew Paris as using the warning discourse of counsel to the king. In his *Chronica Majora* for 1252, he shows Isabella going to Henry (who was at that time in London for de Montfort's counsel on Gascony), to assert her rights over a wardship ('de quadam custodia') belonging to her in which the king, her distant relative, had a small share.[81] Paris reports Henry as refusing to attend to Isabella's grievance,

whereupon the countess, although a woman, replied with an undauntedness beyond a woman, 'Why, my lord King, do you avert your face from justice? One cannot now obtain what is right and just at your court. You are appointed a mediator between the Lord and us, but you do not govern well either yourself or us, neither do you fear to vex and trouble the church in many ways.'[82]

In response Henry is said to have asked her sneeringly if the nobles of England have 'confederated with you and given you a charter to be their spokeswoman and advocate ['advocata et prolocutrix'], as you are so eloquent ['quia eloquens es']?' Paris admiringly represents Isabella, though still a young woman (she would probably have been in her twenties), as silencing the king by replying that not the nobles but Henry's father (King John, d. 1216 before her birth) had given the charter she had, and Henry had affirmed it, though he was now refusing to honour it.

---

[80] For Stephen Segrave (Justiciar from 1232–4), see Turner, *Men Raised from the Dust*, 120–42 (139 for Hugh d'Albini's grant of land to him). Gilbert Basset has a role in Richard Marshal's conflict with Henry III (Richard led Gilbert Basset's defenders against the king in 1233, ibid. 130). Gilbert Clare was married to Isabella's aunt. In the *vita*, Matthew Paris gives only a stock scene between the Archbishop and the king in which Edmund seeks out the king at Woodstock and induces him on grounds of family and religous piety not only to remit his wrath but to restore Gilbert Marshal's holding (Lawrence, *St Edmund of Abingdon*, 240–1). On Edmund's negotiations between the rebellious barons, the king, and the curialists after Richard Marshal's death in Ireland in 1234, see ibid. 87, 91; *Chron. maj.* iii. 273–4.

[81] They were both great-grandchildren of Henry I. Isabella's grandfather Hameline was half-brother of Henry II (W. Blaauw, *The Barons War* (London: Bell and Daldy, 1871), 59). Isabella's brother John, sixth Earl de Warenne, was married to the king's half-sister, Alice de Lusignan. For de Montfort's council on Gascony, see Maddicott, *Simon de Montfort*, 41. Isabella took a similar dispute before Henry in 1256 when she contested the right of Adam de Brymton to marry her ward Joanna de Olneye without her own consent: CR (1254–6), 446.

[82] *Chron. maj.* v. 336–7 (AD 1252). Further quotation by page number in text. Translation modified from Giles.

'whereby it is plainly proved that you have broken your faith and your oath. Where are the liberties of England, so often granted, so often committed to writing ['totiens in scripta redactae'], so often redeemed? I, therefore, although a woman, and all of us your natural ['indigenae'] and faithful subjects, appeal against you, before the tribunal of the awful judge of all.' (p. 337)

Paris thus represents Isabella both as pious patroness and baronial spokesperson. Doubtless he does so partly in the service of the recurrent anxieties of the English court, church, and nobility over Henry III's foreign counsellors and favourites.[83] But his reminder that Isabella as a baron had powers of wardship herself sits interestingly with Bocking's construction of her. Bocking's closing letter to the bishop and canons of Chichester in his *vita* of Richard of Chichester uses (as many medieval women writers do), the topos of female weakness as a sign of divine authorization (though he is also careful to stress Isabella's rank):

Following the prophet's example, I do not consider that I should despise the nourishment which saves souls, albeit supplied by the diligence and devotion of a woman. The story in the book of Kings commends the widow of Zarephath [1 Kgs. 17: 7–24]: this widow [Isabella] is commended by her descent from kings . . . In addition to this, who knows if the Lord wanted this Life to be written through the agency of a woman, for as long as the blessed Richard lived he strove to promote virtue in women and especially in her of whom we speak. She repaid him as best she could and not wanting to seem ungrateful for the benefits conferred upon her by the holy man, achieved through the efforts of others what she was unable to do herself . . . Therefore, as if imitating Him who, despising neither the weakness of the female sex nor the smallness of the offering, singled out the widow's two mites from a treasury abounding in riches [Mark 12: 41–4], have regard to my intentions rather than to any deficiencies [in my work].[84]

Thus Isabella, who in other contexts is an orator in monastery and court, a fearless defier of kings, traveller, foundress, wielder of seigneurial wardships and also of papal letters, licences, and suits, becomes, in Bocking's representation of the noble patroness of Richard's *vita*, a chaste and humble widow, contributing her mite. But even a sketchy outline of her life and texts suggests this rhetoric of piety could be deployed by women and not merely contain them. As an unappended heiress, high-profile use of chastity as pious cultural capital must

[83] Paris invokes the favourite 13th-c. trope of the insider alien (much used in curial and baronial politics against the Savoyards and the Lusignans, whether in the matter of foreign wives or foreign bishops): he has Isabella say: 'I also appeal before the face of Christ against those who are your advisers [*consiliarii*], who bewitch and infatuate you, and turn you from the paths of truth, being eagerly intent only on their own advantage.' The king, however, 'continued incorrigible and would not listen to these or other salutary counsels [*verbis salubribus*].' Between 1225 and 1258 Henry disposed of 50 baronial wards and five of seven heirs of earldoms to foreigners or favourites: for a succinct account of the enormous tensions this provoked in the barony and of the baronial redefinition of disparagement in the rebellion of 1258, see Waugh, 'Marriage, Class, and Lordship', esp. 202–7.

[84] Jones, 232–4, 159.

have helped Isabella's mobility and independence around and through the structures of baronial kin, church, and court. Her profile among monastic chroniclers (notably Paris and the Waverley annalist) and Bocking's approval suggests how successful she was, as indeed does what little can be traced of her life and activities. The rhetorical enthusiasm of thirteenth-century churchmen for textual and social enclosure of women does not mean that women's piety is a purely interior matter.

As the proliferation of late twelfth- and thirteenth-century lives of the saint suggests, Becket's cult engaged a range of lay and ecclesiastical interests around the figure of the ecclesiastical courtier saint from the end of the twelfth century onwards. Ian Short has shown that a member of the gentry, Simon fitz Simon, requested a private copy of the Anglo-Norman Life by Beneit originally designed for [male] monastic use, with an epilogue specifically recommending that Sir Simon should read, and have the life read aloud to, his wife, 'dame Ysabele'.[85] At the other end of the century, another archbishop, the Franciscan John Pecham, translates pseudo-Dionysius (the *Jerarchie*) for Eleanor of Provence (as well as writing the reproaches to her about anti-Semitism discussed in Chapter 3.3 above). The careers and thought of English churchmen of this period have been principally studied through their Latin writings and *vitae* in their ecclesiastical and monastic institutional contexts, but vernacular sources suggest a more complex and varied world where the interests of women and churchmen are interwoven and where the first of these may influence the second. The needs of great noblewomen are a likely source of pressure towards explication and clarification with all its benefits for the writing of the one who teaches in such situations (as is so notably exemplified in the careers of Bocking's cited authority Jerome; and of Abelard, the twelfth-century cleric who in this respect modelled himself on Jerome). Richard of Chichester's *vita* shows the requests of a noblewoman (probably Isabella, since she is described as a close friend) prompting thought and clarification for Richard in his writing and teaching: Edmund's mother, as noted above, is represented as redirecting his mathematical studies to devotional (and Trinitarian) ends. Like the much-studied Continental holy women of Liège who were to become influential models in later Middle English and Anglo-French literature, Richard's noblewoman friend, probably Isabella, is said to have a vision in which he appears.[86]

Edmund of Canterbury was himself an enthusiastic proponent of devotion to the five wounds, to the body of Christ, and to the eucharist. But he shares this style of devotion with the court as the acquisition of passion relics became not only fashionable but a way of asserting national, social, and personal identities in the first half of the thirteenth century: influence may have flowed

[85] 'The Patronage of Beneit's *Vie de Thomas Becket*', 256, vv. 401–3.

[86] Bk. i. 29: Jones, 124, 200 (and see n. 11 above). It is significant that the testimony in this chapter (entitled 'That he was not a novice'—Quod non fuit neophitus—Jones, 122), 'proves' Richard's spirituality by so much reference to a lay noblewoman, rather than to churchmen.

in several directions and circuits. The contemplative, neo-Victorine temper of
Edmund's influential *Mirour* provides a framework for extended meditative practices, but his scheme for the use of the canonical hours in passion meditation
is so admirably suited for psalter and *horae* reading that one may wonder if it
was not so much influenced by women's practice as constitutive of it.[87] Matthew
Paris also subscribed to the devotion to Christ's body (in his case with a nationalizing inflection: the places on earth where that body had lived were in his view
under infidel and pagan threat). In his Life of Edmund, Paris's account of Henry
III's acquisition of Christ's marble footstep is carefully paralleled with Isabella's
following of St Edmund; she by divine grace follows the saint's trace (vv. 1983–
4) where the king cults and acquires Christ's footstep (vv. 2003–16).

The illness and asceticism valued as a sign of sanctity in these lives provides
another preoccupation in which royal and baronial practices can be seen alongside and partly mediated through hagiographic texts. Becket's celebrated illness
from excessive fasting at Pontigny had become a model instance of asceticism.
In the Life by Matthew Paris, Edmund develops asceticism and *imitatio Christi*
a stage further through the voluntary acceptance of illness when he heals a
colleague by prayer and by taking on the pain of the abscess himself (vv. 635–66).
The illnesses of ascetic saints qualified them for thaumaturgical roles alongside
Edward the Confessor, the saint so intensely culted by Henry III. Ela, Countess
of Salisbury and thirteenth-century foundress of Lacock Abbey, was cured by
the blood of Becket, sent from Pontigny by Edmund of Canterbury, who had
been, in 1219, the treasurer of Salisbury, while Eleanor of Provence (d. 1291) had
a relic of Richard of Chichester's arm (she herself took the veil in retirement to
Amesbury 3 July 1276, perhaps having acquired the relic at the translation of
the saint to his new shrine on 16 June 1276, as well as her own relic of Becket's
blood, earlier sent her from Pontigny by Edmund).[88] In his *Chronica Majora*,
Paris celebrates the 1246 acquisition of the *arma Christi*, and in 1247 the procuring
of the Holy Blood of Hailes, donated to the abbey by Richard of Cornwell
(d. 1272), the king's brother and the husband of Sanchia (to whom, as
earlier noted, Matthew Paris asked Isabella to send on the lives of Edward and
Thomas). Richard of Cornwell organized the dedication of the relic in 1251 and
the king himself held a festival of relics on the feast of Edward the Confessor
to celebrate the arrival of the Holy Blood in England.[89] In the rising market of

[87] While treasurer of Salisbury, Edmund was for instance reputed to be friendly with Ela, Countess
of Salisbury and foundress and abbess of the Augustinian canonesses' house of Lacock (he certainly witnessed her foundation charter). On Edmund's innovations see Mother Mary Philomena
SHCJ, 'St Edmund of Abingdon's Meditations'.

[88] For the relic of Richard of Chichester, see *Vie seint Richard*, ed. Russell, M1064n.

[89] M. E. Roberts, 'The Relic of the Holy Blood and the Iconography of the Thirteenth-Century
North Transept Portal of Westminster Abbey', in Ormrod (ed.), *England in the Thirteenth
Century*, 129–42 (137). Grosseteste's *determinatio* on the holy blood (for the problem of how Christ
could be resurrected in perfection yet leave bodily fluids on earth) is reported by Paris, *Chron.
maj.* vi. 138–44.

passion relics, and particularly when seen against the acquisitions of Louis IX of France, this relic was of national and international significance.[90] In his Edmund Life, Paris contextualizes his celebration of Isabella's devotion to the saint and Henry III's acquisition of Christ's footstep in marble (vv. 1983–2016) with the assertion that God has shown himself so munificent and generous to England as to have sent the holy blood itself and that this is an even holier relic than the cross and the nails and crown of thorns (vv. 1995–6, 1999–2000) of French ownership at St Denis, Paris. In Trevet's history for Edward I's daughter Mary at Amesbury, Edmund's holy life and teaching is said to have illuminated the church and made Edmund dearly beloved by King Henry for his sanctity, and Richard of Chichester is described as having lived 'en si grant seintete . . . qe Dieux pur lui moustra grantz miracles, si come piert en l'estoire de sa vie, qe son confessour, frere Rauf de Bokyngham del ordre de freres prechours, escript'.[91] The Dominican Trevet has his own emphases in his representations of English history for the princess, but clearly regarded these saints' lives as part of her world, as they were of her mother's and grandmother's.

Hairshirts and holy blood have their fashions, but need be neither merely cynically acquired or used in a purely private religiosity: they need the social significations of piety that give ascesis its meanings and powers. The figure of the chaste pious baronial widow, strongly assimilated to penance and asceticism, but not simply dissociated from her magnate and family experience, once again suggests the limitations of enclosure as a model for women's lives. Enclosure is a cultural habit of thought and imagery regarding widows, but not at all necessarily definitive of their practices and their piety, or of the roles such women played in literary and cultural history.

[90] Louis IX of France purchased the crown of thorns in 1239 from Baldwin, Emperor of Constantinople, and in 1241 also bought portions of the true cross and other relics from Baldwin: see Roberts, 'Relic of the Holy Blood', 136.

[91] Trivet, *Chronicle*, ed. Rutherford, 330.

6
Virgin Authority and its Transmission

This chapter explores the documentation and representation of virgin authority in the form of abbess sanctity, and especially the availability of models and
precedents for female achievements. It argues that although (as outlined in Chapter 1.5 above) institutional resources for women did not generally support full
versions of the hagiographic and historiographic genres of male monasticism,
there are still some relatively unexplored sources for women both in Latin and
in Anglo-Norman. These suggest that there were ways in which information,
precedents, models, and strategies could be garnered by women, and also that
the late twelfth and thirteenth centuries see immensely varied and individual
female communities in Britain, not (as used to be implied) a single, depressingly
homogenized and failing nunnery culture, notably devoid of interest and
achievement in comparison with the new developments of the late twelfth- and
early thirteenth-century Low Countries. The chapter focuses especially on the
three British virgin abbess lives and miracles which were read in the nunnery of
Campsey. As virgin widows, many abbess saints bridged the worlds of secular
and spiritual households and provided appropriate models for vowesses and for
women who founded and/or entered nunneries later in life. Abbesses and their
powers are represented in a relatively rich way in the texts of twelfth- and thirteenth-
century England and their hagiographic lives can be seen as testimony to women's
interests and achievements in insular female communities.

6.1. FOUNDRESSES AND ABBESSES

The most authoritative institutional form of early female sanctity outside the
passio of the virgin martyr of the universal church is that of abbess. In the early
medieval period, abbesshood and royal status had been virtually inseparable in
insular culture as elsewhere in Europe, and queenliness remained important
in models of female sanctity as also of female patronage, but post-Conquest
abbesshoods and foundations were undertaken by increased numbers of noblewomen, and by a wider class range of foundresses.[1] While Isabella, Countess

---

[1] Robert Folz, *Les Saintes Reines du moyen âge en Occident vi–xiiie siècles* (Brussels: Societé des
Bollandistes, 1992): for the widening range of patronage in the 11th c., see Halpin, 'Women Religious
in Late Anglo-Saxon England'. In the post-Conquest period, only Lillechurch, the refoundation
of Amesbury, and Burnham are allowed as certain royal foundations by Thompson, but there

of Arundel, seems to have chosen not to enter the nunnery she founded, other noblewomen did become abbesses of their own monastic houses, and yet others were abbesses or prioresses in the foundations of their families. Sally Thompson has shown that, excluding mendicant foundations, women are involved in the foundation of some 44 of the 137 (out of 145) post-Conquest nunneries of whose history something is known, and that 20 of these are women acting without the involvement of men, while other women foundresses may be concealed in cases recorded as family foundations.[2] Again, initiatives of women in further cases may well be concealed within the attribution of foundation to male spiritual kin, as when a male founder is said to have responded to female needs or requests.[3]

Many significant foundresses are high-born widows who carry over female roles of mourning, servicing, and spiritual intercession for the patriarchal lineage by founding houses for their husband's and ancestors' souls. Here the chief qualifications for becoming an abbess-foundress are a noble and lengthy widowhood, successful negotiation with male kin and king for fiscal freedom, and retention of dower. But there are other women foundresses who use more fortuitous and meritocratic routes and less extensive personal resources to found smaller communities (often but not invariably hermitages or hospitals). In these cases the absence of a family tradition of foundation was sometimes compensated for by male ecclesiastical patronage in gaining a more permanent form for an initially *ad hoc* situation. A kind of meritocracy was thus possible for foundresses as well (though their foundations would seldom be large enough to include a higher rank than that of prioress). The best-known example from the post-Conquest period is the relationship of Christina of Markyate and Abbot Geoffrey of St Alban's: represented within the conventions of spiritual friendship and holy women's counsel in the monastic *vita* of Christina, it also signals the institutional relations of the wealthy Benedictine monastery and the smaller community that attracted patronage from its grand neighbour as it developed under Christina's leadership from a male eremitic group to a female priory.[4] Less fully documented cases exist: the nunnery at Carrow, for instance, seems to

are numerous foundations by aristocratic widows (*Women Religious*, 166–7, 172). The high status of such foundations is significant: though the great majority of post-Conquest nunneries had only the rank of priory, of the nine which were abbeys, five were the foundations of noblewomen. On the expansion of English monialism in the earlier and later 12th c. see Venarde, *Women's Monasticism*, 76–7.

[2] *Women Religious*, 167–72 and Appendix A. For the occlusion of women's roles in foundations by married couples see ibid. 177; also Janet Burton, *The Monastic Orders in Yorkshire 1069–1215* (Cambridge: Cambridge University Press, 1999), 132–5.

[3] See Thompson, *Women Religious*, ch. 10: for Gilbert of Sempringham's response to women's requests for a religious life, see *Book of St Gilbert*, ed. and tr. Foreville and Keir, ch. 9. For the foundation of Kilburn by a male cleric for female recluses see *Letters of Osbert of Clare*, ed. Williamson, 16–17; Thompson, *Women Religious*, 25–6.

[4] *Life of Christina*, ed. Talbot, 27–9, 138–40, 144–50. Christina of Markyate's importance in the history of her priory is largely subsumed in the credit given to Geoffrey Abbot of St Alban's in Knowles and Hadcock, entry for Markyate (261, 265).

have been 'founded' by two women, Seyna and Lescelina, 'sorores moniales de hospite Sancte Marie et Sanct' Johannie in Norwich'.[5]

Abbesses were often significant landholders, ruled communities, administered complex estates (sometimes including powers of life and death in the manorial courts over which they had jurisdiction), and negotiated with the king and Rome over taxation, rights, and privileges.[6] Noblewomen who managed large secular estates sometimes had estate handbooks written for them: how is the role of abbess recorded and what kinds of images of their predecessors and of female authority in the religious life were there for Anglo-Norman women? Only two or three copies of the Benedictine rule's institutional provisions for electing abbesses (in Latin, early Middle English, and French) survive from provenanced nunnery manuscripts of the twelfth and thirteenth centuries.[7] More must have been extant, but so too will have been more of the individually formulated or adapted rules also characteristic of many female communities. The self-declared informality of the best-known of these latter, *Ancrene Wisse*, is itself something of a rule rather than an exception among *regulae* for women.[8]

[5] On foundress widows of lower rank see Thompson, *Women Religious*, 174–5, and on Carrow, 49. See also for smaller foundations, Gilchrist, *The Other Monasticism*.

[6] Abbesses were none the less forbidden in canon law to preach or read the gospel in public, to veil consecrated virgins, hear confession, or give liturgical blessing. As noted by Gold, abbesses can gain 'educational, spiritual and administrative experience', but experience 'the limitations on the opportunity imposed by an ideology proclaiming feminine weakness' (*The Lady and the Virgin*, 77): see also J. Baucher, *Abbesse* in *Dictionnaire de droit canonique*, ed. R. Naz *et al.* (Paris: Letouzey et Ane, 1935–65), i, cols. 67–79; René Metz, 'Le Statut de la femme en droit canonique médiéval', in id., *La Femme et l'enfant dans le droit canonique médiéval* (London: Variorum Reprints, 1985), art. IV.

[7] Vernacular versions of *regulae* (Benedictine, Augustinian, Franciscan, and Brigittine) from the 14th and 15th c. are more frequent (see Bell, Appendices I–III). For a study of the ideology of later rules in English houses, see Nancy Warren, 'Profession, Visitation, and Everyday Practice: The Construction of Identity in Later Medieval Monasticism', *New Medieval Literatures*, 5 (forthcoming). On Anglo-Norman rules see the introduction to the edition of a Norman (12th-c.) text, *The Anglo-Norman Rule of St Benedict*, ed. Ruth Dean and M. D. Legge (Oxford: Blackwell, 1946). The rule extant in an early 13th-c. manuscript from Wintney, a Cistercian nunnery in Hampshire, is in Latin and early Middle English and adapts the Benedictine rule grammatically and in other ways for a female house: see Mechtild Gretsch, 'Die Winteney-Version der Regula Sancti Benedicti: eine frühmittelenglische Bearbeitung der altenglischen Prosaübersetzung der Benediktinerregel', *Anglia*, 96 (1978), 310–48); Jeanne Krochalis, 'The Benedictine Rule for Nuns: Library of Congress, MS 4', *Manuscripta*, 30 (1986), 21–34 (30–3); *Die Winteney-Version der Regula Sancti Benedicti*, ed. Mechtild Gretsch (Tübingen: Max Niemeyer, 1978). This manuscript also contains Anglo-Norman directions for calculating the calendar, see Introduction, n. 28. Vernacular rules are not limited to women: on French rules for male houses see Hunt, 'Anecdota Anglo-Normannica'; id., 'An Anglo-Norman Rule of St Augustine', *Augustiniana*, 45 (1995), 177–89.

[8] Herbert, 6/31–10/26; Trethewey, 166/25–169/24; Tolkien, f. 26/28–f. 4a/17. Gilbert of Sempringham also adapts and innovates for his new order for women (*Book of St Gilbert*, ed. and tr. Foreville and Keir, ch. 18). The nine major Benedictine Anglo-Saxon nunneries were supplemented by many post-Conquest foundations (of varying and sometimes changing affiliation), and *regulae* were written for anchoritic and hospital communities as well as for convents: see, for instance, 'Anglo-Norman Rules for . . . St Mary de Pré and Sopwell', ed. Hunt, 93–104; id., 'An Anglo-Norman Treatise on the Religious Life', in Peter Rolfe Monks and D. D. R. Owen (eds.), *Medieval Codicology, Iconography, Literature and Translation: Studies for Keith Val Sinclair* (Leiden: E. J. Brill, 1994), 267–75.

Benedictine rules and some others give accounts of the role of the abbess and sometimes of other offices and often include ceremonies for installing abbesses, thus inculcating a certain amount of information about abbesshood. But they are not guides as to who might become an abbess in practice (which involved not only the internal politics of the house over elections but the interests of lay and ecclesiastical patrons). Marilyn Oliva has shown for the later Middle Ages that within female communities meritocratic routes to the office of abbess existed alongside the qualifications of rank and foundress status: able women could progress up the hierarchy of convent administrative roles.[9] Less is known in detail about the inhabitants of twelfth- and thirteenth-century communities, but there are some indications that similar possibilities existed. The view of nunnery history (held by Power for the fourteenth and fifteenth centuries and reluctantly seconded by Thompson for the twelfth and thirteenth) that 'there seem to have been few women of spiritual vision or stature following a religious vocation in the twelfth and thirteenth centuries, or, if there were, they have left no trace on the records' is premature: it is rather, as Thompson's researches show, that stature attained by women is with difficulty made permanent and visible.[10] The sources for female authority are exiguous relative to male ecclesiastical documentation. Nevertheless they are by no means non-existent and the relatively scarce institutional records can be amplified by 'informal' and unofficial genres. When an appropriate range of evidence is taken into account, it is much harder to see declining standards as the essential feature of female community and women's literary culture in this period.

The monastic genre of the hagiographic dossier and *vita* and the institutional propagation of cult, for instance, was seldom applied to notable female achievement, and far more readily open to male churchmen.[11] Since generations of abbesses and prioresses ruled female—and some double—houses (of both male and female foundation), there were in principle a number of opportunities for women to join the ranks of male monastic and ecclesiastical saints as distinguished and canonized religious leaders, whether as foundresses, abbesses, or both. Yet Christina, notable twelfth-century foundress of Markyate, remained uncanonized

[9] 'Aristocracy or Meritocracy', in W. J. Sheils and Diana Wood (eds.), *Women in the Church SCH* 27 (1990), 197–208.

[10] See Thompson, *Women Religious*, 11 for this assessment: also Power, *Medieval English Nunneries*, 29 and ch. 2; Thompson, 'Why the English Nunneries had no History'.

[11] On canonization rates in the early and high Middle Ages, see Schulenberg, 'Sexism and the Celestial Gynaceum'. In post-Conquest insular culture, male saints join church calendars and legendaries, both Latin and vernacular, at a much faster rate than female: earlier Benedictine churchmen such as Duncan and Æthelwold and successful abbots such as St Botolph are joined by contemporary figures in the 12th and 13th c.—Becket, Richard of Chich, Edmund of Pontigny, Thomas Cantilupe of Hereford—as discussed in Ch. 5 above. There are many more types of sanctity exemplified in male ecclesiastical careers (pope, bishop, abbot, scholars and confessors, hermit, ecclesiastical founder, etc.): there are also more efforts to cult laymen (of which Stouck ('Saints and Rebels', cited in Ch. 5, n. 70 above) includes a brief survey).

(although she was given a Latin *vita*); the supremely able early thirteenth-century abbess Euphemia of Wherwell was not culted; nor Ela, Countess of Salisbury, foundress and first abbess of Lacock.[12] Even the rank of abbess does not suffice for women to challenge the very low rates of female canonization. Abbess saints exemplify both the enduring historical presence and the recurrently liminal status of female religious achievement. The pantheon of British abbess saints, as noted in Chapter 2.1, is long-lived (from the twelfth to the sixteenth century) but relatively stable: chiefly composed of Anglo-Saxon princess abbesses, it seldom adds post-Conquest or late medieval women (see Figure 2.2). Yet three of the original ten lives in the manuscript of the Augustinian canonesses at Campsey are of women foundresses, suggesting interest on the part of the women of Campsey themselves, or a sense of such lives as useful reading for them.[13] Unlike the male ecclesiastical careers represented in that manuscript—Isabella of Arundel's thirteenth-century churchmen saints and their late twelfth-century predecessor, Becket—none of the three virgin abbess-foundresses are contemporary women (though, as I shall later argue, this is not to say that they do not figure contemporary concerns).

6.2. ABBESS MODELS AND FEMALE TRANSMISSIONS OF POWER

For all the mythical and cultural resonance of the figure of the virgin in monastic hagiography and historiography, virgin women are very seldom foundresses. As is well known, Robert d'Arbrissel wanted mature women, not cloistered virgins, to head his new double Fontevrault house, while Abelard calls the appointment of 'virgins . . . rather than women who have known men ['quae viros cognoverunt']' a 'pernicious practice', and although this may be special pleading in the light of Heloise's personal history, Abelard could and did point, in his account of the history of women's roles in the church, to the tradition whereby much older women, 'virgins of sixty years', were recommended as deaconesses in the early church, age remedying the ignorance assumed by Abelard as entailed

---

[12] The text of Christina's life survives as an addition to a St Alban's manuscript (s. xiv²) of John of Tynemouth's *Sanctilogium Angliae*: see *Christina of Markyate*, ed. Talbot, 1–6, and, for the argument that another copy of the life must have existed at Markyate by way of providing a biography of their foundress for the nuns there, 3–4. On Euphemia see Ch. 6.2 below. There may have been a *vita* of Ela by her successor Beatrice, but if so, it is now lost: J. C. Russell, *Dictionary of Writers of Thirteenth-Century England*, Bulletin of the Institute of Historical Research Special Supplement, 3 (London, 1936; repr. with additions and corrections 1967), 23. However, this tradition seems to refer rather to a cartulary portrait of Ela and arises from confusion over the extent of the destruction of Lacock records in the Cottonian fire (see W. L. Bowles and John Gough Nichols, *Annals and Antiquities of Lacock Abbey in the County of Wilts with Memorials of the Foundress Ela Countess of Salisbury . . .* (London: Nichols and Son, 1835), pp. vi–vii, 180–1). On the cult of Ela's son, see Ch. 7 n. 69 below.

[13] For editions of these Lives see nn. 43, 44 below.

in not knowing men).[14] In practice women with experience and women who had been married were often foundresses and abbesses and might indeed be explicitly preferred to women without experience of the world. The twelfth- and thirteenth-century foundress in Britain was most likely to be a widow or a wife. Nevertheless, in the Latin and vernacular hagiography with which the representations of charters, cartularies, registers, and *regulae* can be supplemented, virginity and martyrdom, or honorary versions of these gained by penance and asceticism, remain pervasive conventions for representing female monastic leadership.

While there is no known equivalent to the series of letters between Heloise and Abelard on the role of women in the life of the church, and the adaptation and organization of monastic life for women, a number of letters from churchmen to women in England survive, even if the replies of their female correspondents are not always extant.[15] One of the most striking post-Conquest works to propose anything resembling a theorization of the abbesses' position is a letter of Osbert of Clare, prior of Westminster, to Adelidis, abbess of Barking (c.1138–66). Though couched as a personal communication, the letter is also a treatise on virgin authority, history, and rule.[16] Its exemplary female figures are offered as figures of virginity and of continence, but embrace a wider range of female roles, arranged in a careful sequence. Osbert's first exemplary virgin martyr is St Cecilia (who, in addition to being married, was, like an abbess, a preacher in her own household); she is followed by St Etheldreda of Ely (not only a virgin and princess, but a widow and abbess); by Silva (a vestal virgin who became the mother of the founders of Rome through rape by Mars), and by Judith (chaste Old Testament widow, heroine, and saviour of her

[14] On d'Arbrissel see Gold, *The Lady and the Virgin*, 110–13: for Abelard, see *The Letters of Abelard and Heloise*, tr. Betty Radice (Harmondsworth: Penguin Books, 1974), 200; 'Abelard's Rule for Religious Women', ed. T. P. McLaughlin, *Mediaeval Studies*, 18 (1956), 241–92 (252); and for further discussion by Abelard, see 'The Letter of Heloise on Religious Life and Abelard's First Reply', ed. J. T. Muckle, *Mediaeval Studies*, 17 (1955), 240–81 (264). Abelard's phrasing both implies the usual category of non-virgin professed women, i.e. widows, and allows for Heloise's own situation as a separated/abandoned wife.

[15] Nor are such letters restricted to the 12th c.: see e.g. 'Two Opuscula of John Godard, First Abbot of Newenham', ed. C. H. Talbot, *Analecta Sacri Ordinis Cisterciensis*, 10 (1954), 208–67 (one of these is addressed to Godard's sister, Margaret, abbess of Tarrant in the late 13th c.). In addition to well-known letters to women such as those of Anselm, Hildebert of Le Mans, Aelred of Rievaulx, Peter of Blois, and Peter the Venerable, William de Montibus wrote in Latin to nuns (see Joseph Goering, *William de Montibus (c.1140–1213): The Schools and the Literature of Pastoral Care* (Toronto: Pontifical Institute of Mediaeval Studies, 1992), pt. II. 6, 'Epistola ad moniales' [after 1202], 225–6), and Grosseteste corresponded with his sister Yvette, a nun ('Juettae sorori suae', see *Grosseteste Epistolae*, ed. Luard, *Ep.* 8. 43–5).

[16] This was possibly written early in Henry II's reign, *c.*1156–7 and certainly before Adelidis was succeeded as abbess by Marie Becket in 1173. See *Letters of Osbert of Clare*, ed. Williamson, no. 41; Newman, 'Flaws in the Golden Bowl'; for a translation see Morton, *Heavenly Brides and Holy Mothers*, no. I. Further references are by page and line number in Williamson's edition.

people).[17] The final figure offered Adelidis is Ethelburga ('mater tua beata et illustris', p. 176/3), seventh-century foundress of Barking.

In the complex series of negotiations between past and present which shape this treatise, Osbert's Ovidian tale of Silva offers the most remarkable and the central figure. This vestal virgin, 'corrupted' and impregnated in her sleep by Mars, will become the mother of Romulus and Remus, and she dreams of two palm trees. In Osbert's exposition the smaller palm signifies Remus and Julius Caesar, the taller is Romulus and Octavian, Caesar Augustus. Under Augustus's census of the world the journey to Bethelehem is taken, and in Augustus's peace, holy virginity sows most fruitfully on earth. As in the reign of Octavian, 'Christ's birth renews our eternal life, so in [the psalms of] the octave we rise again', says Osbert (p. 160/16–17). A pagan virgin (for examples can be taken not only from the 'daughters of Jerusalem, but . . . the Chaldeans', p. 157/28–30) thus, in her dream, provides the key claim of Osbert's account of virginity's history, like Bede's (see Chapter 2.1. above) a theory of history considered as a site for the production of Christian virginity. Osbert offers Adelidis in effect a mythography of virgin rule, together with examples of considerable (though also carefully curtailed and qualified) virgin power. They are grouped with some care as to their historical and other meanings: Cecilia as an early Roman virgin martyr is a 'mirror' (p. 155) of universal virgin sanctity; Etheldreda its primary insular incarnation. The Old Testament figure of Judith signifies confession and becomes the occasion of a treatise within the treatise: with every point of her story intensely allegorized, she becomes both a tropological mediation of sacred history and personal conduct and an eschatological figure of the soul. Judith is the springboard for a number of counsels and reflections— on humility, charity, hospitality, and chastity—before the letter returns to Ethelburga, historically contemporary with Etheldreda of Ely from the seventh century, but, as the foundress saint of Barking, a continuous presence in the life of Adelidis's own community. The order of Osbert's exemplary figures positions the treatise's audience in a particular temporal and existential moment: the present in which she is addressed looks to apocalypse, is morally informed, and descends from a redeemed past in which history is produced by virginity and the mother of God prepared for by the pagan antitype of the lapsed vestal.

These meanings are public and doubtless, in the manner of most medieval virginity and chastity letters, intended for more than one audience. Adelidis herself becomes a figure within the treatise, addressed as a vidual abbess ruling in the image of her virgin predecessor. The figure of Judith, played on to produce images of Adelidis as widow ('for your bridegroom [i.e. Christ] has surely died for you', p. 164/27–8), also alludes to the widow's status of regained honorary

---

[17] In the case of Cecilia, Osbert cautions that she is the *only* woman ever to perform the office of [public] holy preaching (*Letters of Osbert of Clare*, ed. Williamson, 155/31–2, 156/10). This saint none the less remained popular among women and is cited in several notable cases: see Ch. 1, n. 57 above.

virginity through the link of confession with penance. As Vera Morton has argued, it is also possible that the letter was a form of intervention in the politics of Adelidis's later years as an abbess, when in the course of a dispute between the abbey and a priest of Archbishop Theobald's, a scandalous story was spread about her.[18] Discussion of monastic obligations such as hospitality and charity is oblique in Osbert's treatise, and combined with personal moral exhortation to purity: conceivably Osbert was warning Adelidis or propagating a particular image of her in the dispute with Theobald.

Barking Abbey, which has the lioness's share of extant post-Conquest nun-nery books of Latin learning, owned a twelfth-century manuscript collection of saints' lives including some of the Barking foundress biographies recomposed in the late eleventh century by Goscelin of St Bertin.[19] Here a number of precedents and continuities were available to its abbesses. The extant pro-venanced manuscript includes a Life of Ethelburga, Barking's foundress, and *lectiones* for the feast of St Hildelith, Ethelburga's successor and the presiding abbess of the dedication of Aldhelm's *De Virginitate*.[20] Although two of the lives are dedicated to Maurice, Bishop of London (1086–1107), the occasion for the commission to Goscelin may well have been the building programme of Ælfgyva, abbess from about the time of the Conquest.[21] One of Goscelin's accounts of the *translatio* of the early abbesses' shrines to the enlarged church shows Ælfgyva taking comfort and inspiration from a vision of Ethelburga, Barking's foundress. As Ælfgyva prays alone at night in the abbey's church, the walls of the foundress's shrine seem to move outwards as if to crush her. Ethelburga appears and demands better quarters: when Ælfgyva commits herself to this, the

[18] I draw here on the work of my former student, Vera Morton (forthcoming in *Heavenly Brides and Holy Mothers*, no. I, Introduction). As she points out, at the time of Osbert's letter (if, as is most likely, it was written in 1156/7), Archbishop Theobald warned Adelidis to 'abstain from your notorious familiarity and cohabitation' with Hugh (a lay administrator of the abbey's estates, who continued in office until after the possible date of Adelidis's death in *c*.1166: see *The Letters of John of Salisbury*, ed. W. J. Millor, SJ, and H. E. Butler; rev. C. N. Brooke (Oxford: Clarendon Press, 1986), i, nos. 69 and 132). It seems at least possible that the Archbishop's letter to Adelidis testifies less to her imprudent conduct than to the interests of the Archbishop and his priest Roger of Ingatestone, who was in dispute with Barking over his tithes at the time of Theobald's letter.

[19] The manuscript is Cardiff, Public Library MS I. 381, ff. 81–146 (see Introduction n. 15, above). See Bell, s.v. Barking for a list of provenanced extant Barking books (nos 3, 4, 10, 12 are all or predominantly Latin and from the 12th–13th c.). Since Goscelin also wrote an account of the post-Conquest *translatio* of Barking abbesses, and reworked other Barking *vitae*, the convent very possibly owned other manuscripts of his hagiographic writings.

[20] Ker, *Medieval Manuscripts*, ii. 348–9: 'De virginitate', tr. Lapidge, in *Aldhelm: The Prose Works*, tr. Lapidge and Herren, 51–132 (59).

[21] For Goscelin's work as aimed at the hostile Norman Maurice while enlisting support for the cult and translation of the English saints of Barking as planned by Abbess Ælfgyva, see Paul Hayward, 'Translation-Narratives', 81–3. On the dates of the Barking translations and Goscelin's *vitae* see 'Texts of Jocelyn of Canterbury', ed. Colker, 383–460 (387–8), Hayward, 'Translation-Narratives', 81 n. 60. Ælfgyva had grown up in Barking (as Colker points out, 388): she is said to have been loved for the grace in her and for her intelligence by the mistress of the monastery's school ('scolae monasterialis magistra', 453, (i) ll. 10–11).

awesome figure of her predecessor suddenly shrinks to a tiny girl who leaps into Ælfgyva's arms to be comforted by her embrace.[22] Alfgyva had met initial opposition both within the convent and from the bishop of London for her planned extensions, and Goscelin's account heroicizes her doubts and difficulties, using long-established conventions of monastic vision and authentication to do so. Owing something to convention as it does, his imagery for the relation of Ælfgyva to her predecessors still positions her within a living and dynamic tradition, where she becomes mother to the house that mothers her. It has been pointed out that actual relations of a maternal kind within nunneries (the care of young children, for instance) were officially discouraged and symbolic maternity favoured.[23] Nevertheless, symbolic maternity is not without value for women as a figure for the relations and continuities in female monastic traditions. Goscelin's account of Ælfgyva's vision implicitly recognizes the necessity of precedents, role-models, and traditions of institutional history in enabling change and development, both in the life of a community and in the vision and determination of its leaders.

The Barking lives are much more like the hagiographic dossier of a large male house than anything extant for nunneries thereafter: they are rare both in their survival and in being lives written in relatively close knowledge of an individual nunnery's traditions (Goscelin was able to draw on the memories of at least one older nun within the house as well as on its records).[24] Nevertheless, some female houses seem to have continued to own or acquire collections of Latin saints' lives. In addition to the Barking manuscript containing Goscelin *vitae*, another group of Latin legends is provenanced to a female house. Belonging (certainly in the later Middle Ages) to the Benedictine abbey of Romsey in Hampshire, this manuscript collection, put together *c.*1300 and now London, BL Lansdowne 436, includes twelve abbess lives among its 47 saints.[25]

The thirteenth- and fourteenth-century dates of the Barking and Romsey manuscripts are potentially significant indications of communities with continuing or, perhaps, newly increased Latinity.[26] Such manuscripts may have been

[22] 'Texts of Jocelyn of Canterbury', ed. Colker, 454.
[23] See Power, *Medieval English Nunneries*, ch. 4; on the occlusion of biological maternity in female sanctity, Mulder-Bakker, Introduction to Mulder-Bakker (ed.), *Sanctity and Motherhood*, 3–30; on the problems of authorizing maternity in the monastic 'eschatological' family, see Felice Lifshitz, 'Is Mother Superior? Towards a History of Feminine *Amtscharisma*', in Parsons and Wheeler (eds.), *Medieval Mothering*, 117–38.
[24] 'Texts of Jocelyn of Canterbury', ed. Colker, 418; van Houts, *Memory and Gender*, 52.
[25] For a list of contents, description, and edition of one of the male lives in the manuscript, see P. Grosjean, 'Vita S. Roberti novi monasterii in Anglia abbatis', *AB* 56 (1938), 335–60. For the abbess lives in the manuscript see Figure 2.2 above.
[26] Romsey was among the wealthier nunneries and seems to have had a college of secular canons attached to it (Gilchrist, *Gender and Material Culture*, 38; Henry G. D. Liveing, *Records of Romsey Abbey: An Account of the Benedictine House of Nuns with notes on the Parish Church and Town (AD 907–1558) Compiled from Manuscript and Printed Records* (Winchester: Warren and Son, 1906). For a study of Latin preaching at the Benedictine nunnery of Elstow, see Mary E. O'Carroll, SND, *A Thirteenth-Century Preacher's Handbook* (Toronto: Pontifical Institute of Mediaeval Studies, 1997).

used solely by chaplains in these convents, but there is no direct evidence for this. The Romsey manuscript, a large and handsome, though not luxurious, volume, is suitable for reading aloud, and gives signs of having been carefully compiled for the use of a female community, though probably not initially Romsey, since it gives no special prominence to its joint *vitae* of the tenth-century foundress Ethelfleda and the early abbess Merwenna (her successor, *fl.* 960) and the inscription of ownership is later than the manuscript's texts.[27]

The manuscript begins with a chronicle of British history from the reign of Hengest in which the roles of kings and of abbesses are particularly signalled, both in text and in page layout and decoration, and organized according to genealogy. Rather than being a house dossier or a calendrical legendary, the ensuing legendary is an ecclesiastical history of Britain through its church leaders and some of its saintly Anglo-Saxon kings, beginning with the mission to the Anglo-Saxons of Augustine of Thanet and Canterbury (d. 610), and including churchmen from the tenth-century Benedictine reform. Stress is also laid on eremitic reforming saints: the early hermit Guthlac of Crowland (d. 714) is included and, apart from Bishop Hugh of Lincoln (d. 1200), the manuscript's latest saints are all eremitic figures, Wulfric of Haselbury (d. 1154), Godric of Finchale (d. 1170), Robert of Knaresborough (d. 1218). Of the 43 (originally 47) lives in the manuscript, twelve are women saints, a high proportion relative to many collections. They are all British abbesses and foundresses as well as virgins, and they are not grouped together at the end of the legendary, but occur throughout in what seems to be a mixture of chronological and genealogical/regional grouping.[28] Lives of long-standing attestation, such as Hild of Whitby, are mingled with lives elaborated in the twelfth century (the Cutberga Life, for instance, is almost entirely constituted by the saint's rhetorically developed speeches in favour of virginity as she seeks to convert the husband she has not wanted). All the lives are abbreviated versions, and however spectacularly some of them utilize the rhetoric of the virgin martyr (Cutberga is the most extreme example here, though Osith is like the 'ovis erupta de ore leonis', f. 29v, when her stag

---

[27] Romsey may or may not have owned the manuscript before the 15th-c. inscription of ownership was added to it, but the marking of abbess names (by marginal inscription of their names ringed in different colours) suggests initial compilation for a person or community with a particular interest in them. So, for instance, on f. 4v the East Anglian dynasty of abbesses circles the names of Sexburga, [H]ercongota, [H]ermanilde in red: on f. 5r the Mercian dynasty of Penda notes Ermenburga, Milburga, Mildreda, Mildritha (cf. Figure 2.1 above). Romsey had a long-standing reputation for learning, and had been responsible for the education of Matilda, wife of Henry I and daughter of St Margaret of Scotland: see further n. 42 below.

[28] So, for example, Werburga of Chester, Hanbury, and Repton (ff. 27–9), as daughter of Wulfhere of Mercia, follows the (highly legendary) account of Wulfhad and Rufinus his sons (ff. 23v–27); Osith (ff. 29–30), of whose husband Sighere, Wulfhere was the overlord, follows Werburga. Etheldreda is grouped together with her sisters (in a compilation based on Bede). On the other hand Milburga (d. 715) of Wenlock, daughter of Merewalh, king of Mercia, follows Hugh of Lincoln and precedes Bishop Oswald of York (d. 972). Despite its later 14th-c. index and 15th-c. inscription of Romsey's ownership, the manuscript texts seem to be the fruit of a single act of compilation.

saves her from Siger), it is their historic role in the church which is emphasized in this compilation.

On its own, the Lansdowne manuscript might seem most obviously to be of interest in the configuration where it has always had most attention: as an analogue to the work of John of Tynemouth (d. 1349), compiler of the *Nova Legenda Anglie*, the influential first among the nationalizing legendaries of the fourteenth century.[29] Yet considered alongside the closely contemporary Campsey manuscript (compiled after 1276 and added to in the early fourteenth century), the Lansdowne manuscript looks just as much an expression of female communities' interest in their own ecclesiastical history. If this was a manuscript for pious reading and edification, it is informed edification (not simply moralized and historically decontextualized romance reading: see Chapter 1.3 above). Edburga of Winchester (d. 960), of whom Lansdowne includes a Life, is attributed with the composition of seven songs a day (as Laurel Braswell has shown, this number is itself symbolic, derived from Ps. 119: 164: it partly encodes the ability of a house to carry out its liturgical duties).[30] Lansdowne's early fourteenth-century text of the Life of Ethelfleda of Romsey (*fl.* 960) also continues to testify to the reputation for liturgical competence that is a motif of twelfth-century *vitae*: Ethelfleda is noted for her skills of singing and reading ('in cantendo et legendo', f. 44r) and furthermore, when the light is too poor in winter as Ethelfleda goes up to read to the convent ('ad legendu*m* leccionem', f. 44r), her finger shines with a divine light which ceases only when she has completed the reading.

A reputation for learning remained an important aspect, even if a stereotypical one, of the representation of abbesses and their communities in the late twelfth and thirteenth centuries. Abbesses are frequently shown with a book as well as a staff of office on monastic seals, and in illumination: among their other attributes they are figures of the authority of monastic learning. Ethelfleda is distinguished by her devotion and zeal in prayer and the liturgy and by her refusal to hear or recite the canonical hours anywhere except in church (f. 43v): this resistance to (presumably) the developing laicization of the liturgy in the growth of private use of the psalter and of books of hours and her other virtues commend her to Merwenna, who trains her with motherly zeal for a career in which she will be favoured by God in the church. Yet interestingly this relation is not without its tensions: having had a vision of the abbess Merwenna cutting switches, Ethelfleda intervenes in the discipline of the convent to say that the whole convent will gladly sing and chant and carry out orders, and there is no need for beating (f. 44v). Ethelfleda is thus not only a figure of the house's ability to perform its liturgical function, but a model of contemplative and choir nun priorities as

---

[29] See *Nova Legenda Anglie*, ed. Carl Horstmann (Oxford: Clarendon Press, 1901), pp. ix–x.

[30] Laurel Braswell, 'St Edburga of Winchester: A Study of Her Cult AD 950 with an Edition of the Fourteenth-Century Middle English and Latin Lives', *Mediaeval Studies*, 33 (1971), 292–333 (303, 331).

against the administrative and disciplinary role of her own educator, the abbess Merwenna. In a *vita* shaped in the twelfth century Ethelfleda's intervention over the switches argues for the internalized value of devotion to liturgical practices rather than the use of externally imposed discipline.

Against the continuing and relatively lavish historiography of pre-Conquest foundresses, the records of abbess foundresses in Anglo-Norman England are relatively sparse, or occupy more modest genres of commemoration. Although they do not seem to have produced or owned formal Latin hagiographic dossiers as often as male monastic houses, nunneries continued to commemorate their inhabitants in other genres more directly expressive of the principal spiritual capital of female religious: their role in prayer, commemoration, and intercession. Two extant mortuary rolls of prayers for the dead from the thirteenth century suggest undiminished vigour in comparison with the Continental rolls from the twelfth century in which English nunneries participated.[31] When the mortuary roll of the prioress of Lillechurch was carried round to affiliated houses for the addition of prayers and consolatory verses, 372 houses in England and north-west France added their *tituli*.[32] In the elegantly illustrated roll of about 1230 from Castle Hedingham, Lucy (de Vere?, perhaps the daughter of the first Earl of Oxford, Aubrey de Vere III, d. 1194) is called prioress and first foundress by her successor Agnes in supplicating the prayers of other religious houses.[33] The account of prioress Lucy is a stylized eulogy, and closely modelled on the desiderata of the Rule, yet suggesting the influence of affective piety and other contemporary trends. Outdoing Bede's twice-married Etheldreda, Lucy is said to have been 'seven times bound by the chain of marriage' and to have remained 'uncontaminated and inviolate'. As abbess she is said to have practised an abstinence so strong with so many vigils, fasts, harshness of clothing, and discipline that, like Job, it left her flesh consumed and her skin sticking to her bones. She is also a model for the convent of 'more

[31] It was customary on the deaths of abbesses for messengers to be sent to other monastic houses carrying rolls on which commemorative verses and prayers could be inscribed (see Léopold Delisle, *Rouleaux des morts du ixe au xve siècle* (Paris: Renouard, 1866). For the 12th-c. roll for the Conqueror's daughter Matilda, abbess of Holy Trinity, Caen (extant only in transcriptions by Mabillon), see ibid. 178.

[32] Lillechurch mortuary roll is Cambridge, St John's College MS 271 (ed. G. O. Sayle, 'The Mortuary Roll of the Abbess of Lillechurch, Kent', *Proc. Camb. Antiq. Soc.* 10 (1898–1903), 383–409: Thompson corrects the dating from the later to the earlier 13th c., *Women Religious*, 11 n. 26).

[33] The text of Agnes's letter is printed by Dugdale (*Mon.* iv. 436–7). The letter immediately follows three beautifully executed ink and wash illustrations at the head of the roll: the first shows the crucifixion and the Virgin Mary seated with a lily, the second the ascent of the prioress's soul (not naked, but decorously veiled) to heaven between two angels and the third her funeral (London, BL, MS Egerton 2849, opening of roll). On de Vere's third wife (thought by Leland and others to be the prioress Lucy, but in fact named Agnes), see Cecily Clark, 'La Vie féminine en Angleterre'. Thompson suggests Lucy may have been the daughter of Aubrey de Vere (*Women Religious*, 181). Houses contributing to the roll include Barking, Horsham St Faith, Campsey (nos. 16, 49, 59).

frequent reading, more fervent prayer and more intense emotion' ('lectio fre-
quentior, oratio pinguior et ferventior affectus').[34]

Cartularies are a further source where portraits of abbesses, if not full hagiographic dossiers, may be found. One of the better-documented thirteenth-
century cases is Euphemia, abbess of the Benedictine abbey of Wherwell in
Hampshire from 1226 to 1257. Like her predecessor Matilda (1186–until after
1208), to whom Peter of Blois wrote, Euphemia received Latin letters, including an *epistola consolatoria* and poems on Matilda's death by Guy, prior of
Southwick.[35] A good command of Latin for reading is also suggested by
Euphemia's psalter, and a second Wherwell psalter of *c.*1300 does nothing
to diminish the impression of good Latinity among Wherwell's choir nuns and
its female administrators.[36] No formal hagiographic biographies of foundresses
and abbesses are extant from Wherwell, but its (unedited) early fourteenth-
century cartulary contains a prose account of Matilda and of Euphemia

[34] *Mon.* iv. 436–7 and MS Egerton 2839, ff. 1–2.

[35] Extant as an addition to a 12th-c. Wherwell calendar, now St Petersburg (*olim* Leningrad)
Public Library Qu.v.l.62, f. 12v: see Dom Antonius Staerck, *Les Manuscrits latins du Ve au XIIIe
siècle conservés à la Bibliothèque impériale de Saint Pétersbourg*, I (St Petersburg: Franz Krois, 1910),
274–5 and II, pl. xcvi (f. 4v). Guy of Southwick was author of a treatise on confession commissioned by Bishop William de Vere of Hereford, 1186–98, and dated to 1190–8 ('Opuscule de Guy
de Southwick', ed. André Wilmart, *RTAM* 7 (1935), 337–52 (338)). He died *c.*1217 (Sharpe,
Handlist, 157). Euphemia is addressed by Guy as 'F. uenerabili priorisse Warewella', his letter being
well before her promotion to abbess in 1226. For Peter of Blois's letter to Matilda see *The Latin
Letters of Peter of Blois*, ed. Elizabeth Revell, Auctores Britannici Medii Aevi XIII (London: British
Academy, 1993), no. 17 (I thank Professor Revell for this reference). This letter, addressing Matilda
as an abbess 'of noble stock and a still nobler mind', invokes the appropriately queenly model of
Esther (§6) as a precedent for Wherwell's intercessory prayers for the church during the interdict
(ibid. 100, §6).

[36] On Euphemia's psalter (Cambridge, St John's College MS 68) see Rodney M. Thomson,
Manuscripts from St Alban's Abbey 1066–1235 (Woodbridge and Totowa, NJ: D. S. Brewer for the
University of Tasmania, 1982), i. 37, 56–8; ii, pl. 137. For the obits of Euphemia's mother and
predecessor abbess see ibid. 58–9. In the litany (f. 209v) the virgins are headed by the Magdalen,
Mary of Egypt, Felicitas, and Perpetua. The double appearance of Fides in the litany (Fides Spes
and Karitas and a second 'Fidis' grouped with Eufemia, Katerina, and Margareta just before the
litany concludes with 'Adeldrida' on f. 209vb/12) is considered an error by Thomson (58): but I
am grateful to Professor Pamela Sheingorn (pers. comm.) for confirmation that the second Fides
is more likely to be Foy of Agen and Conques. A prayer for women's use added on f. 1r unusually
specifies female saints (in honore *omnium sanctorum* tuor*um* et *sanctarum* tuar*um*) as well as a
female penitent ('et p*ro* me misera peccatrice'). The other surviving Wherwell psalter (London,
BL, MS Addit. 27866, 14th c.) is a small pocket-book psalter, entirely in Latin, with additions and
corrections of a practised kind—omitted words in psalms, extra (mostly south-western) saints in
the calendar, etc. Part of the late s.xiv/xv inscription of ownership has been erased and replaced
with 'Johanna Stretford' (f. 137v, 121v old numbering) just before the litany. A Jonette de Stretford
was nominated to Romsey in 1333 by Bishop Stratford 'en regard de charite' (Power, *Medieval
English Nunneries*, 189 suggests a poor relative, and see Liveing, *History of Romsey*, 98). The psalter
may have been the personal psalter of a choir nun: personal ownership inscriptions become increasingly common in the 15th c. (Ann Hutchison, pers. comm.). The evidence from Wherwell, such
as it is, thus suggests a continuing Latinity supplemented (rather than replaced *faute de mieux*) by
vernacular works.

herself.[37] Matilda is praised for strength in adversity, for replenishing the house's numbers and multiplying its possessions, and for her gifts of relics, ornaments, precious vestments and, 'for our teaching and learning ['doctrine et erudicione nostra']', six books ('sex libro*rum* volumina', f. 45r), books additional to those noted for the house by Bell.[38] The account of Euphemia is still more informative about what was admired in female leadership. Euphemia increased the number of nuns from forty to eighty and enlarged the funding of their clothing allowance; she constructed a new infirmary with a good drainage system; built a new chapel in honour of the Virgin within a new enclosure which she had planted with trees; built new service buildings; planted vines and gardens; cleared and rebuilt or restored several manors and farms on the nunnery estates, improving fire safety in them and building a new mill; rebuilt the bell tower when it collapsed and replaced the presbytery of the nunnery church on deep and firm foundations, living to see it dedicated to Peter and Paul. She also gave crosses and saints' relics ('reliquiis *sanctorum*', f. 44r) adorned with precious stones, vestments, and books ('vestime*n*tis et libris', f. 44r) to the church of the nunnery. She also 'so conducted herself with regard to exterior affairs that she seemed to have the spirit of a man rather than of a woman': her holy manner of life was exemplary and her achievements an inspiration (f. 43v), while she was also 'zealous in charity and hospitality' (f. 44r).[39] The amenity and efficiency of Euphemia's building, improvement, and expansion is praised throughout the cartulary's account.

Even this formidable level of female achievement (carried out over an unusually lengthy career as abbess) has produced no extant formal monastic hagiography. In the fourteenth-century index to the cartulary, the account of Euphemia is not a life (*vita*), but a 'compilation concerning the excellent rule of Euphemia, abbess of Wherwell' ('compilac*io* Eufemie abb*atisse* de Where*welle* de bona gub*ernatione* sua', f. 3v, no. lviii) and the narrative occupies little more than two sides (ff. 43v/16–45v/23) in the manuscript's small 24-line folios, following the even shorter account of Matilda. These commemorations of successive abbesses suggest a pattern familiar in women's history: that of success established in one generation, briefly built on, and then recontained. Certainly something like a family tradition of female activity is suggested by the fact that Euphemia's mother, Margaret de Walliers, came from St Bertin and that the cartulary calls Euphemia 'our [i.e. the convent's] friend and the compatriot ('*nost*re *amice* et *co*mpat*riota* sue', f. 43v) of Matilda whose family is across

[37] London, BL, MS Egerton 2104 A, item lix, ff. 43v/16–44v/23 (Euphemia); item lx, ff. 44v/23–45r/3 (Matilda). The cartulary, some 460 items, is a fair copy of earlier documents, in Latin throughout except for a sequence of letters (ff. 52v–53r) in French directed to Edward I (see further below). It was calendared in the 17th c. (MS Egerton 1024 B).
[38] Bell, s.v. Wherwell.
[39] The cartulary's account is paraphrased in *VCH, Hampshire* ii. 132–3. Euphemia will be given an updated entry in the new *Oxford Dictionary of National Biography* (pers. comm., *DNB*).

the sea' ('*transmarinis*', f. 44v). Flemish family traditions may be responsible for the post-Conquest conduct and development of this Anglo-Saxon Benedictine house. But the documentary context of the two lives may also be significant. They occur in the cartulary together with the Wherwell foundation story of Queen Ælftrudis (d. 1002), purported murderess of her stepson Edward. However, not only is Ælftrudis represented in the cartulary narrative as lavishly penitent and inspired by a vision to found on the island of Wherwell a church dedicated to the holy cross in memory of Christ's outpouring of redemptive blood, but the positioning of this story in the cartulary suggests that it confers prestige on the house. It is the fifty-eighth item (f. 43r–v) following copies of the charters and confirmations of foundation and the papal privileges of the nunnery, and it precedes the accounts of Euphemia (item lix, ff. 43v–44v) and her predecessor Matilda (item lx, f. 44v), who both died on the same day. The queen's initial foundation gift is followed by the gifts of the Flemish-born abbesses to the house: Euphemia and Matilda are presented here as continuing a tradition of Anglo-Saxon queenly foundation.[40]

Cartularies are not innocently factual documents (Wherwell's cartulary later presents the ladies of this wealthy convent to Edward I as 'ses pauvres nonaynes, labbesse e couent de Wher*well*', f. 52v, apropos his 'ministres' encroachments from the royal forest on the abbey's rights in the neighbouring forest of Harewood). It is tempting to think that this early fourteenth-century copy may reflect a Benedictine reassertion of prestige in response to the major new foundation of Augustinian canonesses at Lacock by Ela, Countess of Salisbury, in 1240. Wherwell's representation of itself as founded on pre-Conquest queenly largess together with lavish Flemish provision would fit with such an assertion. At Lacock, Ela of Salisbury herself evidently also continued earlier traditions, intending a dual foundation in the manner of Anglo-Saxon royal houses or the Caen *abbaye aux hommes* and *abbaye aux dames* of William the Conqueror and his wife. The house for Carthusians begun by her husband William Longespee which she completed was to have been called *Locus Dei* and her own abbey of canonesses at Lacock was to have been *Locus Beatae Mariae*.[41] Regally lavish gift-giving remained an important mark of the foundress, and this tradition was substantially refreshed for the early Anglo-Norman court, as Lois Huneycutt has shown, in Margaret of Scotland's twelfth-century *vita*.[42] Whether Wherwell's cartulary assertions were consciously written against Ela's lavish new foundation

---

[40] See the works cited in n. 1 and Ch. 1, nn. 106–7 above, and, more generally, Jo Ann McNamara, 'Imitatio Helenae: Sainthood as an Attribute of Queenship', in Sticca (ed.), *Saints' Legends*, 51–80.

[41] W. G. Clark-Maxwell, 'The Earliest Charters of the Abbey of Lacock', *Wiltshire Archaeological and Natural History Magazine*, 35 (1907–8), 191–209 (193).

[42] Huneycutt, 'Idea of the Perfect Princess'; also her ' "Proclaiming Her Dignity Abroad": The Literary and Artistic Network of Matilda of Scotland, Queen of England 1100–1118', in McCash (ed.), *Cultural Patronage*, 155–74.

or not, the idea of queenly largess remained important in the representation of abbesses of whatever rank. Such an ideal does not contradict but complements reforming emphasis on the *vita apostolica* and asceticism. The most valued asceticism is that of those who could choose otherwise, the humblest humility that of those who have a long way to stoop.

These traditions are continued but also given further contemporary inflections in the vernacular twelfth- and thirteenth-century hagiographic lives of abbesess. The Campsey manuscript, compiled within twenty years of Euphemia's abbacy, is rich testimony to the cultural and historical interests of women. The manuscript consists of Anglo-Norman lives, and was used by canonesses rather than traditional Benedictine nuns, but there is no cause to read the move into the vernacular here as a sign of decline. Campsey's three foundress-abbess lives are of St Osith, St Etheldreda, and St Modwenna. Osith is the first British abbess saint to appear in an extant Anglo-Norman life: her twelfth-century Latin *vita* was given a late twelfth-century Anglo-Norman reworking, itself added to in the thirteenth century (including an interpolation which links Osith with Modwenna).[43] *Modwenna* and *Audrée* are thirteenth-century lives, the first based on a Latin *vita* which was itself rewritten as part of the twelfth-century revival of Modwenna's cult by the monks of Burton-on-Trent, the second a reworking of the account of St Etheldreda in the twelfth-century *Liber Eliensis*.[44] Unlike *Modwenna* and *Osith*, which are anonymous, the Life of *Audrée* identifies itself as having been composed by a certain 'Marie': her identity is unknown, but she may have been connected with the nunnery of Chatteris near the saint's chief cult in Ely, or perhaps with Barking.[45] All

[43] As noted in Ch. 5.1 n. 52 above, this strengthens the links of the west Midlands Modwenna with the Osith of Hereford and Essex: in the narrative terms important in this chapter it gives Modwenna a prestigious disciple and an opportunity to show her own protective and educative powers. For the interpolation, see 'Anglo-French Life of St Osith', ed. Baker, 476–504; id., 'Episode from the . . . Life of St Modwenna'. There is an additional miracle in the 12th-c. Life concerning either Richard Belmeis, bishop of London and founder of Chich, 1121, or Richard Fitz-Neal, bishop of London, d. 1198 ('Anglo-French Life of St Osith', ed. Baker, 477–8) which may also have been added in the 13th c. (see D. W. Russell, 'Secularization of Hagiography', 13). According to Jean Fournée, Osith was also culted in Normandy at La Lande-de-Goult (Orne) (*Le Culte populaire et l'iconographie des saints en Normandie* (Paris: Société d'histoire et d'archéologie normandes, 1973) t. II, *Étude générale*, 235).

[44] *St Modwenna*, ed. Baker and Bell, pp. xi–xii; Price, '*La Vie de sainte Modwenne*', 172. Robert Bartlett is editing Geoffrey of Burton's *vita* (Oxford University Press, forthcoming). For the Anglo-Norman Etheldreda see *Audrée*, ed. Södergård.

[45] The Audrée text in the late 13th-c. section of the Campsey manuscript is not the original of the Anglo-Norman Life (which may have been composed any time between 1189 and the later 13th c.). On the date, see *Audrée*, ed. Södergård, 55; *ANLB* 264–5. On the identity of the author Marie, see Wogan-Browne, 'Re-routing the Dower', in Carpenter and MacLean (eds.), *Power of the Weak*, 31–2. Legge speculates (on unnamed grounds) that Marie may have been from Barking (*ANCL* 50): see further Blanton-Whetsall (cited in Ch. 5 n. 51 above). A third possible community for the Life's composition is that of the Augustinian canonesses at the refounded house of Canonsleigh in Devon (see further n. 67 below): the 1284 refoundation and dedication to Etheldreda is late, but not completely impossible for the text or for the Campsey manuscript in which its extant copy survives.

three saints figure in the virgin pantheon of male monasticism as discussed in Chapter 2.1 above, but here, in a manuscript containing the Countess of Arundel's saints, two lives composed in and one patronized by Barking Abbey, and itself certainly used in a female community, they become very much texts of female foundation. They represent a further 'informal' source for representing the transmission of powers and precedents between women.

As mentioned above, a virgin wanting to become an abbess is represented within the conventions of virgin martyrdom, a rich body of narrative possibilities which can be deployed with different selections and nuances in different lives. In the well-known Life of Christina of Markyate, the only twelfth-century *vita* we have of a twelfth-century woman aspiring to this career path, Christina is represented as suffering from parental beatings and other cruelties over a long period and from attempted nuptial rape. Hagiography of more legendary figures shows the qualification of the abbess for rule as inscribed on her body in motifs also drawn from the repertoire of virginity topics. In the twelfth-century *vita* of St Winifred of Flintshire, an angry prince-suitor decapitates the saint, after which she is resurrected and becomes, under the tutelage of her spiritual director, a foundress-abbess. Winifred's neck-scar is greatly venerated: focusing attention on her headship of the community, it becomes in effect a badge of office.[46] The virgin martyr's emphatic 'no' to the tyrant suitor encodes the abbess's profession. In the second, longer version of Brigid of Ireland's life (present in several early *South English Legendary* manuscripts), the saint prays for help in repelling the heart of the duke to whom she has been forcibly betrothed.[47] God miraculously removes one of her eyes, and restores it as soon as her father and suitor permit her to take the veil. Losing or gouging out one's eyes is a variant of cutting off one's nose in the stories told by twelfth- and thirteenth-century chroniclers of the resistance of good women to rape.[48]

Viewed within the context of lives in the Campsey manuscript, however, the primary emphasis of such narrative tropes may be not so much that punishment or mutilation as damaged breeding stock is a precondition of women's promotion to abbess-foundress status, as that abbesshood requires some freedom from marital and breeding demands. Winifred of Flintshire bears a scar, but it marks restored wholeness and echoes the famous neck-scar of Etheldreda

[46] See AA.SS. Nov. i (1887), 714 §12: for the later cult see C. de Smedt, 'Documentum de S. Wenefreda', *AB* 6 (1887), 305–52: d'Evelyn, 'Legends of Individual Saints', *Manual of the Writings in Middle English*, ii. 633–4 (no. 293). No Anglo-Norman life is known.

[47] Bridget of Ireland's Middle English Life is extant in two versions (d'Evelyn and Foster, 'Saints' Legends', *Manual of the Writings in Middle English*, ii. 573, no. 50): *Early South English Legendary*, ed. Horstmann, 192–3 and *SEL*, ed. d'Evelyn and Mill, i. 45–6, ll. 221–31, 241–9.

[48] See Schulenberg, 'Brides of Christ and Sacrificial Mutilation', and for a secular representation, Marie de France's *Bisclavret* (in *Marie de France: Lais*, ed. Ewert, 55/235). Carol Neel cites what seems to have been a historical instance of nasal self-mutilation as a defence against enforced betrothal in the 13th c. in the case of Oda of Rivreulle (d. 1257): see her 'The Origins of the Beguines', *Signs*, 14 (1989), 321–41 (336–7).

herself.[49] Brigid of Ireland loses an eye at her prayer for deliverance, but this also signals change in the nature of Brigid's vision. In the Campsey life of Modwenna, the saint twice qualifies a younger woman for succession to her rule. She does so by ageing the one and blinding the other. In the first case, the high-born Orbilla pleads her unworthiness to take charge of the convent (as abbesses and prioresses were conventionally expected to do on election). Her youth and beauty, she says, could 'bring great harm' and make her 'fall into great error'.[50] Modwenna, in what seems almost a version of liturgical exsufflation, blows on Orbilla's fresh complexion and girds her with her own girdle (vv. 572–3). Orbilla's face instantly wrinkles and her hair whitens (vv. 579–80), and Modwenna promises her that she will no longer need to fear *raptus* for the sake of her beauty ('Que pur belté seez ravie', v. 583). Commending a daughter house of her monastery to Orbilla's charge, Modwenna now renames her Servilla (v. 588).[51] To her second spiritual daughter, Brigne, also much loved by her ('sa dame la eime tendrement', v. 5390), Modwenna offers a prophetic vision of ecclesiastical success: Brigne will found a monastery, become an abbess, noble maidens and wealthy ladies will flock there to take the habit with her (v. 5524), and there will be no trouble from robbers and depredations (vv. 5537–40). To guard Brigne better from sin in this career, however, her eyes (with which she has just beheld the heavenly radiance surrounding Modwenna's private nightly collation with angels) will now be blinded so that she will never see anything that could lead her into sin (vv. 5541–6). This is further glossed in a short homily by Modwenna as the fortunate removal of the means by which Eve was deceived in her transgressive gaze on the apple: what are the eyes but 'the messengers who make the heart desire evil?' (vv. 5563–4). Brigne 'must not be troubled if God wishes so to amend her condition' (vv. 5561–2).

Such dramatic scenes of qualification for office seem to encode its powers in far less desirable ways than the sensible provisions of foundresses themselves, who, if faced with an absence of institutional tradition and precedent, borrowed from ancient monastic strategies of expansion and deployed staff from established nunneries to help them in setting up their foundations.[52] In so far as the *Vie sainte Modwenne* is a vernacular source presenting the goals of institutional monasticism, such writing may seem not distant enough from the misogynist dualism familiar from, for instance, the courtly representation of younger and older women in the Dame Ragnell figures associated in insular tradition with

[49] *Audrée*, ed. Södergård, vv. 1919–21 (and vv. 2246–7 for the scar's posthumous healing).

[50] 'Par ma bealté e mun eage | Avenir puet grant damage' (vv. 557–8); 'Par la belté de ma culur | Chair purraie en grant errur' (vv. 561–2). References henceforth by line number in the text.

[51] Since 'orb' means 'blind' in Anglo-Norman, there are a number of possible allegorical meanings in the change of names here.

[52] So Ela of Lacock, for instance, secured a Benedictine prioress, Wymarca, to run Lacock and prepare Ela herself before the foundress took over as abbess (for Wymarca's letter of 1239 see W. R. Jones and W. D. Macray (eds.), *Charters and Documents Illustrating the History of the Cathedral, City, and Diocese of Salisbury*, RS 97 (London, 1891), no. ccxxii. 251–2).

Gawain.[53] Both the incidents in which Modwenna qualifies a younger woman suggest female sexuality as disqualification from office. Yet Modwenna's ageing of Orbilla, targeted at the conventional signs of youthful romance virginity, removes these markers in the creation of a prestigious role for Orbilla. The violence of the transition may mark its stringent demands and the difficulties of female careers as much as antifeminism. If these changes defeminize Orbilla, they also take her beyond the limitations of femininity and into what for many purposes is a third gender. Age had the capacity to confer new authority and new powers of prophecy and counsel on women in the religious life, and Modwenna's actions should perhaps be read less as mutilation than as the liberation they claim to be.[54] Equally, an interiorization of vision away from the world, as in Brigne's case, is reckoned one of the privileges of monastic success and is an image of contemplative monasticism. (In a text written by a woman, Clemence of Barking's St Catherine herself invokes a savage version of the *memento mori* topos as a rebuke to spectators deploring the loss of youth and beauty as Catherine goes to execution.)[55]

Modwenna is the most 'professional' of the three abbesses: she enters the religious life directly in her youth by making a vow to a visiting bishop (vv. 117–18) and meets no difficulty: her royal parents, indeed, are painlessly converted in the space of a quatrain (vv. 205–8). Her Life opens with an account of the value of the religious life in the context of redemption history (vv. 1–40) and with a portrait of female monastic life as a heroic victory over the flesh and human nature (vv. 45–56). However, it also includes an account of Modwenna's education: once veiled, she is sent to a 'good man' to be taught 'lettrure' (v. 184, perhaps here specifically Latin letters), while herself teaching a child of her own charitable fostering 'lettres' ('reading') when he is about 5 or 6 years old (vv. 227–8). Her Life is presented as an exemplary biography by which the labours and victories of religious maidens ('puceles', v. 41) may be better understood, but, in the formidable British scope of Modwenna's foundations and achievements, constitutes, as I have elsewhere argued, an ambitious professional *speculum* for any aspirant abbesses and foundresses among its audiences.[56]

The Lives of Audrée and Osith, on the other hand, are at once abbess lives and lives of virgin spouses entangled with mortal men, not only with the heavenly bridegroom. The most powerful blending of professed and lay religious female lives is found in *Audrée*, one of the few lives of virgin marriage (other than the Barking *Edouard le confesseur* also present in the Campsey manuscript) certainly

[53] See A. G. Rigg, *Gawain on Marriage: The Textual Tradition of the De coniuge non ducenda* (Toronto: University of Toronto Press, 1986); Bartlett J. Whiting, 'The Wife of Bath's Tale', in W. F. Bryan and Germaine Dempster (eds.), *Sources and Analogues of Chaucer's Canterbury Tales* (New York: Humanities Press, 1941), 222–64.

[54] Mulder-Bakker, ' "The Prime of Their Lives" ', in Dor *et al.*, *New Trends in Feminine Spirituality*, 215–36.

[55] *Life of Saint Catherine*, ed. MacBain, vv. 1981–2000.

[56] Price, '*La Vie de sainte Modwenne*', 173–6.

written by a woman.[57] Audrée (Anglo-Saxon: Æthelthryth; Latin: Etheldreda) of Ely, is the most prominent insular abbess in Latin historiographical tradition and more vernacular lives of her were made than of any other native female saint.[58] Reference has been made in Chapter 2.1 to the importance of custody of Etheldreda's intact body as in effect a form of charter for the landholding of the Ely monks and to the role of the twelfth-century *Liber Eliensis* Life of Etheldreda in articulating and propagating this use of the saint. But here the Ely *vita* is reworked by a woman writing for an aristocratic female community (whether Chatteris, Barking, or elsewhere) where some members might well be professed after widowhood or annulment of marriage, and it is read aloud in the Campsey manuscript by women to other women in another such community. The vernacular Life of this holy widowed virgin with its account of virginity, marriage, dower, foundation, and autonomy must have read in a range of ways in these contexts—as English lineage history; as a text of female rule by professed women; as a text for women interested in association with female communities—foundresses, patronesses, vowesses, lay boarders. Indeed, breaking down distinctions between contemplative and active life, Audrée is said in the Life to resemble both Martha and Mary: 'this queen perfected herself in the service of God . . . she followed Martha in labour and Mary in prayer'.[59]

However exemplary, Audrée's career is not unlike the Anglo-Norman noblewomen who, particularly as widows with dower property, were patronesses and foundresses.[60] Some of these, whether or not they preferred what *La vie sainte Audrée* calls 'the spouse who cannot die' (v. 1166), resisted remarriage or, like Isabella, Countess of Arundel, paid large sums to avoid it.[61] Audrée in effect experiences most of the possible roles open to secular Anglo-Norman noble- and gentrywomen: motherhood, the only role not literally experienced by her, is spiritually available, since Audrée's status as virgin foundress and abbess enables

[57] Virgin spouses of special importance in insular hagiography are St Alexis, Christina of Markyate, St Cecilia, Edward the Confessor and his queen Edith. On medieval hagiographic chaste marriage see Elliott, *Spiritual Marriage*; André Vauchez, *Les Laïcs au moyen âge* (Paris: Éditions du cerf, 1987), 4ième partie, ch. xvii. For other Anglo-Norman and French examples, see Janice M. Pindar, 'The Intertextuality of Old French Saints' Lives: St Giles, St Evroul and the Marriage of St Alexis', *Parergon*, 6A (1988), 11–21: for an example which includes the point of view of the bride, see the discussion of the nun of Barking's Life of Edward the Confessor in Wogan-Browne, ' "Clerc u lai, muïne u dame" ', 68–73.
[58] Several of these in later medieval England are associated with female communities, most notably Wilton in the case of the early 15th-c. Life associated with that of St Edith in Cotton Faustina B iii (*S. Editha sive Chronicon Vilodnense in Wiltshire Dialekt*, ed. Carl Horstmann (Heilbronn: Henninger, 1883)), and whatever female house, if any, may have owned the Vernon manuscript, which contains a *SEL* version of the life of St 'Aeldri' (Audrée).
[59] *Audrée*, ed. Södergård, vv. 1223–4, 1229–32 (henceforth referenced by line number in the text).
[60] Some post-Conquest nunneries were founded by widows who later remarried: 'even for those who stayed in the world, founding a nunnery may well have seemed the best way of crystallizing a measure of independence' (Thompson, *Women Religious*, 175, 177).
[61] See Loengard, 'Of the Gift of My Husband', 233–7.

her to propagate a lineage of spiritual successors as well as occupying a maternal spiritual role towards her nuns and handmaidens.

The Life by Marie contains a great deal of explicit reflection on marriage and the constraint of women: the narrator offers reassurance that Audrée showed much greater holiness ('mut greindre sainteté', v. 349) in following her personal desire for a religious career rather than carrying out other people's wishes for her ('acompleir autres volunté', v. 350). Audrée rejoices at her 'deliverance from the servitude . . . of the yoke of marriage' (vv. 369–70); a *vitae patrum* exemplum encourages her and her first husband to virgin marriage; there is an extensive account of her second husband's psychological pressure on her for consummation (rape is not an option considered).[62] Pithy octosyllabics repeatedly sum up or reassert Audrée's determination: 'Meuz vout mener issi sa vie | Ke aver a home compaignie' ('She would rather live her life in this manner than live with a man', vv. 951–2, see also vv. 1263–4): she is burdened ('chargee') by Ecgfrid's suit, and angered ('ennuyee') by his offers (vv. 792–3); her purpose is unshaken (vv. 1049–56), and she conquers both her husbands 'par la *force* Jhesu Crist' (v. 1043, my italics). The narrator invites general reflection on how hard it is to escape the world and 'charnel temptation' (v. 1131) in marriage, and suggests that in her religious life Audrée is both Martha and Mary, combining work and prayer (vv. 1229–32). Once escaped, it is claimed, nothing in religion weighs upon her as heavily as had the miseries of marriage (v. 1240).

Much of the narration of *Audrée* is carried out in the third person, with relatively little direct speech and in a style which embraces some lyricism and exclamation, but which on the whole deploys a register of chronicling facticity: this is very different, for example, from the speeches and spectacle of the Katherine Group. The narrative also includes sustained and detailed attention to the genealogies of Audrée and her family and husbands, and a portrait of her father Anne as a good king, reminiscent of the Haveloc/Havelock portraits of Anglo-Norman and Middle English romance: King Anne treats both clergy and people fairly (vv. 509–10), is a father to orphans, and governs widows 'gently' ('doucement', v. 520), a matter of significance when the king had rights to the remarriage of widows and the ability to insist unless large fines could be afforded.[63] King Anne is also a [biological] father to holy ladies ('seintes dames', v. 561) and an opponent of the pagan Penda by whom he is eventually killed. For all the idealization of the portrait of Audrée's father (none of it incompatible with his own rights to marry his daughter to his preferred suitor, though it is implied that Tonbert is a very persistent suitor, vv. 287–8), this is also a

---

[62] This may be inherited from Bede's portrayal of Egfrid as a virtuous king working closely with Archbishop Wilfrid of York (see Hollis, *Sharing a Common Fate*, 165–7), but since the text follows the *Liber Eliensis* in making Ecgfrid intend to throw Audrée violently out of his aunt's monastery (v. 1286), it seems most likely that the protocol of not showing saints raped combines here with a representation of the difficulties of marriage.

[63] See further the works cited in Ch. 5, n. 2 above.

carefully deployed history, with Audrée's lineage placed as ancient and distinguished within the Christian history of the English people (vv. 37–228). In *Audrée*, the narrator declares, she intends to memorialize the history of the saint in the vernacular ('l'estoire . . . en romanz fas la memoire', vv. 319–20).

La vie sainte Audrée in this way is a blending of hagiography and historiography and has continuities (across Latin and vernacular) with earlier medieval biographies of queens and abbesses. In the prologue, the narrator draws particular attention to Audrée's royal rank: 'I have begun to make this book for St Audrey the queen . . . and before I speak of her marriage, I must describe her lineage' (vv. 29–36). Audrée's virginity is, appropriately, 'queen over all the virtues' (vv. 2801–2), and it is an exemplary element of her humility that this virgin queen can exercise it from a royal height. In addition to the descent from King Anne that gives Audrée earthly royalty, her descent from her mother is detailed. Audrée's mother, Hereswitha, is sister to St Hild and is herself twice married and the producer of four saintly daughters: she spends her widowhood as a professed nun at Chelles in order to have an eternal crown.[64] Audrée's sisters and nieces eventually succeed her at Ely (see Figure 2.1), so that her lineage goes forwards into the future as well as creating her initial position. In the particular fecundity of the virgin body, at once the denial and the perfection of human generation, the virgin foundress simultaneously disrupts biological lines of filiation and creates spiritual genealogies. She thus both evades and reinscribes the pressures of family lineage, and does so in a matrix of kinship and family connections affecting the status and property of her house. The lines of spiritual filiation by which the mother house of Ely passes to Audrée's sister Sexburga and thence to her niece, and in which Sexburga translates Audrée to future generations by moving her to a richer shrine, make for the perpetuation both of an ideal female spiritual community and of a founding family's connections and influence in a major religious house. Later medieval lives of Audrey frequently become collective biographies inclusive of her sisters and nieces.[65]

Audrée's own house of Ely had been, in common with the houses of some other pre-Conquest abbesses, refounded in Æthelwold's tenth-century Benedictine reform as a house for monks only. Refoundation of male houses for women is a rarer phenomenon, but one of the few such refoundations is of a house dedicated to St Etheldreda. Although there is no direct documentary link, Audrée's Life could conceivably have played some role in inspiring such

[64] *Liber Eliensis*, ed. Blake, i. 13, 18; *Audrée*, ed. Södergård, vv. 141–228, 613–24. For Hereswitha's daughters see Figure 2.1 above. Bede says that Hereswitha became a nun at Chelles and that it was her example that inspired Hild as abbess (*Historia Ecclesiastica*, ed. Colgrave and Mynors, iv, ch. 23, p. 406). For brief modern accounts and bibliography of the daughters, see the entries under their names in Farmer, *Oxford Dictionary of Saints*.

[65] The Romsey manuscript discussed above includes a version of this holy kinship: as does the later Middle English Life associated with Wilton (n. 58 above). Bradshaw's *St Werburga* (printed 1521) includes a life of Etheldreda as ch. xviii (*St Werburge*, ed. Carl Horstmann, EETS ES 88 (London, 1887)).

patronage when, in 1284, Maud de Clare, Countess of Gloucester, ejected the Augustine canons from the priory of Canonsleigh in Devon and replaced them with canonesses.[66] Maud had founded, together with her husband Richard, the priory of Clare in Suffolk in 1248; her vigorous and wealthy widowhood extended over twenty-five years, during which time, till her death in 1289, she held one-third of the extensive de Clare estates in dower, and spent time in Cambridgeshire.[67] Previously dedicated to the Virgin and St John the Evangelist, Canonsleigh seems to have addded Etheldreda to its patron saints after Maud's refoundation, the only monastic house to have such a dedication apart from Etheldreda's own abbey of Ely.[68] Maud also gave her new house a fine specimen of the 'informal' rules mentioned above in the form of a manuscript of *Ancrene Wisse* (to which minor French texts and a Latin hymn to Etheldreda were added).[69] In establishing her foundation, Maud was opposed by Archbishop Pecham, who objected to the replacement of the canons, true religious, by '*mulierculae*' ('little women'), but the Countess of Gloucester seems to have drawn very successfully on the help of other powerful widows to defeat him.[70] Ela, Countess of Salisbury and now abbess of her own foundation of Lacock,

[66] On Canonsleigh see George Oliver, *Monasticon Diocesis Exoniensis* (Exeter: Hannaford, 1846), 244. In 1247 the Countess of Seez in Normandy was able, with papal permission, to eject monks from the Cistercian house of Perray near Angers and refound it as Perray-aux-Nonnains (Berman, 'Fashions in Monastic Patronage', 42).

[67] Maud's father, the Earl of Lincoln, offered Henry III 5,000 marks for permission to marry her to the 16-year-old Richard de Clare, heir of the enormous Gloucester estates. They were married in 1238 and Richard died in 1262 (Altschul, *A Baronial Family*, 34, and on Maud's dower, 36). Before turning Canonsleigh into Mynchenlegh ('Nunsleigh'), Maud had spent time (after the battle of Evesham in 1265) in Cambridgeshire with her pluralist son Bogo de Clare annexing further monastic houses from the rebels. One pre-1265 abbess of Chatteris is named as Marie de St Clare in the nunnery's cartulary (though there is nothing to show that she wrote the *Vie sainte Audreé*): see *Mon.* ii. 615; *Cartulary of Chatteris*, ed. Breay, 394–5. Maud had earlier tried to have 40 enclosed nuns under the rule of Augustine and 10 Fontevrault priests take over a priory at Sandleford, but despite a generous endowment and a papal mandate of 1274 directing the fulfilment of her intentions, the Sandleford project did not come to fruition. Eventually, again providing for 40 canonesses, Maud was successful (Charles Spencer Perceval, 'Remarks on Some Early Charters and Documents Relating to the Priory of Austin Canons and Abbey of Austin Canonesses at Canonsleigh in the County of Devon', *Archaeologia*, 40 (1866), 417–50 (417)). The name of Mynchenlegh occurs in later medieval documents, but reverts to Canonsleigh in Knowles and Hadcock. A Clare from an earlier generation was Abbot of Ely (Richard fitz Richard de Clare, d. 1107): see Blake, *Liber Eliensis*, 225–34, 413–14; Jennifer Ward, 'Royal Service and Reward: The Clare Family and the Crown 1066–1154', *ANS* 11 (1989), 261–78 (268–9).

[68] The first written evidence of the new dedication is from 1308: see Perceval, 'Remarks on Some Early Charters', 426.

[69] See *The English Text of the Ancrene Riwle, Cotton Cleopatra C.vi*, ed. E. J. Dobson, EETS os 267 (London, 1972), pp. xx–xxv. Although the canonesses' rule was in Early Middle English, the injunctions of Bishop Stapledon to the house in 1319–20 were issued in French (*Calendar of the Cartulary of Canonsleigh*, ed. V. M. London, *Devon and Cornwall Record Society*, 10 (1965), p. xvii), suggesting (as do the French additions to the Cotton Cleopatra manuscript itself) that the house remained at least partly francophone.

[70] Pecham, *Registrum*, ed. Martin, iii. 939, quoted in *Calendar of the Cartulary of Canonsleigh*, ed. London, pp. xi–xiii.

sent three nuns from Lacock to help initiate Maud's canonesses.[71] The wealthiest widow of all, Isabella de Fortibus, Countess of Aumale and Devon and niece to Maud de Clare by marriage, was involved in rehousing the canons and in some crucial donations to the canonesses of property of which she was overlord.[72] Pecham lost, and Maud established the house in time to garner spiritual benefits for her soul (she died four years later in 1288).

Audrée thus shows a woman writer and female audiences reacting to a rolemodel who had been a paradigmatic saint for male tenth-century Benedictine reform and for twelfth-century male monasticism. Their response is to make Audrée resemble themselves and the conditions of their own lives and aspirations. Both Campsey (where this Life was kept and read) and Canonsleigh (where the Countess of Gloucester commemorated Etheldreda) were houses of Augustinian canonesses, founded or refounded in the thirteenth century. *Audrée's* stress on intermediate forms of life within a female community, on the combination of Mary and Martha, on the addition of female reclusion to Benedictine sanctity, on the modulation of virgin martyr suit and pursuit to vidual asceticism, and its emphasis on dower all fit with the thirteenth century: the *Liber Eliensis's* monastic Benedictine saint has become a life that describes and is part of the vigorous demand for female community on the part of women, especially widows and retired women in thirteenth-century England.

6.3. ABBESS MIRACLES AND THEIR CLIENTS

The life of the abbess is only the first part of her career: her post-mortem gifts, patronage, and power are if anything still more impressive and largely expressed in visionary appearances and miracles. The significance of miracles is further suggested by the way they travel with lives, even out of the geographical range of their initial communities, for whom they might be supposed to serve as direct shrine and house publicity. Miracles, like hagiographic lives themselves, are not simply historiographic, but interpretative and heuristic: they are history, ritual, performance script, and literature all at once. In transmission, miracles tend to become more thematically homogenous and to cohere with the chief characteristics of the saint: their meaning is stylized as it is reworked, though none the less meaningful for that. When St Osith of Chich adds virgin martyr qualifications to her abbess role, her first posthumous miracle is to carry her

---

[71] A letter of 1284 from Alice, abbess of Lacock, consents to Dame Matilda Tablere, Juliana de Bristoll, and Clementia de Ovile going to Leigh and releases them from their oath of obedience to Lacock (Perceval, 'Remarks on Some Early Charters', 424–5). Matilda Tablere became first abbess of Leigh (Oliver, *Monasticon Diocesis Exoniensis*, 225).

[72] The East Anglian estates with which Maud endowed the new house were held of Isabella de Fortibus, who also arranged for Plympton (a large Augustinian priory in Devon) to take in the evicted canons (*Calendar of the Cartulary of Canonsleigh*, ed. London, p. xiii).

own head into church and present it to God on the high altar, after which she embarks on a career of more miracles and visionary appearances.[73] Her dual career is thus marked by an echo between motifs: the laying of Osith's head on the altar is a 'stronger' form of her earlier self-dedication at the altar (vv. 667–78). As Benedicta Ward argues in her fundamental study, 'people asked how miracles related man to God, not how they could be defined in their constituent parts . . . incredulity about a miracle was resolved not by a reference to facts or evidence but by a closer examination of the tale's significance'.[74] The semiotics of miracles respond well to literary interpretation, the more so as these narratives articulate a number of important relations and desires: between patron and client, between numinous and human, between, in an ecclesiastically structured polity, power and its clients. In so far as abbess saints are figures of the holy or figures of a group identity, their actions do not necessarily represent powers directly exercised by or ordinarily attributable to women, but, like any other genre of narrative, they can none the less express the preoccupations and hopes of their composers and audiences.

All three abbess lives in the Campsey manuscript—Audrée, Osith, Modwenna —vary in their selection of miracles from their Latin sources. A full study of these miracles in terms of their textual history and place in the cults of these saints would take a book in itself, the more so as all the lives copied into the manuscript in the late thirteenth century include post-mortem miracles apart from the Life of St Catherine. Nevertheless it is worth noting, if only selectively, certain trends that emerge in the Campsey manuscript's selection and presentation of abbess miracles. All three saints are intensely concerned with the protection and rights of their cults and communities and all also show an interest in the social control exercised by and upon women. Modwenna, the figure among the three most fully constituted by what Felice Lifshitz has called 'Amstcharisma', the power of office, has more miracles of provision and convenience in comparison with the other abbesses.[75] In the posthumous miraculous provision for visitation and for church building with which—like the abbesses of Barking in the *vitae* commissioned from Goscelin of St Bertin—Modwenna aids her successor Derlarra, two major concerns of monastic administration are represented. Transmitted gifts of strategies and conventions empower the monastic successor in learning how to manage institutional inspection and expansion.

Provision miracles of course are accounts of mythic powers. But, read aloud at mealtimes in Campsey, Modwenna's provision miracles will have presented a figure of ideal and inimitable power in the saint, *and* the emplotment of recurrent concerns in the management of nunneries. Provision miracles in

---

[73] 'Anglo-French Life of St Osith', ed. Baker, vv. 825–8.

[74] *Miracles and the Medieval Mind*, 42.

[75] Lifshitz, 'Is Mother Superior?' For the argument that Modwenna's numerous flotation miracles can be understood not only as Celtic archaeological deposits in the textual tradition of her legend but as aspects of 12th- and 13th-c. sanctity, see Price, '*La Vie de sainte Modwenne*', 181.

Modwenna's life partly speak to the necessities of monastic diet: Modwenna's houses must practise heroic austerity in a diet on which prelates cannot ordinarily be fed, and yet find appropriate banquets for visitors as necessary. The visit of a bishop to a nunnery was of no small moment, especially after the council of Oxford in 1222 (when episcopal control over nunneries was extended to include the appointment of the nuns' confessors, the control of nunnery numbers, corrodies, and the admission of secular women) and after 1232, when these responsibilities became a matter of papal interest following Pope Gregory IX's orders to English bishops to carry out formal visits in person or by deputy to all non-exempt houses in their diocese.[76] These usually had a month's notice, but, as with kings, bishops and abbots might also at any time, and perhaps with very little notice at all, descend upon a nunnery. Gifts of wine and venison, as also of building timber, sometimes came from kings to nunneries, and royal goodwill, especially given church–state relations in England for much of the later twelfth and thirteenth centuries, was crucial, just as was that of the diocesan bishop. Hospitality was a matter of honour, necessity, policy, and sometimes anxiety and economic difficulty.[77] Modwenna is several times shown finding emergency provision for visiting bishops and kings (and also providing extra resources for an impoverished lord who must entertain his king: richer abbeys, rather than secular households, might indeed take the burden of hospitality to the king in a particular region).

Questions of provision and diet also encode the socio-economic relations between monasteries and the wider community: when Modwenna establishes a new foundation at Killeevey, the local swineherd perceives her nuns as competition for the herbs and acorns in the woods where he tends his pigs. He is of course converted and persuaded to accept the monastery's presence in the local economy. The reassurance of the swineherd is managed through Modwenna's miraculous restoration of his lost herd, her resurrection and return of his gift of a slaughtered pig, and her eventual acceptance of a crudely slaughtered stag as the swineherd's gift to her community. If the sisters are no threat because they do not consume flesh, or at least require only the aristocratic flesh of stags, the swineherd's original perception of them as a threat to the more basic products of the forest remains less fully incorporated into the monastery's interests than the narrative represents the swineherd himself as being. The possibility that the monastery's relation to local peasant communities is a predatory one is quickly turned into tribute to the virtuous exiguousness of the sisters' diet. This incident may also speak to other concerns—the economic hardship which visited poorly endowed or managed nunneries, for instance, could be seen in the nuns' diet— but it seems primarily concerned with a courtly and aristocratic community's

<hr />

[76] Coldicott, *Hampshire Nunneries*, 52.

[77] For Henry III's gifts of venison and wine on the installation of Hampshire abbesses and particular nuns see ibid. 77, 80: Eleanor de Montfort gave wine to Wintney after entertaining the prioress at Odiham Castle: Henry III kept a cellar at Wherwell, 80.

conversion of a local economy to its own priorities and the role of monastic ideology in securing co-operation.

As a construction of female holy life, indeed, *La vie de seinte Modwenne* is in large part—and unsurprisingly so for women of seigneurial rank—a lesson in class prerogatives. If this text teaches charity and consideration of the poor as a duty of the aristocratic monastery, it is also instructive on the social structures that reproduce poverty and riches. Relations with secular and ecclesiastical power are repeatedly represented at all levels and Modwenna's house is often shown defending itself against members of its own class, but the depredations of lords arouse less horror than the possibility of peasant revolt. So, for example, in a dispute with Roger of Poitiers, Count of Montgomery, over abbey grain supplies, where the monastery has gone so far as to fight and win a battle against sixty of Roger's armed vassals, the greatest ferocity is reserved for two abbey 'villeins' who have absconded to the Count. They die suddenly after the battle, but are subsequently seen carrying their coffins around Count Roger's lands and shape-changing into bears, monkeys, leopards, lions, dragons, while a plague strikes until Roger pays compensation to the abbey. Finally, the villeins' corpses are disinterred (with the bishop's permission, vv. 8465–6), and their hearts cut out and burnt all day until at dusk a black crow is observed to fly from the ashes (vv. 8485–6).

Analogously, Count Roger's forester at Tutbury, Osmund, is represented as keeping a mastiff of Baskervillean dimensions and propensities: by day it feigns humility and love, but at night, off the leash, it has no love for any man, and does not cease howling and barking if it cannot injure men with its teeth (vv. 8525–36). Just so, the narrative explicates, the serf is humble when poor, faithless when empowered: 'maistrie' (v. 8540) causes him to sunder loyal and amicable human relations and to go brutishly and uncontrollably seeking to do damage and evil everywhere (vv. 8541–58). Modwenna makes a personal appearance to Osmund to threaten vengeance for his depredations upon abbey servants and the abbey forest, but Osmund is nevertheless unable to resist carrying off the abbey's pigs, and his eyes fall out within the month (vv. 8647–8). This incident is the culminating representation of the wonders with which God honours Modwenna (v. 8656): it is the end of the poem in the Bodleian manuscript (Digby 34) and the final narrated marvel of the slightly longer text in the Campsey manuscript. In earlier miracles during her lifetime, Modwenna converts the wolfish nature of robbers, turns predatory wolves into cattle dogs, and thieves and marauders into penitents: the servant of the local magnate seems to represent an unconvertible problem, and remains as an assertively monitory summing up of many of the themes deployed in the earlier miracles.[78]

The class-horror expressed in the rebellious villeins' ghoulish animal shape-shifting and the forester's mastiff is as vivid and as intimate to aristocratic

[78] On animal miracles see further Price, '*La Vie de sainte Modwenne*', 183–4.

self-representation here as the *Roman de la rose*'s presentation of Daunger in the Lady as a *vilein* with a club.[79] A comparable near-contemporary insular case is that of Ogger, smith and dissident Gilbertine lay brother, who, in the *vita* of St Gilbert, becomes a focus for the leadership's anxieties over the rebellion of the lay brothers (leading to Henry II's threat to the Pope to withdraw all his own grants to the new order for women).[80] In Modwenna's Life, these rebellious incidents are represented in her posthumous career, when the monastery has become a male house: nevertheless, the tutelary construction of class vengeance and fear here expressed in a female figure can no more be excluded from the reading of the women of Campsey than the gendering of other aspects of sanctity and community expressed in the miracles copied in the manuscript.

Like Modwenna, the Lives of the other two abbesses, Audrée and Osith, assert their saint's ability to defend her house from trespass, plunder, attack, and subversion through miracles of protection and vengeance. The concerns of class and *courtoisie* are encoded in a slightly different, and apparently more beneficent register in *Audrée*. The well-known miracle of the monk who attempted transgressively to inspect Audrée's intact body has been alluded to already (Chapter 2.1): it is a thematically key miracle in the *Liber Eliensis*'s assertions of Etheldreda's continuing presence as an inviolable body of integrity and proprietorship for the monks at Ely. The vernacular Life retains this stress in its handling of Audrée's posthumous career, but remains equally interested in Audrée's queenship. One of Audrée's most widely retold miracles shows a queen quite literally intervening: it bulks largely in the vernacular Life.[81] The miracle concerns the freeing of a prisoner, Bricstan of Chatteris, in the sixteenth year of Henry I's reign (1115–16), in which Queen Matilda took a particular interest. The queen sends her chaplain to investigate (vv. 3222–3), commands bell-ringing and a procession to Westminster in celebration of the miracle, and sends Bricstan to Ely. Later the queen herself takes his fetters to Ely for preservation in the minster and gives thanks to St Audrée for the *pitie* (v. 3237) she had shown, a virtue of courtly and intercessory importance especially relevant for queens.[82] The story as told in the vernacular Life underlines the courtly metaphorics of

[79] As Felicity Riddy has argued, the representation of 'the mercilessness of the beloved woman as a peasant's revolt—attack by a dangerously aggressive "cherl" armed with a club' reveals the predication of pity on hierarchy: see Riddy, 'Engendering Pity', in Evans and Johnson (eds.), *Feminist Readings in Middle English Literature*, 54–71 (59).

[80] *Book of St Gilbert*, ed. and tr. Foreville and Keir, 78–84: see also the appendix by Cecily Clark on the ethnic origin of the name Oggerus, 338–40.

[81] *Audrée*, ed. Södergård, vv. 3166–237; for Orderic's version see *Ecclesiastical History of Orderic Vitalis*, ed. Chibnall, iii, bk. vi. 346–58 (where the miracle is principally credited to St Benedict); *Liber Eliensis*, ed. Blake, bk. iii, ch. 33. 266–9; also told by Gregory of Ely: see Pauline Thompson and Elizabeth Stevens, 'Gregory of Ely's Verse Life and Miracles of St Æthelthryth', *AB* 106 (1988), 373/34–5.

[82] Lois L. Huneycutt, 'Intercession and the High Medieval Queen: The Esther Topos', in Carpenter and MacLean (eds.), *Power of the Weak*, 126–46, and John Carmi Parsons, 'The Queen's Intercession', ibid. 147–77.

imprisonment and grace through women, and the perceived intercessory power of queenship, whether queen of earth ('good queen Maud' who dissented from Henry I's plans for church control) or heaven (Audrée herself, and the Virgin Mary, much illustrated as crowned in heaven from the late twelfth century).[83] An apparently insignificant miracle throws further light on this theme: a man is wounded by a hedge thorn which enters under his skin as he works on Audrée's feast day and makes him diseased and feverish. For all his attentiveness, suffering, and pleas for mercy thereafter (vv. 3772–5), Audrée refuses her mercy for a year, but finally withdraws the thorn and the venom from his wound and makes him whole (vv. 3790–95). This demonstration of Audrée's powers of control and cure reveals by withholding the power of her intercession, and does so in terms that overlap with the *cortois* rhetoric of mercy, as in the man's plea:

> 'Dame de grant pité
> Par un seul jur si te ay peché
> Ne deussez si prendre a ire.
> Mut en ay suffert grant martire.
> Dame, pur Deu regardez moy.
> Je te promet en bone foy
> Ke tut jurs mes te serveray
> Et vostre feste garderay.
> A tuz ceus le fray feirer
> Ke m'amerunt et averunt cher.'
>   (vv. 3780–9)

'Lady of great mercy, if I have sinned against you for a single day you should not be so angry. I have suffered great torment from it. Lady, for God's sake, look [mercifully] on me. I promise you in good faith that I will serve you always from now on and will keep your feast, and I will make all those who love me and hold me dear celebrate it.'

Courtliness and female power here extend beyond personal relations to the social and political powers of seigneurial women in a way that, again, cannot have been lost on an audience such as Campsey.

Not only female figures of sanctity but their female clients are represented in the miracles of these hagiographic lives, although whether it is a matter of publicity for the local miracles of a particular shrine or devotional literary biography of international saints, women will be under-represented in miracle tales and collections. 'Kings have sought him on pilgrimage', says Guernes de Pont-Ste-Maxence in his Life of Becket, 'princes, barons, dukes with their nobles, people from foreign lands, speaking many different tongues, prelates, monks, recluses, people on foot' (vv. 5891–4): everyone, in short, except women. Prohibition and restrictions with regard to sacred spaces; greater difficulties

---

[83] For Matilda's intervention in the investiture controversy see her correspondence with Anselm and Pope Paschal (Walter Fröhlich, tr. and annot., *The Letters of St Anselm of Canterbury*, iii, Cistercian Studies Series 142 (Kalamazoo, Mich.: Cistercian Publications, 1994), e.g. Letters 317, 320, 323, 346–7). Matilda was given the custody of Barking Abbey by Henry I till her death in 1118.

of travel for women; expectations that women should suffer patiently and silently—such factors might well affect women's ability to get to shrines, while access only to outer or subordinate reaches of sacred space might also affect the extent to which women's cures were seen as prestigious and record-worthy. Statistical surveys confirm a general picture of female under-representation (Finucane's study gives 61 per cent men, 39 per cent women at both French and English shrines, for instance) and this can hold even in contexts where one might expect more women.[84] In *Audrée*, a life made by a woman for other women, England's most famous abbess saint performs thirty-five miracles for men, two for particular places, one for a child, and seven for women (these seven are concerned with social control as well as with help and cure). Among Osith's cures in all her Latin and vernacular lives, three women are cured (of infertility, deformity, and paralysis); four men, all clerics, are cured, three of them of paralysis (of whom two have originally had the disease given them by Osith in punishment, as has one of the women).[85]

Restriction, however, can of itself create demand and provoke alternative recourse, and smaller shrines specializing in catering for women develop, precisely because of the unsatisfactoriness of the larger centres. As Jane Tibbetts Schulenberg has shown, in tandem with St Cuthbert's abhorrence of women at Durham, the neighbouring shrine of St Godric began to specialize in female cures: Cuthbert's abhorrence had to be modified to the extent of allowing women access and cures in an area outside the West doors so that Durham could maintain its pilgrimage market-share.[86] Gender-based restrictions can be very quickly overtaken by economic considerations. Class and enterprise can also intersect with gender-based restriction, as with the enforced modifications to the Cistercian ban on women at Edmund of Canterbury's shrine at Pontigny (Chapter 5.1, esp. n. 40 above). Although the women represented in such incidents tend to be upper-class, the Anglo-Norman Life of St Osith includes 400 lines, not in the Latin *vita*, narrating the miraculous cure at Osith's principal shrine at Chich of a paralysed Welsh woman from Hereford (vv. 1065–1416). This is one of three principal miracles narrated in the vernacular Life out of the more numerous incidents available in the varying Latin traditions: they emphasize important and related aspects of Osith's cult. After an unsuccessful visit to Bury, where she is refused permission to pray and watch at King Edmund's shrine by the sacristan, the woman is instructed in a visionary

[84] Ronald C. Finucane, *Miracles and Pilgrims: Popular Beliefs in Medieval England* (London: Dent, 1977), 143.

[85] As analysed by Bethell, 'Lives of St Osyth' (some of the miracles have variants in different lives), 89–96.

[86] See Schulenberg, *Forgetful of Their Sex*, 346–8, also her forthcoming study on gender and sacred space; on healing miracles as a 'ritual of affliction', see Catherine Bell, *Ritual*, 115–20. The case of Alice de Vere suggests women corrodians, at least of high rank, were permitted at Chich (see Barrow, 'A Twelfth-Century Bishop and Literary Patron', 177–8).

appearance by the saint himself to go to Chich. She arrives, helped by her sister, on the eve of Osith's fair, when the canons of Chich are at vespers. At St Osith's, with the sister on the point of desperation and rebellion, access to the shrine is granted. In the morning the canons' matins at the point of the sixth response, 'regnum mundi', are disturbed by the cries of the woman as she leaps up, cured, and moves towards the altar.[87] She tells the canons about her journeys and her special direction to Chich and they now begin, as is conventional in the event of a miraculous cure, the Te Deum. The story has clearly been well told ('tut par ordre lur ad cunté', v. 1265) and the woman now obtains permission to stay on at the site of her cure and dedicate herself to God and St Osith. She works hard, doing as much as she can around the minster, even bringing stone ('trere piere', v. 1300), for a long period.

But the envious devil now decides to divert the strength which has come from God into worthless matters ('en fanfelue', v. 1318), and because woman is such a frail thing by nature, always listens to bad counsel, and leaves the true way for folly and the good for the evil, the young scullion Godwine is able to seduce the cured woman (vv. 1329–38). No sooner are they in bed than St Osith jams the woman's legs immovably one over the other in the form of a cross (i.e. the three-, rather than four-nail crucifix, not much represented in insular sources before the *Guide for Anchoresses*), as strongly 'as if they were fastened with a nail' (v. 1352).[88] The scullion tells all in the morning, and his superiors run to the minster and pray St Osith not to shame and enthrall her handmaid. But the woman remains paralysed until, eventually, the scullion dies. She is cured on the night following the scullion's death, and remains for the rest of her life at Chich serving with great devotion.

In spite of the misogyny topics which, with lavish rhetoric, assimilate the cured woman to Eve at the moment of her fall, this story is most notable for the identity of interest between the woman and the canons.[89] The diversion from the Benedictines and St Edmund at Bury to Chich and the canons for cures suggests an attempt to foster Osith's cult (perhaps, since the woman is denied access at Bury and allowed into the church in Chich, in something like the Cuthbert versus Godric situation, in this case St Osith's against the prestigious neighbouring Benedictine house of Bury and its martyr saint Edmund). The woman's cure is shown in the narrative as integrated with the canons' performance of their offices, and she is called Osith's 'ancele' ('handmaiden', v. 1389) in the canons' prayers for her legs to be unlocked. The seduction story protects their saint from perceived failure in what must have been a prize cure and continuingly present testimony to her powers, and it also protects the woman's

---

[87] For this responsory, see Bethell, 'Lives of St Osyth', 95 n. 2.

[88] Shepherd (ed.), *Ancrene Wisse*, 57 n. 13.

[89] As always in miracle cures, the saint has something to lose as well, as a female client of Audrée's is quick to point out: if her husband is allowed to die, the woman says, no one will visit Audrée's tomb (*Audrée*, ed. Södergård, vv. 3606–11).

status as an accepted shrine pensioner. If Godwine the scullion did not exist, he would probably have had to be invented once the remission of the woman's paralysis ceased.

The canons and their new shrine-attendant solve their problem in a manner thematically consistent with the saint, in a sort of applied reading of her miracles. In all her lives, Osith uses paralysis for vengeance and protection. Bishop Richard de Belmeis of London is paralysed when he tries to oust the canons from Chich (vv. 1521–4), a paralysis only partially alleviated when he sends his ring to be offered on her altar and the property is restored (vv. 1515–16, 1643–7). Some sailors have their ship immobilized when they come to Colne mouth for a favourable wind: only when a piece of marble removed by one of them from Osith's church is restored does the saint confer mobility on their ship (vv. 857–1064). In the earlier of the two lost twelfth-century *vitae*, there is a story, preserved in Tynemouth's version, of a woman with a withered arm, who makes a vow of chastity when cured by Osith, but subsequently marries, and has her legs locked.[90] She is cured again when she repents and leads a better life (presumably to be defined as a voluntary locking of her legs when approached by her husband for anything other than purposes of procreation). These miracles continue to express the powers of a married virgin saint and abbess whose own most spectacular demonstration of mobility consisted of carrying her head into the minster and laying it on the altar after invading Danes cut it off.[91]

Thus an apparently misogynistic account of social control over female sexuality and enterprise can be seen to be telling a different story about the relations between a cult and female devotees. The determination and courage with which women must often have had to embark on seeking cures is also movingly voiced in the mounting desperation of the paralysed woman and her sister, and in the difficulty of their journeys: it takes them twenty days to cover the fifty miles from Bury to Chich (v. 1192) in the 'petites jurnees' to which they are so 'bien acustumees' (vv. 1101–2). This story, preserved only in the vernacular Life, may owe its prominence there to the expectations of a female audience, and provides indirect testimony to the importance, for all their relative under-representation, of female clients.

As well as being notable for sharing a motif with Marie de France's *Eliduc*, one of Audrée's miracles includes an account of a daughter's difficulties in accepting her mother's remarriage. The authoritative figure of St Audrey seems to have mediated the physiological and psychological difficulties felt between the mother and daughter as part of the latter's growing up and acceptance of the

---

[90] Bethell, 'Lives of St Osyth', 96(c).

[91] The play on the boundaries between paralysis and mobility perhaps also owes something to the problematic location of Osith's chief cult centre as between Aylesbury and Chich: several medieval Latin lives circulated making different claims (see Bethell, 'Lives of St Osyth'; Hohler, 'St Osyth and Aylesbury'). The Hereford miracle story discussed above draws on the lost Life by William de Vere, bishop of Hereford.

second marriage: a set of tensions and contradictions that could perhaps only be resolved by a saint who herself is twice married but the proponent of female chastity. The narrative is not always clear, and in addition to extensive abbreviation of the extant Latin account, something may have been lost in transmission. Nevertheless, the vernacular reworking throws the relationship of the mother and daughter into new prominence. After a Cirencester widow has married and moved into Ranulf of Wallingford's house with her daughter, the daughter, 'a noble and well-dressed young woman, but one who contradicted and opposed and insulted her mother' (vv. 3479–81), has a series of dreams in which a visionary woman strikes her, making her nose bleed and damaging her eyes, one nearly being put out and the other's vision impaired, then in three subsequent appearances instructs her to 'carry [her] candle' (v. 3505) to Ely for healing. The girl answers that her mother will not allow her to go (though the distressed mother has in fact been praying to St Audrey for pity on her daughter's condition); the mother interprets her daughter's visions as 'fantasme' (v. 3516) and the girl loses her power of speech. In two further dreams, the visionary woman cures the girl's dumbness by placing a flower in her mouth, and when she continues to be forgetful and does not act on the command to go to Ely, strikes her with a club, making her forehead bleed.[92] The next night Audrée appears, wipes away the blood, and says that, in response to the mother's entreaties, the daughter will be healed at Ely. Mother and daughter make the pilgrimage together, carrying their candles, and both the daughter's 'squinting eye and the better eye were healed and she never had pain from them again' (vv. 3558–9).

The custom of carrying and offering one's candle to a saint's shrine is documented for other shrines, but seems particularly apt to this tale of a troubled adolescence, since the candles were often made to the measure of the suppliant's height.[93] So too does the physical misery of the young woman, the need for many reminders of what she must do, the nosebleeds, the temporary disfigurement and loss of speech followed by submission to an authoritative older woman's instruction—a kind of puberty ritual. Although the mother's second marriage is mentioned in the much longer Latin narrative, it is not so much as a feature of the mother–daughter relationship as a way of identifying the status of the cured girl.[94] The concern with the troubled and rebellious young woman and the saint's mediation in her relation to her mother is particular to the vernacular Life. Adolescent rebelliousness and mother–daughter relations are

[92] The flower motif, common (as Ann Hutchison has pointed out to me) to Audrée and to Marie de France's *Eliduc*, is also found in one of St Gilbert's miracles concerning a young woman, Felicia of Answick, who vows to take the Gilbertine habit if cured of her lameness, and dreams that the flower ('flos rubicundus') falls on her lap from the mouth of a statue of the Virgin Mary (*Book of St Gilbert*, ed. and tr. Foreville and Keir, 270–2).

[93] Finucane, *Miracles and Pilgrims*, 95–6.

[94] The miracle is present in the *Liber Eliensis* (ed. Blake, bk. ii, ch. 60. 307–12), but not in Gregory of Ely or any of the later English vernacular lives.

prominent in thirteenth-century Liège lives of holy women, but again, certainly in the context of a woman's life of a female saint for a female community, this theme also has its insular airing.[95]

For all their stereotypical elements and for all their use, in earlier versions, by male houses, these abbess lives illustrate the power to found, the power to propagate spiritual genealogies and some institutional continuities, the power of vision, the power to keep records, the power to punish, to give counsel and alms, to preach, to intercede, to judge and lead. In their gathering together in the Campsey manuscript they represent in themselves an appropriation and realignment by women of lives conceived as orthodox exemplars of male Benedictine and Augustinian monasticism. Here these rewritten monastic founding virgins stretch the rich and flexible capacities of virginity to the limit, inflecting the ideal with manifold powers, for, at least, women with or aspiring to the class prerogatives also strongly represented in the lives. For audiences connected with or aware of the ecclesiastical and seigneurial families whose foundations shaped the landscape of East Anglia and Essex, the abbess lives and the manuscript as a whole contain a great deal of information about the powers of that world and the powerful roles women could play within and beyond their communities.

---

[95] See Alexandra Barratt, 'Undutiful Daughters and Metaphorical Mothers among the Beguines', in Dor *et al.*, *New Trends in Feminine Sprituality*, 81–104.

7

The Virgin Speaks

This final chapter considers theological issues in hagiography and argues for women's composition in the genre as a mode of theological practice. In twelfth- and early thirteenth-century England, women's interests in the redemption were not exclusively a matter of affective concerns with the body of Christ. The chapter studies the response of Clemence of Barking to Anselmian soteriology in her Life of St Catherine and her use of a pagan role model, the Sibyl, as a legitimating didactic and prophetic female voice. Once a perspective is established for taking Anglo-Norman women's participation in such matters seriously, the chapter sketches some further areas of enquiry into vision and debate where the apparent dearth of evidence from insular culture can be reconsidered. Finally, the Barking Life of St Edward is briefly considered as an example of an intellectual and self-conscious version of these concerns on the part of a woman writer concerned to articulate a particular vision of insular history and a role for the virtues of virginity in it.

7.1. SAINTS' LIVES AND THE PREACHING AND TEACHING OF WOMEN

In many representations of ideal female conduct, women's public speech was restricted in England in the twelfth and thirteenth centuries as in the later Middle Ages. Official, 'authorized' forms of speech, especially preaching and teaching, were particularly interdicted.[1] Yet, as has been noted for other medieval times and places, how restrictive this is depends in part on one's definition of teaching and preaching. Women teach, but the lessons they give are seen as informal anchoritic 'counsel'; women intervene to modify behaviour or policy, but instead of the institutionally authorized and public form of preaching use the charismatic authority of vision and prophecy. Women's public speech is represented in a number of ways during the period, perhaps nowhere more luxuriantly than in saints' lives. We should be cautious about assuming that the representation of speech by women is a representation of women's freedom to speak, and saints are exceptional as well as exemplary for their audiences. Nevertheless, the plenitude and range of female speech in twelfth- and thirteenth-century hagiography, and the thematizing of women's preaching and debating in contemporary

---

[1] See Blamires, 'Women and Preaching'.

lives, hardly suggest that women's speech was securely relegated to the exceptional. The many Catherines and Magdalens of this period function as a locus for the politics of vernacular and lay, not only women's, speech.[2] But in thematizing issues of church and clerical power these figures still represent copious and efficacious speech by women.

The speech of abbess saints, though supposedly confined within their ecclesiastical households, is by definition authoritative and also often didactic, expository, or preaching, as exemplified in Chapter 6 above. An abbess saint such as Modwenna gives homilies to nuns, lay patrons, and to male clerical colleagues. Such representations certainly provide models of women speaking authoritatively to women and men even if this is coded as informal in comparison with male monastic and ecclesiastical speech. Some of the very strategies for providing women with stereotypical roles also encourage a mobility of response, a kind of provisional trying-out of the rhetorical positions from which one could answer as, for instance, 'dame, amie, fille, sorur' in the Anglo-Norman 'Quatre titres' treatise for women religious.[3] Even within its deliberately narrowed compass, the specialized anchoritic legendary of the Katherine Group, for example, offers exceptional aural lushness in the heightened and supple rhythmical alliterative prose of its three lives. These saints share many of the characteristic speech types of hagiography (stinging rebukes to irrationally furious suitors, fathers, and governors, where litotes and syntactic control are mimetic of the saint's superior logic; commanding and monitory speeches to mourning crowds; interrogation and denunciation of demons and pagan tyrants; lyrical declarations of love for God and, in the declamatory and didactic articulations of their own positions, prayer-like praise, visionary intensities of perception, and ranging accounts of human redemptive history and the created universe). Between the three virgins of this group, speech also differs perceptibly, with different registers and figures being used for the distinct thematic emphases of each life: from the gorgeous psalmody with which Margaret hymns her creator God to the plangent lyricism over earthly transience which makes Juliana's account of a typologically informed human history so luminous, to the rhetorical magnificences of denunciation and asseveration of Katherine's attack on classical learning.[4] As Savage and Watson have noted in their translation of this latter, the early Middle English *Katerine* is 'much ruder'—magnificently so—than the Latin *vita's* saint:

---

[2] Susan Crane has argued, for example, that the association of Anglo-Norman with the feminine authorizes it as a mother-tongue ('Social Aspects of Bilingualism in the Thirteenth Century', in Prestwich, Britnell, and Frame (eds.), *Thirteenth Century England VI*, 103–16.

[3] See Ch. 1, p. 31 and, on the role of fantasy in reading, Ch. 1, n. 75, above.

[4] A full account of Katherine Group speech has yet to be written: for some preliminary characterizations of the individually distinct rhetorics and thematics of the three Lives see Jocelyn Price, 'The Liflade of Seinte Iuliene', *Medievalia et Humanistica*, 14 (1986) 37–58, and ead., 'The Demonology of Seinte Margaret', *Leeds Studies in English*, 16 (1985), 337–57.

'Lo[w]! thullich is al that ye thenketh todei forto weorri me with: Homers motes ant Aristotles turnes, Esculapies creftes and Galienes grapes, Filistiones flites and Platunes bokes, and al thes writers writes thet ye wreotheth ow on. Thah [ich beo] in alle of se earliche ilearet thet ich ne font nawt feole neauer min euening, thah, for thi thet ha beoth ful of idel yelp ant empti of thet eadi ant liffule lare, al ich forsake her ant cwethe [ham] al s[k]er up . . .' (p. 46/314–21)

'See, this is all you mean to combat me with today: Homer's discussions, Aristotle's tricks of argument, Aesculapius' lore and Galien's experiments, Philistion's chidings and Plato's books—and all these writers' writings you rely on. Though I became learned in all of them from so early an age that I have found very few my equal, nevertheless, because they are full of idle boasts and empty of the blessed, living teaching, I forsake them all and declare them all useless . . .'

Although opportunities for women's eloquence are less formally offered and less well-resourced, in institutional terms, than the school-exercises for boys and young men which Marjorie Curry Woods has shown to be so interesting as texts of male formation, the rhetorical positions available in saints' lives are unlikely to have been any less encouraging to verbal play and fantasy.[5] It is difficult to believe that the represented denunciation, defiance, prayer, and asseveration in saints' lives offered no models of pleasure and plenitude in speech to their female audiences. For those without access to Latin classes on Ovidian and other classical heroines, vernacular saints' lives constitute a repertoire of authorized speeches by women.

Dealing with a different but comparable intersection between Latin scholasticism and vernacular *rumanz* in her account of medieval models of female verbal response and the *Bestiaire d'amours*, Helen Solterer has argued that medieval prescriptiveness regarding women's responses and those responses as represented do not produce simple ventriloquism for patriarchal concerns, but a locus for examining and politicizing speech.[6] Something of this sort also happens when the virgin saint gazes back at and contests, rebukes, and confounds the pagan. As explored in Chapter 3.2 above, the virgin saint's divinely authorized no-saying is one of the more powerful models of women dealing with flattering or bullying speech. The virgin martyr is indeed a doubled version of Solterer's responding women, for she both debunks flattery and falseness in speech and speaks for and of God, simultaneously engaging in a form of vernacular *disputatio*. She is also often represented as deploying public and official forms of speech, herself appropriating the patriarchal rights of interrrogation practised on her in vain by the pagan tyrant: so, for instance, St Juliana's devil is forced to declare his strategies and is publicly humiliated (in Bozon's Life, the taunt applied alike to courtly seducers and the flatterer of moral treatises is flung at

---

[5] Woods, 'Rape and the Pedagogical Rhetoric of Violence'.
[6] Helen Solterer, *The Master and Minerva: Disputing Women in French Medieval Culture* (Berkeley, Los Angeles, and London: University of California Press, 1995).

him: he is revealed as a 'losengier', v. 796, before he ignominiously flees, v. 1182).[7] So, too, abbess and queen saints, whose rank or age still further authorizes them, are represented as using commanding speech.

St Helena, a widely diffused model of authorized female concern with relics and commemoration, is a powerful and resolute interrogator. In an Anglo-Norman prose Life in one nunnery manuscript, she is said so to have 'occupied herself with the Scriptures and the love of God' and to have 'enquired so much into Scripture that she knew about the passion and the resurrection and said that she would not have peace night or day until she had found the cross'.[8] In command of Jewish sources from her Bible reading, she is measured and firm in her eloquence:

'Jo ai conud par les liueres as prophetes que uus amastes deu. Mes uus estes afolez ker uus avez dit male de celui ki uus uuleit deliurer de mal.' (BL, MS Egerton 613, f. 25v)

'I have known by your prophetic books [the Old Testament] that you loved God, but you are irrational, for you have spoken evil of him who wished to deliver you from evil.'

With the determination of a pagan judge, procurator, or other tyrant, but with more success, she starves information out of the Jew Judas about the whereabouts of the true cross. Helena is a comprehensively empowered seigneurial speaker, authorized both by rank and her use of biblical authority. That she could serve as a precedent is evident in Turgot's Life of Margaret of Scotland (d. 1093): 'it seemed as if a second Helena were present there, for just as [Helena] at one time overcame the Jews by citing passages from the Scriptures, so now did this Queen overcome those who were in error'.[9] Debate and dialectic in defence of the faith were, as Alcuin Blamires notes, regarded as still more difficult for women than preaching.[10] The next section of this chapter explores in more detail Clemence of Barking's creation of authoritative and persuasive female voices in all these practices.

---

[7] *Seven More Lives*, ed. Klenke, 84–91.

[8] '. . . si se trauailler en escriptures e amour deu . . . se enquist tant par les escriptures que ele sout la passiun e la resurrecciun. e dist que pais nen auereit ne de nuiz ne de iurz desque la que truuee auereit la cruiz', BL, MS Egerton 613, f. 25v (a 13th-c. miscellany nunnery manuscript: see Hill, *Notes & Queries*, NS 223 (1978), 394–409 for a description). Helena's British cult dates from before the Conquest: for a full-length study see Antonina Harbus (University of Sydney, forthcoming); for Jocelyn of Furness's *Vita s. Helene regine*, see Grosjean, 'De codice hagiographico gothano', *AB* 58 (1940), 101; there is also a lost Life by Thomas of Hales. See further McNamara, 'Imitatio Helenae'; Emmanuele Baumgartner, 'Sainte(s) Hélènes', in *Femmes: mariages-lignages, xiie–xive siècles: mélanges offerts à Georges Duby* (Brussels: De Boeck-Wesmael, 1992), 43–53: Giles Constable, 'Troyes, Constantinople, and the Relics of St Helen in the Thirteenth Century', in *Mélanges René Crozet* (Poitiers, 1966), 1035–42, repr. in Constable, *Religious Life and Thought (11th–12th Centuries)* (London: Variorum, 1979), no. xiv.

[9] 'Crederes alteram ibi Helenam residere: quia sicut illa quondam Scripturarum sententiis Judaeos, similiter nunc et haec Regina convicerat erroneos', AA.SS. Iun. ii, 1867, 326F. On this life see further Huneycutt, 'Idea of the Perfect Princess'.

[10] 'Women and Preaching', 144.

7.2. SIBYLS AND SOTERIOLOGY:
THE VOICES OF CLEMENCE OF BARKING

Clemence of Barking's late twelfth-century life of St Catherine is an obvious place to find authoritative female speech (a woman composes a life of the virgin patroness of learning for her female community in which she shows a solitary female debater defeating fifty clerks). Both the saint's speech and the narration draw effortlessly and subtly, as several commentators have shown, on lyrical, courtly, didactic, and other registers.[11] Clemence transforms both vernacular and Latin source materials, and challenges or repositions the discourses of other audiences —clerical and seigneurial—beyond the Barking community. Here I will argue that Clemence's most profound achievement is her translation (in the full medieval sense of interpretative rather than simply interlingual transfer) of the thought of Anselm of Canterbury (d. 1109) on the redemption. The themes and arguments of her text depend on a worked-out substratum of Anselmian ideas developed independently of her main Latin source, the mid-eleventh-century 'Vulgate' *vita*. This substratum informs the whole of the *Vie sainte Catherine*, not just its unusually full and central debate, and is in many ways the key to Clemence's aesthetic as well as providing a theological grounding for her saint's powers of gift and martyrdom discussed in earlier chapters. As Anselm himself had said in the opening of the *Cur Deus*, the necessity for God to become man was something about which both lay and lettered longed to know:

By what logic or necessity did God become man, and by his death, as we believe and profess, restore life to the world, when he could have done this through the agency of some other person, angelic or human, or simply by willing it? About this issue not only people who are [Latin] literate, but many also who are unlettered [non solum litterati sed etiam illitterati], ask questions and long for a rational explanation.[12]

Anselm 'naturalizes dialectic' as an instrument for the discussion of central human doctrines, and, like Anselm, Clemence, willingly or not, stands 'aside from the intellectual fashions' of the schools, though evidently aware of them.[13]

---

[11] Duncan Robertson, 'Writing in the Textual Community'. See also Batt, 'Clemence of Barking's Transformations of *courtoisie*', 114; MacBain, 'Anglo-Norman Women Hagiographers', 244–5.

[12] Anselm, *Cur Deus homo*, I. ch. 1, ed. F. S. Schmitt, *S. Anselmi Cantuariensis Archiepiscopi Opera Omnia*, ii (Edinburgh: Nelson and Sons, 1946), 48/2–6; tr. Brian Davies and G. R. Evans, *Anselm of Canterbury: The Major Works* (Oxford and New York: Oxford University Press, 1998), 265.

[13] R. W. Southern, *Anselm and His Biographer* (Cambridge: Cambridge University Press, 1961), 79; id., *Saint Anselm: A Portrait in a Landscape* (Cambridge: Cambridge University Press, 1990), 370. Clemence uses vernacular equivalents of a number of school terms, in many cases the first or only example recorded by the *AND*: for instance, *rhetorien* (vv. 331, 673, *retorien* v. 491), *plaideresse* (v. 335, 479), *pruveure* (v. 428), *clerjastre* (v. 486), *filosophe* (v. 489), *gramaire* (v. 489), *dileticien* (v. 492), *philosophe* (v. 677), *pruvance* (vv. 776, 779, 876), *cuntrairies* (v. 810).

She offers her community and the nearby Angevin court an aristocratic and courtly spirituality which, like Anselm's own, unites theology and devotion. Both authors remain deeply aware throughout their writing of affect, desire, and volition.[14] Clemence was Latinate enough—and so was Barking's culture in the twelfth century—to have composed saints' lives in Latin had she wished.[15] Her choice of the vernacular, in so far as it is a choice to include those without formal literate (i.e. 'Latinate') status, may very well have been both a mode of preaching and of theological reflection on her part. In her work, we can see a further dimension of hagiography: its role, to quote Marc van Uytfanghe, as 'l'expérience tangiblement renovelée et actualisée de l'histoire chrétienne du salut consignée dans la Bible', assimilating simultaneously 'l'Ecriture' and 'l'après-Ecriture' to create 'une symbiose et une acculturation réalisées par l'hagiographie médiévale'.[16]

First, however, it is worth noting that Clemence participates in some other twelfth-century intellectual preoccupations. Unusually among the writers of hagiographic *passiones*, but typically of twelfth-century thinkers, Clemence takes pagan thought seriously. She retains her Latin source's mention of Plato, and develops its account of the Sibyl, the pagan virgin praised by Abelard as superior in prophecy to the evangelists and particularly associated with soteriological knowledge: 'in her prophesying the Sibyl omitted neither the divinity nor the humanity of the Logos'.[17] Clemence frames her expanded account of the Sibyl's sayings with two quotations in direct speech, organized chiastically (the Latin *vita* has only one prophecy). She also shows the Sibyl initiating the pun on the wood (*fust*) of the cross and the preterite of the verb 'to be' (*fust*) out of which the climax of her saint's debate on the redemption will be developed:

[14] Anselm did not regard his work on prayers as disjunct from his philosophical work (see Benedicta Ward, *The Prayers and Meditations of St Anselm* (Harmondsworth: Penguin, 1973)). For the early circulation of the prayers and meditations to Countess Matilda of Tuscany, see Otto Pächt, 'Illustrations of St Anselm's Prayers and Meditations', *Journal of the Warburg and Courtauld Institutes*, 19 (1956), 68–83; Southern, *Saint Anselm*, 110–12. In addition to debate and argument Clemence writes lyrical vision, meditation, and prayer for her saint (e.g. vv. 1666–796, 2491–504, 2558–66) and embraces these genres in the Life's narration (see for instance the meditative account of God's goodness and his pursuit of the clerks, vv. 1211–28).

[15] Barking has the largest number of extant post-Conquest Latin manuscripts among female houses in the 12th and 13th c. (see Bell, s.v. Barking) as well as Latin correspondence to its abbess and nuns in the mid-12th c. (see Ch. 6, n. 16 above).

[16] Marc van Uytfanghe, 'L'Hagiographie', in *Le Moyen Age et la Bible*, ed. Pierre Riché and Guy Lobrichon, *La Collection Bible de tous les temps*, 4 (Paris: Beauchesne, 1984), 449–87.

[17] Peter Dronke, *Hermes and the Sibyls: Continuations and Creations*, Inaugural Lecture, 9 Mar. 1990 (Cambridge: Cambridge University Press, 1991), citing Letters Three and Seven to Heloise (for the quotation see *Theologia Scholarivm*, ed. E. M. Buytaert and C. J. Mews, *Petri Abaelardi: Opera Theologica*, CCCM 13 (Turnhout: Brepols, 1987), 398, §189). Divination was in Abelard's view the reward of the Sibyls' virginity.

(1). Sibille de la croz redit;
—Ço sai, ses diz avez escrit.
Ço dit: 'Cil Deu est boneuré
Ki pent en halt fust encroé.'[18]

The Sibyl says of the cross (I know you have texts of her sayings): 'Blessed', she says, 'is that God who hangs fixed high on a tree' [and/or] 'who hanging high, was crucified'.

(2). Sibille dist 'Boneuré fud
Cil Deu ki el fust est pendu.'
(vv. 915–16)

The Sibyl said: 'Blessed was that God who on the tree was hung.'

Clemence thus integrates the Sibyl's prophecy into the key thematic lexis of her own treatment of the redemption. Authorized pagan predecessors can be useful in recuperating women's heterodox and marginalized status in matters of doctrine and teaching, and the Sibyl had learning and prophetic authority in both Latin and the vernacular.[19] There was an extensive twelfth-century revival of interest in all ten of the Sibyls. The Cumaean Sibyl in the *Roman d'Eneas* has studied a curriculum including all of Catherine's accomplishments and more: she is 'divineresse', 'prestresse', knows 'nigromance, fusique, retorique, musique, dialectique, gramaire', and is a 'profetiseresse'.[20] The Tiburtine Sibyl explicating the collective dream of the Roman senate as a portent of Christ provides an analogy for St Catherine dealing with the emperor's pagan rhetors, as also for female authority about the redemption.[21] And perhaps, given the use of 'the Sibyl'

---

[18] *Life of Saint Catherine*, ed. MacBain, edited text of MS A, vv. 903–6: for the Latin *vita*, see *Seinte Katerine*, ed. d'Ardenne and Dobson, 168/457 (both henceforth referenced by line number and by page and line number respectively in the text). The particularity of what Clemence is doing here is underlined by scribal responses. In (1) the reading of the A manuscript for v. 906 is not understood by the scribe of the Campsey manuscript (MacBain's MS W), even though there is often much to be said for W readings elsewhere. The A reading here is the *lectio difficilior* and W's the more conventional 'en la croiz crucifie'. A's reading of *encroé* also allows a double meaning: *encroé* is 'en-crossed' and 'patterned with roundels' (like Catherine's wheels later in the text and Plato's round sign—see *Timaeus* 40a–d—at v. 901). Again, in (2) the Campsey scribe and also the Picard scribe (MacBain's MS P) are less careful over the pun on *fust* found in A at v. 916: W's reading is 'ken la croiz fu pendu' and P's 'qui en crois penes fu'.

[19] In the legendary history of the cross, the Sibyl becomes a virtuous pagan proto-martyr, beaten by the Jews for her prophecy, put in a dungeon and comforted by angels and her name changed from Sibyl to Susanna; for a 12th-c. Latin text and a 13th-c. prose French version of this story, see R. M. Morris, *Legends of the Holy Rood*, EETS os 46 (London, 1871), Appendix I, 52–3: see further Josiane Haffen, *Contribution a l'étude de la sibylle médiévale: étude et edition du ms BN f. fr. 25407 fol. 160v–172v: Le Livre de Sibile*, Annales Littéraires de l'Université de Besançon (Paris: Les Belles Lettres, 1984).

[20] *Eneas: Roman du XIIe siècle* ed. J.-J. Salverda de Grave, CFMA (Paris: Champion, 1925), vv. 2199–2209, 2257–8.

[21] Bernard McGinn, '"Teste David cum Sibylla": The Significance of the Sibylline Tradition in the Middle Ages', in Julius Kirschner and Suzanne Wemple (eds.), *Women of the Medieval World: Essays in Honor of J. H. Mundy* (Oxford: Blackwell, 1985), 7–35 (24–5, esp. 25 n. 115).

as a soubriquet among the eleventh-century Latin women poets of Le Ronceray convent in Angers and for Muriel of Wilton Abbey, the name Sibyl connoted a specific tradition of women's convent writing for Clemence of Barking.[22] The use of the Sibyl in polemic is also very much a part of Clemence's culture, as in, for example, Peter of Blois (also writing in the ambience of Henry II's court) and his 'Against Jewish Unfaithfulness'.[23] Anglo-Norman Sibyls are also import-ant, as they had been for Augustine, for their role in the 'fifteen signs' of the Day of Judgement (supposedly composed by the Sibyl, extant in numerous manuscripts, and frequently recompiled in encyclopaedias and manuals).[24] That the Sibyl prophesied the fall of Troy and is a figure in Geoffrey of Monmouth is a further possible resonance, while Sibyls also figure in the liturgical *ordo prophetarum*; as a vogue in women's names from the late twelfth century onwards; and in the *Livre de Sibile*, 'the noble queen', the Anglo-Norman version of the prophecies of the Tiburtine sibyl by Philippe de Thaon, perhaps written between 1139 and 1148 and revised in 1154.[25] This work is dedicated to a royal woman, probably the ex-empress Matilda (v. 1211). It explains that 'there were ten Sibyls, well-born noble women [gentils dames nobiles] who had in their lives 'the spirit of prophesy' (vv. 2–4) and that 'all wise women [femmes savantes] who could divine the future were named Sibyls' (vv. 11–14). The Sibyl, that is, will have been a figure of authoritative prophecy for the audiences of the Catherine Life as well as for Clemence herself.

Interest in the Sibyl is congruent with Clemence's treatment of the era of Constantine as one of Christian fulfilment. The Sibyl is characteristically associated with the fate of dynasties, and Clemence locates the action of her narrative in the pagan province of a Christianizing empire and in a history capable of Christian immanence. She shows the emperor Maxentius's kingdom passing away (v. 2430), she has her saint threateningly and powerfully prophesy the emperor's defeat by a man of Christian faith (i.e. Constantine, vv. 1943–8). She adds a reference to Constantine's mother, Helena, thus underwriting Constantine's reign as that in which the true cross is rediscovered (v. 56). In the Life's prologue meditations on the world grown old (vv. 37–44) and (in narrat-ive recapitulation and commentary following the martyrdom of the clerks) on

---

[22] See Bond, *The Loving Subject*. The Sibyl and the vestal virgins figure in Abelard's writings to Heloise, and the vestals are also important in the precedents offered to Adelidis, abbess of Barking by Osbert of Clare (Ch. 6.2 above). In the 13th-c. Picard version of Catherine's life, the Sibyl is called a poetess, 'poetes' (*De Sainte Katerine: An Anonymous Picard Version of the Life of St Catherine of Alexandria*, ed. W. MacBain (Fairfax, Va.: George Mason University Press, 1987), v. 536.

[23] See Maginn, ' "Teste David cum Sibylla" ', and Dronke, *Hermes and the Sibyls*.

[24] Augustine had given particular status to the Erythraean Sibyl, the vehemence with which she countered idolatry, and her prophetic song of the judgement (*City of God*, bk. xviii).

[25] *Le Livre de Sibile* ed. Hugh Shields, ANTS 37 (London, 1979), to whose Introduction on 'The Sibyl in the Middle Ages' I am indebted for much of the information in this paragraph. In a dedicatory epilogue, the book is described as 'Le Livre de Sibile, | La roïne nobile' (vv. 1207–8). Quotation from this edition is henceforth by line number in the text.

the way human nature has changed from its pristine nature in paradise (v. 1204), she locates her audiences' time as also in need of renewal.

Clemence's most striking imaginative engagement with paganity has for many commentators been her treatment of the figure of the pagan tyrant, and especially her use of the courtly registers of Thomas's *Tristan* to show the pagan emperor Maxentius mourning division in his will between his desire and his power.[26] The courtly casuistry of Maxentius's meditation in the latter part of his speech is *Tristan*-like in its dense juxtaposition of the ideas of power ('poeir') and a self-controverted will ('voleir') as Maxentius deplores the necessity of his decision to execute his wife:

> Poi me valdra [puis] mun *poeir*
> Quant perdu avrai mun *voleir*;
> [Kar desque mun *voleir* me faut,
> De ceo ke ne *voil*, mei ke chaut?]
> Quel joie *purrai* jo aveir
> De *poissance* cuntre *voleir*?
> [Las, tut *puis* ceo ke ne ruis,
> Et ceo ke plus *voil*, pas ne *puis*.]
> Cuntre *voleir poeir* acoil
> Mais cest *voleir* senz *poeir* doil.
> Car si jo en usse *poissance*,
> Dunc fust fenie ma grevance.
> Ore ne sai jo a quel fin traire,
> Quant [jo] mun *voleir* ne pois faire.
>
> (vv. 2203–16; my italics)

My *power* will be of little use to me when I have lost what I *want*. For if I cannot have what I *want*, what do I care for what I do not *want*? What joy *can* I have from *power* which contradicts *desire*? Wretch that I am, I *can* do everything I do not care for, and that which I most *want* I cannot do. I amass *power* counter to my *desire*, but I lament this *powerless desire*. For if I had *power* to effect my desire, my trouble would be ended. Now I do not know what to aim for when I *cannot* realize my *desire*.

This is striking enough as the discourse of a hagiographic tyrant, but Maxentius is not the first to use these terms in Clemence's *Life*. Their resonance is earlier established in her saint's conduct of debate in Anselmian terms. As Anselm himself says, 'for a complete treatment [of why God became man] it is essential to have an understanding of power [*potestatis*] and necessity [*necessitas*] and will [*voluntatis*], and certain other things which are so constituted that no one of them can be fully considered without the others'.[27] Late twelfth-century

---

[26] See William MacBain, 'Five Old French Renderings of the *Passio Sancte Katerine virginis*', in Jeanette Beer (ed.), *Medieval Translators and Their Craft*, Studies in Medieval Culture 25, Medieval Institute Publications (Kalamazoo: Western Michigan University, 1989); the works cited in n. 11 above and in Ch. 3, n. 77.

[27] *Cur Deus*, I, ch. 1, ed. Schmitt, ii. 49/7–10; Davies and Evans, 266.

saints' lives often include very full versions of debate between saints and pagans and Clemence's is one of the fullest. Her Catherine defeats Maxentius's fifty philosophers substantively and in detail. In the influential thirteenth-century Latin *Legenda Aurea*, by contrast, we are told only that the saint 'showed that [the Christian redemption] had been predicted by pagans', that she contradicted and 'refuted [the pagan orators] with clear and cogent reasoning . . . reduced them to silence . . . and instructed them in the faith'.[28] Clemence's use of Anselm is most readily apparent in her handling and extension of the debate. The belief that the son of God is 'both God and man' (vv. 730–1) is claimed by Clemence's Catherine from the outset as the 'essence ('sume') of my position' (v. 729) and as her 'filosophie' (v. 731). Clemence makes the pagan clerks' questions of why the Christian God suffers and of how he could die (vv. 785–8) issues to be dealt with by argument, not only by credal statements. Her saint inverts the clerks' boastful account of their role in Anselmian terms: they themselves are to become students/believers ('disciple', v. 819) in order to learn as they listen to Catherine's exposition. In the manner of contemporary theological dialogues (Honorius's *magister* and *discipulus*, or Anselm's own dialogue with Boso in *Cur Deus Homo*, for instance), Catherine, as *magist[ra]* to the pagan clerks' *discipuli*, then uses their objections to develop her argument.

But Clemence uses Anselmian matter as well as Anselmian modes and thought in having her Catherine explain how and why a god would want to become incarnate and die (vv. 951–76).[29] Where her Latin source stresses God's defeat of the devil, Clemence foregrounds a distinction not in her source but

---

[28] Graesse, *Legenda Aurea*, 787–9; tr. William Granger Ryan, *The Golden Legend* (Princeton: Princeton University Press, 1993), ii. 336–7.

[29] Since Clemence may have known Anselm through florilegia, and since the manuscript traditions of Anselm's work in any case added a great deal of pseudo-Anselm material, her thought (in spite of the verbal closeness at vv. 951, 961–4 below) on some points may be Anselmian rather than a direct reading of texts by Anselm. Nevertheless, the interrelation of the crucial points of her thinking (as well as the ways in which she has recast the Latin *vita*) makes it clear that she has absorbed the structure of Anselm's thought and her formulation is much closer to Anselm himself than to the versions of his thought disseminated in, for instance, Honorius's influential *Elucidarius* (composed perhaps at Canterbury as early as 1096 in its first recension (V. I. J. Flint, *Honorius Augustodunensis of Regensburg*, in Historical and Religious Writers of the Latin West, ed. Patrick J. Geary, *Writers of the Middle Ages* (London: Scolar Press, 1995), v. 101)). The further discussion of the redemption by Honorius in his *Inevitabile* was often used as a fourth book of the *Elucidarius* (ibid. 144), but has no phrasing as close to Clemence's as hers is to Anselm's in the *De incarnatione* and the *Cur Deus*.

Recent work suggests that Anselm's work was more swiftly known in the 12th c. than was previously thought, often in ways of possible relevance to Clemence. Yoko Hirata has argued that John of Salisbury's *vita* of Anselm was seen by Becket as a source of parallels for his own life ('St Anselm and the Two Clerks of Thomas Becket', in D. E. Luscombe and G. R. Evans (eds.), *Anselm: Aosta, Bec and Canterbury: Papers in Commemoration of the Nine Hundredth Anniversary of Anselm's Enthronement as Archbishop, 25 September 1093* (Sheffield, Academic Press, 1996), 323–33 (332)), a comparison also made by Michael Staunton ('Trial and Inspiration in the *Lives* of Anselm and Thomas Becket', ibid. 310–22). There were over 60 manuscripts of *Cur Deus homo* before 1220

crucial for Anselm: that between God's nature and his power.[30] It was not through any necessity that God became man, but through his power:

> *Par poesté, nient par nature*
> *Devint li faitres criature.*
> (vv. 837–8; my italics)

(*Through his power, not through his nature*, the maker became a creature).[31]

Nothing in the devil's actions or in God's own nature constrains God to become human: it is an act of supreme free will, grace, and appropriateness, enabling the redemption of man by man.

and in the 12th c. it was at monastic centres in Normandy and England (Michael Robson, 'The Impact of the *Cur Deus homo* on the Early Franciscan School', ibid. 334–47 (338, 335–6)).

At least one copy of Anselm's *De conceptu virginali* is known from a 13th-c. nunnery manuscript (copied by the D scribe of the Canonsleigh manuscript of *Ancrene Wisse*: see Tony Hunt, 'An Anglo-Norman Treatise on the Religious Life', in Monks and Owen (eds.), *Medieval Codicology*, 267–75 (267)): another possibility is Cambridge, Trinity College MS O.2.29, a 13th-c. manuscript containing the *De custodia interioris hominis* attributed to Anselm and an imperfect copy of the *Elucidarius* of his follower Honorius alongside the sermons of Maurice de Sully in French. It also includes a later collect for St Ethelburga and is a possible addition to the books owned by Barking. On Anselm florilegia in England and Normandy see G. R. Evans, 'Abbreviating Anselm', *RTAM* 48 (1981), 78–108.

[30] I am grateful to Sarah Kay for shared drafts and discussions on this point: for her use of it and her discussion of Clemence's deployment of different types of formal argument see her *Contradiction in Medieval Literature* (forthcoming). For the source here, see *Seinte Katerine*, ed. d'Ardenne and Dobson, 165–6 (quotations henceforth referenced by page and line number). Although the Latin *vita* is itself generally Anselmian in its celebration of the redemption's appropriateness, it contains no formulation on the two natures or the power/nature distinction close to Anselm's text. It is not close until *Catherine*, vv. 1001–2, where the *vita* has 'Potens equidem erat Deus, per angelum quemuis aut per aliquam celestem uirtutem, prostrato diabolo hominem eripere, si uoluisset, sed, omnia cum ratione agens, Deus sic modum statuit uictorie ut qui hominem subiugarat per hominem ipse uinceretur' (170/498–502). However, *potens* and *voluisset* here are neither a grammatical pair as in *Catherine*'s *potesté* and *volonté* (vv. 1001–2), nor do they continue a previously established lexis, so that once again Clemence crucially transforms the terms of the argument. Clemence further develops the nature/power distinction in her concluding account of Christ's goodness ('bunté', v. 2654, first used at v. 9), as giving us 'occasion' ('materie', v. 2649) to manifest goodwill ('bone volenté', v. 2650) by himself becoming a created being through his goodness ('bunté'), not his nature (v. 2654).

[31] In the important article to which the present discussion is in many ways a gloss, Duncan Robertson has argued for the Anglo-Norman *Tristan* as a source of this distinction ('Writing in the Textual Community', 18–24). The fragmentary condition of the extant texts of *Tristan* preclude absolute certainty, but there is no such use of *poeir* opposed to *nature* in them (and Robertson's argument cites none, using rather Thomas's general clerkly familiarity with such distinctions as a source, 18–19). One other possible source is the Anglo-Norman Life of St Lawrence (written in the late 12th c. for a 'handmaiden of St Lawrence') which distinguishes God's power and nature in a contrast between human manufacture and divine creation, the tyrant's idols versus the poor as church treasure: 'through his power, and not according to nature, the creator made himself a creature' (v. 478). This passage occurs within a resumé of the fruit and cross argument more extensively dealt with by Clemence, to which it is lexically close enough to suggest that (the Lawrence Life being, probably, earlier) Clemence knew this Life (*La Vie seint Laurent*, ed. D. W. Russell, vv. 464–515, tr. Wogan-Browne and Burgess, 52–3). In the Lawrence Life, however, the power/nature distinction is not linked with other points of Anselm's thinking as it is in *Catherine*.

> Bien *poust Deus par poesté*
> *U par sule sa volenté*
> Guarir le mund de l'Enemi,
> Mais par greinur dreit le fist si,
> Que un hume l'ume venjast
> Ço que hume forfist, hume amendast.
>   (vv. 1001–6; my italics)

God could easily have preserved the world from the enemy *through his power or through his will alone*, but by a greater justice he did it this way, so that man avenged man, for a crime committed by man, man made amends.

God could not die in his impassible immortal nature and suffered death only in the human nature he had assumed in the incarnation. As Anselm says (in phrasing closely followed by Clemence and without equivalent in her source), 'in the incarnation of God it is understood that no humiliation of God came about: rather it is believed that human nature was exalted':[32]

> Pur ço que murir ne poeit
> En la nature u il esteit,
> Se vesti de char e de sanc,
> Qu'il recut d'un virginel flanc.
> *Sa nature pas ne muad*
> *Mais nostre par soe honurad.*
> *La sue ne pot estre enpeirie,*
> *Mais nostre par soe essalcie.*
>   (vv. 957–64; my italics)

Since he could not die in the nature in which he was, he covered himself in flesh and blood, which he received from a virgin's womb. *He did not change his nature, but honoured ours by his own. His could not be harmed, but ours was exalted by his.*

For Clemence, like Anselm, the incarnation is a matter of God freely putting on human nature (neither mingling it with divine, nor using it as a disguise): she follows Anselm both in her account of the two natures and in not linking the incarnation to the question of the devil's rights to fallen humanity.[33]

---

[32] 'Non . . . in incarnatione dei ulla eius humilitas intelligitur facta, sed natura hominis creditur exaltata', *Cur Deus*, I, ch. 8, ed. Schmitt, ii. 59/27–8; tr. Davies and Evans, 275. See also 'In omnibus his non est divina natura humiliata, sed humana est exaltata. Nec illa est imminuta, sed ista est misericorditer adiuta. Nec humana natura in illo homine passa est aliquid ulla necessitate, sed sola libera voluntate' (*Meditatio humanae salvationis*, ed. Schmitt, iii. 87/102–88/104).

[33] In passages dealing directly with the incarnation Clemence shows God as clothing himself in humanity ('se vesti', v. 959 quoted above), not, as for instance in the Early Middle English *Katerine*, veiling and hiding himself in flesh and blood in order to trick the devil ('ischrud and ihud', *Seinte Katerine*, ed. Dobson and d'Ardenne, 62/433, and see *Anchoritic Spirituality*, tr. Savage and Watson, 426, n. 26). For a full account of this debate and the subsequent literary uses of the devil's rights, see Marx, *The Devil's Rights and the Redemption*. Marx cogently refutes Southern's influential view that the incarnation as the deceit and defeat of the devil ceased to be used after

This was by no means a necessary or inevitable position at the time. Guernes de Pont-Ste-Maxence's Life of Becket, its final version completed (with the help of patronage from Barking's abbess Marie Becket) in 1173–5, assumes the 'devil's rights' argument:

> Cil ki sunt a dampner, purveü sunt a mort;
> De lur dampnatiun n'i a mes nul resort.
> E si Deus les salvot, deable fereit tort.

Those who are to be damned are destined for death: there is no reprieve from their damnation. And if God were to save them he would be wronging the devil.[34]

Clemence's expansion of the debate also acknowledges Anselm's argument in which the two natures of the incarnation depend on the nature of the Trinity and imply no inequality of its members (in the unity of God's persons the incarnate person of the Trinity, even though sent by the Father, remains equal to him and mortal only in the human nature he assumes, not in his person).[35] Indeed, she stresses the equality of persons in the Trinity:

> Jo di que Deu nostre salvere
> Est *par nature uel al pere*
> E des qu'il est al pere uel,
> Dunc n'est il pas en sei mortel
> Il ne pot en sei mort suffrir,
> Ne dolur ne peine sentir.
>
> (vv. 951–6; my italics)

My point is that God our saviour is *by nature equal to the father*, and since he is the father's equal he is not himself mortal. He cannot suffer death in himself, nor feel sorrow or suffering.

Anselm's arguments famously (though not finally) shift the emphasis of debate from repayment and justice between God and the devil to God's completely unconstrained and unconstrainable nature and prompt a fresh focus on the grace-enabled reciprocities possible between God and humans. The redemption becomes God's way of allowing humanity to make satisfaction for its

---

Anselm's influence became felt, and shows its importance in vernacular literature from the 13th c. and later. In her maintenance of the Anselmian view, however, Clemence has a trickster devil but not a trickster Christ.

[34] *La Vie de saint Thomas le martyr par Guernes*, ed. Walberg, 25, st. 134, vv. 666–8. It is possible that Guernes alludes to Clemence in his comment on other vernacular lives of Becket, 'composed by clerics or laypeople, monks or a woman' ('clerc u lai, muïne u dame', st. 33, vv. 161–2).

[35] Developed most fully in *Epistola de incarnatione verbi* (second recension, 1093–4): 'Nam qui recte suscipit eius incarnationem, credit eum non assumpsisse hominem in unitatem naturae, sed in unitatem personae', ch. 9 (Schmitt, ii. 24/9–10). See also 'although we declare that the Son in his humanity is less than the Father and the Holy Spirit, yet the latter two persons [*personae*] do not on that account surpass the Son, since the Son also has the same majesty [*eandem maiestatem*] whereby they are greater than the Son's humanity, the same majesty whereby he himself with them is also superior to his humanity' (ibid., ch. 10 (Schmitt, ii. 26/6–9; Davies and Evans, 251)).

sins. In Clemence's work, this provides a framework in which her St Catherine's self-dedication to such a God and her willingness to see martyrdom as a gift in response to God's personal love and his suffering for her sake is rendered intelligible, not masochistic or sensational. This is not simply didactic material thrown into the narrative: more than any other saint's passion, Clemence's lucidly and thoroughly grasps the critical role of Trinitarian theology and its equality of persons for the genre of *passio*. If a saint's passion narrative is to have Christian theological coherence, God must not appear as a filicide and he must be distinguishable from the pagan tyrant in his demand for sacrifice, whether of his son or of his virgin daughters. The parallels between God's and the tyrant's demands for the virgin's ideological and sexual attachment to themselves must be claimed very strongly indeed as oppositional rather than parallel.

From the other side of the country, another, slightly later, twelfth-century Life offers a comparison: the Life of St George, by Simund de Freine (d. 1224 × 8?), canon of Hereford, correspondent of Gerald of Wales and author of a French metrical Boethius, the *Roman de philosophie*.[36] *Georges* shares with *Catherine* a tyrant emperor's destruction of his wife (though in this case it is the wife who uses courtly discourse: she feels 'amur fine' (v. 1366) for Christ following her conversion). At the outset of the saint and the tyrant's contest, Dacien, the pagan emperor, argues that a God cannot be both one and three, that George believes in a hanged man, one who was sold for money and born in a manger (vv. 286, 295); Apollo is the better lord with more to offer. George replies in a single exposition of 'all the points of my belief' ('tuz les poinz de ma creance', v. 416, not *Catherine*'s 'filosofie', v. 731) that God is three persons and one substance through his great power ('il est par sa grant poissance | Treis persones, une substance', vv. 345–6) and became man because

> hom covint que ceo fust
> Qui son tort adrescer peust.
> Dunt estuveit altre nestre,
> Quant Adam nel poeit estre.
> Si fist Deus cum dreitureus,
> Hom pur nus devint morteus;
> Estre voleit hom pur home,
> Pur le trespas de la pome.
> (vv. 365–72)

it was fitting that it should be a man who was able to right [Adam's] wrong. Thus it was necessary that another man should be born when Adam could not be the one to do so. So God acted like a just Lord and became a mortal man for our sake; he wanted to become a man for man's sake because of the forfeit of the apple.

---

[36] *Les Œuvres de Simund de Freine*, ed. John E. Matzke, SATF 59 (Paris, 1909), 61–117; *ANLB* 183–7.

Thus (following a quick 'proof' of the virgin birth by the analogy of sun through glass),

> cil hom sosfrit la peine
> Solunc la nature humeine.
> Solunc ceo que Deu esteit
> Pur ren murir ne poeit.
>   (vv. 411–14)

this man suffered pain only in his human nature. In so far as he was God, he could not die at all.

But there is no further intellectual exchange. Instead, a series of elaborate tortures and miracles thrash out the difference between George's god as creator and Decius's Apollo as provider of riches.

Even though the position announced in George's *credo* is Anselmian to the extent of stressing the role of God's human nature and hence of humanity in the incarnation, the thought and strategies of the text are not Anselmian in the thoroughly assimilated way of Clemence's, and its thematics are very different. They are pivoted around a contrast which for Clemence is obviated by her use of the Anselmian distinction between God's nature and his power (not used in *Georges*). Clemence's Latin source makes the point that God's power in miracles of resurrection and healing is shown not through the incantations of a sorcerer ('magicis carminibus'), but only through divine power ('sola diuina potentia', p. 166/418–19), but she leaves this aside. In *Georges*, on the other hand, this remains a central theme throughout the graphic contest between saint and pagan. To borrow again from Girard's terms (as earlier deployed in Chapter 3.2, 3.3 above), theologically the scapegoat *in* this text is worldliness: the scapegoat *of* the text is the need very firmly to distinguish theology and magical thinking. *Miracula* must be clearly separated from *merveille* (vv. 882, 1236)—Dacien's term for the means by which his queen has been converted—and, above all, saint must be distinguished from sorcerer ('enchanturs', vv. 598, 599). George is very like a weather or fertility god, baptizing with the rain from a convenient cloud, making fruit trees grow where pagan thrones had been. His ability to provide bread and feasts, resurrect dead oxen, and to be three times resurrected from his own bare bones has to be heavily stamped as Trinitarian and the very opposite of the powers of the hideous demon whom he forces to vacate Apollo's statue—and of the pagan sage who cuts a bullock in two and reconstitutes (as opposed to resurrecting) it in a false miracle. The long contest, however, continues without any development of Decius's position, or, for that matter, of George's, beyond the initial statement of the points of Christian belief. Duncan Robertson has suggested that this pre-dragon George is a priest-hero 'of the Word, offering veritable speech-acts . . . and himself as a sacrifice', and certainly, in George's three-day Trinitarian passion of elaborate tortures, miracles, and resurrections, Simund de Freine's text demonstrates the power of the man of

God.[37] It also uses the rhetorical strategies of top-down preaching and teaching (as in, for instance, George's explanation to Dacien of virgin birth as sunlight through glass, offered as 'an analogy you will be able to perceive', vv. 385–6). For Clemence of Barking, argument rather than assertion is at stake: enjoyable as the canon of Hereford's narrative is, the nun of Barking has a more vivid sense of how her audience could be served by hagiographic debate.[38]

Through Clemence's handling of debate, the emperor Maxentius's terms of courtly love and seigneurial sovereignty are contextualized as pagan parodies of the divine versions of love and power articulated by the saint herself.[39] The full significance of Clemence's handling of the pagan tyrant best emerges when seen as integral to her treatment of the life as a whole. In this context, Maxentius becomes part of a contrastive Anselmian analysis of the disordered will alongside the properly disposed one of Clemence's saint. For Anselm,

When a wicked man rages and is driven into the various dangers posed by his evil deeds, we protest that injustice does these deeds; not that injustice is something in itself or does anything, but because the will to which all voluntary movement of every man is

---

[37] *The Medieval Saints' Lives*, 43. George for instance converts a pagan by making fruit trees grow (vv. 584–5): in an early 14th-c. version of the Life (possibly an Anglo-Norman copy) this is a distinguishing mark of Christ ('aorez Jhesucrist | Qui fait aux arbres porter fruit | Et fait croistre tous autres biens': 'you must worship Jesus Christ who makes the trees bear fruit and causes all other good things to grow', vv. 189–91, Phillipps MS 3668, now in Amsterdam, Bibl. Philos Hermetica, ed. John E. Matzke, 'Contributions to the History of the Legend of St George with Special Reference to the Source of the French, German and Anglo-Saxon Versions', *PMLA* 18 (1903), 99–171 (163)).

[38] The typological depth and clarity of Clemence's reworking of the debate has a closer analogue in the *Jeu d'Adam*, the famous mid-12th-c. *Ordo Representacionis Adae* now extant only in a very problematic manuscript from Tours, in which the narratives of Adam and Eve and Cain and Abel are used together with a procession of prophets to create a typologically structured paraliturgical drama for Septuagesima to be played within (not at the door of) a church: see Tony Hunt, 'The Unity of the *Play of Adam* (*Ordo Representacionis Ade*)', *Romania*, 96 (1975), 368–88, 497–527; Willem Noomen, 'Le *Jeu d'Adam*: Étude descriptive et analytique', *Romania*, 89 (1965), 145–93 (90–3). The *Jeu d'Adam* also uses subtle and lucid octosyllabics with many figures of repetition including chiasmus (see e.g. vv. 315–86, Adam's speech of reproach to Eve) but interprets Eve's role very differently from Clemence. Her Catherine strikingly refrains from making the Virgin the answer to Eve: the Virgin is, rather, the bearer of the fruit through whom hell is destroyed ('De ceste eissi le bon fruit, | Dunt li fernal sunt destruit', vv. 1753–4). What the two works do have in common is the development and transformation of Latin forms in vernacular contexts, and a lucid and powerful union of theology and myth (see Jean-Pierre Bordier, 'Le Fils et le fruit: le *Jeu d'Adam* entre la théologie et le mythe', in Herman Braet, Johan Nowé, and Gilbert Tournoy (eds.), *The Theatre in the Middle Ages* (Leuven: Leuven University Press, 1985), 84–102, and, for the background in academic theology see Hunt, 'The Unity of the *Play of Adam*'). The two texts may yet shed more light on each other (particularly if Clemence's text is given the dozen or so editions and the century's work devoted to the *Jeu d'Adam*).

[39] Maxentius's terms of love and sovereignty—'joie . . . poeir . . . voleir . . . poissance . . . honur . . . justice . . . amur' (vv. 2165–2256) require exclusions and divisions, especially in comparison with the courtly-spiritual qualities of the heavenly court, where, as Robertson points out, Clemence pointedly shows charity *and* honour, nobility *and* benevolence, riches *and* humility coexisting ('Writing in the Textual Community', 17).

subject, without justice, inconstant, unrestrained and ungoverned, throws itself and everything subject to it into all kinds of evil.[40]

In the narrative's opening, Maxentius falls out with Constantine's immanently Christian regime, and flees to Alexandria, where the action opens with him sitting in his palace. The first narrative event of the Life is that the emperor conceives the wicked thought ('felun penser', v. 68) of demanding the entire populace's presence in Alexandria to make sacrifices, and that he summons his messengers to translate it into action. In a passage of narrative commentary, Clemence draws attention to Maxentius's behaviour as a grotesque version of the disordered will's urge to create:

a wicked man cannot conceal his nature; when he sees an opportunity for evil deeds he is quite incapable of restraining ['se . . . retraire'] himself. And this is what Maxentius did, since he possessed the power ['ot poesté'] to do so and was unable to conceal his iniquity. (vv. 70–4)

In contrast, good will ('bon vuleir', v. 511), as the narrative later claims, is never without effect. Through it one has the ability ('poeir') to act and ease in doing so (vv. 511–12).

Maxentius duly proclaims his word, which is sent into his whole realm through the messengers who carry and announce it ('nuntier', v. 77). This produces the raucous holocaust by which Catherine is prompted to leave her palace to challenge him (vv. 129–32, 169–84), ultimately to transform his meanings by becoming a sacrifice of her own. Maxentius's irascible and compulsive pouring forth of his will into the world creates only a noisy parody, and his own powers incarnate nothing of worth. For Clemence's Catherine, on the other hand, rewarding God's gift of eternal life with her love to the limit of her power ('poeir', v. 2679) means that 'no part of her will ['voleir'] remained unexpressed' (v. 2684).

Together with Clemence of Barking's transposition and reworking of the intellectual modes of contemporary male academic education goes the creation of a vernacular language in which this doctrine can be thought. At the climax of the debate Clemence has her saint's speech pull all strands of argument and feeling together in what, I would argue, is an Anselmian aesthetic vernacularized. Contemplating the redemptive patterning of human history, Anselm argues in the *Cur Deus Homo* that

it was appropriate that, just as death entered the human race *through a man's disobedience*, so life should be restored *through a man's obedience*; and that, just as the sin which was the cause of *our damnation originated from a woman*, similarly the *originator* of *our justification* and salvation should be born of *a woman*. Also that the devil, who defeated the man whom he beguiled *through the taste of a tree*, should himself similarly be defeated by a man through *tree-induced suffering*, which he [the devil] inflicted. *There are many*

---

[40] *De conceptu virginali et de originali peccate*, ch. 5, Schmitt, ii. 146/13–18; tr. Davies and Evans, 365.

other things, too, which if carefully considered, display the indescribable beauty [pulchritudinem]
of the fact that our redemption was procured in this way. (italics mine)[41]

Clemence's Life of Catherine extends Anselm's union of argument and aesthetics so that the vernacular's own possibilities of patterning and correspondence constitute a trace of the 'indescribable beauty' perceived by Anselm in the mode of the redemption. The crucial puns and paronomasia of Clemence's account work only in French: this is a theology that has to be thought and felt in the vernacular. The dense network of puns and echoes with which Catherine concludes the debate translate the Word very thoroughly into the fruit promised in the life's prologue:

Par le *fruit* del *fust* devée	*fruit wood*
Fud tut le mund a mort livré.	*was*
Jesu *fud* le *fruit* acetable	*was fruit*
E a tut le mund feunable.	
Icist bon *fruit fud* en cròiz mis,	*fruit was*
Si ramenad en pareis	
L'ume ki en *fu* hors geté	*was*
Par le *fruit* ki *fud* devée.	*fruit was*
Par cest *froit fumes* nus guariz	*fruit were*
Ki par l'altre *fumes* periz.	*were*
N'est tei avis que ço dreit *fust*,	*was* (subj.)
Que cil ke venqui par le *fust*,	*wood*
Que par le *fust fust* pois vencu,	*wood was*
Par le *fruit* ki *fud* pois rependu?	*fruit was*
(vv. 977–90; my italics)	

Through the *fruit* of the forbidden *tree* the whole world *was* condemned to death. Jesus *was* the acceptable *fruit* and fecund for the whole world. This good *fruit was* put on the cross and it restored to paradise man who had been [*was*] thrown out because of the *fruit* that *was* forbidden. By this *fruit*, we who *were* destroyed by the other *were* saved. Do you not think it [*was*] right that he who conquered by means of the *tree was* then by the *tree* conquered himself, by the *fruit* which *was* hung on it once more?[42]

---

[41] 'Oportebat namque ut, sicut *per hominis inoboedientiam* mors in humanum genus intraverat, ita *per hominis oboedientiam* vita restitueretur. Et quemadmodum peccatum quod fuit causa *nostrae damnationis, initium habuit a femina*, sic *nostrae iustitiae* et salutis auctor *nasceretur de femina*. Et ut diabolus, qui *per gustum ligni* quem persuasit hominem vicerat, *per passionem ligni* quam intulit ab homine vinceretur. *Sunt quoque multa alia quae studiose considerata, inenarrabilem quandam nostrae redemptionis hoc modo procuratae pulchritudinem ostendunt*' (italics mine), *Cur Deus homo*, I, ch. 3, ed. Schmitt, ii. 51/5–12; tr. Davies and Evans, 268–9.

[42] I have marked here only the interwoven and chiastic patternings of the lexis of 'fruit' (*fruit*, *froit*), 'wood' (*fust*), and verbal forms of 'being' (*fu, fud, fust*): see also vv. 991–1006 where these link with further patterns (Wogan-Browne and Burgess, *Virgin Lives*, p. xlvii). A further example of contemporary punning on the verb 'to be' is the celebrated passage from the *Roman de Renart* of c.1170–80 when Renart pretends—to his enemy and victim, Ysengrim the wolf—to be a jongleur from England in whose speech *fut* and *fout* (respectively from *estre*, 'to be', and *foutre*, 'to fuck'), are indistinguishable (see *Le Roman de Renart*, ed. and tr. Micheline de Combarieu du Grè

Anselm's *Monologion* argues that 'to strive . . . to give expression to this impressed image [of God in man]; to strive to actualize by an act of will this, nature's potential; such above all is . . . the debt that rational creation owes its Creator'.[43] Clemence's aesthetic and ethics of composition make the vernacular the place of actualization.

These concerns are given a small-scale prelude in her prologue, a prologue that is both like Marie de France's to her *lais*, but also significantly different in its exposition of the duty of revelation:

> Cil ke le bien seit e entent
> Demustrer le deit sagement
> Que par le *fruit* de sa *bunté*
> Seient li altre amonesté
> De bien faire e de bien *voleir*
> Sulunc ço qu'en unt le *poeir*.
> (vv. 1–6; my italics)

All those who know and understand what is good have a duty to demonstrate it wisely, so that by the *fruit* of its *goodness* others may be encouraged to do good deeds and to *want* what is good as far as they *are able*.

Like Clemence, Marie de France stresses duty: 'anyone who has received from God the gift of knowledge and true eloquence has a duty not to remain silent: rather should he be happy to reveal such talents' (vv. 1–4), but her metaphor is of the flowering of eloquence in the propagation of knowledge: 'when a truly beneficial thing is heard by many people, it enjoys its first blossom, but if it is widely praised its flowers are in full bloom' (vv. 2, 5–8).[44]

Clemence sees a more instrumental role for the writer, in whom wisdom is even more to be valued than eloquence. The vernacular composer is a channel for the transformative effects on human wills of what is in all senses (as her saint's debate stresses), the fruit of the Word. The incarnate Word manifests a

and Jean Subrenat (Paris: Union Générale d'éditions, 1981), 348–51, branche I, vv. 2387–95). Renart's obscene punning on the verb 'to be' suggests that existence equates with being screwed or screwing (and also, as the pun is extended to Renart's repertoire of stories—of Merlin, Brendan, Noton, Arthur, Tristan, Chevrefeuille, and the 'lay' of Isolt—a matter of screwing representation while representing adulterous screwing). This violent reduction of meaning is the opposite of Clemence's, but Renart's repertoire looks very like that of some of her audiences (the Anglo-Norman St Brendan for instance was dedicated to Henry I's queen, while Clemence herself repositions the language of the Tristan story even more radically than Renart) and arguably contributed to the resonance of the pun. For Renart as royal women's reading in early 14th-c. England see Carter Revard, 'Courtly Romances in the Privy Wardrobe', in Evelyn Mullally and John Thompson (eds.), *The Court and Cultural Diversity* (Cambridge: Brewer, 1997), 297–308 (297–8).

[43] *Monologion*, ch. 68, ed. Schmitt, i. 78/14–16; tr. Davies and Evans, 73.
[44] 'Ki Deus ad duné escïence | E de parler bon'eloquence | Ne s'en deit taisir ne celer, | Ainz se deit volunters mustrer. | Quant uns granz biens est mult oïz, | Dunc a primes est il fluriz, | E quant loëz est de plusurs, | Dunc ad espandues ses flurs' (Marie de France, *Lais*, ed. Ewert, Prologue, vv. 1–8; tr. Burgess and Busby, 41).

God who is not so much invisible as unseeable in ordinary human perception ('Hume devint a tuz *mustrable* | Kar en sei fud Deu *nun veable*', vv. 839–40). So too Catherine prays for power to demonstrate God's truth in her speech ('Dune mei, sire, si parler | Que tun dreit puisse *mustrer*', vv. 547–8), in a usage which takes on the connotations both of dialectic and revelation. So too Clemence, whose text is both a gift to Barking (v. 2692) and also an address to the world of 'seignurs' (v. 1159).

In the debate over the nature and powers of her chosen lover, Clemence's Catherine says nothing of Christ's body on the cross. In her argument, it is fruit that hangs there, an apple replaced.[45] This is an account cognizant of, but not epistemologically focused on, the suffering of Christ (as becomes common in the dolorism of the thirteenth and later centuries). Later lives rarely re-create the Anselmian union of reason and faith, and a more affective and devotional spirituality reigns. When, for instance, in Matthew Paris's early thirteenth-century Anglo-Norman Life of St Alban, St Amphibal converts the saint, Alban first balks at the Trinity.[46] He is finally convinced by a detailed vision of the 'divers turmentz' of Christ (vv. 229–58), concerning which Amphibal congratulates him that it is not by the speech of others, by teaching or language, but by 'avisiun' that God has changed his heart (vv. 295–6).[47] Direct affective contact with his ultimate overlord converts Alban the good *seignur*.

Seen as the fruit, rather than the torment, of the cross in *Catherine*, Christ's passion implies the entire framework of fall and redemption as the context for human choices and behaviour. The soteriological issue of the two natures has implications for the nature of God's creation. Catherine loves Christ not only as the bridegroom for whom she helps the queen to exchange Maxentius, but as her creator ('tun faitre', v. 1853, as he announces himself in her dungeon). Her debate includes an account of free will and a rewriting of Eve, who, in Catherine's account of the fall, is deceived, rather than innately deceptive:

---

[45] There is undoubtedly an intense awareness of body in the Catherine Life, but it is of bodies in society: of the spaces between disputants and of speech as occurring within inhabited social spaces (vv. 195–8, 259, 305, 323, 591–614, 627–30, 1863–76, etc.). Catherine's own body decorum is seemly and expressive of an intact will (in contrast to the physiology of Maxentius's anger and contorted volition, paid close attention in vv. 1109–12, 1239–41, 1427–9, 1957–60, 2116–18, 2155–8). The unblemished state of the burned converted clerks' bodies is God's reward to them (v. 1321); the emperor's decision to leave the queen's body unburied for scavenging animals evokes horror in Porphyiry, captain of his guard (vv. 2369–76 and see Wogan-Browne and Burgess, *Virgin Lives*, pp. xxxiii–xxxiv).

[46] *Vie de seint Auban*, ed. Harden, vv. 191–6 (quotations henceforth referenced by line number in the text).

[47] In Clemence's text, the queen has a dream (vv. 1529–48), before visiting the saint in her dungeon, but this, her crowning as a converted bride of Christ, and the conversion of the attendant captain of Maxentius's guard are mediated and explained by Catherine (vv. 1599–1660). The captain, Porphiry, is converted by the vision evoked by the saint's eloquence when he questions her ('l'araisune', v. 1661) and she replies with an account of heaven (vv. 1666–796). These modes of persuasion supplement rather than, as in *Auban*, cut through debate.

> Humes e femmes raisnables fist
> E pois en pareis les mist.
> L'enemi la femme *enginna*
> Par la pume qu'ele manga.
>
> (vv. 701–4; my italics)

He made men and women as rational beings, and then placed them in Paradise. The enemy deceived the woman through the apple which she ate.

The verb 'enginer' in association with women is otherwise reserved for the pagan emperor, who speaks of his wife's conversion as an example to other women who will also 'enganerunt' their lords (v. 2235). His position is placed both by Catherine's in the debate and by Clemence's narration, with its resonant declaration that God never created anything evil ('Deu ne fist unches male chose', v. 1205) and that human will is accordingly free to choose. God has not put anyone in a position where they must sin against their will ('volenté', v. 1208). Contra Maxentius's misogynist determinism, God's creation, for the saint and the narrative, is itself a gift and good in its nature: all is created essentially good, however much (in the doctrine of the world grown old, invoked in the prologue, vv. 17, 37–40) it may have changed since (vv. 1203–4).

On the indications of responses to her work as we so far have them, Clemence's voice was received as authoritative. Her Life is extant in thirteenth-century insular and Continental manuscripts.[48] In a West Midlands preaching miscellany of the late thirteenth or early fourteenth century, twelve lines of her narratorial commentary in *Catherine* are copied as 'proverbia Marie Magdalene' —that is, as the most authoritative represented female preaching voice of this period—while in an early thirteenth-century Anglo-Norman prose version of the *Historia Karoli Magni et Rotholandi* (*Pseudo-Turpin Chronicle*), a clerk, William de Briane, seems to have drawn closely on Catherine's debate for the theological discussion between his Rollant and the pagan giant Ferraguz.[49]

---

[48] The *Catherine* Life appears with the *Brendan*, *Alexis* and Herman de Valenciennes' *Romanz de Dieu et de sa mere* in an Anglo-Norman manuscript (BN nouv. acq. fr. 4503); is copied in north-west France (see Robertson, *Medieval Saints' Lives*, Appendix, for the female scribe of this manuscript); and copied again in the Campsey manuscript.

[49] See *Catherine*, vv. 599–610, quoted without identification from Cambridge, Trinity College MS B.14.39 in *Religiöse Dichtung im Englischen Hochmittelalter*, ed. Reichl, 107. Reichl assigns the lines (corresponding to vv. 599–610 of the Catherine Life, though not identified as such) to his Scribe C with the title added by Scribe E (463). Scribe C copied 5 items, in both French and English, and came from north of Gloucester (ibid. 21). It is, of course, not necessary for *sententiae* to have a separate existence as proverbs in order to be perceived as such and extracted from narrative.

For William de Briane's dependence on Clemence see *The Anglo-Norman Pseudo-Turpin Chronicle*, ed. Ian Short (Oxford: Blackwell for ANTS, 1973), 53/792–810: I hope soon to publish a detailed study of the close verbal parallels between the two texts. (It may be significant that the patrons of the earlier Continental French *Turpin* of the late 12th c. were the Count and Countess of St Pol (*Anglo-Norman Pseudo-Turpin*, ed. Short, 2), the same family who later owned the Continental French prose *remaniement* of the Barking *Vie d'Edouard le confesseur*, and who retained their

In the thirteenth century, the incarnation is increasingly apprehended through the nativity as well as through the crucifixion and the redemption.[50] The fruit of the cross becomes flesh-fruit in later thirteenth- and fourteenth-century Anglo-Norman and Middle English devotional meditation and lyric, often mediated by the Virgin's gaze on the cross.[51] But a focus on the whole redemptive framework around the divine and incarnate Christ is a feature of much writing for women and lay people in the twelfth and earlier thirteenth centuries, and the cross-apple figures not only flesh-fruit for affective consumption but the scriptural study of Anglo-Norman women patrons.[52] The soteriological interests of medieval women have, until recently, received less attention than their affective devotions, partly because these interests are seldom stressed by medieval clerical writers of women's biography.[53] Jacques de Vitry, for instance, in the midst of constructing a new and influential model of affective female holiness in his early thirteenth-century *vita* of Marie d'Oignies in the diocese of Lièges, sees consideration of both God's natures as the exception in d'Oignies's piety: 'sometimes', he says, 'she moderated her sorrow and restrained

cross-channel links (see Paul Meyer, 'Notice du ms Egerton 745 du Musée Britannique', *Romania*, 39 (1910), 532–69 and *Romania*, 40 (1911), 45–62); on Marie de St Pol, see Hilary Jenkinson, 'Mary de Sancto Paulo'.)

A full study of Clemence's influence on other Catherine hagiographers has yet to be made, though there are some hints that suggest it as worthwhile. Her version, for instance, is the earliest of the vernacular Catherine lives to take up the Vulgate's Sibyl and it has been suggested that the Poitevin and other versions of the life may have been influenced by hers (*La Passion de Sainte Catherine d'Alexandrie*, ed. Olivier Naudeau (Tübingen: Niemeyer, 1982), 8). Certainly the 13th-c. Poitevin version by Aumeric has an occasional Clemence-like crispness (for instance 'Aiso dit Sibilla de Dé | Si tu non m'en cres, si crei lé', 125, vv. 833–4), but it seems to owe her no wider intellectual debt. MacBain suggests that in the Western French 13th-c. version, Gui (whose principal source is the shorter Vulgate) may also be following Clemence or Clemence's French source (*De Sainte Katherine*, p. ix). Gui picks up Clemence's emphasis on *fust* ('Et si dist que beneoist *fust* | Ci qui seroit penduz en *fust*', vv. 758–9, 782–807), though the pun is not sustained and Gui's emphasis on the reasonableness of God's justice reverts to the Vulgate rather than taking Clemence's Anselmian approach to the issue: see H. A. Todd (ed.), 'La Vie de sainte Catherine d'Alexandrie', *PMLA* 15 (1900), 17–73 (39). The insular dramatic version of the life extant as a fragment in Manchester, John Rylands Library, MS French 6 (ff. 9r–10r) is not running at these points (and is probably of earlier date), and Catherine's *passio* is not included in the 14th-c. Anglo-Norman life in London, BL, MS Addit. 40143 (an early account of the saint's mystical marriage). For a copy of this life, I thank Professor MacBain, who is preparing an edition of it and others in a full study of vernacular Catherine lives: meanwhile see his 'Five Old French Renderings of the *Passio sancte Katerine virginis*', Beer (ed.), *Medieval Translators and Their Craft*, 41–65.

[50] In the late 13th-c. Campsey copy of Clemence's Life of Catherine, the scribe goes with the grain of these developments, and loses Clemence's precision about the Sibyl's prophecy by substituting 'nessence' (MS W)—'birth'—for 'sainte croiz', at v. 898.

[51] See *Moral Love Songs*, ed. Fein, 87–100; Sarah Stanbury, 'The Virgin's Gaze: Spectacle and Transgression in Middle English Lyrics of the Passion', *PMLA* 106 (1991), 1083–93.

[52] These issues and texts are studied in more detail in a study I am preparing, 'Whose Bible Is It Anyway?: Women and Holy Writings in Anglo-Norman England'.

[53] But see now Else Marie Pedersen, 'The In-carnation of Beatrice of Nazareth's Theology', in Dor *et al.*, *New Trends in Feminine Spirituality*, 61–80; Amy Hollywood, *The Soul as Virgin Wife: Mechthild of Magdeburg, Marguerite Porete, and Meister Eckhardt* (Notre Dame, Ind.: University of Notre Dame Press, 1995), ch. 2.

the flood of her tears and would raise her consciousness to the divinity and majesty of Christ, and by thus leaving behind consideration of his humanity, tried to find consolation in his impassibility'.[54] But Clemence's *Catherine*, even without further reference to the many rich variations in the reading models offered to Anglo-Norman women in twelfth- and thirteenth-century devotional writings, shows that the texts of female and vernacular audiences do not have to be seen as limitingly corporeal and literal. In this case, vernacular hagiography is more, not less, theologically aware than clerical Latin hagiography.

7.3. THE VIRGIN'S BODY: VISION AND HISTORY IN ENGLAND

Doctrinal and theological functions for saints' lives may be relatively readily conceded, but it is generally assumed that there is little visionary material in women's insular sources between Christina of Markyate and Julian of Norwich.[55] For women in north-west Europe on the other hand, vision in the late twelfth and thirteenth centuries is well recognized as an increasingly important marker of holy status and an authorizing convention of speech and composition. As much recent writing has shown, vision is both the legitimation and the site of theological and other forms of praxis for women.[56] While Anglo-Norman texts do not give us a tradition of hitherto-unknown insular women visionaries, there are some indications that we could frame questions and investigations in insular culture in different ways from those posed for modern scholarship by the large and rich body of Continental women's writing. In an insular culture strongly aware, as I have argued in Chapter 2, of *translatio imperii* and with a large investment in legitimating Anglo-Saxon virgin bodies, the state and whereabouts of the Virgin's own body was an issue of some moment, all the more highlighted by contemporary promotion of the feasts of the Assumption and the Immaculate Conception.[57] Wace's *La Concepcion Nostre Dame* narrates the Virgin's life

[54] *Vita Mariae Oigniacensis* AA.SS. Iun. v (1867), 542–72 (551A, §16); tr. Margot King and Hugh Feiss, *Two Lives of Marie d'Oignies* (Toronto: Peregrina Press, 3rd edn., 1993), pp. 50, 16.

[55] Peter Dinzelbacher surveys the mystical experiences of saints in 12th-c. insular Latin *vitae*: Christina of Markyate is the only woman included ('The Beginnings of Mysticism Experienced in Twelfth-Century England', *The Mystical Tradition in England IV*, ed. Marion Glasscoe (Cambridge: Brewer, 1987), 111–31).

[56] See Elizabeth Alvilda Petroff (ed.), *Medieval Women's Visionary Writing* (Oxford: Clarendon Press, 1986), Introduction. Carol Zaleski notes that vision at this period less often gains its protagonist access to an otherwise inaccessible environment and becomes more frequently experienced as the visit of an authoritative person divulging privileged information: *Otherworld Journeys: Accounts of Near Death Experience in Medieval and Modern Times* (New York: Oxford University Press, 1987).

[57] Osbert of Clare, Prior of Westminster and author of several Latin letters to Barking (see Ch. 1, n. 8 and Ch. 6.1 above), was, among others, committed to the establishment of this feast: see A. Wilmart, 'Les Compositions d'Osbert de Clare en l'honneur de Saint Anne', *Annales de Bretagne*, 37 (1925–6), 15–32; Donald Nicholl, *Thurstan, Archbishop of York* (York: Stangate Press, 1964), 186–7; Edmund Bishop, 'On the Origins of the Feast of the Conception of the Blessed Mary', in his *Liturgica Historica: Papers on the Liturgy and Religious Life of the Western Church* (Oxford: Clarendon Press, 1918), 238–59 (242–5, 248–9).

while remaining noncommital on the issue of corporeal assumption.[58] The Anglo-Norman version of Elizabeth of Schönau's visions is extant in a miscellany manuscript of the twelfth and thirteenth centuries at one stage of its career addressed to women. It includes, immediately before the vision of Elizabeth (here become a nun called 'Ysabel', v. 50), an 'explication de pater [noster]' addressed to a mother, 'ma doce mere'.[59] Isabel asks the Virgin Mary whether her body was glorified with her spirit in the Assumption: 'for anyone who could know this, a great doubt would be removed' (vv. 97–8). A year later she is answered in a vision: God wanted fully and openly to glorify the Virgin when he took body and soul to be in heaven with himself (vv. 194–6). Isabel at first says little by way of proclaiming this doctrine, because she fears that people will say this is an 'idea madly invented for novelty' (vv. 235–6). Other questions, as, for instance, how old the Virgin was when Gabriel came and she conceived and became pregnant, suggest the assimilation of doctrine to women's own lives and concerns: visionaries, as Alexandra Barratt has pointed out a propos Elizabeth of Töss, mould the figure of the Virgin to their own concerns (and in the case of this manuscript, as with many others, their information is used by other women).[60]

As Anne Clark has suggested in her study of Elizabeth of Schönau, a theme of great importance to women visionaries is the role of purgatory.[61] Marie de France's *Espurgatoire saint Patriz*, largely received within a framework privileging her collections of *lais* and *fables*, has been found an uninspiring text. Yet, especially since Yolande de Pontfarcy's edition with its apparatus of variants and sources, it has been possible to treat Marie de France as a theorist, open-minded, if not sceptical, of purgatorial vision.[62] Her distinctions are taken ultimately from Augustine via Gregory the Great (*Dialogues*, lib. IV, cap. 28–9, PL 77.365, 368), retained and identified by Marie in her handling of her Latin source, Henry of Saltrey's *Tractatus*. Before quitting the body, her narrative explains, many souls see what is to happen to them, many *par revelaciun*, and others *par avisiun*, or

---

[58] 'Ne puis dire ne afermer, | Ne je nel vueil ci aconter, | Que hom ne feme qui vesquist | Puis cele here le cors veïst . . . Bien pot [God] dunques resusciter | Sa mere vive en ciel porter' ('I cannot say or affirm, nor do I wish to recount here that any man or woman who ever lived saw her body since that hour . . . God *could* well resurrect his mother and carry her to heaven'), *The Conception Nostre Dame of Wace*, ed. William R. Ashford (Mensha, Wis.: Banta, 1933), vv. 1721–4, 1793–4.

[59] 'Poem on the Assumption', ed. J. P. Strachey, in J. P. Strachey, H. J. Chaytor, and O. H. Prior (eds.), *Poem on the Assumption, Poem on the Day of Judgement, Divisiones Mundi*, Cambridge Anglo-Norman Texts (Cambridge: Cambridge University Press, 1924), 13–26. For the manuscript (Cambridge, Pembroke College MS 112) see James, *Catalogue*, 108–9: Tony Hunt notes the expunction of the female address and its replacement by 'beau sire' ('An Anglo-Norman Treatise on Female Religious', 207).

[60] *Women's Writing in Middle English*, ed. Alexandra Barratt (London and New York: Longman, 1992), 71–2.

[61] Anne L. Clark, *Elisabeth of Schönau: A Twelfth-Century Visionary* (Philadelphia: University of Pennsylvania Press, 1992), esp. ch. 6; see also Newman, 'On the Threshold of the Dead', in ead., *From Virile Woman to WomanChrist*.

[62] *L'Espurgatoire Seint Patriz: Nouvelle édition critique accompagnée du De Purgatorio Sancti Patricii*, ed. Yolande de Pontfarcy (Louvain: Peeters, 1995).

par lur dreite consciënce (direct knowledge divinely sent) (vv. 65–7).[63] Some souls see visions before their deaths: they are ravished from their bodies and then they return and show what they have seen of torment or salvation ('ou de turment ou de salu', v. 74). They see spiritually what appears to them corporeally ('Il veien espiritelment | ço ke semble corporelment', vv. 77–8). Many people want to know about what happens to souls, but since we can have no certainty, we should rather fear asking and trying to find out (vv. 93–110). What we can know is that according to their deeds, souls suffer to greater or lesser degrees the tortures of purgatory (vv. 111–13, with v. 113 apparently the earliest known use of 'purgatory' as a noun).[64] Thus purgatory at its first vernacular appearance becomes, in a woman writer's hands, a kind of third term to handle epistemological uncertainty without abrogating final judgement.

The sense of an issue needing clarification here is very strong in comparison with, for example, the translation of Gregory's *Dialogues* by Angier, thirteenth-century canon of St Frideswide's, Oxford, for an audience of 'seignurs and dames', where the same material is prefaced by literary topoi of apology inscribing clerical service to the audience rather than any kind of direct thematic focusing.[65] In Marie's work, the initial questions concerning corporeality and the afterlife are further pursued: what the returning visionaries describe is said to be a demonstration of spiritual essence in which what is seen spiritually is similar to the corporeal ('la mustrance | de cele espiritel substance | ke semblable est a corporel, | ço k'il veient espiritel', vv. 173–6). Mortal and corporeal men have seen the purgatorial torments applied to the form and appearance of living corporeal substance ('en forme e en semblance | de home corporel sustance', vv. 179–80), just as, earlier, St Gregory has been said to say of incorporeal spirits (i.e. spirits outside their bodies) that they *can* be 'roasted and burned by fire in the world' ('ars e bruïz | el siecle, del feu corporel', vv. 153–6). In the Latin source this is 'quod uero . . . incorporeos spiritus dicunt pena corporalis ignis posse cruciari, narratione etiam ista hoc uidetur affirmari', but the last clause is not translated by Marie, and the prologue concludes in a question: 'who would truly believe, if they did not have a demonstration of it, that what we have to show here is true?' (vv. 181–4). She thus, as Michael J. Curley argues, submits

---

[63] This is Augustine's theory of three kinds of vision (*reuelatio, uisio, demonstratio*): see Martine Dulaey, *Le Rêve dans la vie et la pensée de saint Augustin* (Paris: Études Augustiniennes, 1973), 111–13.

[64] *L'Espurgatoire*, ed. Pont Farcy, Introduction and n. to v. 113.

[65] Paris, BN f. fr. MS 24766, ff. 2r–10v. In this manuscript, the prologue to Angier's *Dialogues* includes advertisements of the scope and merits, for all lay people, of Gregory's book, and a table of contents in Latin with, as is carefully explained, glosses 'en Romanz en la marge escrit' where one may find 'quei li chapitre dit' (f. 3rb), together with a rich deployment of prologue topoi. But all this is directed to creating and placing a lay audience for the book: there is no discussion of its theology as such. Of the two texts, Marie de France's is much more one of theological enquiry and reflection. For the Life of Gregory (composed by Angier after translating the *Dialogues*), see 'La Vie de saint Grégoire le Grand traduite du Latin par Frère Angier, religieux de Sainte-Frideswide', ed. Paul Meyer, *Romania*, 12 (1883), 145–208.

theology to experience and reverses Henry of Saltrey's priorities.[66] Both the Anglo-Norman text of Elizabeth's visions and Marie's *Espurgatoire* thus suggest active engagement by women in insular literary culture in contemporary debate as to the ultimate nature and meaning of human corporeality.

The genres in which visions are recorded as well as the kinds of people who have, or appear in, visions suggest, unsurprisingly, that the boundaries between lay and professed female vision are permeable. Women's relations with the after-life, and in particular their commemorative and intercessory responsibilities of continuing care for the dead of households and lineages, were common to nuns and laywomen alike. According to the *Book of St Gilbert*, both a Cistercian prioress, Agnes of Nunappleton, and the wife of Ralph de Hauteville saw visions of St Gilbert of Sempringham's death.[67] St Edmund of Canterbury's mother, a townswoman and pious widow, makes a visionary appearance to her son while he studies at Oxford and, in vernacular lives of Edmund, is herself sometimes suggested as a subject of cult, while Isabella of Arundel seems to have had a vision of Richard of Chichester.[68] In 1250 Ela of Lacock (d. 1261), foundress, widow, and abbess, has a premonitory vision of the death of her son William Longespee in the siege of Damietta, and is reported as a woman of constancy and maternal piety by Matthew Paris for doing so.[69] Some time after 1235, Loretta, Countess of Leicester, a widow and anchoress, tells the abbot of Vaux de Cernay of a dead woman's visionary appearance to her friend, also by then a religious, to explain the power of devotion to the five joys of Mary.[70] According to Wherwell's

[66] *Saint Patrick's Purgatory: A Poem by Marie de France*, tr. Michael J. Curley (Binghamton: SUNY, 1993), 25 (a discussion which I saw after this chapter had been written and with which I am pleased to be in agreement). For an account of Marie's creation of a new vernacular audience for the poem see ibid. 22–4.

[67] *Book of St Gilbert*, ed. and tr. Foreville and Keir, chs. 53, 54, 124–8.

[68] For her conversion of Edmund from arithmetic to the Trinity, see *Vie seint Edmund*, vv. 469–506. For the *SEL*'s representation of her as a holy woman, see Ch. 5, n. 68 above. For Isabella of Arundel's vision see Ch. 5 n. 11 above.

[69] *Chron. maj.* v. 153–4, 173: see further, Simon Lloyd, 'William Longespee II: The Making of an English Crusading Hero', *NMS* 35 (1991), 41–69; Simon Lloyd and Tony Hunt, 'William Longespee II: The Making of an English Crusading Hero: Part II', *NMS* 36 (1992), 79–125. Ela is represented as thanking God for allowing her, an unworthy sinner ('indignae peccatricis'), to bear in her body a son whom He has shown to be worthy of the crown of martyrdom (*Chron. maj.* v. 173). The cult seems to have been better known on the Continent and remained, as far as is known, unpromoted by Ela herself, though Lacock Abbey made some attempt (Lloyd and Hunt, 'William Longespee II', 99–100).

[70] Powicke, 'Loretta of Leicester', 269–70: the narrative was added to a Marian miracle collection at Vaux de Cernay (a house favoured by the de Montforts) sometime after 1235. Powicke suggests that the abbot to whom the 'reclusa cantuariensis quondam comitissa leycestre' told the story was Thibaut de Marly (abbot 1235–47), and, more speculatively, that the woman who smiled five times on her deathbed and who returned to reassure her friend was Annora de Braose, Loretta's sister, sometime prisoner of King John and herself a recluse for many years. The story and the communication between the two women is reminiscent of better-known Continental visionaries of the period. It is also one of several events testifying to the stature of Loretta's counsel *qua* holy woman (counsel also given to the king and to the newly arrived friars): the documentary traces for Loretta are a small part of the career of a woman whose influence was through speech.

cartulary, Ælftrudis had a penitential vision leading to the house's foundation, and she is, of course, far from being along among foundresses in this.[71] In Denis Piramus's late twelfth-century life of Edmund of East Anglia, a pious widow's vision is portrayed as a crucial intervention in the decision of the king of Saxony to allow his saintly son Edmund to take up the English crown.[72] In the anonymous Anglo-Norman *Passiun* of the same saint, another woman caring for Edmund's body (she trims the fingernails and beard) is the witness to a divine sign of the king's martyrdom.[73] Most of these women visionaries are widows (the widow in Piramus's *Edmund* is explicitly stated to be 'de grant aage' (v. 1158) and hence above suspicion in King Offa's many visits to her for counsel), and vision is represented as strategic or revelatory but not occupational for them: none has a full or early career as *mulier sancta*.[74] If we draw a very sharp line between contemplative and mystic vision and other kinds, such representation remains outside accounts of women's literary history in England, but it is by no means clear that we should draw such lines.[75] At all events, though clerical and monastic *vitae* of contemporary holy women are largely absent in England, vernacular (and Latin) hagiography and historiography show that vision was a mode associated with and used by women in insular literary culture.

In this context it is worth focusing once more on Barking to consider briefly the vision of history in its hagiography. The nun of Barking's Life of Edward the Confessor presents a saint-king who is a virgin visionary and contemplative, given to intense corporeal identification with poverty and suffering, and with special abilities in healing blindness and partial-sightedness, 'no matter how [the power of vision] had been lost' (v. 3284).[76] Edward is the focus of a sacralizing mystique of kingship, but the Life is also deeply embedded in English history,

---

[71] Wherwell cartulary, item 57 (London, BL, Egerton MS 2104A, f. 43r–v).

[72] *La Vie seint Edmund le rei*, ed. Hilding Kjellman (Göteborg: Elander, 1935), quoted by line number in the text. For the Roman matron's credentials as widow, semi-religious or vowess, and prophetess, see vv. 1116–24; for Offa's high regard for her counsel, vv. 1147–52. Her narration to the king of Saxony of her prophetic vision of his son Edmund's glory is at vv. 1225–94, followed by the king's command that a written text of the vision be explicated by a bishop, vv. 1295–1304.

[73] *La Passiun de seint Edmund*, ed. Judith Grant, ANTS 36 (1978), vv. 1153–1200 (esp. 1189–92).

[74] Clemence of Barking is usually assumed to be a professed career nun, a proponent of the professionally virgin life (and her learning and her achievement as a writer do seem consistent with someone with long-standing opportunities for systematic reading and writing). But if we had any evidence that Clemence herself had been married before entering Barking, it would be equally possible to see her as a widow writing a vision of virginity's superiority, especially in the queen's dream of Catherine and of her own crowning by Catherine as an honorary virgin (vv. 1533–50, 1605–7).

[75] For a recent analysis of the ways in which 'mysticism' has been conceived and deployed in English scholarship see Nicholas Watson, 'The Middle English Mystics', ch. 20 in Wallace (ed.), *Cambridge History*, 539–65.

[76] See W. MacBain, 'The Literary Apprenticeship of Clemence of Barking' for the argument that this Life is by Clemence of Barking (the apology for insular French and the refusal to name the author in the Barking Life cannot be confidently read as apprenticeship in the context of Anglo-Norman hagiographic prologues: for a male writer's apologies see Ch. 2.2 above; further on prologue conventions see Wogan-Browne, 'Wreaths of Thyme').

as well as in Barking's own history and position in the English realm, and seems to have been perceived as such in contemporary reception.[77]

The principal source for the Barking Life, Aelred's *Vita Edwardi Regis*, was composed for the saint's 1163 translation in the presence of Henry II, and, as Robert Stein has argued, constructs the saint as a 'celebration and guarantee of the legitimacy of [Henry's] rule'.[78] Aelred's *vita* replaced a Life of *c*.1138 by a writer well known to the mid-century abbess and nuns of Barking, Osbert of Clare.[79] Rosalind Ransford has illuminated Aelred's own experience of the manifold ethnic and national complexities over which Henry reigned, and shown the ex-courtier of David of Scotland presenting to Henry II a vision of specifically English kingship.[80] The Barking Life retains the prominence Aelred gives Alfred and Edgar as kings of the English, but precedes this with a vision of the unending plenty of the creator's presence as it is devoured in the gaze of the angels. Their desire continually grows by what it feeds on, but will never be sated or exhausted (vv. 24–38). The nun's Life, then, unlike Aelred's *vita* or Matthew Paris's later reworking of it, opens the narrative with an image of transcendent kingship as a focus for the desires of a celestial court.[81] It is tempting to see this not only as an image for Edward's kingship and, through him, Henry's, but as testimony to the direction of the Barking community's own gaze. In insular hagiographic tradition, the figure of Edward had already been deployed by one woman as protection for her own position: Edward's queen, Edith, commissioned the first Latin hagiographic biography of her husband when left vulnerable (especially as a childless consort) by the king's death.[82] At the likely period of the Anglo-Norman Life's composition, following the death of Adelidis,

[77] Paris, BN f. fr. 1416, a late 13th-c. manuscript containing the *Roman d'Eneas* (ff. 1r–63r) followed by Wace's *Brut* (ff. 63v–184v), replaces Wace's text at ff. 157r–181v with *Edouard*, vv. 69–4482. As Södergård points out, there are lacunae and intercalations in the treatment of the *Edouard* lines (*Vie d'Edouard*, ed. Södergård, 48), but they are not marked in the manuscript as material from another text. (The narrative uses standard formulae for narrative transitions—'De saint edward larrai atant | dirai de calewadre [Cadwalader] avant', f. 181rb/29–30, for instance—but, palaeographically and in every other way, the *Edouard* is received in this manuscript as historiography.)

[78] 'The Trouble with Harold: The Ideological Context of the *Vita Haroldi*', *New Medieval Literatures*, 2 (1998), 181–204 (190).

[79] Ed. Marc Bloch, *AB* 41 (1923), 5–131, and see further Barlow, *Life of King Edward*, pp. xxxiii–xxxvii.

[80] 'A Kind of Noah's Ark: Aelred of Rievaulx and National Identity', in Stuart Mews (ed.), *Religious and National Identity*, SCH 18 (1982), 137–46, and see Short, 'Tam Angli quam Franci', 168–72.

[81] For the Aelred *vita* see PL195.738–90: for Matthew Paris's version see *L'Estoire seint Aedward le rei*, ed. Wallace, henceforth referenced by line number in the text (the opening of the life is quoted above, Ch. 1.5 and see n. 128). For another vivid image of kingship (in a text dedicated to the queen of either Henry II or Henry III), see Merlin's vision of poets feeding from Arthur's breast (*Laȝamon's Brut*, ed. G. L. Brook and R. F. Leslie, EETS es 277 (London, 1978), 600, Caligula MS, ll. 11494–8).

[82] Stafford, *Queen Emma and Queen Edith*. Barking's own connections with London pre-date the Conquest: in Edward's day it owned twenty-eight houses and half a church within the City of London, with which its communication (by water) was good (*The Early Charters of Eastern England*, ed. C. R. Hart (Leicester: Leicester University Press, 1966), 117–45 (143, 145)).

abbess of Barking from, probably, *c.*1155–1166,[83] the abbacy remained vacant and in the king's hands until 1173 when he appointed Marie Becket.[84] A portrait from Barking of the holier aspects of the lineage of which Henry wanted to be seen as the continuator may have had its tactical value. The Aelred *vita*, of which the Barking Life is a very full vernacularization, provided an admirable vehicle for an exemplary account of kingship in England. The Anglo-Norman text also retains a full account of Edward's posthumous cure of a nun from Barking, living still 'in good health and high esteem' at the abbey (v. 6447). Although given a vision in which she and some companions walk towards Westminster and seek refreshment there, the nun prays for healing in her own abbey, since she is unaccustomed to travel and does not want to organize horses and travelling companions (vv. 6500–9). In the nun's cure, Edward's power thus extends out, benevolently, to Barking.

For Matthew Paris's thirteenth-century vernacularization of the same Aelred *vita*, dedicated to Queen Eleanor and written for the different conditions of Henry III's court, the great point of Edward's return from exile to England is that he establishes a series of European allegiances (vv. 876–89) and that he loves his indigenous barony ('baruns natureus', v. 914), while banishing 'flatterers and aliens of uncertain loyalty' (vv. 916–18).[85] Edward is the king whose courtesy transforms roughness and dissent, whose court teaches good manners and whose honour is unparalleled since Arthur (vv. 896–909). The nun of Barking's narrative is more interested in the sacredness of the bond between the visionary, prophetic, virgin king and his land. In exile, Edward is 'rich in chastity' (v. 941), and the harder he seeks to recover his land, the harder he practises his chastity ('plus enforça sa chasteé', v. 949). His gift of prophecy is both God's reward for this chastity and the proof of its perfect integrity (vv. 1451–62). Just as 'Christ the king | Freed Holy Church when he suffered death' (vv. 791–2), so Edward messianically liberates 'religion, | Knowledge ['science'], faith, goodness ['bunté'] and reason' (vv. 795–6). The earth is more readily cultivated, the air

[83] For the charges of scandalous conduct brought against Adelidis by Archbishop Theobald, see Ch. 6, n. 18, above. Adelidis's brother fought in the Battle of the Standard and was defended by Aelred in his *Relatio* for going over to King David. He died in 1157 and his son was favoured by Henry II: see Paul Dalton, 'Eustace Fitzjohn and the Politics of Anglo-Norman England: The Rise and Survival of a Twelfth-Century Royal Servant', *Speculum*, 71 (1996), 358–83 (380). As with Clemence's *Catherine*, the Barking *Edouard* will have been composed in a milieu with many long-lived interconnections with the court.

[84] Södergård's argument (*Vie d'Edouard*, 23–4, 25–6) that the nun of Barking could not speak benevolently of Henry II after the murder of Becket is not conclusive (*Catherine*, ed. MacBain, p. xxv). After the murder may be exactly when a reworking of the Aelred *vita* would be most wanted by the king. Södergård's argument assumes that 'the attitude of a woman in religion [to Henry II]' 'must be the same' as Guernes de Pont-Ste-Maxence in his Becket Life (*Vie d'Edouard*, 23), but see p. 235 above.

[85] On Henry III's foreign favourites, as perceived by the English barony, see the works cited in Ch. 5, nn. 77, 83 above. For the model of kingship in Paris's *Aedward* see Binski, 'Reflections on *La Estoire de Seint Aedward le Roy*'.

healthier, and the sea more tranquil' (vv. 803–4; see also vv. 2273–8) because of his return (a theme of Aelred's not retained by Matthew Paris).

Edward's vision shortly before his death of a severed tree which rejoins its trunk and begins fruiting is interpreted in the nun's narrative as signifying that the tree flowered again at the birth of the empress Matilda, and first truly bore fruit of which 'the land received the comfort' when Henry II was born and made two peoples and lineages one (vv. 4985–92). Matthew Paris unsurprisingly finds that the tree first fruited with the arrival of Henry III ('li terz Henri', v. 3846), who has made kings and barons and kingdom share one common blood of England and Normandy (vv. 3851–3), but it is noteworthy that the bond here is one of blood and lineage. This once more shows by contrast how insistent the nun of Barking is on the sacred relation between king and land (vv. 4988 and 4993–8).[86] In her narrative, the enemies of the realm, the events of the reign, and Edward's qualities are viewed as a series of typological figures for the reign and providence of Christ. One might here adapt Barbara Newman's felicitous term 'la mystique cortoise'.[87] Here the regnal mystique of a saintly king's court is used to provide a vision of sacral kingship—and possibly also a template of behaviour for a contemporary royal family, one perhaps (depending on whether *Edouard* was written before or during the various quarrels between Henry II and his sons from 1172 to 1189) facing a series of potential lineage and succession crises.[88]

In the nun's text Edward rules not in spite of but through holiness and his saintly powers. The Danes, for instance, are explicitly aligned with the devil (much as they are in virgin martyr *passio*) and declared eventually to have returned to their own territory, hell (vv. 762–3). Rather as in virgin *passio*, they are subjugated less by military and diplomatic means than by Edward's virtues and prophetic insights. His gift of prophecy is used like a weapon against them, predictions and their narrative confirmation succeeding each other so rapidly that the prophecy begins to seem causative. Thus Edward, his heart rapt to God in the mass one day, smiles a spontaneous and beatific smile (vv. 1509, 1521–6) which is subsequently carefully enquired about by the court. It turns out to have been caused by Edward's vision of the Danish leader preparing his ships for war and falling from one of them to a watery grave (the narrative, in keeping with its account of Edward's messianic and living relation to the land, elaborates Aelred's account of devilish Danish death-by-water to explain that the sea

---

[86] On Matthew Paris's treatment of the source here see Françoise Laurent, '"A ma matere pas n'apent de vus dire . . .": *La Estoire de seint Aedward le rei* de Matthieu Paris ou la "conjointure" de deux écritures', *Hagiographie*, 3 (1998), 125–53 (139–40).

[87] 'La Mystique cortoise: Thirteenth-Century Beguines and the Art of Love', in ead., *From Virile Woman to WomanChrist*.

[88] Södergård argues that *Edouard*'s invocation of blessing on Henry II's heirs could not have been written during this period of fraternal and paternal enmity (*Vie d'Edouard*, 22–3), but it could equally be argued that this is exactly when such monitory and even apotropaic invocations might be uttered.

'without pride' receives the proud [Danish] king—and keeps him: 'Ele l'ad senz orguil receu | L'orguillus rei e retenu', vv. 1599–1600). The death of the Danish king is immediately confirmed and the times matched between the event in Denmark and the vision in England (vv. 1619–28). Not only is God fighting on Edward's side, but he can be seen to be doing so, and the Danes at once seek peace agreements with Edward (vv. 1633–4).

Edward's personal virtues include complete devotion to 'true religion' (v. 870): his great goodness ('bunté', vv. 903, 5333, a word also much used of Christ) is manifest in the sweetness of his face and bearing and his deportment (in a simile not in Aelred) as ordered 'as if he had been trained in a cloister' (vv. 909–10). Through him a model in which God unites the best of *cortoisie* and religion is visible: 'sa [God's] justise fud fin amur' (v. 1675), as Edward explains to his people. As William MacBain has pointed out, 'fin'amor', 'refined love', is used in *Edouard* in a range of contexts to indicate trust in social relationships (so that, for instance, the treacherous English have none towards each other before Edward takes the throne, vv. 529–31), and to invoke the codified courtly love of southern France.[89] 'Fin'amor' is also used of God's love for humanity (as in v. 1675 already quoted), and of the saintly king's love for St John (of whom the more he hears the more he desires to drink in—'li reis beit tot cum fin amanz', v. 4458), while, in the poem's celebration of virginity, 'delit de sa fin amur' (v. 1360) characterizes the relation between God and his glorious spouse, Chastity, and between Edward and his queen.[90] The 'fin'amor' of virginity is here not confined to heterosexual *Brautmystik*. Cementing a range of relations in a holy reign, it can indeed be seen as 'la mystique cortoise' (in both more literal and wider senses than usual)—as the love that holds courtly society together in its attempts to express God's model of social as well as personal relations. The development of 'the royal love' (the formula *pro amore Dei* or *pro amore x* in adminstrative documents) in the reign of Henry I has been argued to show complementary emotional and fiscal meanings, understood by contemporaries as testifying to the interdependence of love and patronage, and may have made the term especially resonant in the Anglo-Norman context.[91]

In Clemence of Barking's Life of Catherine, the passage of time is carefully marked both on a diurnal and an epochal scale: the sun rises on the successive days and various events of Catherine's passion and the Christianization of Constantine's realm moves closer, the more so as Catherine so convincingly manifests the Word in the Alexandrian province Maxentius has sought to subdue to

---

[89] 'Some Religious and Secular Uses'; and his 'Courtliness in Some Religious Texts of the Twelfth Century', in Giovanna Angeli and Lucian Formisano (eds.), *L'Imaginaire courtois et son double* (Naples: Edizioni scientifiche italiane, 1992), 371–86.

[90] On Edward's celibate marriage in the Barking Life, see Wogan-Browne, ' "Clerc u lai, muïne u dame" ', 70–3. In *Catherine*, on the other hand, fin'amor is not mentioned, but for the Bernardine 'sweet' love between Catherine and Christ see Ch. 2, n. 88 above.

[91] Christelow, 'The Royal Love in Anglo-Norman England', 28–9: see Ch. 2, n. 48 above.

his pagan will. For the *Vie d'Edouard* history is also informed by hagiography (metonymically as well as figurally, in that events are both historical events and signs), and regnal power is a place for *imitatio Christi*. This concern with typology makes *Edouard* in some ways a more abstract and stylized text (especially as against the more quotidian politics of Matthew Paris's later version of the life).

Yet the *Edouard* narrative dramatizes its own concerns too. In two further examples of Edward's insight, for instance, it enacts the transforming power of Edward's holiness. Earl Godwin swears that he has not slain Edward's brother, and calls God to witness that the morsel in his hand will not pass unobstructed down his throat if he has ever done treason to Edward (vv. 3881–94). Edward makes the sign of the cross over Godwin's mouthful and, as Godwin duly chokes to death, calmly orders 'this dog' taken out (v. 3916). There follows immediately an account of an Easter feast, which is described in great detail twice. First is the narrative's account of the rich clothing of the king, nobles, and the hall itself, the hierarchical seating-order, the rich vessels and cups of gold. Edward, fearing pleasure in all this worldly glory, is 'ravished' in his heart to God ('tut raviz en Deu esteit', v. 3984), while the anxious court, not daring to disturb the beatific smile on the king's face, continue with the feast to satiation, the removal of cloths and tables and the provision of songs and story-telling (vv. 3993–4004). Later on in the king's chamber, the feast is redescribed by Edward, who tells Count Harold and two churchmen how he had internally turned away from the great cups, good dishes, silver platters, good wine, and noble company to God (vv. 4025–36). He has been rewarded with the illumination of 'the eyes of the heart' (v. 4039) in which he saw a prophetic vision of the Seven Sleepers of Ephesus turning over onto their other side (vv. 4017–76).

The vivid diptych of the two feasts confronts the relation between sign and meaning in several ways. Earl Godwin's denial of God's meaning provokes the power of the cross as sign, in a kind of reverse eucharist. As the narrative comments, the perfect virtue of the king's holy hand has changed the nature of the food he blessed so that it 'cruelly killed the body | That it should by nature have fed' (vv. 3923–4). The perjurer chokes on God's incarnate creation in the act of denial. God is in himself glorious and marvellous ('merveillus') in revealing his secrets and reasons to his faithful (vv. 3933–6) and has the power to exercise his will (v. 3937):

> esmerveillier n'estuet,
> S'il merveillus, merveilles fait.
> (vv. 3939–40)

it is not a cause for marvel that [God], being marvellous, works marvels,

as he does with King Edward, himself the worker of so many 'merveilles' (vv. 3941–2). The successful consumption of the court amidst the hierarchical lavishness of its Easter feasting, on the other hand, becomes suddenly spectral in the face of the 'dulurus signe e mortel' (v. 4052) seen by Edward. His vision of the Seven Sleepers turning over preludes plague, starvation, and pagan conquest for the realm (vv. 4063–68). The mode of narration itself flexibly participates here in the revelation of meaning and form: in the first case it represents God's vengeance on Godwin with mimetic suddenness, but with Godwin distanced as a traitor and a perjurer, and the difficulties of identification with his viewpoint reinforced by Edward's cool response. In the second half of the diptych, the narrative heaps up details of a feast with which audience identification is far more likely, only to change its meaning and value with great suddenness, this time for the entire court and audience.

Thus, in *Edouard*, narrative qualities themselves participate in and articulate the nun of Barking's negotiations between historical event and significance, outer form and inner meaning. The purity of the virgin king's being, underscored by the perceptiveness of his own visionary gaze and his power to correct the sight of others, enables right reading and response to historical contingency. Edward himself functions as a sign of God's abundant grace ('sa plentive grace', v. 5328) for what the narrative, in an addition to Aelred, calls an England 'freed ['franchie'] and a church enriched ['enrichie']' (vv. 109–10) by Henry II, scion of this 'holy lineage' (v. 108).

Among the texts of the 'foyer' of vernacular hagiography provided by the women of Barking themselves, together with texts associated with the abbey (Adgar's Marian miracle collection and Guernes's Life of Becket), the *Vie d'Edouard* deserves a higher place and more discussion than the assumption of its apprenticeship status and derivative closeness to Aelred has generally allowed it to be given. There is still much work to be done on the interrelations of the texts and their manuscript and social contexts: there may well be a whole world of allusions and interplay between them which in the current state of knowledge can only be guessed at.[92] Recalling the presence of a de Valoignes abbess at Barking (d. 1213) and the presence, later in the thirteenth century, of three Barking texts in the hagiographic manuscript owned at the de Valoignes's family foundation of Campsey, it is also impossible not to hope that a great deal more remains to

---

[92] For example, Guernes de Pont-Ste-Maxence, writing at the start of the 1170s and in England to revise his Life of Becket with the patronage of Marie (Becket's sister and abbess of Barking 1173–5), proclaims that the nuns of Barking have fed him up and the abbess has given him an excellent palfrey (Walberg, *La Vie de saint Thomas le martyr par Guernes*, Appendix 2). Adgar's *Gracial* (a Marian miracle collection addressed to a knowledgeable female audience ('bone gent senee', v. 63) and especially to 'dame Mahaut' (*Gracial*, ed. Kunstmann, v. 65: probably Maud, natural daughter of Henry II, and abbess of Barking, appointed 1175–98 in succession to Marie Becket), shares its prologue topos of the communal nature of grace (vv. 36, vv. 37–40) with Clemence's *Catherine* (where Christ distributes his grace and goodness *in common*, vv. 3, 9, 10, 12) and also plays (against Guernes?) with the theme of the gifts he could expect from noble patrons—an expensive horse, an ermined tunic. These, Adgar says, are merely transitory compared with the grace he can receive by his dedication to God and the Virgin (vv. 51–9). See also Matthew Paris's description of the Countess of Arundel as a spur to the production of a saint's life (cited in Ch. 5, n. 20 above).

be said of the relations between these two houses and their texts.[93] Outside *Ancrene Wisse* and its manuscripts and associated texts there are few more important textual clusters in women's twelfth- and thirteenth-century literary culture in Britain than the Barking–Campsey nexus. But my immediate purpose in this chapter has been to point to some insular women's voices we are not yet hearing fully and to the high level of accomplishment at which they speak, through virgin hagiography, about the theology and the events of their time.

---

[93] Christiania de Valoignes was abbess 1200–13 (Loftus and Chettle, *History of Barking*, 34; *VCH, Essex* ii. 120).

Conclusion

By the time full account is taken of Anglo-Norman book production and readership, questions of women's literacies and literature will become still more complicated. The increase in Middle English records and texts in the fourteenth and fifteenth centuries has begun to be seen as a renaissance in female literacy. But not only are linear models of progress inadequate to the complexities of the late medieval period in themselves (under a conservative episcopal programme of controlled reading, the early fifteenth century, for instance, saw intellectual contraction as well as increased numbers of texts), but such models ignore the state of women's literary culture in the earlier period.[1] If there is a renaissance of women's writing in Middle English, is there a decline of women's writing in Anglo-Norman? of women's knowledge of texts composed in Continental French? And (especially in the light of Anglo-Norman-Latin mixes in nunnery documentation) how certain are we of the shape of the history of women's Latinity in insular culture?

Given the nature of the extant records, questions of mapping remain complex and unsettled. The modes and contexts of women's reading are not as susceptible to histories of institutional ownership as male monastic records and the 'unofficial' networks of women's families and friendships need to be included for a full account. But, in addition to this, the losses from the libraries and the records of female communities have been disproportionately large and what records remain have been given disproportionately low attention. David Bell's invaluable catalogue of books certainly provenanced to female communities between the ninth and the sixteenth centuries totals 144 manuscript books for all houses (excluding the Gilbertines) with a subtotal of 32 for the period between the eleventh century and the early fourteenth century: this is, notoriously, fewer than many single male monasteries possessed.[2] As Bell suggests, however, these figures are both conservative and disproportionately small in comparison with what will once have existed in nunnery libraries: moreover, among extant medieval books there are large numbers which were highly probably compiled for or owned by female communities but for which there happens to be no known provenance. Not only the richness of this literary culture, but the extent to which we can examine and estimate it is greater than has been thought. Other

---

[1] Nicholas Watson, 'Censorship and Cultural Change in Late-Medieval England: Vernacular Theology, the Oxford Translation Debate, and Arundel's Constitutions of 1409', *Speculum*, 70 (1995), 822–64.

[2] For these figures, which exclude printed books, see Bell, 34.

scholars have shown the importance of orality in women's literary culture and demonstrated new ways in which it can shape our understanding and add to our knowledge.[3]

The absences from our maps have both to be remembered and kept provisional. In medieval studies at large, one extant manuscript can make an enormous difference: in medieval women's writing one swallow has often to represent the summers of decades. An example of a house with, as far as is known, no surviving texts composed by women can none the less serve to exemplify a miniature diachronic history from the earlier to the later Middle Ages, even though a very small proportion of what must once have been extant is all that now survives. Amesbury, one of post-Conquest Britain's four nunneries of royal Anglo-Saxon foundation, remained of interest to post-Conquest royal houses. As noted in Chapter 1.5, Henry II refounded Amesbury as a Fontevrault house in 1177 as part of the price for dispensation from his vow of pilgrimage to Jerusalem. An episcopal visitation ordered by Henry conveniently discovered the nunnery to be scandalously mismanaged, and, after deposing the abbess and sacking many of the nuns, he allowed the remainder to join a group of twenty or so nuns imported from Fontevrault.[4] The Plantagenet and Lancastrian royal families continued to visit and to grant donations to the house. Alpesia, cousin of Henry III, became a nun there before 1233 and Eleanor of Brittany, Prince Arthur's sister, bequeathed her body to Amesbury, where it was taken when she died in 1241.[5] Eleanor of Provence and two of her granddaughters entered the house: Mary, fourth (or sixth) daughter of Edward I, on 15 August 1285 at the age of 6 and Eleanor, daughter of Beatrice of Brittany, on 25 March 1285, at the age of 10, while their grandmother took the veil in 1286.[6] Isabel, daughter of Henry of Lancaster, entered Amesbury in 1327, when Princess Mary, now in her early forties, was still there (they subsequently went on pilgrimage together).[7] Joan, daughter of Margaret Despencer and Piers Gaveston, died at Amesbury and was buried there by Mary.[8] Mary died in 1332, having acted as Fontevrault's vice-regent in England.[9] She is also supposed to have had a lover and to have been fond of gambling.[10] She provides a good example of how class privilege may mean that the experience even of a woman enclosed as a very young child involves more of a history than virgins are supposed to have.

[3] See, for example, Riddy, ' "Women talking about the things of God" '.
[4] See Ch. 1, n. 116 above.   [5] *VCH, Hampshire* ii. 245.
[6] On Eleanor's retirement and her arangements for her granddaughters, see Howell, *Eleanor of Provence*, 300–11.
[7] Mrs Mary Anne Everett Green, *Lives of the Princesses of England* (London: Colburn, 1849–55), ii. 434–5.
[8] Trivet, *Chronicle*, ed. Rutherford, 351.   [9] *VCH, Hampshire* ii. 249.
[10] These allegations were made in the divorce suit of John de Warenne (d. 1347), seventh earl of Surrey and courtier of Edward II: see Constance Bullock-Davies, *Menestrellorum multitudo: Minstrels at a Royal Feast* (Cardiff: University of Wales Press, 1978), 86–7.

As a Fontevrault house, Amesbury continued an already established inter-nationalism. Its contribution to the mortuary roll of Matilda, abbess of La Trinité in Caen and daughter of William the Conqueror, suggests that the nunnery early had international networks of contact in female houses.[11] These continued in dealings, correspondence, and the movement of royal and noble women between Fontevrault and the English house. Yet, even though William of Malmesbury spent so much of his life in a monastery some thirty miles distant, his only men-tion of Amesbury states that he knows only that, like Wherwell, it was founded in penance by Queen Ælftrudis, 'the murderess of St Edward', and that it had the relics of St Melor.[12]

Rather than expiating a female crime, however, Amesbury's pre-Conquest pro-minence and possible tenth-century refoundation is more likely to be linked to the deposit of relics, presumed to be St Melor's, at Amesbury church by preachers from Brittany.[13] The life of St Melor survives not only in several insular Latin versions of the eleventh and twelfth centuries, but in a fragmentary Anglo-Norman version almost certainly written for the nunnery.[14] The child prince and saint is mutilated at his uncle's command and loses his right arm and left foot. These are miraculously replaced with flexible silver prostheses (used by the saint to crack nuts for his playmates) and the uncle eventually decides that only decapitation will do. Melor's head produces springs wherever it touches the ground. The trans-formation of the limbs by which feudal fealty is sworn into reliquary-like silver and the fecundity of the martyred head certainly seem to encode the nunnery's economic improvement via the translation of relics. They also perhaps figure and thereby claim one of the functions of the old royal nunneries (which, in addition to their acting as *gynacea* for women due to produce the lineages of the future, also, as custodians to major relics and important burials, guarded and transmitted sources of wealth from the past).

Unlike Barking, Campsey, Romsey, and other female houses, Amesbury has no extant Latin theological books of learning and only one late Middle English manuscript is definitely provenanced to it. However, the numerous and lavish thirteenth-century psalters in Latin and Anglo-Norman made for the nunnery and for the noblewomen associated with it suggest a much richer textual and visual culture than is apparent from the relatively short list of surviving

[11] Delisle, *Rouleaux des morts*, 188–9, Titulus 13 (where, under the abbesses Heahfleda and Rachenilda, seven nuns, fifteen men, five women, and 'others of our friends' are named).

[12] 'Sancti Eduardi interfectrice' (*GP* i. 188). Melor's lineage and sanctity is also an unknown quantity ('cuius prosapiae cuiusve sanctimoniæ incertum mihi', ibid.).

[13] On the Amesbury relics see A. H. Diverres, 'An Anglo-Norman Life of St Melor', *The National Library of Wales Journal*, 15 (1967–8), 167–76 (168). On the Breton connections see further G. H. Doble, *The Saints of Cornwall*, part 3, 'Saint Melor, Patron of Mylor and Linkinhorne' (Oxford: Holywell Press, 1966), 20–52.

[14] The extant manuscript, the Bettisfield roll, is mid 14th c., but the Life was written earlier: Diverres, 'Life of St Melor', 167, 174.

manuscripts definitely provenanced to the house, a culture in which female vertical and horizontal networks of book ownership and transmission can be glimpsed.[15] A London psalter of *c*.1270 with scenes from the passion, a portrait of St Dunstan, and a feast of Melor was probably made for Eleanor of Provence (perhaps for her entry to Amesbury as a widow after the death of Henry III), and was given or bequeathed by her to her granddaughter, Eleanor of Brittany, who became Abbess of Fontevrault.[16] The early thirteenth-century Imola Psalter, probably made in Winchester, includes, in addition to its Amesbury Litany, a controversial illustrated genealogy of St Anne and ends with the death of Eleanor of Aquitaine in 1204: it may have spent part of its history at Amesbury.[17] The early thirteenth-century Oxford Psalter and Hymnal with its highly graded Melor feast, and a thirteenth-century psalter and a fourteenth-century Breviarium, both now only fragmentary, were Amesbury books.[18] One surviving book adapted for Amesbury, the Amesbury Psalter of *c*.1250–5, constitutes as interesting a 'vision of history'—that is, of salvation history—as many more 'literary' texts. The manuscript has four opening full-page miniatures which alternate a nun (or, perhaps, as appropriate for the Fontevrault order, a widow, or vowess) kneeling to the Virgo lactans and to Christ in Majesty with the Annunciation and the Crucifixion interspersed. Explicit salvation history is also available in the miniatures of a Tree of Jesse, with David harping, the Virgin, Christ, prophets, Moses, and a Sibyl.[19]

In a fourteenth-century Amesbury Book of Hours, French devotions and prayers supplement the offices (so, for instance, a prayer to 'seinte anne gloriouse', 'Seietz mamie 7 mon escu | En ceste pilgrimage' on f. 10r col. b–f. 10v col. a).[20] Eleanor of Provence was a strong supporter of the Dominicans and also of the Franciscans, both of whom continued to have patronage from royal British women: in a house so closely associated with the Plantagenet royal family, it is not surprising to find, preceding the Hours of the Virgin (f. 18v), a courtly and affective prayer addressed to St Francis of Assisi:

[15] See Bell, s.v. Amesbury for a list of provenanced books.

[16] Eleanor of Provence died in 1291, a year after her daughter-in-law Eleanor of Castile: Howell, *Eleanor of Provence*, 307. On her books, chivalric and devotional, see ibid., 80–99; for Eleanor of Castile, see Parsons, 'Of Queens, Courts, and Books'. Eleanor of Provence is also thought to be the patron of a psalter possibly made in London *c*.1270 with an illustrated calendar including Melor: see *EGM [II] 1250–85*, iv. 2, no. 152a and b, 140–1 (New York, Metropolitan Museum Acc. 22. 24. I + Cleveland, Museum of Art Acc. 24.427).

[17] See *EGM [I] 1190–1250*, iv. 1, no. 26, 74–5 (Imola, Biblioteca Comunale MS 100).

[18] *EGM [I] 1190–1250*, iv. 1, no. 27, 75 (Oxford, Bodleian Library MS Liturg. 407; Windsor Castle, Jackson collection 3: see Ker, *Medieval Libraries* s.v. Amesbury, and Watson, *Supplement*, 1); the Breviarium (4 folios) is in London in the ownership of Christopher de Hamel.

[19] Oxford, All Souls MS 6: the calendar includes two feasts for Melor with high grading, but Morgan argues that the book was adapted rather than made for Amesbury as it does not have a full Amesbury Calendar: *EGM [II] 1250–85*, iv. 2, no. 101, 59–61 (60–1).

[20] Cambridge University Library MS Ee.6.16 (the Amesbury Hours). 'Audree' is included in the calendar (f. 16v) and 'Edeldreda' in the litany (f. 66r).

Doux sire seint franceis ke ihu tant amastes
Et de sa seinte passiun nuit e iour pensastes
ke en *vos*tre seintisme corps lenpreinte portastes
Lamour ihu crist tant vous eschaufa
Et *vos*tre cuer de pite gracious eslumina
ke en meins e pies e coste dehors se moustra
Et lui amant en semblance de ami conforma . . .

(f. 171r)[21]

Sweet lord saint Francis who loved Jesus so much and thought night and day of his passion so that in your holy body you bore its imprint: the love of Jesus Christ so kindled you and so illumined your gracious heart with pity that it was manifested in your hands and feet and side, and, loving him, conformed you to the appeareance of your beloved . . .

It was not until 1334 or later, when Princess Mary was in her forties, that Trevet wrote his Chronicle for her. The Chronicle extends from creation to 1334, and maintains simultaneous international and regional and sacred and secular perspectives throughout. It combines detailed accounts of Mercian, Wessex, Kentish, and Essex regnal families with Roman and other Continental concerns. The Chronicle includes a transmission story for the text explicated to Mary's mother, Eleanor of Provence, by John Pecham, Archbishop of Canterbury, in his Anglo-Norman version of Pseudo-Dionysius: the emperor of Constantinople in the time of the emperor Lewis (son of Charlemagne)

maunda les livres Seint dionis de Arriopage, q'il escript des ordres et *gerarchies* de aungles. Ceux livres a grant joie furent resceu a Paris en la feste Seint Dionis, et mesmes la nyt estoient sanez dis e neof malades.[22]

[Louis] sent the books of St Dennis the Areopagite which he wrote on the orders and hierarchies of angels. These books were received with great joy in Paris at the feast of St Dennis and that very night nineteen sick people were cured.

It is to Mary that the Anglo-Latin and Anglo-French traditions, whose co-presence is obscured in our literary histories, are made visible: in the time of the same emperor, Trevet continues, 'Seint Kenelm, le fitz Kenulf, fu occis et martirize treiterousement en sa enfaunce par Ascabert, procuratour du roialme de Merce, par l'abett et l'envie Quendrithe sa soer' ('St Kenelm, the son of Kenwulf, was treacherously killed and martyred in infancy by Ashbert, procurator of the realm of Mercia, through the prompting and because of the jealousy of his

---

[21] From f. 199v of the Amesbury Hours, prayers and visualizations of the passion in French, interspersed with Latin quotations and exclamations, continue to present Christ's suffering and feminized body to their audiences: thus for instance, Christ is visualized as 'si descolorez *que vus* resemblastes un vil mesel, *vn* ord leprous. *vus* q*i* les eungeles e totes creatures en ciel e en tere enbelisez e enluminez e choisez de vostre gloriose beaute' (f. 203v).

[22] *Chronicle*, ed. Rutherford, 251–2; henceforth referenced by page number in the text. (The patron saint Denys and the earlier Areopagite are routinely conflated in later medieval French lives of the saint.)

sister Quendritha', p. 253). For Mary too, Elizabeth of Schönau is also a presence, although her translation into Anglo-Norman culture has remained relatively hidden from us: as Trevet explains,

En le temps cist Eugenie [Pope Eugene III, 1145–53], en l'evesche de Trevers en un abbeie q'est appelé Stonange [Schönau], estoit famous une nonayne Elizabeth, qe vivoit en grande seintete, et veoit plusours avisions, en quels lui estoient mouustréz multz des merveilles, qe d'autres morteus n'estoient conues, de queles ele escript un livre, mes la court de Rome ne le voleit autorizer ne confermer. Entre autres choses disoit ele qe par revelacion lui fu moustré que le corps Noster Dame fu pris en ciel le qarauntisme jour apres qe dieuz avoit pris a lui sa alme. (p. 305)

In the time of this Eugene, in the bishopric of Trier in an abbey called Schönau, there was a famous nun Elizabeth, who lived in great holiness and saw several visions, in which there were shown to her many marvels unknown to other mortals, and about which she wrote a book, but which the papal curia did not want to authorize or confirm. Among other things she said that it had been shown to her as a revelation that the body of Our Lady had been taken into heaven the fortieth day after God had taken her soul to himself.

   Under Mary's protection, Isabel, daughter of Henry of Lancaster, also entered Amesbury in 1327 (her father's authorship of the penitential treatise *Livre des seynts medicines* still some eighteen years ahead in 1352). Apart from the psalters associated with Amesbury and its inhabitants, no further texts are known from the house in the fourteenth and fifteenth centuries, though it is difficult to suppose that its inmates had no other texts than psalters and no awareness of courtly literature. Amesbury certainly retained its associations with royalty, since it is there that Gwenevere is shown, dying in her black and white habit, in the fourteenth-century stanzaic *Morte Arthure* and in Malory's fifteenth-century reworking of this in the final book of his *Morte d'Arthure*. But it is difficult to associate any further texts with Amesbury until the late fifteenth or early sixteenth century when an English homiletic letter was composed for two sisters there.[23] This work's exegesis of the vows of stability, obedience, and chastity postulates seamlessly ahistorical conduct and aspirations. Its explication of double cloister, for instance, is not dissimilar, though less brilliantly developed and rhetoricized, to the *Guide for Anchoresses'* inner and outer rules:

ye know wel yf a gardyn be well closyd abowte and surely, nothyng can cume theryn but from above. Soo in to that person whych is wel closyd wyth bodely chastyte shold non thoughte cum but heuynly and from aboue. For yff a gardyn wer neuer [f. 24r] so well closyd yf hit be full of swyne and vnclene bests the closure prophyte nothyng to the clenys of the gardyn. Soo yff bestly mouyng of vnclennys hayue domynacion and rome in oons mynd, the bodely chastity profytyth lytill or nothyng. Therfore hit was not only seyd, 'ortus conclusus soror mea sponsa', that is to sey that that person wych

---

[23] Yvonne Parrey, 'Devoted Disciples of Christ: Early Sixteenth-Century Religious Life in the Nunnery at Amesbury', *Bulletin of the Institute of Historical Research*, 67 (1994), 240–8.

is sust*er* to C*r*ist by his yncarnac*i*on and chosyn by g*ra*ce to be his spouse may not be oonly as a gardyn closyd w*i*t oon closur*e*, that is to sey chastyte of bodey, but also 'ort*us* conclus*us*' a geyne: that is to sey closyd also w*i*t chastyt*e* of mynd a*nd* thowghte. (Oxford, Bodleian Library, MS Add. 42, ff. 23v–24r, abbreviations expanded, punctuation mine)

This is further illustrated by Seneca's story of a vestal virgin whose mental dwelling on the pleasure of marriage caused her to lose 'the m*e*ryt of hure v*i*rginyte' (f. 26r).[24] The *longues durées* of virginity writing continue in evidence here, though the inscribed authorial figure (a priest) and his audience (his 'deare susterys' Mary and Anne, in their 'scole of Cryste') carry different class implications and intertextualities than the works with which this book began.[25]

Amesbury suggests both a partially lost history of textual production and reception and the possibility of different positionings for more visible texts. It also raises the question of differing continuities and rates of change in different textual communities. The surface presented to modern literary histories by St Kenelm, for instance, has been very small for so important a figure in the post-Conquest historiography of the ancient Mercian dynasty: his brief appearance in the *Nun's Priest's Tale* as an exemplum of the prophetic power of dreams is barely visible, contained as it is within a series of narrative frames (an exemplum retold by a cock to a hen within an exemplum told by a priest to pilgrims within a tale told by a pilgrim called Chaucer within a poem called *The Canterbury Tales*).[26] Melor, the child patron of Amesbury, brings with him a Breton heritage far less visibly and prolifically captured than the appropriation of Arthur by neighbouring Glastonbury, and he too occupies an almost invisibly small place in modern literary history. Yet both these child saints were key figures of *translatio*, linguistic, economic, and political: they can figure the alternative narratives of those who were not history's victors, though they may have been very far from being its victims.

As this book has suggested, many strands contribute to the literary histories to be investigated here. The gathering of texts and social and cultural networks around Barking and Campsey is particularly important, but many other individual female communities would repay further literary study attentive to all the linguistic registers traceable within them: so too would further comparative considerations of the literary culture of women within particular orders. (It is, for instance, striking that so high a proportion of extant Latin nunnery cartularies are from the thirteenth-century houses of Augustinian canonesses at a period

---

[24] *Excerpta Controversiarum*, VI, no. 8 (ascribed to Seneca, 'Libro declamacionum sexto', in the manuscript, f. 26r), see *L. Annaei Senecae oratorum et rhetorum*, ed. H. J. Müller (Vienna, 1887), 264.
[25] See further *The Idea of the Vernacular*, ed. Wogan-Browne, Watson, Taylor, and Evans, where the prologue to this letter is edited in Part 2, no. 9.
[26] On the Latin traditions for Kenelm see Rosalind Love, *Three Eleventh-Century Anglo-Latin Saints' Lives*, pp. lxxxix–cxxxix.

of vigorous foundation by noblewomen and that many of these houses owned extant manuscripts of French and, later, Middle English texts.) England had no known beguine communities, but it does have many communities formed and/or inhabited by women that share some aspects of the characteristically 'intermediary' nature of communities in the Continental thirteenth-century 'women's movement'.[27] Since so many nunnery documents (even of the relatively small proportion that survive) still remain unedited and there is no history of the Augustinian canonesses in England such possibilities must remain speculative for some time.

As well as house literary histories, the literary histories of more families than the relatively well-studied royal women of England and their reading and patronage should repay investigation. There are signs, for instance, that high literacy was a tradition among the women born or married into the de Vere family over several generations in the thirteenth century: Alice de Vere, though a laywoman, owned one of the most liturgically complex of the extant early books of hours, while the prioress of Hedingham commemorated in the elegantly illustrated mortuary roll of the thirteenth century was Lucy (almost certainly a de Vere daughter).[28] Both synchronic studies of particular groups and texts and diachronic studies of families' and monastic houses' literary histories have contributions to make to the intricate mosaic that needs building up.

Apart from their copying into the Campsey collection, the other directions of dispersal for the Barking lives suggest, however, that there is not just a vertical chronology of devotional and theological texts and books to be considered here. Clemence of Barking's *Catherine* appears in a late thirteenth-century Picard version at about the same time as the Campsey manuscript, suggesting that one context of women's literary culture in this period must be that of the monastic, court, and family networks criss-crossing the channel.[29] The Campsey and the Picard version of *Catherine*, that is, take place not only at the same date, but arguably within the same cultural framework, rather than in the two different nations and disciplines to which the categories of modern scholarship have assigned them. The Barking Life of the Confessor, for instance, not only replaces part of Wace's narrative in a manuscript of the *Roman de Brut*, but is given a fourteenth-century prose *remaniement* in a manuscript belonging to the counts of St Pol (a family with many insular connections and later to become, via one of its wealthy widows, Marie de St Pol, patron to Jesus College, Cambridge).[30]

---

[27] For these terms see Grundmann, tr. Rowan, *Religious Movements in the Middle Ages*.

[28] For the de Vere family, see *CP* x, s.v. Oxford. For Alice de Vere (d. 1310) and her high liturgical literacy see Claire Donovan, 'The Mise-en-Page of Early Books of Hours in England', in Brownrigg (ed.), *Medieval Book Production*, 147–61 (150) and *The de Brailes Hours*, 196–200 (197); for an earlier Alice de Vere see Barrow, 'A Twelfth-Century Bishop and Literary Patron', 177–8; for Lucy de Vere see *Mon.* iv. 436–7; for Anne de Vere, abbess of Barking 1295–1318, see Loftus and Chettle, *History of Barking*, 36–8 and *VCH*, Essex ii. 121.

[29] See p. 230 n. 22 above.

[30] For this copy of Wace's *Brut* see Ch. 7, n. 77. On the prose *remaniement* see Ch. 7, n. 49.

This speaks again to the way in which eastern England and north-west France and Flanders are a single region for many purposes, and also to the intertextuality of hagiography and history which remains a part of women's texts and literary culture as it does of hagiographic writing in general. Comparisons with women in neighbouring regions (and in an era where waterborne transport is the most efficient and swift, north-west France and the Low Countries can be counted as neighbouring) may be illuminating not only for the contrasts that have traditionally been made between insular and Continental women's religious lives, but for the connections and continuities.

Indeed, it is a question how far trends and generalized changes can usefully be observed in the current state of knowledge: rather than global pictures, we may do better to think of many specific literacies of different kinds within various social networks and in different mixes of linguistic registers. It is thus more helpful at the moment to think of women's literary culture rather than their literary history in the period: a sense of the possible, the probable, and the securely documentable and arguable will take a great deal of further research to establish. The scratching of surfaces represented by the present book is both premature and long overdue.

Bibliography

PRIMARY SOURCES

Note: Editions of saints' lives and works are listed under the name of the saint in question; medieval authors are listed under their first name; anonymous medieval texts are usually listed alphabetically according to their title followed by their editor, even when the edition appears in a journal: collections and anthologies and non-medieval titles are listed under editors' names.

Brussels, Bibl. royale, MS 2057–62
Cambridge:
  St John's College MS 68
  Trinity College MS B.14.39
  Trinity College MS O.2.29
  Trinity College MS R.14.7
  University Library MS Addit. 7220
Cardiff, Public Library MS 1. 381, ff. 81–146.
London, British Library:
  Additional 70513 (*olim* Welbeck I C 1)
  Additional 27866
  Cotton Claudius D.III
  Cotton Domitian A.XI
  Cotton Vitellius F.VII
  Egerton 613
  Egerton 2104A
  Egerton 2104B
  Egerton 2710
  Egerton 2849
  Lansdowne 436
  Royal 17A xxvii
Oxford, Bodleian Library:
  Addit. A. 42
  Bodley 82
  Bodley 654
  Bodley 779
  Bodley 870
  Digby 34
  Dugdale 18
  Rawlinson poet. 234
Paris, Bibliothèque Nationale:
  fonds fr. 902
  fonds fr. 1038

fonds fr. 1416
fonds fr. 6276
fonds fr. 19525
fonds fr. 24766
nouv. acq. fr. 4503

Abbey of the Holy Ghost, in N. F. Blake (ed.), *Medieval English Religious Prose*, York Medieval Texts (London: Edward Arnold and Evanston, Ill.: Northwestern University Press, 1972), 88–102.

ABELARD and HELOISE, 'The Fifth and Sixth Letters of Abelard and Heloise', ed. J. T. Muckle, *Mediaeval Studies*, 17 (1955), 240–81.

—— 'Letter Seven from Abelard to Heloise', ed. T. P. McLaughlin, *Mediaeval Studies*, 18 (1956), 241–92.

The Letters of Abelard and Heloise, tr. Betty Radice (Harmondsworth: Penguin Books, 1974).

Acta sanctorum quotquot toto orbe coluntur . . . , ed. J. Bollandus and G. Henschenius (Antwerp, 1643–): *Acta sanctorum: Editio novissima*, ed. J. Carnandet *et al.* (Paris: Palmé, 1863–).

ADAMS, NORMA and DONEHUE, CHARLES, JR. (eds.), *Select Cases from the Ecclesiastical Courts of the Province of Canterbury c.1200–1301* (London: Selden Society, 1981).

ADGAR, *Le Gracial*, ed. Pierre Kunstmann (Ottawa: Editions de l'Université d'Ottawa, 1981).

Ælfric's Lives of Saints, ed. W. W. Skeat, EETS os 76 and 82 (London, 1881 and 1885; repr. as one vol. 1962).

AELRED, *Vita Aedwardi*, PL195.738–90.

AGNES, ST, *The Old French Lives of Saint Agnes and Other Vernacular Versions of the Middle Ages*, ed. A. J. Denomy (Cambridge, Mass.: Harvard University Press, 1938).

ALAIN DE LILLE, *De arte praedicandi*, PL210.109–98.

—— *Alain de Lille: The Art of Preaching*, tr. Gillian Evans, Cistercian Studies Series 23 (Kalamazoo, Mich.: Cistercian Publications, 1981).

ALBAN, ST, *see* James, M. R.; Matthew Paris.

ALDHELM, *De virginitate*, in *Aldhelm: The Prose Works*, tr. Michael Lapidge and Michael Herren (Ipswich and Totowa, NJ: Brewer, 1979).

AMBROSE, *De virginibus*, PL16.187–232.

—— *Ep.* V, PL16.891–8.

Amys e Amyllyoun, ed. Hideka Fukui, ANTS Plain Texts Series (London, 1990).

ANGIER OF ST FRIDESWIDE, 'La Vie de saint Grégoire le Grand traduite du Latin par Frère Angier, religieux de Sainte-Frideswide', ed. Paul Meyer, *Romania*, 12 (1883), 145–208.

Anglo-Norman Lapidaries, ed. Paul Studer and Joan Evans (Paris: Champion, 1924).

ANSELM, ST, *S. Anselmi Cantuariensis Archiepiscopi Opera Omnia*, ed. Franciscus Salesius Schmitt, 5 vols. (Edinburgh: Nelson and Sons, 1946).

—— *Anselm of Canterbury: The Major Works*, tr. Brian Davies and Gillian R. Evans (Oxford and New York: Oxford University Press, 1998).

—— *The Letters of Anselm of Canterbury*, tr. and annot. Walter Fröhlich (Kalamazoo, Mich.: Cistercian Publications, 1994).

The Ancrene Riwle: A Treatise on the Rules and Duties of Monastic Life Edited and Translated from a Semi-Saxon MS of the Thirteenth Century, ed. James Morton, Camden Society Publications 57 (London, 1853).

The English Text of the Ancrene Riwle, Cotton Cleopatra C.vi, ed. E. J. Dobson, EETS os 267 (London, 1972).

Ancrene Riwle: Introduction and Part One, ed. R. W. Ackermann and Roger Dahood, Medieval and Renaissance Texts and Studies (Binghamton: SUNY, 1984).

The French Text of the 'Ancrene Riwle': Trinity College Cambridge MS R.14.7, ed. W. H. Trethewey, EETS os 240 (London, 1958).

The French Text of the 'Ancrene Riwle': British Museum MS Cotton Vitellius F vii, ed. J. A. Herbert, EETS os 219 (London, 1944).

Ancrene Wisse, Parts Six and Seven, ed. Geoffrey Shepherd (London: Nelson, 1959; rev. edn. Exeter: Exeter University Press, 1985).

Ancrene Wisse: MS Corpus Christi College Cambridge 402, ed. J. R. R. Tolkien, EETS os 249 (London, 1962).

Annales monastici, ed. H. R. Luard, RS 36 (London, 1864–9).

AQUINAS, *Summa theologiae* (London and New York: Blackfriars with Eyre and Spottiswoode and McGraw-Hill, 1964–), various editors and translators.

ASPIN, I. T. (ed.), *Anglo-Norman Political Songs*, ANTS 11 (Oxford, 1953).

AUDREY, ST, *Vie sainte Audrée, see* Marie [of ?Chatteris, of ?Barking].

AUGUSTINE, *City of God*, tr. H. Bettenson (Harmondsworth: Penguin, 1984).

—— *De civitate Dei*, PL41.13–804.

—— *De sancta virginitate*, PL40.395–427.

—— *De trinitate*, PL42.818–1098.

—— *Summa virtutem de remediis anime*, ed. Siegfried Wenzel (Athens: University of Georgia Press, 1984).

BARING-GOULD, SABINE, *Virgin Saints and Martyrs* (London: Hutchinson, 1900).

BARLOW, *see* Edward, the Confessor, St.

BARRATT, ALEXANDRA (ed.), *Women's Writing in Middle English*, Longman Annotated Texts (London: Longman, 1992).

Bede's Ecclesiastical History of the English Church and People, ed. Bertram Colgrave and R. A. B. Mynors (Oxford: Clarendon Press, 1969).

BELL, ALEXANDER, 'The Anglo-French *De Sanctis*', *Notes and Queries*, 12th ser. 5 (1919), 281–3.

BENEDICT, ST, *The Anglo-Norman Rule of St Benedict*, ed. Ruth Dean and M. D. Legge (Oxford: Blackwell, 1946).

BENEIT, *La Vie de saint Thomas le Martyr par Beneit, poème anglo-normand du XIIème siècle publié d'après tous les manuscrits*, ed. Börje Schlyter, Études romanes de Lund 4 (Lund: C. W. K. Gleerup, 1941).

BLAAUW, *see* Richard of Chichester, St.

BOZON, *see* Nicholas Bozon.

BRENDAN, ST, *The Anglo-Norman Voyage of St Brendan*, ed. Ian Short and Brian Merrilees (Manchester: Manchester University Press, 1979).

BUCKLAND, ROBERT, *Lives of Women Saints of Our Contrie of Englond (c.1610–1615)*, ed. Carl Horstmann, EETS os 86 (London, 1886).

BUTLER, ALBAN, *Lives of the Saints*, ed. Herbert Thurston and Donald Attwater (Westminster: Christian Classics, 1956).

Calendar of the Close Rolls Preserved in the Public Record Office (London: PRO Texts and Calendars, 1896–).

Calendar of Entries in the Papal Registers Relating to Great Britain and Ireland, ed. W. H. Bliss, C. Johnson, and J. A. Twemlow (London: HMSO, 1890–).

Calendar of Papal Bulls, ed. W. H. Bliss and C. Johnson (London: HMSO, 1890–).

Calendar of the Patent Rolls Preserved in the Public Record Office (London: PRO Texts and Calendars, 1891–).

Cartulaire de l'Abbeye de Conques en Rouergue, ed. Gustave Desjardins, Documents historiques publiés par la Société de l'École des chartes (Paris: Picard, 1879).

The Cartulary of Canonsleigh Abbey: Harleian MS no. 3660: A Calendar, ed. V. M. London, *Devon and Cornwall Record Society* 10 (Torquay: Devonshire Press, 1965).

The Cartulary of Chatteris Abbey, ed. Clare Breay (Woodbridge and Rochester, NY: Boydell, 1999).

CATHERINE, ST, *La Passion de sainte Catherine d'Alexandrie par Aumeric, éditée d'après le ms 945 de la Bibliothèque de Tours*, ed. Olivier Naudeau, Beihefte zur Zeitschrift für Romanische Philologie 186 (Tübingen: Max Niemeyer, 1982).

—— 'La Vie de sainte Catherine d'Alexandrie', ed. H. A. Todd, *PMLA* 15 (1900), 17–73. *See also* Clemence of Barking; Katherine, St.

Charters and Documents Illustrating the History of the Cathedral, City, and Diocese of Salisbury, ed. W. R. Jones and W. D. Macray, RS 97 (London, 1891).

CHRISTINA OF MARKYATE, *The Life of Christina of Markyate, a Twelfth-century Recluse*, ed. and tr. C. H. Talbot (Oxford: Clarendon Press, 1959, repr. with additions, 1987).

The Chronicle of Bury St Edmunds 1212–1301, ed. Antonia Gransden (London and Edinburgh: Nelson, 1964).

The Chronicle of the Election of Hugh, Abbot of Bury St Edmunds and Later Bishop of Ely, ed. R. M. Thomson (Oxford: Clarendon Press, 1974).

CLEMENCE OF BARKING, *The Life of Saint Catherine by Clemence of Barking*, ed. William MacBain, ANTS 18 (Oxford, 1964).

—— *The Life of St Catherine*, in Wogan-Browne and Burgess (trs.), *Virgin Lives*.

CLEMENT, ST, 'La Vie de seint Clement pape', ed. Nora K. Willson, Ph.D. thesis (Cambridge University, 1952).

La Court de Paradis: Poème anonyme du xiiie siècle, ed. Eva Vilamo-Pentti, Annales Academiae Scientiarum Fennicae Ser. B, t. 79.1 (Helsinki: Société de la littérature finnoise, 1953).

Corset, see Rober le chapelain.

CYPRIAN, *De habitu virginum*, PL4.451–78.

DAY, MILDRED LEAKE (ed.), *The Rise of Gawain, Nephew of Arthur (De ortu Walwanii nepotis Arturi)* (New York: Garland, 1992).

DEMBOWSKI, *see* Mary of Egypt, St.

DENIS PIRAMUS, *La Vie Seint Edmund le Rei, poème anglo-normand de XIIème siècle par Denis Piramus*, ed. Hilding Kjellman (Göteborg: Elander, 1935).

The Early Charters of Eastern England, ed. C. R. Hart (Leicester: Leicester University Press, 1966).

EDITH, ST, *S. Editha sive Chronicon Vilodunense im Wiltshire Dialekt*, ed. Carl Horstmann (Heilbronn: Henninger, 1883).

EDMUND OF CANTERBURY, ST, *Mirour de seinte eglyse (St Edmund of Abingdon's Speculum Ecclesiae)*, ed. A. D. Wilshere, ANTS 40 (London, 1982).
See also Matthew Paris.

EDMUND, KING and MARTYR, ST, *La Passiun de Seint Edmund*, ed. Judith Grant, ANTS 36 (London, 1978).
See also Denis Piramus.

EDWARD THE CONFESSOR, ST, *The Life of King Edward Who Rests at Westminster*, ed. Frank Barlow (London and New York: Nelson, 1962; 4th edn. Oxford: Clarendon Press, 1992).

—— *La Vie d'Edouard le confesseur, poème anglo-normand du XIIe siecle*, ed. Östen Södergård (Uppsala: Almqvist & Wiksell, 1948).
See also Matthew Paris.

EDWARD, KING and MARTYR, ST, *Edward King and Martyr*, ed. Christine E. Fell, Leeds Texts and Monographs, NS (Leeds University: School of English, 1972).

ELISABETH OF HUNGARY, ST, 'La Vie de sainte Elisabeth d'Hongrie', ed. Ludwig Karl, *ZRPh* 24 (1910), 295–314.
See also Nicholas Bozon.

ELIZABETH OF SCHÖNAU, 'Poem on the Assumption', ed. J. P. Strachey, in J. P. Strachey, H. J. Chaytor, and O. H. Prior (eds.) *Poem on the Assumption, Poem on the Day of Judgement, Divisiones Mundi*, Cambridge Anglo-Norman Texts (Cambridge: Cambridge University Press, 1924), 13–26.

Eneas: Roman du XIIe siècle, ed. J.-J. Salverda de Grave, 2 vols., CFMA (Paris: Champion, 1925–9).

Eructavit: An Old French Metrical Paraphrase of Psalm XLIV, ed. T. A. Jenkins, Gesellschaft für romanische Literatur, Bd. 20 (Dresden: Gesellschaft für romanische Literatur, 1909).

FAITH, ST, 'Vie anglo-normande de sainte Foy par Simon de Walsingham', ed. A. T. Baker, *Romania*, 66 (1940–1), 49–84.

—— *Liber Miraculorum Sancte Fidis: Edizione critica et commento*, ed. Luca Robertini (Spoleto: Centro italiano di studi sull'alto medioevo, 1994).

—— *The Book of Sainte Foy*, tr. Pamela Sheingorn (Philadelphia: University of Pennsylvania Press, 1995).

FEIN, SUSANNA GREER (ed.), *Moral Love Songs and Laments* (Kalamazoo, Mich.: Medieval Institute Publications, 1998).

Flores Historiarum, ed. H. R. Luard, RS 95 (London, 1890).

FRANCIS, ST, *The Life of Saint Francis of Assisi: A Critical Edition of the Ms Paris, Bibl. Nat. fonds françaises 2094*, ed. Janice M. Pindar (Rome: Archivum Franciscanum Historicum, 1995).

—— 'The Lives of St. Francis of Assisi contained in MSS BN fr. 19531, 2094, 13505', ed. Janice M. Pindar, D.Phil. thesis (University of Oxford, 1985).

—— 'Fragments d'une Vie de saint François d'Assise en vers anglo-normands', ed. Louise Stone, *Archivum Franciscanum Historicum*, 31 (1938), 48–58.

French Text of the Ancrene Riwle, see Ancrene Riwle.

GAIMAR, *L'Estoire des Engleis*, ed. Alexander Bell, ANTS 14–16 (Oxford, 1960).

—— *Lestorie des engles solum la translacion Maistre Geffrei Gaimar*, ed. T. D. Hardy and Charles Trice Martin, RS 91 (London, 1888).

GAUTIER DE COINCI, *Le sermon en vers de la chasteé as nonains de Gautier de Coinci*, ed. Tauno Nurmela (Helsinki: Société de la littérature finnoise, 1937).

Gesta Abbatum monasterii Sancti Albani, ed. H. T. Riley, RS 28 (London, 1867–9).

GEOFFREY OF BURTON, *Life of St Modwenna*, ed. Robert Bartlett (Oxford: Oxford University Press, forthcoming).

GEOFFREY OF MONMOUTH, *The Historia Regum Britannie of Geoffrey of Monmouth*, ed. Neil Wright, vol. 1 (Cambridge: Brewer, 1985).

GEORGE, ST, 'La Vie de saint George', in John E. Matzke (ed.) *Les Œuvres de Simund de Freine*, SATF (Paris, 1889), 61–117.

GILBERT OF SEMPRINGHAM, ST, *The Book of St Gilbert*, ed. and tr. Raymonde Foreville and Gillian Keir (Oxford: Clarendon Press, 1987).

[GILES OF ROME, tr. Henri de Guachi], *Li Livres du gouvernement des rois*, ed. Samuel P. Molenaer (London: Macmillan, 1899).

GILES, ST, *La Vie de saint Gilles*, ed. G. Paris and A. Bos, SATF (Paris, 1881).

—— 'Un fragment de *La vie de saint Gilles*', ed. L. Brandin, *Romania*, 33 (1904).

GODARD, *see* John Godard.

GOSCELIN OF ST BERTIN, 'Texts of Jocelin of Canterbury which Relate to the History of Barking Abbey', ed. Marvin L. Colker, *Studia Monastica*, 7 (1965), 383–460.

—— *The Liber Confortatorius of Goscelin of St Bertin*, ed. C. H. Talbot, *Analecta monastica*, ser. 3, Studia Anselmiana 37, ed. M. M. Lebreton, J. Leclercq, and C. H. Talbot (Rome: Pontifical Institute of St Anselm, 1955), 1–117.

Des granz geantz, ed. Georgina Brereton (Oxford: Blackwell, 1937).

GREGORY OF ELY, 'Gregory of Ely's Verse Life and Miracles of St Æthelthryth', ed. Pauline Thompson and Elizabeth Stevens, *AB* 106 (1988), 333–90.

GREGORY, ST, *see* Angier of St Frideswide.

GROSJEAN, P., 'Codicis Gothani Appendix', *AB* 58 (1940), 177–204.

GROSSETESTE, *see* Robert Grosseteste.

GUERNES DE PONT-SAINTE-MAXENCE, *La Vie de saint Thomas le Martyr par Guernes de Pont-Sainte-Maxence*, ed. E. Walberg (Lund: Gleerup; Oxford: Oxford University Press, 1922).

GUILLAUME LE CLERC, *Le Besant de Dieu de Guillaume le clerc de Normandie*, ed. Pierre Ruelle (Brussels: Éditions de l'Université de Bruxelles, 1973).

—— 'La Vie de Madeleine', ed. R. Reinsch, *Archiv*, 64 (1880), 85–94.

GUILLAUME LE MARÉCHAL, *see* William Marshal.

Hali Meiðhad, ed. Bella Millett, EETS os 284 (London, 1982).

HENRY OF HUNTINGDON, *Historia Anglorum: The History of the English People*, ed. Diana Greenway (Oxford: Clarendon Press, 1996).

HERBERT DE BOSHAM, *Homilia in festo S. Thomae*, PL190.1403–14.

HERMAN DE VALENCIENNES, *Li Romanz de Dieu et de sa mère de Herman de Valenciennes*, ed. Ina Spiele (Leyde: Presse Universitaire de Leyde, 1975).

HILDEBERT OF LAVARDIN, *Ep.* 19, PL171.191–2.

HILL, BETTY, *see* 'Salut et solace de l'amour Jesu'.

HONORIUS 'AUGUSTODUNENSIS', *Elucidarium*, PL172.1109–75.

—— *Speculum ecclesie*, PL172.807–1108.

HORRALL, SARAH M. (gen. ed.), *The Southern Version of the Cursor Mundi*, 5 vols. (Ottawa: University of Ottawa Press, 1978–2000).

Horstmann, Carl (ed.), *Sammlung Altenglischer Legenden* (Heilbronn: Henninger, 1878).

Hugh of Lincoln, Little St, *Hugues de Lincoln: Recueil de ballades anglo-normandes et écossaises relatives au meurtre de cet enfant commis par les juifs en mcclv*, ed. F. Michel (Paris: Silvestre; London: Pickering, 1834).

Hugh of Lincoln, St, *Magna Vita Sancti Hugonis (The Life of St Hugh of Lincoln)*, ed. and tr. Decima L. Douie and David Hugh Farmer (Oxford: Clarendon Press, 1961, repr. with corr. 1985).

Hugh of St Victor, *De arrha anime*, PL176.950–70.

Hunt, Tony (ed.), 'An Anglo-Norman Treatise on Female Religious', *Medium Ævum*, 64 (1995), 205–31.

—— 'Anglo-Norman Rules for the Priories of St Mary de Pré and Sopwell', in Stewart Gregory and D. A. Trotter (eds.), *De mot en mot: Aspects of Medieval Linguistics: Essays in Honour of William Rothwell* (Cardiff: University of Wales Press and MHRA, 1997), 93–104.

—— 'An Anglo-Norman Treatise on the Religious Life', in Peter Rolfe Monks and D. D. R. Owen (eds.), *Medieval Codicology, Iconography, Literature, and Translation: Studies for Keith Val Sinclair* (Leiden: Brill, 1994), 267–75.

Jacobus de Voragine, *Legenda Aurea, vulgo Historia Lombardica dicta*, ed. T. Graesse (Bratislava, 1890, 3rd edn.).

—— *The Golden Legend: Readings on the Saints*, tr. William Granger Ryan, 2 vols. (Princeton: Princeton University Press, 1993).

Jacques de Vitry, *The Exempla of Jacques de Vitry*, ed. T. F. Crane (London: Nutt for the Folklore Society, 1890).

—— *Vita Mariae Oigniacensis*, AA.SS. June t. 5 (1867).

—— *Two Lives of Marie d'Oignies*, tr. Margot King and Hugo Feiss (Toronto: Peregrina Press, 3rd edn., 1993).

James, M. R., Jacob, E. F., and Lowe, W. R. L., *Illustrations to the Life of Saint Alban in Trinity College Dublin MS E.i.40* (Oxford: Clarendon Press, 1924).
See also Matthew Paris.

Jameson, Anna, *Sacred and Legendary Art*, 2 vols. (London, 1848; Boston and New York, 3rd edn.: Houghton Mifflin, 1857).

Jerome, *Ep.* 54, Ad Furiam, 'De viduitate servanda', PL22.550–60.

—— *Select Letters of St Jerome*, ed. F. A. Wright (London: Heinemann, 1933).

—— *Traduction en vers français du xiie siècle de l'épître de saint Jérôme à Eustochium*, ed. Tauno Nurmela (Helsinki: Société de la littérature finnoise, 1947).

Le Jeu d'Adam, ed. W. van Emden, British Roncesvals Society Publications I (Edinburgh: Société Ronscesvals, 1996).

Jocelin of Brakelond, *Chronica Jocelini de Brakelonda*, ed. J. G. Rokewode (London: Camden Society, 1840).

John the Almsgiver, St, *The Life of St John the Almsgiver* I, ed. Kenneth Urwin, ANTS 38 (London, 1980); II, *Notes, Introduction and Glossary*, ANTS 39 (London, 1981).

John Godard, 'Two Opuscula of John Godard, First Abbot of Newenham', ed. C. H. Talbot, *Analecta Sacri Ordinis Cisterciensis* 10 (1954), 208–67.

John Pecham, *Jerarchie*, in M. Dominica Legge (ed.), 'John Pecham's *Jerarchie*', *Medium Ævum* 19 (1942), 77–84.

—— *Registrum Epistolarum Fratris Johannis Peckham Archiepiscopi Cantuarensis*, ed. Charles Trice Martin, 3 vols., RS 77 (London, 1882–5).

—— *The Register of John Pecham, Archbishop of Canterbury 1279–1292*, 2 vols., Canterbury and York Society, 64–5: vol. 1, ed. Decima L. Douie, vol. 2, ed. F. N. Davis (Torquay: Devonshire Press, 1968, 1969).

JOHN OF SALISBURY, *The Letters of John of Salisbury*, ed. W. J. Millor, SJ, and H. E. Butler, rev. C. N. Brooke (Oxford: Clarendon Press, 1986).

JULIANA, ST, 'Vie sainte Juliane' in *Li ver del Juïse*, ed. Hugo von Feilitzen (Uppsala: Edv. Berling, 1883), Appendix 1, 1–24.

—— *Þe Liflade ant te Passiun of Seinte Iuliene*, ed. S. R. T. O. d'Ardenne, EETS OS 248 (London, 1961).

KATHERINE, ST, *De Sainte Katerine: An Anonymous Picard Version of the Life of St Catherine of Alexandria*, ed. William MacBain (Fairfax, Va.: George Mason University Press, 1987).

—— *Seinte Katerine*, ed. S. R. T. O. d'Ardenne and E. J. Dobson, EETS SS 7 (London, 1981).

See also Catherine, St; Clemence of Barking.

Laȝamon's Brut, ed. G. L. Brook and R. F. Leslie, vol. 2, EETS ES 277 (London, 1978).

LAWRENCE, ST, *La Vie de saint Laurent: An Anglo-Norman Poem of the Twelfth Century*, ed. D. W. Russell, ANTS 34 (London, 1976).

—— 'The Life of St Lawrence', in Wogan-Browne and Burgess (trs.), *Virgin Lives*.

Le Légendier apostolique anglo-normand, ed. D. W. Russell (Montréal: Presses de l'Université de Montréal, 1989).

Legends of the Holy Rood, ed. R. M. Morris, EETS OS 46 (London, 1871).

LEVY, BRIAN, and JEFFREY, DAVID L. (eds.), *The Anglo-Norman Lyric: An Anthology* (Toronto: Pontifical Institute of Mediaeval Studies, 1989).

Libellus de dictis quatuor ancillarum S. Elisabethae sive examen miraculorum eius, I. B. Menckenii Scriptores Rervm Germanicarvm praecipve Saxonicarvm, tomvs II (Lipsiae, Ioannis Christiani Martini, 1728).

Libellus de diversis ordinibus et professionibus qui sunt in aecclesia, ed. Giles Constable and Bernard Smith (Oxford: Oxford Medieval Texts, 1972).

Liber Eliensis, ed. E. O. Blake, Camden Society, 3rd ser. 92 (London, 1962).

LIEBERMANN, FELIX (ed.), *Die Heiligen Englands: Angelsächsisch und Lateinisch* (Hanover: Hahn'sche, 1889).

Le Livre des Manières, ed. R. A. Lodge (Geneva: Droz, 1979).

Li Livres du gouvernement des rois, *see* Giles of Rome.

LOVE, ROSALIND C. (ed. and tr.), *Three Eleventh-Century Anglo-Latin Saints' Lives: 'Vita Sancti Birini', 'Vita et miracula Sancti Kenelmi' and 'Vita Sancti Rumwoldi'* (Oxford: Clarendon Press, 1996).

Le Mantel mautaillié, ed. F. A. Wulff, *Romania*, 14 (1885), 343–80.

MARBODE OF RENNES, 'Ad reginam Anglorum', PL171.1660.

—— *Marbode of Rennes (1035–1123): De Lapidibus considered as a Medical Treatise with Text, Commentary and C. W. King's Translation; together with Text and Translation of Marbode's Minor Works on Stones*, ed. John M. Riddle (Wiesbaden: Franz Steiner, 1977).

MARGARET, ST, *see* Wace; Millett and Wogan-Browne.

MARIE [OF CHATTERIS? OF BARKING?], *La Vie sainte Audrée: poème anglo-normand du XIIIe siècle*, ed. Östen Södergård (Uppsala: Almqvist & Wiksell, 1955).

MARIE DE FRANCE, *L'Espurgatoire seint Patriz: Nouvelle édition critique accompagnée du De Purgatorio Sancti Patricii*, ed. Yolande de Pontfarcy (Louvain and Paris: Peeters, 1995).

—— *Saint Patrick's Purgatory: A Poem by Marie de France*, tr. Michael Curley (Binghamton: SUNY, 1993).

—— *Marie de France: Lais*, ed. Alfred Ewert (Oxford: Blackwell, 1944; repr. with Introduction and Bibliography by Glyn S. Burgess, London: Bristol Classical Press, 1995).

—— *The Lais of Marie de France*, tr. Glyn Burgess and Keith Busby (Harmondsworth: Penguin Classics, 1986).

MARIE D'OIGNIES, *see* Jacques de Vitry.

MARTÈNE, EDMUND, and DURAND, URSINUS (eds.), *Thesaurus novus Anecdotorum* (Paris, 1717; repr. Farnborough, Hants: Gregg, 1968–9).

MARY OF EGYPT, ST, *La Vie de sainte Marie l'Egyptienne*, ed. Peter Dembowski, Publications romanes et françaises 144 (Geneva: Droz, 1977).

MARY MAGDALEN, ST, 'Die Episode aus der Vie de Madeleine', ed. Ludwig Karl, *ZRPh* 34 (1910), 363–70.

See also Guillaume le clerc.

MATTHEW PARIS, *La Vie de seint Auban. An Anglo-Norman Poem of the Thirteenth Century*, ed. A. R. Harden, ANTS 19 (Oxford, 1968). *See also* James, M. R.

—— *Chronica Majora*, ed. H. R. Luard, RS 57, 7 vols. (London, 1872–83).

—— 'La Vie de saint Edmond, archevêque de Cantorbéry', ed. A. T. Baker, *Romania*, 55 (1929), 332–81.

—— *Vita Edmundi*, ed. C. H. Lawrence, *see under* Secondary Sources, in *St Edmund of Abingdon*.

—— *The Life of St Edmund by Matthew Paris*, tr. C. H. Lawrence (Stroud: Alan Sutton in association with St Edmund Hall, Oxford, 1996).

—— *La Estoire de seint Aedward le rei*, ed. Kathryn Young Wallace, ANTS 41 (London, 1983).

—— *La Estoire de Seint Aedward le Rei . . . together with some pages of the Manuscript of the Life of St Alban at Trinity College, Dublin*, ed. M. R. James (London: Roxburghe Club, 1920).

—— *Flores historiarum*, ed. H. R. Luard, Rerum Britannicarum medii aevi scriptores 95 (London: Eyre and Spottiswoode, 1890).

Maurice de Sully and the Medieval Vernacular Homily, ed. C. A. Robson (Oxford: Blackwell, 1952).

MELOR, ST, 'The Life of St Melor', ed. A. H. Diverres, in Ian Short (ed.), *Medieval French Textual Studies in Memory of T. B. W. Reid*, ANTS OP 1 (London, 1984), 41–53.

MEYER, PAUL, 'Bribes de littérature anglo-normande', *Jahrbuch für romanische und englische Literatur*, 7 (1866), 37–57.

Middle English Lyrics, ed. Maxwell S. Luria and R. L. Hoffman (New York: Norton, 1974).

MILLETT, BELLA and WOGAN-BROWNE, JOCELYN (ed. and tr.), *Medieval English Prose for Women: Extracts from the Katherine Group and 'Ancrene Wisse'* (Oxford: Oxford University Press, 1990; pbk. 1992).

'Le Miracle de Sardenai', ed. Gaston Paris, *Romania*, 11 (1882), 519–37: *(suite) Romania*, 14 (1885), 82–93.

'*Miroir des Bonnes Femmes*: A New Fragment of the *Somme le Roi* and a *Miroir des Bonnes Femmes*, a hitherto unnoticed text', ed. John L. Grigsby, *Romania*, 82 (1961), 458–81.

Miroir ou Évangile des domnées, see Rober le chapelain.

Mirour de seinte eglyse, see Edmund of Canterbury, St.

MODWENNA, ST, *Saint Modwenna*, ed. A. T. Baker and Alexander Bell, ANTS 7 (Oxford, 1947).

See also Geoffrey of Burton.

Monasticon Anglicanum, ed. William Dugdale, rev. J. Caley, H. Ellis, and B. Bandinel (London: Bohn, 1846).

Monumenta Franciscana, ed. J. S. Brewer, 2 vols., RS 4a, 4b (London, 1858–82).

MOORE, ROBERT IAN (ed.), *The Birth of Popular Heresy: Documents of Medieval History* (London: Arnold, 1975).

MORGAN, NIGEL J. (ed.), *The Lambeth Apocalypse: Manuscript 209 in Lambeth Palace Library: A Critical Study*, 2 vols. (London: Harvey Miller, 1990), facsimile and study.

MORTON, VERA (tr.), *Heavenly Brides and Holy Mothers: Texts from Twelfth-Century Convents in England and France* (Brewer, forthcoming).

NICHOLAS BOZON, *Three Saints' Lives by Nicholas Bozon*, ed. Sr. M. Amelia Klenke, Franciscan Institute Publications History Series 1 (St Bonaventure, NY: Franciscan Institute, 1947).

—— *Seven More Poems by Nicholas Bozon*, ed. ead., Franciscan Institute Publications Historical Series 2 (New York: Franciscan Institute, and Louvain: Nauwelaerts, 1951).

—— 'Lettre de l'empereur Orgueil', in *Deux poèmes de Nicholas Bozon: Le char d'orgueil; La lettre de l'empereur Orgueil*, ed. Johann Vising (Göteborg: Elander, 1919).

NICHOLAS, ST, *see* Wace.

NICHOLAS TREVET, 'The Anglo-Norman Chronicle of Nicholas Trivet', ed. A. Rutherford, Ph.D. thesis (University of London, 1932).

NICHOLS, JOHN A. (ed.), 'The History and Cartulary of the Cistercian Nuns of Marham Abbey, 1249–1536', Ph.D. diss. (Kent State University, 1974).

Nova Legenda Anglie, ed. Carl Horstmann, 2 vols. (Oxford: Clarendon Press, 1901).

OLIVER, GEORGE (ed.), *Monasticon Diocesis Exoniensis* (Exeter: Hannaford, 1846).

ORDERIC VITALIS, *The Ecclesiastical History of Orderic Vitalis*, ed. Marjorie C. Chibnall, 6 vols. (Oxford: Oxford University Press, 1969–80).

L'Ornement des Dames. Ornatus mulierum: Texte anglo-normand du xiiie siècle, ed. Pierre Ruelle, Université libre de Bruxelles, Travaux de la Faculté de philologie et de lettres t. 36 (Brussels: Presses Universitaires de Bruxelles, 1967).

OSBERT OF CLARE, *The Letters of Osbert of Clare, Prior of Westminster*, ed. E. W. Williamson (London: Oxford University Press, 1929).

OSITH, ST, 'An Anglo-French Life of St Osith', ed. A. T. Baker, *Modern Language Review*, 6 (1911), 476–502.

PAPHNUTIUS, ST, 'Vie de saint Panuce', ed. A. T. Baker, *Romania*, 38 (1909), 418–24.

PAUL THE HERMIT, ST, 'An Anglo-French Life of Saint Paul the Hermit', ed. A. T. Baker, *MLR* 4 (1908–9), 491–504.

PETER OF BLOIS, *The Latin Letters of Peter of Blois*, ed. Elizabeth Revell, Auctores Britannici Medii Aevi XIII (London: British Academy, 1993).

La Plainte d'amour, poème anglo-normand, ed. Johan Vising (Göteborg: Göteborg Högskola Aarsskrift Text XI, App. crit XIII, 1905–7).

'Poème anglo-normand sur le mariage, les vices et les vertus par Henri (XIII siècle)', ed. Jacques Monfrin, *Mélanges de langue et de littérature du Moyen Age et de la Renaissance offerts à Jean Frappier, par ses collègues, ses élèves et ses amis* (Geneva: Droz, 1970), ii. 845–67.

Le Poème moral, ed. Alphonse Bayot, Académie Royale de langue et de littérature françaises de Belgique, Textes anciens, I (Brussels: Palais des Académies, 1929).

The Anglo-Norman Pseudo-Turpin Chronicle, ed. Ian Short, ANTS 25 (Oxford, 1973).

PYNSON, *see* Richard Pynson.

Quadrilogus, PL190.346–70.

RALPH OF COGGESHALL, *Chronicon Anglicanum,* ed. J. Stevenson, RS 66 (London, 1875).

RANULPH HIGDEN, *Polychronicon Ranulphi Higden Monachi Cestrensis,* ed. J. Rawson Lumby, RS 41 (London, 1846).

Registrum Anglie de Libris Doctorum et Auctorum Veterum, ed. R. H. Rouse and M. A. Rouse, Latin text est. R. A. B. Mynors, Corpus of British Medieval Library Catalogues, II (London: British Library in association with the British Academy, 1991).

'Regulae reclusorum Angliae et quaestiones tres de vita solitaria saec. xii–xiv', ed. Livarius Oliger, *Antonianum,* 9 (1934), 37–84.

REICHL, KARL, *Religiöse Dichtung im englischen Hochmittelalter: Untersuchung und Edition der Handschrift B.14.39 des Trinity College in Cambridge,* Texte und Untersuchungen zur englischen Philologie, Bd. I (Munich: Wilhelm Fink, 1973).

RICHARD OF CHICHESTER, ST, *Vita S. Richardi Episcopi Cistrensis,* AA.SS April t. 1 (Antwerp, 1675; Paris and Rome, 1865).

—— 'Vita sancti Ricardi Episcopi Cycestrensis', ed. and tr. David Jones, in id., 'St Richard of Chichester: The Sources for His Life', *Sussex Record Society,* 79 (1995), 83–159.

La Vie seint Richard evesque de Cycestre, ed. D. W. Russell, ANTS 51 (London, 1995).

—— 'The Will of Richard de la Wych', ed. W. H. Blaauw, *Sussex Archaeological Collections,* 1 (1848), 164–92.

RICHARD PYNSON, *The Kalendre of the Newe Legende of Englande from Pynson's Printed Edition of 1516,* ed. Manfred Görlach, Middle English Texts, 27 (Heidelberg: Winter, 1994).

ROBER LE CHAPELAIN, *Corset,* ed. K. V. Sinclair, ANTS 52 (London, 1995).

—— *Étude sur le Miroir ou les Évangiles des Domnées de Robert de Gretham,* ed. M. Y. Aitken (Paris: Champion, 1922).

—— *Miroir ou Les Évangiles des domnées: edizione di otto domeniche,* ed. Severio Panunzio (Bari: Adriatica Editrice, 1967).

ROBERT OF BRUNNE, *see* William Waddington.

ROBERT GROSSETESTE, *Epistolae Roberti Grosseteste episcopi,* ed. H. R. Luard, RS 25 (London, 1861).

—— *Rotuli Roberti Grosseteste episcopi Lincolniensis,* AD mccxxxv–mccliii, ed. F. N. Davis, Canterbury and York Record Society, 10 (London, 1913).

—— *The Middle English Translations of Robert Grosseteste's Chateau d'amour,* ed. Kari Sajavaara, Mémoires de la Société Néophilologique de Helsinki 32 (Helsinki, 1967).

ROBERTINI, *see* Faith, St.

Roman d'Eneas, see Eneas.

Le Roman de Troie par Benoît de Sainte-Maure: publié d'après tous les manuscrits connus, ed. Léopold Constans, SATF iv (Paris, 1898).

Li Romanz de Dieu, *see* Herman de Valenciennes.

Rotuli de dominabus et pueris et puellis de XII comitatibus (1185), ed. J. H. Round, Publications of the Pipe Roll Society 35 (London: St Catherine's Press, 1913).

Rouleaux des morts du ixe au xve siècle, ed. Léopold Delisle (Paris: Renouard, 1866).

'Salut et solace de l'amour Jésu', ed. Betty Hill in ead., 'British Library Ms. Egerton 613—I', *Notes and Queries*, ns 25/223 (Oct. 1978), 394–409; 'British Library Ms. Egerton 613—II', ibid. (Dec.), 492–501.

SAVAGE, ANNE, and WATSON, NICHOLAS (tr. and annot.), *Anchoritic Spirituality: 'Ancrene Wisse' and Associated Works*, The Classics of Western Spirituality (New York and Mahwah, NJ: Paulist Press, 1991).

SAYERS, JANE E. (ed.), *Original Papal Documents in England and Wales from the Accession of Pope Innocent III to the Death of Pope Benedict XI (1198–1304)* (Oxford: Oxford University Press, 1999).

SAYLE, G. O. (ed.), 'The Mortuary Roll of the Abbess of Lillechurch, Kent', *Proc. Camb. Antiq. Soc.* 10 (1893–1903), 383–409.

SHARPE, M. (ed.), *Bristol Accounts of the Castle Constables*, Bristol Record Society 34 (Bristol, 1982).

SHEINGORN, *see* Faith, St.

SHIELDS, HUGH (ed.), *Le Livre de Sibile*, ANTS 37 (London, 1979).

The Early South English Legendary: MS Laud 108, ed. Carl Horstmann, EETS os 87 (London, 1887).

The South English Legendary, ed. Charlotte d'Evelyn and Anna J. Mill, 3 vols., EETS os 235, 236, 244 (London, 1956–9).

STENGEL, E., 'Handschriftliches aus Oxford', *Zeitschrift für französische Sprache und Literatur*, 14 (1892), 127–60.

TANQUERAY, F. J. (ed.), *Deux poèmes moraux anglo-français: Le Roman des romans et le Sermon en vers* (Paris: Champion, 1922).

—— (ed.), *Recueil des lettres anglo-françaises 1265–1399* (Paris: Champion, 1916).

TERTULLIAN, *De Virginibus Velandis*, PL2.887–914.

THAÏS, ST, in 'Henri d'Arci: The Shorter Works', ed. R. C. Perman, in E. A. Francis (ed.), *Studies in Medieval French Presented to Alfred Ewert* (Oxford: Clarendon Press, 1961), 279–321.

THOMAS BECKET, ST, *The Becket Leaves*, introd. Janet Backhouse and Christopher de Hamel (London: British Library, 1988).

—— *Fragments d'une vie de saint Thomas de Cantorbéry en vers accouplés*, ed. Paul Meyer, SATF (Paris, 1885).

See also Beneit; Guernes de Pont-Sainte-Maxence; *Quadrilogus*.

Thomas of Britain: Roman de Tristan, ed. Stewart Gregory (New York: Garland, 1991).

THOMAS OF HALES, 'Thomas of Hales' Sermon', ed. M. Dominica Legge, *MLR* 30 (1935), 212–18.

La Vengeance de Nostre Seigneur: The Old and Middle French Prose Versions: The Version of Japheth, ed. Alvin Ford, Studies and Texts 63 (Toronto: Pontifical Institute of Mediaeval Studies, 1984).

La Vengeance de Nostre Seigneur: The Old and Middle French Prose Versions, ed. Alvin Ford, Studies and Texts 115 (Toronto: Pontifical Institute of Mediaeval Studies, 1993).

The Book of Vices and Virtues, ed. W. N. Francis, EETS os 217 (London, 1942).
Vices and Virtues, ed. F. Holthausen, EETS os 89 (London, 1888).
Vitas patrum: A Thirteenth-Century Anglo-Norman Rimed Translation of the Verba senio-rum, ed. Bro. B. A. O'Connor (Washington DC: Catholic University of America Press, 1949).
WACE, *Wace: La Conception Nostre Dame*, ed. W. R. Ashford (Mensha, Wis.: Banta, 1933).
—— *La Vie de sainte Marguerite*, ed. Elizabeth A. Francis, CFMA (Paris: 1934).
—— *La Vie de saint Nicolas par Wace*, ed. Einar Ronsjö (Lund and Copenhagen: Gleerup and Munksgaard, 1942).
—— *Le Roman de Brut de Wace*, ed. Ivor Arnold, SATF, 2 vols. (Paris, 1938–40).
WALTER MAP, *De nugis curialium. Courtiers' Trifles*, ed. and tr. M. R. James, rev. C. N. L. Brooke and R. A. B. Mynors (Oxford: Clarendon Press, 1983).
WERBURGA, ST, *The Life of Saint Werburge of Chester by Henry Bradshaw*, ed. Carl Horstmann, EETS os 88 (London, 1887).
WILMART, ANDRÉ, 'Une lettre inédite de St Anselme à une moniale inconstante', *Rev. Bén.* 41 (1928), 319–32.
WILLIAM OF MALMESBURY, *De gestis pontificum Anglorum libri quinque*, ed. N. E. S. A. Hamilton, RS 52 (London, 1870).
—— *De gestis regum Anglorum libri quinque*, ed. W. W. Stubbs, 2 vols., RS 90 (London, 1887–9).
WILLIAM MARSHAL, *Guillaume le maréchal, comte de Striguil et de Pembroke, régent d'Angleterre de 1216 à 1219*, ed. Paul Meyer, 3 vols., SATF (Paris, 1891–1901).
WILLIAM DE MONTIBUS, 'Epistola ad moniales', ed. Joseph Goering, in *William de Montibus c.1140–1213: The Schools and the Literature of Pastoral Care* (Toronto: Pontifical Institute of Mediaeval Studies, 1992), Part II.6, 225–6.
WILLIAM WADDINGTON, *Robert of Brunne's 'Handlyng Synne' AD 1303, with those parts of the Anglo-French Treatise on which it was founded, William of Waddington's 'Manuel des pechiez . . .'*, ed. F. J. Furnivall (London: Paul, Trench, Trübner and Co. for EETS, 1901).
WILMART, ANDRÉ, 'Opuscule de Guy de Southwick', *RTAM* 7 (1935), 337–52.
WILSON, H. A. (ed.), *The Pontifical of Magdalen College*, HBS 39 (1910).
Die Winteney-Version der Regula Sancti Benedicti, ed. Mechtild Gretsch (Tübingen: Max Niemeyer, 1978).
WOGAN-BROWNE, JOCELYN, and BURGESS, GLYN (trs.), *Virgin Lives and Holy Deaths: Two Exemplary Biographies for Anglo-Norman Women* (London: Everyman, 1996).
WULFSTAN, *Die 'Institutes of Polity, Civil and Ecclesiastical': Ein Werk Erzbischofs Wulfstans von York*, ed. K. Jost (Bern: Francke, 1959).

SECONDARY SOURCES

ALBERTI, GIOVANNI, *Maria Goretti: Storia di un piccolo fiore di campo* (Rome: no publisher, 1985; 2nd edn. 1990).
ALLEN, HOPE EMILY, 'Eleanor Cobham', *Times Literary Supplement* (22 Mar. 1934), 214.
—— 'Wynkyn de Worde and a Second French Compilation from the *Ancrene Riwle* with a Description of the First', in *Essays and Studies in Honor of Carleton Brown* (New York: New York University Press, 1940).

ALTSCHUL, MICHAEL, *A Baronial Family in Medieval England: The Clares 1217–1314* (Baltimore: Johns Hopkins University Press, 1965).

ARNOULD, E., *Le Manuel des péchés: étude de littérature religieuse anglo-normande* (XIIIe siècle) (Paris: Droz, 1940).

ASHLEY, KATHLEEN, and SHEINGORN, PAMELA, 'An Unsentimental View of Ritual in the Middle Ages or, Sainte Foy was no Snow White', *Journal of Ritual Studies*, 6 (1992), 63–85.

—— —— *Writing Faith: Text, Sign, and History in the Miracles of Sainte Foy* (Chicago: University of Chicago Press, 1999).

ASHTON, MARGARET, 'Gold and Images', in W. J. Sheils and Diana Wood (eds.), *The Church and Wealth*, SCH 24 (1987), 189–207.

ATKINSON, CLARISSA W., ' "Precious Balsam in a Fragile Glass": The Ideology of Virginity in the Later Middle Ages', *Journal of Family History*, 8 (1983), 131–43.

D'AVRIL, FRANÇOIS and STIRNEMAN, PATRICIA, *Manuscrits enluminés d'origine insulaire viie–xxe siècle* (Paris: Bibliothèque Nationale, 1987).

BAKER, A. T., 'An Episode from the Anglo-French Life of St Modwenna', in Mary Williams and James A. de Rothschild (eds.), *A Miscellany of Studies in Romance Languages and Literatures Presented to Leon E. Kastner, Professor of French Language and Literature in the University of Manchester* (Cambridge: Heffer, 1932), 9–21.

BAKER, DEREK (ed.), *Medieval Women* (Oxford: Blackwell, 1978).

BARNES, GERALDINE, *Counsel and Strategy in Middle English Romance* (Cambridge: Brewer, 1993).

BARRATT, ALEXANDRA, 'Anchoritic Aspects of *Ancrene Wisse*', *Medium Ævum*, 49 (1980), 32–56.

—— 'Books for Nuns: Cambridge University Library MS Additional 3042', *Notes and Queries*, NS 45 (Sept. 1997), 310–19.

—— 'Flying in the Face of Tradition: A New View of *The Owl and the Nightingale*', *University of Toronto Quarterly*, 56 (1987), 471–85.

—— 'Undutiful Daughters and Metaphorical Mothers among the Beguines', in Dor et al. (eds.), *New Trends in Feminine Sprituality*, 81–104.

BARROW, JULIA, 'A Twelfth-Century Bishop and Literary Patron: William de Vere', *Viator*, 18 (1987), 175–89.

BARTLETT, ROBERT, 'The Hagiography of Angevin England', in P. R. Coss and S. D. Lloyd (eds.), *Thirteenth-Century England V* (Woodbridge: Brewer, 1995), 37–52.

—— *Trial by Fire and Water: The Medieval Judicial Ordeal* (Oxford: Clarendon Press, 1986).

BASWELL, CHRISTOPHER, 'Latinitas', in Wallace (ed.), *Cambridge History*, 122–51.

BATT, CATHERINE, 'Clemence of Barking's Transformations of *courtoisie* in *La Vie de sainte Catherine d'Alexandrie*', in Roger Ellis (ed.), *Translation in the Middle Ages, New Comparisons*, 12 (1991), 102–33.

BAUMGARTNER, EMMANUELE, 'Sainte(s) Hélènes', in [Duby], *Femmes: mariages*, 43–53.

BECKWITH, SARAH, 'Passionate Regulation: Enclosure, Ascesis, and the Feminist Imaginary', *South Atlantic Quarterly*, 93 (1994), 803–24.

BELL, CATHERINE, *Ritual: Perspectives and Dimensions* (New York and Oxford: Oxford University Press, 1997).

BELL, DAVID N., *What Nuns Read: Books and Libraries in Medieval English Nunneries*, Cistercian Studies Series 158 (Kalamazoo, Mich.: Cistercian Publications, 1995).

BENNETT, ADELAIDE, 'A Book Designed for a Noblewoman: An Illustrated *Manuel des Péchés* of the Thirteenth Century', in Brownrigg (ed.), *Medieval Book Production*, 163–81.

BENSON, ROBERT L., and CONSTABLE, GILES, with LANHAM, CAROL D. (eds.), *Renaissance and Renewal in the Twelfth Century* (Oxford: Clarendon Press, 1982).

BENTON, J. F., 'The Court of Champagne as Literary Center', *Speculum*, 36 (1961), 551–91.

BERMAN, CONSTANCE, 'Fashions in Monastic Patronage: The Popularity of Supporting Cistercian Abbeys for Women in Thirteenth-Century Northern France', *Proceedings of the Annual Meeting of the Western Society for French History*, 17 (1990), 36–45.

—— 'Cistercian Nuns and the Development of the Order: The Abbey at Saint-Antoine-des-Champs outside Paris', in E. Rozanne Elder (ed.), *The Joy of Learning and the Love of God: Studies in Honor of Jean Leclercq* (Kalamazoo, Mich.: Cistercian Publications, 1995), 121–56.

BERNARDS, MATTHÄUS, *Speculum virginum: Geistigkeit und Seelenleben der Frau im Hochmittelalter*, Beihefte zum Archiv für Kulturgeschichte, Heft 16, Forschungen zur Volkskunde, Bd. 36/38, (Cologne: Graz, 1955; 2nd edn. Cologne and Vienna, 1982).

BESTUL, THOMAS H., *Texts of the Passion: Latin Devotional Literature and Medieval Society* (Philadelphia: University of Pennsylvania Press, 1996).

BETHELL, DENIS, 'The Lives of St Osyth of Essex and St Osyth of Aylesbury', *AB* 88 (1970), 75–127.

BILLER, PETER, 'The Earliest Heretical Englishwomen', in Wogan-Browne *et al.* (eds.), *Medieval Women*, 363–76.

BINNS, ALISON, *Dedications of Monastic Houses in England and Wales 1066–1216* (Woodbridge and Wolfeboro, NH: Boydell Press, 1989).

BINSKI, PAUL, 'Reflections on the *Estoire de seint Aedward*: Hagiography and Kingship in Thirteenth-Century England', *JMH* 16 (1990), 333–50.

—— 'Abbot Berkyng's Tapestries and Matthew Paris's Life of St Edward the Confessor', *Archaeologia*, 109 (1991), 81–100.

BISHOP, EDMUND, 'On the Origins of the Feast of the Conception of the Blessed Mary', in id., *Liturgica Historica: Papers on the Liturgy and Life of the Western Church* (Oxford: Clarendon Press, 1918), 238–59.

BLAAUW, WILLIAM HENRY, *The Barons War: Including the Battles of Lewes and Evesham* (London: Bell and Daldy, 1871).

BLACKER, JEAN, *The Faces of Time: Portrayal of the Past in Old French and Latin Historical Narrative of the Anglo-Norman Regnum* (Austin: University of Texas Press, 1994).

—— '"Dame Custance La Gentil": Gaimar's Portrait of a Lady and her Books', in Evelyn Mullally and John Thompson (eds.), *The Court and Cultural Diversity* (Cambridge: Brewer, 1997), 109–19.

BLAMIRES, ALCUIN, 'Women and Preaching in Medieval Orthodoxy, Heresy, and Saints' Lives', *Viator*, 26 (1995), 135–52.

BLANTON-WHETSALL, VIRGINIA, 'St Aethelthryth's Cult: Literary, Historical, and Pictorical Constructions of Gendered Sanctity', Ph.D. thesis (SUNY Binghamton, 1998).

BLOCH, R. HOWARD, 'The Poetics of Virginity', in id., *Medieval Misogyny and the Invention of Western Romantic Love* (Chicago and London: University of Chicago Press, 1991), 93–112.

BLUMENFELD-KOSINSKI, RENATE, *Not of Woman Born: Representations of Caesarean Birth in Medieval and Renaissance Culture* (Ithaca and London: Cornell University Press, 1990).

—— and SZELL, TIMEA (eds.), *Images of Sainthood in Medieval Europe* (Ithaca and London: Cornell University Press, 1991).

BOND, GERALD A., *The Loving Subject: Desire, Eloquence and Power in Romanesque France* (Philadelphia: University of Pennsylvania Press, 1995).

BORDIER, JEAN-PIERRE, 'Le Fils et le fruit. Le *Jeu d'Adam* entre la théologie et le mythe', in Herman Braet, Johan Nowé, and Gilbert Tournoy (eds.), *The Theatre in the Middle Ages* (Leuven: Leuven University Press, 1985), 84–102.

BOSWELL, JOHN EASTBURN, '*Expositio* and *Oblatio*: The Abandonment of Children and the Ancient and Medieval Family', *American Historical Review*, 89 (1984), 10–33.

BOUILLET, A., and SERVIÈRES, L., *Sainte Foy. Vierge et martyre* (Rodez: E. Carrere, 1900).

BOUREAU, ALAIN, *La Légende dorée: le système narratif de Jacques de Voragine (+1298)* (Paris: Éditions du Cerf, 1984).

BOWLES, W. L., and NICHOLS, JOHN GOUGH, *Annals and Antiquities of Lacock Abbey in the County of Wilts with Memorials of the Foundress Ela Countess of Salisbury* (London: Nichols and Son, 1835).

BRASWELL, LAUREL, 'St Edburga of Winchester: A Study of Her Cult AD 950 with an Edition of the Fourteenth-Century Middle English and Latin Lives', *Mediaeval Studies*, 33 (1971), 292–333.

BRAY, JENNIFER, 'The Mohammetan and Idolatry', in W. J. Sheils (ed.), *Persecution and Toleration*, *SCH* 21 (1984), 89–98.

BROADHURST, KAREN M., 'Henry II of England and Eleanor of Aquitaine: Patrons of Literature in French?', *Viator*, 27 (1996), 53–84.

BROWNRIGG, LINDA L. (ed.), *Medieval Book Production: Assessing the Evidence* (Los Altos, Calif.: Anderson-Lovelace, 1990).

BULLOCK-DAVIES, CONSTANCE, *Menestrellorum multitudo: Minstrels at a Royal Feast* (Cardiff: University of Wales Press, 1978).

BURGESS, GLYN S., *Marie de France: An Analytical Bibliography* (London: Grant and Cutler, 1977) and *Supplements* no. 1 (1986), no. 2 (1997).

BURGIN, VICTOR, DONALD, JAMES, and KAPLAN, CORA (eds.), *Formations of Fantasy* (London: Methuen, 1986).

BURTON, JANET, *Monastic and Religious Orders in Britain 1000–1300* (Cambridge and New York: Cambridge University Press, 1994).

—— *The Monastic Orders in Yorkshire 1069–1215* (Cambridge: Cambridge University Press, 1999).

—— 'Yorkshire Nunneries in the Middle Ages: Recruitment and Resources', in John C. Appleby and Paul Dalton (eds.), *Government, Religion and Society in Northern England 1000–1700* (Stroud: Sutton, 1997), 104–16.

BYNUM, CAROLINE WALKER, *Jesus as Mother: Studies in the Spirituality of the High Middle Ages* (Berkeley and London: University of California Press, 1982).

—— *Fragmentation and Redemption: Essays on Gender and the Human Body in Medieval Religion* (New York: Zone Books, 1991).

—— *The Resurrection of the Body in Western Christianity 200–1336* (New York: Columbia University Press, 1995).

CALDICOTT, DIANA K., *Hampshire Nunneries* (Chichester: Phillimore, 1989).

CALIN, WILLIAM W., *The French Tradition and the Literature of Medieval England* (Toronto: University of Toronto Press, 1994).

The Cambridge History of Medieval English Literature, see Wallace, David (ed.).

CAMILLE, MICHAEL, 'The Book of Signs: Writing and Visual Difference in Gothic Manuscripts', *Word and Image*, 1 (1985), 133–48.

—— 'Seeing and Reading: Some Visual Implications of Medieval Literacy and Illiteracy', *Art History*, 8 (1985), 26–49.

—— *The Gothic Idol: Ideology and Image-Making in Medieval Art* (Cambridge: Cambridge University Press, 1989).

CANNON, CHRISTOPHER, 'The Style and Authorship of the Otho Revision of Laȝamon's *Brut*', *Medium Ævum*, 62 (1993), 187–209.

CARPENTER, JENNIFER, and MacLEAN, SALLY-BETH (eds.), *Power of the Weak: Studies on Medieval Women* (Urbana and Chicago: University of Illinois Press, 1995).

CARRUTHERS, MARY, *The Book of Memory: A Study of Memory in Medieval Culture* (Cambridge: Cambridge University Press, 1990).

CASTERAS, SUSAN P., 'Virgin Vows: The Early Victorian Artists' Portrayal of Nuns and Novices', *Victorian Studies*, 24 (1981), 157–84.

CHANTER, TINA, 'Female Temporality and the Future of Feminism', in John Fletcher and Andrew Benjamin (eds.), *Abjection, Melancholia and Love: The Work of Julia Kristeva*, Warwick Studies in Philosophy and Literature (London and New York: Routledge, 1990), 63–79.

CHIBNALL, MARJORIE, 'L'Ordre de Fontevrauld en Angleterre au XIIe s.', *Cahiers de civilisation médiévale*, 29 (1986), 41–7.

CHODOROW, NANCY, *The Reproduction of Mothering: Psychoanalysis and the Sociology of Gender* (Berkeley: University of California Press, 1978).

CHRISTELOW, STEPHANIE MOOERS, 'The Royal Love in Anglo-Norman England: A Fiscal and Courtly Concept', *HSJ* 8 (1996), 29–42.

CHRISTIE, A. G. I., *English Medieval Embroidery* (Oxford: Clarendon Press, 1938).

CLANCHY, MICHAEL T., *England and Its Rulers: Foreign Lordship and National Identity 1066–1272* (Totowa, NJ: Barnes and Noble, 1983).

—— *From Memory to Written Record: England 1066–1307* (London: Edward Arnold, 1979; 2nd edn. Oxford and Cambridge, Mass.: Blackwell, 1993).

CLARK, ANNE L., *Elisabeth of Schönau: A Twelfth-Century Visionary* (Philadelphia: University of Pennsylvania Press, 1992).

CLARK, CECILY, 'La Vie féminine en Angleterre au temps d'Aliénor d'Aquitaine', *Cahiers de civilisation médiévale*, 29 (1986), 49–51.

CLARK-MAXWELL, W. G., 'The Earliest Charters of the Abbey of Lacock', *Wiltshire Archaeological and Natural History Magazine*, 35 (1907–8), 191–209.

CLOVER, CAROL, *Men, Women and Chain Saws: Gender in the Modern Horror Film* (Princeton: Princeton University Press, 1992).

COAKLEY, JOHN, 'Friars as Confidants of Holy Women: Medieval Dominican Hagiography', in Blumenfeld-Kosinski and Szell (eds.), *Images of Sainthood in Medieval Europe*, 222–46.

COHN, JAN, *Romance and the Erotics of Property: Mass-Market Fiction for Women* (Durham, NC: Duke University Press, 1988).

CONSTABLE, GILES, 'Troyes, Constantinople, and the Relics of St Helen in the Thirteenth Century', in *Mélanges René Crozet* (Poitiers, 1966), 1035–42, repr. in Constable, *Religious Life and Thought (11th–12th Centuries)* (London: Variorum Reprints, 1979), no. xiv.

—— 'Renewal and Reform in the Religious Life: Concepts and Realities', in Benson and Constable (eds.), *Renaissance and Renewal*, 37–67.

—— *Three Studies in Medieval Religion and Social Thought: The Interpretation of Mary and Martha, the Ideal of the Imitation of Christ, the Orders of Society* (Cambridge: Cambridge University Press, 1995).

COOKE, KATHLEEN, 'Donors and Daughters: Shaftesbury Abbey's Benefactors, Endowments and Nuns *c.*1086–1130', *ANS* 12 (1989), 29–45.

COON, LYNDA L., *Sacred Fiction: Holy Women and Hagiography in Late Antiquity* (Philadelphia: University of Pennsylvania Press, 1997).

COOPER, KATE, *The Virgin and the Bride: Idealized Womanhood in Late Antiquity* (Cambridge, Mass. and London: Harvard University Press, 1996).

COSS, PETER R., *Lordship, Knighthood, and Locality: A Study in English Society 1180–c.1280* (Cambridge: Cambridge University Press, 1991).

—— and LLOYD, S. D. (eds.), *Thirteenth-Century England I* (Woodbridge: Brewer, 1995).

CRANE, SUSAN, *Insular Romance: Politics, Faith and Culture in Anglo-Norman and Middle English Literature* (Berkeley: University of California Press, 1986).

—— *Gender and Romance in Chaucer's Canterbury Tales* (Princeton: Princeton University Press, 1994).

—— 'Social Aspects of Bilingualism in the Thirteenth Century', in Prestwich *et al.* (eds.), *Thirteenth Century-England VI*, 103–16.

—— 'Anglo-Norman Cultures in England, 1066–1460', in Wallace (ed.), *Cambridge History*, 35–60.

CROSS, J. E., 'Pelagia in Medieval England', in *Pélagie la pénitente: métamorphoses d'une légende* (Paris: Études Augustiniennes and CNRS, 1984), ii. 281–93.

CROUCH, DAVID, *William Marshal: Court, Career and Chivalry in the Angevin Empire, 1147–1219* (London and New York: Longmans, 1990).

—— 'The Culture of Death in the Anglo-Norman World', in C. Warren Hollister (ed.), *Anglo-Norman Political Culture and the Twelfth-Century Political Renaissance* (Woodbridge: Boydell Press, 1997), 157–80.

CUBITT, CATHERINE, 'Virginity and Misogyny in Tenth- and Eleventh-Century England', *Gender and History*, 12 (2000), 1–32.

DALTON, PAUL, 'Eustace Fitz John and the Politics of Anglo-Norman England: The Rise and Survival of a Twelfth-Century Royal Servant', *Speculum*, 71 (1996), 358–83.

D'AVRAY, D. L., and TAUSCHE, M., 'Marriage Sermons in *ad status* Collections of the Central Middle Ages', *AHDLMA* 47 (1980), 71–119.

DEAN, RUTH J., with the collaboration of BOULTON, MAUREEN B. M., *Anglo-Norman Literature: A Guide to Manuscripts and Texts*, ANTS OP 3 (London, 1999).

DEARAGON, RAGENA C., 'Dowager Countesses 1069–1230', *ANS* 17 (1994), 87–100.

DENHOLM-YOUNG, N., 'An Early Thirteenth Century Anglo-Norman Manuscript', *Bodleian Quarterly Record* (1929–31), 225–30.

DERRIDA, JACQUES, 'Given Time: The Time of the King', *Critical Inquiry*, 18 (1992), 161–87.

DIAMOND, ARLYN, 'Engendering Criticism', *Thought*, 64 (1989), 298–309.

DIEKSTRA, F. N. M., 'Some Fifteenth-Century Borrowings from the *Ancrene Wisse*', *English Studies*, 71 (1990), 81–104.

DINZELBACHER, PETER, 'The Beginnings of Mysticism Experienced in Twelfth-Century England', in Marion Glasscoe (ed.), *The Medieval Mystical Tradition in England: Exeter Symposium IV, Papers Read at Dartington Hall, July 1987* (Cambridge: Brewer, 1984), 111–31.

DIVERRES, A. H., 'An Anglo-Norman Life of St Melor', *The National Library of Wales Journal*, 15 (1967–8), 167–76.

DOBLE, G. H., *The Saints of Cornwall* (Oxford: Holywell Press, 1966).

DOBSON, ERIC J., *The Origins of Ancrene Wisse* (Oxford: Clarendon Press, 1976).

DOBROWOLSKI, PAULA, 'Women and their Dower in the Long Thirteenth Century, 1265–1329', in Prestwich *et al.* (eds.), *Thirteenth Century England VI*, 157–64.

DONOVAN, CLAIRE, 'The Mise-en-Page of Early Books of Hours in England', in Brownrigg (ed.), *Medieval Book Production*, 147–61.

—— *The de Brailes Hours: Shaping the Book of Hours in Thirteenth-Century Oxford* (London: British Library, 1991).

DOR, JULIETTE, 'Post-Dating Romance Loan-words in Middle English: Are the French Words of the *Katherine* Group English?', in Matti Rissanen, Ossi Ihalainen, Terttu Nevalainen, and Irma Taavitsainen (eds.), *History of Englishes: New Methods and Interpretations in Historical Linguistics*, Topics in English Linguistics, 10 (Berlin and New York: Mouton de Gruyter, 1992), 483–505.

—— JOHNSON, LESLEY, and WOGAN-BROWNE, JOCELYN (eds.), *New Trends in Feminine Spirituality: The Holy Women of Liège and their Impact* (Turnhout: Brepols, 1999).

DORAN, JOHN, 'Oblation or Obligation? A Canonical Ambiguity', in Wood (ed.), *The Church and Childhood*, SCH 31 (1994), 127–41.

DRONKE, PETER, *Hermes and the Sibyls: Continuations and Creations*, Inaugural Lecture, 9 Mar. 1990 (Cambridge: Cambridge University Press, 1991).

[DUBY, GEORGES], *Femmes: mariages-lignages xii–xiv siècles: mélanges offerts à Georges Duby* (Brussels: De Boeck-Wesmael, 1992).

DULAEY, MARTINE, *Le Rêve dans la vie et la pensée de saint Augustin* (Paris: Études Augustiniennes, 1973).

DUNBAR, AGNES B. C., *A Dictionary of Saintly Women*, 2 vols. (London: Bell, 1904–5).

EALES, R., 'Henry III and the End of the Earldom of Chester', in Coss and Lloyd (eds.), *Thirteenth-Century England I*, 100–13.

ELKINS, SHARON K., *Holy Women of Twelfth-Century England* (Chapel Hill and London: University of North Carolina Press, 1988).

ELLIOTT, ALISON, *Roads to Paradise: Reading the Lives of the Early Saints* (Hanover, NH: University Press of New England for Brown University Press, 1987).

ELLIOTT, DYAN, *Spiritual Marriage: Sexual Abstinence in Medieval Wedlock* (Princeton: Princeton University Press, 1993).

—— 'The Physiology of Rapture and Female Spirituality', in Peter Biller and A. J. Minnis (eds.), *Medieval Theology and the Natural Body*, York Studies in Medieval Theology I (York: York Medieval Press, 1997), 141–74.

ELLIS, ROGER, and EVANS, RUTH (eds.), *The Medieval Translator* 4, Medieval and Renaissance Texts and Studies 123 (Exeter: University of Exeter Press, 1994).

ENGEN, JOHN VAN, 'Professing Religion: From Liturgy to Law', *Viator*, 29 (1998), 323–43.

ERLER, MARY, 'English Vowed Women at the End of the Middle Ages', *Mediaeval Studies*, 57 (1995), 155–203.

ESMEIN, A., *Le Mariage en droit canonique*, 2nd edn. with R. Genestal (Paris: Recueil Sirey, 1929–35).

EVANS, GILLIAN R., 'Abbreviating Anselm', *RTAM* 48 (1981), 78–108.

EVANS, MICHAEL, 'An Illustrated Fragment of Peraldus's *Summa* of Vice: Harleian MS 3244', *Journal of the Warburg and Courtauld Institute*, 45 (1982), 14–68.

EVANS, RUTH, and JOHNSON, LESLEY (eds.), *Feminist Readings in Middle English Literature: The Wife of Bath and All Her Sect* (London: Routledge, 1994).

EVE, JULIAN, *A History of Horsham St Faith, Norfolk: The Story of a Village* (Norwich: Catton Printing, 1992; rev. edn. 1994).

D'EVELYN, CHARLOTTE, and FOSTER, FRANCES A., 'Saints' Legends', in Albert E. Hartung (gen. ed.), *A Manual of the Writings in Middle English*, ii (New Haven: Connecticut Academy of Arts and Science, 1970), 410–57; 553–649.

FARMER, D. H., *The Oxford Dictionary of Saints* (Oxford: Oxford University Press, 4th edn., 1997).

FARMER, SHARON, 'Persuasive Voices: Clerical Images of Medieval Wives', *Speculum*, 61 (1986), 517–43.

FINUCANE, RONALD C., *Miracles and Pilgrims: Popular Beliefs in Medieval England* (London: Dent, 1977; repr. Macmillan, 1995).

FLETCHER, ALAN J., 'The Dancing Virgins of *Hali Meiðhad*', *Notes and Queries*, NS 40 (1993), 437–9.

FLINT, V. I. J., *Honorius Augustodunensis of Regensburg*, in Patrick J. Geary (ed.), Historical and Religious Writers of the Latin West, *Writers of the Middle Ages*, v (London: Scolar Press, 1995).

FOLLIET, GEORGES, 'Les Trois Catégories de chrétiens: suivie d'un thème augustinien', *L'Année théologique augustinienne*, 14 (1954), 81–96.

FOLZ, ROBERT, *Les Saintes Reines du moyen-âge en Occident vi–xiiie siècles* (Brussels: Société des Bollandistes, 1992).

FOURNÉE, JEAN, *Le Culte populaire et l'iconographie des saints en Normandie*, 2 vols. (Paris: Société d'histoire et d'archéologie normandes, 1973).

FRANKIS, P. JOHN, 'Laȝamon's English Sources', in Mary Salu and Robert T. Farrell (eds.), *J. R. R. Tolkien, Scholar and Storyteller: Essays in Memoriam* (Ithaca and London: Cornell University Press, 1979), 64–75.

—— 'The Social Context of Vernacular Writing in Thirteenth Century England: The Evidence of the Manuscripts', in Coss and Lloyd (eds.), *Thirteenth Century England I*, 175–84.

—— 'Views of Anglo-Saxon England in Post-Conquest Vernacular Writing', in Pilch (ed.), *Orality and Literacy*, 227–47.

FULTON, RACHEL, 'Mimetic Devotion, Marian Exegesis, and the Historical Sense of the Song of Songs', *Viator*, 27 (1996), 85–116.

GAFFNEY, WILBUR, 'The Allegory of the Christ-Knight in *Piers Plowman*', *PMLA* 46 (1931), 155–68.

GALLOWAY, ANDREW, 'Chaucer's *Legend of Lucrece* and the Critique of Ideology in Fourteenth-Century England', *ELH* 60 (1993), 813–32.

GARDEIL, A., 'Dons du seint esperit', in A. Vacant, E. Mangenot *et al.* (eds.), *Dictionnaire de théologie catholique* (Paris: Letouzey et Ané, 1908–50), iv, pt. 2.

GAUNT, SIMON, *Gender and Genre in Medieval French Literature* (Cambridge: Cambridge University Press, 1995).

GEARY, PATRICK, *Furta Sacra: Thefts of Relics in the Central Middle Ages* (Princeton: Princeton University Press, 1978).

GEHRKE, PAMELA, *Saints and Scribes: Medieval Hagiography in its Manuscript Context* (Berkeley, Los Angeles, and London: University of California Press, 1993).

GEORGIANNA, LINDA, *The Solitary Self: Individuality in the 'Ancrene Wisse'* (Cambridge, Mass. and London: Harvard University Press, 1982).

GEROULD, G. H., *Saints' Legends* (Boston and New York: Houghton Mifflin, 1916).

GILBERT, JANE, ' "Boys will Be . . . What?" Gender, Sexuality, and Childhood in *Floire et Blanceflor* and *Floris et Lyriope*', *Exemplaria*, 9 (1997), 39–62.

GILCHRIST, ROBERTA, ' "Blessed art thou amongst women": The Archaeology of Female Piety', in P. J. P. Goldberg (ed.), *Woman is a Worthy Wight: Women in English Society, c.1200–1500* (Stroud: Sutton, 1992), 212–26.

—— *Gender and Material Culture: The Archaeology of Religious Women* (London and New York: Routledge, 1994).

—— *Contemplation and Action: The Other Monasticism* (London and New York: Leicester University Press, 1995).

GILLINGHAM, JOHN, 'Love, Marriage, and Politics in the Twelfth Century', in id., *Richard Coeur de Lion: Kingship, Chivalry and War in the Twelfth Century* (London and Rio Grande: Hambledon Press, 1994), 243–55.

GILLOW, JOSEPH, *Bibliographical Dictionary of the English Catholics* (London: Burns and Oates, 1885–1902).

GIRARD, RENÉ, *La Violence et le sacré* (Paris: Grasset, 1972), tr. Patrick Gregory as *Violence and the Sacred* (Baltimore and London: Johns Hopkins University Press, 1977).

—— *Le Bouc émissaire* (Paris: Grasset, 1983), tr. Yvonne Freccero as *The Scapegoat* (Baltimore: Johns Hopkins University Press, 1986).

GODBOUT, JACQUES T., with CAILLÉ, ALAIN, TR. DONALD WINKLER, *The World of the Gift* (Montreal, Kingston, London, and Ithaca: McGill-Queen's University Press, 1998).

GOLD, PENNY SCHINE, *The Lady and the Virgin: Image and Experience in Twelfth-Century France* (Chicago: Chicago University Press, 1985).

GOLDING, BRIAN, 'Anglo-Norman Knightly Burials', in Christopher Harper-Bill and Ruth Harvey (eds.), *The Ideals and Practice of Medieval Knighthood* (Woodbridge: Boydell Press, 1986), 35–48.

—— 'Burial and Benefactions: An Aspect of Monastic Patronage in Thirteenth-Century England', in Ormrod (ed.), *England in the Thirteenth Century*, 64–75.

—— *Gilbert of Sempringham and the Gilbertine Order c.1130–c.1300* (Oxford: Clarendon Press, 1995).

—— 'The Hermit and the Hunter', in John Blair and Brian Golding (eds.), *The Cloister and the World: Essays in Medieval History in Honour of Barbara Harvey* (Oxford: Clarendon Press, 1996), 95–117.

GOODICH, MICHAEL, *Vita Perfecta: The Ideal of Sainthood in the Thirteenth Century* (Stuttgart: Anton Hiersemann, 1982).

—— *Violence and Miracle in the Fourteenth Century: Private Grief and Public Salvation* (Chicago: University of Chicago Press, 1995).

GOODY, JACK, *The Development of the Family and Marriage in Europe* (Cambridge: Cambridge University Press, 1983).

GÖRLACH, MANFRED, *The Textual Tradition of the South English Legendary*, Leeds Studies in English Texts and Monographs, NS 6 (University of Leeds: School of English, 1974).

—— *Middle English Saints' Lives* (Tübingen: Franke, 1998).

GOUGAUD, DOM LOUIS, *Devotional and Ascetic Practices in the Middle Ages*, English edition prepared by G. C. Bateman (London: Burns, Oates and Washbourne, 1927).

GRAHAM, ROSE, *St Gilbert of Sempringham and the Gilbertines: A History of the Only English Monastic Order* (London: Elliot Stock, 1901).

GRANSDEN, ANTONIA, *Historical Writing in England c.550–c.1307* (London: Routledge & Kegan Paul, 1974).

GRAVDAL, KATHRYN, *Ravishing Maidens: Writing Rape in Medieval French Literature and Law* (Philadelphia: University of Pennsylvania Press, 1991).

GREEN, JUDITH A., *The Aristocracy of Norman England* (Cambridge: Cambridge University Press, 1997).

GREEN, MRS MARY ANNE EVERETT, *Lives of the Princesses of England*, 6 vols. (London: Colburn, 1843–55).

GRETSCH, MATHILDE, 'Die Winteney-Version der Regula Sancti Benedicti: eine frühmittelenglische Bearbeitung der altenglischen Prosaübersetzung der Benediktinerregel', *Anglia*, 96 (1978), 310–48.

GROSJEAN, PAUL, 'Vita S. Roberti novi monasterii in Anglia abbatis', *AB* 56 (1938), 335–60.

—— 'De Codice hagiographico gothano', *AB* 58 (1940), 177–204.

—— 'Saints Anglo-Saxons des marches Gauloises', *AB* 79 (1961), 161–9.

GRUNDMANN, HERBERT, *Religiöse Bewegungen im Mittelalter* (Hildesheim: Olms, 1961), tr. Steven Rowan as *Religious Movements in the Middle Ages: The Historical Links between Heresy, the Mendicant Orders, and the Women's Movement in the Twelfth and Thirteenth Centuries with the Historical Foundation of German Mysticism* (Notre Dame, Ill. and London: University of Notre Dame Press, 1995).

HAFFEN, JOSIANE, *Contribution à l'étude de la sibylle médiévale: Étude et edition du ms BN f. fr 25407 fol. 160v–172v: Le Livre de Sibile*, Annales Littéraires de l'Université de Besançon (Paris: Les Belles Lettres, 1984).

HALL, EDWIN, and UHR, HORST, *'Aureola super auream*: Crowns and Related Symbols of Special Distinction for Saints in Late Gothic and Renaissance Iconography', *Art Bulletin*, 67 (1985), 567–603.

HALLISSY, MARGARET, *Venomous Woman: Fear of the Female in Literature*, Contributions in Women's Studies (Westport, Conn.: Greenwood, 1987).

HALPIN, PATRICIA A., 'Women Religious in Late Anglo-Saxon England', *HSJ* 6 (1994), 97–109.

HANEY, KRISTINE E., 'The Saint Alban's Psalter and the New Spiritual Ideals of the Twelfth Century', *Viator*, 28 (1997), 145–73.

HARF-LANCNER, LAURENT, *Les Fées au Moyen Age: Morgane et Mélusine. La Naissance des fées* (Paris: Champion, 1984).

HASENOHR, GENEVIÈVE, 'Aperçu sur la diffusion et la réception de la littérature de spiritualité en langue française au dernier siècle du Moyen Age', in Norbert R. Wolf (ed.), *Wissensorganisierende und wissensvermittelnde Literatur im Mittelalter*, Wissensliteratur im Mittelalter, Schriften des Sonderforschungsbereichs 226 Würzburg/Eichstatt (Wiesbaden: Reichart, 1987), 57–90.

HASKINS, SUSAN, *Mary Magdalene* (London: Harper Collins, 1993).

HAYWARD, PAUL A., 'The Idea of Innocent Martyrdom in Late-Tenth- and Eleventh-Century Hagiography', in Diana Wood (ed.), *Martyrs and Martyrologies*, *SCH* 30 (Oxford: Blackwell for the Ecclesiastical History Society, 1993), 81–92.

—— 'Suffering and Innocence in Latin Sermons for the Feast of the Holy Innocents', in Wood (ed.), *The Church and Childhood*, 67–80.

—— 'Translation-Narratives in Post-Conquest Hagiography and English Resistance to the Norman Conquest', *ANS* 21 (1999), 67–93.

HEAD, THOMAS, *Hagiography and the Cult of the Saints: The Diocese of Orléans 800–1200* (Cambridge: Cambridge University Press, 1990).

—— 'The Marriages of Christina of Markyate', *Viator*, 21 (1990), 75–101.

—— 'Saints, Heretics, and Fire: Finding Meaning through the Ordeal', in Sharon Farmer and Barbara H. Rosenwein (eds.), *Monks and Nuns, Saints and Outcasts: Religion in Medieval Society: Essays in Honor of Lester K. Little* (Cornell University Press, 2000), 220–38.

HERRMANN-MASCARD, NICOLE, *Les Reliques des saints: Formation coutumière d'un droit* (Paris: Klincksieck, 1975).

HILL, BETTY, *see* 'Salut et solace de l'amour Jésu' under Primary Sources.

HILL, JOYCE, 'The Dissemination of Ælfric's *Lives of Saints*: A Preliminary Survey', in Szarmach (ed.), *Holy Men and Holy Women*, 235–60.

HINNEBUSCH, W. A., *The Early English Friars Preachers* (Rome: Santa Sabina, 1951).

HIRATA, YOKO, 'St Anselm and the Two Clerks of Thomas Becket', in Luscombe and Evans (eds.), *Anselm*, 323–33.

HOHLER, CHRISTOPHER, 'St Osyth and Aylesbury', *Records of Buckinghamshire*, 18 (1966), 61–72.

HOLLIS, STEPHANIE, *Anglo-Saxon Women and the Church: Sharing a Common Fate* (Woodbridge and Rochester, NY: Boydell Press, 1992).

HOLLYWOOD, AMY, *The Soul as Virgin Wife: Mechthild of Magdeburg, Marguerite Porete, and Meister Eckhardt* (Notre Dame, Ind.: University of Notre Dame Press, 1995).

HOLT, J. C., 'Feudal Society and the Family in Early Medieval England: The Heiress and the Alien', *Transactions of the RHS*, 5th ser. 35 (1985), 1–28.

VAN HOUTS, ELISABETH M. C., *Memory and Gender in Early Medieval Europe 900–1200* (Basingstoke: Macmillan, 1999).

HOWELL, MARGARET, *Eleanor of Provence: Queenship in Thirteenth-Century England* (Oxford and Malden, Mass.: Blackwell, 1998).

HUDSON, JOHN, *Land, Law, and Lordship in Anglo-Norman England* (Oxford: Clarendon Press, 1994).

HUNEYCUTT, LOIS L., 'The Idea of the Perfect Princess: The *Life of Saint Margaret* in the Reign of Matilda II, 1100–1118', *ANS* 12 (1990), 81–97.

—— 'Intercession and the High Medieval Queen: The Esther *topos*', in Carpenter and MacLean (eds.), *Power of the Weak*, 126–46.

—— ' "Proclaiming her dignity abroad": The Literary and Artistic Network of Matilda of Scotland, Queen of England 1100–1118', in McCash (ed.), *The Cultural Patronage of Medieval Women*, 155–74.

HUNT, TONY, 'The Unity of the *Play of Adam, Ordo Representacionis Adé*', *Romania*, 96 (1975), I. 368–88, II. 497–527.

—— 'The Song of Songs and Courtly Literature', in Glyn S. Burgess (ed.), *Court and Poet: Selected Proceedings of the Third Congress of the International Courtly Literature Society (Liverpool, 1980)* (Liverpool: Francis Cairns, 1981), 189–96.

—— 'Anecdota Anglo-Normannica', *Yearbook of English Studies*, 15 (1985), 1–17.

IOGNA-PRAT, DOMINIQUE, 'La Geste des origines dans l'historiographie clunisienne des xi et xii siècles', *Rev. bén.* 102 (1992), 135–91.

JAEGER, C. STEPHEN, *The Envy of Angels: Cathedral Schools and Social Ideals in Medieval Europe, 950–1200* (Philadelphia: University of Pennsylvania Press, 1994).

JAMBECK, KAREN K., 'Patterns of Women's Literary Patronage in England, 1200–ca. 1475', in McCash (ed.), *The Cultural Patronage of Medieval Women*, 228–65.

JAMES, M. R., *A Descriptive Catalogue of the Manuscripts in the Library of St. John's College* (Cambridge: Cambridge University Press, 1913).

—— *A Descriptive Catalogue of the Manuscripts in the Library of Pernbroke College, Cambridge* (Cambridge: Cambridge University Press, 1905).

—— *The Western Manuscripts in the Library of Trinity College, Cambridge: A Descriptive Catalogue* (Cambridge: Cambridge University Press, 1900–4).

JANKOFSKY, KLAUS P., 'Public Executions in England in the Late Middle Ages: The Indignity and Dignity of Death', *Omega*, 10 (1979), 43–57.

JANSEN, K. L., 'Mary Magdalen and the Mendicants: The Preaching of Penance in the Later Middle Ages', *JMH* 21 (1995), 1–25.

JAVELET, ROBERT, *Image et ressemblance au douzième siècle* (Paris: Letouzey et Ané, 1967).

JENKINSON, HILARY, 'Mary de Sancto Paulo, Foundress of Pembroke College, Cambridge', *Archaeologia*, 66 (1914–15), 401–46.

JOHN, ERIC, *Orbis Britanniae and Other Studies* (Leicester: University of Leicester Press, 1966).

JOHNSON, LESLEY, 'Return to Albion', *Arthurian Literature*, 13 (1995), 19–40.

—— and WOGAN-BROWNE, JOCELYN, 'National, World and Women's History', in Wallace (ed.), *Cambridge History*, 92–121.

JOHNSON, PENELOPE D., *Equal in Monastic Profession: Religious Women in Medieval France* (Chicago: University of Chicago Press, 1991).

—— 'Pious Legends and Historical Realities: The Foundations of La Trinité de Vendôme, Bonport and Holyrood', *Rev. bén.* 91 (1981), 184–93.

JOHNSON, PHYLLIS, and CAZELLES, BRIGITTE, *Le Vain Siècle guerpir: A Literary Approach to Sainthood through Old French Hagiography of the Twelfth Century*, North Carolina Studies in the Romance Languages and Literatures 205 (Chapel Hill: University of North Carolina Press, 1979).

JONES, CHARLES W., *Saint Nicholas of Myra, Bari and Manhattan: Biography of a Legend* (Chicago: Chicago University Press, 1978).

JONES, DAVID, see Richard, St, under Primary Sources.

KAPLAN, CORA, '*The Thornbirds*: Fiction, Fantasy, Femininity', in Burgin *et al.* (eds.), *Formations of Fantasy* (London: Methuen, 1986), 142–66.

KAPPELER, SUZANNE, *The Pornography of Representation* (Cambridge: Polity Press, 1986).

KARRAS, RUTH MAZO, *Common Women: Prostitution and Sexuality in Medieval England* (Oxford and New York: Oxford University Press, 1996).

—— 'Sex, Money, and Prostitution in Medieval English Culture', in Jacqueline Murray and Konrad Eisenbichler (eds.), *Desire and Discipline: Sex and Sexuality in the Pre-Modern West* (Toronto: University of Toronto Press, 1996).

KASTNER, JÖRG, *Historiae fundationum monasteriorum* (Munich: Arbeo Gesellschaft, 1974).

KAY, SARAH, *The Chansons de Geste in the Age of Romance: Political Fictions* (Oxford: Clarendon Press, 1995).

—— *Contradiction in Medieval Literature* (Stanford, forthcoming).

KELLY, HENRY ANSGAR, 'Meanings and Uses of *Raptus* in Chaucer's Time', *Studies in the Age of Chaucer*, 20 (1998), 101–65.

KER, N. R., *Catalogue of Manuscripts Containing Anglo-Saxon* (Oxford: Clarendon Press, 1957; reissued 1990).

—— *Medieval Libraries of Great Britain: A List of Surviving Books* (London: RHS; 2nd edn. 1964).

KER, N. R., *Medieval Libraries of Great Britain: Supplement to the Second Edition* ed. ANDREW G. WATSON (London: RHS, 1987).

—— *Medieval Manuscripts in British Libraries*, i–iii (Oxford: Clarendon Press, 1969, 1977, 1983); iv with A. J. Piper (Oxford: Clarendon Press, 1992).

KLEINBERG, AVIAD M., *Prophets in Their Own Country: Living Saints and the Making of Sainthood in the Later Middle Ages* (Chicago and London: University of Chicago Press, 1992).

KLENKE, AMELIA, 'Steventon Priory and a Bozon Manuscript', *Speculum*, 30 (1955), 218–22.

KNOWLES, D. and HADCOCK, R. N., *Medieval Religious Houses, England and Wales* (2nd edn., London, 1971).

KOSMER, ELLEN VIRGINIA, 'A Study of the Style and Iconography of a Thirteenth-Century *Somme le roi* (British Museum MS Add. 54180) with a consideration of other illustrated *Somme* Manuscripts of the Thirteeth, Fourteenth and Fifteenth Centuries', Ph.D. thesis (Yale University, 1973: University Microfilms, Ann Arbor, Mich.).

KRISTEVA, JULIA, 'Women's Time', in Catherine Belsey and Jane Moore (eds.), *The Feminist Reader: Essays in Gender and the Politics of Literary Criticism* (London: Macmillan, 1989).

KROCHALIS, JEANNE, 'The Benedictine Rule for Nuns: Library of Congress, MS 4', *Manuscripta*, 30 (1986), 21–34.

KRUEGER, ROBERTA, 'Love, Honor and the Exchange of Women in *Yvain*: Some Remarks on the Female Reader', *Romance Notes*, 25 (1985), 302–17.

—— *Women Readers and the Ideology of Gender in Old French Verse Romance* (Cambridge: Cambridge University Press, 1993).

KRUGER, STEVEN F., 'Conversion and Medieval Sexual, Religious, and Racial Categories', in Karma Lochrie, Peggy McCracken, and James A. Schultz (eds.), *Constructing Medieval Sexuality*, Medieval Cultures 11 (Minneapolis and London: University of Minnesota Press, 1997), 158–79.

LABARGE, MARGARET WADE, 'Three Medieval Widows and a Second Career', in Michael M. Sheehan (ed.), *Ageing and the Aged in Medieval Europe* (Toronto: Pontifical Institute of Mediaeval Studies, 1990), 159–72.

LACHAUD, FRÉDÉRIQUE, 'Embroidery and the Court of Edward I', *NMS* 37 (1993), 33–52.

LADNER, GERHARDT, 'Images and Terms of Renewal', in Benson and Constable (eds.), *Renaissance and Renewal*, 1–33.

LANGMUIR, GAVIN I., *History, Religion and Antisemitism* (London and New York: Tauris, 1990).

—— 'The Knight's Tale of Young Hugh of Lincoln', *Speculum*, 47 (1972), 459–82.

—— 'Thomas of Monmouth: Detector of Ritual Murder', *Speculum*, 59 (1984), 820–46.

LAPLANCHE, JEAN and PONTARLIS, J.-B., 'Fantasy and the Origins of Sexuality', tr. and repr. in Burgin *et al.* (eds.), *Formations of Fantasy*.

LAURENT, FRANÇOISE, '"A ma matere pas n'apent de vus dire . . .": La Estoire de seint Aedward le rei de Matthieu Paris ou la "conjointure" de deux écritures', *Hagiographie*, 3 (1998), 125–53.

LAWRENCE, CLIFFORD HUGH, *St Edmund of Abingdon: A Study in Hagiography and History* (Oxford: Clarendon Press, 1960).

—— 'St Richard of Chichester', in M. J. Kitsch (ed.), *Studies in Sussex Church History* (London: Leopard's Head Press: 1981), 35–55.

See also Matthew Paris under Primary Sources.

LECLERCQ, JEAN, 'Monachisme et pérégrination au IX et XII siècles', *Studia Monastica*, 3 (1961) 33–52.

LEES, CLARE A., 'Engendering Religious Desire', *JMEMS* 27 (1997), 17–45.

LEWIS, KATHERINE J., *The Cult of St Katherine in Later Medieval England* (Cambridge: Brewer, 1999).

—— '"Lete me suffre": Reading the Torture of St Margaret of Antioch in Late Medieval England', in Wogan-Browne *et al.* (eds.), *Medieval Women: Texts and Contexts*, 69–82.

—— MENUGE, NOËL JAMES, and PHILLIPS, KIM M. (eds.), *Young Medieval Women* (Gloucester: Sutton, 1999).

LEYSER, HENRIETTA, *Medieval Women: A Social History 450–1500* (New York: St Martin's Press, 1995).

LIFSHITZ, FELICE, 'Is Mother Superior? Towards a History of Feminine *Amtscharisma*', in Parsons and Wheeler (eds.), *Medieval Mothering*, 117–38.

LIVEING, HENRY G. D., *Records of Romsey Abbey: An Account of the Benedictine House of Nuns with notes on the Parish Church and Town (AD 907–1558) Compiled from Manuscript and Printed Records* (Winchester: Warren and Son, 1906).

LLOYD, SIMON, 'William Longespee II: The Making of an English Crusading Hero', *NMS* 35 (1991), 41–69.

—— and HUNT, TONY, 'William Longespee II: The Making of an English Crusading Hero: Part II', *NMS* 36 (1992), 79–125.

LOENGARD, JANET S., '"Of the Gift of My Husband": English Dower and its Consequences in the Year 1200', in Julius Kirschner and Suzanne Wemple (eds.), *Women of the Medieval World: Essays in Honor of John H. Mundy* (Oxford: Blackwell, 1985), 215–55.

—— '*Rationabilis dos*: Magna Carta and the Widow's "Fair Share" in the Earlier Thirteenth Century', in Walker (ed.), *Wife and Widow in Medieval England*, 59–80.

LOFTUS, E. A. and CHETTLE, H. F., *A History of Barking Abbey* (Barking: Wilson and Whitworth, 1932).

LOGAN, F. DONALD, *Runaway Religious in Medieval England c.1240–1540* (Oxford: Clarendon Press, 1996).

LUSCOMBE, D. E., and EVANS, G. R. (eds.), *Anselm: Aosta, Bec and Canterbury: Papers in Commemoration of the Nine Hundredth Anniversary of Anselm's Enthronement as Archbishop, 25 September 1093* (Sheffield: Academic Press, 1996).

LUTTRELL, CLAUDE A., *The Creation of the First Arthurian Romance: A Quest* (Evanston, Ill.: Northwestern University Press, 1974).

—— 'The Medieval Tradition of the Pearl Virginity', *Medium Ævum*, 31 (1962), 194–200.

LYNCH, JOSEPH H., *Simoniacal Entry to Religious Life 1000–1260* (Columbus: Ohio State University Press, 1976).

MACBAIN, WILLIAM, 'The Literary Apprenticeship of Clemence of Barking', *AUMLA* 9 (1958), 3–22.

—— 'Some Religious and Secular Uses of the Vocabulary of *fin'amor* in the Early Decades of the Northern French Narrative Poem', *French Forum*, 13 (1988), 261–76.

—— 'Five Old French Renderings of the *passio Sancte Katerine virginis*', in Jeanette Beer (ed.), *Medieval Translators and their Craft*, Studies in Medieval Culture, 25 (Kalamazoo, Mich.: Western Michigan University, Medieval Institute Publications, 1989), 41–63.

—— 'Courtliness in Some Religious Texts of the Twelfth Century', in Giovanna Angeli and Luciano Formisano (eds.), *L'Imaginaire courtois et son double* (Naples: Edizioni scientifiche italiane, 1992), 371–86.

—— 'Anglo-Norman Women Hagiographers', in Short (ed.), *Anglo-Norman Anniversary Essays*, 235–50.

McCASH, JUNE HALL (ed.), *The Cultural Patronage of Medieval Women* (Athens and London: University of Georgia Press, 1996).

McCRACKEN, PEGGY, 'The Body Politic and the Queen's Adulterous Body in French Romance', in Linda Lomperis and Sarah Stanbury (eds.), *Feminist Approaches to the Body in Medieval Literature* (Philadelphia: University of Pennsylvania Press, 1993), 38–64.

McCULLOCH, FLORENCE, 'Saints Alban and Amphibalus in the Works of Matthew Paris: Dublin, Trinity College MS 177', *Speculum*, 56 (1981), 761–85.

—— 'Saint Euphrosine, Saint Alexis and the Turtledove', *Romania*, 98 (1977), 168–85.

McDONNELL, COLLEEN, and LANG, BERNARD, *Heaven: A History* (New Haven and London: Yale University Press, 1988).

McGINN, BERNARD, ' "Teste David cum Sibylla: The Significance of the Sibylline Tradition in the Middle Ages', in Julius Kirschner and Suzanne Wemple (eds.), *Women of the Medieval World: Essays in Honor of John H. Mundy* (Oxford: Blackwell, 1985), 7–35.

McNAMARA, JO ANN, 'Imitatio Helenae: Sainthood as an Attribute of Queenship', in Sticca (ed.), *Saints*, 51–80.

—— 'The Need to Give: Suffering and Female Sanctity in the Middle Ages', in Blumenfeld-Kosinski and Szell (eds.), *Images of Sainthood in Medieval Europe*, 199–221.

MADDICOTT, JOHN ROBERT, *Simon de Montfort* (Cambridge: Cambridge University Press, 1994).

MAGENNIS, HUGH, 'St Mary of Egypt and Ælfric: Unlikely Bedfellows in Cotton Julius E.vii?', in Poppe and Ross (eds.), *The Legend of Mary of Egypt*, 91–112.

MAKOWSKI, ELIZABETH, *Canon Law and Cloistered Women: Periculoso and its Commentators 1298–1545* (Washington, DC: Catholic University of America Press, 1997).

MANDACH, ANDRÉ DE, '*The Creation* of Hermann de Valenciennes: An Unpublished Anglo-Norman Mystery Play of the Twelfth Century', in Short (ed.), *Anglo-Norman Anniversary Essays*, 251–72.

MARCHESIN, ISABELLE, 'Les Jongleurs dans les psautiers du haut moyen âge: nouvelles hypothèses sur la symbolique de l'histrion médiéval', in *Cahiers de civilisation médiévale*, 41 (1998), 123–39.

MARGHERITA, GAYLE, *The Romance of Origins: Language and Sexual Difference in Middle English Literature* (Philadelphia: University of Pennsyvania Press, 1994).

MARX, W. C., *The Devil's Rights and the Redemption in the Literature of Medieval England* (Cambridge: Brewer, 1995).

MARY PHILOMENA SHCJ, MOTHER, 'St Edmund of Abingdon's Meditations Before the Canonical Hours', *Ephemerides Liturgicae*, 3 (1964), 33–57.

MATTER, E. ANN, *The Voice of My Beloved: The Song of Songs in Medieval Western Christianity* (Philadelphia: University of Pennsylvania Press, 1990).

MATZKE, JOHN E., 'Contributions to the History of the Legend of Saint George, with special reference to the Sources of the French, German and Anglo-Saxon Metrical Versions', *PMLA* 18 (1903), 99–171.

MAUSS, MARCEL, *The Gift: Forms and Functions of Exchange in Archaic Societies*, tr. Ian Cunnison, introd. E. E. Evans-Pritchard (London and New York: Norton, 1967).

MEALE, CAROL M., 'The Miracles of Our Lady: Context and Interpretation', in Derek Pearsall (ed.), *Studies in the Vernon Manuscript* (Cambridge: Brewer, 1990), 115–36.

—— (ed.), *Women and Literature in Britain 1150–1500* (Cambridge: Cambridge University Press, 1993; repr. with additional material 1996).

MENACHE, SOPHIA, 'The King, the Church and the Jews: Some Considerations on the Expulsions from England and France', *JMH* 13 (1987), 223–36.

—— 'Matthew Paris's Attitudes Toward Anglo-Jewry', *JMH* 23 (1997), 139–62.

METZ, RENÉ, *La Femme et l'enfant dans le droit canonique médiéval* (London: Variorum Reprints, 1985).

MEYER, PAUL, 'Légendes hagiographiques en français', *Histoire Littéraire de la France*, Académie des Inscriptions et Belles Lettres (Paris: Imprimerie Nationale, 1906), xxxiii. 328–458.

—— 'Notice du MS Bibl. Nat. Fr. 6447', repr. from *Notices et Extraits des manuscrits de la Bibliothèque Nationale et autres bibliothèques* 35 (Paris: Imprimerie Nationale, 1896), 68–73.

—— 'Notice du ms. Egerton 745 du Musée Britannique', *Romania*, 39 (1910), 532–69.

—— 'Notice du ms. Egerton 745 du Musée Britannique (suite)', *Romania*, 40 (1911), 41–69.

—— 'Notice du ms. Egerton 2710 du Musée Britannique', *Bulletin de la Société des Anciens Textes Français* 15 (1889), 72–97.

—— 'Notice du ms. Sloane 1611 du Musée Britannique', *Romania*, 40 (1911), 541–558.

—— 'Notice d'un manuscrit de Trinity College Cambridge contenant les vies en vers français de Saint Jean L'Aumônier et de Saint Clément, pape', *Not. et Ext.* 38 (1903), 293–339.

MILLER, EDWARD, *The Abbey and Bishopric of Ely: The Social History of an Ecclesiastical Estate from the Tenth Century to the Fourteenth*, Cambridge Studies in Medieval Life and Thought, NS 1 (Cambridge: Cambridge University Press, 1951).

MILLER, JAMES L., *Measures of Wisdom: The Cosmic Dance in Classical and Christian Antiquity* (Toronto: University of Toronto Press, 1985).

MILLETT, BELLA, 'The Saints' Lives of the Katherine Group and the Alliterative Tradition', *JEGP* 87 (1988), 16–34.

—— 'The Origins of *Ancrene Wisse*: New Answers, New Questions', *Medium Ævum*, 61 (1992), 206–28.

—— ' "Women in No Man's Land": English Recluses and the Development of Vernacular Literature in the Twelfth and Thirteenth Centuries', in Meale (ed.), *Women and Literature*, 86–103.

—— '*Ancrene Wisse*', the Katherine Group and the Wooing Group: A Bibliographical Guide, in T. L. Burton (gen. ed.), Annotated Bibliographies of Old and Middle English Literature ii (Cambridge: Brewer, 1996).

—— '*Ancrene Wisse* and the Book of Hours', in *Writing Religious Women*, ed. D. Renevy and Christiania Whitehead (Cardiff: University of Wales Press, forthcoming).

MILLINGER, SUSAN J., 'Humility and Power: Anglo-Saxon Nuns in Anglo-Norman Hagiography', in Nichols and Shank (eds.), *Distant Echoes*, 115–28.

MILSOM, S. F. C., 'Inheritance by Women in the Twelfth and Early Thirteenth Centuries', in M. S. Arnold, T. A. Green, S. A. Scully, and S. D. White (eds.), *On* the Laws and Customs of England: Essays in Honour of S. E. Thorne (Chapel Hill: University of North Carolina Press, 1981), 60–89.

MITCHELL, LINDA E., 'Noble Widowhood in the Thirteenth Century: Three Generations of Mortimer Widows 1246–1334', in Louise Mirrer (ed.), *Upon My Husband's Death: Widows in the Literature and Histories of Medieval Europe* (Ann Arbor: University of Michigan Press, 1992), 169–90.

MOLIN, JEAN-BAPTISTE, and MUTEMBE, PROTAIS, *Le Rituel du mariage en France du XIIe au XVIe siècle* (Paris: Beauchesne, 1974).

MOREY, JAMES H., 'Peter Comestor, Biblical Paraphrase and the Medieval Popular Bible', *Speculum*, 68 (1993), 6–35.

MORGAN, NIGEL J., *Early Gothic Manuscripts [I] 1190–1250*, A Survey of Manuscripts Illuminated in the British Isles IV, Part I (London: Harvey Miller, 1982).

—— *Early Gothic Manuscripts [II] 1250–1285*, A Survey of Manuscripts Illuminated in the British Isles IV, Part II (London: Harvey Miller, 1988).

—— 'The "Life of St Thomas Becket" ', *Burlington Magazine*, 1019 (1988), 85–96.

—— and LASKO, PETER, *Medieval Art in East Anglia 1300–1520* (London: Thames and Hudson in association with Jarrold, 1974).

MOORE, HENRIETTA L., *Feminism and Anthropology* (Cambridge: Polity, 1988).

MOORE, JOHN S., 'The Anglo-Norman Family: Size and Structure', *ANS* 14 (1991), 153–96.

MOORE, ROBERT IAN, *The Origins of European Dissent* (London: Allen Lane, 1977).

—— *The Formation of a Persecuting Society: Power and Deviance in Western Europe 950–1250* (Oxford and New York: Blackwell, 1987).

MORTON, VERA, *Heavenly Brides and Holy Mothers: Texts from Twelfth-Century Convents in England and France* (Boydell and Brewer, forthcoming).

MUESSIG, CAROLYN, 'Paradigms of Sanctity for Thirteenth-Century Women', in Beverley Mayne Kienzle et al. (eds.), *Models of Holiness in Medieval Sermons*, Textes et études du Moyen Age 5 (Louvain-la-Neuve: Fédération internationale des instituts d'études médiévales, 1996).

MULDER-BAKKER, ANNEKE B. (ed.), *Sanctity and Motherhood: Essays on Holy Mothers in the Middle Ages* (New York and London: Garland, 1995).

—— 'Was Mary Magdalen a Magdalen?', in R. I. A. Nip, E. M. C. van Houts, C. H. Kneepkes, and G. A. A. Kortekaas (eds.), *Media Latinitas: A Collection of Essays to mark the occasion of the Retirement of L. J. Engels* (Turnhout: Brepols and Stenbrugis in abbatia S. Petri, 1996), 269–74.

—— 'Lame Margaret of Magdeburg: The Social Functions of a Medieval Recluse', *JMH* 22 (1996), 155–69.

—— 'The Prime of Their Lives: Women and Age, Wisdom and Religious Careers in Northern Europe', in Dor et al. (eds.), *New Trends in Feminine Spirituality*, 215–36.

NEEL, CAROL, 'The Origins of the Beguines', *Signs*, 14 (1989), 321–41.

NELSON, JANET, 'Parents, Children, and the Church', in Wood (ed.), *The Church and Childhood*, 81–114.

NEWMAN, BARBARA, *From Virile Woman to WomanChrist* (Philadelphia: University of Pennsylvania Press, 1995).

NEWMAN, CHARLOTTE A., *The Anglo-Norman Nobility in the Reign of Henry I: The Second Generation* (Philadelphia: University of Pennsylvania Press, 1988).

NICHOLL, DONALD, *Thurstan, Archbishop of York* (York: Stangate Press, 1964).

NICHOLLS, JONATHAN W., *The Matter of Courtesy: Medieval Courtesy Books and the Gawain-Poet* (Woodbridge: Brewer, 1985).

NICHOLS, JOHN A., 'Medieval Cistercian Nunneries and English Bishops', in Nichols and Shank (eds.), *Distant Echoes*, 237–49.

—— and SHANK, LILLIAN T. (eds.), *Distant Echoes: Medieval Religious Women* I, Cistercian Studies Series 71 (Kalamazoo: University of W. Michigan Press, 1984).

NOOMEN, WILLEM, 'Le *Jeu d'Adam*: Étude descriptive et analytique', *Romania*, 89 (1965), 145–93.

NOONAN, JOHN T., 'Power to Choose', *Viator*, 4 (1973), 419–34.

O'CARROLL, SND, MARY E., *A Thirteenth-Century Preacher's Handbook* (Toronto: Pontifical Institute of Mediaeval Studies, 1997).

OLIVA, MARILYN, 'Aristocracy or Meritocracy', in W. J. Sheils and Diana Wood (eds.), *Women in the Church*, SCH 27 (1990), 197–208.

—— *The Convent and the Community in Late Medieval England: Female Monasteries in the Diocese of Norwich, 1350–1540*, Studies in the History of Medieval Religion, 12 (Woodbridge and Rochester, NY: Boydell Press, 1998).

OLIVER, GEORGE, *Monasticon Diocesis Exoniensis* (Exeter: Hannaford, 1846).

O'REILLY, JENNIFER, ' "Candidus et rubicundus": An Image of Martyrdom in the "Lives" of Thomas Becket', *AB* 99 (1981), 303–14.

ORMROD, W. M. (ed.), *England in the Thirteenth-Century: Proceedings of the 1984 Harlaxton Symposium* (Woodbridge and Dover, NH: Boydell Press, 1986).

OTTER, MONIKA, 'The Temptation of St Æthelthryth', *Exemplaria*, 9 (1997), 139–64.

PARK, DAVID, 'Wall Painting', in Jonathan Alexander and Paul Binski (eds.), *The Age of Chivalry: Art in Plantagenet England 1200–1400* (London: Royal Academy of Arts in association with Weidenfeld & Nicolson, 1987), 125–36.

PARKER, CATHERINE INNES, 'Fragmentation and Reconstruction: Images of the Body in *Ancrene Wisse* and the Katherine Group', *Comitatus*, 26 (1995), 27–52.

PARREY, YVONNE, 'Devoted Disciples of Christ: Early C16th Religious Life in the Nunnery at Amesbury', *Bulletin of the Institute of Historical Research*, 67, no. 164 (1994) 240–8.

PARSONS, JOHN CARMI (ed.), *Medieval Queenship* (Stroud: Alan Sutton, 1994).

—— 'The Queen's Intercession in Thirteenth-Century England', in Carpenter and MacLean (eds.), *Power of the Weak*, 147–77.

—— 'Of Queens, Courts, and Books: Reflections on the Literary Patronage of Thirteenth-Century Plantagenet Queens', in McCash (ed.), *The Cultural Patronage of Medieval Women*, 175–201.

—— and WHEELER, BONNIE (eds.), *Medieval Mothering* (New York: Garland, 1996).

PAYEN, JEAN-CHARLES, *Le Motif du repentir dans la littérature française médiévale* (Geneva: Droz, 1968).

PEDERSEN, ELSE MARIE WIBERG, 'The In-carnation of Beatrice of Nazareth's Theology', in Dor *et al.* (eds.), *New Trends in Feminine Spirituality*, 61–80.

PERCEVAL, CHARLES SPENCER, 'Remarks on Some Early Charters and Documents Relating to the Priory of Austin Canons and Abbey of Austin Canonesses at Canonsleigh in the County of Devon', *Archaeologia*, 40 (1866), 417–50.

PETERS, EDWARD M., *The Magician, the Witch and the Law* (Hassocks: Harvester, 1978).

—— *Torture* (Oxford: Blackwell, 1985).

PETERS, EDWARD M., 'Destruction of the Flesh—Salvation of the Spirit: The Paradoxes of Torture in Medieval Christian Society', in Alberto Ferreiro (ed.), *The Devil, Heresy and Witchcraft in the Middle Ages: Essays in Honor of Jeffrey B. Russell* (Leiden: Brill, 1998), 131–48.

PHILIPPART, GUY (ed.), *Hagiographies*, Histoire internationale de la littérature hagiographique latine et vernaculaire en Occident, des Origines à 1550, I (Turnhout: Brepols, 1994–).

PHILLIPS, KIM M., 'Maidenhood as the Perfect Age of Women's Life', in Lewis *et al.* (eds.), *Young Medieval Women*, 25–46.

PILCH, HERBERT (ed.), *Orality and Literacy in Early Middle English*, ScriptOralia 9 (Tübingen: Gunter Narr, 1996).

PINDAR, JANICE M., 'The Intertextuality of Old French Saints' Lives: St Giles, St Evroul and the Marriage of St Alexis', *Parergon*, 6A (1988), 11–21.

POPPE, ERICH, and ROSS, BIANCA (eds.), *The Legend of Mary of Egypt in Medieval Insular Hagiography* (Dublin and Portland: Four Courts Press, 1996).

POSTLEWATE, LAURIE, 'Vernacular Hagiography and Lay Piety', in Sticca (ed.), *Saints*, 115–30.

POWER, EILEEN, *Medieval English Nunneries c.1275–1535* (Cambridge: Cambridge University Press, 1922).

POWICKE, F. M., 'Loretta, Countess of Leicester', in J. Goronwy Edwards, V. H. Galbraith, and E. F. Jacob (eds.), *Historical Essays in Honour of James Tait* (Manchester: private subscription, 1933), 247–72.

—— *The Thirteenth-Century 1216–1307: The Oxford History of England IV* (Oxford: Clarendon Press, 1953).

PRESTWICH, MICHAEL, BRITNELL, R. H., and FRAME, ROBIN (eds.), *Thirteenth Century England VI* (Woodbridge and Rochester, NY: Boydell Press, 1997).

PRICE, JOCELYN, 'Inner and Outer: Conceptualizing the Body in *Ancrene Wisse* and Aelred's *De institutione inclusarum*', in Gregory Kratzmann and James Simpson (eds.), *Medieval English Religious and Ethical Literature: Essays in Honour of G. H. Russell* (Cambridge: Brewer, 1986), 192–208.

—— 'The Demonology of Seinte Margaret', *Leeds Studies in English*, 16 (1985), 337–57.

—— 'The *Liflade of Seinte Iuliene* and Hagiographic Convention', *Medievalia et Humanistica*, 14 (1986) 37–58.

—— '*La Vie de sainte Modwenne*: A Neglected Anglo-Norman Hagiographic Text', *Medium Ævum*, 57 (1988), 172–89.

PURCELL, DOMINIC, 'The Priory of Horsham St Faith and Its Wall Paintings', *Norfolk Archaeology*, 35 (1970–3), 469–73.

RADWAY, JANICE A., *Reading the Romance: Women, Patriarchy, and Popular Literature* (Chapel Hill: University of North Carolina Press, 1984).

RANSFORD, ROSALIND, 'A Kind of Noah's Ark: Aelred of Rievaulx and National Identity', in Stuart Mews (ed.), *Religious and National Identity*, SCH 18 (1982), 137–46.

RASTETTER, SUSAN J., '"Bot mylde as maydenes seme at mas": The Feast of All Saints and *Pearl*', *Bull. John Rylands Lib.* 74 (1992), 141–54.

RAYMO, ROBERT R., 'Works of Religious and Philosophical Instruction', in Albert E. Hartung (gen. ed.), *Manual of the Writings in Middle English*, vii (1986), 2255–2378.

RAYNAUD, GASTON, 'Le Miracle de Sardenai', *Romania* 11 (1882), 519–37; *Romania* 14 (1885), 82–93.

REINBURG, VIRGINIA, 'Remembering the Saints', in Nancy Netzner and Virginia Reinburg (eds.), *Memory and the Middle Ages* (Chestnut Hill, Mass.: Boston College Museum of Art, 1995), 17–33.

RELIHAN, ROBERT J., '*Les Peines de purgatorie*: The Anglo-Norman and Latin Manuscript Traditions', *Manuscripta*, 22 (1978), 158–68.

REMENSNYDER, AMY G., 'Legendary Treasure at Conques: Reliquaries and Imaginative Memory', *Speculum*, 71 (1996), 884–906.

—— *Remembering Kings Past: Monastic Foundation Legends in Medieval Southern France* (Ithaca: Cornell University Press, 1995).

REVARD, CARTER, 'Courtly Romances in the Privy Wardrobe', in Evelyn Mullally and John Thompson (eds.), *The Court and Cultural Diversity* (Cambridge: Brewer, 1997), 297–308.

REYNOLDS, PHILIP LYNDON, 'The Dotal Charter as Theological Treatise', *RTAM* 61 (1994), 54–68.

RICHARDS, MARY P., 'MS Cotton Vespasian A. XXII: The Vespasian Homilies', *Manuscripta*, 22 (1978), 97–103.

RIDDY, FELICITY, ' "Abject odious": Feminine and Masculine in Henryson's *Testament of Cresseid*', in Helen Cooper and Sally Mapstone (eds.), *The Long Fifteenth Century: Essays for Douglas Gray* (Oxford: Clarendon Press, 1997), 229–48.

—— 'Engendering Pity in the *Franklin's Tale*', in Evans and Johnson (eds.), *Feminist Readings in Middle English Literature*, 54–71.

—— ' "Women talking about the things of God": A Female Sub-Culture in Late Medieval England', in Meale (ed.), *Women and Literature*, 104–27.

RIDGWAY, HUW, 'Henry III and the Aliens, 1236–1272', in P. R. Coss and S. D. Lloyd (eds.), *Thirteenth-Century England II* (Woodbridge: Boydell, 1988), 88–99.

RIDYARD, SUSAN J., *The Royal Saints of Anglo-Saxon England: A Study of West Saxon and East Anglian Cults* (Cambridge: Cambridge University Press, 1988).

RIGG, A. G., *A History of Anglo-Latin Literature, 1066–1422* (Cambridge: Cambridge University Press, 1992).

RIQUET, S. J., MICHEL, 'Christianity and Population', in Orest Ranum and Patricia Ranum (eds.), *Popular Attitudes to Birth Control in Pre-Industrial France and England* (New York: Harper & Row, 1972), 21–44.

ROBERTS, M. E., 'The Relic of the Holy Blood and the Iconography of the Thirteenth-Century North Transept Portal of Westminster Abbey', in Ormrod (ed.), *England in the Thirteenth Century*, 129–42.

ROBERTSON, DUNCAN, 'Poem and Spirit: The Twelfth-Century French "Life" of St Mary the Egyptian', *Medioevo Romanzo*, 7 (1980), 305–27.

—— *The Medieval Saints' Lives: Spiritual Renewal and Old French Literature* (Lexington, Ky.: French Forum Publishers, 1995).

—— 'Writing in the Textual Community: Clemence of Barking's Life of St Catherine', *French Forum*, 21 (1996), 5–28.

—— 'The Anglo-Norman Verse Life of St Mary the Egyptian', *Rom. Phil.* 52 (1998), 13–44.

ROBINSON, PAMELA, 'A Twelfth-Century Scriptrix', in Pamela R. Robinson and Rivkah Zim (eds.), *Of the Making of Books: Medieval Manuscripts, their Scribes and Readers. Essays Presented to M. B. Parkes* (Aldershot: Scolar Press, and Brookfield, Vt.: Ashgate Publishing Co., 1997), 73–93.

ROBSON, MICHAEL, 'The Impact of the *Cur Deus homo* on the Early Franciscan School', in Luscombe and Evans (eds.), *Anselm*, 334–47.

ROLLASON, DAVID W., 'Lists of Saints' Resting Places in England', *ASE* 7 (1978), 61–94.

—— *The Mildrith Legend: A Study in Early Medieval Hagiography in England* (Leicester: Leicester University Press, 1982).

—— *Saints and Relics in Anglo-Saxon England* (Oxford: Blackwell, 1989).

ROSENTHAL, CONSTANCE L., 'The *Vitae Patrum* in Old and Middle English', University of Pennsylvannia diss. (Philadelphia, 1936).

ROSENTHAL, JOEL T., *The Purchase of Paradise: Gift Giving and the Aristocracy, 1307–1485* (London: Routledge & Kegan Paul, 1972).

ROSOF, PATRICIA J., 'The Anchoress in the Twelfth and Thirteenth Centuries', in John A. Nichols and Lillian T. Shank (eds.), *Peaceweavers: Medieval Religious Women*, ii, Cistercian Studies Series 72 (Kalamazoo: University of Michigan Press), 123–44.

RUBIN, GAYLE, 'The Traffic in Women: Notes on the Political Economy of Sex', in Rayna R. Reiter (ed.), *Towards an Anthropology of Women* (New York and London: Monthly Review Press, 1975), 157–210.

RUDD, W. R., 'The Priory of St Faith', *Norfolk Archaeology*, 23 (1929).

RUSSELL, D. W., 'The Secularization of Hagiography in the Anglo-Norman *Vie seinte Osith*', *Allegorica*, 12 (1991), 3–16.

RUSSELL, JOSIAH COX, *Dictionary of Writers of Thirteenth-Century England*, Bulletin of the Institute of Historical Research Special Supplement 3 (London: Longmans, 1936; repr. with additions and corrections 1967).

SAENGER, PAUL, 'Books of Hours and the Reading Habits of the Later Middle Ages', in Roger Chartier (ed.), *The Culture of Print: Power and the Uses of Print in Early Modern Europe*, tr. Lydia G. Cochrane (Cambridge: Polity Press: 1988), 141–73.

SALIH, SARAH, 'Performing Virginity: Sex and Violence in the Katherine Group', in Cindy L. Carlson and Angela Jane Weisl (eds.), *Constructions of Widowhood and Virginity in the Middle Ages* (New York: St Martin's Press, 1999), 95–112.

—— 'Queering *Sposalia Christi*: Virginity, Gender, and Desire in the Anchoritic Texts', *New Medieval Literatures*, 5, ed. Rita Copeland (forthcoming).

SALTER, ELIZABETH (ed. Derek Pearsall and Nicolette Zeeman), *English and International: Studies in the Literature, Art and Patronage of Medieval England* (Cambridge: Cambridge University Press, 1988).

SALZMAN, L. F., *Building in England Down to 1542: A Documentary History* (Oxford: Clarendon Press, 1952).

SAVAGE, ANNE, 'The Solitary Heroine: Aspects of Meditation and Mysticism in *Ancrene Wisse*, the Katherine Group and the Wooing Group', in W. Pollard and R. Boenig (eds.), *Mysticism and Spirituality in Medieval England* (Woodbridge and Rochester, NY: Brewer, 1997), 63–84.

—— 'The Translation of the Feminine: Untranslatable Dimensions of the Anchoritic Works', in Ellis and Evans (eds.), *The Medieval Translator*, 181–99.

SAXER, VICTOR, *Le Culte de Marie Magdalene: des origines à la fin du Moyen Age* (Auxerre and Paris: Publications de la Société des fouilles archéologiques et des monuments historiques de l'Yonne, 1959).

SCHAEFER, URSULA, 'Twin Collocations in the Early Middle English Lives of the Katherine Group', in Pilch (ed.), *Orality and Literacy*, 179–98.

SCHMID, ELISABETH, *Familiengeschichten und Heilsmythologie: Die Verwandtschaft-strukturen in den französischen und deutschen Gralromanen des 12 und 13 Jahrhunderts* (Tübingen: Niemeyer, 1986).

SCHULENBERG, JANE TIBBETTS, *Forgetful of Their Sex: Female Sanctity and Society ca. 500–1100* (Chicago: University of Chicago Press, 1998).

—— 'The Heroics of Virginity: Brides of Christ and Sacrificial Mutilation', in Mary Beth Rose (ed.), *Women in the Middle Ages and the Renaissance* (Syracuse: Syracuse University Press, 1986), 26–72.

—— 'Sexism and the Celestial Gynaeceum, from 500–1200', *JMH* 4 (1978), 117–33.

—— 'Strict Active Enclosure and its Effects on the Female Monastic Experience, ca. 500–1100', in Nichols and Shank (eds.), *Distant Echoes*, 51–86.

SCRAGG, D. A. G., 'The Corpus of Anonymous Lives and Their Manuscript Content', in Szarmach (ed.), *Holy Men and Holy Women*, 209–23.

—— and TREHARNE, ELAINE, 'Appendix: The Three Anonymous Lives in Cambridge, CCC 303', ibid. 231–4.

SEARLE, ELEANOR, 'Women and the Legitimization of Succession at the Norman Conquest', *ANS* 3 (1980), 159–70.

SHARPE, RICHARD, *A Handlist of the Latin Writers of Great Britain and Ireland before 1540*, Publications of the Journal of Medieval Latin I (Turnhout: Brepols, 1997).

SHEEHAN, MICHAEL M. (ed.), *The Will in Medieval England* (Toronto: Pontifical Institute of Mediaeval Studies, 1963).

—— 'Choice of Marriage Partner in the Middle Ages: Development and Mode of Application of a Theory of Marriage', *Studies in Medieval and Renaissance History*, NS I (1978).

—— (ed.), *Ageing and the Aged in Medieval Europe* (Toronto: Pontifical Institute of Mediaeval Studies, 1990).

—— (ed. James K. Lafarge), *Marriage, Family, and Law in Medieval Europe: Collected Studies* (Toronto: University of Toronto Press, 1996).

SHEINGORN, PAMELA, 'The Maternal Behavior of God: Divine Father as Fantasy Husband', in Parsons and Wheeler (eds.), *Medieval Mothering*, 77–99.

SHORT, IAN, 'An Early Draft of Guernes' *Vie de Saint Thomas Becket*', *Medium Ævum*, 46 (1977), 20–34.

—— 'The Patronage of Beneit's *Vie de Thomas Becket*', *Medium Ævum*, 56 (1987), 239–56.

—— 'Patrons and Polyglots: French Literature in Twelfth-Century England', *ANS* 14 (1991), 229–49.

—— (ed.), *Anglo-Norman Anniversary Essays*, ANTS, OP 2 (London, 1993), 235–50.

—— 'Gaimar's Epilogue', *Speculum*, 69 (1994), 323–43.

—— '*Tam Angli quam Franci*: Self-Definition in Anglo-Norman England', *ANS* 18 (1995), 153–75.

SINCLAIR, FINNUALA, *Blood and Milk: Motherhood and Matrix in Old French and Occitan 'chansons de geste'* (Peter Lang, forthcoming).

SINCLAIR, KEITH VAL, 'The Anglo-Norman Patrons of Robert the Chaplain and Robert of Gretham', *FMLS* 27 (1992), 193–208.

—— 'The Translations of the *Vitas Patrum, Thaïs, Antichrist*, and *Vision de saint Paul* made for Anglo-Norman Templars: Some Neglected Literary Considerations', *Speculum*, 72 (1997), 741–62.

SISSA, GIULIA, *Le Corps virginal: la virginité féminine en Grèce ancienne* (Paris: Vrin, 1987); tr. A. Goldhammer as *Greek Virginity* (Cambridge, Mass. and London: Harvard University Press, 1990).

—— 'Une virginité sans hymen: le corps féminin en Grèce ancienne', *Annales économies sociétés civilisations*, 39 (1984), 1119–39.

SMITH, JACQUELINE, 'Robert of Arbrissel: *procurator mulierum*', in Baker (ed.), *Medieval Women*, 175–84.

SOLTERER, HELEN, *The Master and Minerva: Disputing Women in French Medieval Culture* (Berkeley, Los Angeles, and London: University of California Press, 1995).

SOUTHERN, RICHARD W., *Saint Anselm: A Portrait in a Landscape* (Cambridge: Cambridge University Press, 1990).

—— *Grosseteste: The Growth of an English Mind in Europe* (Oxford: Clarendon Press, 1986).

—— *Anselm and His Biographer* (Cambridge: Cambridge University Press, 1961).

SPEED, DIANE, 'The Saracens of *King Horn*', *Speculum*, 65 (1990), 564–95.

STAERCK, DOM ANTONIUS, *Les Manuscrits latins du Ve au XIIIe siècle conservés à la Bibliothèque impériale de Saint Pétersbourg*, I (St Petersburg: Franz Krois, 1910).

STAFFORD, PAULINE, 'The King's Wife in Wessex 800–1066', in Helen Damico and Alexandra Hennessy Olsen (eds.), *New Readings on Women in Old English Literature* (Bloomington and Indianapolis: Indiana University Press, 1990), 56–78.

—— *Queen Emma and Queen Edith: Queenship and Women's Power in Eleventh-Century England* (Oxford: Blackwell, 1997).

—— 'Women and the Norman Conquest', *Transactions of the RHS*, 6th ser. 4 (1994), 221–49.

STANBURY, SARAH, 'The Virgin's Gaze: Spectacle and Transgression in Middle English Lyrics of the Passion', *PMLA* 106 (1991), 1085–93.

STANILAND, KAY, *Embroiderers*, Medieval Craftsmen Series (London: British Library, 1991).

STAUNTON, MICHAEL, 'Trial and Inspiration in the *Lives* of Anselm and Thomas Becket', in Luscombe and Evans (eds.), *Anselm*, 310–22.

STEIN, ROBERT M., 'The Trouble with Harold: The Ideological Context of the *Vita Haroldi*', *New Medieval Literatures*, 2 (1998), 181–204.

STENGEL, E., 'Handschriftliches aus Oxford', *Zeitschrift für französische Sprache und Literatur*, 14 (1892), 127–60.

STICCA, SANDRO (ed.), *Saints: Studies in Hagiography*, Medieval and Renaissance Studies 141 (Binghamton, NY: SUNY, 1996).

STOCK, BRIAN, *The Implications of Literacy: Written Language and Models of Interpretation in the Eleventh and Twelfth Centuries* (Princeton: Princeton University Press, 1983).

STOUCK, MARY ANN, 'Saints and Rebels: Hagiography and Opposition to the King in Late Fourteenth-Century England', *Medievalia et Humanistica*, NS 24 (1997), 75–94.

STRATHERN, MARILYN, *The Gender of the Gift: Problems with Women and Problems with Society in Melanesia* (Berkeley: University of California Press, 1988).

STRINGER, K. J., *Earl David of Huntingdon: A Study in Anglo-Scottish History* (Edinburgh University Press, 1985).

SULLIVAN, MATTHEW T., 'The Original and Subsequent Audiences of the *Manuel des Pechés* and its Middle English Descendants', D.Phil. thesis (University of Oxford, 1990).

SUMMERSON, H. R. T., 'The Early Development of the *peine forte et dure*', in E. E. Ives and A. H. Manchester (eds.), *Law, Litigants, and the Legal Profession* (London: RHS, 1983), 116–25.

SUTCLIFFE, SEBASTIAN, 'The Cult of St Sitha in England: An Introduction', *NMS* 37 (1993), 83–9.

SWANSON, JENNY, 'Childhood and Childrearing in *ad status* Sermons by Later Thirteenth-Century Friars', *JMH* 16 (1990), 309–31.

—— *John of Wales: A Study of the Works and Ideas of a Thirteenth-Century Friar* (Cambridge: Cambridge University Press, 1989).

SYMONS, THOMAS, '*Regularis concordia*: History and Derivation', in David Parsons (ed.), *Tenth-Century Studies: Essays in Commemoration of the Millennium of the Council of Winchester and the 'Regularis Concordia'* (London and Chichester: Phillimore, 1975), 37–59.

SZARMACH, PAUL E. (ed.), *Holy Men and Holy Women: Old English Prose Saints' Lives and Their Contexts* (Albany, NY: SUNY Press, 1996).

TANNER, NORMAN, *The Church in Medieval Norwich 1370–1532* (Toronto: Pontifical Institute of Mediaeval Studies, 1984).

TAYLOR, ANDREW, 'Into His Secret Chamber: Reading and Privacy in Late Medieval England', in James Raven, Helen Small, and Naomi Tadmor (eds.), *The Practice and Representation of Reading in England* (Oxford: Oxford University Press, 1986), 41–61.

THIRY, CLAUDE, and THIRY-STASSIN, MARTINE, 'Mariage et lignage dans l'histoire de Guillaume le maréchal', in [Duby], *Femmes: mariages*, 349–59.

THIRY-STASSIN, MARTINE, 'L'Hagiographie en Anglo-Normand', in Philippart (ed.), *Hagiographies*, 407–28.

THOMAS, MARCEL, 'Une compilation anglo-normande de la fin du xiiie siècle: "La vie de gent de religion"', in *Recueil de travaux offerts à M. Clovis Brunel* (Paris: Société de l'École des chartes, 1955), ii. 586–98.

THOMPSON, JOHN, 'The Cursor Mundi and its French Tradition', in O. S. Pickering (ed.), *Individuality and Achievement in Middle English Poetry* (Cambridge: Brewer, 1997), 19–37.

THOMPSON, SALLY, 'The Problem of the Cistercian Nuns', in Baker (ed.), *Medieval Women*, 227–52.

—— 'Why English Nunneries had no History: A Study of the Problems of the English Nunneries Founded after the Conquest', in Nichols and Shank (eds.), *Distant Echoes*, 131–49.

—— *Women Religious: The Founding of English Nunneries After the Norman Conquest* (Oxford: Clarendon Press, 1991).

THOMSON, RODNEY MALCOLM, *Manuscripts from St Alban's Abbey 1066–1235*, 2 vols. (Woodbridge: Brewer for the University of Tasmania, and Totowa, NJ: Biblio Distribution, 1982).

—— *William of Malmesbury* (Woodbridge and Wolfboro, NH: Boydell Press, 1987).

TILLOTSON, JOHN, 'Visitation and Reform of the Yorkshire Nunneries in the Fourteenth Century', *Northern History*, 30 (1994), 1–21.

TOLKIEN, J. R. R., '*Ancrene Wisse* and *Hali Meiðhad*', *Essays and Studies*, 14 (1929), 104–26.

TOWNSEND, DAVID, 'Anglo-Latin Hagiography and the Norman Transition', *Exemplaria*, 3 (1991), 385–433.

TRUAX, JEAN A., 'From Bede to Orderic Vitalis: Changing Perspectives on the Role of Women in the Anglo-Saxon and Anglo-Norman Churches', *HSJ* 3 (1991), 35–51.

TURNER, RALPH V., *Men Raised From the Dust: Administrative Service and Upward Mobility in Angevin England* (Philadelphia: University of Pennsylvania Press, 1988).

TYSON, DIANA B., 'The Adam and Eve Roll in Corpus Christi College Cambridge MS 98', *Scriptorium*, 52 (1998), 301–16.

—— 'Patronage of French Vernacular History Writers in the Twelfth and Thirteenth Centuries', *Romania*, 100 (1979), 180–222.

UITTI, KARL, 'Women Saints, the Vernacular, and History in Early Medieval France', in Blumenfeld-Kosinski and Szell (eds.), *Images of Sainthood in Medieval Europe*, 247–67.

VAUCHEZ, ANDRÉ, 'Beata stirps: sainteté et lignage en occident aux XIIIe et XIVe siècles', in G. Duby and J. Le Goff (eds.), *Famille et parenté dans l'Occident médiéval* (Paris: 1974), 397–406.

—— 'Les Fonctions des saints dans le monde occidental (IIe–XIIIe siècle)', *Actes du colloque organisé par l'École française de Rome avec le concours de l'université de Rome 'La Sapienza'* (Rome: École Française de Rome, 1991), 161–72.

—— *Les Laïcs au moyen âge: pratiques et expériences religieuses* (Paris, 1987); tr. Margery J. Schneider as *The Laity in the Middle Ages* (Notre Dame, Ind.: University of Notre Dame Press, 1993).

DE VEGVAR, CAROL NEUMANN, 'Saints and Companions to Saints: Anglo-Saxon Royal Women Monastics in Context', in Szarmach (ed.), *Holy Men and Holy Women*, 51–93.

VENARDE, BRUCE L., *Women's Monasticism and Medieval Society: Nunneries in France and England 890–1215* (Ithaca and London: Cornell University Press, 1997).

VICINUS, MARTHA, *Independent Women: Work and Community of Single Women 1850–1920* (London: Virago, 1985).

Victoria County History of England: volumes for individual counties under county names:

VCH *Bedfordshire* ii, ed. William Page (London: Constable, 1910).

VCH *Cambridgeshire* ii, ed. L. F. Salzman (London: Oxford University Press, 1948).

VCH *Essex* ii, ed. William Page and J. Horace Round (London: Constable, 1907).

VCH *Dorset* ii, ed. William Page (London: Constable, 1908).

VCH *Hampshire* ii, ed. H. Arthur Doubleday and William Page (Westminster: Constable, 1903).

VCH *Norfolk* ii, ed. William Page (London: James Steel, 1902).

VCH *Suffolk* ii, ed. William Page (London: Constable, 1907).

VCH *Sussex* ii, ed. William Page (London: Constable, 1907).

VCH *Wiltshire* iii, ed. R. B. Pugh and Elizabeth Crittall (London: Oxford University Press for Institute of Historical Studies, 1956).

VINCENT, NICHOLAS, *Peter des Roches: An Alien in English Politics 1205–1238*, Cambridge Studies in Medieval Life and Thought, 4th ser. 31 (Cambridge: Cambridge University Press, 1996).

VITZ, EVELYN BURGE, 'Re-reading Rape in Medieval Literature: Literary, Historical and Theoretical Reflections', *Romanic Review*, 88 (1997), 1–26.

VOADEN, ROSALYNN (ed.), *Prophets Abroad: The Reception of Continental Holy Women in Medieval England* (Cambridge: Brewer, 1996).

WALKER, SUE SHERIDAN, 'Free Consent and Marriage of Feudal Wards in Medieval England', *JMH* 8 (1982), 123–34.

—— 'Punishing Convicted Ravishers: Statutory Strictures and Actual Practice in Thirteenth and Fourteenth-Century England', *JMH* 13 (1987), 237–50.

—— 'Litigation as Personal Quest: Suing for Dower in the Royal Courts, circa 1272–1350', in Walker (ed.), *Wife and Widow in Medieval Europe*, 81–108.

—— (ed.), *Wife and Widow in Medieval Europe* (Ann Arbor: University of Michigan Press, 1993).

WALLACE, DAVID (ed.), *The Cambridge History of Medieval English Literature: Writing in Medieval Britain 1066–1547* (Cambridge: Cambridge University Press, 1999).

WALLACE-HADRILL, J. M., 'Bede and Plummer', in Gerald Bonner (ed.), *Famulus Christi: Essays in Commemoration of the Thirteenth Century of the Birth of the Venerable Bede* (London: SPCK, 1976), 366–85.

WALMSLEY, JOHN, 'The Early Abbesses, Nuns, and Female Tenants of the Abbey of Holy Trinity, Caen', *Journal of Ecclesiastical History*, 48 (1997), 425–44.

WARD, BENEDICTA, *Harlots of the Desert: A Study of Repentance in Early Medieval Sources* (Oxford: Mowbray, 1987).

—— *Miracles and the Medieval Mind: Theory, Record and Event 1000–1215* (Aldershot: Wildwood House; rev. edn. 1987).

WARD, JENNIFER C., 'Royal Service and Reward: The Clare Family and the Crown 1066–1154', *ANS* 11 (1988), 261–78.

—— *Women of the English Nobility and Gentry 1066–1500* (Manchester: Manchester University Press, 1995).

WARREN, ANN K., 'The English Anchorite in the Reign of Henry III, 1216–1272', *Ball State University Forum*, 19 (1978), 21–8.

—— *Anchorites and their Patrons in Medieval England* (Berkeley, Los Angeles, and London: University of California Press, 1985).

WARREN, NANCY BRADLEY, 'Pregnancy and Productivity: The Imagery of Female Monasticism Within and Beyond the Cloister Walls', *JMEMS* 28 (1998), 531–52.

WATSON, NICHOLAS, 'The Methods and Objectives of Thirteenth-Century Anchoritic Devotion', in Marion Glasscoe (ed.), *The Medieval Mystical Tradition in England: Exeter Symposium IV* (Cambridge: Brewer, 1987), 132–53.

—— 'Censorship and Cultural Change in Late-Medieval England: Vernacular Theology, the Oxford Translation Debate, and Arundel's Constitutions of 1409', *Speculum*, 70 (1995), 822–64.

—— 'The Middle English Mystics', in Wallace (ed.), *Cambridge History*, 539–65.

WAUGH, SCOTT L., 'Marriage, Class and Royal Lordship in England under Henry III', *Viator*, 16 (1985), 181–207.

—— 'Women's Inheritance and the Growth of Bureaucratic Monarchy in Twelfth and Thirteenth-Century England', *NMS* 34 (1990), 71–92.

WEISS, JUDITH, 'The Date of the Anglo-Norman *Boeve de Humtone*', *Medium Ævum*, 55 (1986), 237–41.

—— 'The Metaphor of Madness in the Anglo-Norman Lives of St Mary the Egyptian', in Poppe and Ross (eds.), *The Legend of Mary of Egypt*, 161–73.

—— 'The Power and Weakness of Women in Anglo-Norman Romance', in Meale (ed.), *Women and Literature*, 7–23.

WERTHEIMER, LAURA, 'Adeliza of Louvain and Anglo-Norman Queenship', *HSJ* 7 (1995), 101–15.

WHATLEY, E. GORDON, *The Saint of London: The Life and Miracles of St Erkenwald* (Binghamton: SUNY, CMERS, 1989).
—— 'Late Old English Hagiography, ca. 950–1150', in Philippart (ed.), *Hagiographies*, 429–99.
WHEELER, BONNIE (ed.), *Listening to Heloise: The Voice of a Twelfth-Century Woman* (New York: St Martin's Press, 2000).
WELTER, J. TH. *L'Exemplum dans la littérature religieuse et didactique du Moyen Age* (Paris and Toulouse: Occitania, 1927), 83–108.
WHITE, STEPHEN D., *Custom, Kinship, and Gifts to Saints: The 'laudatio parentum' in Western France* (Chapel Hill: University of North Carolina Press, 1988).
WHITEHEAD, CHRISTIANIA, 'Making a Cloister of the Soul in Medieval Religious Treatises', *Medium Ævum*, 67 (1998), 1–29.
WIGRAM, S., *Chronicles of the Abbey of Elstow* (Oxford and London: Parke and Co., 1885).
WILMART, ANDRÉ, 'Les Compositions d'Osbert de Clare en l'honneur de Saint Anne', *Annales de Bretagne*, 37 (1925–6), 15–32.
—— 'Une lettre inédite de St Anselme à une moniale inconstante', *Rev. bén.* 40 (1928), 319–32.
—— 'L'Histoire ecclésiastique composée par Hugues de Fleury et ses destinataires', *Rev. bén.* 50 (1948), 293–305.
WINSTEAD, KAREN, *Virgin Martyrs: Legends of Sainthood in Late Medieval England* (Ithaca: Cornell University Press, 1997).
WOGAN-BROWNE, JOCELYN, 'Saints' Lives and the Female Reader', *FMLS* 27 (1991), 314–32.
—— 'Queens, Virgins, and Mothers: Twelfth and Thirteenth Century Hagiographic Representations of the Abbess in Medieval Britain', in Louise Fradenburg (ed.), *Women and Sovereignty* (Edinburgh: Edinburgh University Press, 1992), 14–35.
—— 'The Apple's Message: Some Post-Conquest Hagiographic Accounts of Textual Transmission', in A. J. Minnis (ed.), *Late Medieval Religious Texts and their Transmission: Essays in Honour of A. I. Doyle*, York Manuscripts Conferences, Proceedings Series 3 (Cambridge: Brewer, 1994), 39–54.
—— 'Wreaths of Thyme: *Translatio* and the Female Narrator in Anglo-Norman Hagiography', in Ellis and Evans (eds.), *The Medieval Translator*, 46–65.
—— 'The Virgin's Tale', in Evans and Johnson (eds.), *Feminist Readings in Middle English Literature*, 165–94.
—— '"Bet . . . to . . . rede on holy seyntes lyves . . .": Romance and Hagiography Again', in Carol M. Meale (ed.), *Readings in Medieval English Romance* (Cambridge: Brewer, 1994), 83–97.
—— 'Chaste Bodies: Frames and Experiences', in Sarah Kay and Miri Rubin (eds.), *Framing Medieval Bodies* (Manchester University Press, 1994), 24–42.
—— 'Re-routing the Dower: The Anglo-Norman Life of St Audrey by Marie (of Chatteris?)', in Carpenter and MacLean (eds.), *Power of the Weak*, 27–56.
—— '"Clerc u lai, muïne u dame": Women and Anglo-Norman Hagiography in the Twelfth and Thirteenth Centuries', in Meale (ed.), *Women and Literature*, 61–85.
—— 'Outdoing the Daughters of Syon?: Edith of Wilton and the Representation of Female Community in Early Fifteenth-Century England', in ead., Rosalynn Voaden, Arlyn Diamond *et al.* (eds.), *Medieval Women: Texts and Contexts in Late Medieval Britain: Essays for Felicity Riddy* (Turnhout: Brepols, 2000), 399–415.

—— WATSON, NICHOLAS, TAYLOR, ANDREW, and EVANS, RUTH (eds.), *The Idea of the Vernacular: An Anthology of Middle English Literary Theory, 1280–1530* (University Park, Pa.: Penn State University Press, 1999).

WOLFTHAL, DIANE, *Images of Rape: The 'Heroic' Tradition and Its Alternatives* (Cambridge and New York: Cambridge University Press, 1999).

WOLPERS, THEODOR, *Die englische Heiligenlegende des Mittelalters: eine Formengeschichte des Legendenerzählen von der spätantiken lateinischen Tradition bis zur Mitte des 16 Jahrhunderts* (Tübingen: Niemeyer, 1964).

WOOD, DIANA (ed.), *The Church and Childhood: Papers Read at the 1993 Summer Meeting and the 1994 Winter Meeting of the Ecclesiastical Society*, SCH 31 (Oxford: Blackwell for the Ecclesiastical History Society, 1994).

WOOD, SUSAN MERIEL, *English Monasteries and Their Patrons in the Thirteenth Century* (London: Oxford University Press, 1955).

WOODS, MARJORIE CURRY, 'Rape and the Pedagogical Rhetoric of Sexual Violence', in Rita Copeland (ed.), *Criticism and Dissent in the Middle Ages* (Cambridge: Cambridge University Press, 1996), 56–86.

YORKE, BARBARA,'Sisters under the Skin', *RMS* 15 (1989), 95–117.

ZALESKI, CAROL, *Otherworld Journeys: Accounts of Near Death Experience in Medieval and Modern Times* (New York: Oxford University Press, 1987).

Index

Note: *Italic* page numbers refer to illustrative material; works are entered under their author's name if known; critics and scholars are usually indexed only if mentioned in the text.